Encyclopedia of
the United States
in the Twentieth Century

Editorial Board

Encyclopedia of
The United States
in the Twentieth Century

Stanley I. Kutler
Editor in Chief

Robert Dallek
David A. Hollinger
Thomas K. McCraw
Associate Editors

Judith Kirkwood
Assistant Editor

Volume II

CHARLES SCRIBNER'S SONS
Macmillan Library Reference USA
Simon & Schuster Macmillan
New York

SIMON & SCHUSTER AND PRENTICE HALL INTERNATIONAL
London   Mexico City   New Delhi   Singapore   Sydney   Toronto

Charles Scribner's Sons
Macmillan Publishing Company
1633 Broadway
New York, New York 10019

Library of Congress Cataloging-in-Publication Data

Encyclopedia of the United States in the twentieth century
    / Stanley I. Kutler, editor in chief; Robert Dallek,
    David A. Hollinger, Thomas K. McCraw, associate
    editors; Judith Kirkwood, assistant editor.
        p.   cm.
    Includes bibliographical references and index.
    ISBN 0-13-210535-7 (set: hc: alk. paper). —
0-13-307190-1 (vol. 1: hc: alk. paper). — 0-13-307208-8
(vol. 2: hc: alk. paper). — 0-13-307216-9 (vol. 3: hc:
alk. paper). — 0-13-307224-X (vol. 4: hc: alk. paper).
    1. United States—Encyclopedias.   I. Kutler, Stanley
I.
E740.7.E53 1996
973'.003–dc20   95-22696
                                                  CIP

5 7 9 11 13 15 17 19   20 18 16 14 12 10 8 6 4
PRINTED IN THE UNITED STATES OF AMERICA

The paper in this publication meets the requirements of
ANSI/NISO Z39.48-1992 (Permanence of Paper)

Contents

Contents of Other Volumes

CONTENTS OF OTHER VOLUMES

Alphabetical Table of Contents

ALPHABETICAL TABLE OF CONTENTS

Common Abbreviations Used in This Work

Ala.	Alabama	Me.	Maine
Ariz.	Arizona	Mich.	Michigan
Ark.	Arkansas	Minn.	Minnesota
Art.	Article	Miss.	Mississippi
b.	born	Mo.	Missouri
c.	*circa*, about, approximately	Mont.	Montana
Calif.	California	n.	note
cf.	*confer*, compare	N.C.	North Carolina
chap.	chapter (plural, chaps.)	n.d.	no date
Cong.	Congress	N.D.	North Dakota
Colo.	Colorado	Neb.	Nebraska
Conn.	Connecticut	Nev.	Nevada
d.	died	N.H.	New Hampshire
D	Democrat, Democratic	N.J.	New Jersey
D.C.	District of Columbia	N.Mex.	New Mexico
Del.	Delaware	no.	number (plural, nos.)
diss.	dissertation	n.p.	no place
ed.	editor (plural, eds); edition	n.s.	new series
e.g.	*exempli gratia*, for example	N.Y.	New York
enl.	enlarged	Okla.	Oklahoma
esp.	especially	Oreg.	Oregon
et al.	*et alii*, and others	p.	page (plural, pp.)
etc.	*et cetera*, and so forth	Pa.	Pennsylvania
exp.	expanded	P.L.	Public Law
f.	and following (plural, ff.)	pt.	part (plural, pts.)
Fla.	Florida	R	Republican
Ga.	Georgia	Rep.	Representative
ibid.	*ibidem*, in the same place (as the one immediately preceding)	rev.	revised
		R.I.	Rhode Island
Ida.	Idaho	S.C.	South Carolina
i.e.	*id est*, that is	S.D.	South Dakota
Ill.	Illinois	sec.	section (plural, secs.)
Ind.	Indiana	Sen.	Senator
Kan.	Kansas	ser.	series
Ky.	Kentucky	ses.	session
La.	Louisiana	supp.	supplement
M.A.	Master of Arts	Tenn.	Tennessee
Mass.	Massachusetts	Tex.	Texas
Md.	Maryland	UN	United Nations

COMMON ABBREVIATIONS USED IN THIS WORK

U.S.	United States		Vt.	Vermont
U.S.S.R.	Union of Soviet Socialist Republics		Wash.	Washington
v.	versus		Wis.	Wisconsin
Va.	Virginia		W. Va.	West Virginia
vol.	volume (plural, vols.)		Wyo.	Wyoming

ENCYCLOPEDIA OF
THE UNITED STATES
IN THE TWENTIETH CENTURY

Part 3

GLOBAL AMERICA

INTRODUCTION

Robert Dallek

The publication of this encyclopedia in 1996 marks nearly a hundred years of America as a world power. Beginning with the Spanish-American War and extending through the Cold War and the crises in the Persian Gulf, Somalia, Korea, and Bosnia, the United States has played a major part in overseas affairs.

To be sure, in the first forty years of the century, most Americans hoped that we would continue to enjoy the freedom from international burdens that had largely characterized the first hundred years of our life as a nation. But from the perspective of 1996, we can see how futile that expectation was. Once we acquired an island empire in 1898, which projected U.S. power into the Caribbean and the far reaches of the Pacific, we were inextricably enmeshed in foreign affairs. And even if we had not taken control of Cuba, Puerto Rico, Guam, the Philippines, and Wake Island, America's growing involvement in world trade made our national well-being partly dependent on traditional power struggles around the globe. Whether Germany or Great Britain became the dominant power in Europe, whether Soviet communism expanded across Europe and into Asia, whether Japan succeeded in creating an East Asian coprosperity sphere, whether China had a government capable of creating domestic stability and committed to friendship with or antagonism to the United States, whether cooperative or hostile regimes controlled Middle Eastern oil supplies, whether stable development or unpredictable changes dominated the life of Western Hemisphere nations mattered far more than Americans in the first half of the twentieth century were willing to allow.

The articles in this part of the Encyclopedia try to make sense of the developments that shaped the country's response to the world beyond our shores. The first two articles, on pacifism and arms limitation and on foreign policy, are essentially discussions of the domestic influences on U.S. views of overseas affairs. They lead the section because they are a bridge between nineteenth- and twentieth-century influences on America's role in international relations.

As a nation favored by a geography that allowed it to shun involvements in overseas conflicts and large defense expenditures, Americans identified their country with the rule of law, disarmament, and nonmilitary solutions to world conflicts. As David S. Patterson shows in his article, arms control and pacifism retained a hold on the American imagination throughout the century, even after the country had assumed the burden of being a superpower and had begun spending billions of dollars annually on the defense of its national security. Patterson's essay is the story of America's idealistic and moralistic approach to foreign affairs. He demonstrates that in spite of the country's nuclear arsenal, refusal to give up a first-strike option, and its record of military interventions in every corner of the globe, its desire for pacifist solutions to overseas struggles and collective security, as opposed to traditional balance-of-power diplomacy, was a sincere expression of national opinion. There is good reason why Woodrow Wilson's highly unrealistic characterization of World War I as the war to end all wars and the war to make the world safe for democracy, Franklin Roosevelt's depiction of Yalta as representing the end of spheres of influence, and George Bush's appeal for a new world order had so much resonance among so many Americans during this century.

Melvin Small's article effectively relates the interaction between domestic politics and America's foreign actions. Though he emphasizes that partisan politics has consistently shaped our responses to external challenges, Small explains that this was only one of many elements shaping U.S. foreign policy. Nevertheless, his essay is a demonstration of how important and consistent an element domestic politics has been in explaining what we did abroad. Small shows us that despite the declaration of American political leaders that politics ends at the water's edge, the truth is that except at the start of a war, when the great majority of Americans rally 'round the flag, partisan political advantage is as much a part of foreign affairs as it is of domestic ones.

The next three articles on national security, the world wars, and limited wars form a second thematic discussion of Global America. These three essays reflect on the ways in which Americans have dealt with threats to the country's national survival in the twentieth century. Mark Lowenthal's discussion of the national security state analyzes what has gone into the making of U.S. defense policy. Specifically, it dissects competing ideas on where and how the country wished to use its resources to defend itself from external threats. It also explains how America shifted from being a nation without a clear vision of its security needs to one with commitments to the international status quo and, at the end of the century, back again to an uncertain perspective of what will best serve the nation's long-term safety. Lowenthal's essay is also a thoughtful discussion of bureaucratic politics or the struggle between Congress and the executive for control of foreign and defense policies.

David Kennedy's discussion of American participation in the two world wars persuasively argues that both conflicts were partly struggles over how America defined its relationship with the outside world. In a word, the two global conflicts in the twentieth century not only redefined European and Asian relations but went far to transform America from an insular, marginal power into the most important nation in world affairs. Moreover, the two great wars are a study in the importance of evangelism in American foreign policy. Both wars were crusades for democracy, free enterprise, and the American way of life. Kennedy's essay does not neglect the many important issues that surrounded U.S. involvement in the wars and the debates over postwar peacemaking. But the underlying themes of his essay provide a broad picture of how truly important these two conflicts were in shaping the long-term course of twentieth-century U.S. foreign affairs.

George Herring's article on limited wars is a thoughtful discussion of the differences between America's approach to traditional large-scale conflicts, the Civil War, World Wars I and II, and the more limited struggles it fought in the Philippines, Central America and the Caribbean, and Korea and Vietnam (its most important limited wars), and the Persian Gulf. Herring skillfully shows the tensions and internal anguish these limited conflicts have pro-

voked throughout American history. These struggles have left Americans confused and shouting at each other over the wisdom and consequences of fighting with "one hand tied behind our backs." Herring concludes that "the future of limited wars remains murky." His essay is a welcome addition to the literature on the subject and may help to produce some needed discussion of how we wish to deal with future military actions of this sort.

The last three articles in this part are discussions of what Akira Iriye sensibly calls the "globalization of the United States." In an article on world regions Iriye analyzes America's strategic, political, economic, and cultural transformation into a global nation. Through its interactions with Latin America, Europe, Africa, the Middle East, South and East Asia, and the Pacific, the United States has changed the countries of each of these regions at the same time that they have altered the course of America's internal life. There was nothing linear about this process. Nor is it necessarily fixed in concrete. It is an ongoing dynamic process that will continue to shape U.S. and overseas affairs for as far into the future as anyone can see.

Emily Rosenberg echoes and expands upon Iriye's argument by describing the cultural interactions that have characterized American relations with the rest of the world from the beginning of the century. Rosenberg shrewdly points out that the influence of American music and films abroad is essentially a continuation of the way in which religious and social reformers previously spread the American gospel around the world. Rosenberg's article is a demonstration of how much the last hundred years, in Henry Luce's phrase, has indeed been the American century.

The final article, Jeffry Frieden's on America's interaction with the world economy, is a brilliant analysis of the conflicting impulses that have dominated the country's approach to overseas markets, investments, and competitors. The twentieth century has seen a contest between advocates of greater and lesser U.S. integration into the world economy. At the same time, international economic developments beyond our control have made some of these debates irrelevant. Frieden convincingly shows that "what happens inside the United States is as important for the world economy as the world economy is for the future of the United States." Frieden's essay will leave no doubt in readers' minds that an essential part of any encyclopedia on twentieth-century America is the discussion of why and how the United States changed and was changed by the outside world.

PACIFISM AND ARMS LIMITATION

David S. Patterson

Many social scientists believe that public opinion can have a significant impact on U.S. government policy. Its influence on foreign policy, however, is less clear than it is in the area of domestic politics. In the latter, civil rights and environmental groups, for example, have often turned to the courts to advance their causes, but the courts have eschewed involvement in foreign policy. Moreover, the president plays a much larger role in foreign affairs than in domestic policy.

Nevertheless, American presidents over time have derived information on public opinion from several sources—polls, the media, Congress, interest groups (including peace, internationalist, and antiwar movements), friends and advisers, and mail—and the interaction of these sources can influence the president's national security and foreign policies. Peace movements promoting pacific, internationalist, and antimilitaristic goals in twentieth-century America have had an impact on U.S. foreign policies, which would have been somewhat different if the groups had not existed. They were also more effective in those periods, such as the 1920s and 1930s, when "peace" had wider support in Congress and among the media and American public.

It is difficult to determine how much impact the peace cause had on any issue or era, for it is generally unclear whether a policymaker's decision was made in response to public pressures or for unrelated reasons. The problem is compounded in cases where policymakers discounted the role or influence of peace movements, even though the documentary record, while often inferential and fragmentary, suggests otherwise. Because of these constraints, historians, though utilizing the best available evidence and social science techniques, such as public opinion polling data and voting behavior of Congress, have been able to measure the relative success of these movements only intuitively rather than precisely.

The core belief underlying the American peace movement was "pacifism," which initially derived from the Christian reforming tradition. While pacifists in colonial America advanced many theological and philosophical justifications for their pacifist faith, they all advocated ending or avoiding war and controlling militarism. Not surprisingly, many of the earliest proponents of pacifism were Protestant ministers, and the religious impulse continued to motivate pacifist activity in the twentieth century. In organized form pacifism was limited at first mainly to the historical peace churches (Brethren, Mennonites, and Quakers) in North America from the early settlements.

Peace activism developed only gradually as an organized secular phenomenon in the modern world after about 1815. The thirteen colonies had revolted against Great Britain in the 1770s in part because of the arbitrary actions of the mother country's military authorities. The newly independent nation expressed its antimilitarist biases by making the military subject to civilian authority, opposing a large standing army, and recognizing the right of citizens to bear arms in their own defense.

The religious pacifist position also drew support at various times from more secular sources in response to the brutality and horrors of warfare. Moral revulsion against armaments and war had of course existed from early recorded history, and these same ethical concerns also inspired the antiwar and antimilitarist movements in twentieth-century America. These movements grew in response to peace workers' perception of America's emergence as the dominant world power and the crucial role of their nation in fostering a peaceful world order. Whether opposed to large standing armies, naval armaments, chemical warfare, the bombing of defenseless noncombatants, or nuclear weapons, pacifists and their allies sought to limit, if not end arms races and develop new, authoritative international institutions for peacemaking and peacekeeping. Throughout the century the peace movement was composed disproportionately of the well-educated middle and upper classes, especially among women reformers, liberals, and intellectuals. Following the development of the atomic bomb, scientists increasingly joined the antinuclear movement that came to be known as "nuclear pacifism."

ANTI-IMPERIALISM, ANTIMILITARISM, AND INTERNATIONAL ARBITRATION

In the first century of the new nation, antimilitarism was more a state of mind than conscious national policy, and it was not seriously debated. Indeed, antimilitarism did not begin to attain even the semblance of an organized entity outside the religious pacifist sects until the end of the nineteenth century. At that point two seemingly unrelated developments served as catalysts for new interest in the regulation of armaments.

The first development was the emergence of the United States as a major world power and accompanying public debate over America's proper place in the international arena. Many Americans believed that the onrush of events over Cuba that led to the Spanish-American War and the acquisition of new possessions—especially the Philippine Islands, thousands of miles from the continental United States—enabled the United States, belatedly but fortuitously, to join the European imperial powers (and Japan) in the extension of Western power and ideals to the non-Western world. In addition, the takeover of the Philippines was seen as a God-given opportunity to uplift and civilize the Filipino natives.

At the same time, however, many Americans were disturbed by what they perceived as profound changes in their nation's place in world politics. War and the imperial aftermath at the end of the century, they believed, meant a dramatic repudiation of America's ideals of democracy ("consent of the governed"), antimilitarism, and anticolonialism. These events, together with President Theodore Roosevelt's navalism and imperialism in the Caribbean and Central America in the first years of the new century, galvanized many Americans into organized opposition to militaristic and aggressive foreign policies.

At the end of the nineteenth century, the American peace movement was still very small. Only a few peace groups, notably the American Peace Society (APS), founded in Boston in 1828, and the Universal Peace Union, headed by Philadelphia Quaker Alfred H. Love, who had taken a nonresistant position during America's Civil War, consistently resisted the McKinley administration's drift toward war with Spain. Love undertook a personal campaign to avert war

with Spain but failed completely. Indeed, when news of his antiwar efforts appeared in the press, he was publicly denounced, and threats were made on his life.

The anti-imperialist movement after the war was somewhat larger but was centered almost entirely in the Northeast and a few urban centers. Many of the prominent anti-imperialist spokesmen had formerly participated in or were influenced by the antislavery cause during the Civil War era. Others, like Andrew Carnegie, who increasingly made peace his central concern in the first decade of the twentieth century, also drew upon the British free trade tradition, especially the anti-imperialist liberals William Gladstone and John Bright. Domestically, most anti-imperialists were spokesmen for the ethical verities associated with the preindustrial America of their youthful years, and their opposition to imperialism was essentially a culmination of their rising disillusionment with the emerging urban-industrial era. They were profoundly conservative on economic and social questions, and some railed against the wave of "new" immigrants from southern and eastern Europe pouring into what they perceived as America's increasingly dirty, depersonalized cities. Politically, many were independent Republicans (Mugwumps) who deplored corruption in American political life but offered no reform program beyond honesty and high-minded leadership in government.

Compared with the imperialists, who offered a vision of an adventuresome role for the United States in a more complex, interdependent world, the antiimperialists appeared backward-looking to a more secure, isolationist America. Strategically, they warned that American annexation of the Philippines would mean abandonment of its secure international role and increasing involvement in diplomatic intrigue and power politics. And the economic consequences, they predicted, would be drastic increases in the army and navy, creation of a colonial bureaucracy, and enlarged administrative expenses, all of which would be economically ruinous to the homeland.

The anti-imperialists' appeals to tradition might have carried the day if the Senate had rejected the peace treaty with Spain, which ceded Puerto Rico, Guam, and the Philippines to the United States. But William Jennings Bryan, leader of the Democratic party, urged Democratic senators to consent to the treaty. A future leader of the peace cause, he argued seemingly inconsistently that ratification of the treaty would bring about legal peace and give the U.S. government freedom of action in solving the Philip-

Peace advocates William Jennings Bryan and Henry Ford, December 1915. Bryan resigned as secretary of state in June 1915. PRINTS AND PHOTOGRAPHS DIVISION, LIBRARY OF CONGRESS

pine issue. Persuaded by Bryan (as well as the affront to the nation's honor with news of the loss of American lives in a skirmish with Filipino forces in the Philippines), a few antiannexationist Democrats voted for the accord in February 1899, which narrowly received the necessary two-thirds majority. Bryan apparently thought he could blame the McKinley administration for American imperialism in the 1900 presidential campaign. If this was his strategy, it failed; many Americans, believing that ratification of the treaty resolved the issue, were more interested in domestic matters than in a "great debate" on imperialism.

The main contribution of the American peace movement during the debate over imperialism was the ethical underpinnings its spokesmen brought to the anti-imperialist protest. Whether drawing upon the uncompromising moralism of the Christian pacifist, British anti-imperialist, or antislavery traditions, they repeatedly stressed that the rule of subject peoples without their consent was immoral. Quakers like APS secretary Benjamin F. Trueblood consistently argued that American rule of unconsenting foreigners was un-Christian and should be abandoned. The pacifists also protested the U.S. military's rigorous suppression of the Filipino insurrection from 1899 to 1902, with the resulting deaths on both sides. If less religious American friends of peace drew from

other traditions, they nonetheless emphasized that imperialism was ethically wrong and should be abandoned. They maintained their position in the face of President Theodore Roosevelt's "Big Stick" diplomacy in the Caribbean and his "rape of Panama."

As anti-imperialists predicted, the nation's new far-flung empire required a much larger navy to protect its new possessions and shipping routes. Under President Roosevelt (1901–1909), an avowed proponent of a big navy, the United States embarked on an ambitious naval-building program. He drew support from the Navy League of the United States, a new naval preparedness group. The more ardent pacifists attacked the "follies," "absurdities," and "delusion" of large armaments, but their modest antipreparedness campaign had little effect in Congress, which obligingly approved Roosevelt's request for two battleships each year. As a gesture to growing sentiment for a respite to the escalating armaments race, Roosevelt requested only one battleship before the Second Hague Peace Conference (1907). Following the failure of that conference on disarmament and faced with rising Japan-American tensions, however, Roosevelt increased his request for battleships to four in late 1907 and 1908. Congress approved only two each year, but Roosevelt still managed to increase the military budget more than 600 percent during his presidency.

For his part, Roosevelt believed that power, not paper, was what mattered most in world politics. Although his awareness of the highly charged imperial rivalries in Europe tempered his militaristic proclivities, he sharply criticized the peace movement. He attacked the peace workers' "shortsightedness," "folly," "sentimentality," and "hysterical pseudo-philanthropy," and singled out Carnegie, Trueblood, and APS president Robert Treat Paine for special censure.

Roosevelt's successors as president, William Howard Taft and Woodrow Wilson, though much more sympathetic to the peace movement, largely continued America's naval-building program in undiminished form before World War I. In consequence, by 1914 the number of U.S. battleships patrolling the oceans ranked second in the world only to Britain's.

More important than the reaction against imperialism and navalism was a second, more hopeful development: the movement for peace and arbitration. Actually, antimilitarism and peace sentiment began to coalesce in the origins of the initial major event in this process, the First Hague Peace Conference (1899). Tsar Nicholas II of Russia initiated the moves for this international meeting when he issued a re-script in August 1898 to major governments to meet to discuss the arms race. Because the real, though unstated reason for Nicholas's initiative was to prevent the deployment of a new field gun the rival Austrians had invented, his purposes were more cynical than altruistic. Nevertheless, he posed as a farsighted statesman anxious to halt the escalating burden of land and naval armaments that fueled international tensions and the threat of war.

The delegates from the twenty-six participating nations at the Hague Conference, quickly perceiving that they could make no progress on disarmament, turned to discussions about international mechanisms to reduce the risk of war. Andrew D. White, head of the American delegation, actively encouraged these discussions. He revered the seventeenth-century Dutch jurist Hugo Grotius, often called the father of international law, and believed that the Hague meeting could advance international law and arbitration. Most peace workers believed that if a good plan of arbitration could be agreed upon, disarmament would follow.

Despite its meager achievements, the First Hague Peace Conference signed conventions defining procedures for arbitration, mediation, and the establishment of commissions of inquiry and reiterating "civilized" rules of warfare. Most important for the peace movement, it created the Permanent Court of International Arbitration, the first world tribunal in history. The new body was not really "permanent" or a "court" and involved no compulsion. It simply allowed nations to appoint arbiters from which they could voluntarily select their adjudicators.

Americans' earlier aggressive behavior toward Indians, Mexicans, and others suggests little commitment to peacemaking. Many idealistic Americans professed to believe in fair play and faith in law, however, and creation of the court revived support for the pacific settlement of international disputes, which had traditionally been a basic principle of U.S. foreign policy. The court also sparked new interest in the peace movement. As early as 1885, the Rev. Edward Everett Hale had predicted the establishment of a world court in the twentieth century, and he almost single-handedly organized American support for the court idea before the Hague Conference. Following that meeting, proponents of the Permanent Court argued that this body would gradually increase in stature and eventually lead to more authoritative international institutions and a new world order. Among the new recruits to the peace cause after 1900 was the German-American representative, Richard Bartholdt (R-Mo.). Working through the

Interparliamentary Union, an organization of American and European lawmakers, Bartholdt lobbied President Roosevelt to support the Union's initiative for a second conference at The Hague. Roosevelt obliged, though he deferred the actual invitation to Tsar Nicholas II. By that time Bartholdt, the journalist Hamilton Holt, and others were campaigning for a more authoritative judicial body as well as the establishment of an international executive and legislature. These optimists were temperamentally and ideologically forerunners of Woodrow Wilson's vision of a league of nations, though Wilson later developed his ideas on world organization largely independently.

With international tensions in Europe rising, the Second Hague Peace Conference (1907) failed to agree on any concrete measures for improving the machinery of international organization, much less arms limitation. But the peace workers' initial discouragement was only skin deep. Increasingly before 1914 they gave enthusiastic perorations of the achievements of the two conferences and reaffirmed the Western dream as the poet Albert Tennyson had penned it a half-century earlier, of "The Parliament of Man, the Federation of the World."

In working toward that ideal, the peace movement continued to encourage American leadership in international arbitration. Still isolated from European and Asian politics, the peace leaders perceived no threat to the security of the nation if it agreed to arbitrate its disputes. The rapid rapprochement with Britain around the turn of the century revived enthusiasm for an arbitral accord between the two nations. The U.S. Senate had defeated an earlier Anglo-American arbitration agreement in 1897, but Roosevelt's secretary of state, John Hay, negotiated arbitration treaties with Britain and several other powers in 1904 and 1905. Because these accords excepted questions involving "vital interests," "independence," and "honor" of either party, and "the interests of third parties," they were very limited in scope, but the Senate further weakened them. Objecting to a clause in them that allowed the governments to sign a "special agreement" whenever they needed to interpret the provisions of a treaty before beginning arbitration, the Senate changed the words "special agreement" to "treaty," thereby requiring its consent to an additional treaty before arbitration could commence. Believing this amendment rendered the treaties innocuous, Roosevelt pigeonholed them. He accepted similar reservations, however, in twenty-five arbitration accords in 1908–1909 negotiated by Hay's successor, Elihu Root.

The arbitration cause was joined more directly during Taft's presidency. Taft's support for the peace cause derived from his lifelong passion for justice. As he said in 1911, "International Law is really a wonderful creation." He supported law groups that urged the transformation of the Hague Court into a truly permanent court of international justice and, like Elihu Root, James Brown Scott, and other legalists, wanted to create a truly permanent international court composed of eminent jurists who would replace or take over the functions of temporary arbitral tribunals like the Hague Court. Taft hoped to extend jurisdiction of an international prize court, which the Second Hague Peace Conference had recommended, as an opening wedge for a more authoritative international court of arbitral justice. This hope dissolved when Britain rejected the prize court in 1911.

Despite this setback Taft went ahead with treaties with Britain and France, which provided that all "justiciable" disputes would be submitted to The Hague or some other international tribunal. When one government disputed the other's contention of a "justiciable" question, a joint commission of inquiry would investigate; and if it decided affirmatively, it would be referred to arbitration. The scope of the treaties was potentially far-reaching. Taft intended that they would make "a long step forward by demonstrating that it is possible for two nations at least to establish . . . the same system of due process of law that exists between individuals under a government," and he valued them less as a preventer of war (which was unlikely with Britain and France) than as a precedent toward the peaceful settlement of all international controversies.

The American peace movement was well prepared to campaign for these treaties. In the years from 1906 to 1912 the cause grew rapidly, as new peace societies were formed in New York, Chicago, and several other cities. Most impressive were the establishment of two new liberally endowed foundations in 1910, the Carnegie Endowment for International Peace (CEIP) in Washington, D.C., and the World Peace Foundation, founded by Edwin Ginn, a Boston book publisher. Although Carnegie selected extremely cautious trustees to manage his $10 million endowed fund, they had no difficulty in supporting the conservative Taft administration's arbitration treaties. The endowment underwrote the costs of public meetings and publications favoring the treaties. Numerous business, church, and college groups also endorsed the accords, and all measurable indices of public opinion suggested solid support for them.

The Senate again demonstrated, however, that it was more concerned with protecting its prerogatives and its nationalistic biases than in extending the principle of arbitration. Many senators attacked the provisions for the commission of inquiry as too vague, and they called for clarifying and restrictive amendments. Partisan politics also hurt the treaties, with both progressive Republican senators and Democrats eager to embarrass the administration in the upcoming presidential election of 1912.

Taft conceded that his treaties indicated his willingness to assume moderate risks to national interests in order to advance the arbitration principle in world politics. "We cannot make an omelet without breaking eggs," he argued. "We cannot submit international questions to arbitration without the prospect of losing." He believed the commission of inquiry provided an additional check on unrestrained arbitration and was a concession to senators' nationalistic concerns. Unconvinced, however, the Senate proceeded to approve the treaties only after passing several amendments which eliminated the joint commission and excluded many kinds of controversies, and a disappointed Taft refused to proceed with ratification of the emasculated accords.

Despite this setback peace workers had high hopes for the incoming Wilson administration. In promoting conciliation treaties, Secretary of State William Jennings Bryan continued Taft's emphasis on conflict resolution. Bryan's treaties called for the signatory powers to refer all their differences that diplomacy or arbitration could not resolve to a permanent commission of inquiry. The commission would report on the dispute within a year, during which the parties would agree not to use force. Bryan believed that the delay would allow passions to cool and avert war. By 1915 he had negotiated thirty "cooling off" accords with foreign governments, twenty of which were ratified.

Because Bryan's treaties contained no provisions for enforcement and also permitted the signatories to resort to war after the commission had submitted its report, they did not advance internationalists' efforts to develop legal and moral restraints to nations' abilities to wage war. Most peace workers, however, welcomed the laudable pacifist ideal that inspired them.

THE PEACE MOVEMENT AND WORLD WAR I

The onset of the European war came as a rude shock to peace leaders everywhere. To be sure, they were not entirely innocent of the European hatreds and recognized the possibility of a European war. But unwilling to assume man's irrationality, they had tended to blame an impersonal factor, the armaments race, for world tensions. And even after general war developed, they continued to assert that the conflict was the inevitable result of the escalating armaments race rather than of more fundamental economic and imperial rivalries that contributed to European insecurity and in turn to the arms buildup.

World War I shattered the superficial unity among the peace workers. The programs of the prewar peace organizations, which had emphasized mediation, arbitration, arms limitation—all moderate international reforms—were inadequate in a wartorn world. The lawyers continued during the maelstrom to work for the codification of international law and the creation of a world court, and the conservative Carnegie Endowment moved in that direction. But even these legalists conceded that the belligerents' blatant violations of the law of "civilized" warfare dealt international law a sharp setback.

The American Peace Society was fairly typical of the paralysis of the peace groups during the war. The society had grown remarkably in the decade before 1914, but its new members were much more cautious on peace questions. In a time when domestic reform was pervasive and respectable, many may have turned to the peace movement as a safe moral reform. To many of these newcomers, peace did not connote nonresistance or challenges to the status quo but order and stability, and they were inclined to accept "adequate" armaments, though they never defined what was meant by that word. The APS's activist, antimilitarist faction was further diluted when some of its older liberals resigned because of their disenchantment with the society's conservatism.

The American Peace Society's ties to the Carnegie Endowment (CEIP) also constrained it. The society had begun to accept annual subventions from the endowed group before 1914 and became increasingly dependent on CEIP's good will for its financial health. When CEIP's powerful directors urged the peace organization to "withdraw within itself . . . to limit its program consciously," the society's conservative leadership obliged. It thus failed to take positions on the questions of military preparedness, mediation, and U.S. entry into the war during American neutrality. The society ultimately endorsed American military involvement in the war and membership in a postwar world organization while expressing reservations about specific features of Woodrow Wilson's League of Nations.

But the American peace movement did not entirely collapse after 1914; rather it was reorganized. As its leaders began to perceive their real differences, they gradually transformed the movement into several autonomous organizations, each of which promoted clearly defined programs. Women became much more active in the reorganized movement. Before the war "new women" reformers had been involved in the settlement house movement, suffrage, temperance, and other domestic reforms; after 1914 many of them became interested in peace questions. To be sure, many women reformers later supported the American war effort for patriotic reasons or because they correctly perceived that women's contributions to the war on the domestic front would faciliate the attainment of women's suffrage. But a large number of them showed a tenacious, even lifelong commitment to the peace cause, and probably a higher percentage of female than male reformers were active in it. It is debatable whether the "maternal instinct," women as the biologically "weaker sex," or social conditioning underlay this interest, but the commitment of the new peace activity to other reform causes compatible with women's rights encouraged their participation.

With the intensification of the European war, several reformers started a movement for neutral mediation of the conflict. Fanny Garrison Villard, daughter of the nonresistant pacifist and abolitionist William Lloyd Garrison, veteran peace worker Lucia Ames Mead, settlement house workers Lillian D. Wald, Emily Greene Balch, and Jane Addams, and suffragist Carrie Chapman Catt actively participated in this effort. They were early joined by European women reformers from each belligerent side. The fiery Hungarian suffragist and pacifist Rosika Schwimmer and Emmeline Pethick-Lawrence, a British suffragist, for instance, came to the United States in late 1914 to campaign for neutral mediation of the war. The women's efforts created a groundswell of support for a separate female group; the result was the founding of the Woman's Peace Party (WPP) in early 1915.

Among the planks of the new organization, many of which anticipated the liberal peace principles later enunciated in Woodrow Wilson's Fourteen Points, the first proposed "the immediate calling of a convention of neutral nations in the interest of early peace." Along with Schwimmer, Julia Grace Wales, an instructor of English at the University of Wisconsin, initiated the neutral conference plan. Wales drafted a paper exploring how a conference of neutral nations could continuously serve as a clearing house

Jane Addams at the fortieth anniversary of Hull House, the settlement house she founded in 1889 in Chicago. PRINTS AND PHOTOGRAPHS DIVISION, LIBRARY OF CONGRESS

for peace feelers from both belligerent sides and also offer its own proposals to them.

Many European women shared the American women's concerns. Distressed by the appalling human suffering, the Dutch physician Aletta Jacobs and like-minded European women reformers called an international women's congress at The Hague in late April 1915. Many of these European women had been active in suffrage work, and the International Woman's Suffrage Alliance, founded shortly before the war, became the organizational vehicle for bringing together the women participants at The Hague. Despite imposing difficulties, more than 1,100 women from almost all the European belligerent and neutral nations attended the meeting. They were joined by forty-seven Americans, including many from the WPP.

The delegates passed several resolutions calling for open diplomacy, democratic control over foreign policies, self-determination of subject peoples, non-recognition of conquered territories, some form of postwar disarmament, and the creation of a new authoritative world organization to develop practical proposals for promoting international amity. These resolutions provided the best early international expression for a "new diplomacy" in world affairs.

More important for the mediation movement, the congress approved a resolution urging the formation of a neutral conference for continuous mediation. It also dispatched delegations to present their resolutions to the European governments and to promote a neutral mediation conference. The delegates representing neutral nations met with the leaders of the belligerent nations and the Vatican, while women envoys from both belligerent sides and neutrals talked with the war leaders. Altogether, the women talked to twenty-nine heads of government and foreign ministers. Although most of the political leaders expressed only polite interest in their scheme, none was openly hostile, and the women concluded that they should continue to promote the neutral conference idea vigorously.

They then sought the endorsement of Woodrow Wilson, the leader of the one large neutral. Over the next year Wilson had sixteen meetings with pacifist leaders. Wilson praised the liberal peace principles in the women's program, which he said he had studied carefully; and while he deferred endorsement of any specific mediation scheme, he indicated his strong interest in mediation when the proper opportunity arose.

The President's temporizing yet sympathetic attitude appeased most peace workers on the mediation issue. Many in fact had already become more concerned about the President's call for military preparedness. Amos Pinchot, Paul Kellogg, Lillian Wald, Oswald Garrison Villard, Crystal Eastman, and others founded the Anti-Preparedness Committee in late 1914, soon renamed the American Union Against Militarism (AUAM), to resist Wilson's plan for a 400,000 man "Continental Army" and an accelerated naval rearmament program. Although a small group with only about 1,000 members, by 1916 the AUAM had offices in twenty-two American cities. The new organization took some credit when the administration abandoned the "Continental Army" scheme, but Congress approved the other parts of the President's preparedness program.

One mediation proponent who was dissatisfied with Wilson's inaction on mediation was the automobile magnate Henry Ford, who in November 1915 agreed to finance an unofficial conference composed of prominent neutral citizens in the hope that Wilson and other neutral leaders would give it official status. If the idea, however idealistic, had any promise, it was immediately obscured when Ford chartered a "peace ship" packed with pacifistic enthusiasts who

Lillian D. Wald. PRINTS AND PHOTOGRAPHS DIVISION, LI-
BRARY OF CONGRESS

would, in Ford's naive words, "get the boys out of
the trenches by Christmas day." Although his conference of neutral citizens soon convened in Scandina-
vian capitals, it was not endorsed by neutral governments.

Wilson campaigned during the 1916 election on
a platform of peace and progressive reform. He had
kept the country out of the European conflict and
had drawn back from full-scale invasion of Mexico
following border clashes between American troops
and Mexican rebels led by Francisco Villa. Moreover,
he had hinted at his desire to serve as peacemaker
among the belligerents. Wilson had in fact adroitly
handled the peace advocates, keeping them at arm's
length while showing strong sympathies for mediation and reform, and most of them endorsed his
reelection. Believing his electoral triumph in November 1916 showed solid public backing for a peace
initiative, he offered his independent mediation, culminating in his "peace without victory" address in
January 1917 in which he outlined the liberal principles that should serve as the basis of any peace settlement.

Wilson's mediation bid failed when the German
government shortly announced submarine warfare
against all neutral and enemy belligerent shipping.
Germany's decision galvanized the peace movement
into opposition against U.S. entry into the war. The
WPP, AUAM, American Neutral Conference Committee, and other peace groups formed an Emergency Peace Federation (EPF) to lobby Congress
against American participation. With the strong support of Bryan, Sen. Robert La Follette (R-Wis.),
and other antiwar legislators, the peace forces urged
an advisory public referendum on the war. Their rationale was an extension of the progressive notion
among domestic reformers that the vote of the people
was more to be trusted than that of their representatives in Congress. This effort failed, and Congress
voted decisively for war against Germany on 6 April.

In the decade or so before the European war,
the word "pacifist" had been applied generously to
anyone advocating international amity, but its mean-

Robert M. "Fighting Bob" La Follette, Republican representative from Wisconsin (1885–1891), governor (1901–1907),
and United States senator (1906–1925). La Follette was one
of five senators to vote against the declaration of war in April
1917; after World War I he opposed U.S. participation in
the League of Nations and the World Court. PRINTS AND
PHOTOGRAPHS DIVISION, LIBRARY OF CONGRESS

ing narrowed considerably during the war to apply only to those who refused to endorse the war effort. Pacifists became objects of opprobrium and often had to endure charges of treason. After the war its meaning broadened again and became more respectable in proportion to popular disillusionment with the war experience.

Of the 3 million draft-eligible young American men, about 65,000 claimed noncombatant service during World War I. The Selective Service Act (May 1917) limited exemption to members of the historic peace churches, however, and local draft boards granted this status to only 20,873. The draft law required even these to report to army camps for noncombatant military service. Faced with the prospect of army encampments along with the military's use of patriotic arguments to persuade war objectors to enlist, only 3,989, or .14 percent of those drafted, continued to maintain their position after reaching training camp. The War Department court-martialed and imprisoned about 450 of these. Congress later allowed objectors to be furloughed to alternate civilian service, and an executive order belatedly exempted those who could demonstrate to a board of inquiry their "conscientious scruples" against war.

There were also a number of "absolutists" who refused even to register under the terms of the law or to report for medical examinations. It is not certain how many were in this category, but some 100 to 150 of them were sentenced by civil courts. Much more numerous were those evading the draft, roughly estimated at 171,000. If draft dodgers were caught, they were subject to a prison sentence, but it is not known how many were actually tried and convicted.

The sources of conscientious objection in the United States were religious, philosophical, or political. Religiously, the historic peace churches, especially the Quakers, led the way, and the American Friends Service Committee (AFSC) was created in 1917 to provide alternatives for Quaker objectors. In addition, the Social Gospel movement in the first decades of the twentieth century had infused organized Protestantism with a critical awareness of social injustice and the obligation of the churches to promote social reform. This reform impulse merged with traditional ethical notions of individual Judeo-Christian conscience in fostering war resistance among some liberal Protestant clergymen and lay people. The best organized expression of the liberal pacifists' position was the American branch of the Fellowship of Reconciliation, which British pacifists had founded.

Philosophical anarchism also influenced some objectors. Various prewar European thinkers, especially Leo Tolstoy, had expounded this view, which rejected the state as materialistic, repressive, and militaristic and instead emphasized the absolute integrity of the individual soul and the development of voluntaristic communal societies. A few Americans, notably Henry David Thoreau, had earlier advanced this philosophical position, while the youthful rebel Randolph Bourne perhaps best expressed it in his writings opposing U.S. involvement in the world war.

The strongest root of conscientious objection was political. By the turn of the century European Socialists, influenced by Marxist theory of war and revolution, had vigorously argued that international wars were the result of competing capitalist states and that workers should call a general strike rather than provide cannon fodder for the imperial and materialistic aspirations of the capitalist classes. Because of their geographical isolation, American Socialists before 1914 had said virtually nothing about international conflict and shunned the peace movement. The prospect of U.S. involvement in the European war, however, sparked fresh debate among American Socialists on the conflict. Shortly after the U.S. decision for war, the Socialist party at its annual convention in Saint Louis voted to oppose the war. This decision split the party, but the majority faction provided support for conscientious objectors.

For a time antiwar Socialists and pacifists from the AUAM and the EPF cooperated in founding a new left-wing group, the People's Council for Peace and Democracy in America, whose message was that war and militarism endangered democracy. Advocating an early peace on liberal terms, protection of civil liberties, and repeal of conscription, the People's Council held large rallies in many American cities and seemed to be forging a coalition among farmers, labor unions, and liberal pacifists. In the superpatriotic upsurge following American entry, however, the People's Council was branded as treasonous, and law enforcement agencies broke up its meetings and hounded its members. These agencies also moved to suppress the antiwar activities of the Industrial Workers of the World and the Socialist party.

Alarmed at the increasing radicalism of the People's Council, a minority in the AUAM led by Paul Kellogg and Lillian Wald split off to work with prowar liberals for democratic terms in the peace treaty. The more pacifistic majority, including the social worker Roger Baldwin, the socialist Norman Thomas, and Crystal Eastman, focused on the plight of conscientious objectors. From their efforts came the founding of the Civil Liberties Bureau, renamed the American Civil Liberties Union in 1920.

The cordial relations between Woodrow Wilson and the mediation proponents during neutrality unraveled during American belligerency. There was in fact irony in the relationship, because Wilson never promoted their specific peace proposal but became the foremost champion of their other liberal principles for international reform after he had carried the nation into a war that all the peace workers viewed with strong misgivings and in some cases opposed completely. Wilson became contemptuous of pacifist opponents of American involvement, and in late 1917 he said of them: "I want peace, but I know how to get it, and they do not." Such criticism, together with his endorsement of the Espionage Act (1917) and other repressive wartime measures that restricted civil liberties, dampened much of the pacifists' respect for the President.

Not surprisingly, these pacifists were henceforth reluctant to support Wilson's peace program. The defection of pacifists from Wilson's camp was never complete, but it was an early sign that the war would severely test the progressive coalition he had so painstakingly put together before American belligerency.

WOODROW WILSON, INTERNATIONALISTS, AND THE LEAGUE OF NATIONS

The transformation of the American peace movement during the war also resulted in bold initiatives for a new postwar international order. The conflict particularly sharpened awareness among internationally minded Americans of the need for permanent authoritative institutions for prevention of war. The blatant violations of international law by the European belligerents convinced many nonpacifists that the pre-1914 emphasis on juridical institutions and nonenforceable sanctions had proven inadequate and that new approaches were required. In June 1915, Hamilton Holt, William H. Short, and Theodore Marburg associated with like-minded peace, business, and professional people in founding the League to Enforce Peace (LEP). William Howard Taft, a convert to the need for more authoritative international institutions, became its president.

The LEP envisioned a world organization whose member states would pledge the use of their economic and military forces against any of their number that refused to submit its justiciable disputes to a world court or its nonjusticiable ones to a council of conciliation for decision before resorting to force.

These conciliation measures might fail to prevent war, the league's spokesmen conceded, but they were confident that the cooling-off period would deter hostilities in almost every case. Convinced that Germany was the aggressor in 1914, they also assumed that the new organization could identify the outlaw in future disputes and could move quickly to punish the violator. Claiming 300,000 members by early 1919, it was easily the most influential private internationalist group in the United States.

At the same time, pacifists as well as nonpacifists who had reservations about the potential distasteful effects of compulsory sanctions rejected the LEP program. Many of them joined instead with international lawyers in promoting the creation of a permanent world court after the war. James Brown Scott, John Bassett Moore, and other well-known legalists especially attacked the league's assumption that an authoritative world body could always define the aggressor in a given war, pointing to the American conflicts of 1812 and 1898 and the Franco-Prussian war of 1870 as examples of debatable war origins.

The internationalists helped to nourish President Wilson's commitment to a new world order based on substituting collective security for the balance of power in international politics, but his proposals for what became the League of Nations were largely his own. When he first publicly espoused his conception of postwar collective security in an address to the LEP in May 1916, he refused to discuss details, and he privately labeled the internationalist leaders "butters in" and "woolgatherers." He particularly had a low opinion of international lawyers and rejected House's and Lansing's advice to support the creation of a world court as a juridical complement to his proposed league.

Essentially, President Wilson sought to project American liberal principles onto the international stage. His attempt to "internationalize" American values and institutions was utopian, but he displayed considerable practical negotiating skills in working toward his goal. He expounded eloquently on his liberal peace principles in his "Fourteen Points" address in January 1918, including the final point urging the formation of "a general association of nations," but he completed the details of his proposed League of Nations only in the course of drafting its Covenant with the Allied leaders at the Paris Peace Conference in 1919. He was willing to compromise on freedom of the seas, reparations, and other of his points to win the Allied leaders' acceptance of the League of Nations, which became part of the peace treaty signed at Versailles. Mainly because of British persistence, he also reluctantly agreed to the inclusion of an article in the Covenant providing for a Permanent Court of International Justice (World Court).

Despite Wilson's successes in Europe, he failed to persuade the required two-thirds of the Senate to approve the Treaty of Versailles. There are various explanations for his failure: his partisan appeal to elect loyal Democrats in the November 1918 congressional election which backfired, his decision to attend the Paris Peace Conference which left his political fences unmended at home, his decision not to include any senators or Republican leaders in his peace delegation, his few efforts to compromise which might have won over moderate Republican senators to the treaty, and his ill-fated Western speaking tour on behalf of the treaty when he suffered a stroke leaving him incapacitated and the protreaty forces leaderless.

Wilson's personal failings, political partisanship on both sides, and the Senate's traditional concern for its prerogatives all contributed to the defeat of the treaty, but equally important was the role of ideas. The heart of the Covenant was Article 10, under which the League of Nations pledged to preserve members' territorial integrity and existing political independence against external aggression, and the League Council, consisting of the great powers, would decide what collective actions would be taken in case of such threats or actual attacks. The vague and indefinite obligations of this article worried many senators. They particularly feared that nations would be unwilling to relinquish their sovereignty in practice when vital interests were involved and that the guarantees of collective action under Article 10 therefore offered only an illusory hope of security.

Sen. Henry Cabot Lodge, Republican majority leader, proved successful in uniting Republican senators to insist on several reservations to the treaty, including one that required congressional approval of any obligations undertaken by the League to preserve the territorial integrity or political independence of any other country. Together with a small number of senators in both parties irreconcilably opposed to the treaty, well over one-third of the Senate was prepared to reject the Versailles accord without significant reservations. Wilson opposed these reservations, however, and succeeded in persuading most Democratic senators not to desert him to join the Republican majority. The LEP itself split on the question of reservations and proved ineffective in influencing the debate. Thus, the treaty both with and without reservations failed to win even a majority, let alone the required two-thirds, vote in the

Senate in late 1919, and the treaty with reservations again fell seven votes short in March 1920. In the end, Wilson believed, it was better that the United States did not join the League of Nations if it was unwilling to make major commitments to it.

PEACE INITIATIVES IN THE 1920s AND 1930s

The enormous material destruction and human carnage of the world war created widespread public interest in new peace initiatives. The main manifestation of this interest was the rising insistence on disarmament. One of Wilson's Fourteen Points had called for limitation of armaments, and he believed that the League of Nations would provide the security nations required before they would consider reductions in armaments.

The defeat of the Versailles Treaty in the United States increased pressures on the incoming Harding administration for a larger U.S. navy; but Sen. William E. Borah (R-Idaho) introduced a joint resolution urging the new President to convene an international disarmament conference. Hearings on Borah's initiative attracted broad public support. Partly in response to this popular sentiment but also because of the new administration's fiscal conservatism and Secretary of State Charles Evans Hughes's perception of the other major powers' aversion to a costly arms race, Harding invited the major powers to attend the Washington Conference of 1921–1922.

In a dramatic address to the opening session of the conference, Hughes proposed that the United States, Britain, and Japan stop construction on many of their battleships and battle cruisers and scrap others. With his speech, one pundit commented, "Hughes sank in thirty-five minutes more ships than all the admirals of the world have sunk in a cycle of centuries."

Actually, Hughes's proposals were more calculated than utopian. Because the Americans' "Black Chamber" intelligence operation had broken the Japanese code, he knew in advance what naval reductions the Japanese delegates would accept, and the American negotiators worked them down to that level. In return for its smaller naval ratio, Japan demanded security, and Hughes accepted no further fortifications for the U.S. possessions of Guam, the Aleutian Islands, Samoa, and the Philippines. Because Congress was unwilling to authorize funds for the improvement of U.S. defenses in the western Pacific, Hughes gave up nothing that the United States was not prepared to sacrifice in any event. For this concession Hughes won agreement for the Washington Five-Power Treaty that established a ten-year "naval holiday" on the construction of new battleships and aircraft carriers. It also provided limits for their total tonnage until 1936 according to a ratio of 5 (United States and Great Britain), 3 (Japan), and 1.7 (France and Italy), though the latter two were allowed a slightly higher ratio for carriers. The treaty was the first time major powers had agreed voluntarily to arms reductions.

The United States also promoted a ban on chemical warfare. At the 1899 Hague Peace Conference, the U.S. delegation alone had voted against a convention prohibiting the use of asphyxiating gases. This convention had been violated during the world war and prompted demands for its reaffirmation. The peace treaties after the war forbade Germany and its allies from manufacturing or importing poisonous gases, and at the Washington conference the United States unsuccessfully called for a convention on the nonuse of asphyxiating gases.

The Coolidge administration advanced a similar initiative at a conference on arms trafficking. The resulting Geneva Protocol of 1925 reiterated the ban on the use of chemical weapons and added one for bacteriological weapons. Although the United States signed the protocol, fierce lobbying against it caused the Senate to defer its consent. It soon entered into force without U.S. ratification, which did not occur until a half-century later.

Coolidge also supported disarmament. In 1927 he invited nations to a disarmament conference in Geneva to stop an impending naval race by extending the 5:5:3 tonnage ratios for capital ships to the remaining classes of "auxiliary" warships: cruisers, destroyers and torpedo-boats, and submarines. Britain and Japan accepted, but France and Italy refused to participate.

The Geneva conference failed mainly because of Anglo-American disagreements. Naval officers and technical experts who were more interested in their own nation's naval prowess than in disarmament strongly influenced both delegations. Moreover, unwilling to adjust to its declining power after the war, the British adopted a tough negotiating position.

President Herbert Hoover persisted by cooperating with British leaders in advancing far-reaching proposals at a disarmament conference in London. The resulting London Naval Agreement of 1930 extended the "naval holiday" on construction of capital ships to 1936 and provided for the same naval ratios to all categories of vessels not covered under the Washington treaty, except for equality in submarines.

The Washington and London treaties were the only significant accords providing for real disarmament, as opposed to management of the arms race, until the Intermediate-range Nuclear Forces Treaty (INF) of 1987.

The London agreement almost immediately began to unravel, however. France refused to sign the treaty because Britain and the United States had rejected agreements guaranteeing French security; and with France opposed, Italy also refused to sign. Japan wanted a higher naval ratio and was disappointed with the treaty, which strengthened Japanese extremists and precipitated domestic violence, including the assassination of the prime minister and the fall of the government.

In 1932, fifty-nine nations, including the Soviet Union and Germany, sent delegations to a world disarmament conference in Geneva called by the League of Nations to negotiate major limitations on land as well as naval armaments. Seven years in the making, the conference might have succeeded in 1930 or early 1931, but Japan's military incursion into Manchuria from 1931 to 1933 seriously undermined hopes for further disarmament. Moreover, France again insisted on security pacts with Britain and the United States as the price for its support. Britain refused, and, more removed from European embroilments, the consistent American position was that security would come not from defense pacts but from disarmament. Hoover proposed a one-third reduction in all "offensive" armaments, but the conference failed to reach any agreement. When it adjourned in the summer of 1933, Hitler, now in power, had already announced that Germany would disregard the armament restrictions imposed on Germany in the Versailles Treaty.

The Washington and London treaties expired in 1936 after Japan gave notice that it would no longer comply with them. A second London Naval Treaty in 1936 retained or reduced limits for the size and firepower of individual capital ships but did not stop new naval construction, which quickly accelerated.

All American peace advocates strongly supported disarmament after World War I. In April 1931, for instance, twenty-eight peace organizations formed the Interorganization Council on Disarmament to lobby for disarmament at the White House, Congress, and the State Department, hold demonstrations, and send observers to the world disarmament conference. But the disparate groups could not agree on a broader program; and as the campaign for disarmament faltered, the peace coalition became increasingly irrelevant and dissolved in early 1933.

Far from unified in the interwar years, the peace movement took three distinctive approaches to war prevention: legalist, functionalist, and reformist. The Carnegie Endowment for International Peace, the American Society of International Law, and the American Peace Society championed the conservative legalist position, which advocated American membership in the World Court but not the League of Nations. The Harding and Coolidge administrations supported U.S. adherence to the Court. But because isolationists and other opponents of collective security believed that internationalists' promotion of U.S. adherence to the Court was part of a larger strategy to get the nation to join the League of Nations, they also proposed reservations stating that even with membership in the Court the United States would assume no obligations under the League Covenant.

The functionalists also wanted the United States to join the Court but felt, correctly, that emphasis on the codification of international law and judicial decisions was inadequate for war prevention. Through such groups as the Foreign Policy Association and the League of Nations Association (LNA), its leaders—Columbia University history professor James T. Shotwell, the prominent lawyer Raymond B. Fosdick, and other members of the eastern establishment—promoted American membership in the League of Nations. These internationalists considered peace to be a problem of social engineering and believed that the League provided the institutional basis for managerial control over foreign affairs. They had almost no organizational roots outside the Northeast, and when they ventured into the American heartland, they reported widespread apathy toward foreign affairs. More likely, the public was confused or uncertain about America's role in the world, but the internationalists' elitist perspective restricted their ability to develop much rapport with the ordinary citizenry.

The reformists were mostly liberal pacifists who shared the legalists' faith in law, but unlike the lawyers they viewed its strength not in its sanction for order but as a vehicle for social and political change. Just as piracy, dueling, slavery, and the saloon had been outlawed, they argued, so could war. The newly founded Women's Peace Union even proposed a constitutional amendment that would make war for any purpose illegal. Pacifist reformers also established a number of other new peace groups after the world war, including the Women's International League for Peace and Freedom (WILPF, the U.S. section absorbed the Woman's Peace Party), National Council for the Limitation of Armaments, and National Council for Prevention of War.

The most prominent nonpacifist spokesman for the outlawry of war idea in the 1920s was Salmon O. Levinson, a wealthy Chicago lawyer, who personally financed the movement. In branding war a crime, outlawry suggested collective action by law-abiding states against lawbreakers, but Levinson opposed the League of Nations and international sanctions. In supporting America's traditional freedom of action in foreign affairs, he won for his outlawry of war idea broad support from antiwar progressive reformers and anti-League senators, and in 1923 he persuaded Senator Borah to introduce a resolution calling upon nations to outlaw war.

Outlawry received a boost in April 1927 when French Foreign Minister Aristide Briand proposed a bilateral treaty with the United States which would renounce war as an instrument of national policy and settle all disputes by pacific means. Suspicious that such an accord would amount to a negative military alliance committing the United States to the security of France against Germany, Secretary of State Frank Kellogg balked at a bilateral arrangement. Well aware of the strong support for the measure, however, he intimated that he would sign the accord if it included other major powers. Under the terms of the resulting multilateral Pact of Paris (or Kellogg-Briand Pact) signed in August 1928, the parties renounced war and agreed to settle all disputes by "pacific means." The treaty also allowed wars for "self-defense," however, and contained no enforcement provisions, and many signatory states attached unilateral reservations or interpretations. But because of the popular enthusiasm for peace as well as the treaty's innocuous and general provisions, the Kellogg-Briand Pact breezed through the U.S. Senate, and soon more than sixty nations had agreed to it.

Meanwhile, in January 1926, the Senate voted 76–17 to join the World Court, but it added five "reservations and understandings," the last of which would have prevented the Court from making advisory opinions involving the United States without the advance consent of two-thirds of the Senate in each case. Though the advisory opinions would have no legal force, Court opponents argued that such opinions—on questions involving the Monroe Doctrine, high tariffs, immigration restriction, and war debts, for example—would be embarrassing. The members of the World Court refused to accept that reservation, however, and subsequent efforts at compromise failed.

When the Roosevelt administration revived the

World Court issue in January 1935, the Senate again added the fifth reservation on advisory opinions. Although this time Roosevelt and Senate proponents of the Court defeated attempts to require Senate approval of each proposed advisory opinion, their victory was illusory. Irish Americans and the popular "radio priest" Father Charles E. Coughlin were joined by powerful isolationists senators Hiram Johnson (R-Calif.), Gerald P. Nye (R-N.D.), Arthur Vandenberg (R-Mich.), George W. Norris (R-Nebr.), and Borah in condemning U.S. adherence to the Court, and the agreement failed 52–36, or seven votes short of the required two-thirds majority.

In retrospect, the defeat of the World Court in 1935 can be seen as a significant barometer of the rising American mood of noninvolvement in political and military commitments. The Court itself was only a very modest internationalist effort, but its defeat revealed the real weakness of internationalism. Isolationism was deeply ingrained in the American tradition but for several reasons it increased in intensity in the early 1930s. For one thing, the rising threats of war or actual war in Europe and Asia strengthened Americans' aversion to foreign involvement. For another, with the deepening Great Depression Americans focused inward on domestic problems; interest in foreign affairs seemed almost a luxury by comparison. Public opinion polls in the mid-1930s, however unsophisticated, consistently showed that jobs, business prosperity, and taxes were the most important issues to Americans. In consequence, those Americans who wanted their government actively to support collective efforts against the aggressor states made little headway. In 1935, for example, LNA director Clark Eichelberger joined the National Peace Conference, an umbrella coalition of peace and internationalist groups, in hopes of gaining support among the participating pacifist organizations for collective security; but finding the pacifists firmly in control of the coalition and committed to keeping the nation out of war at any cost, he soon resigned.

Moreover, the conventional view of America's high-minded reasons for intervening in World War I had given way to revisionist arguments that America's entry had been brought about by Allied pressures and the machinations of brokers, bankers, and businessmen who had unwisely tied the cause of the United States to the benefit of Britain and France. As the world moved closer to war in the 1930s, many more Americans came to believe that World War I had been a futile, tragic conflict, which had not made the world safe for democracy or ended the threat of

Senator Gerald P. Nye. PRINTS AND PHOTOGRAPHS DIVISION, LIBRARY OF CONGRESS

war, and that all modern wars would be the same. Pacifist writers like Kirby Page and Sherwood Eddy as well as revisionist historians popularized these themes in books and articles.

How could pacifists who were internationalist, even transnationalist, in their thinking become leading spokesmen for isolationism in the 1930s? Actually, at first many pacifists had publicly condemned Japan's invasion of Manchuria and had urged the United States and the League of Nations to impose economic sanctions on Japan. They understood the differences between totalitarian states and the Western democracies and identified with the victims of fascist aggression in Manchuria and later in Ethiopia and Spain.

But they also believed that power politics and economic interests motivated Western nations. In their view the victors had humiliated Germany in 1919 and made it a have-not nation, and the present struggle was a continuation of the conflict between the haves and have-nots. Given their perspective and their perception of the League's and American public's unwillingness to support collective action, many American pacifists retreated to a neutralist stance as an alternative to war.

In their search for scapegoats for American involvement in the world war, peace activists accused greedy, prowar businessmen, particularly the munitions makers and bankers. Dorothy Detzer, WILPF executive secretary, persuaded Senator Nye to head a special committee to investigate the organizations engaged in arms manufacturing or trafficking. The Nye Committee held extensive hearings from 1934 to 1936. While unable to substantiate charges of influencing the decision for U.S. military intervention in 1917, it publicized the abuses of the armaments industry and popularized the image of "merchants of death" and the rising isolationist temper in the nation.

Pacifists found willing allies among progressive-pacifist members of Congress. Drawn almost entirely from the midwestern and Plains states, these isolationist congressmen were sympathetic to the antiwar movement and the conspiratorial view of the role of eastern bankers and businessmen in war causation. In trying to keep the nation out of another world war, they were prepared to relinquish America's traditional neutral rights. They did so by sponsoring the successful strict neutrality legislation from 1935 to 1937 that imposed bans on arms sales and loans to all belligerents, prohibited other trade with them unless the goods were paid for and transported by the purchaser, and made it unlawful for Americans to travel on belligerent ships. Actively supported by pacifist groups, isolationists also revived the war referendum idea when Rep. Louis Ludlow (D-Ind.) proposed a constitutional amendment stating that except for attack or invasion any declaration of war by Congress would not take effect until confirmed by a nationwide popular vote. In January 1938 the amendment narrowly failed in the House, 188–209.

President Roosevelt privately criticized the pacifists' "wild-eyed measures to keep us out of war" but was reluctant to alienate isolationist members of Congress whose strength was formidable and whose support he needed for his domestic programs. He acquiesced in the neutrality laws, which gave him discretionary authority to invoke them, and he only belatedly opposed the Ludlow Amendment. As Axis aggression escalated, Roosevelt became more outspoken in favor of U.S. support for the Western democracies. As late as August 1941, however, he stayed in the background on the debate over extension of the draft law of 1940, which passed the House by only a one-vote margin.

Support for strict American neutrality eroded from 1938 to 1941 partly because of the continued totalitarian belligerency, which steadily discredited the pacifists' assumption that moral issues, while significant, did not warrant an active U.S. diplomacy.

Just as important for the decline of the isolationist coalition, however, were the inherent weaknesses in it. The progressive-pacifist noninterventionists drew support from right-wing nationalists, who opposed collective actions with the League and the Western democracies and insisted upon U.S. freedom of action to defend U.S. interests. In the mid-1930s the combination of pacifism and unilateralism seemed logical; entanglements and war seemed virtually synonymous terms. But the two were in fact incompatible as long-term foreign policy strategies because on the question of peace or war pacifism sacrificed freedom of action by always choosing peace over the risks of a foreign policy that might bring war, while the nationalists insisted on freedom of choice. Pacifists' attempts at cooperation with the nationalistic America First Committee in 1940–1941, which contained neofascist and anti-Semitic elements, further undermined the capacity of pacifists to present a united front. Thus, to the already eclipsed peace movement, Pearl Harbor, despite its shock, was almost an anticlimax.

PACIFISTS IN WARTIME, 1941–1945

Under the provisions of the Selective Training and Service Act (1940), conscientious objector status was given to anyone "who, by reason of religious training and belief, is conscientiously opposed to participation in war in any form." This definition covered all religious pacifists but still excluded nonreligious objectors. In reality, the local Selective Service boards interpeted the provisions, and practice varied from place to place. The total number of conscientious objectors (COs) in World War II was nearly 43,000, or .42 percent of those drafted. Curiously, this percentage was three times higher than that for World War I, although there had been much more vocal opposition to the earlier conflict. Perhaps because the nation had already experienced COs in the first war and because the second was so overwhelmingly popular, the government and the general public were more inclined to tolerate war opponents. Even with their somewhat larger numbers, however, COs in World War II still constituted a tiny minority, had no effect on the war effort, and felt isolated. (See table 1.)

Of the COs, more than 25,000 conscientious objectors served in the military as noncombatants during the war years. Another 12,000 joined Civilian Public Service camps, which were overseen by the Selective Service Administration and financed by the War Resisters League, Fellowship of Reconciliation (FOR), other pacifist groups, and churches. The purpose of the camps was fair enough: to provide useful alternative service for pacifists in forestry work, public hospitals, road construction, volunteers for

Table 1.   EXEMPTION RATES FOR
CONSCIENTIOUS OBJECTORS IN THE
UNITED STATES IN THE TWO WORLD
WARS AND DURING THE VIETNAM WAR

War or Year	Ratio of CO Exemptions to Actual Inductions, per 100 Inductions
World War I	0.14
World War II	0.15
1966	6.10
1967	8.10
1968	8.50
1969	13.45
1970	25.55
1971	42.62
1972	130.72
1973	73.30

SOURCES: Table reprinted from *The New Conscientious Objector: From Sacred to Secular Resistance*, edited by Charles C. Moskos and John Whiteclay Chambers (Oxford University Press, 1993), p. 42. Ratios compiled by Stephen M. Kohn, *Jailed for Peace: The History of American Draft Law Violators, 1658–1985* (1986), p. 93, Copyright © 1986, 1987 by Stephen M. Kohn, Praeger Publishers, an imprint of Greenwood Publishing Group, Inc., Westport, Conn. Reprinted with permission.

medical experiments, and other projects unrelated to the war. It would have been difficult in wartime to try to balance the public's demands for national security and the pacifists' insistence on personal liberty and conscience, but the Civilian Public Service encountered problems from the start. The participants received no compensation, and many pacifists found the work demeaning. To make the situation worse, the military assumed increasing control over the camps, which further alienated the pacifists.

In addition, by 1945 some 6,000 absolutists, almost three-fourths of whom were Jehovah's Witnesses, were serving terms in prison or were out on parole under restrictions imposed by the Department of Justice. Almost all of them were subject to severe civil and political disabilities.

In response to increasing public demands for amnesty, President Truman finally appointed an amnesty board to make recommendations for executive clemency for those convicted of violating the draft. Guided by the recommendations of this board, Truman selectively pardoned about 3,000 of the 15,805 who had been convicted under the draft law. The board labeled about 10,000 of the larger total "willful violators," meaning all nonreligious objectors and draft evaders. As during World War I, many more draft dodgers, perhaps nearly 350,000 according to a government figure, were not caught. This large number made no distinction between the many tech-

nical violations (e.g., filling out forms incorrectly) and outright desertion. In any case, the figure constituted a proportional decline from World War I evaders, because the number of inductees in World War II more than tripled, while the number of dodgers only doubled.

FOUNDING OF THE UNITED NATIONS

Meanwhile, ardent internationalists worked assiduously to create a new world organization after the war. The failure of the democracies to act collectively to stop fascist aggression strongly pointed to the need for a new authoritative body to preserve world peace after the war. The United Nations Association (successor to the defunct League of Nations Association), the Commission to Study the Organization of Peace, and the Commission to Study the Bases of a Just and Durable Peace, a study group composed of Protestant ministers and laymen, were a few of the more influential new internationalist societies founded during the late 1930s and early 1940s. Along with other surviving internationalist groups, they emphasized the necessity of world organization for war prevention. Vice President Henry A. Wallace and Under Secretary of State Sumner Welles were administration advocates of internationalism, while Wendell Willkie, Roosevelt's Republican opponent in 1940, eloquently expressed this ideal in his best-selling book, *One World* (1943).

Despite the groundswell of support for a world organization, the politicians remained cautious. In 1943, for instance, the Republican party and a Senate resolution sponsored by Tom Connally (D-Tex.) endorsed American participation in a postwar cooperative world body to prevent aggression but were vague on the important issue of the use of force to maintain the peace.

Ultimately, Allied leaders Roosevelt, Churchill, and Stalin had to negotiate the question of a postwar world organization. Roosevelt's credentials as a champion of internationalism were shaky, to say the least. While he had supported the League of Nations, he was flexible and ready to accept reservations. In the interwar years he had drifted away from support for collective security, and during the 1932 presidential campaign he opposed U.S. membership in the League. During the war he enunciated the "Four Policemen" concept, which would have required the United States, the Soviet Union, Britain, and China rather than a more broadly representative international police force to maintain the peace after the war.

While agreeing on the need for a new world

body, the members of the Grand Alliance had to deal with concrete issues relating to its scope and powers. One question was what nations would be initially represented in both the Security Council and the General Assembly. At the Dumbarton Oaks conference in Washington in 1944, Allied delegates agreed on an assembly of all member states, an eleven-seat security council with five permanent members (including France), an Economic and Social Council, and an International Court of Justice to succeed the Permanent Court of International Justice.

A second crucial question was what voting procedures would be followed in the Security Council. At the Yalta Conference in early 1945, the three Allied leaders accepted a formula allowing only the permanent five member nations on the Security Council—the United States, Soviet Union, Britain, France, and China—to veto enforcement decisions, but not procedural matters.

The question of what constituted procedural matters was not resolved until the San Francisco Conference in April–May 1945. Determined to avoid Woodrow Wilson's mistakes, Roosevelt had appointed a bipartisan delegation to the conference, which included the senior Republican senator Arthur Vandenberg (R-Mich.), a recent convert to internationalism. Roosevelt died a few weeks before the opening of the conference, but Truman's first major decision as president was to go forward with it. At San Francisco small nations, fearing limitations of discussion of important issues in the Security Council, raised questions about the Yalta formula. When the Soviet delegation argued that a great power veto could also be used to prevent discussion of disputes, the United States objected, and Truman, reminding Stalin of the Yalta formula, successfully appealed to the Soviet leader to drop insistence on an absolute veto. Because the Big Five refused to give up the right to veto recommendations for the peaceful resolution of disputes, small nations remained dissatisfied. U.S. leaders realized, however, that the veto also served to protect their own nation's vital interests. As Vandenberg wrote in his diary, "the irony of the situation, is that the greater the extent of the 'veto,' the more impossible it becomes for the new League to involve America in anything against our own will."

Despite much idealistic rhetoric in favor of an authoritative United Nations, the new body was a modest internationalist undertaking. Besides the veto, other features of the UN Charter revealed the predominance of the great powers' national interests. It created an ambiguous trusteeship system that paid lip service to eventual self-government of colonial peoples but did not dismember the British and French empires and gave the United States control over Japanese possessions in the western Pacific. Moreover, in permitting individual and collective acts of self-defense, the United Nations preserved the Monroe Doctrine, allowed for regional pacts, and exempted domestic questions like immigration restriction and the tariff from UN jurisdiction. With these safeguards, the U.S. Senate consented to the UN Charter without reservations in late July 1945 by a vote of 89–2, only nine days before the dropping of the first atomic bomb on Hiroshima.

The United Nations was in fact a creature of big power politics and was based on the assumption of continuing harmony among the major nations. Stalin's main concern was a Soviet veto in the Security Council to protect Soviet interests. Once he got it, he was willing to compromise on other details, such as scaling back his earlier demands for sixteen votes in the General Assembly to three.

NUCLEAR PACIFISM AND THE COLD WAR

Articles in the UN Charter directed the Security Council and General Assembly to draw up disarmament plans and recommend principles governing the regulation of armaments. The General Assembly created the UN Atomic Energy Commission to serve as a clearing house for the exchange of information on peaceful uses of atomic energy and to develop plans for atomic disarmament.

Debate in the new commission first focused on a U.S. proposal for international control of atomic energy, which U.S. delegate Bernard Baruch put forward in 1946. Superficially, the Baruch plan seemed bold and generous. The United States was prepared to give up its atomic monopoly, destroy or dispose of its atomic stocks, and turn over atomic secrets to an international atomic control authority. But it also provided for a step-by-step internationalization, with no time limit on each stage, and only at the very end would the United States give up its atomic monopoly. The Baruch plan went further in proposing that no nation would have a veto power in the proposed atomic control agency or in enforcement decisions in the Security Council against violators.

The Soviets objected to elimination of their right to veto proposed sanctions or punishment and countered by urging immediate cessation of the production of atomic weapons, which would precede control measures. Enforcement would come through the Security Council where the big powers' veto favored the Soviet Union. Perhaps to make their proposal more acceptable, the Soviets conceded that controls and sanctions could be developed by majority decision in the commission.

Because even the most pessimistic American estimates indicated that the Soviets could not develop an atomic bomb for another three to five years, probing of the Soviets' offer would have done no immediate harm to U.S. security. But Baruch, with Truman's approval, took no chances and rejected the Soviet proposition. A. J. Muste, whose well-developed radical nonviolent views made him known to the Cold War generation as "Mr. Pacifist," noted agreement of the two sides on one point: "Both say to the other 'I don't trust you and will not take any chances, but I ask you to trust me and take the chances which that involves.' " With the escalating Cold War tensions during the remainder of the Truman presidency, the hopes for arms control treaties faded.

Implicit in the Baruch plan were certain basic principles that would underlay all future U.S. arms control initiatives during the Cold War. The first was that arms control was subordinate to national security policy. During the 1920s and 1930s the United States had promoted disarmament as an end in itself, but in the less secure nuclear world arms limitation proposals became only a means to an end and had to be weighed against their effects on U.S. worldwide security interests.

Second, arms control accords had to include strict verification procedures to ensure compliance. Again, the interwar disarmament treaties contained no formal inspection requirements; but because of pervasive mistrust of the Soviet Union's intentions during the Cold War, the United States required inclusion of ongoing verification in arms control accords. A related principle was greater openness. From the U.S. perspective, Soviet secrecy resulted in uncertainty and fear of war. Thus the Americans consistently advocated more candor in disclosing the nature, size, and deployment of military forces. Such openness would reduce the fear of war from miscalculation. Finally, with the formation of regional alliances like the North Atlantic Treaty Organization (NATO), the United States treated its security as indivisible from that of its friends, and arms control accords could not compromise allied security.

The incredible destructive force of the atomic bombs dropped on Hiroshima and Nagasaki resulted in the formation of a new peace movement that came to be known as "nuclear pacifism." This antinuclear movement persisted throughout the Cold War era, rising and declining in rough proportion to the per-

ceived threat of nuclear annihiliation. The dangers to civilization became more real following the Soviet Union's successful test of an atomic bomb in 1949 and the prospect of the proliferation of these weapons to other nations. Even before these events, a concerted movement to abolish nuclear weapons was spearheaded by the older liberal pacifist and internationalist groups, especially the FOR, AFSC, and WILPF, which were joined by two new ones, the Federation of American Scientists (FAS) and the United World Federalists (UWF).

Many Americans turned to the UWF, which campaigned for the establishment of some form of supranational government as the only alternative to the end of humanity in a third world war. Formally organized by the writer-editor Norman Cousins, the war hero and author Cord Meyer, Jr., the New York lawyer Grenville Clark, and others in 1947, the UWF within two years had enrolled 45,000 members in more than 700 chapters.

In the 1950s, however, support for the movement fell off markedly. Part of the decline was internal. The UWF's position on the United Nations, for instance, was never clear, with some wanting to strengthen the organization as the embryonic world government while others, seeing it as a creature of entrenched nation-state interests, wanted to start anew. Moreover, most were pragmatic liberals who, in the face of ultranationalist critics, compromised their principles by excluding Communists from their supposedly universalist organization and by increasingly supporting the U.S. government's policy of containing Soviet power. Meyer even resigned from the UWF to join the Central Intelligence Agency.

More important in the UWF's decline, however, was the escalating Cold War, and many lost interest in the cause when it became clear that world government required a global consensus, which was not remotely possible in a polarized world. Henceforth world federalism became more academic, focusing particularly on the influential book by Grenville Clark and Louis B. Sohn, *World Peace through World Law* (1958), which proposed a series of specific steps for transforming the United Nations into a genuinely authoritative world body.

Founded in 1946, the FAS was composed primarily of scientists, many of whom had helped develop the atomic bomb, and concerned laymen who were shocked by the horrific effects of atomic weapons and worried about their proliferation. Its early leaders included Albert Einstein, Hans Bethe, Leo Szilard, and Linus Pauling. The bomb convinced them that scientists had a moral responsibility to prevent another war.

The FAS carried weight beyond its modest membership because of the high prestige of its leaders. Moreover, the FAS was closely linked to the influential journal *Bulletin of the Atomic Scientists*, whose readership extended beyond the scientific community.

Scientific opinion was not united, however. Edward Teller and other physicists, some of whom were associated with the atomic weapons laboratories, believed the Soviet menace was real and lasting and that the United States had to be prepared to develop more and larger weapons. As the Cold War intensified, the influence of these hardliners grew, and in early 1950 President Truman decided to develop the H-bomb. The sharp cleavage in the scientific community persisted, and President Eisenhower noted in 1957 that "some of the mutual antagonisms among the scientists are so bitter as to make their working together almost an impossibility."

Continued atmospheric nuclear testing by both sides served as the catalyst in a second wave of antinuclear activity. The two new groups in 1957, the Committee for Non-Violent Action (CNVA) and the National Committee for a Sane Nuclear Policy (SANE), which led this movement, were deliberately complementary. While Muste, Lawrence Scott, and others formed CNVA to engage in Gandhian nonviolent direct action tactics, including demonstrations at American testing sites, SANE, initially led by Cousins, Homer Jack, and AFSC secretary Clarence Pickett, organized an educational campaign against nuclear testing.

For the next thirty-five years SANE was arguably the most consistently influential American peace organization. In its first years it focused on the deleterious effects of nuclear testing on human health and in fueling the arms race. For publicity it held peace rallies and published full-page advertisements in major metropolitan newspapers. The latter often cited the mounting scientific evidence that the fallout from atmospheric nuclear tests contained the radioactive substances iodine 131 and strontium 90, which were taken up by cows and ended up in milk. These substances in milk would cause unborn children to be born dead or be much more likely to die of leukemia or cancer.

To be sure, SANE experienced problems, such as the alienation of many radical pacifists in 1960 when a majority of its executive committee required chapters to discourage leadership by pro-Soviet sympathizers. But overall SANE, benefiting from the mounting apprehensions among Americans over the dangers of nuclear testing and war, grew phenomenally to 150 chapters. Its advertisements were signed by prominent scientists, intellectuals, and entertainers, and it won the active support of Dr. Benjamin Spock, Martin Luther King, Jr., and Norman Thomas, among others.

ARMS CONTROL FROM EISENHOWER TO JOHNSON

Eisenhower perceived the growing fears of the arms race in general and nuclear testing in particular. He said in 1955, "the people of the world are thoroughly scared of the implications of nuclear war," and four years later he added, "I think that people want peace so much that one of these days governments had better get out of their way and let them have it."

Eisenhower made arms control a high priority of his administration. He had personally experienced the totality of the Second World War and was deeply committed to preventing another major conflict. He also realized that the arms race, if unchecked, could produce disastrous economic consequences. A staunch fiscal conservative, he believed that an overburdened military budget would undermine the nation's health and in the long run erode its ability to preserve its security.

Perhaps most important, however, was the news of the Soviet Union's successful test of a hydrogen bomb in August 1953, less than a year after the U.S. first test of a thermonuclear weapon. Eisenhower correctly perceived that Soviet air power and its growing stockpile of H-bombs would soon make the United States vulnerable to massive surprise attack, and he was convinced that in a nuclear war American casualties, even in a single attack and with advance warning, might number close to 100 million. His disarmament initiatives were efforts to reduce the numbers of nuclear weapons and the prospects of a Soviet knock-out blow.

Following Stalin's death in March 1953 and the end of the Korean War, Eisenhower launched several arms control initiatives that were designed to foster détente with the new Soviet leadership. First, in late 1953 he announced his "atoms for peace" plan in which the U.S. and Soviet governments would donate fissionable materials to an international agency with safeguards for the peaceful development of nuclear power. The diversion of these materials from military to civilian uses, he hoped, would end the nuclear arms race. Then at the four-power Geneva summit in July 1955, he unveiled his "open skies" proposal, which called for mutual aerial reconnaissance of Soviet and U.S. military installations and the exchange of blueprints of them.

He also appointed Harold Stassen, a liberal Republican, to a newly created position to develop arms control proposals, and he supported Stassen's subsequent efforts to forge a new U.S. disarmament negotiating position. Eisenhower and Stassen also wanted a nuclear test ban with the Soviet Union. Failing formal agreement, Eisenhower announced a moratorium on testing in late 1958, and the Soviets for a time reciprocated.

Despite these initiatives the Eisenhower presidency achieved no major arms control agreements with the Soviet Union. The one possible exception, the multilateral Antarctic treaty (1959), which banned all military measures from that continent, was hardly a big breakthrough. The numbers of nuclear weapons in the U.S. and Soviet arsenals actually increased markedly during his presidency. Ironically, his administration contributed to the influence of the military-industrial complex against which he so eloquently warned in his farewell address of January 1961.

Soviet intransigence may help to explain the absence of substantive progress on arms control. Despite Nikita Khrushchev's rhetoric of "peaceful coexistence," it may be that the Kremlin was uninterested in arms control agreements and was stalling until it had gained parity or superiority in nuclear weaponry. Soviet officials probably perceived the Eisenhower administration's arms control policies as confused or contradictory and thus not worthy of serious negotiation. Some contradictions in the U.S. position are fairly obvious. If Eisenhower really wanted détente, then why was Secretary of State John Foster Dulles calling for "massive retaliation" with nuclear weapons in the event of a Soviet attack? Moreover, despite his disdain for nuclear weapons, Eisenhower indicated that he might use them, if necessary, in limited wars, and his administration made tactical nuclear weapons for this purpose.

Even Eisenhower's disarmament initiatives were one-sided. Because the United States had considerably more fissile material than the Soviet Union, he knew that under his "atoms for peace" initiative the United States could reduce its atomic stockpile by two or three times the amounts of the Russians and still improve U.S. security. Although "open skies" would have helped to allay the security concerns on both sides, it probably did not appear as an equitable proposition to the Soviet Union, which had much more military-related information to reveal than the relatively more open United States. Moreover, interagency bickering as well as difficulties in achieving a coordinated position with America's NATO allies delayed agreement on a U.S. negotiating position on a comprehensive arms control initiative until the last years of his second term. Finally, he was inconsistent in authorizing intelligence flights over the Soviet Union, and the downing of a U-2 plane over Soviet territory in May 1960 ended hopes for détente at an East-West summit meeting.

Actually, the incongruity between his professions for peace and disarmament and his actual policies was more apparent than real. Despite his dovish instincts Eisenhower was a Cold Warrior. He believed the Soviet totalitarian government was determined to communize the world. Such suspicions compromised the prospects for far-reaching arms control accords with the Soviet Union. Moreover, Eisenhower craved popular approval. This desire to be liked made him more reluctant to risk hardliners' opposition by advancing bolder, more equitable arms control proposals to the Soviets.

In the long term, Eisenhower's main influence was as an educator. He used his position to try to improve communication with the Soviet Union, which would reduce misunderstanding and possible miscalculation and prepare the way for arms control. In essence, he emphasized confidence-building, which soon became part of the established lexicon of arms controllers.

In speaking about arms limitation, Eisenhower almost always used the word "disarmament," but his policy initiatives, which really tried to slow and manage the escalating arms race, were closer to "arms control." In response to John F. Kennedy's 1960 campaign promise, Congress created the Arms Control and Disarmament Agency (ACDA) in 1961. The use of both terms in the title suggested the lingering tension between the idealistic hopes and more realistic expectations of proponents of arms limitation, but "arms control" increasingly expressed the more modest view of what was possible in the field.

ACDA's mandated functions included the formulation of arms control proposals and policy options for discussion by the other involved department heads leading to eventual decision by the president. In practice, however, ACDA was only one of several players in the formulation of arms control policy, and its actual influence depended on the relationship between the ACDA director and the secretary of state and president. Because some chief executives—Lyndon Johnson and Richard Nixon, for example—paid little attention to the new agency, ACDA's impact was often minimal. By contrast, Paul Warnke, President Carter's ACDA director, had more influence because he was a confidant of Secretary of State

Cyrus Vance and had Carter's respect, but even Warnke's influence was gradually undercut by National Security Adviser Zbigniew Brzezinski, who advocated a much tougher line toward the Soviet Union. ACDA's longer term significance was its expertise in technical, scientific areas, such as the details of verification and inspection procedures.

Kennedy occasionally pursued détente with the Soviets but found the road rough, even rocky at times. When the Soviet Union resumed testing of nuclear weapons in September 1961, Kennedy felt obliged to authorize U.S. tests as well. A year later the Cuban missile crisis threatened to plunge the world into nuclear holocaust, but cooler heads on both sides prevailed.

Second thoughts following the confrontation over Cuba helped to clear the air for Soviet-American relations, and the arms talks made progress. In June 1963 the two sides reached agreement on a direct communications link, or "hot line," to allow the government heads in Moscow and Washington to transmit messages back and forth instantly. Although not an arms limitation measure, it was an important confidence-building step in reducing the chances of miscalculation in crises and possible nuclear war. This agreement was amended in 1971, 1984, and 1988 to add advanced facsimile transmission capabilities.

The sticky issue on testing was inspections, which the U.S. side required to verify compliance but which the Soviet Union resisted as incursions on its sovereignty. Finally, American and British emissaries went to Moscow to deal directly with Khrushchev. Once the parties agreed to narrow the focus to atmospheric nuclear weapons tests, agreement was reached quickly. The resulting Limited Test Ban Treaty (1963) banned tests in the atmosphere, outer space, and underwater but not underground. Because the signatories agreed that modern scientific instruments could easily detect all but underground tests, the treaty provided for no control posts or inspections. Ultimately, more than one hundred nations signed the treaty, but two nuclear powers, France and China, have not adhered to it.

The hopes for a comprehensive test ban proved more elusive. U.S. negotiators insisted that it was not always possible to distinguish between natural seismic shocks and underground nuclear tests, and thus a comprehensive ban required on-site inspections. Continued underground testing facilated the arms race by permitting the modernization of nuclear weapons. U.S. and Soviet negotiating efforts finally resulted in the Threshold Test Ban Treaty in 1974,

which limited underground tests to a yield of 150 kilotons. While the two nations adhered to this limit, neither President Nixon, beleaguered by the Watergate scandal, nor his immediate successors risked submitting it to the Senate for approval, and the Senate's consent and ratification were achieved only in 1990. A companion accord, the Peaceful Nuclear Explosions Treaty (1976), extending the threshold to nontest areas, also was not ratified until 1990.

Lyndon Johnson also pursued arms accords. In 1967 the United States, Britain, and the Soviet Union signed the Outer Space Treaty, which prohibited the sending of objects containing nuclear weapons or weapons of mass destruction around the earth or the stationing of such weapons on the moon, other celestial bodies, or in outer space. In 1960 Eisenhower had proposed an extension of the principles of the Antarctic treaty to outer space. Following the limited test ban accord, the Soviet Union dropped its insistence on tying outer space to other disarmament questions, and agreement became possible. Again, verification was no issue because the parties' space-tracking facilities could monitor unauthorized launchings.

A year later the same three powers signed the Nuclear Non-Proliferation Treaty. The desire to stop the spread of nuclear weapons was in the interest of all the nuclear weapons states, and many nonnuclear states also emphasized nonproliferation as a priority issue in various international forums. Dean Rusk took the lead in this area. Although often depicted as a rather unimaginative secretary of state, he initiated a series of meetings on "nondissemination" with Soviet ambassador Anatoliy Dobrynin as early as 1962. The main stumbling block was the planned multilateral nuclear force which the United States and its NATO allies were considering. The Soviets objected to the nuclear sharing implications of this force which, they claimed, would give West Germany access to or control of nuclear weapons. Despite the Soviet Union's skepticism the two sides finally agreed on a treaty prohibiting the transfer and acquisition of nuclear weapons to nonnuclear states. The Soviets in effect accepted U.S. assurances on the control and use of its weapons in Western Europe, but were successful in adding a provision requiring all nonnuclear parties to negotiate safeguard agreements with the International Atomic Energy Agency, which would verify compliance on the peaceful transfer and uses of nuclear materials and technology.

U.S. diplomats then won approval from their European allies who worried that the treaty would compromise NATO defense arrangements. The Americans argued successfully that it would still permit U.S.-owned and -controlled nuclear weapons on the soil of nonnuclear allies, and would not prevent nonnuclear members from later becoming nuclear weapons states.

The nonnuclear states were unwilling to renounce nuclear weapons unless the nuclear powers agreed to reduce their nuclear stockpiles. The three nuclear powers thus included in the treaty assurances of good faith in negotiating arms reductions. They also agreed to a UN Security Council resolution (France abstained) calling for Security Council actions to assist any nonnuclear state party to the agreement that was the victim of nuclear aggression or threat of aggression. Sixty-two states participated in the signing ceremony in 1968. Today there are more than 150 signatories, including nuclear states France and China, both of which signed in 1992, but some nations believed to have nuclear weapons capabilities—India, Pakistan, and Israel, for example—have not signed.

THE ANTI–VIETNAM WAR MOVEMENT

Besides fear of nuclear annihilation, another root of peace action was war itself, particularly if its methods and purposes seemed immoral. The latter was the case of the Vietnam War, which was increasingly perceived as an unethical and illegal U.S. military incursion. As American involvement in Vietnam escalated in the mid-1960s, the antiwar reaction grew to massive proportions. For many the peace cause became the vehicle for larger changes in American culture. The movement came to include New Left elements—the Students for a Democratic Society, for instance—as well as civil rights activists from the Southern Christian Leadership Conference and the Student Nonviolent Coordinating Committee among others, new religious groups, and hippies and counterculture advocates. It even spurred antiwar sentiment among disenchanted military veterans, many of whom organized the activist Vietnam Veterans Against the War. Active-duty troops marched in antiwar demonstrations, and desertions from the armed forces grew rapidly, totaling more than 90,000 for the years 1968 and 1969. Among government workers, Daniel Ellsberg, a former Defense Department analyst, became a hero of the movement for his release of the *Pentagon Papers* in 1971, which exposed the government's unrelenting pursuit of the war.

The disparate groups cooperated erratically in organizing national demonstrations against the Vietnam War, several of which were the largest in American history. Nearly 100,000 protesters participated in a march on the Pentagon in October 1967, for example, and two years later 500,000 demonstrated against the war in the nation's capital. Profound internecine quarrels in the peace movement developed, however, on the degree to which the energies of the cause should also be redirected toward broader social and political change. Antiwar liberals wanted to focus solely on the war as a policy issue. Perhaps its best expression was the Vietnam Moratorium Committee, which was composed mainly of respectable middle-class citizens and intellectuals. Aimed at "middle America," it was most effective in organizing local rallies and teach-ins at colleges and universities against the war. The more radical elements by contrast perceived the antiwar movement as a vehicle for revolutionary social change. Many of its proponents coalesced in the Mobilization Committee (later the New Mobilization), whose organizing strategy was massive public demonstrations in the nation's capital. Even these diverse coalitions did not work particularly well and soon disintegrated.

There is no clear-cut judgment on the impact of the anti–Vietnam War movement. On the one hand, some observers have claimed that it had virtually no influence on government policy and may even have been counterproductive in its effects on public opinion. While the peace movement emphasized the immorality of the war, most Americans were much more pragmatic and did not identify closely with its ethical appeals. On the other hand, the relentless antiwar protests unquestionably put Johnson and Nixon on the defensive and may have limited their military options, and it made more possible the peace talks with the North Vietnamese and the gradual withdrawal of U.S. troops. Nixon and National Security Adviser Henry Kissinger blamed Congress for the failure in Vietnam but did not acknowledge that Congress was responding to the powerful antiwar movement.

One part of the antiwar effort focused on the issue of military conscription. Some peace groups provided counseling on conscientious objection and other alternatives to military service, and many young men opposed to the war resorted to conscientious objection, draft resistance, avoidance, or evasion. Major draft-card burning ceremonies around the nation became symbolic protests against the war and U.S. militarism. At the end of the war President Ford created a program of conditional clemency for some 131,000 draft resisters and military deserters in return for alternative service, but fewer than 20 percent joined the program. President Carter followed with a grant of blanket amnesty to the countless thousands of draft evaders who had fled to Canada, Sweden, or elsewhere.

FROM THE STRATEGIC ARMS TALKS TO THE END OF THE COLD WAR

Meanwhile, nuclear arms talks continued in spite of the Vietnam conflict. Though other arms accords were negotiated in the 1970s, notably a multilateral Biological Weapons Convention (1972), which banned the development, production, stockpiling, or acquisition of biological agents or toxins, the primary focus throughout the decade was on ballistic missiles. The introduction of these new weapons systems greatly complicated arms control negotiations. For one thing, the Soviet and American systems were asymmetical, with the former concentrating on heavy intercontinental ballistic missiles (ICBMs) and sea-launched missiles (SLBMs) with enormous throw-weights and the latter emphasizing a more balanced array of land- and submarine-based systems and bombers. In addition, the United States decided not to increase the number of its missiles but to develop a system in which many nuclear warheads, known as multiple independently targeted reentry vehicles (MIRVs), could be placed on a single missile and directed to separate targets.

Moreover, the two sides had different views of "strategic," defined as weapons that could reach the other's territory. Because the United States had positioned short- and medium-range missiles and bombers in Western Europe, which could reach the Soviet Union, the Soviets wanted to include them in the strategic talks, while excluding their own shorter range systems which could not reach U.S. soil. The United States, however, refusing to compromise its NATO security commitments, argued that its forward-based systems in Europe countered Soviet short- and medium-range systems and insisted that only intercontinental systems should be covered. The development of defensive antiballistic missile (ABM) systems, which were designed to intercept incoming missiles before they could reach their targets, further complicated the problem. When the Soviets began to deploy an ABM system in 1966, the United States reluctantly followed.

As early as 1964 the United States had proposed bilateral discussions on a possible freeze on strategic nuclear offensive and defensive weaponry, but the Strategic Arms Limitation Talks (SALT), delayed because of the Soviet invasion of Czechoslovakia in 1968, did not begin until the onset of the Nixon presidency. Then it took more than two years of negotiations before the two sides signed two SALT I agreements in May 1972. One was the ABM treaty of unlimited duration, which limited ABM deployments for each power to two areas (later reduced to one) and imposed qualitative and quantitative limits, including prohibitions on the development, testing, or deployment of more advanced ABM technology. The other was the interim agreement on strategic arms for five years, which basically froze the number of ICBM and SLBM launchers. Both agreements provided for assurance of compliance with the provisions by "national technical means" (photoreconnaissance satellites, for example), rather than inspections, and within these limits each nation agreed not to interfere with the other's verification efforts.

As the term "interim" suggested, the SALT I accord on offensive weapons was essentially a holding action until the two sides could reach a more comprehensive accord. This commitment, though clearly stated in the SALT I treaty, resulted only in bilateral acceptance of a framework for the SALT II talks before the Carter administration. Jimmy Carter, genuinely committed to nuclear disarmament, stated in his inaugural address that he wanted "to banish nuclear weapons from the earth," but the Soviet Union was reluctant to make deep cuts in its strategic arsenals. The SALT II treaty (1979) established equal aggregate limits of 2,400 nuclear delivery vehicles (ICBMs, SLBMs, and bombers), with sublimits of 1,320 on MIRVed ballistic missiles and bombers with long-range cruise missiles, 1,200 launchers of MIRVed ballistic missiles, and 820 launchers of MIRVed ICBMs, and banned certain new delivery and weapons systems. Verification again would be by national technical means.

SALT II immediately came under attack by conservatives and Republicans as too accommodating to the Soviet arms buildup and indicative of the softness of the Carter administration on Cold War issues. When the Soviet military invaded Afghanistan in December 1979, Carter withdrew the treaty, which was already in deep trouble, from the Senate, and it was not ratified. For most of the 1980s, however, the Reagan administration agreed with the Soviets to adhere to its provisions.

The Republican attacks on SALT II were part of its broad-scaled campaign to discredit the Carter administration for its pursuit of détente with the Soviet Union. The incoming Reagan administration launched a major rearmament program, which included the development of the new MX missile and a 500-ship navy. Soviet-American relations deteriorated to a low point following the Soviet shootdown of a Korean Airlines plane in 1982 with the loss of many American lives and President Ronald Reagan's depiction of the Soviet Union the following year as the "evil empire." Arms talks likewise got nowhere. Although Reagan came forward with a "zero option" that offered the elimination of U.S. ground-launched cruise and Pershing II missiles if the Soviet Union eliminated its short- and medium-range missiles threatening Western Europe, the Soviets were unwilling to go that far. Indeed, they walked out of the talks in late 1983 in protest against the deployment of the ground-launched missiles in Europe. Reagan's announcement the same year of the Strategic Defense Initiative, which sought to develop a sophisticated defensive system to intercept incoming ballistic missiles, also jeopardized the strategic arms talks. While many knowledgeable observers argued that this "star wars" concept was in violation of the ABM agreement or unworkable, Reagan continued to promote it. His administration also produced periodic reports detailing the Soviets' noncompliance with arms control accords, and Soviet leaders later conceded that one of their radar installations at Krasnoyarsk was in violation of the ABM treaty.

The escalating arms competition produced a third surge of antinuclear activism in the early 1980s. SANE, the Physicians for Social Responsibility, and other established groups cooperated with an activist coalition in favor of an immediate "freeze" on the production and deployment of nuclear weapons on both sides. Randall Forsberg, Helen Caldicott, and other women were prominent in this new movement, which consisted of nearly 9,000 peace and nuclear freeze groups. Moreover, the Catholic bishops issued a pastoral letter calling for a halt in the nuclear arms race. Congress also became restless, and the Reagan administration engaged in a public relations effort to defend the buildup while claiming that it too wanted to curb the arms race.

The impact of the antinuclear movement, then and earlier, was mixed. Far from a mass movement, it surely increased public awareness of the dangers of nuclear weapons. It did not stop the arms race but probably slowed its pace. In the early 1980s freeze resolutions passed in eight out of nine states and the House of Representatives and forced the media and the government to respond to its program. Polling data at the time indicated that public opinion, which had become much more pessimistic about the chances of survival in a nuclear war, rejected higher defense budgets and wanted nuclear disarmament.

The pressures of the nuclear freeze movement did not push the Reagan administration into the arms talks but likely made it willing to begin them earlier. It also toned down its strident rhetoric and adopted more flexible negotiating positions. In order to save the MX even in truncated form from concerted lobbying against it, the administration accepted an agreement with Congress in which it promised a vigorous commitment to the arms talks. Opposition from the scientific community to SDI and arms control proponents in Congress also led to a congressional ban on antisatellite development and testing.

Ironically, the greatest achievements in nuclear disarmament came in the next decade when the peace movement was relatively quiescent. In 1985 the new Soviet leader Mikhail Gorbachev clearly signaled his desire for improved relations, and the bilateral relationship began to improve dramatically. Talks on medium-range and strategic nuclear forces resumed in earnest, and Reagan and Gorbachev held four summits to advance the negotiations. At the Washington summit in December 1987, the two sides signed the Intermediate-range Nuclear Forces (INF) treaty, which eliminated all ground-launched nuclear missiles with a range capability between 300 and 3,400 miles and permitted U.S. and Soviet inspectors to verify compliance on each other's soil. In the following few years, the two sides destroyed more than 2,700 INF missiles in Europe and the Soviet Union. Several supplementary agreements have since clarified details of the INF treaty.

The INF treaty presaged real disarmament in other areas. Among the many subsequent arms-related agreements were the treaty on conventional arms forces in Europe (CFE), the Strategic Arms Treaties (START I and II), and the Chemical Weapons Convention. The multilateral CFE agreement (1990), which reduced and set limits on a large number of conventional weapons from the Atlantic to the Urals, culminated nearly twenty years of intermittent talks. It was complemented two years later by a CFE1A agreement, which set limits on military personnel and by the Treaty on Open Skies. Reminiscent of Eisenhower's rejected initiative thirty-seven years earlier, the Open Skies treaty permits unarmed observation flights over Eurasian and North American soil from Vancouver to Vladivostok to build confidence against military movements and surprise attack. START I (1991) reduces U.S. and former Soviet Union's strategic nuclear delivery systems and their warheads by about one-third, while START II (1993) cuts U.S. and Russian nuclear warheads by another one-third as well as eliminates all heavy ICBMs, regarded as the most destabilizing strategic weapons, and MIRVed ICBMs. START II places limits of 3,000 to 3,500 strategic nuclear warheads for each side. As of early 1994, the Open Skies and START II treaties had not been ratified. (See table 2.)

POST–COLD WAR PROBLEMS AND CHALLENGES

With the end of the Cold War, the fear of nuclear annihilation that had earlier generated urgent peace activity seems to have declined significantly. To be sure, during the Gulf War there were scattered dissenting voices and many demonstrations, but the antiwar movement, consisting of a disparate collection of liberals and socialists, church groups, free market libertarians, and ideological conservatives, was not well organized. Although vaguely reminiscent of the liberal pacifists and isolationist conservatives who formed the anti-interventionist coalition from 1939 to 1941, fifty years later the Left and Right were too far apart to consider common antiwar action.

Moreover, during the 1992 presidential campaign Bush argued that the United States "won" the Cold War because of its "peace through strength" policies, and he castigated the "nuclear freeze" position as a failed alternative. Bill Clinton, elected president in 1992, did not challenge that view, but some peace advocates have responded that unless it was Germany or Japan, which avoided major military commitments, no nation "won" the Cold War and that both the Russian and American people are the losers. Besides a shaky American economy, they assert, the Cold War brought government secrecy and a skewed measurement of national strength in terms of military hardware and technology instead of educational and other non-military achievements. The internal changes in the Soviet Union, they emphasize, resulted less from U.S. external pressures than from indigenous factors, including generational change and the desire to reduce military spending to improve the peoples' standard of living. In addition, the 1986 nuclear accident at Chernobyl probably hastened Russians' disillusionment with nuclear technology. Finally, they give some credit to Gorbachev and other Soviet reformers for their courageous roles in ending the Cold War.

Questions persist, and the so-called "new world order" will remain elusive until they are resolved. A serious issue is the nuclear stockpiles in the republics of the former Soviet Union. Except for Russia, which will retain a nuclear capability, and Ukraine, the other new states have agreed to ship their warheads to Russia and to sign the Non-Proliferation and START agreements. All tactical nuclear warheads were shipped from the other republics to Russia in mid-1992, but other promises have not yet been carried out. In January 1994 Ukraine, Russia, and the United States signed a "swords into plowshares" accord in which over a roughly three-year-period Ukraine's dismantled nuclear warheads would be shipped to Russia where the enriched uranium would be extracted from the warheads and converted to nuclear fuel rods or sold to the United States for the same purposes. Many of those fuel rods would be returned to the Ukraine for use in the nation's civilian nuclear power plants. A nationalistic Ukrainian parliament, which has opposed past international nuclear agreements, still must approve this pact. Given the enormous numbers of weapons and the instability of the new republics, there is also the possibility of the clandestine sale of nuclear weapons to black marketeers and atomic theft by terrorists. If real security is to be achieved, improved and more elaborate verification methods for the destruction and cut-off of fissionable materials will be required.

In any event, even after the completion of the present destruction of warheads containing nuclear weapons as well as the silos containing the missiles, the total number of nuclear weapons worldwide could be as many as 16,000. This is because the START treaties do not cover the nuclear forces of the United Kingdom, France, and China.

The Chemical Weapons Convention (1993) is also at risk. Chemical weapons are relatively cheap and easy to make, and enforcement may be difficult. The challenge inspections permitted under the treaty may entail negotiations to implement in practice. Moreover, the absence of immediate and effective international sanctions in the treaty may hamper its effectiveness. It is also possible that some producers of chemical weapons— Iraq and Libya, for instance— may not sign the accord, and without their adherence it will not cover many of the actual or potential pariahs in the chemical weapons field.

The end of the Cold War also resulted in rising demands for an end to nuclear testing. Truly effective arms control, critics have contended, required curtailing the arms race, and getting control of the technology that testing had fostered was the way to stop it. When Russia and France separately declared moratoriums on testing in 1992 (to last until mid-1993), the pressures for U.S. testing eased. To an appropriations bill passed in the fall of 1992, Congress included a provision to suspend all nuclear tests for nine months followed by strict limits on testing and a total ban by 1997 unless other countries resumed testing.

Table 2.   LANDMARK ARMS CONTROL TREATIES

Title	Year Enacted	Description
Washington Naval Treaty (Five-Power Naval Limitation Treaty)	1922	First treaty to achieve genuine arms reductions. The United States, Great Britain, France, Italy, and Japan agreed to reduce the tonnage of their capital ships (primarily battleships) and to keep these units in strict tonnage ratios to one another.
Kellogg-Briand Pact (Renunciation of War as an Instrument of National Policy)	1928[a]	Pledge to forswear war by the United States, Great Britain and its major dominions, France, Germany, Japan, et al.; typified idealistic interwar arms control.
Arms Control and Disarmament Act	1961	Under congressional impetus, created Arms Control and Disarmament Agency and established formal goals for U.S. arms control policy.
Limited Test Ban Treaty	1963	First treaty affecting nuclear weapons, in which the United States, Great Britain, and the Soviet Union agreed to forgo testing in the atmosphere, outer space, and under water; Senate debate also reflected presidential need to pledge continued strong defense programs to ensure passage.
Nuclear Non-Proliferation Treaty	1968[b]	Banned the spread of nuclear weapons, provided for safeguard arrangements, and ensured nondiscriminatory access to peaceful uses of nuclear energy. Signators included the United States, the Soviet Union, and 60 other nations.
Antiballistic Missile Systems (ABM) Treaty; Strategic Arms Limitation Talks (SALT I, Interim Agreement on Strategic Offensive Arms)	1972	First U.S.-U.S.S.R. arms control agreements under détente, serving to "cap" nuclear arms race quantitatively by limiting deployments of ABM systems, initially to two sites, and setting upper limits on the number of strategic nuclear missile launchers; also led to Jackson amendment, requiring equal levels in future agreements. ABM treaty was also the subject of a constitutional debate between the Reagan administration and the Senate over treaty interpretation as it related to Strategic Defense Initiative (SDI; Star Wars) testing.
SALT II Treaty	1979[c]	Follow-up to SALT I, extending limits to include bombers, and beginning qualitative limits as well; never brought to vote in Senate because of Soviet invasion of Afghanistan, signaling the end of détente.
Intermediate Nuclear Forces (INF) Treaty (Treaty on the Elimination of Intermediate-Range and Shorter-Range Missiles)	1987	First U.S.-U.S.S.R. arms control agreement to eliminate (rather than cap or reduce) an entire class of nuclear weapons systems.
Strategic Arms Reduction Treaty (START)	1991	Perhaps the last of the classic U.S.-U.S.S.R. arms control treaties, negotiated at the end of the Cold War and on the eve of the Soviet collapse, reducing launchers and setting weapons-loading and other qualitative limits. The four nuclear-armed Soviet successor states (Russia, Ukraine, Belarus, and Kazakhstan) undertook to fulfill the same obligations in the Lisbon Protocol (23 May 1992) and the U.S.-Russian-Ukrainian agreement (January 1994).

[a] Year concluded; ratified in 1929.
[b] Year concluded; ratified in 1969.
[c] Year concluded; it was not ratified.
SOURCE: Adapted from *Encyclopedia of the United States Congress* (New York: Simon & Schuster, 1995), p. 98.

In the interim it is expected that the Clinton administration will try to negotiate agreement on a global ban.

Finally, the U.S. government will have to decide what kind of security system it desires in the new world order. Several options are available. Will it continue, for example, to choose to act as the world's policeman and begin to level off the recent scaled-back defense budgets? Or will it decide to promote a cooperative international security system, working through a strengthened United Nations, in which the United States assumes a much smaller portion, perhaps even less than half, of the cost for multilateral peacemaking and peacekeeping activities? The answers to these kinds of questions will have far-reaching implications not just for defense spending but for the future role of disarmament in U.S. policy.

SEE ALSO The National-Security State; The World Wars; Limited Wars; Foreign Policy (all in this volume).

BIBLIOGRAPHY

Broad surveys of the American peace movement include Charles DeBenedetti, *The Peace Reform in American History* (1980); and Charles Chatfield, *The American Peace Movement: Ideals and Activism* (1992). Two collections of articles focusing on organized activities of twentieth-century peace movements are Charles Chatfield, ed., *Peace Movements in America* (1973); and Chatfield and Peter van den Dungen, eds., *Peace Movements and Political Cultures* (1988).

Standard works of the peace movement for selected periods are C. Roland Marchand, *The American Peace Movement and Social Reform, 1898–1918* (1972); Charles Chatfield, *For Peace and Justice: Pacifism in America, 1914–1941* (1971); and Lawrence S. Wittner, *Rebels Against War: The American Peace Movement, 1941–1960* (1969). The role of SANE is covered in Milton S. Katz, *Ban the Bomb: A History of SANE, the Committee for a Sane Nuclear Policy, 1957–1985* (1986). A carefully researched analysis of the impact of opposition to the Vietnam War on government policies is Melvin Small, *Johnson, Nixon, and the Doves* (1988). The most comprehensive treatment of the movement is Charles DeBenedetti, with the assistance of Charles Chatfield, *An American Ordeal: The Antiwar Movement of the Vietnam Era* (1990).

Two workmanlike monographs by Calvin DeArmond Davis, *The United States and the First Hague Peace Conference* (1962), and *The United States and the Second Hague Peace Conference: American Diplomacy and International Organization, 1899–1914* (1976), develop the interrelationships between American internationalists and policymakers before World War I. A broader treatment of American internationalism can be found in Warren F. Kuehl, *Seeking World Order: The United States and International Organization to 1920* (1969). The role of internationalists in the founding of the United Nations is perceptively treated in Robert A. Divine, *Second Chance: The Triumph of Internationalism in America during World War II* (1971).

Two recent books evaluating the influence of the peace movement on government policies during the Cold War are Lawrence S. Wittner, *One World or None: A History of the World Nuclear Disarmament Movement through 1953* (1993); and David Cortright, *Peace Works: The Role of the Peace Movement in Ending the Cold War* (1993). Wittner's volume is the first of a projected trilogy.

Interpretive essays on the ideas and activities of many prominent twentieth-century internationalists and peace advocates appear in two unique reference works, Warren F. Kuehl, ed., *Biographical Dictionary of Internationalists* (1983); and Harold Josephson, ed., *Biographical Dictionary of Modern Peace Leaders* (1985).

There is no comprehensive survey of the U.S. government's arms control policies in the twentieth century. A useful interpretation of naval disarmament in the interwar period is Robert G. Kaufman, *Arms Control in the Pre-Nuclear Era: The United States and Naval Limitation between the Wars* (1990). Glenn T. Seaborg, Chairman of the Atomic Energy Commission from 1961 to 1971, has written two "insider" accounts of U.S. arms control policies in the 1960s, *Kennedy, Khrushchev, and the Test Ban* (1981), and *Stemming the Tide: Arms Control in the Johnson Years* (1987). A collection of the formal treaties still in force is reproduced in U.S. Arms Control and Disarmament Agency, *Arms Control and Disarmament Agreements: Texts and Histories of the Negotiations* (1990 edition), which also provides summary histories of the negotiations leading to each treaty.

FOREIGN POLICY

Melvin Small

When Alexis de Tocqueville visited the United States in the 1830s, he saw much to admire in the unique political system that was barely a half-century old. He expressed concern, however, about the potential for disaster in the way foreign policy had been conducted in the new republic.

> Foreign policies demand scarcely any of those qualities which a democracy possesses; and they require, on the contrary, the perfect use of almost all of those faculties in which it is deficient. . . . It cannot combine measures of secrecy, and it will not await their consequences with patience. . . . [D]emocracies . . . obey the impulse of passion rather than the suggestions of prudence . . . and abandon a mature design for the gratification of a momentary caprice.

Further, Tocqueville did not see ahead to the problem of dual loyalties in a multiethnic nation. At the time that he wrote, most European Americans were of Anglo-Saxon extraction. After massive Irish immigration in the 1840s and 1850s, as well as the arrival of other groups through the decades such as Germans and Jews, hyphenates become an important factor in the determination of certain foreign policies.

Tocqueville was not the first to worry about the abilities of democratic polities to conduct effective foreign policies. Over two thousand years earlier, Thucydides expressed similar concerns about leaders in the Greek city states who permitted domestic political considerations to affect questions of national security. To be sure, such considerations affect leaders in authoritarian societies as well, but they are better able to conduct secret diplomacy than their democratic counterparts. Moreover, they are not compelled to stand for periodic elections during which time often uninformed voters evaluate their foreign policies.

Other governments complain about the lack of continuity in America's foreign relations. Every four or eight years they have to deal with a new president, who has his own programs and different emphases in the international sphere. In addition, because of

the ability of the Senate to reject or amend treaties, those other governments cannot be certain that agreements initialled by the president will be accepted by the senators. Even societies with freely elected parliaments have been spared some of the problems in the American system created by the inherent conflict between an independent executive and an independent legislature, each of which has overlapping, constitutionally prescribed responsibilities in the international arena.

From 1789 through most of the nineteenth century, however, few worried about these difficult—and in many ways unprecedented—problems. The United States, secure behind its oceanic barriers, was not an important player in the Eurocentric international system. Nevertheless, even during its first one hundred years, the unique nation-state became involved in several major foreign crises. In all of them, domestic political considerations figured prominently in the development of strategies to meet external threats.

In the discussion that follows, I look briefly at some celebrated cases of the influence of domestic politics on the foreign policies of the United States during the early years and then turn to the twentieth century for a more detailed analysis. There are those who claim that one domestic variable in particular, the economic needs of the nation-state, explains not just American foreign relations but all nations' foreign relations. Although I discuss a variety of economic issues in my survey, I also examine many other domestic matters. One should bear in mind, however, that they constitute one set of variables among many that help to explain the contours of American foreign policy. As in all countries, rational, self-interested security concerns figure prominently in the decision making much of the time.

Any survey of the relationship between American domestic and foreign politics must be incomplete. Domestic components lurk behind virtually every American interaction in the international system.

Consequently, I will highlight only the most celebrated cases as well as those that illustrate general themes in this issue area.

THE FIRST 125 YEARS

Almost from the start, domestic politics influenced American foreign policies and vice versa. When the emerging Federalist and Democratic-Republican factions adopted opposing positions on the French Revolution in the middle 1790s, some who chose sides did so for partisan reasons. Indeed, the development of the American two-party system itself was affected significantly by this issue. The activities of French agents in the United States, particularly in the election of 1796, contributed to this epochal schism. No doubt James Madison's policies toward England, which led ultimately to the war of 1812, were also shaped by domestic politics, with, for example, the 1812 election weighing heavily upon him as he decided for war in the spring of that year.

Although foreign policies have rarely played the paramount role in elections at any time in American history, they were a factor on occasion in the nineteenth century with each party accusing the other of not being nationalistic enough or of truckling to foreign enemies. In 1844, for instance, when Democratic candidate James Knox Polk's claims to all of the Oregon country up to the 54° 40′ line stirred up jingoistic Americans, his party's campaign rhetoric made it more difficult to accept the reasonable compromise of the 49th parallel, and with some help from a bumbling British envoy, almost led to war with England. Fortunately, even though exaggerated campaign rhetoric could exacerbate international tensions during and after elections, foreign powers learned to discount the rhetorical bellicosity and xenophobia they experienced every four years.

Most of the United States' nineteenth-century conflicts and crises involved Great Britain, often over issues unresolved from the American Revolution. The fisheries question was prominent among them. Seamen from New England periodically broke British laws regulating their limited rights to fish off the coast of British North America. Acting independently of Washington, they were concerned about their livelihood. That understandable but relatively narrow economic concern brought the United States and England to the brink of general war on several occasions and led to moves and countermoves involving other unresolved issues such as disputed boundaries and trade.

The Civil War, the nation's most severe domestic crisis, was intimately related to foreign affairs in many ways. For example, in April 1861, at the start of the war, Secretary of State William Seward concocted an aborted plot to provoke a foreign war in order to unite North and South against a common enemy. Two years later, President Abraham Lincoln issued his Emancipation Proclamation in part as an attempt to curry favor with foreign observers who were tilting toward the Confederacy. Finally, during the months following the war Irish American Fenians created an Anglo-American crisis when they launched several invasions of Canada to free Ireland from British rule.

Twenty years later, in a case of unsolicited foreign interference in American domestic politics, the intemperate statements of the British minister, Sir Lionel Sackville-West, influenced the election of 1888 when he made it appear that his country was rooting for the Republicans. In general, from that point on, foreign governments have been careful about revealing their favorites in American election campaigns for fear of assisting the other party, and have refrained from taking specific actions that could be interpreted as assisting one party.

As the century came to a close and the United States was granted membership in the major-power club, foreign policies became more important for the entire international system. By that juncture, the dimensions of the problem posed by the role domestic politics played in American diplomacy were clear. Whether the issues involved elections, partisan conflict between a legislature of one party and a president of another, hyphenate Americans, or local economic issues, diplomats in Washington and around the world had become well aware of the peculiar political system that had developed in the United States.

THE PROGRESSIVE ERA, 1898–1920

American precipitation of the Spanish-American War, an event that symbolized its arrival on the world scene as a major player, was deeply influenced by domestic factors, which included the "psychic crisis" of the 1890s, reactions to the most severe depression in American history, yellow journalism, and especially, the perception that President William McKinley was a weak leader. In fact, had McKinley not asked Congress for a declaration of war in April 1898, the Democrats, with their eyes on the by-elections that fall, might have introduced a war resolution themselves. Although it has never happened, the Constitution certainly permits Congress to declare war without the president's approval.

The colonies aquired in that "splendid little war"

Secretary of State John Hay, c. 1898. PRINTS AND PHOTO-GRAPHS DIVISION, LIBRARY OF CONGRESS

became an issue in the election of 1900 when the Democratic candidate, William Jennings Bryan, ran as an anti-imperialist against the alleged imperialist McKinley. To counter Bryan, Republicans boasted about the Open Door notes that Secretary of State John Hay had issued in 1899 and 1900. To the untutored observer, those anti-imperialist "paper bullets" seemed to have saved China from foreign aggression. In reality, Hay's notes, virtually ignored by the powers, had little to do with their decision to halt the carving up of the Chinese Empire. Although Hay took credit for his party for saving China, he privately called his notes "mere flapdoodle."

Hay was less interested in Chinese independence than in keeping the door open to American trade and investment in a seemingly unlimited market of 500 million Chinese. Business and government leaders, who accepted the notion that overproduction led to periodic recessions, believed that they could begin to solve that problem by gaining a strong foothold in China. The Open Door policy, which par-

tially explains American entry into World War II, as well as into the Korean and Vietnam wars, was based primarily upon the need to find markets to avert the sort of depression that devastated the country from 1893 to 1896. Had Hay or McKinley informed Americans that the notes were not terribly significant, they might have nipped the ultimately disastrous Open Door policy in the bud.

Interest in the China trade related closely to the need to build a transoceanic canal in Central America. The debates over that canal offer another example of domestic business considerations determining foreign policy. Agents of the New Panama Canal Company, which owned the rights to a canal built in Panama, exercised considerable—and to some degree nefarious—influence on the congressional decision for a Panamanian instead of a Nicaraguan route. Had the canal been built in Nicaragua, the United States would not have been forced to sponsor a revolution in Panama (then a province of Columbia), would have owned a canal closer to its own ports, and would have avoided much of the ill will caused by the fact, as Senator S. I. Hayakawa (R-Calif.) boasted over seventy years later, that "we stole it fair and square."

President Theodore Roosevelt, who may not have stolen the canal, but who did claim that he "took the canal while Congress debated," confronted several major international crises during his seven years as president. Two of the most important dealt with immigration laws that reflected the United States' anti-Asian biases. In 1904, Congress made permanent the exclusion of Chinese from immigration to the United States. Congress had passed the first temporary Chinese exclusion act in 1882 in response to hostility in the western states to cheap Chinese labor. The new and permanent legislation outraged young Chinese nationalists, who responded with a successful boycott of American goods and businesses in their country. Although Roosevelt sympathized with the Chinese, the only nationality excluded from immigration to the United States, he would not challenge the popular congressional bill. When the boycott continued through 1905, the trustbuster threatened the Chinese government with punitive measures unless it compelled its citizens to cease their actions in restraint of trade.

The Japanese, against whom American racism was directed one year later, were not the Chinese. When the San Francisco school board decided to segregate its schools to keep often older Japanese students away from their American counterparts, Tokyo, fresh from a smashing triumph in the Russo-

Japanese War, protested vigorously. Roosevelt, who did not want to irritate the Japanese unduly over what was to him a petty domestic issue, was constrained by the fact that the states controlled their own educational systems. He ultimately worked out a compromise, the Gentleman's Agreement of 1907, in which in exchange for San Francisco's rescinding the segregation policy the Japanese promised informally to keep their citizens from emigrating to the United States. Six years later, the California legislature drew Woodrow Wilson into a comparable crisis with Japan when it barred aliens from owning land.

As he analyzed the prospects for a Japanese-American war that might begin over conflict in China, Roosevelt began to back away from a vigorous defense of the Open Door. He realized that the United States could not protect its power so many miles from its shores, considering that the Philippines, in a military sense, was "a heel of Achilles." This realistic approach to the limits of American power might have headed off the almost inevitable clash between the United States and Japan in 1941. Yet he was reluctant to use his bully pulpit to denounce the fast-becoming-hallowed Open Door policy. Thus his little-understood executive agreements of 1905 and 1908 were forgotten when William Howard Taft and Woodrow Wilson expressed support for the Open Door and ignored the drift of their predecessor's policy. No doubt Roosevelt's fear of the political implications of appearing to truckle to Tokyo kept him from trying harder to keep the United States from meddling in what some on both sides of the Pacific had begun to consider the Japanese Caribbean.

Although the term "military-industrial complex" did not come into vogue until the 1960s, such a complex existed during the Progressive Era, centering around naval development. Roosevelt was one of the chief popularizers of the idea that the United States needed a first-class navy to protect its interests around the world. Others in the United States, including members of the prominent lobby, the Navy League, promoted naval building for their own pecuniary interests. However, most Americans saw little need to incur the costs of building a large navy since their country not only was impregnable but was little involved in international politics. Thus, during the yearly debates over naval appropriations, legislators and administration aides often warned about the dramatic growth of the German and Japanese navies, two aggressive commercial rivals in Asia and Europe. The emphasis upon those two countries as nations against whom the United States should be arming

contributed to growing feelings of mutual hostility. The same sort of thing happened during the Cold War when the Soviet threat was depicted in the darkest possible terms whenever Congress considered defense appropriations.

Not as strong as the armaments lobby, a peace lobby, which involved many influential Americans, also flourished during the Progressive Era. Its spirited activities on behalf of the disarmament and arbitration movements helped to promote those causes in the United States.

The Taft administration made a gesture toward international amity when the United States and Canada concluded a reciprocity treaty in 1911. In the debates in both countries, business and agricultural leaders in different regions naturally took positions for or against the agreement depending upon its impact upon them. Most important, however, was the support for the agreement expressed in many American newspapers. They rarely pointed out their own self-interest in editorials awash with arguments about how it would improve the economy. The newspaper industry itself stood to gain dramatically if Canadian lumber for newsprint entered the United States duty-free. Although Canadians ultimately rejected the treaty, American newspapers influenced the more positive outcome of the debate in the United States.

All of America's international problems during the Progressive Era paled before those posed by World War I. From the start of the war in 1914 to the failure of the Senate to approve the peace treaty in 1920, domestic, partisan, ethnic, and economic considerations affected virtually every international issue.

Even during the interregnum between his election in November 1912 and his assumption of the presidency in March 1913, partisan politics impacted upon Wilson's diplomatic strategies. The academic specialist in domestic politics who said "it would be the irony of fate" if he had to concentrate on foreign policy, first was compelled to select William Jennings Bryan as his secretary of state. A three-time loser for the presidency, completely inexperienced in foreign relations, Bryan was still Mr. Democrat. Tradition demanded that he be offered the most prestigious position in the new administration.

In addition, although Wilson initially opposed the tradition, unique to the United States, of rewarding inexperienced party loyalists with major diplomatic appointments, he bowed to party pressures and posted amateur diplomats to several key European capitals. No doubt he thought he had not sacrificed his principles too much since he expected few major problems to arise on the continent during his tenure that would involve the United States. He was not alone. After resolving peacefully a series of crises between 1905 and 1913, European leaders thought they would also be able to finesse the latest crisis created by the assassination of Austrian Archduke Franz Ferdinand in Sarajevo on 28 June 1914.

When the big war finally came six weeks later, Wilson, like the rest of the world, was shocked. Even more shocking was the fact that it did not end in a month or two but continued on for four years, affecting the United States even more dramatically than it had been affected during the last world war from 1793 to 1815.

At the onset of the Great War, most Americans were mildly Anglophilic with the establishment, including Wilson, strongly Anglophilic. But as much as 20 percent of the population was strongly pro-German because of links to mother countries. The intensity of European Americans' feelings towards the combatants in 1914, compared to that of the somewhat more indifferent general population, posed problems for Wilson's neutrality policies.

Economic factors weighed heavily on Wilson as well. The United States was sliding from a recession in 1913 toward a depression in early 1914. The economy began to turn around when the most prominent neutral in the world became the prime supplier of the belligerents, in this case, mostly the Allies since the British Navy controlled the Atlantic.

When the British began to violate American neutrality, as they had done in previous wars, Wilson naturally protested. As the violations increased, the intensity of his formal written protests increased to a point where wags suggested that the State Department was running out of stationery. But he could never threaten to sever economic links to the British if they did not cease their illegal activities on the high seas. Had they called his bluff, the United States would have been catapulted back into recession.

Wilson's approach to the loan issue illustrates the crucial relationship between his neutral strategies and the economy. When the war began, he adopted a new and highly moralistic policy of prohibiting American bankers from loaning money to belligerents. When, in late 1914, the British began to run out of cash to buy American products, Wilson reversed himself on credits and then, in early 1915, on loans. He had concluded that the traditional legal practice of permitting belligerents to make loans in neutral countries, which he had earlier opposed, had suddenly become a practical necessity considering the positive effect the war trade was having on the American economy—and his electoral prospects.

Most of those credits and loans went to one side, the Allies. Of course, the Germans could have contracted loans as well if they could have found bankers to deal with them, in much the same way that they could have purchased munitions in the United States if they could have found a way to get them across the British-controlled Atlantic. With money and war supplies flowing primarily to the British, the Germans claimed, not without reason, that Wilson's holier-than-thou neutrality was skewed.

Further, when they introduced limited submarine warfare in early 1915 in order to challenge British control of the seas, Wilson declared that he was going to hold the Germans to a greater degree of responsibility for submarine infractions than for the less lethal infractions committed by the British Navy. Although by the end of 1916, Wilson had become exasperated with British infractions, which increased in quantity and quality throughout the war, he—and London—realized that while he could threaten the Germans with a severance of relations or worse if they did not halt the illegal aspects of their submarine warfare, he could not threaten the British in the same manner because their trade was essential to American prosperity.

Wilson's neutrality policies could not keep the United States out of World War I. After the Germans declared unlimited submarine warfare on 31 January 1917 and then began sinking American ships on purpose, not by mistake as had been the case during the previous two years, Wilson asked Congress for a declaration of war on 2 April. In an eloquent and stirring address to a nation that harbored a sizeable minority opposed to war entry, the President stressed issues broader than just submarine warfare, the presumed *casus belli*. Above all, he promised that American belligerency would lead to a more progressive international system. Instead of telling his constituents that the war had been caused by such evils as nationalism, arms races, and alliance systems, and that all parties were to some degree to blame, Wilson painted the Germans in the darkest of terms. On the other hand, the Allies, including the new tsarless but-not-yet-Leninist Russia ("a fit partner for a league of honor"), appeared as virtually blameless progressive democracies. Americans were thus set up for disillusionment when they found out later about their imperialist allies and, especially, when a new world order did not replace the old one as Wilson had promised. Yet the President felt he had to "sell" the war in idealistic and black-and-white terms in order to rally as much of the population as possible around the idea of accepting that "fearful thing."

Even more than the entry into the war, the conflict over entry into the League of Nations became mired in domestic politics. Wilson contributed to his own difficulties when he made several political blunders, beginning with his call for a vote of confidence for his foreign policies in the congressional elections of 1918. As is usually the case in by-elections, the party in power lost, although not because of foreign-policy issues. Nevertheless, Republicans could argue that he no longer represented American opinion on foreign policy since his politically unwise call for a mandate had been rejected. In addition, his failure to send a truly bipartisan delegation to Paris made the resulting Treaty of Versailles "Wilson's treaty" and thus a major issue of partisan contention as the election of 1920 neared.

When the Republicans won the Senate by one seat in 1918, they organized the committees, including the key Foreign Relations Committee. From that powerful post, the Republican chairman, Henry Cabot Lodge, developed a clever strategy of parliamentary delay until he was able to rally opposition nationwide and enough votes to defeat Wilson's treaty.

Hyphenate Americans were among those most vocal in their denunciations to the peace treaty. Irish Americans disliked the fact that England had not only her vote but the vote of five commonwealth nations in the proposed League of Nations. German Americans were angry with the harsh peace that blamed the Fatherland for the entire war. In addition, liberals and progressives, upset about the end of domestic reform in 1917 and the reactionary Red Scare of 1919, saw the peace as a vindictive one that supported the imperialist policies of America's allies.

When the treaty finally reached the floor of the Senate in November 1919 and then again in March 1920, more than two-thirds of the senators voted for American entry into some sort of League of Nations. However, the issue had become so politicized that a stubborn and seriously ill Wilson in effect said no League unless you accept my unadorned document, and the Republicans said no League unless you accept our treaty laden with reservations.

Critics have assailed Wilson for committing the "supreme infanticide" by refusing to permit Democrats to desert his ship when it appeared that the only way the United States was going to enter the League was with the Republican-amended document. At the time, however, he felt that the vote

Senator Henry Cabot Lodge (*right*) with John Taylor Adams.
PRINTS AND PHOTOGRAPHS DIVISION, LIBRARY OF CONGRESS

in March 1920 would not be the last vote on the issue—the American public would have a chance to opt for his League in the election of 1920. Here, former professor Wilson, one of the nation's greatest experts on the American political system, made another tactical blunder. Rarely had foreign policy figured prominently in previous presidential elections. The election of 1920 was no exception, with domestic issues deciding the outcome as they had in the 1918 by-elections.

FROM WAR TO WAR, 1920–1945

The United States did not join the League and was relatively inactive in international politics during the 1920s. Major foreign-policy problems did arise, nonetheless, including recognition of the Soviet Union, and immigration restriction. Domestic political considerations colored the United States' posture on both issues.

Whatever American leaders thought about the wisdom of recognizing the Soviet Union, so many groups had come out for nonrecognition that it would have been political suicide for either the Democrats or Republicans to suggest it. Fearful of enhancing the status of radicalism and communism in the United States through recognition of the Bolsheviks, the American Federation of Labor, the American Legion, and the Catholic church, among others, opposed opening the door to communist diplomats. No influential organizations or leaders suggested otherwise as the issue was put on hold until the onset of the Depression when the prospect of increased Russian trade helped to win converts to the cause of recognition.

In a far more important action against foreigners, for the first time in American history, except for Chinese exclusion, Congress enacted legislation in 1921 and 1924 to restrict immigration on the basis of national origin. At issue was the perceived watering down of America's Anglo-Saxon and northern European stock by the peoples of southern and eastern Europe who had flocked to this country during the three decades prior to World War I. The new laws established quotas that discriminated against those who wanted to emigrate to the United States from such countries as Greece, Italy, Russia, Rumania, and Poland. Although none of those discriminated against reacted the way that China and Japan did during Theodore Roosevelt's administration, immigration restriction on the basis of national origin affected American relations with those countries and its image abroad.

This race-based approach to immigration, which remained firmly in place until 1965, led to the American refusal to accept many Jews from Hitler-dominated Europe in the late 1930s, the war years, and even the postwar years. The three-cornered conflict among Arabs, Jews, and the British over Palestine was exacerbated from 1945 through 1947 when the United States, among others, refused to accept the remnant of European Jewry languishing in displaced persons camps. Some DPs, who preferred to emigrate to the United States, had no choice but to try to get into Palestine illegally, despite a British blockade and Arab hostility provoked by the fear that they would soon be outnumbered by Jews in the Holy Land.

During the twenties, the United States generally practiced isolationism when it came to political, if not economic, relationships with the powers and their new institutions. Nevertheless, the experiences of World War I spurred the development of internationalist and dovish groups that exerted pressure on the administrations of Harding and Coolidge. In 1918, both the Council on Foreign Relations and the Foreign Policy Association were founded as citizens' lobbies to produce greater awareness about the world and the United States' role in it. Peace groups such as the World Peace Foundation and the Carnegie Endowment for International Peace were even more important. Their leaders and members wrote letters and signed petitions to buttress American support for the Washington Naval Disarmament Conference of 1921–1922 and the Kellogg-Briand Pact.

The Great Depression of the thirties created immense pressures on American politicians to alleviate unemployment and economic stagnation. The policies they adopted affected other countries struggling to improve the lot of their own citizens, and ultimately affected international politics in general. For example, the United States tried to protect sectors of its economy against lower cost foreign competition in order to save American jobs. The Smoot-Hawley Tariff of 1930, primarily aimed at improving the domestic economy, obviously had a significant impact abroad. American economic nationalism made it much harder for other nations to sell their goods here and, for that reason, to buy goods as well. The high tariff, which did little to boost the American economy, increased the severity of the depression around the world. Not surprisingly, it was paralleled by comparable economic nationalist policies from the major powers. Later on in the thirties, American diplomats like Secretary of State Cordell Hull, linked the deleterious impact of economic nationalism not just to the world's economy but also to the rise of fascism and Nazism in Europe. Allied post–World War II planning envisaged the erection of a series of multilateral institutions, such as the International Monetary Fund and the General Agreement on Tariffs and Trade, to foster cooperation and lower tariffs.

The weakness of the virtually unregulated American banking system during the go-go years of the twenties also contributed substantially to the world-wide economic downturn. The World War I reparations and loan redemption system that developed during that decade began with loans from American banks to the Germans to repay the British and French who repaid the Americans. When the American banking system self-destructed after the Crash in the fall of 1929, the international repayment system collapsed.

However one evaluates the relationship between economic nationalism and rising international tensions, from 1931 on the United States confronted an unprecedented series of crises that led ultimately to its entry into World War II. Throughout the period, as might be expected, domestic considerations played

Secretary of War Henry L. Stimson reaches for the first capsule in the selective service lottery, 15 October 1940. PRINTS AND PHOTOGRAPHS DIVISION, LIBRARY OF CONGRESS

a major role in determining Washington's responses to those crises. Moderate interventionists, from Secretary of State Henry L. Stimson during the Manchurian Crisis of 1931–1933 through Roosevelt as late as the fall of 1941, were severely constrained by what they perceived to be pervasive isolationist sentiments.

The United States was not alone. Politicians in England and France also confronted a public that was not enthusiastic about collective security. Only one power consistently called for joint action against German and Japanese aggression—the Soviet Union. Although the United States finally recognized the Russians in 1933, the lukewarm response to their pleas for collective security against fascism after 1935 was affected by domestic anticommunism. For many Americans, communism was the ultimate enemy. Whereas Japanese militarism and German fascism posed only military threats to their neighbors and no threat to the United States, communism, directed by conspirators in Moscow, could come to the United States through its ideology, not just with the Red Army and Navy.

Domestic anti-Semitism also affected American policies during the thirties. Anti-Semitism, then widely shared, made many Americans easy prey for those who contended that interventionist sentiment was influenced, as the isolationist spokesperson

Charles A. Lindbergh charged in 1941, by the Jews, whose "greatest danger to this country lies in their large ownership and influence in our motion pictures, our press, our radio, and our government." Lindbergh's wildly exaggerated charges had some basis in fact. As Hitler's persecution of the Jews increased exponentially after the enactment of the Nuremberg Laws of 1935, the small but disproportionately influential American Jewish community was undoubtedly among the most fervent opponents of his regime.

Finally, in terms of general influences on American policymakers dealing with the crises of the late thirties, Roosevelt had created his sweeping and unprecedented New Deal reform and recovery programs through strong presidential leadership in partnership with Congress. The President knew that he risked the survival of those programs, and even his political future, if he challenged the general isolationist mood in the country. Even within his party, Democrats were poised to oppose him if he moved too quickly into the European and Asian maelstroms. Liberals remembered what had happened to Progressive reform when the United States entered World War I.

Aside from these general influences, specific domestic considerations figured prominently in Roosevelt's responses to the series of crises that shook Europe from 1935 to 1939. When the Italians invaded Ethiopia in 1935, a year before the 1936 election, the President weighed his options with one eye on the Italian American vote. Italian Americans, who generally supported Democrats, were split in terms of their approval of Italian dictator Benito Mussolini.

There was no doubt, as well, that the American Catholic community, generally supportive of the fascist revolution in Spain, affected Roosevelt's cautious policy toward the social democratic Republic, the legitimate government in Madrid. Catholics, who were more often found in the Democratic than Republican columns, had been told by their hierarchy that the war in Spain, which some saw as a conflict between democracy and fascism, was a war between communism and Christianity.

Whatever domestic pressures he felt, Roosevelt coordinated his policies with the British and French, who, in their attempt to localize the conflict, instituted an arms embargo against the Loyalists and turned a blind eye toward the Italian and German violations of nonintervention pledges. These two policies, acceded to by the Americans, spelled doom for the Madrid government, which though supported by the Soviet Union, was never its puppet, until perhaps the last days of the war.

As Roosevelt and his aides contemplated responses to fascist aggression in Europe and Africa, and Japanese militarism in Asia, they were able to evaluate their constituents' attitudes with a new tool, the modern public opinion poll. Although polls are blunt tools that provide unsubtle snapshots of opinion at a discrete point in time, their availability increased the confidence of leaders in their abilities to determine more accurately the peoples' policy preferences.

Americans made those preferences abundantly clear from 1935 through 1941—Americans wanted to stay out of war. When World War II broke out in September 1939, Roosevelt began a cautious policy of moral, political, and economic support for the British and French that began with cash-and-carry neutrality and moved through the Destroyer Base Deal in September 1940 and Lend-Lease in February 1941. Undoubtedly he wanted to do more to aid the democracies but was hampered by strong isolationist sentiment, which might have affected the 1940 presidential election in which he ran for an unprecedented third term.

In that election, Roosevelt and the Republican nominee, Wendell Willkie, maintained an informal gentleman's agreement to leave foreign policy out of the campaign. Willkie, a moderate and something of an internationalist, generally approved of Roosevelt's policies of aid to the Allies. But, in October, when it appeared that he was going to lose, the Republican candidate broke the agreement and began to charge that a vote for Roosevelt was a vote for war.

At the time, the president did expect to be in the war in the near future because of the threat to American national security posed by expansionist Germany and Japan. Yet he understood that realistic talk about the possibility—not even probability—of future American intervention might result in the loss of the election. Thus, he promised the "mothers and fathers of America" that "your boys are not going to be sent into any foreign wars." This was pure demagoguery, since Roosevelt expected that American boys would soon have to fight in World War II.

Roosevelt's position was understandable given Willkie's cheap shot. Nevertheless, many of the same people who accepted his white lie in 1940 would not accept a white lie in 1964 when Lyndon Johnson told prospective voters that the war in Southeast Asia would be fought by Asian, not American, boys.

The Roosevelt-Willkie election marks a turning point in the influence of foreign relations on presidential elections and, of course, vice versa. Reflecting

the United States' leadership in the international system, issues relating to foreign affairs were important factors in every campaign from 1940 through 1988. Aware of this development, other nations began paying special attention to the domestic content of American foreign policy as early as a president's third year in office.

This could be seen, for example, in Roosevelt's diplomacy in 1943 and 1944. Critics have objected to the way he deferred political decisions concerning the postwar world until final military victory. Thus he may have lost the opportunity to limit the Soviets' spheres of influence when they were still battling the Nazis inside their own country. Roosevelt preferred to keep the issue of postwar Eastern Europe out of the headlines because of the votes of hyphenate Americans, especially Polish Americans, who would take umbrage if some of the fatherland were "given away" to the Soviet Union in a hard-nosed bargain. Indeed, when the Republicans raised that very issue in the 1944 election, the president announced that he was supportive of Polish territorial claims. His support weakened substantially at the Yalta Conference, three months after he had been elected to a fourth term.

Even after the election, Roosevelt and then Harry S. Truman could not accept publicly a spheres-of-influence settlement, as proposed by Joseph Stalin and Winston Churchill, even had they wanted to, for fear of alienating European Americans whose fatherlands were about to disappear behind the fast-lowering Iron Curtain. It was easier for Churchill to accept such an amoral deal not only because his public was more realistic but also because he did not fear the political power of such groups in England.

Similarly, Roosevelt was severely constrained in posing any sort of postwar counterweight to the Red Army by the unwillingness of Americans to maintain a peacetime military establishment. He led his allies to believe that the United States would retreat to its shores once the war was over, confronted by demands to balance the budget and return to "normalcy." Here he was mistaken, with anticommunism ultimately defeating isolationism and budget-balancing during the late 1940s.

Several of the themes developed by Roosevelt and his aides to rally maximum support for the war effort came home to haunt postwar administrations. For example, the constant attempt to make China an equal member of the Big Four and to sell its struggle against Japan as part of the fight of democracies against dictatorships affected domestic politics during the early 1950s. If the Chinese were so democratic and so strong, how could it be that they fell to communism only four years after the end of World War II?

The depiction of Russia as a fit partner again for a league of honor, a depiction reinforced by Moscow's heroic military effort and rhetorical liberalization during the conflict, led to recriminations later about naive or fellow-traveling American diplomats being too soft on the Reds at places like Yalta. Roosevelt felt compelled to offer periodic exaggerated praise for the brave Russians because many in this country spoke out in public against the alliance of necessity. Such vocal anticommunism reinforced Stalin's paranoia about the capitalists delaying a second front and led to his veiled threats of a separate peace with Berlin. Although Roosevelt had good reasons to paint an overly pleasant view of the Soviet Union, his strategy backfired spectacularly during the Cold War era when it was brought up against the Democratic standard-bearer, Adlai Stevenson, in the election of 1952.

The war did produce a good measure of bipartisanship, beginning with Roosevelt's appointments of Republicans Henry L. Stimson as secretary of war and Frank Knox as secretary of the Navy in 1940. All was not exactly sweetness and light between the parties during the global conflict, however. As the election of 1944 approached, Republicans attacked Roosevelt's conduct of foreign and military affairs. When late in the campaign, à la Willkie four years earlier, the Republican candidate, Thomas E. Dewey, began criticizing Roosevelt's wartime policies, the President lashed back, calling his opponent and supporters isolationists—a label that had come to be associated with defeatism and appeasement in the thirties.

In addition to the general issue of Roosevelt's competence, some Republicans accused the Democratic leadership of being unprepared for the Pearl Harbor attack. Although Dewey had been told by Gen. George C. Marshall about the ability of the United States to decode Japanese messages in 1941, an ability that was still contributing significantly to the success of the naval war in the Pacific, he took the high road and did not reveal this information during the campaign. Certainly the Republicans would have been even more aggressive on the Pearl Harbor issue had they known about the codebreaking.

The future of the British mandate in Palestine was another potentially contentious issue that arose during the war. Both parties were concerned about the Jewish vote, which was sizeable in several large states, especially New York. The result was that politicians who felt that the idea of a Jewish state in Palestine may not have been in America's national interest were compelled to deal carefully with this matter. With New York Republican Dewey running for president in 1944 and 1948, Palestine became embroiled in electoral politics as each party vied for the Jewish vote by adopting platforms attractive to Zionists.

Jewish Americans were not passive observers on this issue. They began to develop a powerful Zionist lobby with which American presidents and legislators had to deal from the election of 1944 to the end of the century. And although some in the Jewish community still opposed a Jewish state as World War II came to a close, once Israel was established in 1948, almost all Jewish Americans became strong supporters of its continued existence.

THE EARLY COLD WAR YEARS, 1945–1962

When, in 1943, Franklin Roosevelt told Joseph Stalin that the American public would not accept the stationing of American troops abroad in peacetime, he, like most of his fellow citizens, assumed that the United States would return to the sort of normalcy that marked the twenties. He could not have imagined that six years later hundreds of thousands of American soldiers, integral parts of a huge peacetime military-industrial complex, would still be on guard in Europe and Asia; nor could he have imagined that his country would become the leader of a permanent peacetime military alliance and give away billions of dollars in foreign aid. Of course, in 1943, he did not foresee the Cold War with the Soviet Union, which produced the state of extreme tension that necessitated those unprecedented actions from the most insular of major powers.

The transformation of American attitudes from isolationism to interventionism in all areas of the globe is one of the most important developments in modern history. American policymakers accomplished that transformation through constant and sometimes hysterical appeals to their constituents to convince them that the United States had to assume leadership of the democracies and their empires in the postwar world.

The general suspicion and hostility that Americans felt toward domestic communists and fellow-travelers made the job of the interventionists somewhat easier. As tensions with the Soviet Union increased, so too did repression of communists at home; the more closely they were linked to Moscow, the easier it became for politicians to persecute them and for conservative isolationists to accept interventionism.

The government's propaganda assault against communists—and their ideas—at home and abroad pervaded all aspects of American life and culture from the end of the war to the sixties. In the private sector, without much prodding, journalists and film, radio, and television producers struck patriotic and anti-communist themes. And it worked. An insular, antimilitarist, penny-pinching people became an interventionist, internationalist, generous nation almost overnight. But that remarkable conversion, based upon a caricature of world politics, came with some costs.

One cost was paid by the State Department. Although there were not many former members of the Communist party in the department, or other branches of government for that matter, the Cold War at home led to the dismissal of experts who were allegedly soft on communism and the resignation of others who were demoralized by the party line to which they had to adhere or risk being branded subversive. Further, the gutting of the State Department produced timidity on the part of those who remained who might have challenged hard-line policies in the Third World in particular. More important, the government lost the services of many experts who understood the history and culture of countries like China and Vietnam, for example, who might have suggested alternate policies in the fifties and sixties.

The Red Scare was not manufactured out of whole cloth. Through its actions abroad and even in the United States, the Soviet Union made it easy for Americans to fear and hate communism. From 1946 through 1950, the West was rocked by a series of spy scandals in Canada, the United States, and Great Britain involving domestic communists who allegedly stole the "secret" of the atomic bomb among other classified materials.

Yet even such sensational events would not have aroused the American public sufficiently had it not been for the Truman administration's efforts to demonize the Soviet Union. Americans were shocked by Winston Churchill's Iron Curtain speech at Fulton, Missouri in 1946. President Truman, who had seen the speech in advance, privately endorsed the popular British leader's clarion call for vigilance and unity to meet the threat to world peace.

Even more dramatic was Truman's impassioned 1947 request to Congress for $4 hundred million to aid Greece and Turkey in their struggles against the Soviet Union and their surrogates. The Truman Doctrine address was meant, as Sen. Arthur S. Vandenberg (R-Mich.) advised the president to "scare the hell out of the country" so that Americans would finally realize how seriously the Soviet Union threatened national security and Congress would foot the bill for the containment program. The selling of the program became a major activity for the foreign-policy establishment.

The problem with these early strident propaganda campaigns, which may have been necessary to secure passage of the Truman Doctrine, the Marshall Plan, and the Point 4 programs, and to assure American entry into the North Atlantic Treaty Organization, was that the selling of the Red Menace in the late forties made it harder to unsell that image after the death of Stalin in 1953. In addition, the notion that most anticolonial activity in the world was the product of the puppet masters in the Kremlin made it more difficult for Americans to accept later that there were places in the Third World where the locals had legitimate grievances against western overlords. The constant repetition of such themes had an impact on the president and his advisers, who came to believe their own propaganda in a subconscious feedback process. Finally, by depicting the enemy in such apocalyptic terms, Truman increased Soviet fears of an aggressive America and justified their legendary paranoia.

If the many exaggerated alerts to the Soviet danger were not bad enough in terms of contributing to the Kremlin's fear of the United States, the election of 1948 certainly reenforced it. As early as January 1947, presidential aide Clark Clifford told Truman that as the next election approached, he should stress foreign affairs–in times of national crisis, the public generally supports the president.

Clifford was also instrumental in convincing the President, against the judgment of Secretary of State Marshall and others, to take the lead in recognizing Israel in May 1948. Whatever foreign-policy rationale he advanced for such an approach, Clifford was concerned about the Jewish vote in the fall election. The Democratic party, which was in difficult financial shape in the 1948 campaign, relied on the fundraising of Abraham Feinberg, a strong supporter of Israel, who, with Truman aide David Niles and the President's former business partner, Eddie Jacobson, exercised influence in the Oval Office. Israel needed that influence to balance pro-Arab sentiments in the State Department, which revolved around Western Europe's need for Middle East oil as well as the long-term interests of American oil companies.

As in most elections, domestic issues dominated the political debate in 1948, but one of those issues, the Democratic party's alleged dalliances with communists and fellow travelers, clearly had foreign-policy overtones. The Democrats had used that same issue to assail their competitors on the Left in the Progressive party. The Republican candidate, Dewey, also criticized Truman's apparent appeasement of communism in places like Greece and China although he did not exploit the Berlin crisis, which had begun in June. Other Republican leaders lambasted Roosevelt's wartime diplomacy, especially his actions at the Yalta Conference. Although the conference was not a major issue in 1948, it became a potent one for Republicans in the years to follow.

Nevertheless, confident of winning, Dewey did not veer too far from bipartisanship on foreign policy, aside from raising the issue of Israel's borders in late October as the Jewish state and its Arab enemies wrangled over terms to end the Israeli War for Independence. Truman responded by calling for an even larger part of the Negev desert for Israel than demanded by Dewey, as each candidate jockeyed for advantage with Jewish voters.

Clark Clifford had been correct when he suggested that foreign affairs was one area in which a president could rally the population. Truman and his successors were aided immeasurably in that area by the development of new institutions such as the Central Intelligence Agency and the National Security Council in 1947, which increased their control over foreign-policy making. In addition, the availability of radio, and then television, made it easier for the president to go directly to the public to explain matters of national security. The electronic media willingly surrendered airtime to presidents when they wanted to tell their constituents, in presumably nonpartisan speeches, about dangers that loomed abroad. Ironically, since the country did not have an official government newspaper or television station, as is the case in more authoritarian countries, the public accepted such messages over "free" airwaves more readily than overt propaganda that might have come through government channels.

As had been the case since World War I, Congress was not pleased with its diminished role in foreign policy. The period from the end of World War II through the seventies long has been considered as dominated by healthy congressional bipartisanship, except for election years, with both parties accepting presidential leadership in the vitally important international sphere. A careful analysis of this common assumption suggests otherwise, with Republicans and Democrats often splitting along partisan lines on foreign affairs. Indeed, Truman enjoyed less support from Congress during the Korean War than did Johnson during the Vietnam War.

The Korean War itself, a limited war, was tailor-made for partisan wrangling when the battle lines became fixed around the 38th parallel in the late winter of 1951. With the conflict stalemated, it no longer seemed to be as serious a threat to national security and thus became fair game for the Republicans. General Douglas MacArthur exacerbated the situation when, on several occasions, he appealed over the head of the President to Republicans to support more aggressive strategies to defeat the communists. Whether or not MacArthur's demands to bomb and maybe even invade China were sound, when he appealed publicly to the opposition, Truman finally had to relieve him of his duty. Aside from the general's clear insubordination, his call for escalation, eagerly accepted by many Republicans, frightened America's allies and enemies alike.

By the time the 1952 presidential election came around, the MacArthur affair had blown over. Yet the Democrats' conduct of the war was a powerful issue for Republicans. Americans had been reluctant to switch leaders in the middle of previous wars. The Korean War was another matter. As the conflict continued through 1951 and 1952, more and more citizens expressed dissatisfaction with the administration's military and diplomatic strategies.

Even without the unprecedented no-win war or limited war, the odds were stacked against the Democrats in 1952. They had been in power for twenty years, it appeared to be time for a change, and their candidate, Adlai E. Stevenson, was no match for the popular World War II hero, Dwight David Eisenhower. The allegedly sorry diplomatic record of the Democrats, which included the "loss" of China, the Russian "theft" of the atomic bomb, and the no-win war, contributed to Republican confidence. Two of the three main themes in their election equation—K_1C_2 or Korea, Communism, and Corruption— involved foreign-policy issues. In addition, Republican spokespersons, although not Eisenhower, attacked the defensive policy of containment and called for the offensive policy of rollback. That policy, which became an important part of Republican rhetoric, created false hopes among East Europeans that the United States would come to their aid when they rebelled against the Soviet-installed regimes, as was the tragic case with Hungary in 1956.

The general assault on the Democrats as being too soft on communism became a common theme in all elections from 1952 to 1988. The Democrats came to be associated with people for whom peace was more precious than defending national security, people who were interested in disarmament and shied away from military confrontation, even though, ironically, they were also the "party of war" with their war entries in 1917, 1941, 1950, and in Vietnam.

Eisenhower also promised to go to Korea if elected. This meant very little in practice but held out the hope that if he made the trip, the war might end sooner. Unlike rollback, this campaign pledge was redeemed, although the trip that the President-elect took in late November did not accomplish as much in ending the war as did the death of Stalin in March 1953 and Eisenhower's veiled threat to use nuclear weapons against the North Koreans and Chinese if the war dragged on much longer.

The Korean War ended in July 1953. The fact that the Chinese "volunteers" had fought alongside the North Koreans made it impossible for the United States to normalize relations with Beijing for the foreseeable future. With the cries of "who lost China" from the campaign of 1952 still ringing in American ears, and the powerful China Lobby committed to restoring the Chinese Nationalists to the mainland, the question of recognition was put off not just during the Eisenhower administration but through the Kennedy and Johnson administrations as well. As with the opposition that developed in the United States to the Soviet revolution, once the communists had been demonized, it was difficult to undemonize them without paying a heavy political price.

During the Eisenhower administration, the Central Intelligence Agency, headed by Secretary of State John Foster Dulles's brother, Allen, expanded its covert activities dramatically. It enjoyed "victories" in Iran and Guatemala as well as "losses" in Egypt, Tibet, Indonesia, Ukraine, and Eastern Europe, among other places. The CIA kept knowledge of these victories and defeats, and the means used to pursue them, from the public. During World War II, Americans accepted the idea that their intelligence services should be engaged in covert activities, including murder and sabotage, which seemed justified to protect national security. Such activities in peacetime, like the overthrow of a freely elected government in Guatemala, were another matter. In 1954, the Doolittle Commission reported to the President, but not to the public, that "We must learn to subvert, sabotage, and destroy our enemies by more clear, more sophisticated and more effective methods than those used against us. It may become necessary that

Allen Dulles, Director of Central Intelligence, 1953–1961. ARCHIVE PHOTOS

the American people will be made acquainted with, understand and support this fundamentally repugnant philosophy." Presidents from Eisenhower to the present chose not to discuss this issue with the public, or with most members of Congress for that matter. They determined that not only would national security be endangered by revealing such activities but that the public might not understand how such "repugnant" and undemocratic actions were vital to national survival.

Whereas the Republicans were on the offensive in the election of 1952, the Democrats, again led by Stevenson, played that role in 1956. Stevenson called for a ban on the testing of hydrogen bombs and also attacked the Eisenhower-Dulles strategy of brinkmanship. Eisenhower objected strongly to the injection of the nuclear issue into the election. When the Soviet premier wrote to the President during the campaign calling for an H-bomb test ban, he inadvertently hurt Stevenson, much to the defensive Republicans' pleasure.

The election also affected foreign policy in terms of both Anglo-French and Russian calculations in the Middle East and Hungary, respectively, in Octo-

Secretary of State John Foster Dulles (*right*) with French foreign minister Georges Bidault.
ARCHIVE PHOTOS

ber. The British and French, and their Israeli ally, hoped that they could get away with an invasion of Egypt during the campaign. They reasoned that Eisenhower could not afford to oppose them given the unpopularity of the anti-Western Egyptian leader, Gamal Abdul Nasser, and the importance of the Jewish vote. Similarly, the Russians thought they could smash the Hungarian rebellion not only because of the attention given to the Suez Crisis but also because Eisenhower would be reluctant to take risky actions in the international sphere during the height of the campaign. Although Eisenhower was furious at his allies and the Russians, albeit for different reasons, both crises contributed to his victory margin, since voters usually rally around experienced presidents during crises.

Throughout much of Eisenhower's two terms,

the Democrats controlled Congress. Because of this, he was forced to work closely with the opposition on his foreign programs. Indeed, as an internationalist who subscribed to the general bipartisan consensus that had obtained since the late forties, in many cases the Democrats were his most supportive allies against the isolationists and unilateralists on Capitol Hill.

The National Highway Act of 1956 was one program both parties could agree upon. Those concerned about the expense were brought on board somewhat disingenuously by the argument that the act was a defense measure that would enable the military and the citizenry to move about more efficiently if they were at war with the Soviet Union.

All Americans, regardless of foreign policy orientation, were shocked in 1957 when the Soviet Union launched *Sputnik* into orbit. They had long been secure in the knowledge that the United States was a clear number one in scientific innovation. When the Russians beat the Americans into space, observers blamed the failures of the American educational system. The result was massive new spending for higher education, including the $5 billion National Defense Education Act.

The Russians again demonstrated their advances in military technology when they shot down an American U-2 spy plane on 1 May 1960. Eisenhower first denied that the plane was a spy plane and then, when confronted by the evidence that the Russians had been holding back, not only admitted it but maintained that the United States was correct in pursuing its U-2 program. Both Eisenhower and Russian premier Nikita S. Khrushchev had high hopes for the Paris summit meeting, which was to take place just after the shootdown. Khrushchev apparently expected that Eisenhower would not take responsibility for the program and blame his aides. Not realizing how Eisenhower's admission of lack of control over his underlings might disturb the American electorate, the Russian leader miscalculated and then made things worse by demanding an apology before the summit could formally begin.

Because of the way that Khrushchev appeared to be the disrupter of the summit conference, its failure and the administration's blundering did not become issues in the election of 1960. But this was the first election in which the inexperience in foreign relations of one of the candidates, the youthful senator from Massachusetts, became a significant issue. As vice president, Richard M. Nixon had traveled around the world, debated with Khrushchev in Moscow, and had been stoned by mobs in Venezuela. John F. Kennedy had to demonstrate that he could manage American foreign policy in the dangerous nuclear age. He succeeded in allaying American fears about his inexperience in the first televised presidential debate in which he appeared to be as mature and knowledgeable as Nixon. In a comparable situation in 1976, Americans became more confident about candidate Jimmy Carter's foreign policy expertise when President Gerald R. Ford "liberated" Poland during a televised debate.

The issue of Cuba also arose during the Kennedy-Nixon debates when the Democrat attacked the Republicans for not doing more to remove Castro from Cuba. Even if they had not been briefed specifically about the matter, Kennedy and his advisers knew in general that plans were afoot to assist anti-Castro Cubans to overthrow the Cuban leader. When Ken-

Soviet premier Nikita S. Khrushchev, 1958–1964. ARCHIVE PHOTOS

nedy made the charge, Nixon was at a disadvantage because he could not explain all that he knew about Eisenhower's secret anti-Cuban policy, including the training of a rebel army to invade the island. Kennedy endangered national security by cynically using the issue for partisan purposes during the campaign. Of course, as we have seen, that was not unprecedented.

On the other hand, although the United States was not in crisis in 1960, Khrushchev's truculent speech at the United Nations in September, as well as his famous shoe-banging temper tantrum, helped Nixon on the grounds that he had already established his ability to deal with the fiery leader of the Soviet Union. Khrushchev later claimed that because he wanted Kennedy to beat the hard-line Nixon, he delayed until after the election the planned release of two American RB-47 pilots who had been shot down over the Soviet Union. He feared that such welcome news during the campaign might contribute to Nixon's chances for victory.

Before Kennedy took office, President Eisenhower offered a valedictory to his constituents. His farewell address ranks second only to Washington's in terms of its impact. Eisenhower warned about the "grave implications" of the growing influence of the military-industrial complex in "every city, every State house, every office of the Federal government." He had fought for eight years, not always successfully, to balance the budget and, especially, to curtail the military's spending and economic and political power. Hundreds of millions of dollars each year went to fighting the Cold War, hundreds of millions that meant jobs in congressional districts and corporate profits. Congress, the Department of Defense, and the corporations constituted the triumvirate of the military-industrial complex, which engaged in a weapons procurement program often driven by domestic political considerations, not foreign or military policy needs.

Eisenhower's call for restraining this powerful behemoth, while thrilling liberals and others who shared his concerns, ultimately fell on deaf ears. At least when the Democrats came into office in January 1961, American military procurement policies, aside from new budgeting systems, remained essentially in place.

The new president, however, introduced structural changes in his foreign-policy-making machine, which were to impact dramatically on the course of events over the next two decades. In order to maintain tighter executive control over foreign policy, Kennedy increased substantially the role of the president's adviser for national security affairs. Under Truman and Eisenhower, that post had been almost clerical, with the adviser serving as a coordinator and facilitator. Under Kennedy, National Security Adviser McGeorge Bundy began to develop an independent policy-making function, which slowly began to rival that of the secretary of state. Unlike the secretary, the national security adviser did not have to appear before Congress when summoned. With a small staff insulated from the huge State Department bureaucracy, Bundy and, in particular, his successors Walt Whitman Rostow and Henry Kissinger, fashioned policies in relative secrecy. This development made it more difficult for Americans and their representatives to know just what the president was up to in the international sphere.

FROM THE MISSILES OF OCTOBER TO THE NEW WORLD ORDER, 1962–1992

Few Americans knew what was going on in the White House during those thirteen days in October 1962 that constituted the Cuban missile crisis, the most dangerous crisis of the Cold War. At the time, participants in the crisis estimated the chances for a nuclear exchange at anywhere from 33 to 50 percent. Given what we now know about Russian strategies, some of those same participants believe the odds for war were even shorter.

Domestic politics helped to determine the way that Kennedy responded to the Soviet introduction of offensive missiles into Cuba. In the first place, as congressional elections approached, he perceived himself a failure as president. Congress had enacted little of his New Frontier program and, in foreign affairs, he had lost at the Bay of Pigs, been bullied by Khrushchev at the Vienna Summit, accepted the neutralization of Laos, and stood by while the Russians built a wall between East and West Berlin. In addition, the first rumors about the missiles in Cuba came from a Republican Senator, Kenneth Keating of New York.

Thus, when the time came to act, Kennedy was concerned about his political prospects, as well as national security interests. To be sure, as in all crises, few speak even in private about such selfish considerations. Nevertheless, they had to be a factor, for example, when Kennedy refused to trade outmoded and soon-to-be dismantled missile bases in Turkey for the bases in Cuba. Had he agreed to do so at the onset of the crisis, the United States would not have risked nuclear war, either by invading or bombing Cuba, or even by enforcing the naval quarantine that was decided upon at the eleventh hour.

In fact, the missile trade was part of the ultimate deal that resolved the crisis. Kennedy kept that information from the American public because it would have given the impression that Khrushchev's alleged aggression paid—and that the President had lost the diplomatic duel. One wonders whether Kennedy would have moved so close to the brink if he knew, as we later learned, that warheads might have already arrived in Cuba and that Soviet commanders may have been given orders to use them if necessary to repel an invasion.

After that most dangerous of Cold War crises, when Kennedy and Khrushchev retreated from the abyss Soviet-American relations improved, symbolized by the signing of the Partial Test Ban treaty in 1963. Since 1957, the National Committee for a Sane

Nuclear Policy (SANE) had been lobbying effectively for disarmament. A small group with never more than 25,000 members, SANE, along with allies like Women Strike for Peace, popularized the argument that the testing of nuclear weapons was polluting the environment and pressured Kennedy to do something about the problem.

He did not confront the same sort of pressure about his Vietnam policies, with only 16,000 "advisers" in the country by the fall of 1963 and most Americans unconcerned about the apparently limited commitment to prop up the Saigon regime. Despite the lack of public attention to Southeast Asia, Kennedy had become nervous about the prospect of a greater American commitment. He allegedly told several of his advisers that he would contemplate de-escalating but only after the 1964 election. He did not want to run for reelection as the president who lost Vietnam to the communists. Later, both Lyndon Johnson and Richard Nixon made similar calculations as they considered the relationship between withdrawal from Vietnam and their electoral prospects in 1968 and 1972 respectively.

Relatively free to escalate modestly in Vietnam, Kennedy was hobbled by Congress's Hickenlooper Amendment, which restrained a president's ability to conduct diplomacy in other parts of the Third World. Comparable to the Jackson-Vanik Amendment of 1974, which tied trade with the Soviet Union to its treatment of Soviet Jews, and the Clark Amendment of 1976, which prohibited aid to American friends in the Angolan civil war, the Hickenlooper Amendment of 1962 warned that foreign aid would be cut off to recipients who nationalized American properties without compensation or otherwise discriminated against American businesses. Presidents did not appreciate these examples of congressional assertiveness. Yet as the branch of government that approves spending and trade legislation, Congress had every right to attach such codicils to its bills, even if they did decrease executive flexibility in foreign-policy making.

In the election of 1964, domestic issues were paramount with Kennedy's successor, Lyndon Johnson, a liberal Democratic reformer running against Barry Goldwater, a conservative Republican candidate who allegedly threatened to dismantle the Welfare State. There was, however, one foreign-policy issue that did become important—the escalation of the Vietnam War. Because of several comments from the loose-lipped Goldwater, he appeared as a mad bomber, willing to use nuclear weapons to win the war. One famous television ad for Johnson, which

was so offensive that it was pulled after a few days, showed a little girl counting the petals she plucked from a daisy. Her innocent exercise ultimately turned into a countdown for a nuclear explosion. For his part, Sen. J. William Fulbright (D-Ark.), who ram-rodded the Gulf of Tonkin Resolution through the Senate in August, only to become a leading dove less than a year later, explained his enthusiastic support for Johnson in terms of his fear that the dangerous Goldwater might make it to the White House and precipitate a world war.

To distance himself even more from the hawkish Arizona senator, Johnson promised that the war in Vietnam would be a war fought by Asian boys, suggesting that a vote for him was a vote against further escalatory moves in Southeast Asia. During the nine months from his election in November 1964 to July 1965, Johnson approved the bombing of North Vietnam and the assumption by American boys of the main ground combat role in Vietnam. Johnson's escalation in the air in February and on the ground in July belied his campaign statements about the war. As the conflict continued through 1966 and 1967, those statements contributed to the decline in his credibility, a key factor explaining why he lost public support for his Vietnam policies.

The escalation of 1965, particularly the bombing, contributed to the growth of the largest antiwar movement in American history. Through mass one-city demonstrations attracting as many as 500,000 participants, letter and petition writing, electoral politics, and draft resistance, the movement affected all aspects of the Southeast Asian policies of both Johnson and Nixon. Indeed, two specific Vietnam foreign-policy decisions were influenced by the movement, which—though it never captured the loyalties of a majority of citizens—had great strength among upper- and upper-middle-class citizens and their college-age children.

The first decision occurred in the Johnson administration. After the world was astonished by the spectacle of more than 35,000 young people besieging the Pentagon on 21 October 1967, the president felt compelled to launch a major public relations campaign in November and early December, which emphasized that the ever-more-costly war was being won and that there was light at the end of the tunnel. When on the heels of this propaganda blitz, the communists launched their Tet Offensive on 31 January 1968, Americans found it difficult to understand how, if things were going so well, the enemy was able to put together such a large, and initially successful, operation. Although by the middle of February the offensive had failed, many were skeptical when Johnson proclaimed victory. This skepticism was a factor in declining public support for the President's policies in Vietnam and contributed to his monumental decisions of 31 March 1968 not to escalate and not to seek reelection.

Johnson's decisions related clearly to the decline in approval ratings for his handling of foreign relations. Critics later claimed that he brought this upon himself because of his failure to rally support for the war in Southeast Asia. One of the main lessons drawn from America's failure in Vietnam was the folly of becoming involved in another such limited war without first securing popular support for the long haul. But Johnson faced a difficult problem. When he and his advisers made the war an American war in 1965, they viewed it as the prototype of the wars of the future in the Third World. The United States had to learn how to fight such wars with its nuclear arms tied behind its back. Had Johnson aroused passionate support for the war, perhaps by emphasizing the serious threat posed to the national security by the Vietnamese communists, how could he have contained those who would have demanded the use of all available weaponry? Yet by not arousing Americans, Johnson made it difficult for them to support him in what appeared to be an endless war.

Domestic factors alone go a long way toward explaining the President's March 1968 speech. For one thing, the activities of the antiwar movement and other protest movements of the era had contributed to one of the most turbulent few years in American history. The antiwar movement in particular, strongest on elite college campuses, threatened to destroy the American establishment, as Johnson was told by his advisers both within, and especially, outside of the Washington Beltway.

This instability, coupled with Johnson's reluctance to cut his Great Society programs or raise taxes, contributed to a weakening economy that worried Wall Street in the late winter of 1968. As with the French in 1954, although the United States had not been defeated on the ground and still had the physical resources to continue to fight in Vietnam, the establishment and much of the public demanded de-escalation and withdrawal.

Both candidates in the 1968 campaign, Johnson's vice president, Hubert H. Humphrey, and Republican Richard M. Nixon, contended that if elected they would accede to those demands. Democrats, especially, were not convinced that Nixon, the old Cold Warrior, would beat such a hasty retreat from Southeast Asia. In a situation comparable to Senator Fulbright supporting the Gulf of Tonkin resolution in 1964 because he feared the election of Barry Goldwater, the chief negotiator at the Paris peace talks, W. Averell Harriman was so distressed at the prospect of a Nixon victory that he went beyond his instructions in an attempt to secure a settlement before election day.

Johnson was not entirely pleased with Humphrey's campaign. Nevertheless he helped him on 31 October, six days before the election, with the announcement of a complete bombing pause over North Vietnam in order to get the peace talks moving. The Republicans countered this "October surprise" with the secret employment of intermediaries who urged the South Vietnamese to resist any new peace moves until after the election of their friends in the Republican party. Although Richard Nixon was not directly involved, he knew in general about this gambit. According to his camp, such intervention was legitimate because of Johnson's allegedly cynical use of a national security issue to help elect Humphrey.

The second major Vietnam policy decision influenced by the powerful antiwar movement occurred during the Nixon administration. Upon taking office in 1969, the new president initiated a program of covert escalation, including the bombing of Cambodia, to force the communists to adopt more conciliatory positions at the peace talks. In July, he sent communist leader Ho Chi Minh a secret ultimatum—be more forthcoming at Paris or face escalation. Within the White House, aides discussed a variety of escalatory "savage blows," which included the mining of Hanoi and Haiphong harbors and the bombing of the flood control systems in the north.

As Washington and Hanoi considered their options, and after Nixon had failed to announce initiatives to hasten an end to the war, antiwar leaders began planning a new type of demonstration for 15 October 1969, two weeks before the ultimatum deadline about which they knew nothing. This demonstration, the Moratorium, ultimately involved over four million Americans in over two hundred cities who attended vigils and rallies to protest the pace at which Nixon was withdrawing from Vietnam. The numbers involved were so large, and the millions of not just young people but middle-class adults who took part were so impressive, that Nixon had to take them into account when he permitted the 1 November deadline to pass without any action from the United States, even though Hanoi had not budged. In fact, he was so concerned about his deteriorating position on the home front that he went to work on his Silent Majority speech of 3 November, the most important speech of his presidency to that time, to rally the alleged majority of administration supporters against the antiwar crowds in the streets. The Silent Majority speech was coupled with a fierce attack, led by Vice President Spiro T. Agnew, against the elite media, which the administration claimed was liberal and unpatriotic.

Aside from the impact of the movement on Johnson's 31 March 1968 decision and on Nixon's 1 November 1969 nondecision, it influenced the war in at least one other important way. Vietnamese communists counted upon opponents of the war in the United States to influence their country's policies. Thus, even though both Johnson and Nixon claimed repeatedly that American policy was not made in the streets by antiwar demonstrators, the fact that they knew that Hanoi took the movement into account in its own calculations certainly affected Washington's calculations.

The relative success of the antiwar movement, supported after 1968 by more and more prominent reference figures, spelled the end of the bipartisan Cold War consensus. This development led to increased politicization in the American foreign-policy-making process in the 1970s and 1980s, which was marked by congressional muscle flexing, the pervasiveness and aggressiveness of the electronic media, the weakness of the political parties, and the proliferation and power of well-funded interest groups.

Although the antiwar movement declined in influence after the spring of 1971, in part because fewer and fewer American soldiers were participating in the combat in Southeast Asia, the war did figure in the election of 1972. In the first place, the Democratic candidate, Sen. George McGovern (D-S.D.), was nominated in part because of rule changes in his party that were precipitated by the riots at the 1968 convention in Chicago when antiwar activists and others were excluded from the political process.

More important, as in the election of 1952, Republicans labeled their Democratic opponent with a negative alphabetic slogan—he was the AAA candidate, an alleged supporter of abortion, appeasement, and amnesty for draft dodgers. The only thing McGovern had going for him was a promise to end the war more quickly than Nixon. That promise lost its salience when Nixon's popular national security adviser, Henry Kissinger, announced on 31 October, four years to the day from Johnson's October surprise, that he had a peace agreement with the communists.

Although Kissinger had struck a deal with Hanoi, he did not have one with the South Vietnamese, who rejected the terms he had negotiated. Only after the election did the President inform Americans that Kissinger's deal had come unglued because the *North Vietnamese* had reneged. This alleged reneging led to the bombing of Hanoi and Haiphong with B-52s for thirteen days in December in order to force the communists back to the negotiating table.

Almost as soon as he was reelected, Nixon's administration began to unravel. The Watergate affair, which started with a simple break-in in June 1972 at Democratic party headquarters in Washington by a group working for the Committee to Reelect the President and ended with Nixon's resignation in August 1974, also had its foreign component. As the indictment against the president built through 1973, charges that he ordered the break-in of the office of the psychologist of the leaker of the *Pentagon Papers,* Daniel Ellsberg, sold ambassadorial appointments, and, especially, harassed and illegally put under surveillance thousands of alleged enemies in the antiwar movement contributed to his downfall. Indeed, the first such illegal activity began over a Vietnam War issue when a *New York Times* reporter wrote about the secret bombing of Cambodia in March 1969. This led Nixon to wiretap journalists and government officials to identify the leak.

On the other side of the equation, the pressures of the year-and-a-half long Watergate scandals significantly affected the President's foreign policies. He was compelled to downplay détente with the Soviet Union in order to maintain conservative support in Congress, and during some crises, such as the Yom Kippur War in 1973, he was physically or emotionally unable to exert his authority in the White House.

Nixon's illegal use of the CIA and the FBI, brought to light during the Watergate investigations, led to the Rockefeller and Church committee investigations of American intelligence agencies in 1975. Because of those investigations, citizens learned for the first time of assassination plots against foreign leaders as well as innumerable violations of their rights to assemble, petition, and protest. The outrage produced by these revelations led to new congressional oversight legislation and a change in the leadership of the CIA that affected all covert intelligence activities.

Congress regained power in the foreign-policy sphere in other ways as well. In 1973, seeking to restore some of its original constitutional authority, it passed the War Powers Act over the veto of the Watergate-emasculated Nixon. In order to tether Cold War presidents who had moved the United States into undeclared wars, the act compelled the

Secretary of State Henry Kissinger (*second from left*) meeting with Egyptian President Anwar Sadat (*third from right*), 1975. PRINTS AND PHOTOGRAPHS DIVISION, LIBRARY OF CONGRESS

president to inform Congress within forty-eight hours after committing troops to a war zone and also to ask for Congress's permission to keep them in that zone beyond a sixty-day period.

The controversial act had little to do with Jimmy Carter's record of nonintervention in pursuit of his diplomatic goals. Despite the fact that his administration was the first of the Cold War to keep the United States out of war or large-scale covert military interventions, the election of 1980 was one of those most influenced by foreign affairs. The growing reaction against the détente policies of the Nixon-Ford administrations, which were continued to some degree under Carter, lurked in the background. Carter also stressed human rights, albeit inconsistently, in an attempt to pursue a foreign policy that reflected American democratic values. In 1976, a group of conservative and neoconservative politicians and intellectuals formed the Committee on the Present Danger to combat the alleged softness in U.S. policy toward the Soviets. Especially concerned about their country's approach to arms negotiations, this group lobbied successfully against the SALT II agreements.

Supported by many members of the committee, Ronald Reagan ran against Carter as a candidate who would restore American power and prestige in the world. He claimed that under the weak Democratic leader, the United States had permitted communism to expand in Central America and Africa. Moreover, from November 1979 through the campaigning season and beyond, Americans were held hostage in Tehran by Iranian militants apparently working for the fiercely anti-American Ayatollah Ruhollah Khomeini. The issue of the hostages in Tehran, kept alive by constant media attention, was the main reason Carter launched a disastrous rescue mission in March 1980. In addition, during the difficult primary campaign he waged against Sen. Edward M. Kennedy (D-Mass.), the President hinted that he was on the verge of achieving a diplomatic breakthrough on the morning of an important primary in Wisconsin. There was no diplomatic breakthrough.

For Reagan and his supporters, the hostage issue demonstrated how feeble the powerful United States had become, unable to free its citizens held captive by a Third World nation. He also assailed the Democrats for giving the Panama Canal and the Canal Zone to the Panamanians, an issue that was used successfully against several targeted Democratic senators, including the influential Frank Church (D-Idaho).

In this campaign, as in 1968, Republican operatives interfered with a Democratic president's diplomacy. At the least, they purloined or otherwise obtained classified government documents to make certain that Carter had no October surprises for them in terms of a sudden release of the hostages. Some intriguing but unsubstantiated evidence suggests as well that Republicans may have struck deals with Tehran not to release the hostages until Reagan was safely elected in exchange for arms they desperately needed for their war against Iraq that began in 1980.

Iran figured prominently in the most serious scandal of the Reagan administration, the Iran-Contra affair. Had it not been for the fact that the genial President, according to Oliver North's *Under Fire,* "did not always know what he knew," the United States might have experienced its second impeachment hearing in little more than a decade.

The scandal began when Congress, through the 1984 Boland Amendment, prohibited the Reagan administration from sending military aid to the Contras in their war against the Sandinista regime in Nicaragua. At the same time, the administration, under pressure to liberate Americans taken hostage by terrorists in Lebanon, engaged in secret negotiations with Iranians to trade arms for hostages. Although no Boland Amendment prohibited such a transaction, the president and his aides had earlier taken strong positions against such a policy. When the complicated trade turned up a dividend or "residuals" in terms of money left over from arms purchases, they were channeled by North to the Contras. He later claimed that the Boland Amendment did not apply to the National Security Council where he worked.

Even though many Americans thrilled to Reagan's patriotic and tough speeches and approved of his invasion of Grenada in 1983, not all were enthusiastic about the intensification of the Cold War, symbolized by his use of the phrase "evil empire" to characterize the Soviet Union. A nuclear freeze movement, which enjoyed popularity throughout the country and in Congress in 1983, threatened to make foreign policy a key issue in the election of 1984. This perceived dovish pressure, as well as pressure from U.S. allies and his wife, Nancy, caused Reagan to soften his rhetoric as the 1984 campaign began and his policies after reelection.

Despite the gradual warming of Soviet-American relations after Mikhail Gorbachev's accession to power in 1985, new problems relating to the failings of the American economy impinged on both Reagan's and George Bush's abilities to construct an American foreign policy based upon purely strategic considerations.

America's economic conflict with Japan in the eighties and into the nineties was an excellent example of an "intermestic" issue. For over a decade, the United States' automobile industry had been battered by Japanese competition. The main reason, despite administration and auto executive complaints of an unlevel playing field, was the simple fact that they were making better cars than Americans. Ronald Reagan and George Bush were free traders. But they could not ignore the clamor from their constituents to do something about Japanese automobiles. Economic conflict between Detroit and Tokyo, stemming primarily from the failure of the American automobile industries to compete, led to increasingly tense Japanese-American diplomatic relations.

Ironically, on his January 1992 trip to Japan and Australasia, Bush encountered Australian farmers who complained about government subsidies to American farmers, which enable them to undersell the Australians. Bush countered by talking about the subsidies that the European Community gave to their farmers as the reason for American price supports. Bush, like the Europeans, could not afford to alienate such an important sector of the economy and the electorate, even though he theoretically opposed all subsidies.

In a comparable vein, voters in the normally anticommunist Farm Belt were enraged when Jimmy Carter embargoed wheat shipments to the Soviet Union to punish the communists for their invasion of Afghanistan. The fiercely anti-Soviet Ronald Reagan championed the farmers' cause in the election of 1980, in another example of the complexities of intermestic politics.

Several of the major events that accompanied the end of the Cold War illustrate intermestic politics as well. When the nations of eastern Europe and the old Soviet Union moved toward capitalism and democracy, Americans cheered. They were less enthusiastic, however, when their new friends asked for billions of dollars in loans and credits to make it through the difficult transition to a free-market economy. As Republicans and Democrats warily approached the election of 1992 during a serious recession, they were nervous about offering the much-needed massive aid to foreigners while their own economy was in the doldrums.

As for defense cutbacks in the early nineties, many observers assumed that once the Cold War was over, the United States would enjoy a huge peace dividend that would come with a downsizing of its military-industrial complex. That dividend would have to wait, however, at least until the 1992 election, because downsizing meant the closing of factories and bases, which had an enormous impact on local economies. All Americans supported defense cuts in the abstract until they involved installations in their cities or counties. Even the simple reduction of armed forces personnel threatened economic stability since it would throw tens of thousands of young men on the job market during a time of high unemployment. Thus, the United States reached a position in the early 1990s where it had built up a massive military-industrial complex to fight an enemy that no longer existed; but that complex had become so important politically and economically that it could not be dismantled without creating a domestic tidal wave of opposition.

Foreign-policy symbols, if not foreign policy itself, figured prominently in the 1988 election. Both candidates, Republican George Bush and Democrat Michael Dukakis tried to demonstrate that they were not "wimps." Dukakis, in particular, assailed for appearing to be too peaceful a fellow to succeed Ronald Reagan, took a ride in a tank at a plant in Michigan to demonstrate he was tough enough to command the American military. Unfortunately, the Massachusetts governor looked so silly in the tank that his well-publicized sound bite backfired against him. George Bush was far more successful demonstrating that despite his preppie image, he was a red-blooded American who would defend the nation against foreign enemies as well as domestic flag burners.

Bush's foreign-policy expertise and contacts with leaders all over the world contributed to his relative success in the global crisis precipitated by Iraq's invasion of Kuwait in August 1990. As during the Vietnam War, the home front was a major factor in the President's ability to wage the political, and ultimately, military, battles in the Gulf crisis of 1991–1992. Learning from some of the failures of Johnson and Nixon during the Vietnam War, Bush made certain that he had the support of the population before he introduced escalatory policies. For example, although he did not ask for a declaration of war, he did ask Congress for approval to use force if necessary to remove Iraq from Kuwait.

By this time, most Americans believed the myth that they lost the war in Vietnam in part because of weakness at home produced by the media, which allegedly supported antiwar positions. Concerned about their negative image during the Gulf crisis, the media undercovered dissenting activities and also generally accepted the strict constraints placed upon them in combat areas.

George Bush himself ended the war once the Iraqis had surrendered in Kuwait, not only because of pressures from his international coalition but be-

cause he felt that any attempt to take Baghdad and throw Saddam Hussein from power would lead to a much longer war with many more casualties. Given the Vietnam and Korean War experiences, he feared a rapid diminution of his widespread popular support had the war dragged on for a while. Ironically, the fact that the coalition did not depose Hussein made it more difficult for Bush to boast about his achievements in the Gulf War during the 1992 presidential campaign. His opponent, Bill Clinton, avoided military service in a somewhat controversial manner and even participated in the antiwar movement during the Vietnam War. Only a small percentage of the electorate claimed that Clinton's activities in the late sixties and early seventies affected their votes. It may well be that the 1992 election marked the beginning of the end of the Vietnam War as a volatile issue in American politics.

CONCLUSION

For over two centuries, American presidents have had to concern themselves with an unusually wide variety of domestic influences as they developed and conducted foreign policies. Whether those influences included the imminence of elections, partisan opposition from Congress, parochial economic considerations, or the lobbying of hyphenate groups, the presidents frequently found themselves constrained from pursuing policies they considered to be in the national interest. Of course, they themselves often cloaked their own partisan policies, directed toward their reelections, in the mantle of national interest.

Writing in the 1830s, when the United States was a marginal player on the international scene, Alexis de Tocqueville was prescient when he worried about the ability of the unusual new nation to operate a rational and effective diplomacy. Nevertheless, although the United States did not always opt for the wisest foreign policy once it joined the major-power club at the turn of the century, it did survive its international crises and wars, while many other nations that operated with fewer domestic constraints on their foreign policies did not.

Obviously the nation's impregnability until the 1950s contributed to its relative success, as did its admirable position in terms of economic power and political stability. It may be true, as well, that the need to cover all domestic bases in times of crisis made American foreign policy stronger because it generally was supported by most citizens. In the short run, undemocratic systems and even those democratic systems in which diplomats operated on longer leashes, appeared to have the advantage in diplomatic duels in which secrecy and dispatch were prime considerations. Such freedom, however, did not necessarily result in more rational or successful policies than those produced by the cumbersome American system.

With the end of the Cold War and the elimination of the major-power enemy against whom most Americans would rally in a crisis, domestic influences may become even more problematic for American foreign-policymakers. Complicating matters is the dramatic increase in the number of democratic states in eastern Europe, the former Soviet Union, and in Latin America, Africa, and Asia. On one hand, they too will have to deal with a more cumbersome political system, often involving legislative-executive conflict, irredentist hyphenate groups, local economic concerns, and periodic elections. On the other hand, those domestic issues may not be as important as they once were since a new world order may be more peaceful than the last. At the least, over the past two hundred years democratic states have rarely engaged in war with one another.

To be sure, they have not always produced the most effective foreign policies. The great American realist, George F. Kennan, was not the first to be concerned about the inability of such polities to operate abroad according to the principles of realpolitik established by the Metternichs and the Bismarcks. Yet as one examines the American diplomatic experience, it is clear that presidents committed more blunders when they tried to operate secretly and in an undemocratic fashion than when they produced programs that were influenced by and acceptable to the wide variety of often insular groups outside the State Department, the Oval Office, and the National Security Council. Further, much of the time, they were unable to employ traditional diplomatic strategies that would have pleased the most rigorous "realpolitican." Perhaps Tocqueville was not so prescient after all.

SEE ALSO The National-Security State; The World Wars; Limited Wars; Pacifism and Arms Limitation; World Regions; Cultural Interactions (all in this volume).

BIBLIOGRAPHY

A sweeping survey of cultural themes and popular moods that have influenced foreign policies is Robert Dallek, *The American Style of Foreign Policy: Cultural Politics and Foreign Affairs* (1983). Richard J. Barnet, *The Rockets Red Glare: When America Goes to War: The Presidents and the People* (1990), is an informed critique of the way presidents have misled the public since the early days of the republic. Although somewhat outdated, Barry B. Hughes, *The Domestic Context of American Foreign Policy* (1978), remains the best textbook in the field.

Edward W. Chester, *Sectionalism, Politics, and American Diplomacy* (1975), meticulously examines how the various sections have reacted to foreign policy initiatives throughout American history. For the important role of the ethnicity of American foreign relations, Louis L. Gerson, *The Hyphenate in Recent American Politics and Diplomacy* (1964), can now be supplemented with Alexander DeConde, *Ethnicity, Race, and American Foreign Policy: A History* (1992).

For skeptical views about the ability of the United States to conduct an effective foreign policy, Walter Lippmann, *Essays in the Public Philosophy* (1955), retains its value for the prominent journalist's thoughtful musings; and George F. Kennan, *American Diplomacy: 1900–1950* (1951), is one of the most influential statements of the realist position. Both authors would disagree with the arguments presented by Charles Chatfield, *The American Peace Movement: Ideals and Activism* (1992), the best overview of the movement.

Ralph B. Levering, *The Public and American Foreign Policy, 1918–1978* (1978), offers a brief, intelligent survey of the public attitudes and interest groups, undertaken for the Foreign Policy Association. Also concentrating on the recent period are "Democracy and Foreign Policy: Community and Constraint," *Journal of Conflict Resolution* 35 (June 1991), a special issue of the journal that features articles from a social-science perspective; and Charles W. Kegley, Jr., and Eugene R. Wittkopf, eds., *The Domestic Sources of American Foreign Policy: Insights and Evidence* (1988), another valuable collection from social scientists.

For the debate over intervention in World War II, Wayne S. Cole, *Roosevelt and the Isolationists: 1932–*

1945 (1983), exhaustively describes the fierce rhetorical battle. To understand how foreign policy affected the election of 1940 and subsequent elections to 1960, Robert A. Divine, *Foreign Policy and U.S. Presidential Elections* 2 vols. (1974), is an essential source. Walter Lafeber, "American Policymakers, Public Opinion, and the Outbreak of the Cold War," in Yonosuke Nagai and Akira Iriye, eds., *The Origins of the Cold War in Asia* (1977), pp. 43–65, is an insightful essay. Two specialized studies on the early Cold War are Richard M. Freeland, *The Truman Doctrine and the Origins of McCarthyism: Foreign Policy, Domestic Politics, and Internal Security, 1946–1948* (1972); and Athan Theoharis, *The Yalta Myths: An Issue in U.S. Politics, 1945–1955* (1970). During the same period, Michael Cohen, *Truman and Israel* (1990), analyzes one of the most complicated cases of the domestic influences on foreign policy. Edward Tivnan, *The Lobby: Jewish Political Power and American Foreign Policy* (1987), is a fair-minded study of the most important hyphenate lobbying group in contemporary America.

Bernard C. Cohen, *The Public's Impact on Foreign Policy* (1973), is a leading political scientist's view of the way the public and foreign policy officials interacted during the 1950s and 1960s. For congressional activity, James M. McCormick and Eugene R. Wittkopf, "Bipartisanship, Partisanship, and Ideology in Congressional-Executive Relations, 1947–1988," *Journal of Politics* 52 (November 1990): 1077–1100, relies heavily on analysis of roll-call votes to reveal that the bipartisanship of the early Cold War has been exaggerated; and Cecil V. Crabb and Pat M. Holt, *Invitation to Struggle: Congress, the President, and Foreign Policy* (1989), concentrates on the more recent period.

Fen Osler Hampson, "The Divided Decision-Maker: American Domestic Politics and the Cuban Crises," in Kegley and Wittkopf, eds., *The Domestic Sources of American Foreign Policy*, pp. 222–247, explains how domestic variables came into play during two Cuban-American crises. Among the most useful of the many books on the Vietnam War are David Levy, *The Debate Over Vietnam* (1991), for a general survey; John E. Mueller, *War, Presidents, and Public Opinion* (1973), which uses polling data from both the Korean and Vietnam wars to show how they lost public support; Charles Debenedetti with Charles Chatfield, *An American Ordeal: The Antiwar Movement of the Vietnam Era* (1990), a well-researched and sensitive study of the controversial movement; and Melvin Small, *Johnson, Nixon, and the Doves* (1988), which relates antiwar activities to policy making. Jack Snyder, *Myths of the Empire: Domestic Politics and International Ambition* (1991), is a sophisticated study of the many ways domestic issues interacted with foreign issues in recent American history.

Analyzing forces that worked against detente in the late 1970s is Dan Caldwell, *The Dynamics of Domestic Politics and Arms Control: The SALT II Treaty Ratification Debate* (1991). Some of those forces were involved in intermestic politics, a concept in Ryan J. Barilleaux, "The President, 'Intermestic' Issues, and the Risks of Leadership," in Kegley and Wittkopf, eds., *The Domestic Sources of American Foreign Policy*, pp. 178–188. In a paean to democracy, Miroslav Nincic, *Democracy and Foreign Policy: The Fallacy of Political Realism* (1992), concludes that the public's preference in recent American foreign policies have generally been wise and prudent.

THE NATIONAL SECURITY STATE

Mark M. Lowenthal

In the late 1960s and early 1970s, largely as an offshoot of opposition to the Vietnam War, the term *national security* took on a pejorative meaning as used by critics, denoting not only their dissent against the war, but their view that national security concerns and organs were too powerful and out of control. This essay takes a more objective stance. As used here, *national security state* means the necessary joining of various policies, interests, and concerns—foreign policy, defense policy, labor and industrial capabilities, economics, internal security—that focus on the ability of a nation to respond to threats to its survival and to advance what it sees as legitimate policy goals.

The term *national security* only came into broad usage during and immediately after World War II. But even during the earlier part of the century, U.S. policymakers were concerned with concepts of the United States as a power in relation to the rest of the world, how to define fundamental national interests, and how to assess potential threats to those interests and available U.S. responses. Similarly, there are antecedents early in the twentieth century for the various organizational issues involved in national security—largely dealing with the best way disparate policies and resources can be brought together, and touching not only on responses by the executive branch but also on the balance of power between the president and Congress in foreign and defense policy. Changing levels of national effort devoted to the problem of security as indicated by military manpower, defense spending, overseas bases, and—not so obviously—by education, propaganda, domestic programs, although evident to some degree in the earlier part of the century, only became more closely integrated with a robust national security structure in the period following 1941.

Thus, the history of national security in the twentieth century is a combination of nascent policy concepts and new policy decisions, along with issues of organization and the proper allocation of national effort broadly conceived.

THE IMPERIAL UNITED STATES, 1898–1914

All wars, regardless of the initial purposes for which they are fought, have unintended outcomes. So it was with the United States' "splendid little war" with Spain in 1898. Ostensibly fought over the future of Cuba, the war resulted in the United States occupying and then taking long-term control over a number of territories, many of them in the Pacific. For Theodore Roosevelt, as assistant secretary of the Navy the man perhaps most responsible for the taking of the Philippines, and several of his like-minded friends—Sen. Henry Cabot Lodge, Capt. Alfred Thayer Mahan, and others—imperial expansion was necessary for reasons of morality, honor, and world power. This last point is important conceptually, because it meant that at the beginning of the twentieth century the United States had a group of political leaders with some sense of a broader world role for the nation and of the accoutrements of power that such a role required.

One such need was for a larger army. Before the war with Spain, the army had numbered 28,000, expanding to 210,000 during the hostilities. After the war, the authorized size was 89,000, although the actual average for the period from 1902 to 1911 was 75,000—still a large increase for the peacetime establishment. More significantly, one-third of these troops were now stationed outside North America, a major change.

The role of these troops overseas was also new. First, the outbreak of the Philippine Insurrection in February 1899 gave the army a war to fight whose purpose differed from past conflicts, including the various campaigns against the Indians. In those cases, the ultimate goal was pacification as a prelude to American settlement; in the Philippines, it was the defeat of an independence movement opposed to U.S. sovereignty over territory that political leaders had already decided would never be made part of the United States proper. The Philippines experience (along with Cuba and Puerto Rico) also thrust soldiers into the role of governors, again in a way different from that encountered in either former U.S. territories or in the occupied South during Reconstruction. This role turned out to be short-lived, as civil government was instituted in 1901, albeit with recurrent civil-military frictions until the insurrection ended in 1902. Interestingly, the army role in the Philippines included the first large-scale use of soldiers in what would now be called civic-affairs programs—health, sanitation, education, and public works.

The conduct of the war and the subsequent requirements of empire also buttressed the arguments of "Big Navy" advocates, again including Theodore Roosevelt and other Mahanists. Although even American isolationists had long focused on the navy as the first line of defense, the emphasis of these new advocates was different. They urged a "blue-water navy" of battleships and cruisers, rather than smaller ships devoted to coastal defense. Under President Roosevelt such a fleet came into being. By 1905 Congress had built or authorized ten battleships. Roosevelt initially believed a fleet of twenty-eight battleships would suffice; with the sudden revolution in naval architecture created by Britain's 1906 launching of HMS *Dreadnought,* Roosevelt increased his annual request from one new battleship to four. Roosevelt eventually used the Great White Fleet as an interesting politico-military tool, its 1906–1907 global cruise serving to demonstrate the United States' arrival on the world stage, to argue in favor of completing what might be termed the United States' first strategic program—the Panama Canal—and as a specifically pointed message to another power emerging on the world stage, Japan, with whom relations were difficult at best.

Finally, the aftermath of the war saw the first steps toward a more modern military administrative system to respond to its new responsibilities. The first step came with the Navy's creation of a General Board in 1900, an advisory group focusing on war plans and fleet composition and deployment. Army reform was more fundamental. That service had long been plagued by the division of authority between the secretary of war and the commanding general, and by the absence of any long-range planning capability. In 1903, despite stubborn opposition in Congress and within the Army bureaucracy, Secretary Elihu Root succeeded in getting passed legislation that created a chief of staff of the Army, with authority over the various Army bureaus and departments

(which the Navy's General Board did not have and which Congress rejected when Roosevelt proposed a similar reform), and a General Staff Corps. That same year the Army War College was established (the Naval War College had been created in 1884), which took on an important planning function. In the summer of 1903 the two services created the Joint Board to achieve some level of coordination on issues of mutual concern. It took another nine years before the chief of staff actually gained supremacy over the internal Army opposition, led by the adjutant general. Despite the limited immediate effect of these various steps (which should also be seen as part of the Progressive Era's fascination with improved organizational methods), they were a keystone to a military better able to cope with its new responsibilities and with the global visions of the political leaders.

There was an effort mounted during the Taft administration to take this coordination one step further, with the Army and Navy's suggestion that a Council of National Defense be created to coordinate military planning with national policy. (As Richard Challener notes in *Admirals, Generals, and American Foreign Policy, 1898–1914,* the military also hoped that such a scheme of military planners buttressed by executive policies would also ease the appropriations process in Congress.) Members of Congress raised objections about an undue role for the military; the opposition of Secretary of State Philander C. Knox and his department, a necessary participant in such a scheme, was fatal.

Defining interests and assessing potential threats are difficult and sometimes dangerous enterprises, as the lists can be drawn too narrowly or too broadly, and can even generate a certain amount of wish fulfillment. The one geopolitical interest that was most clear in this period was that of U.S. hegemony over the Caribbean. Such a concept was not entirely new: Secretary of State Richard Olney's 1895 interpretation of the Monroe Doctrine said as much, but the circumstances had changed. War with Spain had brought the United States actual possessions in the Caribbean; construction of the Panama Canal had raised the strategic importance of the region to the United States. One reflection of this concern was the 1902 creation of the Caribbean Squadron of the U.S. Navy. The United States' interests in Europe were largely unrecognized, Roosevelt's participation in the 1905–1906 Moroccan crisis notwithstanding. East Asian interests were more complex, given the new U.S. acquisitions and the presence of both regional and colonial competitors. The McKinley administration's Open Door remained the overarching theme, but one that flew in the face of power realities in Asia.

The definition of threats during this period is striking for its ultimate irony. Military planners and some political leaders tended to focus most on Japan and Germany. Japan's status as a threat arose from the advent of the U.S. colonial empire in the Pacific—Hawaii, Guam, and the Philippines—with the Philippines much closer to Tokyo than they were to San Francisco, and Japan's own meteoric appearance on the world stage, punctuated by its victories over China and Russia. Domestic concerns over Japanese immigration and the treatment of Japanese already in the United States sharpened the issue. Relations with Germany were not as difficult, but repetitive clashes of interest in the Pacific and the Caribbean gave them threatening status. The military developed a series of COLOR plans to deal with these threats, the remarkably long-lived ORANGE Plan for Japan and Plan BLACK for Germany.

Finally, just as U.S. policymakers at the turn of the century saw an increasing consonance of United States and British interests and effected a diplomatic rapprochement with its "traditional enemy," military planners began to think along similar friendly lines about Britain. Thus U.S. military concerns about Germany were mirrored by the Anglo-German rivalry in Europe and, more importantly, rapprochement with Britain offered the hope that concerns about Japan could be ameliorated via the 1902 Anglo-Japanese alliance.

WORLD WAR I, 1914–1919

The predominant view in the United States of the outbreak of war in Europe in 1914 was that this conflict posed no threat to vital U.S. interests. President Woodrow Wilson certainly held and reflected this view, perhaps even longer than most of his advisers. The initial dilemma posed for the United States by the war was traditional—the rights of neutrals on the high seas—with both Britain and Germany giving cause for concern and offense at the outset of the war. This even-handed view remained prevalent until the first diplomatic crisis with Germany over its submarine warfare. Although, after the *Lusitania*'s sinking in 1915, Germany backed down from attacks without warning, this initial diplomatic confrontation created a shift in the opinions of some, leading to the preparedness debate.

Actually, there was already a burgeoning movement to improve the trained military manpower base in the United States. Led by Chief of Staff General

Leonard Wood, voluntary summer military training at colleges had begun in 1913. The outbreak of war gave Wood—probably the most politically minded U.S. general between George McClellan and Douglas MacArthur—and his supporters, including Theodore Roosevelt, added impetus. At stake here was an old issue in U.S. military manpower policy, the adequacy of the militia— now known as the National Guard—to fill out the small Regular Army in wartime. The War Department exercised little control over Guard training and had little power to call upon it. Congress, reflecting local interests that controlled Guard units, opposed greater federal control. Limited progress had been made by Root in 1903 when

Leonard Wood, Governor General of the Philippines, 1921–1927. PRINTS AND PHOTOGRAPHS DIVISION, LIBRARY OF CONGRESS

Congress passed the Dick Act (replacing the antiquated 1792 Militia Act), but the Guard remained an uncertain contributor to national defense.

The nation was sharply divided by the preparedness debate. Many supported Wilson's principled stand against greater preparedness; members of the influential economic and social establishment who gathered for further summer military training at Plattsburg, New York, in 1915 urged greater defense measures, forming the prodefense Plattsburg movement. Wilson, attuned to public opinion, shifted his position in 1915 and came out for an increased defense program—a five-year naval building program for what would be a high-seas battle fleet and support for the Army plan to increase the size of the Regular force and to scrap the National Guard in favor of a 400,000-man, purely federal (versus state-based) reserve called the Continental Army. Congress altered both plans. Although it authorized an increase in the size of the peacetime Regular Army to 175,000 over five years (wartime strength was authorized at 300,000), Congress killed the Guard-threatening Continental Army; in addition Congress passed the largest naval bill in U.S. history.

A potentially significant part of the 1916 National Defense Act was the creation of a Council of National Defense to coordinate the industries and resources necessary for national security. Comprised of the secretaries of war, navy, interior, agriculture, commerce, and labor (but not state), and given civilian industry and labor leaders as advisers, the Council had little role in the coming war, although it was the first recognizable effort to bring together the various strands of what would later be termed national security. The 1916 act also authorized the president to place orders for defense production and to force industry compliance, another major change in U.S. attitude.

The shift in Wilson's position on preparedness was a domestic political decision and did not reflect a change in his view of what was at stake in Europe. But by 1915 his influential foreign policy adviser, Col. Edward M. House, had concluded that a German victory would threaten U.S. interests, a view eventually shared by Secretary of State Robert Lansing. Wilson's goal, rather consistently, remained one of avoiding belligerency and thus serving to help mediate a victoryless end to the war. His desire to mediate reached the point in late 1916 that House and Lansing feared that a positive German response to Wilson's initiatives might force the United States to side with Germany in the war.

Ultimately, Germany's January 1917 calculation that the advantages of unrestricted submarine warfare outweighed the disadvantages of U.S. belligerency tipped the scales for Wilson. Arthur Link, in *Wilson the Diplomatist,* argues that, had Germany exempted U.S. shipping from this new order, Wilson might still have seen fit to avoid belligerency, although the political costs in terms of the preparedness groups would have been high. Link suggests that Wilson also feared a German victory, but his war message was couched entirely in terms of reaction to the German submarine-warfare decision.

The effects of World War I on the home front were dramatic. The realities of war revealed the inadequacies of the 1916 act; much more manpower than 300,000 Regulars and 400,000 National Guardsmen was needed. In May 1917 the Selective Service Act was passed. Unlike the baneful Civil War experience, however, the 1917 draft was administered locally and by civilians; it also eliminated enlistment bounties, substitutes, and purchased exemptions but allowed exemptions for essential occupations or family conditions. Moreover, draftees were to serve "for the duration." This draft was successful (despite a significant evasion rate), ultimately registering over 22 million men and selecting over 3.6 million.

The economic and industrial requirements of the war also saw unparalleled intrusion by the government in the economy. The first requirement was money. Although income taxes had begun in 1913, Treasury officials preferred not to raise rates dramatically or to impose other new taxes, although both of these did occur to some extent. Instead, some two-thirds of war costs ($15.5 billion) were financed by highly successful Liberty Bond drives; the remaining third ($8.8 billion) came from taxes.

In quick succession in the months following U.S. entry into the war, a plethora of boards was created to control or coordinate various aspects of the economy needed to prosecute the war. Some, like the Food Administration under Herbert Hoover, which oversaw the production, allocation, and conservation of food, were successful. Others, like the Shipping Board and Fleet Corporation, charged with providing the merchant fleet needed to keep U.S. troops and the Allies supplied, were not. Some industries tried voluntary or cooperative organization, which many business advisers of the government favored. In the case of the railroads, this failed; in January 1918 the government took control of the rails.

Most central was the issue of industrial mobilization and war production, to which little advance planning had been devoted by the military. In April 1917 the Council of National Defense created a General Munitions Board (GMB) to coordinate military requirements and industry production. The GMB proved to be too unwieldy and lacked any real authority beyond its effort to coordinate. Moreover, the military, particularly the Army, was extremely reluctant to yield to civilians any authority over procurement and was hampered by ongoing turf battles within its own organization. Robert D. Cuff, in *The War Industries Board,* characterized the GMB as "an adjunct of the War Department."

Some four months after its creation, the GMB was superseded by the War Industries Board (WIB). Initially, it was a minor improvement over the GMB, still lacking real authority and still competing with the Army and Navy for control over supplies and priorities. By the winter of 1917–1918 there were supply crises in several sectors. The situation improved in March 1918 with the accession of Bernard Baruch to the WIB chairmanship, empowered by Wilson with authority over all issues except prices. Although the WIB still lacked as much power as some thought necessary, Baruch used his authority to set priorities to gain some control over both resources and production. Germany's collapse in November 1918 precluded both a second supply crisis and any extension of WIB authority.

Propaganda is probably as old as war itself, but organized propaganda by the U.S. government was another novel aspect of the World War I experience. Under the leadership of journalist George Creel, the Committee on Public Information effectively—in the view of many critics, overzealously—whipped up patriotism. Driven by the notion of "100 percent Americanism"—which John Higham points out in *Strangers in the Land* was a blend of traditional nativism, ongoing political moralizing, and more recent wartime nationalism—there were also excesses against various manifestations of German culture and people of German background. Wilson used the 1798 Alien Enemies Act to jail 1,200 German aliens without trial. Conscientious objectors fared poorly, helping give rise to the National Civil Liberties Bureau, predecessor to the American Civil Liberties Union. Various acts passed after the United States entered the war curtailed First Amendment rights of pacifists and political radicals; socialist leader Eugene V. Debs was sentenced to ten years imprisonment under the broadly cast 1917 Espionage Act for protesting some of these very laws.

Much has been written about Wilson at Versailles and the subsequent debate in the United States over the League of Nations. Three points are relevant to this discussion. First, Wilson remained true to his personal desire to serve as an impartial mediator, despite U.S. belligerency. There was a clear clash between his ideals and traditional European diplomacy; Wilson, with the war over, had little leverage over France and Britain. It is also questionable whether any type of diplomacy was well-suited to the political chaos that had descended upon Europe. Second, it is unclear whether Wilson's goals were simply his own or reflected a wider U.S. view. The political repudiation of the 1918 congressional elections called into question Wilson's mandate. Moreover, having failed to enunciate any compelling national security goals upon entering the war, it was difficult to claim that any of the Fourteen Points (except the second, freedom of the seas) reflected broadly agreed upon U.S. wartime goals. Third, as Link points out in *Wilson the Diplomatist,* the debate over the League was not over U.S. entry versus no entry, but over unconditional entry versus conditions, this latter position being supported by many Americans and a majority of the Senate. Wilson, whose attitude toward Congress regarding defense and foreign policy was imperious, found any tampering with the treaty to be anathema and let it die rather than be changed.

One organizational innovation related to Versailles should be noted. In 1917, at Wilson's request, House organized the Inquiry, a group of academic advisers, to help formulate the peace. Although not as influential as they had hoped to be, the Inquiry was the forerunner of the large-scale involvement of academicians in national security policy that burgeoned after World War II.

THE INTERWAR YEARS, 1919–1939

The collapse of the old order in Europe raised a new specter, bolshevism. Wilson opposed Lenin's regime on moral grounds and ordered U.S. troops into northwestern Russia to guard war supplies and into Siberia mainly as a counter to a large Japanese intervention. But in the immediate postwar period, bolshevism appeared to many to pose a domestic threat. With the onset of peace, there was, predictably, a breakdown of industry-labor unity, with a rash of strikes in 1919. This, combined with the lingering effects of the wartime efforts against political radicals, led to the Red Scare, fought and abetted by Attorney General A. Mitchell Palmer. A largely failed series of bombings allowed the politically ambitious Palmer to exaggerate the threat. In 1919 and 1920, federal and local raids against foreign-born radicals led to their deportation. By the end of 1920 Palmer fell

The Big Four. British prime minister David Lloyd George, Italian prime minister Vittorio Orlando, French premier Georges Clemenceau, and President Woodrow Wilson, Paris, May 1919. PRINTS AND PHOTOGRAPHS DIVISION, LIBRARY OF CONGRESS

victim to his own exaggeration and overreaching, including efforts for a peacetime sedition law. A lasting legacy of the Red Scare, however, was the creation of the General Intelligence Division (GID) within the Justice Department's Bureau of Investigation—the forerunner of the Federal Bureau of Investigation—and the naming of attorney J. Edgar Hoover to the GID's number-two position.

The end of the war saw the traditional U.S. effort to demobilize quickly. The Army released 3.25 million troops in nine months. Interestingly, some nine divisions took part in occupation duties in the Rhineland, although by 1920 this force was down to 15,000 and continued to dwindle until its withdrawal in 1924.

Debate over the postwar role of the Army led to the National Defense Act of 1920, which rejected the traditional model of an expansible Regular Army and relied instead on the Regular Army, and civilian National Guards and Organized Reserves, both of which were capable of meeting wartime emergency needs and were trained by the Regular Army—a system that has survived to the end of the twentieth century. The act also assigned the War Department responsibility for contingency war plans and industrial mobilization plans, a dramatic change. Finally, the act authorized Regular Army and National Guard strength to be, respectively, 280,000 and 436,000. But, the absence of any visible threat led Congress to limit appropriations and Army size, so that by 1922 the Regulars numbered 137,000 and the National Guard 180,000.

The Army was less successful in dealing with its fledgling air capability. Although officers in the Army Air Service and some members of Congress advocated a separate air force, the most the Army would agree to in 1926 was an upgrade to the Army Air Corps, greater representation for Air officers on the General Staff and creation of a new assistant secretary of war for "aeronautics." In a move of rare organizational foresight, the Navy created a Bureau of Aeronautics in 1921. As Vincent J. Davis points out in *The Admirals Lobby*, the Navy's desire to coopt its aviators and keep them firmly under control was a prime motivator in this move.

The Navy was, traditionally, the first line of defense. It faced reductions too, albeit by disarmament. This was not an entirely new concept. Theodore Roosevelt had called for a second Hague Conference in 1904, and a reduction in armaments had been one of Wilson's Fourteen Points. There was also congressional interest, led by Senator William Borah. Thomas Buckley notes in *The United States and the Washington Conference* that congressional support for disarmament grew as support for the League fell.

The 1921–1922 Washington Conference actually represented a merging of two disparate national interests: the U.S. goal to reduce naval levels and British concerns over the Far East. The composition of the U.S. delegation is worth noting. Apparently learning from Wilson's mistake at Versailles, Secretary of State Charles Evans Hughes included two Republican senators (Lodge and Root) and one Democrat (Oscar Underwood).

Hughes's dramatic opening speech calling for major naval disarmament was largely successful and also recognized the likelihood that Congress would not fund the ambitious 1916 naval program that was still underway. The Five-Power Naval Treaty instituted a 5:5:3:1.67:1.67 naval ratio for the United States, Britain, Japan, France and Italy, limited future capital-ship design and construction, and froze fortifications on the Pacific islands. Some critics, largely with hindsight, held that the fortifications freeze left U.S. possessions vulnerable and the Philippines a hostage but, again, it was unlikely that Congress would approve major spending here. The Four-Power Treaty negotiated at the conference recognized the status quo in the Pacific and also achieved the U.S. goal of ending

the Anglo-Japanese alliance, which the Navy's General Board saw as potentially threatening. The Nine-Power Treaty theoretically upheld the Open Door in China. All told, the United States had achieved a number of interrelated defense and foreign policy goals in very short order. The treaties, especially the Naval Treaty, were also important psychologically because they solidified the prevailing view in the United States that now there were no serious foreign threats.

A little noticed addition to national security at this time was cryptanalysis, the making and breaking of codes. The United States had a fledgling capability during World War I, but U.S. cryptanalysis really got underway in 1919. Using joint War Department and State Department funds, Herbert O. Yardley set up what became known as the Black Chamber. The cryptographers' first major contribution to U.S. foreign policy came during the Washington Conference, when Yardley's group provided Hughes with decrypted Japanese cables, revealing their bargaining positions.

As would be the case with later arms control, the Washington Treaty sparked a race in uncontrolled arms, in this case, cruisers. After an abortive 1927 effort to contain this new race, the powers agreed to a new treaty in London in 1930. Japan won a 10:7 ratio in cruisers and destroyers and parity in submarines; there was also a further reduction in capital-ship tonnage. U.S. Navy officers viewed the increase in the Japanese ratio as potentially fatal to the defense of the Pacific.

Perhaps no treaty quite caught the temper of the times as well as the 1928 Kellogg-Briand Pact. Eventually, over sixty nations renounced war "as an instrument of national policy"—albeit with reservations about the right to self-defense and, in the case of the United States, the proviso that adherence carried with it no obligations for enforcement. In reality, as noted in Thomas Buckley's *American Foreign and National Security Policies*, the pact arose from a tortuous diplomatic minuet of French eagerness for and U.S. unwillingness to give some commitment to French security. Still, the wild enthusiasm that greeted the treaty and the naive belief in its efficacy said much about the predominant view of the proper U.S. role in the world.

Given this view, it is not surprising that the Army and Navy had to scramble even for meager funding. The total of all U.S. armed forces averaged around 250,000 for the period 1923–1933; spending averaged $3.2 billion annually. Deprived of sufficient shipbuilding funds to reach even treaty limits, the

Navy devoted some resources to modernization, including lighter armor and the conversion from coal to oil, which would prove crucial in World War II. The onset of the Depression worsened these parsimonious trends, given the propensity of Presidents Herbert Hoover and, initially, Franklin D. Roosevelt, for balanced federal budgets as part of their economic response.

Roosevelt, however, soon changed his view, quickly coming to see shipbuilding as one facet of a jobs program. In June 1933, by Executive Order 6174, Roosevelt transferred $238 million in National Industrial Recovery Act funds to begin bringing the Navy up to London Treaty limits, a total of thirty-one ships. Roosevelt was surprised when no one objected to this bureaucratic legerdemain. The Navy's own appropriations were also increased. Roosevelt found a ready ally in Representative Carl Vinson, chairman of the House Naval Affairs Committee. Vinson had urged such a step on the unwilling and virtually pacifistic Hoover, during whose term not a single new ship was built. The result was the 1934 Vinson-Trammell Act, an authorization (a program) rather than an appropriation (actual money) to build up to the London limits. The ships that eventually were built formed the basis of the World War II Navy.

Interestingly, one of the rationales in the debate over Vinson-Trammell was Japan's increasingly aggressive foreign policy. Japan's seizure of Manchuria from China in 1931–1932 had resulted in the Stimson Doctrine, a pronouncement by Hoover's secretary of state, Henry L. Stimson, that the United States would not recognize changes brought about by actions in violation of Kellogg-Briand. Beyond that statement the United States did little, although Japan remained the only likely foe for which the U.S. had a valid war plan, the resilient ORANGE plan, whose antecedents dated back to 1906.

The Roosevelt administration also saw the revival of U.S. code-breaking efforts, which had been suspended in 1929, when the Hoover administration closed the Black Chamber, based largely on the view that such an activity was incompatible with Hoover and Stimson's views of the moral basis of U.S. foreign policy. (Stimson's oft-quoted and likely apocryphal remark was: "Gentlemen do not read each other's mail.") The Army and Navy maintained their own code-breaking offices and, based on their own reading of international affairs, concentrated on Japan as a target. In 1932 U.S. analysts began working on Japan's diplomatic code; the first decrypted solutions, called MAGIC, were produced in 1940.

These developments in minimal naval rearma-

ment and codebreaking hardly reflected the temper of Congress and the public. The putative "lessons" of the United States' entry into the Great War remained much more important than any apparent breakdown of the postwar settlement. Beginning in 1934, hearings chaired by Sen. Gerald P. Nye blamed profit-seeking bankers and munitions makers, the so-called "merchants of death," for U.S. involvement in the war. In 1935, as the postwar settlement showed its first signs of crumbling in Ethiopia, Congress passed a Neutrality Act. This empowered the president, when proclaiming the existence of a war, to forbid the sale or transportation of munitions to the belligerents and to warn U.S. citizens that they traveled on belligerent vessels at their own risk. The 1937 Neutrality Act forbade travel on belligerents' ships, but allowed the president to list certain items that belligerents could buy if they paid cash and carried them in their own ships, the "cash-and-carry" provision. A 1939 act was less restrictive, but retained restrictions on loans and travel.

These various acts were important not only for what they said about the prevailing sentiment in the United States, but also for their twofold effect on President Roosevelt. First, he tended to overemphasize the strength and depth of what came to be called isolationist sentiment, fostering a certain timidity in him as the prewar crisis deepened. Second, this view drove him to be more devious than usual about certain decisions and their effects, sometimes to the point of self-denial, leading in turn to certain clandestine actions that served as poor precedents for future presidents during the decades to follow.

By 1937 various parts of the foreign policy and defense apparatus began to respond to evident changes in the international environment. Under Army prodding, the services undertook a revision of War Plan ORANGE, which revealed both the deep and longstanding Army and Navy differences over strategy in the Pacific and the plan's irrelevance vis-à-vis the growing uncertainties in Europe. In December 1937 Roosevelt agreed to secret naval talks with Britain about possible war plans in the Pacific. In the aftermath of the Munich conference, about which Roosevelt was first supportive and then perturbed, the President decided to emphasize a massive air power buildup as the best way to increase demonstrable U.S. might. As was often the case with Roosevelt, however, he was more interested in the psychological effects that such a program would have rather than its practicality or military balance. News of the program was more important than any practical effect it had on improving military capabilities.

WORLD WAR II, 1939–1945

The Army-inspired revision of War Plan ORANGE led the military to assess the overall global political situation and its implications for the United States. This willingness—or, from the military's point of view, necessity—was significant because as the Axis threat to the United States increased the military would find itself in the position of having to define not only threats, but plans and options that had important political implications, largely because Roosevelt himself did not do so. In April 1939 the military's Joint Planners saw Germany as the main threat, focusing on potential subversion in Latin America. By June 1939 the Joint Planners had crafted the RAINBOW plans (as opposed to the old COLOR plans), with five different cases depending on the strategic scenario. These ranged from the most basic plan, RAINBOW 1 (defense of the Western Hemisphere) to RAINBOW 5 (war in alliance with Britain and France; projection of U.S. forces to Europe to defeat Germany and Italy). Uncharacteristically, Roosevelt gave verbal approval to RAINBOW 1—a plan still beyond U.S. military capabilities—in October 1939.

The Army, which under the 1920 act had responsibility for industrial mobilization planning, also began a series of revised mobilization plans, resulting in the 1939 Protective Mobilization Plan. Building on a nucleus of 80,000 Regulars and 180,000 National Guardsmen, the plan envisaged an expansion to 420,000 upon mobilization and then up to 740,000 (volunteers and draftees) in eight months, a figure roughly comparable to the existing forces of Britain, France, or Germany.

When war in Europe came in September 1939, Roosevelt reacted far differently than had Wilson. Roosevelt had no aspirations toward and made no pretension of neutrality; still, he felt that efforts to support the Allies were constrained by the neutrality laws and by his interpretation of congressional and public opinion. But whatever expectations he had about the course of the war were undone by Germany's *Blitzkrieg* in May 1940, which defeated France and left Britain fighting alone. The German victory opened up a deep but often halting debate among Roosevelt and his advisers as to the best course for U.S. national security, paralleling a much broader and more vociferous debate taking place in Congress and among the public.

The public side of this debate differed, however, from the preparedness debate that preceded World War I. Few on either side of the issue in 1940 questioned the need to improve U.S. defenses. What was at issue was the national security choice between entering the war against Germany versus armed neutrality. Congress had voted $552 million for defense at the beginning of 1939. In June 1940, hard on the heels of Germany's victory over France, Congress passed a National Defense Tax Bill to raise $994 million, which included provisions for a "two-ocean" navy. More significant was the Selective Training and Service Act, passed in September 1940. This first-ever peacetime draft was in large measure a result of lobbying by private citizens via the Military Training Camps Association (MTCA), many of whom had been part of the Plattsburg movement in the last war. Despite Roosevelt's usual inconstancy and the War Department's initial opposition, the MTCA got the bill introduced and passed. The one-year call-up of 1.2 million troops included an amendment limiting their service to U.S. possessions and territories and the Western Hemisphere, a caveat that actually accorded well with the current state of planning. National Guard mobilization also began that month, thus creating a large expansion of what was still a peacetime force.

The military, assuming Britain was doomed and painfully aware of their own lack of resources, initially urged concentration on Hemispheric Defense (RAINBOW 1). Roosevelt was both more optimistic and, as usual, wanted to keep open as many options as possible. He had already decided that Britain's continued resistance was the key issue and that by keeping Britain in the war he might even stave off the need for U.S. entry. Carrying out this policy was made more difficult by the fact that every major step Roosevelt took—such as the 1940 destroyer-for-bases agreement and Lend-Lease in 1941—actually narrowed his options and made the need for U.S. belligerency more likely if the ultimate goal, Germany's defeat, were to be obtained. The military came to such a conclusion by September 1940; Roosevelt apparently had not.

The military took this conclusion one step further in November 1940, when Adm. Harold R. Stark, chief of naval operations (CNO), wrote a memo that asked the most basic question: What are U.S. interests in the war? Stark, again in advance of the President, accepted the possibility of a two-front war and argued that U.S. interests dictated a strategy of defeating Germany first while maintaining a defensive stance against Japan. Indeed, ongoing Japanese aggression against China greatly complicated planning, leading to a policy aimed at deterring Japan from venturing out into the Pacific. In order to achieve this aim, the U.S. fleet was ordered, in May

1940, to remain in Hawaii after its war games rather than return to the west coast of the U.S., the first attempted use of a strategic deterrent by the United States.

In January 1941, in a step that could hardly be called neutral, the Joint Board, with Roosevelt's permission but with little guidance, convened war planning talks with their British counterparts. These ABC (American-British Conversations) talks, the first of many such conferences, accepted Stark's "Germany first" strategy should the United States, in Roosevelt's words, "be compelled to resort to war." It is not clear when, if ever, Roosevelt accepted the necessity of U.S. entry into the war. Robert Dallek, in *Franklin D. Roosevelt and American Foreign Policy, 1932–1945,* argues that by August 1941, when Roosevelt met Winston Churchill at Argentia Bay, the President had reached such a conclusion. Certainly, the Atlantic Charter—largely a statement of postwar aims—was a remarkable document for a supposedly neutral nation to promulgate alongside a belligerent. But Roosevelt's subsequent inactivity, even in the face of welcome naval incidents with Germany, leaves the issue open. Further, even if Dallek's assessment is correct, by that point Roosevelt likely lagged behind the majority of public opinion on this issue. This is not to suggest that isolationist sentiment was insignificant; the August 1941 vote in the House to extend military service of draftees and National Guardsmen from one year to eighteen months (versus "for the emergency" as Roosevelt requested) only passed by a vote of 203 to 202. The point remains, however, that Roosevelt was not providing leadership to either his planners or the nation.

As was the case before World War I, the very effort to be prepared required a new look at the issue of organization for economic mobilization. This effort began just before the outbreak of war in Europe, with the creation of the War Resources Board, a prominent civilian advisory adjunct to the Army-Navy Munitions Board. Asked to review the Industrial Mobilization Plans, this new panel soon ran afoul of Roosevelt's unwillingness to delegate broad economic authority and was dissolved.

Roosevelt turned next to the old NDAC (National Defense Advisory Council), first authorized in 1916, choosing a mixture of prominent industrialists and union leaders. Marvin A. Kreidberg and Merton G. Henry note in *History of Military Mobilization in the United States Army, 1775–1945,* that Roosevelt had the NDAC report directly to him rather than to the statutory cabinet-level members. Administratively unwieldy, lacking a director, central coordination, or any real authority, NDAC also passed from the scene. Several alphabet-soup agencies followed each other in quick succession, a vivid replay of Roosevelt's administrative methods as experienced during the height of the New Deal. The Office of Production Management (OPM) replaced NDAC, but soon faced a rival in the Office of Price Administration and Civilian Supply (OPACS). OPACS soon split into the Office of Price Administration (OPA) and the Supply Priorities and Allocation Board (SPAB).

It is difficult to see how any coherent organization for economic mobilization was possible at that point. First and foremost, Roosevelt greatly disliked delegating authority to subordinates and preferred to create situations in which they had to compete with one another in policy and administrative areas. Second, as long as Roosevelt was unwilling to accept the absolute necessity of U.S. belligerency, he was not willing to allow the types of dislocation that economic mobilization would entail.

The debate over U.S. policy came to an end with the Japanese attack on Pearl Harbor and the obliging declaration of war four days later by Adolf Hitler, against whom Roosevelt was still reluctant to act. Fanciful theories of U.S. complicity aside, Pearl Harbor stands out as the most massive intelligence failure in U.S. history. Roberta Wohlstetter's *Pearl Harbor: Warning and Decision* points out that the United States committed a number of intelligence errors vis-à-vis Japan, including the failure to coordinate data collection that allowed disparate but significant pieces of information to remain apart, gross underestimates of Japanese capabilities, and mirror-imaging—assuming that Japanese policymakers were motivated by and responded to the same processes of thought and decision as did those in Washington.

Pearl Harbor also served as a largely unappreciated lesson in deterrence: it is impossible to tell whether or not a presumed deterrent is working, as this involves knowing why another nation is *not* doing something. Ironically, the only time that one can be sure that a force has been a deterrent is precisely at that moment when it no longer deters. Thus Japan clearly saw the presence of the U.S. fleet at Hawaii as a problem, which they attempted to solve by attacking it preemptively.

The details of military campaigns are beyond the scope of this essay, but it is important to note the extent to which the World War II effort influenced all aspects of life in the United States and helped create the basic forms of the national security structure and practice that would emerge during the Cold War.

Domestically, the United States went to total mobilization, to an extent that beggared the effort of 1917–1918. Price controls were imposed early in 1942. Strict rationing of food, unknown in the last war, was also imposed. Gasoline was rationed, largely to ameliorate the rubber shortage. According to Richard Polenberg in *War and Society,* by mid-1942 almost one-third of the production of consumer goods had ceased. The military gained broad control over procurement. Some antitrust laws were revised, and the military was allowed to negotiate contracts rather than place them with the lowest bidder and to seek exemptions from some price controls.

The war required an unprecedented level of federal spending. Polenberg notes that government expenses for 1940–1945 were almost twice as much as the total from 1789 to 1940. Roosevelt and his secretary of the Treasury, Henry Morgenthau, preferred taxes to borrowing. Broadening the base of those who had to file income taxes and increasing corporate and excess-profits taxes paid for half of World War II costs, up from 30 percent in 1917–1918. Bonds were issued once again, both to raise revenue and to sop up money so as to control inflation. The bulk of bond sales went to corporate buyers rather than individuals.

Manpower became a major problem, which had not been the case in World War I. Interestingly, in July 1941 Roosevelt had asked the Army and Navy to calculate what the United States would need to do to defeat its presumed enemies. Beyond that task, he gave no guidance, again leaving major definitions and assumptions up to the military. In the Army, the so-called Victory Program devolved down the chain of command to Maj. Albert C. Wedemeyer. Taking into account the needs of industry and the other services, he came up with the prescient figure of 8,795,658 troops (the actual total was 8,291,366). But even with this advance warning, allocating manpower between industry and the front lines became extremely difficult. Ultimately, over 12 million people were in the military at maximum strength, or 8.6 percent of the population (compared to almost 2.9 million or 2.8 percent in World War I).

As always, part of the problem lay in Roosevelt's administrative methods. Paul V. McNutt was given control over manpower (via the War Manpower Commission), which included the Selective Service System, but as this was done by executive order rather than by legislation he lacked real authority. The military, torn between the needs for industrial production and for troops, always came down in favor of troops. In January 1943 McNutt issued a "work or fight"

order as a means of forcing more men into war-related jobs. Predictably, this created domestic political problems from labor and from the powerful farm bloc, which continued to be exempt.

Labor was especially displeased by the instances in which the government took over war-related plants hobbled by strikes under authority of the Smith-Connally Act, passed over Roosevelt's veto. Ultimately, there were some fifty seizures (including coal mines in 1943), half of them carried out by the War Department.

The problems that had bedeviled economic mobilization before the war continued through late 1942, when Roosevelt named associate justice and former senator James Byrnes to head the Office of Economic Stabilization. In 1943 he took over the Office of War Mobilization (which later had the words "and Reconversion" added to its title) and became, in effect, the "assistant president," a title that irked Roosevelt. Rather than running any specific program, Byrnes served as the ultimate coordinator of all the programs. Unlike virtually every other appointee, however, Byrnes had the backing of the President and spoke with final authority.

The demands of a truly global war also necessitated major changes in military organization. Prewar conferences with their well-organized and always united British counterparts made it clear to Admiral Stark and his successor, Admiral Ernest King, and to Army Chief of Staff General George C. Marshall, that their Joint Board apparatus did not compare favorably. In essence, the Joint Board only offered unity at the very top, in the presence of the two chiefs. Below that there remained two (or three, if the Army Air Force was counted separately) parallel but competing organizations of planners, logisticians, etc.

Therefore, in February 1942 the military leaders constituted themselves as the Joint Chiefs of Staff (JCS). By mid-1942 their wartime membership had been set: Marshall; King, who was both chief of naval operations (CNO) and commander in chief, U.S. Fleet; Gen. Henry H. Arnold, commanding general, U.S. Army Air Forces; and Adm. William D. Leahy, a former CNO, whom Roosevelt named to the new position of chief of staff to the commander in chief. Operating without any formal charter, the JCS served as the corporate group responsible for U.S. strategy, the direction of U.S. military operations, and for consultations with military allies, primarily Britain. Leahy was the senior member, although he did not serve as a formal chairman. Rather, he was the principal link between the JCS and the President.

The JCS official history, *The Evolving Role of the Joint Chiefs of Staff in the National Security Structure,* notes that Roosevelt met and dealt with the JCS directly and not through the intermediaries of the secretaries of war and the Navy. As could be expected, an organization to serve the new JCS grew up rapidly, called the Joint Staff.

Much has been written about Roosevelt's relations with the JCS. Unlike Wilson, Roosevelt did not leave the strategy and running of the war entirely to the military. Kent Roberts Greenfield, in *American Strategy in World War II,* holds that Roosevelt overruled the JCS over twenty times, primarily in the earlier stages of the war. Greenfield argues, however, that Roosevelt did so for reasons consistent with his own strategic view of how to win the war and that these concepts largely made sense militarily. There were several motives behind the President's behavior. First, Roosevelt did not hold himself aloof from U.S. allies, as had Wilson, but saw himself as a full and willing partner with Churchill and later with Josef Stalin. Thus, the demands of various wartime conferences and allied unity necessitated a different behavior. Second, Roosevelt enjoyed military issues, while Wilson almost seemed to feel they were abhorrent.

William "Wild Bill" Donovan, director of the Office of Strategic Services in World War II. NATIONAL ARCHIVES

Finally, as noted, Roosevelt rarely delegated full authority in any sphere.

A further organizational innovation came in the area of intelligence. In July 1941 Roosevelt heeded the advice of one of his many informal advisers, William J. Donovan, and created the Office of the Coordinator of Information, with Donovan as coordinator. Like the JCS, Donovan was deeply influenced by British organization. His charter made him responsible for collecting and analyzing "all information and data, which may bear upon national security." As was usual under Roosevelt, however, Donovan was not the sole operator in his field, although he aggressively built and enlarged his fiefdom.

This was soon endangered by the advent of war. Donovan and most of his organization survived, renamed the Office of Strategic Services (OSS) but placed under the jurisdiction and direction of the JCS. This was unfortunate for OSS, as the JCS much preferred its own intelligence units and had little use for OSS clandestine operations as a viable means of

General George C. Marshall. NATIONAL ARCHIVES

winning the war. Nor was the military the only competitor. There was also the Federal Bureau of Investigation (FBI), formally created in 1935 but with a much longer history, and still under the direction of J. Edgar Hoover. Before the war Hoover had been of service to Roosevelt, passing along useful information and gossip on prominent figures of all stripes that the FBI learned via its assiduous but sometimes questionable collection of information on subversives, real or supposed. The President both condoned and abetted this, creating a dangerous precedent for years to come. During the war, the FBI was made responsible for combating Axis subversion in both the United States and Latin America, further dividing intelligence responsibilities.

Despite the aura that developed around the OSS, neither its operations nor its analysis made major contributions to winning the war. Ongoing cryptanalysis efforts by the military—later termed signals intelligence—were of major significance. The ability to read Japanese codes contributed to the stunning victory at Midway in 1942, which abruptly turned the tide in the Pacific. In the European theater, U.S. analysts joined the ongoing British code-breaking effort that produced the equally useful Ultra messages.

One organizational concept significant by its absence was any attempt to coordinate formally at higher levels—beyond the person of the President himself—the various aspects of war-related policy. In 1938, the secretaries of state, war, and the Navy formed the Standing Liaison Committee, but this body's coordinative work was restricted to Latin America. During the war, these three secretaries met at informal weekly lunches, but given how far removed they all were from wartime policies decisions, these meetings were of little significance. Toward the end of the war a more formal mechanism, the State, War, Navy Coordinating Committee (SWNCC), was formed. SWNCC had a formal secretariat and committee structure and was intended to provide the leadership of the three departments with coordinated views on relevant issues. Although it was an important precedent, SWNCC came about too late to have any influence on the conduct of the war.

Unwilling—and, given the Japanese attack, not needing—to go to the extremes of domestic propaganda that had been used by George Creel, Roosevelt established a much less powerful Office of War Information (OWI). Hampered not only by Roosevelt's own desired limits, but also, as Allan M. Winkler argues in *The Politics of Propaganda,* by the absence of specific war aims, OWI was left with no one

version of the war to sell. Again in contrast to World War I, the Roosevelt administration was much more chary about prosecutions under the sedition laws, although the administration did pressure the Catholic Church to silence the right-wing radio priest Father Charles Coughlin. However, the war also saw what is probably the largest violation of civil liberties in U.S. history, the forced relocation of over 110,000 Japanese Americans to isolated and guarded camps.

This internment came about in piecemeal fashion in the frightening months after Pearl Harbor. First, Japanese aliens were differentiated from the more numerous, politically important and less geographically concentrated German and Italian aliens. Political and racial considerations soon came to the fore, including pressure from the California state government, one of whose leading spokesmen in favor of relocation was Attorney General Earl Warren. Responding to unfounded concerns about espionage and subversion, and possible assaults from the Caucasian population, Roosevelt signed the vaguely worded Executive Order 9066, authorizing the Army to remove people from certain designated areas, without ever specifically designating Japanese Americans. Twice during the war the Supreme Court upheld government actions.

The war created a wholly new relationship between the federal government and the academic and scientific communities. The most obvious aspect of this was the Manhattan Project, which produced the atomic bomb, based on what was then a new and unusually close collaboration between the best minds in the community of U.S. and émigré physicists and engineers and Army program managers. It also resulted in a vast complex of facilities that would form much of the basis of the postwar national laboratory and nuclear weapons establishment.

This was but one area of this new relationship. The usual succession of organizations (the National Defense Research Committee, the Office of Scientific Research and Development) oversaw a much wider range of weapons-related work, including radar, fuses, and antisubmarine warfare. Further, as Polenberg notes, there was a large influx of money to major universities so they could do their part in the scientific component of the war effort.

Although the war saw a tremendous accretion of power to the executive, Congress was not entirely supine. On several occasions Congress and the President came into conflict, but these clashes were largely confined to the domestic ramifications of the war and not its conduct or strategy. As noted, the Smith-Connally Act authorizing seizure of strike-bound

British Prime Minister Winston Churchill, President Franklin D. Roosevelt, and Soviet General Secretary Joseph Stalin at Yalta, 4–11 February 1945. Gen. George C. Marshall (in light coat) stands behind Roosevelt. NATIONAL ARCHIVES

plants was passed over Roosevelt's veto. In 1944 FDR vetoed a tax bill that he found to favor the well-off. Senate Majority Leader Alben Barkley went so far as to resign in protest (only to be swiftly reelected), and the bill was passed over Roosevelt's veto, the first time that a tax bill had ever been so enacted. Finally, although Congress was unstinting in providing the necessary financial support for the war, it did not allow this money to be spent without oversight. Most conspicuous was the Senate's Special Committee to Investigate the National Defense Program, created in March 1941 as rearmament efforts stepped up. Chaired primarily by Sen. Harry S. Truman (and often referred to as the Truman Committee), this committee investigated issues of waste and inefficiency in a number of industries and probably resulted in sizable defense savings. Even with an investigatory committee, however, there were limits on

how far Congress would go. When Truman began asking about spending related to the secret Manhattan Project, he accepted Stimson's request to drop the subject.

The war ended in 1945 as a triumph both for the early military plans and for Roosevelt's political-military vision of how the Allies should prosecute the war. Once again, however, U.S. postwar goals were less clear. Roosevelt never articulated a clear vision of what he expected after the war, except references to the four "great powers" (the U.S., Britain, China, and the USSR) having some sort of supranational police role via the new United Nations. This had little form, in part because Roosevelt, as he intimated to Stalin at Yalta, had little expectation that the United States would be able to sustain a large overseas presence once the war was over.

No war that the United States has fought, with

the arguable exception of the Civil War, had such a transforming effect on the nation as did World War II. It had widespread social and economic ramifications and, in terms of the issues important to this analysis, laid the basic groundwork for much of the national security apparatus that would follow in the Cold War. Although it may not have been apparent on V-J Day, nascent or maturing structures already existed in the military, intelligence, and high-level policy coordination. Roosevelt worked largely through an apparatus that he created via numerous executive orders, which gave him much necessary latitude, but also greatly curtailed Congress's role and its ability to carry out effective oversight. Moreover, as Samuel P. Huntington points out in *The Soldier and the State,* the military held a new, more revered place in the nation and had greatly broadened its area of influence from narrow military issues to more comprehensive foreign policy ones.

APOTHEOSIS OF THE NATIONAL SECURITY STATE, 1945–1965

At the end of 1945, the United States held a position of unrivaled world power that few nations have ever achieved wittingly, let alone by default. Its enemies were all defeated and occupied, and even its most powerful allies had to cope with the devastating effects of the war. The U.S. economy was not only intact, but clearly had put the Great Depression behind it. The U.S. military was the most capable, balanced force in the world and had sole possession of the atomic bomb.

Much as Roosevelt had predicted, a rapid demobilization began almost as soon as the war ended, propelled by popular and congressional pressure. By 1946, some three-quarters of the troops had been demobilized, leaving the United States with just over 3 million in the military, a peacetime high but still a dramatic reduction. By 1947 this had been cut in half again, bringing the total below that of 1941. The Navy, during that same period, went from 1,194 major combatant vessels to 267. President Truman also moved quickly to dismantle other wartime structures. Lend-Lease ended abruptly on V-J Day, a step that some critics felt helped alienate the weak and suspicious Soviet Union. In October 1945 Truman disbanded the OSS and, disregarding Donovan's plans for a peacetime successor agency, dispersed its remnants to the State and War departments.

Given the absence of concrete aims beyond the defeat of the Axis, little existed in the way of postwar planning or strategy. The individual services had done some work in 1943–1944 but, as Michael Sherry's *Preparing for the Next War* indicates, the JCS did not begin work on postwar strategic needs until May 1945. When this study emerged in August, it had been greatly affected by the atomic bomb. Reflecting a new sense of vulnerability in an age of ocean-leaping strategic bombers, the JCS's preferred stance was one of sufficient military strength to deter a major war against the United States. Failing that, secret consideration was given to preemptive strikes. But, as Melvyn P. Leffler notes in *A Preponderance of Power,* the United States had trouble sorting out the right course of action vis-à-vis the still chaotic and devastated postwar Eurasian landmass, which was seen as the key to international power.

The issue of "responsibility" for the Cold War has engaged two generations of scholars and lies beyond the bounds of this essay. What is important here are the perceptions and concepts that led to U.S. policies. The United States was caught between its own state of well-being, both inherent and comparative, and the recognition that current international conditions contained potential long-term threats to that well-being. The most likely sources of such threats were seen as twofold but closely connected: postwar devastation in Western Europe offered opportunities for an otherwise weak but potentially exploitative Soviet Union.

An initially wary view of Soviet goals turned bleaker by early 1946. Contributing to this, as Leffler notes, was the alteration of many of the mainstays of the prewar international situation, particularly a vibrant Britain, but also growing communist electoral strength in France and Italy, increasing unrest in the colonial world, and China's ongoing civil war. Thus, the United States was faced with the specter of increasing chaos as well as isolation, being the only power now capable of inhibiting and denying Soviet opportunities for exploitation. George Kennan's famous "long telegram" from Moscow in February 1946 brought together many of these somewhat disparate threads and fears into a coherent whole, in effect offering a single focus for concerns and for policy, the Soviet Union.

The crisis of the winter of 1946–1947, especially Britain's economic collapse and its ramifications for the Greek civil war, brought this search for policy to a head. It is important to note that virtually all Truman's key advisers had held important defense or foreign policy positions during World War II and derived from that a shared mindset. Ernest R. May shows how, in *"Lessons" of the Past,* these policymakers believed that only a firm stand now could stop an otherwise aggressive Soviet Union, a direct reaction to the failure of appeasement in the 1930s. Leffler adds a second prevalent historical "lesson": Versailles and Weimar taught the importance of dealing less harshly with German moderates lest new demagogues be encouraged. It is also important to appreciate the sense of threat and virtual siege that these statesmen felt themselves to be under as they made their decisions.

From this emerged the policy called containment, as outlined in Kennan's July 1947 "X" article, "The Sources of Soviet Conduct," in *Foreign Affairs*. Containment was a multifaceted effort to deny the Soviet Union opportunities for expansion beyond its periphery, by opposing such expansion with "unalterable counterforce," in the expectation that such prolonged opposition would lessen the foreign appeal of Soviet communism and eventually force the USSR to adjust its policies or face breakup.

In terms of actual policies, the Truman administration, working in close collaboration with Congress—which from 1947 to 1949 reverted to Republican control of both houses for the first time in sixteen years—pursued containment along a number of fronts. The March 1947 Truman Doctrine pledged economic and military aid to nations threatened by communism, with an initial request to support Turkey and Greece. In June 1947 Marshall, now secretary of state, proposed the European Recovery Program (the Marshall Plan), to assist Europe in recovering economically from the war. This plan, enacted in March 1948, was based on the belief that if Europe could recover economically and socially, then the appeal of communism would decrease. The plan was made available to all European countries, although the Soviet Union and its satellites declined, arguing that providing the data the plan required violated their sovereignty. Some analysts have suggested that this reluctance actually stemmed from Kremlin concerns about revealing current Soviet weakness, and the perception that they were making gains in Europe.

The assumptions behind the Marshall Plan proved correct and it was a tremendous success in stabilizing Western Europe. Other efforts throughout the remainder of the Cold War to use the new program of foreign aid beyond Europe did not show similar success. First, none of the Third World regions had the same infrastructure or economic expertise that still existed in industrialized Europe in 1947. Second, foreign aid became the victim of too many goals, torn chiefly between predominant military assistance programs and those of a more humanitarian bent. Third, foreign aid became an increasing liability in terms of U.S. domestic politics and never enjoyed the same consensus that supported the Marshall plan.

Tensions over jointly occupied Germany continued through 1948, culminating in the Soviet Union's abortive Berlin Blockade and the successful Allied airlift. This confrontation was important psychologically because it served as the first real crisis test—and potential military clash—of all that had come before.

Simultaneous with the creation of containment was the overhauling of the entire national security structure for dealing with these problems. This process actually began during the war, in 1943, when the Army raised the issue of "unification"—bringing the services into one department rather than their current two (Army and Air Force in War; Navy and Marines in Navy). Congress also showed interest in the idea, in part in the hope that it might allow greater efficiencies and thus savings. The Navy adamantly opposed the idea and, at the request of Secretary of the Navy James Forrestal, the issue was put off until after the war.

Realizing the need to help shape the debate rather than just oppose it, in June 1945 Forrestal asked Ferdinand Eberstadt, a business associate and wartime member of both the Army-Navy Munitions Board and the short-lived War Production Board, to study the entire issue of postwar national security organization. Eberstadt's prescient report suggested creating a third military department, the Air Force; continuation of the JCS, with a statute defining their duties; a National Security Council (NSC) to improve coordination between the State Department and the military; a National Security Resources Board (NSRB) to plan and oversee industrial mobilization; and a Central Intelligence Agency (CIA) to coordinate national intelligence.

Various lessons of the wartime experience are evident in Eberstadt's design, paramount among them the difficulties in coordinating foreign and defense policy, in organizing for economic mobilization, and in coordinating disparate intelligence efforts. In terms of the military, Eberstadt was splitting the difference, acquiescing to the division of the Army and Air Force but not joining all services into one department.

New congressional hearings revealed deep rifts in the military, with the Army and Air Force versus the Navy. In part, the stance of each service was dictated by its views of its primary mission and the degree of dependence on the other services. The Army, the strongest unification advocate, needed the Navy for transport to theaters of war and the Air Force for close air support of ground combat, and thus advocated some degree of unification. The Navy, however, viewed its primary role as power

Secretary of the Navy James Forrestal with admirals William D. Leahy, William F. "Bull" Halsey, Jr., and Chester W. Nimitz. PRINTS AND PHOTOGRAPHS DIVISION, LIBRARY OF CONGRESS

projection via its carrier fleet and preferred to remain apart. Air Force leaders were most interested in the new art of strategic bombing and would favor any plan that resulted in their achieving fully independent status.

An often wearisome debate ground on until 1947. President Truman settled some interservice disputes himself. The reorganization of Congress that year, merging the Military and Naval Affairs Committees of both houses into two Armed Services Committees, also helped. But Demetrios Caraley, in *The Politics of Military Unification*, gives major credit to the shift in Forrestal's position, as he realized that ongoing opposition could only hurt the Navy.

The National Security Act of 1947 largely followed Eberstadt's concept, creating the NSC, with the CIA under it, the short-lived NSRB, a statutorily mandated JCS, and three military departments. The major change was the creation of a secretary of defense, who presided over the National Military Establishment, which included the three departments (the Marines remained in the Navy Department).

Building on both the structure and lessons of the war, this act created an enduring national security structure for the United States. Given the longevity of this structure, it is interesting to note which issues in the congressional debate were or were not para-

mount. In terms of the central issue of military unification, two major concerns were the possibility of a "Prussian general staff" developing and of the services losing their individuality. But several features in the act served to allay such fears: strict limits on the size of the Joint Staff and on the size of the secretary of defense's staff, including a ban on his having a military staff; and the fairly broad independence of the three military departments, including individual seats on the new NSC and the right of budget appeal to the president.

In terms of the NSC, there was even less controversy. There was some debate over its mechanics and membership, with the former proving to be totally vague and fluid, and the latter centering on whether or not the NSC would be dominated by the new secretary of defense, and on whether the Senate would have approval of any new NSC positions. Finally, regarding the CIA, there was also little debate. The main concerns were over the provision allowing the director of Central Intelligence (DCI) to be a serving military officer, CIA coordination with military intelligence, and the possibilities of intrusions into domestic affairs. Yet, few questions were raised about the powers of the new agency, only whether these should be spelled out.

Thus, overall, there was no detailed examination

of the new structure. In part this is understandable, since many of its implications would not be apparent until it had begun to function. Also, much of the debate over the major facets had been going on for years, so there was little new to be said. It could also be argued that good organizations require flexibility, especially in their formative period. However, with the perspective of hindsight, it is also possible to see that key questions were not asked or were not apparent. Finally, and perhaps most striking, the act never attempted to define what was meant by the key phrase and title of the bill, "national security." It remained vague and all-encompassing at the same time.

The remaining aspects of U.S. containment policy came into being in the next few years. Two events in 1949 signaled major changes for U.S. national security policy. In April 1949 an ongoing process of European collective-security arrangements culminated with the formation of the North Atlantic Treaty Organization (NATO), which included the United States. Although a defensive treaty, NATO was an open-ended U.S. military commitment to Western Europe. Given the disparity of West European versus Soviet military forces, it also meant the necessity of deploying large numbers of U.S. troops overseas in peacetime, a decision that some, including Sen. Robert A. Taft, thought beyond the power of the president without reference to Congress. Between the end of the Korean War in 1953 and the beginning of the end of the Cold War in 1989, U.S. peacetime overseas troop strength never fell below some 430,000.

As a regional security treaty, NATO had been preceded by the 1948 Rio Pact and by the Organization of American States. But NATO was the first of many regional security commitments into which the United States entered (followed by SEATO, 1954; the Baghdad Pact, 1955; CENTO, 1959, which the U.S. fostered but did not join; and bilateral treaty commitments to Japan, South Korea, and Pakistan) aimed at bolstering states on the Soviet periphery.

In September 1949 the United States detected evidence of the first Soviet atomic test, ending the U.S. monopoly upon which a number of military assumptions and plans had been based. No one had believed that the U.S. atomic monopoly would last forever, but estimates had foreseen mid-1950 or 1951 as likely dates for a Soviet capability. Although there is a big difference between testing an atomic device and having actual weapons with a means of delivering them, for the first time since the mid-nineteenth century, the United States faced the prospect of a direct military threat.

The advent of the Soviet test led to a reexamination of U.S. policy. It helped settle President Truman's decision, amid much conflicting advice, about whether to develop thermonuclear weapons, referred to at the time as the super bomb. Knowledge and fear that the Soviets could do the same was a decisive point; the nuclear arms race was now on.

A broad examination of the implications of the Soviet atomic capability took place in the State Department's Policy Planning Staff, once Kennan's bailiwick, but now directed by Paul Nitze. The seminal Cold War policy paper they produced, NSC-68 ("United States Objectives and Programs for National Security"), was both evolutionary and revolutionary. It was evolutionary in that it reaffirmed the policies that had been developed since 1947, primarily thwarting Soviet expansion and thus forcing a change in their behavior. But it was revolutionary in that it advocated a great increase in military spending, along with such things as economic assistance and intelligence operations. Critics of NSC-68 have argued that Nitze overmilitarized Kennan's containment strategy. But given the psychological effects of the Soviet atomic test, along with their acknowledged conventional arms superiority and the belief that such advantages tended to embolden them, it is difficult to see how U.S. planners could have come to a different conclusion. Moreover, Secretary of State Dean Acheson admitted to a degree of hyperbole in NSC-68 in order to galvanize policymakers. Kennan had warned that containment would be a prolonged and draining struggle; Nitze's paper suggested its cost and potential risk.

The JCS found themselves in a difficult position in the Cold War. Having been pushed into the center of policy in World War II, the JCS could not retreat to the former peacetime quiescence the military had enjoyed. In a struggle that was neither war nor peace, the lines between military advice and policy tended to blur. Indeed, as C. Wright Mills noted in *The Power Elite,* many senior World War II commanders served in postwar diplomatic positions.

Despite gaining desired statutory authority via the National Security Act, the JCS also lost the intimacy they had had with Roosevelt, as Richard Betts details in *Soldiers, Statesmen, and Cold War Crises.* Instead, they were now part of a much larger Defense Department, as the National Military Establishment became in 1949, which included a strong civilian component supporting the secretary. The Cold War also increased the strains on civil-military relations. Twice Truman had to dismiss a senior officer for insubordination. In 1949 senior admirals "revolted"

General Douglas MacArthur makes his farewell address to a joint session of Congress, 19 April 1951, after his dismissal by President Harry S. Truman on 11 April. Behind him sit Vice President Alben W. Barkley (left) and House Speaker Sam Rayburn (right). Photograph by Mark Kauffman. PRINTS AND PHOTOGRAPHS DIVISION, LIBRARY OF CONGRESS

when faced with defense budget cuts and plans that favored the Air Force bomber program (and thus atomic weapons) over a new super carrier. Their revolt involved both bureaucratic opposition (including allegations of financial wrongdoing by Secretary of Defense Louis Johnson) and congressional testimony opposing Johnson's decisions. CNO Admiral Louis Denfeld was forced to step down as a result.

More dramatic was Truman's clash with General Douglas MacArthur over policy in Korea. The Korean War (1950–1953) was important in defining Cold War policy for a number of reasons. First, it represented the expansion of the Cold War from Europe into Asia, following hard on Mao Zedong's 1949 victory in China. Second, the Truman administration's strategy was that of a limited war, seeking to contain this one flashpoint of communist aggression without allowing it to expand to a wider war. This concept, although appropriate to the circumstances in Korea and within the broader Cold War, ran counter to the longer U.S. military tradition of an unremitting offensive aimed at the total defeat of the enemy. Psychologically, it probably was more difficult to pursue in terms of garnering and maintaining strong public support. MacArthur, bridling at his setback at the Yalu River when China intervened in Korea, stepped far beyond the bounds of military dissent, writing to congressional leaders of his frustration and his desire to broaden U.S. military action in East Asia ("there is no substitute for victory"). Truman, with the concurrence of the JCS and George Marshall, who was now secretary of defense, fired MacArthur, setting off an intense but short-lived political firestorm.

But the Denfeld and MacArthur incidents were exceptions in Cold War military behavior. As Betts documents, through most of the Cold War crises the military were no more hawkish than most of their civilian counterparts. Indeed, some critics of the JCS complained that its corporate behavior tended to show reluctance to use force, a not uncommon preference for those experienced in its risks and costs. At the same time, when force was the preferred decision, the military would then advocate using the maximum force at the earliest opportunity, which ran counter to Cold War preferences for limited conflicts and measured escalation. But the real power in the Defense Department passed to the secretary, acting through the Office of the Secretary of Defense (OSD), his civilian staff. This probably reached its apogee under Secretary Robert McNamara (1961–1968) and his staff of relatively young subordinates (the "whiz kids"), who introduced new management techniques and concepts, such as program budgeting and systems analysis, and thoroughly dominated the JCS.

Institutionally, the JCS often tried to band together against the civilians in the OSD; however, there were often intense internal military rivalries as well. The advent of nuclear weapons gave the Air Force ascendancy over the former first line of defense, the Navy. During the pre–Korean War period of tight defense budgets, there were repeated clashes over roles and missions, that is, which service was responsible for which task. These debates, whose winners could look forward to bigger budgets, often pitted the Air Force against the Navy, or the Army against the Marines. In 1948, Forrestal had to adjudicate the Key West Agreement regarding service roles and missions among the JCS, essentially a peace treaty.

This interservice rivalry also affected the development of nuclear weapons. The Air Force's supremacy via strategic bombers went unchallenged by the advent of missiles, which it also controlled. The Navy developed submarine-borne missiles, allowing it back into the strategic game. The Army managed to keep its finger in via two programs: battlefield nuclear weapons and efforts at strategic defense. It is important to note, however, that the strategic nuclear triad (i.e., weapons on land-based and sea-based missiles, and on bombers) also served to ensure deterrence via retaliation by making a totally disarming Soviet first strike virtually impossible.

The militarization of the Cold War also required a new defense buildup after the World War II demobilization and Truman's efforts to hold down military spending. Defense outlays increased slightly in 1949,

and then went up dramatically with the outbreak of the Korean War. Defense outlays increased steadily throughout the Eisenhower administration (1953–1961), ending at $49.6 billion in 1961, although the effects of these figures are more difficult to assess. Eisenhower, like his mentor Marshall, was greatly concerned about the economic and domestic effects of too much military spending. Thus, in terms of real growth (i.e., taking into account inflation) or as a percentage of total federal outlays, defense spending actually declined.

The size of the armed forces also increased, from 1.5 million in 1950 to over 3.6 million in 1952, and then declined again after Korea but averaged over 2.7 million annually up to the Vietnam buildup. This was unprecedented for what was ostensibly peacetime, and relied on the nation's second peacetime draft, which began in June 1948 at the onset of the Cold War. Over the next twenty-five years almost 5 million draftees were inducted, creating a new and uncontroversial national rite of passage.

The great increase in defense spending was not reflected in the size of the armed forces, which remained much smaller than during World War II. Part of this had to do with the growing complexity and thus expense of weapons. (For example, the cost of fighter planes expressed in constant dollars—that is, of equal value when adjusted for inflation—soared: a P-40 (1940) cost $200,000; an F4U (1944), $350,000; an F86 (1950), $760,000; and an F-4 (1961), $3.8 million. The relative expense of conventional forces and the very real political limits on defense spending for the United States and its NATO allies helped spur increased reliance on nuclear weapons that were, comparatively, cheaper. Thus the Eisenhower administration opted for the doctrine of massive retaliation as the ultimate response to Soviet aggression. As some critics warned, however, this strategy was viable only as long as the United States had unmatched nuclear superiority. This was certainly the case during the classic and most threatening Cold War confrontation, the Cuban missile crisis of 1962.

Reliance on nuclear weapons and the advent of missile-borne warheads, which dramatically reduced warning time, also gave rise to the entirely new field of nuclear strategy. Unlike past strategic schools, civilians tended to predominate in nuclear planning. Using such new intellectual tools as operational analysis and games theory, they thought about such "unthinkable" (in Herman Kahn's words), complex, and often arcane concepts as deterrence theory, ladders of escalation, retaliatory exchanges, counterforce versus countervalue targeting, and mutual assured destruction (MAD). "Defense intellectuals" such as Bernard Brodie, Albert Wohlstetter, Kahn, and Thomas Schelling became important and influential figures in their own right. Many of them initially worked at the Air Force-sponsored think tank, RAND. Many other such organizations developed, largely centered on Washington, D.C. (RAND is in California). This was an entirely new phenomenon, an intellectual class and the resultant business of consultants virtually dependent on U.S. government research contracts, specifically from the Defense Department, for their livelihood.

U.S. nuclear strategy went through several changes. As noted, the U.S. went from secret plans for selected strikes during the brief period of U.S. nuclear monopoly to the Eisenhower administration's public massive retaliation concept. But some questioned the credibility of that strategy, which apparently allowed the United States few options. In the Kennedy administration, McNamara scaled this back to damage limitation, meaning a targeting of Soviet military forces—especially those that could attack the United States—rather than of Soviet cities. McNamara shifted again a few years later to assured destruction, meaning a strategy that deterred the Soviet Union by promising unacceptable levels of damage to their population and industries (as opposed to all-out devastation) should they attack the United States or its allies. McNamara also unilaterally stopped the deployment of ICBMs (intercontinental ballistic missiles, the land-based missile force) when he felt that a level of "sufficiency" had been reached.

Nuclear weapons spurred renewed interest in arms control. Initially, the United States tried to use its leverage as the only atomic power to foster international controls, pledging to forgo its own capabilities once a system of inspections, safeguards, and sanctions was in place. This 1946 offer, known as the Baruch Plan, was predictably—and, some have argued, much to U.S. satisfaction—rejected by the Soviet Union. For the next several years the United States pursued "comprehensive" arms control, attempting to link both conventional and nuclear arms to strike a balance with the Soviet Union. This, too, failed. Ultimately, the greatest spurs to arms control came as a result of Cold War crises. Thus, in the aftermath of the Cuban missile crisis, the United States and the USSR negotiated the Hot Line Agreement to improve communications and the Limited Test Ban Treaty, which Britain also signed, banning above-ground or atmospheric nuclear tests.

Just as nuclear weapons gave rise to a new school of strategy, so too did arms control give rise to a new field of policy with its own language, logic, and imperatives. Spurred by Sen. Hubert H. Humphrey, the Kennedy administration tried to centralize this in 1961 in the Arms Control and Disarmament Agency (ACDA). But ACDA never achieved the status of primus inter pares, as both the State and Defense departments remained the dominant arms-control players.

Arms control proved to be a difficult policy to pursue. First, neither side would willingly negotiate away any weapons or capabilities deemed essential to its security. Second, it was politically difficult to justify entering into agreements with the Soviet Union while it was being simultaneously portrayed as the main threat to peace. Finally, arms control agreements had a tendency to channel weapons development more vigorously into those areas not being limited, as had been the case in pre–World War II naval arms control as well.

The continuing need for advanced weapons and for a competitive weapons research and development program also meant a much closer relationship between the military and the scientific and industrial communities. The Defense Department expanded its own research and development capabilities. Moreover, the World War II complex that had evolved largely around the Manhattan Project grew rapidly in the 1950s and became a large nuclear weapons complex of laboratories, production facilities, and test sites. Defense contracting also became an important source of revenue for many universities.

For most of the century, the low state of U.S. preparedness and less sophisticated weaponry had limited the appeal of military contracting to very few corporations. But the broader relationships established in World War II survived and grew during the Cold War, with comparative concentrations among the larger corporations. For example, of the 100 largest U.S. industrial corporations as ranked by sales in 1970, the top 15 were among the largest 100 defense contractors; a total of 41 of the corporations were among the largest defense contractors.

The presence of this military-industrial complex was made most famous by Eisenhower's warning in his January 1961 farewell address about its potential for "unwarranted influence," although some critics believed this warning came too late. But, in the federal government, it was not just the Defense Department that had an interest in this complex. For Congress, defense contracts and U.S. facilities were also a means of channeling funds and jobs into favored localities. This gave a political dimension to the

613

growth of such a complex and also made it more difficult to cut it back at any given time.

Intelligence represented a near total departure from past U.S. practices and traditions. The CIA, created by Truman to be a coordinator, quickly evolved into a producer of intelligence, competing with the older military and State Department efforts. Increasing abilities to intercept and break codes were brought together in 1952 in the National Security Agency (NSA), which became the largest intelligence component. But prosecution of the Cold War also involved intelligence operations. These included the first centrally organized espionage efforts and a variety of programs usually referred to collectively as covert action. Although these differed widely in scale and scope, the main covert actions involved either support to friendly but threatened governments (such as various anticommunist electoral efforts in Western Europe) or attempts to depose unfriendly ones (Iran, Guatemala, Cuba, and Indonesia among the more prominent). Such activities raised several issues, including the propriety of such efforts and their consonance with the broader goals of U.S. foreign policy vis-à-vis Soviet communism, the degree to which such operations produced long-lasting results that justified the risks, the ability of the United States to control such operations, especially the larger paramilitary ones, and the ability and desire of Congress to provide effective oversight of necessarily covert activities. Covert actions operated on the principle of plausible deniability, that is, a credible stance of no U.S. involvement. Although this was necessary for domestic and international politics, it also tended to divorce policymakers from accountability for their decisions.

One intelligence activity that went from a covert to an overt program was the CIA's foray into psychological operations against the Soviet Union and its allies in the late 1940s that evolved into Radio Free Europe and Radio Liberty. Similar to the function of the British Broadcasting Corporation against Nazi-occupied Europe, these two "private" corporations, funded by the intelligence community, beamed news and propaganda into the Soviet bloc, which vigorously tried to jam the signals. In the mid-1970s, under strong congressional pressure, the two outlets came under the oversight of the Board for International Broadcasting, a new corporation with overt funding. In addition, the wartime Voice of America continued through the Cold War as the nation's official voice overseas and, in 1953, Eisenhower created the U.S. Information Agency, which had the role of disseminating information about the United States and promoting cultural exchanges, scholars' visits, and such, under the overall guidance of the State Department.

As had been the case during the two world wars, the Cold War also produced civil liberties strains, perhaps the most severe other than the Japanese relocation. Part of the problem stemmed from both the reality and the perception of the Soviet and communist threats. The United States and its allies were combating not just a foreign power, but also an ideology that both proselytized overtly and operated within other countries clandestinely. Thus, subversion and espionage became both real and exaggerated concerns.

Sen. Joseph McCarthy became the symbol for this era, and in many ways the period was much like the post–World War I Red Scare. However, McCarthy did not approach his anticommunist campaign with the same cold calculation as had Palmer. Rather, McCarthy's venture appears more like an opportunistic and uncharted ego trip and joy ride that temporarily rescued a foundering senatorial career. But, like Palmer, McCarthy ultimately overreached himself, in his confrontation with the Army, destroying his own credibility. By 1956 the phenomenon had largely burnt itself out, without significantly damaging basic support for containment.

Containment also prompted a tremendous expansion of the definition of U.S. areas of interest overseas. Through the early nineteenth century the main, if not sole concern had been the sanctity of the Western Hemisphere. This changed in the twentieth century; both world wars were fought to preserve a balance in Europe. But World War II also extended that concept to Asia and the Pacific. The pattern of the Cold War was similar. It began with concern over Europe and then spread, via the Chinese communist victory and the Korean War, to Asia. This led to a debate, most pronounced among the senior military, between "Asia-firsters" and "Europe-firsters."

The rapid decolonization of Asia and Africa in the 1960s made each new nation a potential gain or loss in what was essentially a "zero-sum" U.S.-Soviet competition. John Foster Dulles, Eisenhower's secretary of state, found the concept of neutral nations in the midst of the Cold War anathema to his view of a Manichean struggle. Thus, many Third World nations became cockpits of U.S.-Soviet rivalry simply because they existed, rather than because they represented genuine U.S. national interests.

It is difficult to appreciate, especially in the aftermath of the Cold War, the ways in which this struggle affected so many other aspects of U.S. life as well, beyond the new weapons, new strategies, new agencies, and new policies. Three of the most prominent examples were the national highway system, the National Defense Education Act (NDEA), and the space program. As Dwight Eisenhower noted in his memoir, *Mandate for Change,* national security was one reason he supported a massive highway-building program. He refers to the possible need to evacuate large numbers of people from cities; the need to move war matériel from the industrial heartland to ports was another spur. The launching of Sputnik by the USSR in 1957 helped goad the United States into a major investment in education to close an apparent gap. The NDEA, passed in 1958, authorized $1 billion in grants and loans over seven years, emphasizing science, mathematics, and foreign languages. The very title of the act underscored its purpose. Finally, Sputnik also prompted the race for space, beginning with satellites, but moving into manned programs and, eventually, the race to land a man on the moon. Although there were many predictions about the likely militarization of space, these proved to be unfounded, largely because space-based weapons were not militarily efficient. The Outer Space (1967) and Antiballistic Missile (1972) treaties formally limited some types of weapons in space. Indeed, the main contribution that space exploration made to security was the advent of a panoply of reconnaissance satellites, which served to improve greatly intelligence collection and strategic warning against missile attacks, and proved to be the necessary underpinning for arms control agreements.

Finally, for the first time in U.S. history, foreign policy became the major preoccupation of the government. This, in turn, affected the balance of power between the president and Congress. To a certain degree each president was building on the precedents first set by Franklin Roosevelt during World War II. These included increased use of executive orders and of executive office agencies not subject to congressional oversight, such as the NSC. Indeed, the NSC proved to be an extremely malleable entity that reflected the distinct working methods of each president, from Eisenhower's well-delineated staffing pattern to John Kennedy's and Lyndon Johnson's barebones apparatus. The Kennedy and Johnson NSCs saw the emergence of the so-called national security adviser (formally, the assistant to the president for national security affairs), beginning with McGeorge Bundy and Walt Rostow. This position, not subject to Senate confirmation and theoretically responsible only for supervising the NSC's small staff, became a key policy player, often advocating and managing policies within the White House rather than coordinating the view of the other departments. This allowed presidents to manage and direct policy more closely and without the "encumbrance" of the slower moving bureaucracies. Such an approach could reduce the breadth of policy discussions and represented a clear challenge to the secretary of state's primacy in foreign policy; it also definitely limited Congress's oversight.

Other areas where similar patterns blossomed included deployment of troops overseas and into combat without consulting Congress and allowing intrusions by intelligence agencies among domestic political groups. The ongoing sense of threat, which increased as weapons became more sophisticated, and the persistent crises necessarily gave the president, as commander in chief, the need for greater latitude and freedom of action. Moreover, at times Congress abetted this imbalance. For example, on the issue of intelligence operations, members of Congress largely preferred not to know exactly what the CIA was doing.

The underlying support for this imbalanced relationship was what became known as the Cold War consensus. Beginning with Truman's close collaboration with Sen. Arthur Vandenberg in 1947, successive presidents crafted policies that would have bipartisan support. This effort was largely successful, although foreign and defense issues usually became part of election-year rhetoric. Indeed, twice the party seeking control of the White House used erroneous arguments about the nuclear balance as part of its political attack. Thus in 1960 Democrats decried the "missile gap"; in 1980 Republicans warned about the "window of vulnerability." In both cases, the doomsayers largely declared the problem solved after taking office.

Despite different specific policies and strategies (massive retaliation and rollback under Eisenhower, counterinsurgency under Kennedy), and changes in political control of both the White House and Congress, the U.S. maintained a remarkably steadfast adherence to the broad concept of containment.

DEFEAT AND VICTORY, 1965–1991

The Cold War consensus came apart in Vietnam. U.S. involvement progressed from an advisory role to counterinsurgency to increasing U.S. responsibility for ground and air combat. By 1969 the U.S. had 543,000 troops in Vietnam. Johnson, like Truman in Korea, set limits on U.S. strategy and operations. Also, much to the dismay of the military, he pursued a strategy of gradual escalation. Given Johnson's management style, this also meant presidential involvement at a fairly low level of operational planning, to the extent that Johnson personally approved bombing targets. Senior military officials may have resented Johnson's direct involvement and undoubtedly bridled at some operational limits, but these differences only surfaced publicly in a very limited way late in Johnson's term. In a war without stark frontlines and against an opponent embedded in the civilian population and using guerrilla tactics, it became increasingly difficult to demonstrate success. Instead, the war seemed to be an open-ended commitment without any foreseeable end.

The erosion of the Cold War consensus became apparent in several areas. The most evident were the widespread protests against the war, which then spread to deeper questions about the entire national security apparatus and its policies. Potential draftees sought legitimate deferments or chose to flee the United States; critics called into question the equity of a draft that drew more heavily on the less-privileged portion of society. The draft ended in 1973, to be replaced by the All Volunteer Force (AVF). By that time, the armed forces, particularly the Army, were experiencing many of the tensions evident in American society—increased use of drugs and internal friction and clashes along racial lines. These had considerable detrimental effects on military discipline and readiness in the early and mid-1970s.

Politically, debate over the war severely divided the Democratic party and fostered a shift in the position of both major parties. For years the Democratic party had been the internationalist party, while the Republican party coped with a vocal isolationist wing. By the early 1970s the Democrats had a substantial and influential noninterventionist wing in contrast to the Republicans, who now more uniformly defended anticommunist containment.

The inauguration of Richard Nixon in 1969 tended to cast much of this debate in stark partisan terms vis-à-vis a Democrat-controlled Congress. Congress took steps to regain some of its lost powers, passing the War Powers Act in 1973 to require congressional approval of prolonged U.S. troop deployments overseas in areas of potential combat. But loopholes in the act made the required presidential notification an ex post facto exercise in most cases.

Under Nixon containment policy became more subtle. First, the United States pursued a series of agreements with the USSR under the rubric of détente, which operated, in part, on the concept that negotiations and agreements could also help ameliorate Soviet behavior. Second, the United States opened relations with China, thus exploiting the rift in the communist world. In 1972 Nixon concluded two arms control agreements with the USSR, the ABM (Antiballistic Missile) Treaty and SALT (Strategic Arms Limitation Talks) I. This put a cap on both sides' strategic offensive forces, an important step as the Soviets had achieved strategic parity with the United States through a combination of a dogged Soviet arms program and McNamara's decision that U.S. forces had reached a level of sufficiency.

Nixon, more than any of his predecessors, ran policy out of the NSC, under the control of Henry Kissinger. In 1973 Kissinger became secretary of state while keeping his NSC post, a unique combination. Interestingly, the main critics of détente were on the right, claiming that the Soviets were taking advantage of the United States both in the agreements that were negotiated (including arms control and items like wheat sales), and in not changing their international behavior appreciably. These critics pointed to continued—and successful—Soviet support for "wars of national liberation" in Vietnam and Angola, which had a new feature, substantial Cuban military involvement.

The apparent unraveling of the national security consensus continued through two successive crises. The first was the Watergate break-in and the subsequent attempt by the Nixon administration to cover it up. Significantly, Nixon attempted to curtail the FBI investigation of the burglary on alleged national security grounds, citing the one-time CIA connections of some of the operatives. This became the so-called smoking gun that led to Nixon's resignation.

The second crisis was the 1975–1976 executive and then congressional investigation into the intelligence community, which revealed a long history of violations of charters by intrusions into domestic affairs, including the FBI's COINTELPRO and the CIA's CHAOS programs against domestic dissidents and misuse of the Internal Revenue Service; extremely questionable activities, such as surreptitious drug experiments and attempted assassinations overseas; lapses in executive control; and analyses on key issues that were sometimes wide of the mark. The end result was threefold: the intelligence community, but especially the CIA, lost much of its luster and suffered severe morale problems; goaded by the revelations, Congress took steps to improve oversight; intelligence agencies and activities lost much of the license under which they had operated and were never able to retreat entirely from the glare of publicity.

From its withdrawal from Vietnam in 1973 to the Soviet invasion of Afghanistan in 1979, the United States seemed to many to be losing the Cold War. Soviet leaders spoke confidently of the "correlation of forces" favoring the socialist world; so-called Eurocommunists appeared to be close to achieving government ministries in Italy and perhaps France. Communism no longer appeared to be contained.

A sea change in U.S. policy came with the election of Ronald Reagan in 1980, who campaigned not only against the Carter administration, whose foreign policy suffered a series of reverses (seizure of the U.S. embassy in Tehran, the Soviet brigade in Cuba, the Soviet invasion of Afghanistan) and thus was seen as weak if not naive, but also against the détente policies of the Nixon and Ford administrations. In rhetoric not heard since the Eisenhower and Kennedy administrations, there evolved the Reagan Doctrine. This somewhat undefined concept essentially meant countering Soviet expansion on its own terms, that is, supporting guerrillas in Soviet-dominated states. Reaction to this policy by Congress was mixed, with broad support for efforts in Afghanistan, which had been invaded by the Soviets, and growing opposition to support for the Contras fighting the self-avowed Marxist-Leninist Sandinista government in Nicaragua.

These policies contributed to the third great national security apparatus crisis, Iran-Contra. The Reagan NSC was a tumultuous place, with a total of six national security advisers in eight years. Iran-Contra involved revelations that NSC staffers had run a series of covert operations aimed at bargaining with Iran to free U.S. hostages in Lebanon, and had funneled money to the Contras despite congressional prohibitions. A prolonged and detailed congressional inquiry resulted in new restrictions on NSC staff activities and a further strengthening of oversight of intelligence.

Reagan also oversaw a major increase in defense spending, after over a decade of budgets that had meant a decline in real terms. In Reagan's first term (1981–1985), real defense growth averaged 10 percent each year. He also took steps to "reinvigorate" the CIA, increasing its budget and placing it under the direction of the controversial William Casey. But Reagan's strong anti-Soviet line changed with the advent of Mikhail Gorbachev to Soviet leadership in 1985. The two nations negotiated the Intermediate Nuclear Forces (INF) Treaty (1987), which elimi-

U.S. President Ronald Reagan and Soviet President Mikhail S. Gorbachev. ARCHIVE PHOTOS

nated that class of weapons entirely and made great progress toward completing further cuts in strategic arms.

We are still too close to these events to understand all Gorbachev's motivations, but he apparently came to the realization that the Soviet Union could not afford to maintain either its highly active interventionist role overseas or its incredibly high level of defense spending, perhaps reaching 30 to 40 percent of GNP (versus 5 to 6 percent of gross domestic product for the United States under Reagan). The degree to which the U.S. defense buildup and the operations supported under the Reagan Doctrine may have contributed to these Soviet decisions remains uncertain.

Gorbachev's sometimes half-hearted efforts at reform and openness (perestroika and glasnost) had the effect of revealing many of the inadequacies and disaffections of the Soviet system. Although Reagan and later George Bush attempted to deal with Gorbachev as a viable partner, Soviet power and cohesion continued to unravel. In 1991, Gorbachev resigned and the Soviet Union dissolved into its constituent republics. The Cold War was over.

THE NATIONAL SECURITY STATE BEYOND THE COLD WAR

Ironically, the Cold War had been waged and won much along the lines that Kennan had predicted in 1947. Ultimately, the Soviet Union had been forced to turn inward. It had taken not the fifteen years some had predicted at its outset, but forty-five years.

For the United States this was a significant but muted victory. As had been the case in the two world wars, the U.S. had no postwar plans. Indeed, it is doubtful that any policymakers ever expected to see the Cold War end in their lifetimes. The bipolar rivalry had become a fact of international life. Thus the United States now needed to redefine its national security goals. Bush proposed a "new world order," but the concept lacked much definition. In part, policymakers were trapped by the precedent of containment, with many looking for a similar all-embracing concept for the future. Others argued that in a more multipolar world, in which economic and social issues might replace traditional politico-military ones, such a single concept might not be achievable or appropriate.

Part of this reexamination involved a general recognition that the Cold War national security apparatus would have to be reduced. The Defense Department planned for a 25 percent reduction over five years, although increasing numbers of localities and their representatives and senators in Washington began to comprehend—and to contest—the economic effects of such a reduction in both bases and defense contracts. In short, the so-called military-industrial complex had become a central part of their lives. Similarly, plans were made to reduce intelligence spending, although some argued that the world was now less stable than it had been during the Cold War.

To a certain extent the United States had come full circle. Having spent the entire twentieth century as a status quo power, and having shaped each of its national security concepts around efforts to defend that status quo, it found itself again without direct security threats and without a clear sense of how best to pursue U.S. interests within a largely favorable global situation.

SEE ALSO The World Wars; Limited Wars; Pacifism and Arms Limitation; Foreign Policy; World Regions; Cultural Interactions (all in this volume).

BIBLIOGRAPHY

Several works that analyze overarching issues discussed in this essay are worthwhile. U.S. Army, Center of Military History, *American Military History* (1989), the official history of the U.S. Army, is a useful and objective resource. Russell F. Weigley, *History of the United States Army* (1984), is an insightful "unofficial" book on this same topic. There is no official history of the Navy, but Stephen Howarth, *To Shining Sea* (1991), is recommended. Marvin A. Kreidberg and Merton G. Henry, *History of Military Mobilization in the United States Army, 1775–1945* (1955), is an extremely useful discussion of manpower and industrial mobilization issues through the end of World War II. Paul Y. Hammond, *Organizing for Defense: The American Military Establishment in the Twentieth Century* (1961), is an excellent history of the development of defense organization through the Eisenhower administration. Finally, Samuel P. Huntington, *The Soldier and the State* (1957), remains the classic study of civil-military relations.

Howard K. Beale, *Theodore Roosevelt and the Rise of America to World Power* (1956), is still the essential work on prevailing views in the post-1898 emergence of the United States as a world power. Richard Challener, *Admirals, Generals, and American Foreign Policy, 1898–1914* (1973), assesses the blending of military and foreign policy for this formative but rarely studied period.

Arthur S. Link, *Wilson the Diplomatist* (1957), is the premier Wilson scholar's succinct analysis of Wilson's foreign policy views and goals. John Patrick Finnegan, *Against the Specter of a Dragon* (1974), is a good discussion of the pre–World War I preparedness movement and the draft. On the economic aspects of waging World War I, see Charles Gilbert, *American Financing of World War I* (1970), on financial and industrial organization issues, and Robert D. Cuff, *The War Industries Board* (1973), a history of wartime economic mobilization. Finally, David M. Kennedy, *Over Here* (1980), discusses the various effects of the war on the home front, including economic and propaganda issues.

Thomas H. Buckley, *The United States and the Washington Conference, 1921–1922* (1970), is a concise but insightful analysis of U.S. goals and tactics in the Washington Conference.

Robert Dallek, *Franklin D. Roosevelt and American Foreign Policy, 1932–1945* (1979), is the best overview of this broad topic. Mark M. Lowenthal, *Leadership and Indecision: American War Plans and Policy Process, 1937–1942* (1988), emphasizes the differences in view and gaps between Roosevelt and his military advisers and the effect this had on pre–World War II planning. On FDR's role as wartime commander in chief and his relations with the JCS see Kent Roberts Greenfield, *American Strategy in World War II* (1963). Herman M. Somers, *Presidential Agency: OWMR, the Office of War Mobilization and Reconversion* (1969), describes the central role played by James Byrnes and his agency in World War II economic mobilization. The manpower problem can be seen from McNutt's viewpoint in George Q. Flynn, *The Mess in Washington: Manpower Mobilization in World War II* (1979); and from the Army's in Byron Fairchild and Jonathan Grossman, *The Army and Industrial Manpower* (1959). Richard Polenberg, *War and Society: The United States, 1941–1945* (1972), is an excellent canvas of the various domestic effects of World War II.

Vincent C. Jones, *Manhattan: The Army and the Atomic Bomb* (1985), is the Army's official history of its role in developing the atomic bomb. See also James Phinney Baxter III, *Scientists against Time* (1946), a history of the mobilization of scientists and the range of their work during World War II, encompassing much more than just the Manhattan Project.

Michael S. Sherry, *Preparing for the Next War: American Plans for Postwar Defense, 1941–1945* (1977), is a very useful discussion of postwar planning. See also Perry McCoy Smith, *The Air Force Plans for Peace, 1943–1945* (1970), for the important role that the Air Force played in this process; and Vincent Davis, *Postwar Defense and the U.S. Navy*, 2 vols. (1962, 1966), for the Navy's view. Demetrios Caraley, *The Politics of Military Unification* (1966), analyzes the key organizational and political issues surrounding the 1947 National Security Act. Mark M. Lowenthal, *U.S. Intelligence: Evolution and Anatomy* (1992), is a succinct history of the creation and subsequent role of the U.S. intelligence community.

Melvyn P. Leffler, *A Preponderance of Power: National Security, the Truman Administration and the Cold War* (1992), is a detailed and broad-ranging discussion of the goals and perceptions behind the creation of containment. Richard M. Fried, *Nightmare in Red: The McCarthy Era in Perspective* (1990), is one of the few nonpolemical (pro or con) books on the subject, and is especially useful in placing McCarthy in the broader context of the ongoing anticommunist fever.

Richard Betts, *Soldiers, Statesmen, and Cold War Crises* (1977), analyzes the policy role played by the JCS in the Cold War, coming to conclusions about supposed military "hawkishness" that many will find counterintuitive. John Baylis and John Garnett, eds., *Makers of Nuclear Strategy* (1991), assess the intellectual contributions of several leading nuclear strategists. See also, Gregg Herken, *Counsels of War* (1987), a history of the Cold War role played by "defense intellectuals" and the nuclear-scientific community.

THE WORLD WARS

David M. Kennedy

When the peace of Europe exploded into war in the summer of 1914, President Woodrow Wilson, on 4 August, issued a proclamation of American neutrality. Two weeks later he urged his countrymen to remain "impartial in thought as well as in action." Wilson thus invoked one of the oldest of American diplomatic traditions: the isolation of the United States from the conflicts of Europe.

That tradition had roots in George Washington's famous proclamation of neutrality in 1793, in his no less famous Farewell Address of 1796, and in Thomas Jefferson's First Inaugural Address in 1801, with its plea for "peace, commerce, and honest friendship with all nations, entangling alliances with none." The viability of the policy of isolation had been sorely tested in the Napoleonic Wars, as the efforts of Jefferson and his successor, James Madison, to preserve American neutrality ultimately failed when the United States was sucked into the global conflict known to Americans as the War of 1812. In 1823 James Monroe proclaimed again the doctrine of separation between the affairs of Europe and those of the New World. By skillful diplomacy and military good fortune, Abraham Lincoln had maintained that separation by forestalling European intervention in the American Civil War.

Then in 1898 the recently reunited, rapidly industrializing, and newly confident United States appeared to violate its own most venerated diplomatic canons by going to war against Spain. In a few theatrically satisfying and relatively bloodless weeks—the "splendid little war" Secretary of State John Hay called it—the United States liberated Cuba from Spanish imperial rule and became itself an imperial proprietor of the former Spanish colonies in the Philippine Islands, Puerto Rico, and Guam.

Many observers then and since have viewed the Spanish-American War as a pivot-point in American diplomatic history, the moment at which isolationism was forsaken and internationalism—even, in some definitions, imperialism—embraced. But that judgment is surely exaggerated. The acquisition of the Philippines in particular proved enormously controversial, fueling the emergence of a strong anti-imperialist movement. Anti-imperial sentiment played a role in the presidential campaign of 1900 and operated thereafter to check and even roll back the imperialist advances of 1898. As early as 1899 a government commission recommended eventual American withdrawal from the Philippine archipelago, a proposal formally ratified by Congress in the Jones Act of 1916. To be sure, retention of Puerto Rico, as well as American insistence on rights of intervention in Cuban affairs and the acquisition of the Panama Canal Zone in 1903, signaled the clear intention of the United States to assert its paramountcy in the Caribbean basin. But on the larger world stage, where the great European powers dominated, the United States remained in the wings. In the ways in which such things were measured, America was a trivial and peripheral power as the twentieth century opened. Americans were newly assertive in the Western Hemisphere, perhaps, but incapable of projecting their influence beyond that region and apparently uninterested in developing the capacity to do so.

By 1914 the continental European powers had for at least a generation maintained huge standing armies. France, Germany, Russia, and Austria-Hungary each kept half a million men or more under arms. The U.S. Army, by contrast, numbered fewer than 100,000 men in the decade and a half between 1900 and 1915. The U.S. Navy was even smaller, with some 50,000 officers and men on the eve of World War I.

Those numbers reflected not only conscious political choice but also the public's uncritical assumption that isolationism was the touchstone of American foreign policy. At war's outbreak in 1914, the *Chicago Herald* tendered "a hearty vote of thanks to Columbus for having discovered America." The *Literary Digest* crowed that "our isolated position and freedom from entangling alliances [guarantee] that

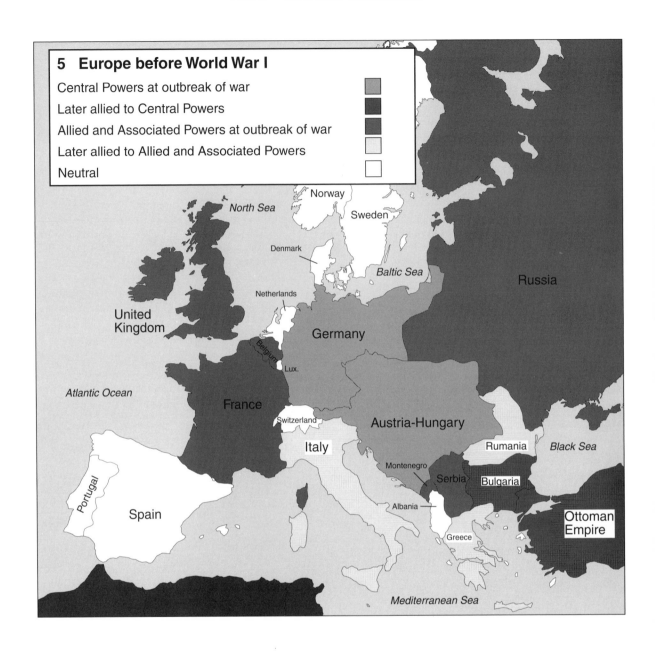

we are in no peril of being drawn into the European quarrel."

Yet the potential heft of the United States in global affairs was large, if for no other reason than the size, vitality, and changing composition of its economy. For the first century of its national existence, the United States was a debtor country, running chronically negative trade balances. Americans in the nineteenth century imported capital and manufactured goods, and annually exported somewhat lesser dollar-valued amounts of raw materials and foodstuffs. Mounting debt to foreign creditors, usually British, accounted for the difference in the values of those trade flows. Yet by 1896 America had

achieved a positive annual balance of trade on current account and by 1914 had liquidated much of its foreign-held debt. By 1913, finished manufactured goods for the first time edged out raw materials and agricultural products as the highest-value American exports. On the eve of World War I, the United States accounted for 11 percent of world trade—close behind Britain at 15 percent and Germany at 13 percent. At the very least, these gross economic facts made access to American markets and control of American exports a crucial factor in any prolonged conflict among the great powers. Whatever its own attitude, therefore, the United States unavoidably became an object of intense diplomatic and military

Table 1. EXPORTS TO BELLIGERENTS, 1914–1916

Belligerent	1914	1915	1916	Percentage Relation of 1916 Figure to 1914 Figure
Britain	$594,271,863	$911,794,954	$1,526,685,102	257%
France	159,818,924	369,397,170	628,851,988	393
Italy[a]	74,235,012	184,819,688	269,246,105	364
Germany	344,794,276	28,863,354	288,899	0.08

[a] Italy joined the Allies in April 1915.
SOURCE: David M. Kennedy and Thomas A. Bailey, *The American Pageant* (1986), p. 716.

interest to the belligerent states when World War I began in 1914.

THE DIPLOMACY OF AMERICAN NEUTRALITY, 1914–1917

For Britain, the supreme object of diplomacy was to maintain secure access to American resources—especially foodstuffs but also munitions and, eventually, credits— while denying that access to the Central Powers, Germany and Austria-Hungary. The Central Powers, largely self-sufficient in food and munitions, were less concerned with maintaining their own access to American markets but highly interested in denying American supplies to Britain.

The Americans, for their part, insisted on exercising the rights of neutrals, as guaranteed in international law, to trade with all the belligerent states. Both Britain and Germany violated those rights. Britain, declaring on 3 November 1914 a blockade of the North Sea gateways to Germany, intercepted Germany-bound American merchant vessels on the high seas, forced them into British ports, often held them for long periods of time, and confiscated both military and nonmilitary cargoes as contraband of war. All these practices were at variance with the accepted procedures of a blockade, which was traditionally conducted at or near the entrances to enemy ports, involved at-sea inspections of cargoes, and was confined to a tightly defined list of contraband goods. The United States government repeatedly protested these British actions, while American trade with Germany shrank by 1916 to about 1 percent of its 1914 value. American trade with Britain, on the other hand, approximately tripled in value in the same period (table 1).

Germany regarded the loss of its trade with the United States as a nuisance but watched with mounting alarm as the output of American farms and factories began to feed the swelling British and French war machines. Accordingly, the German imperial government declared a war zone around the British Isles on 4 February 1915 and announced its intention to interdict merchant shipping within that zone. Yet circumstances left Germany with few and problematic means for implementing this counterblockade. Because the German surface fleet was bottled up in its North Sea and Baltic ports by the British navy, Germany had little alternative to employment of the submarine as its means of denying American supplies to Britain and France.

The submarine was a new and peculiar weapon, not easily fitted into existing international law. It was designed for underseas operation (hence its German name, *Unterseeboot,* or U-boat) and was extremely vulnerable when surfaced. By their very nature, therefore, U-boats could not normally observe the established rules of search and seizure that were recognized in international law as the accepted means of conducting a blockade.

The fearful implications of this new naval technology were soon apparent. On 7 May 1915, off the southern coast of Ireland, a single torpedo, fired without warning from the German submarine U-20, scored a perfect hit on the British passenger liner *Lusitania.* Just eighteen minutes later the giant liner was on the bottom: 1,198 persons aboard were killed, 128 of them Americans.

Five days later the British government published a provocative—and dubiously accurate—report on alleged German atrocities in Belgium. The combined effect of the *Lusitania*'s sinking and this British propaganda initiative excited ferocious anti-German feeling in the United States. And yet that sentiment stopped short of a demand for war. The pugnacious American general, Leonard Wood, noted with disgust in his diary the public's preference for robust rhetoric rather than military action: "Rotten spirit in the *Lusitania* matter. Yellow spirit everywhere." President Wilson reflected the national mood when he observed in a speech at Philadelphia on 15 May that "there is such a thing as a man being too proud to fight. There is such a thing as a nation being so right that it does not need to convince others by force that it is right."

Wilson nevertheless complained vigorously to the German government about the submarine tactics that had produced the *Lusitania* catastrophe. He remonstrated so strongly, in fact, that Secretary of State William Jennings Bryan resigned in protest. But the Germans, grudgingly and belatedly, acceded to Wilson's requests. Following another sinking of a British passenger ship, the *Arabic,* with a loss of two American lives, the German government announced on 5 October 1915 that it had tightened its orders to submarine commanders to prevent a recurrence.

So matters stood until 24 March 1916 when yet another passenger ship, the unarmed French vessel *Sussex* was torpedoed (though not sunk) in the English Channel, in flagrant violation of the *Arabic* pledge. After another stiff protest from Washington, Germany announced the *Sussex* pledge on 4 May 1916. The Germans committed themselves to cease sinking unarmed merchant vessels and passenger liners without warning and provision for the safety of passengers and crews. But there was a string attached to this promise. In return for its restrictions on submarine warfare, Germany demanded the relaxation of the British blockade. If the blockade continued, Germany could pull on this string at any time and instantly unravel the *Sussex* agreement.

Relations with Germany remained tranquil for the remainder of 1916. In November of that year, President Wilson won re-election, partly because, as his campaign slogan proclaimed, "He Kept Us Out of War." He bid for the role of global peacemaker on 22 January 1917 in a memorable address to the Senate in which he called upon the belligerent states to forge a "peace without victory"—a negotiated settlement in which Wilson himself would presumably play the role of mediator.

Meanwhile, American shipments of foodstuffs and munitions flowed copiously to Britain and France, paid for increasingly with credits from private American banks. By early 1917 the house of Morgan, Britain's chief fiscal agent in the United States, held some $400 million in British debts incurred for war purchases. Germany could hardly overlook America's growing role as its enemies' chief supplier and financier. Desperate to break the two-and-one-half-year military stalemate, the German high command repudiated the *Sussex* pledge on 31 January 1917 and announced that it would undertake submarine warfare without restriction against all shipping, neutral or belligerent, bound for Britain or France. By declaring

unrestricted submarine warfare, Germany took a calculated risk that its opponents could be forced into submission before the virtually inevitable entry of the United States into the war could make a difference. This gamble nearly paid off.

The Americans had gambled too. In essence, Wilson had wagered that he could claim all the economic benefit of trade with the British and French belligerents without forcing belligerency on the United States itself. No doubt Wilson's declared commitment to the principles of international law, which guaranteed neutral trading rights, played a part in shaping his policy. Many of his critics, notably George F. Kennan, have seized upon this element in his thinking to condemn him for a formalistic moralism and legalism that, so the argument runs, has no place in the hard world of politics among nations. But more mundane considerations also molded Wilson's thinking. He was the first Democratic president since Grover Cleveland, whose fate it had been to preside over the disastrous depression of the 1890s. Determined not to repeat Cleveland's catastrophe, Wilson was eager to secure the profits from the war trade that began to swell in volume in 1914. To be sure, his insistence on participating in that trade carried risks, but for more than two years he had successfully averted the ultimate peril. Now, however, the Germans had called his bluff: either cease supplying Britain and France, and retire American vessels from the ocean war zone, or face direct attacks on American ships.

Still, even at this late date, Wilson hoped for a solution short of fighting. He broke diplomatic relations with Germany on 3 February but declined to ask Congress for a declaration of war. Instead, he asked Congress on 26 February for the authority to arm American merchant vessels as protection against submarine attacks. The persistent strength of pacifist and isolationist sentiment was evident in the Senate filibuster against Wilson's Armed Ship Bill, prompting Wilson's famous outburst that "a little group of willful men had rendered the great government of the United States helpless and contemptible."

Then, on 1 March, newspapers published a telegram, intercepted by British intelligence, from the German foreign minister, Arthur Zimmermann, to his representative in Mexico, suggesting a German-Mexican alliance against the United States. Mexico's reward would be the recovery of the territories lost to the Americans in the 1840s, including Texas, California, and other states in the Southwest. These revelations inflamed American public opinion against Germany. Further provocation immediately followed, as the U-boats sank several American vessels in the first weeks of March: *Algonquin* on 12 March, *City of Memphis, Illinois,* and *Vigilancia* on 16 March. At his cabinet meeting on 20 March, Wilson found all his advisers in favor of war with Germany. The following day the President summoned the newly elected Congress into special session on 2 April to receive his war message. Four days later, on 6 April 1917, Congress declared war. Six senators and fifty representatives (including the first congresswoman, Jeannette Rankin of Montana) voted against the war resolution.

THE UNITED STATES AS A BELLIGERENT, 1917–1918

"It is a fearful thing to lead this great peaceful people into war," Wilson declared in his war message. No one appreciated better than he just how fearful it was. A careful student of history, Wilson was especially anxious not to repeat the mistake of James Madison (the only other Princeton man to serve as president, Wilson ruefully noted), who had led a disunited people into war in 1812 with nearly disastrous results. "It was necessary for me," Wilson wrote a friend on 4 April 1917, "by very slow stages indeed and with the most genuine purpose to avoid war to lead the country on to a single way of thinking." And yet, even at this late date, and after the flagrant incitements of the Zimmermann telegram and the U-boat attacks on American ships, Wilson still could not count on unanimous support for the war. Nothing more graphically illustrated the stubborn persistence of reservations about America's relation to the war than the fifty-six votes cast on 6 April against the war resolution.

Many factors, in addition to the ancient and honored tradition of isolation, fed those reservations. Conspicuous among them was the astonishingly polyglot character of American society at this historical moment. The census of 1910 enumerated a higher proportion of foreign-born persons in the population—nearly 15 percent—than at any other time in American history. As America went to war in 1917, one of every three Americans was either foreign-born or the child of a foreign-born parent. Ten million of those persons traced their ancestry to what were now the enemy countries of Germany and Austria-Hungary. Millions more derived from Ireland, still under the thumb of Britain, with whom Wilson was now proposing to make common cause. None of these peoples' devotion to the war effort could be taken for granted (see table 2).

Wilson harbored his own suspicions about both British and French war aims and was determined, even as the United States became the cobelligerent of Britain and France, to preserve his country's distinct political identity and his own diplomatic independence. Accordingly, he refused to allow the United States to become a formal ally of the nations fighting against the Central Powers. Instead, the anti–Central Powers coalition was known after 6 April 1917 as the Allied and Associated Powers, with the latter term reflecting America's peculiar detachment. That detachment was further reflected in repeated wartime plans to use American financial power to compel the Allies to conform their war aims to American wishes. In July 1917 Secretary of the Treasury William Gibbs McAdoo proposed making further Treasury loans to Britain contingent on British agreement with American postwar policies. Wilson was not unsympathetic

Table 2. PRINCIPAL FOREIGN ELEMENTS IN THE UNITED STATES, 1910[a]

Country of Origin		Foreign-Born	Natives with Two Foreign-Born Parents	Natives with One Foreign-Born Parent	Total
Central Powers	Germany	2,501,181	3,911,847	1,869,590	8,282,618
	Austria-Hungary	1,670,524	900,129	131,133	2,701,786
Allied Powers	Great Britain	1,219,968	852,610	1,158,474	3,231,052
	(Ireland)[b]	1,352,155	2,141,577	1,010,628	4,504,360
	Russia	1,732,421	949,316	70,938	2,752,675
	Italy	1,343,070	695,187	60,103	2,098,360
Total (for all foreign countries, including those not listed)		13,345,545	12,916,311	5,981,526	32,243,282

[a] Census of 1910; total U.S. population: 91,972,266.
[b] Ireland was not yet independent.
SOURCE: David M. Kennedy and Thomas A. Bailey, *The American Pageant* (1986), p. 714.

with that notion but believed that the timing was wrong. "England and France have not the same views with regard to peace that we have by any means," he told his adviser, Edward M. House, on 21 July. "When the war is over, we can force them to our way of thinking, because by that time they will, among other things, be financially in our hands; but we cannot force them now." McAdoo was instructed to continue extending Treasury loans to the British without attaching political conditions. By war's end he had extended some $10 billion in U.S. Treasury loans to the Allied governments.

At home, Wilson's anxieties about national unity spawned an enormous propaganda campaign to convince the country that American participation in what was still called the "European War" was necessary and just. In the absence of any material threat to a substantial national interest—such as invasion or seizure of an American colony—Wilson took the high ground of principle in his war message. America would fight, he said, "to make the world safe for democracy." Of necessity, Wilson thus tried to shape an image of the war as a crusade, a "war to end war." These were large promises indeed.

Under the energetic leadership of George Creel, an experienced publicist and journalist, the Committee on Public Information (CPI) was created to carry this message to the nation—and the world. Creel blanketed the country with prowar posters, speakers, films, and expositions. The CPI mobilized some 75,000 "Four-Minute Men" to declaim patriotically to audiences in movie theaters, churches, and schools. It distributed millions of pamphlets in dozens of languages explaining the rationale of the American war effort. It assisted the Treasury Department in staging enormous bond-buying rallies featuring bellicose exhortations by popular film stars. At the same time, other government agencies, acting under the authority of the Espionage Act of 15 June 1917 and the so-called Sedition Act of 16 May 1918, moved vigorously to silence antiwar protesters. In all these ways, the Wilson administration hoped to suppress dissenting voices and to manufacture the kind of enthusiasm for the war whose existence was only conjectural in the spring of 1917.

Doubts about the public's commitment to the war effort shaped many aspects of mobilization. In sharp contrast to the experiences of other belligerent states, which had long since resorted to devices like food rationing and centralized governmental control over manufacturing and commerce, the United States preferred persuasion and exhortation to coercion and regimentation. Food administrator Herbert Hoover,

for example, repeatedly rebuffed Allied suggestions that he impose rationing on American consumers, instead urging housewives to observe "meatless Mondays" and "wheatless Wednesdays" in order to conserve food. To be sure, the distance of the United States from the fighting, and the relative brevity of American belligerency (nineteen months, from April 1917 to November 1918), go far toward explaining why the country was spared more draconian mobilization measures. But an important part of the explanation for the relative lightness with which the war bore down on the American economy and American society is to be found in the conscious worries of the Wilson administration that the American people, if pushed too hard, would repudiate the entire war effort and revert to their historic attitude of isolationism.

America's detachment from the war aims of its cobelligerents, and Wilson's worries about the willing cooperation of the American people in the war effort, were both reflected in the measures adopted to raise an American army and field it in France. Although many young men did clamor to volunteer for the armed forces in the spring of 1917, the only practical means to create a mass army in short order was by conscription. To that end, the cohort of males in the designated age group between twenty-one and thirty had somehow to be induced to come forward voluntarily and register themselves. Considerable anxiety attended the preparations for Registration Day on 5 June 1917. Civil War conscription, administered by military officers who had been frequently harassed and even killed, provided a frightful precedent for what might happen. Senator James Reed of Missouri starkly predicted that the streets would run red with blood on Registration Day.

In the event, registration proceeded in an orderly and peaceful fashion, surrounded by all the brass bands, bunting, hoopla, and deliberate cultivation of emotion that informed the food conservation and bond-selling campaigns. Wilson tried to maintain the fiction that the draft was not compulsory at all, but simply "selection from a nation which has volunteered in mass." But within a year Justice Department agents were conducting "slacker raids" in many eastern cities to round up draft dodgers. These dragonnades netted tens of thousands of delinquents in the summer of 1918. Even after these dramatic sweeps, it was estimated that some 337,000 men liable for service managed to avoid it. These numbers rudely qualified Wilson's assertion that the army was formed from a people who had "volunteered in mass."

General John J. Pershing, accompanied by the Duke of Connaught, inspects an honor guard as he enters Westminster Abbey to pay respects at the tomb of Britain's unknown soldier, 1921. PRINTS AND PHOTOGRAPHS DIVISION, LIBRARY OF CONGRESS

The American army of 200,000 grew slowly throughout 1917. The process of registering, inducting, equipping, training, and shipping a huge military force took time. By the end of the year only about 175,000 members of the American Expeditionary Force (AEF), were in France under the leadership of Gen. John J. Pershing. Training facilities were so overcrowded by this time that draft calls were virtually suspended. Then, suddenly, inductions and troop shipments shot up in the first weeks of 1918, eventually producing a 4-million-man army, of whom 2 million went to France with the AEF.

A series of Allied military and diplomatic reverses accounted for this sudden ballooning of the American army. The Italians, allied with France and Britain since 1915, came under especially punishing attack from their Austro-Hungarian foes in October 1917. They retreated in wild disarray from their front on the Isonzo River. In November, the British advance in Flanders had ground to a sickening halt at Passchendaele after an advance of barely two miles, bought with 300,000 casualties. Worse still, the Bolshevik revolution in Russia in November was preparing the ground for an armistice between Germany and the newly formed Soviet Russian government. Woodrow Wilson's famous Fourteen Points address on 8 January 1918 was in part an effort to keep the buckling Bolsheviks—and other dissident leftist and socialist groups in the Allied countries themselves—committed to the war effort by promising an eventual liberal settlement with Germany and the creation of a League of Nations to guarantee the peace.

Wilson's proposal fired the hopes of liberals the world over but failed to keep Russia in the war. The Soviets signed an armistice with the Central Powers in December 1917, and a formal peace settlement

627

was concluded in the Treaty of Brest-Litovsk on 3 March 1918. German troops were now shifted in swelling numbers from the eastern (Russian) to the western front. Newly reinforced, the German western command launched a massive offensive on 21 March 1918. The war had now become a race, testing whether the Americans could throw enough troops across the Atlantic in time to stem the rising German tide from the east.

Allied military leaders wanted American troops as fast as they could get them. They had been dunning Washington for those troops since April 1917, proposing to amalgamate them directly into Allied military units under British or French command. They had even suggested at one point that they be allowed to send their recruiters to the United States to induct Americans directly into their armies. Faced with this new German offensive in the spring of 1918, they clamored still more loudly for access to American manpower. But General Pershing insisted that Americans should fight only under American command. United States troops arriving in France would be held behind the lines until such time as they composed a sufficient force to be deployed independently, with responsibility for their own sector of the front. Even as the German threat mounted in intensity, Pershing held firm. This so-called amalgamation controversy dragged on for months. Pershing at one point icily told Supreme Allied Commander Marshal Ferdinand Foch that he was willing to risk a German advance as far as the Loire River rather than let American troops be amalgamated into Allied units. Here was yet another example of America's stubborn refusal to make a full commitment to the Allied cause, even in the thick of military crisis.

The amalgamation controversy was finally laid to rest in August 1918 when the First U.S. Army was formed and assigned to a sector of the front stretching from the area around Verdun eastward to the Vosges Mountains. Pershing had in fact slightly compromised his adamant refusal to allow amalgamation by permitting a few American units to be thrown into the line under Allied command in May and June 1918. American troops thus contributed to halting the German advance at Cantigny in late May, and at Château-Thierry and Belleau Wood in early June. Perhaps as many as 70,000 American doughboys had tasted battle by mid-July. By that time, the great German offensive was halted, and the initiative passed to the Allied and Associated Powers, now massively reinforced by the American presence.

The Americans had a dual assignment in the counteroffensive that was about to be launched: to reduce the German salient behind the village of Saint-Mihiel to the east of Verdun and then to strike northwest of Verdun toward the German rail center of Sedan. The way to Sedan led through the forbiddingly fortified terrain bounded by the Meuse River on the east and the Argonne Forest on the west.

On 12 September 1918, half a million American troops, preceded by a four-hour artillery barrage, easily overran a German force about half that size in the Saint-Mihiel salient. Four days later, the Saint-Mihiel engagement was over. It scarcely deserved to be called a battle. German resistance was mercifully slight, inflicting about 7,000 casualties on the Americans—largely because the attack had caught the Germans in the midst of a planned evacuation. Pershing had flung his enormous force on the backs of a retreating army.

The swift and easy success of the Saint-Mihiel campaign contrasted sorrowfully with the other major American action, the Meuse-Argonne offensive, launched on 26 September 1918. The Germans in the Meuse-Argonne sector were deeply entrenched in several defensive lines, including the formidable *Kriemhilde Stellung,* which laterally traversed the Meuse-Argonne corridor along the contours of the Romagne Heights, just north of the village of Montfaucon. The rolling hills around Montfaucon bristled with German observation posts and well-registered gun batteries. The attacking force would be subjected to murderous enfilading fire as it struggled up the two narrow defiles leading to the Romagne Heights.

If topography favored the Germans, numbers favored the Americans. Pershing was able to hurl some 1.2 million men into the Meuse-Argonne attack, a force that outnumbered the German defenders by about eight to one. Inexperienced American troops suffered appalling losses in the Meuse-Argonne— some 120,000 casualties before the battle's (and the war's) end on 11 November 1918. But their sheer quantity proved decisive. Nothing struck Allied observers of the American operation with greater force than the prodigiousness of the American effort. "One is much impressed with the extravagance of the Americans," a British officer reported, "both in men and material." To a significant degree, Pershing overcame enemy resistance largely by smothering the Germans with American flesh.

It was the prospect of more such smothering that induced the Germans to sue for an armistice, which was finally concluded on 11 November 1918. When the armistice negotiations had begun on 29 September, Pershing's force was stalled in front of the *Kriemhilde Stellung,* where it remained stuck for more than

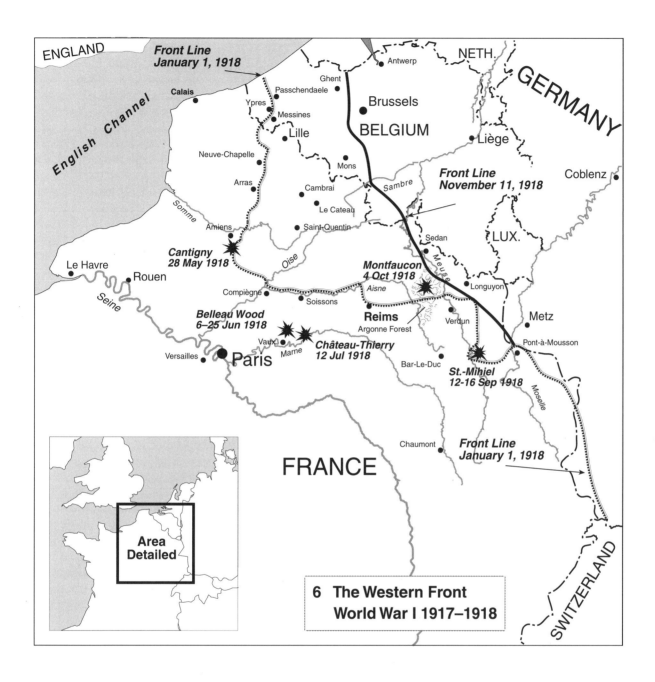

ENGLAND

Front Line
January 1, 1918

English Channel

NETH.

Antwerp

Ghent

Passchendaele

Calais

Ypres

Messines

Brussels

BELGIUM

GERMANY

Lille

Mons

Liège

Neuve-Chapelle

Arras

Cambrai

Le Cateau

Sambre

Front Line
November 11, 1918

Coblenz

LUX.

Somme

Amiens

Saint-Quentin

Sedan

Cantigny
28 May 1918

Oise

Montfaucon
4 Oct 1918

Meuse

Longuyon

Le Havre

Rouen

Compiègne

Soissons

Aisne

Reims

Verdun

Metz

Belleau Wood
6–25 Jun 1918

Vaux

Marne

Château-Thierry
12 Jul 1918

Argonne Forest

Pont-à-Mousson

Versailles

Paris

Bar-Le-Duc

St.-Mihiel
12-16 Sep 1918

Seine

Moselle

Chaumont

Front Line
January 1, 1918

FRANCE

Area
Detailed

**6 The Western Front
World War I 1917–1918**

SWITZERLAND

a fortnight. Pershing never did reach his objective at Sedan. His contribution to the final victory thus owed far less to his troops' performance on the Meuse-Argonne battlefield than it did to the cold calculus of attrition. German reserves were exhausted after the spring 1918 offensive, but the Allies could now draw upon the nearly endless reservoirs of American manpower to reinforce the western front. The Germans had lost their gamble that unrestricted submarine warfare would conclude the war before American strength could be brought to bear.

American war deaths totaled 112,432, more than half from disease. War-related government expenditures came to $26 billion during wartime and eventually mounted to $112 billion when interest payments and veterans' benefits were reckoned with. The main American contributions to the ultimate victory had been foodstuffs, munitions, credits, and manpower—not battlefield victories. Ironically enough, Pershing in some ways had depended more on the Allies than they had depended on him. His AEF had purchased more of its supplies in Europe than it had shipped from the United States. Fewer than five hundred of the AEF's artillery pieces, for example, were of

American manufacture. Virtually all its aircraft were provided by the French and British. A majority of the ships used to transport the AEF both to and from Europe were of French and British registry. America, in short, was no "arsenal of democracy" in this war; that role awaited the United States in the next global conflict, some two decades later.

PEACEMAKING, 1919–1920

The war was now over; it remained to shape the peace. The world's eyes turned to Woodrow Wilson. He had emerged by war's end as the chief spokesman for a liberal peace settlement. He had urged the reintegration of all the belligerent states into a healthy international economy; the recognition of the aspirations of various subject nations for self-determination; and the creation of a new international body, the League of Nations, to guarantee international comity. On 4 December 1918, President Wilson sailed from New York on an unprecedented voyage to champion these causes in person at the Paris Peace Conference.

Yet in a sense, from Woodrow Wilson's perspective the war had ended too soon. As the President had explained in the summer of 1917 when he ordered McAdoo to continue extending Treasury loans to the Allies, he had looked forward to having the Allied governments "financially in our hands" at war's end. Shortly before his journey to Europe in 1918, he had told his cabinet of his intention "to go into the Peace Conference armed with as many weapons as my pockets will hold so as to compel justice." But the war's swift end had in effect struck from Wilson's hand many of the economic weapons he had hoped to flourish, as the Allies retained a significant measure of financial resilience. Neither had the AEF played a military role sufficient to confer much diplomatic authority on the American president.

Wilson nevertheless retained the force of his ideals and his enormous popularity among the war-weary peoples of the world. "If necessary," he remarked in July 1918, "I can reach the peoples of Europe over the heads of their rulers." As his ship headed toward France, he reflected that "the men whom we were about to deal with did not represent their own people." Yet neither, in an important sense, did Woodrow Wilson represent his own people. They were still largely isolationist in sentiment, ill-informed and skeptical about Wilson's grand plans to reshape the world order and to redefine America's place in it. Within days of the war's end, American voters had delivered a sharp rebuke to Wilson's leadership by defying his personal plea for a Democratic Congress. They instead elected Republican majorities to both House and Senate. If the United States had been the sort of parliamentary democracy that Wilson so admired, he would no longer have been entitled to lead his country.

Wilson thus held a weak hand when he sat down at the Paris negotiating table on 18 January 1919. The wonder is that he managed to shape the final settlement as much as he did. His principal accomplishment was the incorporation of the League of Nations covenant as section 1 of the peace treaty. But to secure that aim, Wilson was forced to agree to several articles in the treaty that violated his own ideals, including French annexation of Germany's coal-rich Saar Basin, Japan's absorption of German holdings in China's Shantung peninsula, and Italy's control over the Adriatic seaport of Fiume. The European victors also forced upon Germany, contrary to Wilson's supposed wartime assurances, a punitive settlement that stripped the conquered Germans of their overseas territories, foreign investments, and merchant marine and restricted their control of their own waterways and tariffs. Germany was also compelled to accept a colossal bill for some $33 billion in reparations payments to the victors. Adding insult to injury, the treaty's article 231—the notorious "guilt clause"—forced the Germans to acknowledge sole responsibility for the outbreak of the war.

By the time the final treaty was handed to the Germans at Versailles in June 1919, Wilson was condemned alike by traditional conservatives who resented his idealistic meddling and by disillusioned liberals who scorned his compromising. Europe had hailed Wilson as a savior on his arrival in December 1918. On his departure in July 1919, he was a fallen idol. He had also, as events soon demonstrated, lost his ability to control events at home.

During a brief return to the United States in February and March 1919, Wilson had witnessed a preview of the treaty's eventual fate among his own countrymen. Thirty-nine Republican senators or senators-elect declared that they would not approve the treaty in its present form. They easily commanded enough votes to prevent the two-thirds majority necessary for the treaty's ratification by the United States Senate, which was constitutionally required to approve the document before it became binding on the United States. Conspicuous in this effort was Republican senator Henry Cabot Lodge of Massachusetts, a Harvard Ph.D. in history, Senate majority leader, chairman of the Foreign Relations Committee, and a longtime critic of Wilson. The treaty "might get by at Princeton, but not at Harvard," Lodge sniffed, in a personal slap at Princetonian Wilson. Even more adamantly antitreaty than Lodge were such intractable isolationists as Senators William Borah of Idaho and Hiram Johnson of California, known as "irreconcilables," or "the Battalion of Death."

The treaty's critics focused their fire on article 10 of the League covenant, which obligated signatory states to defend "the territorial integrity and existing political independence of all Members." That article, isolationists charged, constituted a blank check on American men and guns, and unconstitutionally surrendered America's sovereign independence.

Lodge at first stalled for time by holding extensive hearings through the summer of 1919. Wilson, seeing the treaty's prospects dimming in the Senate, resorted yet again to his favorite political tactic—a direct appeal to the people over the heads of their elected representatives. On 3 September 1919, Wilson set out by train from Washington on a barnstorming tour to drum up support for the treaty. Shadowed through the mid-western and western states by Senators Johnson and Borah, a self-constituted "truth squad" that contradicted all Wilson's claims, Wilson collapsed from exhaustion in Colorado on 25 September. Whisked back to Washington, several days later the President suffered a stroke that left him thick of speech and partly paralyzed. He became a recluse in the White House.

At this critical juncture Lodge reported the treaty out of the Committee on Foreign Relations with fourteen reservations attached—a cruel personal slap at Wilson's Fourteen Points. Wilson now faced the prospect of accepting a treaty with the Lodge reservations or having no treaty at all. He chose the latter, urging Democratic senators to vote against the Lodge version. On 19 November 1919, and again on 19 March 1920, the Senate rejected the treaty, principally because of the persistent power of isolationism. But Wilson himself, stubbornly refusing to countenance senatorial amendments to his handiwork, drove the final stake through the treaty's heart.

THE AFTERMATH, 1920–1933

Bloodied by the war and disillusioned by the peace, America turned inward in the 1920s. Republican senator Warren G. Harding astutely captured the national mood in a speech at Boston in May 1920, when he declared that "America's present need is . . . not nostrums but normalcy." "Normalcy" meant, above all, a return to isolation. Indeed, in some ways the war's aftermath witnessed not merely a restoration but a strengthening of isolationist sentiment. In May 1921, for example, Congress passed the first immigration quota law, a major step on the way to the drastic limitation of immigration in 1924. Long a refuge and beacon for the world's huddled masses, the United States now signaled its determination to seal itself off from the rest of the globe.

Tariff policy, too, reflected this new determination to shield America from the world. After two decades of progressively opening American ports to foreign goods, Congress in 1922 passed the Fordney-McCumber Tariff, raising import duties to forbidding levels. Eight years later, Congress passed the Smoot-Hawley Tariff, establishing the highest rates in over a century.

These tariff policies had especially perverse economic implications in the circumstances of the 1920s. The war had definitively reversed the historic position of the United States as an international borrower. High protective tariffs had made a measure of sense when the United States was a debtor nation, struggling to retain its earnings at home. But now that the United States had become a net creditor to the world, foreign merchants needed to sell their goods into American markets if they were ever to acquire the dollars with which to repay American loans. American tariff policies in the 1920s reflected the persistence of a debtor's mentality long after the debtor had become a creditor.

No American credits were more controversial than the $10 billion in wartime Treasury loans to Allied governments. The war-loan issue overshadowed all other foreign-policy matters in the 1920s. France and especially Britain resented their loan obligations. The Americans, they argued, should write off the loans as war costs, equivalent to the blood and treasure the Europeans had consumed while waiting for isolated America to join the battle. Britain and France also complained that the real effect of their borrowed dollars had been to fuel the wartime boom in the American economy, where nearly all their purchases had been made. And to make matters worse, the American tariff laws made it next to impossible to earn the dollars with which to repay the loans.

The Allies repeatedly offered to scale back their reparations demands from Germany if only the United States would forgive its war loans to the Allies. The French Chamber of Deputies made a dramatic point of this offer in 1929, when it explicitly resolved to cover its payments to the United States with its receipts from German reparations. But successive American administrations throughout the 1920s unrealistically maintained that there was no connection between German reparations and Allied debts. Although the Americans took the lead in efforts to reschedule and reduce the German obligations—notably in the Dawes Plan of 1924 and the Young Plan of 1929—Washington held unflinchingly to its tight-fisted insistence on full repayment of the monies owed the American Treasury. "They hired the money, didn't they?" was Calvin Coolidge's curt dismissal of suggestions that the war debts be canceled.

This apparently heartless American indifference to the world's financial health reflected a stubborn fact about the American economy: its asymmetric relation to the international economic system. The United States accounted for 15 percent of world trade in the 1920s, more than any other nation. But the American economy itself was so vast and robust that foreign trade never amounted to as much as 10 percent of America's gross national product. Consequently, American bankers and merchants and shippers were much more attracted by the domestic market than they were by the prospect of international trade and investment. Despite its huge importance to the world economy, therefore, the United States still behaved like the provincial and peripheral power it had been in the nineteenth century. Among the implications of these economic circumstances was the absence of any appreciable constituency in the United States with a powerful material interest in an engaged, internationalist foreign policy. While it was true that the United States clung to its Philippine colony and continued to meddle in Caribbean affairs, these were the policies of a hesitant, regional power, not the signs of a robust international vision. Thus Washington shut the immigration gates, kept tariff barriers high, ignored the havoc that its debt policies wreaked upon its former comrades-in-arms, continued to shun the League, and refused even to join the World Court.

Washington did assume a leadership role in the Washington Naval Conference of 1921–1922, which limited the size of the world's navies, and in the Pact of Paris, or Kellogg-Briand Pact, of 1928, by whose terms sixty-two nations foreswore war as an instrument of national policy. But at bottom both of those initiatives were also premised on the ancient isolationist dream that legal and moral commitments could somehow contain the seething ambitions of the world's desperadoes—or at least keep them safely distant from America's shores.

Even when faced with Japanese armed aggression against China in 1931, the United States refused to act in concert with the League of Nations to impose economic sanctions against Japan. Deprived of American cooperation, the League proved utterly unable to prevent the Japanese from establishing in Manchuria the puppet state of Manchukuo. America's only response to that transparently aggressive move came in 1932, when the Hoover administration proclaimed the Stimson Doctrine. Named for Secretary of State Henry Stimson, it declared that Washington would not formally recognize territorial accessions achieved by force. Fearing that stronger measures might provoke Japanese retaliation against the United States, President Herbert Hoover warmly endorsed this policy. So, apparently, did most of the Depression-weary American public. "The American people," said the *Philadelphia Record,* "don't give a hoot in a rain barrel who controls North China."

Thus, more than a decade after its historic intervention in the European War, and at the beginning of a frightful decade that would spawn a second and still more ghastly global conflict, the United States huddled smugly in a fool's paradise of cultural, economic, and political isolation.

THE APPROACHING SHADOW OF WAR, 1933–1939

On 4 March 1933, Franklin D. Roosevelt was inaugurated as president of the United States. His country was floundering in the economic slough of the Great Depression. Thirteen million workers had no jobs and every bank in the land was closed. Abroad, no less ominous events were gathering. On 27 March, Japan withdrew from the League of Nations to free itself for further exploitation of Manchuria. "This step," the American ambassador to Japan, Joseph Grew, cabled to Roosevelt, "indicates the complete supremacy of the military." On 30 January 1933, Adolf Hitler became chancellor of Germany. He proceeded with ruthless efficiency to build the fearsome Nazi Wehrmacht that would engulf the planet in a second world war before the decade's end. Hitler, Roosevelt privately confided to the French ambassador in Washington, was "a madman."

Yet publicly President Roosevelt appeared at first to be little concerned with these international developments. Preoccupied with the domestic crisis of the Depression, he effectively turned his back on the world in 1933. Roosevelt had served as assistant secretary of the Navy in Woodrow Wilson's cabinet during World War I, and presumably shared his chief's internationalist vision. He had emphatically promoted American membership in the League of Nations in his campaign for the vice-presidency in 1920. But in 1932, under pressure from isolationists, he had repudiated his earlier support of the League. And in his inaugural address he had pointedly declared that "our international trade relations, though vastly important, are in point of time and necessity secondary to the establishment of a sound national economy."

On 16 May 1933, Roosevelt briefly revivified his internationalist inclinations in his "Appeal to the Nations of the World for Peace and for the End of Economic Chaos." Calling attention to the ongoing international Disarmament Conference in Geneva, and the upcoming World Economic Conference in London, Roosevelt declared that "any strong Nation" that refused to participate in these two cooperative efforts would stand indicted by the world community for "responsibility for failure." Praising Roosevelt's speech, the *San Francisco Chronicle* said "This is the end of isolation, or it is nothing."

It was nothing. Within a few months Hitler torpedoed the Geneva disarmament talks and Germany, like Japan, withdrew from the League of Nations. Roosevelt, mocking his own words of 16 May but faithful to the declaration of nationalistic economic priorities in his inaugural address, scuttled the London economic conference so as to free himself to pursue inflationary policies at home. As the British chargé d'affaires in Washington reported to his government in August 1933, "From President downwards immediate interest and sentiment of the country is concentrated on recovery programme and its domestic results . . . . Situation here seems to render isolation and nationalism inevitable."

Other factors beyond the pressing crisis of the Great Depression reinforced American isolation and nationalism in the 1930s. Indeed, this decade of impending global catastrophe witnessed what were arguably the strongest expressions of American isolationism in the nation's history.

On the list of items that nurtured this robust isolationism, disillusionment with American involvement in World War I ranks high. By the 1930s most Americans deeply regretted Woodrow Wilson's break with diplomatic precedent in taking his country into the European war. Regret was fed by a spate of popular histories of that conflict, including C. Hartley Grattan's *Why We Fought* (1929) and Walter Millis's *The Road to War* (1935). Those authors contended that America had been duped into entering the war by British propaganda and by Wall Street financiers. The United States had no substantial in-

terests at stake in 1917, so the argument ran, and should have stayed out of the fray. Wilson was indicted as a mulish moralist and legalist whose stubborn insistence on neutral trading rights had led the country to disaster.

The Senate Munitions Investigating Committee, chaired by North Dakota Democrat Gerald P. Nye, further buttressed these sentiments. From 1934 to 1936, the committee's hearings revealed the lavish profits of American financiers and munitions manufacturers during the neutrality and war periods, and insinuated—though never proved—that somehow those interests had covertly pressured the Wilson administration into war.

The Nye Committee's hearings furnished the backdrop for both public opinion and political initiatives regarding foreign policy in the 1930s. When President Roosevelt proposed in January 1935 that the United States might join the World Court, a Niagara of letters and telegrams fell upon the Capitol, and the Senate decisively rejected the proposal. This repudiation sobered the President, who was from about this date seeking for ways to return to his own earlier internationalist views and to position his country to play a role in checking the growing strength of potential aggressor states like Germany and Japan. But defeat on the World Court issue vividly reminded Roosevelt of the depth of isolationist feeling. He seemed, for the moment, to have no alternative to acquiescing in that feeling. "I fear common sense dictates no new method for the time being," he wrote to Henry Stimson in February 1935. To another correspondent at the same time he predicted: "We shall go through a period of noncooperation in everything . . . for the next year or two."

The period of noncooperation persisted well beyond a year or two. Beginning in 1935, isolation hardened from mere indifference to the world into active repudiation of anything that smacked of international engagement. That repudiation took on institutionalized form in a series of "neutrality" laws enacted between 1935 and 1939.

The first such act, prompted by the Italian invasion of Ethiopia in May 1935, became law on 31 August 1935. It authorized the president, after proclaiming that a state of war existed between foreign states to impose a mandatory embargo on arms shipments from the United States, and to inform American citizens that they traveled on belligerent vessels at their own risk. The statute was clearly precipitated out of the political atmosphere created by the Nye Committee hearings. It represented an effort to avoid the perceived mistakes of Woodrow Wilson by removing the possibility of both the economic and the emotional provocations of 1914–1917. In effect, the United States was formally denying itself certain "neutral rights," even with their attendant economic benefits, as the price for staying out of war. The 1935 statute ran for only six months, but it was extended for fourteen additional months in February 1936. The 1936 law additionally prohibited American loans and credits to belligerent powers, again reflecting the Nye Committee's alleged "lessons" of the 1914–1917 experience.

The neutrality statute was again revised in May 1937. The ban on munitions, loans, and credits was reaffirmed, and travel by American citizens on belligerent vessels was now absolutely prohibited. Regarding commodities other than munitions, the law defined a compromise of sorts. It permitted the legal export to belligerents of certain nonmilitary items on two conditions: that the buyers pay cash and that they carry the goods away from American shores in their own vessels. This cash-and-carry provision worked in practice to favor seafaring nations with extensive dollar reserves—notably Britain, and, more troublesomely, Japan.

The European democracies in the 1930s were still recovering from the bloodletting of the Great War and were themselves reeling from the same economic depression that blighted the United States. Even with American cooperation, they would have been weakly positioned to check Hitler's increasingly brazen maneuvers. Without that cooperation, they proved utterly powerless.

Sensing his adversaries' irresolution, Hitler in 1935 repudiated the Versailles settlement and inaugurated compulsory military service. In 1936 he marched a military force into the Rhineland frontier zone with France, in direct violation of the Versailles agreement, and sent other military units to fight on the side of fascist dictator Francisco Franco in the Spanish civil war. In March 1938 Hitler's Germany annexed neighboring Austria, the Führer's birthplace. In September of the same year he demanded the German-speaking Sudetenland area of Czechoslovakia. At an infamous conference in Munich, Germany, France and Britain abjectly agreed to Hitler's demand, which he described as his "last territorial claim." Six months later his troops overran the remainder of Czechoslovakia. In August 1939, Germany signed a nonaggression pact with the Soviet Union. One week later, on 1 September 1939, Germany invaded Poland. Hitler's modern, mechanized divisions swept across the Polish plain with astonishing speed, giving rise to the term *Blitzkrieg* (lightning war).

Britain and France, at last aroused, declared war on Germany. In Washington, D.C., Franklin Roosevelt was awakened at 3 A.M. by a telephone call from his ambassador to France, William Bullitt, who reported that several German divisions were deep into Polish territory and bombers were over the city of Warsaw. "Well, Bill," Roosevelt replied, "it has come at last. God help us all."

THE ROAD TO WAR IN EUROPE, 1939–1941

The *Blitzkrieg* that subdued Poland in three weeks in 1939 gave way to six months of *Sitzkrieg*—a period of sitting war or phony war during which Hitler consolidated his gains and prepared to deliver the next blows. They finally fell on Denmark and Norway in April 1940, and on Holland and Belgium the following month. *Blitzkrieg* tactics again proved lethally effective. Airborne German troops nullified Holland's historic defense of flooding the invasion routes; mechanized *Panzer* (armored) divisions thrust swiftly into Belgium. On 14 May they penetrated the French defenses near Sedan—the old, unreached, AEF objective of 1918. More than a quarter of a million British troops, in danger of encirclement, were hurriedly evacuated from the French port of Dunkirk. On 22 June 1940, France surrendered to the Germans. In early August, Hitler began air attacks against Britain, preparatory to launching a barge-borne invasion force across the English Channel, scheduled for late September. For months thereafter, the Battle of Britain raged in the air over the British Isles and the Channel. The Royal Air Force's tenacious defense of its native island caused Hitler to postpone his planned invasion indefinitely.

These stunning events in Europe reverberated in the United States. President Roosevelt had issued the ritual neutrality proclamation on 5 September 1939, though on 4 November the Neutrality Act was revised to repeal the mandatory embargo on arms shipments to belligerents. The cash-and-carry provisions, however, were retained. Particularly after the fall of France in June 1940, and during the precarious weeks of the Battle of Britain that followed, debate intensified in the United States over what foreign policy to embrace. Radio broadcasts from London brought the drama of the Battle of Britain directly into millions of American homes. Sympathy for Britain grew but was not yet sufficient to push the United States into war.

The Roosevelt administration faced a historic decision: whether to hunker down in the Western Hemisphere, assume a "Fortress America" defensive posture, and let the rest of the world go to smash, or to seek by all means short of war itself to bolster the beleaguered British. Both sides had their advocates. The Joint Planning Board of the War and Navy Department recommended in June 1940 that Britain be written off and a hemispheric defense be prepared. This position was loudly supported by the America First Committee, an arch-isolationist body that formed in September 1940.

On the opposing side was the Committee to Defend America by Aiding the Allies, sometimes known as the White Committee, after its founder, journalist William Allen White. White had formed the group at Roosevelt's behest in May 1940 to lobby for more actively pro-Allied policies. Among the White Committee's first assignments was the cultivation of public and congressional support for the so-called destroyer-for-bases agreement. Announced by the President on 3 September 1940, the agreement provided for the transfer to Britain of fifty World War I–era U.S. destroyers, to be used for defense against the anticipated cross-Channel invasion. In exchange, Britain granted the Americans the right to lease various Western Hemisphere air and naval base sites.

Hitler and American isolationists alike regarded this transfer of warships as tantamount to an act of war. Indeed, the destroyer-for-bases agreement constituted an unambiguous statement of sympathy for the British cause and came perilously close to a de facto declaration of cobelligerency. This was a decided departure from the incidentally pro-British bias in American policy during the 1914–1917 period, which was in some ways an accidental product of the warring powers' relative naval strengths. Roosevelt had now set himself on a path of deliberate assistance to Britain, a conscious policy of differential neutrality that made no pretense to legal impartiality—though he still hoped to avoid being drawn directly into conflict with Germany.

Roosevelt hoped as well to avoid the bitter partisanship that had wrecked the internationalist policies of his former chief, Woodrow Wilson. Accordingly, in June 1940 he appointed two international-minded Republicans to key positions in his cabinet—Frank Knox as secretary of the Navy, and the venerable Henry Stimson as secretary of War. Partisan wrangling over foreign policy was further muffled in that same month when the Republican party nominated the internationalist Wendell Willkie as its candidate

for president. Only late in the campaign did a desperate Willkie try to make an issue out of foreign policy differences with Roosevelt. His attacks on FDR as a warmonger had little effect, other than pressuring the President into some regrettably unkeepable promises about not sending American boys into foreign wars.

Safely reelected in November 1940, Roosevelt continued with his policies of differential neutrality. In December 1940, British prime minister Winston Churchill wrote to Roosevelt asking for credits with which to purchase war supplies—credits that were prohibited by the Neutrality Act still on the books. The President devised an artful solution, which he explained to the public in a fireside chat radio address on 29 December. America, he said, must become "the great arsenal of democracy," and must in this hour of peril forget about the "silly, foolish old dollar sign." Instead, the President proposed to lend needed equipment to the British, who would theoretically return it after the war. Known popularly as the Lend-Lease Act, and symbolically numbered House Resolution 1776, the Act Further to Promote the Defense of the United States became law on 11 March. By war's end it furnished over $50 billion in military aid to the British and, eventually, to the Soviets and other allies as well.

Germany was already accusing the United States of "moral aggression." But Roosevelt persisted in his effort to provide Britain all aid short of war. As he said in explaining the Lend-Lease proposal to a national radio audience on 29 December 1940: "Emphatically we must get these weapons to them in sufficient volume and quickly enough, *so that we and our children will be saved the agony and suffering of war which others have had to endure*" (emphasis added). That explanation in fact faithfully reflected his strategy at this stage.

But whatever Roosevelt's hopes of avoiding a shooting war, his policies brought the United States to the very brink of armed involvement. Even as the Lend-Lease Bill was making its way through Congress in early 1941, a delegation of British military planners arrived in Washington for joint talks with their American counterparts. Their final report, commonly known as the ABC-1 agreement, provided that in the event of American engagement in a two-front war against both Germany and Japan, priority would be given to the defeat of Hitler. When the United States at last became a formal belligerent in late 1941, this "Europe-first" doctrine formed the foundation of America's war strategy.

An immediate problem in mid-1941 was how to

deliver Lend-Lease supplies safely to the British—and, after the June 1941 German invasion of the Soviet Union, to the Russians as well. In the month of April 1941 alone, German U-boats sank some 650,000 tons of British shipping. All naval authorities agreed that only armed convoys could provide adequate protection against German submarines. Yet the Lend-Lease legislation had specifically declared that "nothing in this Act shall be construed to authorize or permit the authorization of convoying by naval vessels of the United States." Roosevelt writhed for months on the horns of this dilemma. Neither the British cause nor his arsenal-of-democracy strategy would be well served if the Lend-Lease goods destined for Britain ended up on the bottom of the Atlantic.

Roosevelt met with British prime minister Winston Churchill at Argentia Bay, Newfoundland, in early August 1941. On 14 August the two leaders issued a joint statement of principles that should govern the postwar world. Known as the Atlantic Charter, the document reflected many of the ideals that Woodrow Wilson had championed a generation earlier, including self-determination, liberalization of international trade, freedom of the seas, and creation of a successor organization to the ill-starred League of Nations. At the Argentia Conference, Roosevelt also pledged to provide armed escorts for British ships as far eastward as Iceland, which, by agreement with the Icelandic government, had been occupied by American troops in July 1941.

The decision to allow convoying by U.S. naval vessels thrust the United States into nothing less than an undeclared naval war against Germany in the Atlantic. Winston Churchill, for one, believed that this new American policy would constitute but a brief preface to a formal American declaration of war. As Churchill reported to his cabinet on 19 August 1941, Roosevelt at Argentia "said that he would wage war, but not declare it . . . . Everything was to be done to force an 'incident.' . . . The President . . . made it clear that he would look for an 'incident' which would justify him in opening hostilities."

Incidents were not long in coming. A German submarine fired (without effect) on the American destroyer *Greer* off the coast of Iceland on 4 September. Roosevelt used the occasion to make a public announcement of his new convoying policy, but not to ask for a declaration of war. In a replay of Woodrow Wilson's deliberate, even hesitant, policies of February and March 1917, the President instead asked Congress for the authority to arm American merchant vessels and to allow them to enter combat

zones (in effect repealing the "carry" portion of the 1937 Neutrality Act's cash-and-carry provision). In a further reprise of the Zimmermann Telegram episode of 1917, Roosevelt also claimed, without convincing proof, that the Nazis had a secret plan to divide all of South America into five vassal states and to abolish existing religions. Spurred by these provocations, and by torpedo attacks on the U.S. destroyers *Kearny* on 17 October, killing eleven men, and *Reuben James* on 30 October, with the loss of the ship and one hundred lives, in early November, Congress, by thin margins, revised the neutrality statutes in accord with FDR's proposal.

But none of these "incidents" in the Atlantic proved sufficiently provocative to precipitate a declaration of war. After the spate of attacks in October, Hitler, preoccupied with his massive invasion of the Soviet Union, acted with restraint in the "undeclared naval war." And the close votes in Congress on the revision of the neutrality laws strongly suggested to Roosevelt that it would take more than a few naval clashes to push the country into a formal declaration of war. The President had seen another reminder of the persistence of isolationist sentiment on 18 August, when a bill extending the term of service for Selective Service draftees passed the House by a margin of just a single vote. So, as the war entered its third year in the last months of 1941, America was still officially neutral, though strongly and openly supportive of both the British and the Soviets. In the gray expanse of the North Atlantic, the Germans and the Americans faced each other through periscope and gunsight in a tense stand-off, with neither side quite willing to take the next step toward full-blown hostilities. So things might have remained indefinitely but for another "incident," replete with drama and consequence, in the blue waters of the Pacific.

THE ROAD TO WAR IN THE PACIFIC, 1937–1941

If the tangle of issues that eventually led to war between Japan and the United States were reduced to a single word, that word would be *China*. Japan had a long and keen interest in expropriating and developing Chinese resources for its own benefit. Beginning with the Stimson Doctrine in 1932, the United States tenaciously opposed those Japanese designs on China. American policy both frustrated and baffled the Japanese, since the United States had no appreciable economic or strategic stake in China. The historian Herbert Feis aptly dubbed the Stimson

Doctrine "an attitude rather than a program." It did little material good for the Chinese—nor, for that matter, for the Americans—but it did succeed in irritating the Japanese. Eventually, it provoked a war.

In July 1937 Japan moved from its colonial base in Manchuria and launched a full-scale attack on China. President Roosevelt declined to declare that a "state of war" existed between the two belligerents, thus precluding the invocation of the Neutrality Acts. In theory, Americans remained free to supply both combatants; in practice, they did. Japan became increasingly dependent on American goods, especially strategic metals and petroleum, to carry on its war effort.

American sentiment, including that of the President, strongly favored China. But how could that sentiment be translated into policy? Several circumstances constrained Roosevelt's freedom of action. Isolationism and military unpreparedness ruled out any possibility of armed intimidation of Japan. Moreover, Roosevelt's military chiefs agreed that in the event of a two-ocean war, the Atlantic and Europe had strategic priority. The U.S. Navy was especially cautious about pursuing policies that might provoke Japan into fighting. In July 1941 the Navy's War Plans Division, reflecting the ABC-1 agreement struck with the British earlier that year, explicitly advised Roosevelt not to embargo oil shipments to Japan because "an embargo would probably result in a fairly early attack by Japan on Malaya and the Netherlands East Indies, and possibly would involve the United States in early [the implication was premature] war in the Pacific." As it happened, the Japanese navy, apprehensive about conflict with the Americans, was also a fairly consistent voice of restraint in Japanese war councils. It was ironic, therefore, that it was the two naval services that were destined to carry most of the burden of fighting in the Pacific War that began in December 1941.

Debate divided American policy-making circles virtually until the eve of war. Secretary of the Treasury Henry Morgenthau, Jr., and Secretary of War Henry Stimson urged economic sanctions as a means of restraining Japan. Secretary of State Cordell Hull, generally backed by the Navy, prophetically argued that sanctions would simply force the Japanese into seeking alternative sources of supply, by military force if necessary, in Southeast Asia, Indonesia, and the Philippines. For a long season Hull's views prevailed, dampening the tempo of anti-Japanese policy and delaying the final showdown. Washington progressively tightened the economic screws on Japan but did not fully clamp down until July 1941.

The German subjugation of the Netherlands and the fall of France in mid-1940 left the Dutch and French colonies in Indonesia and Indochina, rich in oil and strategic metals, tantalizingly vulnerable to Japanese penetration. To discourage Japanese ambitions in that region, Washington, on 31 July 1940, prohibited the shipment of aviation-grade gasoline to Japan. An embargo on iron and steel scrap followed on 26 September. The Japanese reacted by joining the Tri-Partite Pact with Germany and Italy on 27 September 1940, a move transparently intended to menace the Americans with the prospect of a two-ocean war. On 24 July 1941, Japan forced the collaborationist French Vichy government to allow Japanese troops to enter French Indochina. This was a pivotal move because it cinched the final knot in the American embargo of strategic materials.

On 26 July 1941, over the strenuous objections of the U.S. Navy, President Roosevelt froze all Japanese assets in the United States, effectively cutting off all shipments of any kind to Japan, including, most crucially, oil. The die was now all but cast. The cessation of American oil shipments foreclosed Japan's peaceful options. On 6 September 1941 a Japanese Imperial Conference stipulated that if an agreement with the United States was not in prospect by early October, Japan should move toward war. Japanese prime minister Fumimaro Konoye sought a personal meeting with Roosevelt to hammer out an accord. From Tokyo, American ambassador Joseph Grew advocated the meeting as a last chance to avoid war. But the American government saw no hope for significant Japanese concessions—especially respecting China—and spurned the offer. Konoye's government fell on 16 October 1941, and the military leader General Hideki Tojo became prime minister. Another Imperial Conference on 5 November directed that war plans go forward, to be confirmed on 25 November if a last effort to secure American agreement to Japanese terms for a settlement failed.

China remained the sticking point. Washington simply would not concede any kind of official recognition to the Japanese incursion in China. Secretary Hull, forewarned of the details of Japanese ambassador Nomura's positions, thanks to the success of American cryptanalysts in cracking the Japanese diplomatic code, made this point repeatedly to Nomura during their final, fruitless round of talks in Washington in late November 1941.

At a White House meeting on 25 November 1941, administration officials acknowledged that little room for negotiation remained. War, in some form, seemed inevitable. The question, as Secretary

Stimson recorded in his diary, "was how we should maneuver them into firing the first shot without allowing too much danger to ourselves." The second half of that statement is no less important than the first. Despite decades of investigation, no reliable evidence has ever been adduced to support the charge that the Roosevelt administration deliberately exposed the fleet at Pearl Harbor to attack in order to precipitate war. Risking the entire Pacific Fleet in order to create a casus belli surely constituted "too much danger" to be even remotely imaginable. Moreover, the administration's clear priority by this time was the European and Atlantic theater. So far as Roosevelt was concerned, a Pacific naval war with Japan in 1941 was the wrong war, in the wrong place, with the wrong enemy, at the wrong time.

On the same day that Roosevelt and his advisers were acceding to the virtual inevitability of conflict, 26 November 1941, Tokyo time, a Japanese naval strike force sortied from Tankan Bay in the Kuril Islands, bound for Pearl Harbor.

Another coincidence of dates provides even deeper ironies. On 5 November, as Tojo's government slipped its war machine into gear, the American Joint Board of the Army and Navy advised that "considering world strategy" further Japanese aggression in China "would not justify intervention by the United States against Japan." Thus at the very moment that Japan was finalizing its plans to cripple the American Pacific Fleet at Pearl Harbor—a necessary prelude to expanding its aggression into the South Pacific—American military planners were privately conceding that they were powerless to affect events in China. Well might the question be pondered: Why not publicly accept the implications of this reasoning? Why not acquiesce, however complainingly, in the Japanese presence in China, continue to supply Japan with raw materials, thereby relieving the pressure on Japan to strike southward for other sources of supply, and thus prevent—or at least significantly delay—war between the United States and Japan?

One man who so reasoned in 1941 was American ambassador to Japan Joseph Grew. With few exceptions, the burden of his counsel in 1940 and 1941 was to work out some kind of modus vivendi with Japan. He had much logic on his side. American economic interests in Japan, he repeatedly pointed out, were several times greater than in China. The real danger to the United States, he argued, was Germany. All resources, without stint or let, should therefore be concentrated in that direction. Confrontation with Japan should be avoided or delayed.

Grew's views contended against both popular sentiment in favor of China and an entrenched pro-China group in the State Department. His counsel did not prevail. On the morning of 7 December 1941, aircraft from the Japanese attack force appeared over the American naval base at Pearl Harbor, Hawaii. In two hours of bombing and strafing the Japanese sank or disabled 19 ships, destroyed about 150 aircraft, and killed some 2,400 American soldiers, sailors, and civilians. The following day, with only a single dissenting vote (cast by the same Jeannette Rankin who had voted against war in 1917), Congress declared war on Japan. On 11 December, Germany and Italy, somewhat inexplicably, since the strict terms of their treaty obligations to Japan did not require them to do so, declared war on the United States, which then recognized a state of war with those nations.

THE WAR IN THE PACIFIC, 1941–1945

From the outset of American belligerency, popular passion ran much higher against Japan than against Germany. A legacy of racial animosity toward the Japanese, combined with the humiliating surprise attack on Pearl Harbor, led many Americans to favor a "Japan-first" strategy, in direct contradiction of American strategic doctrine as ratified in the ABC-1, or Europe-first agreement with the British in early 1941.

The master American plan in the event of war with Japan, code-named the ORANGE Plan, had first been formulated in the opening decade of the century. The ORANGE Plan assumed early Japanese capture of the Philippines, and made relief of the Philippines the main American objective. The American garrison in the Philippines was supposed to hold out for three or four months, while the U.S. fleet crossed the Pacific, engaged the main body of the Japanese fleet, destroyed it, and thereby ended the war. Always unrealistic, the plan was revised in 1934 to provide for the capture of the Marshall and Caroline Islands as staging areas for the main engagement with the Japanese fleet—a tacit admission that the war would last years, not months. But whatever its flaws, the ORANGE Plan remained the foundation of the United States' Pacific War strategy right down to 1945. In the two interwar decades, war games were fought at the Naval War College on these assumptions no fewer than 127 times.

Japanese strategic doctrine was virtually the mirror image of this American plan. Known as the doctrine of decisive battle, it envisioned the swift capture of the Philippines and Guam, thus forcing the U.S. fleet to battle. As the American Navy transited the

Pearl Harbor. The USS *Arizona* under attack, 7 December 1941. ARCHIVE PHOTOS

broad Pacific, it would be harassed by submarines and land-based aircraft. Near Guam, or perhaps near the Philippines, the enervated American fleet would be engaged and decisively defeated.

To this basic doctrine the Japanese added some formidable refinements. Their fleet was highly trained for night battle. Its submarines and surface ships alike were armed with the fearfully destructive "long lance" torpedo, capable of speeds up to forty-nine knots, and with a range of up to twenty-four miles. Nothing comparable existed in the American naval arsenal. Most important, in 1940 and 1941 the idea gained ascendancy in Japanese naval circles that rather than lie in wait for the American fleet, Japan should go after it directly at Pearl Harbor. With the U.S. Pacific fleet knocked out, Japan would have an enormous defensive perimeter, stretching from the North Pacific through midocean to the South Pacific.

Within that perimeter, as hostages, would lie Guam and the Philippines, perhaps even Hawaii, Australia, and New Zealand. Safely behind this impregnable barrier, Japan could assume a strategically defensive posture and sue for a negotiated peace on terms it dictated.

This was the prospect of success on which the Japanese gambled in 1941. But it was a faint prospect, dependent on swift and overwhelming initial victories. "If I am told to fight regardless of the consequences," Japanese Combined Fleet Commander Admiral Isoruku Yamamoto told prime minister Konoye in September 1940, "I shall run wild for the first six months or a year, but I have utterly no confidence for a second or third year . . . . I hope that you will endeavor to avoid a Japanese-American war."

At first Yamamoto's fragile hope for victory

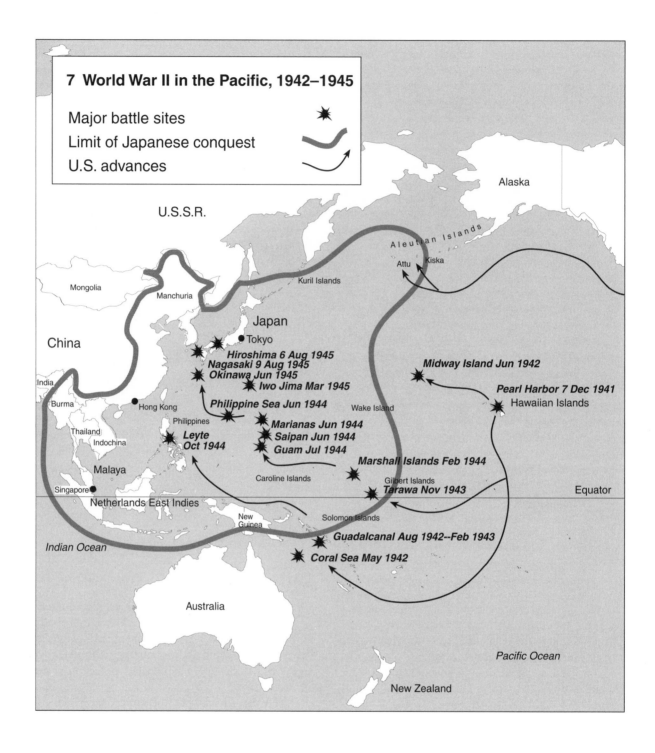

7 World War II in the Pacific, 1942–1945

Major battle sites

Limit of Japanese conquest

U.S. advances

seemed about to be realized. In the first six months of the war, the Japanese did "run wild" from the Kuril Islands in the North Pacific to the Indian Ocean in the south. Guam, Wake Island, and Hong Kong fell to Japanese forces within weeks of Pearl Harbor. The British stronghold of Singapore, "Gibraltar of the Pacific," surrendered on 15 February 1942. Burma and Java succumbed in March. And on 6 May 1942, after a gallant but punishing show of

resistance, General Jonathan Wainwright surrendered the American garrison in the Philippines. The Japanese push southward toward Australia was slowed, but not conclusively checked, at the Battle of the Coral Sea in May 1942. For the first time in naval history the fighting was all done by carrier-based aircraft; the ships involved were separated by 175 miles of sea, and never fired directly on one another.

What should the next Japanese step be? Yamamoto

answered that Japan should finish the job begun at Pearl Harbor by attacking Midway Island northwest of Hawaii. Taking Midway would secure the eastern boundary of the huge Japanese defense perimeter and menace Hawaii itself with the threat of invasion. Colonel James Doolittle's carrier-launched bombing raid on Tokyo in April 1942 added urgency to these Japanese calculations. Thus in late May a Japanese strike force sortied for Midway—into the jaws of a trap.

Unknown to the Japanese, American cryptanalysts had cracked the Japanese naval code; the U.S. Navy thus knew in advance when and where the Japanese strike would fall. On 4 June the Japanese invasion fleet approached Midway from the west and was met with repeated waves of air assaults launched from U.S. carriers hiding to the east of the island. Once again the ships were separated by nearly 200 miles of ocean and never saw each other. At first the American attackers fared badly. Torpedoes misfired, bombs missed their targets, and wandering American aircraft fell from the sky for want of fuel. Then at 10:25 A.M. a dive bomber group from the carrier *Enterprise* found the Japanese carrier force in the most vulnerable of situations, with aircraft strewn about the flight decks in the midst of rearming and refueling. Within five minutes, the dive bombers inflicted mortal damage on four Japanese carriers. The Americans had reversed the element of surprise and had at least partially avenged Pearl Harbor.

The Battle of Midway was a turning point in the Pacific War. It dramatically heralded the new age of naval warfare in which aircraft carriers, not battleships, were the decisive elements. Before the battle the Japanese had six fleet carriers in the Pacific, and the Americans three. With the loss of just one American and four Japanese carriers, Midway inverted that ratio and put the Japanese at a disadvantage from which they never recovered. The stage was now set for Yamamoto's worst nightmare: a battle of production between the behemoth American economy and the much tinier Japanese industrial plant. In the next two years, Japanese shipyards were able to produce only six additional fleet carriers. The United States added fourteen to its fleet, as well as nine light carriers and sixty-six escort carriers. Those kinds of numbers, which could be repeated in countless categories of war matériel, went far toward explaining the reasons for ultimate American victory.

After the Battle of Midway, both Japan and the United States were in strategic transition, though neither fully realized it at the time. Japan was passing onto the defensive after its string of initial victories; the United States began groping for a place to begin an offensive.

That place was found in the jungle of Guadalcanal, in the Solomon Islands of the southwest Pacific. The immediate objective was to prevent the Japanese from completing an airfield from which they could threaten the shipping lifeline to Australia and New Zealand. The further objective was to secure a forward air base from which to attack the large Japanese fortress at Rabaul, on the island of New Britain in the Bismarck Sea.

The first American troops splashed ashore at Guadalcanal on 7 August, meeting only light resistance. The next night, however, a Japanese naval force swept into the narrow waters around Savo Island, just off the Guadalcanal landing beaches, and within minutes sank four U.S. heavy cruisers without itself suffering any significant damage. The Battle of Savo Island ranks as possibly the worst defeat in American naval history. It provided a grim reminder that the Japanese navy still packed a powerful wallop, even after Midway. The losses at Savo also deprived the troops already landed at Guadalcanal of needed supplies.

After six months of grueling air, sea, and land combat the Japanese evacuated Guadalcanal in February 1943. About 1,700 American lives were lost on the island, and about 20,000 Japanese—a casualty ratio that persisted throughout most of the other battles in the Pacific War.

Victory at Guadalcanal opened the path up the Solomon chain toward the Japanese naval fortress at Rabaul. American forces inched their way up the ladder of the Solomons throughout 1943, seizing the northerly island of Bougainville in November. Meanwhile, Australian and American forces under General Douglas MacArthur slogged northwestward along Papua New Guinea's north coast, taking the key position of Buna in January 1943. Plans now called for MacArthur's forces to land on New Britain, just off the Papuan coast, and converge on Rabaul from the west while another force attacked from Bougainville in the south.

But at this juncture American military planners decided to bypass Rabaul, while reducing its effectiveness with air attacks and isolating it by blockade. MacArthur's ground forces were ordered to continue northwestward along the New Guinea coast, ultimately positioning themselves for an invasion of the Philippines. But there would be no invasion of fortress Rabaul. Instead, American planners deflected resources to a new Central Pacific naval campaign under Admiral Chester Nimitz. It opened with a costly amphibious landing on Tarawa, in the Gilbert Islands, in November 1943. It continued into the Marshall Islands with landings on Kwajalein and Eniwetok in February 1944, and into the Marianas with assaults on Saipan in June and Guam in July 1944. MacArthur, meanwhile, landed in the Philippines in October 1944, and the islands were at last liberated from Japanese domination in July 1945.

That the United States mounted two major Pacific drives, under two separate commands—MacArthur's ground campaign in the southwest Pacific, and Nimitz's naval campaign in the central Pacific—reflected an inability to resolve differences of opinion among major commanders, and among competing strategic concepts. Moreover, the simultaneity of those two Pacific campaigns, along with a smaller one under the command of General Joseph Stilwell on the mainland of Asia and the much larger one in the European theater, also reflected the fact that the United States, unlike all other combatants, was only weakly constrained in its military strategies by the availability of physical resources. The United States in World War II illustrated once again, as it had in World War I, that the American way of war was, simply, more—more men, more weapons, more machines, more technology, and more money.

The Central Pacific campaign also reflected the persistent grip of the old ORANGE Plan on the thinking of American strategists. It envisioned piercing the center of the Japanese mid-ocean defense perimeter, thus luring the main Japanese fleet to battle, where it could be destroyed. Something approximating that result occurred in June 1944, in the Battle of the Philippine Sea. That engagement opened with "The Great Marianas Turkey Shoot" on 19 June, when a combination of the combat superiority of the recently developed American "Hellcat" fighter plane and the new technology of the anti-aircraft proximity fuse destroyed nearly 250 Japanese aircraft, with a loss of only 29 American planes. The following day American forces sank one Japanese carrier and damaged two others, as well two heavy cruisers. The Japanese navy never recovered from these massive losses of planes, pilots, and ships.

The Marianas also provided launching bases for the new B-29 "superbombers," whose striking range of 1,500 miles put the Japanese home islands within reach. From November 1944 on, huge flights of B-29s struck Japan almost daily. Beginning in 1945, they carried incendiary bombs that devastated Japan's wooden cities. One raid on Tokyo in early 1945 touched off a firestorm that immolated more than 80,000 people. To secure the air-route from the Marianas to Japan, the Americans took the tiny island of Iwo Jima in March 1945, in a desperate battle that claimed some 7,000 American lives.

The invasion of Okinawa the following month was even more costly. The Japanese had by this time learned how to inflict terrible losses on amphibious landings by forming their defensive lines not on the beachheads but well inland, out of the range of naval guns. At Okinawa the Japanese also made extensive use of the fanatical kamikaze aerial suicide attacks on American ships. When Okinawa was at last secured on 21 June, more than 11,000 Americans had perished.

Extrapolating from those grisly numbers, American planners in mid-1945 calculated that the anticipated invasion of the Japanese home islands, where even more ferocious resistance could be expected, might run as high as 268,000 dead and wounded. That chilling calculus formed part of the context in which the war's atomic end game would be played out.

THE WAR IN EUROPE, 1941–1945

Like the war against Japan, the war against Germany began at sea. During 1942, German submarines inflicted appalling losses on American and British ships in the Atlantic. The U-boats prowled just miles off the American eastern seaboard, easily picking off targets silhouetted at night against the lights of coastal cities. The Germans called it "the happy time." But eventually a combination of improved convoy tactics and better antisubmarine weapons eliminated the U-boat menace. The Allied antisubmarine campaign was greatly bolstered by Ultra, the code name for a British counterintelligence effort that enabled Allied commanders to intercept enemy radio communications and identify the locations of the German submarine wolf packs that lay in wait for Allied convoys in the Atlantic. (See figure 1.)

At home in America, the nation's Depression-dormant industrial plant roared to life and poured forth an avalanche of weaponry: 300,000 aircraft, 76,000 ships, 86,000 tanks, 2.6 million machine guns, and more than 40 billion bullets. The decade-long scourge of unemployment was lifted as some 15 million men and more than 200,000 women entered the armed services. Manpower needs in the booming war plants were so great that the war proved to be a great demographic cauldron, churning and shifting the American people. More than 1.5 million blacks moved out of the Old South to toil in the weapons plants and shipyards of the North and the West. Six million women went to work for wages, half of them for the first time. To harvest the fruit and grain crops of the West, thousands of agricultural workers, called *braceros,* were recruited from Mexico. The national debt rocketed from $49 billion in 1941 to $259 billion in 1945, as no expense was spared to make America

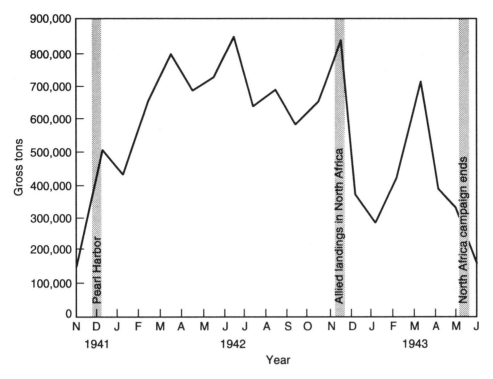

Figure 1.   Merchant tonnage sunk by German U-boats, November 1941–June 1943.
(Source: David M. Kennedy and Thomas A. Bailey, *The American Pageant* [1986], p. 861.)

the "arsenal of democracy." Total wartime expenditures came to nearly $300 billion, and the eventual bill exceeded $650 billion.

While it stocked the Allied arsenal and gathered and trained its growing army and navy, the United States made its first direct military contribution to the war against Hitler in August 1942, when the Eighth Air Force flew from its British bases to bomb railroad marshaling yards in German-controlled Rouen, France. For the next two and one half years, lumbering American B-17 Flying Fortresses joined the British Bomber Command in relentless raids against German targets on the European continent.

Allied bombing harassed the Germans, eventually reducing many of their cities to rubble; but in 1942 the bombers did not appreciably slow Hitler's advance into the Soviet Union. Stalled just short of Moscow in late 1941, the Germans resumed their offensive in the spring of 1942, striking southward into the Russian breadbasket in the valleys of the Don and the Volga, and toward the oil fields of the Caucasus. For weeks the Nazi Panzers raced across the Russian steppes. Then, its supply lines dangerously extended, the apparently invincible Wehrmacht met its match at the Volga River city of Stalingrad in November 1942. A crushing counterattack took more than 200,000 German prisoners and unleashed a Soviet offensive that was never seriously reversed.

Stalingrad was a decisive turning point in the war; but the Russian success was dearly bought. The Soviets already counted their losses in the millions; Anglo-American casualties by this time numbered in the thousands. By war's end some 20 million Soviet soldiers and civilians were to perish. Understandably, Soviet leaders pleaded with the British and American allies to open a second front in the west to drain German strength away from the east.

American leaders, including President Roosevelt, were eager to open a second front with an invasion from England across the Channel into Nazi-dominated France. Lack of shipping and other resources, including trained troops, necessarily meant that the front could not be opened immediately. Moreover, the British, stung by the humiliating retreat from Dunkirk and remembering the bloody stalemate of World War I, preferred to delay an invasion until an absolutely overwhelming force could be thrown ashore. As an alternative for the immediate future, they suggested that the Americans join in the two-year-old battle against German and Italian forces in North Africa.

In November 1942 American troops under General Dwight D. Eisenhower landed at several sites in French Morocco and Algeria. Within six months the Anglo-American forces had defeated the Germans and Italians, taking some 260,000 prisoners. North

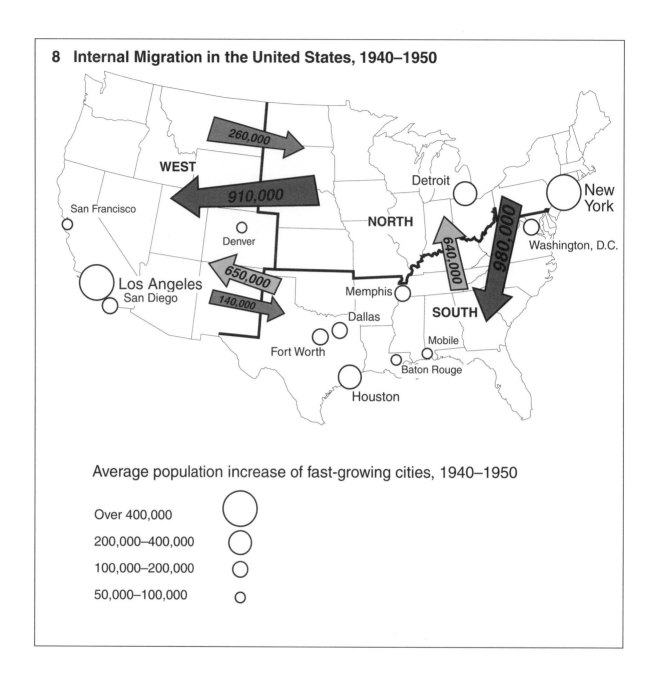

8 Internal Migration in the United States, 1940–1950

260,000

910,000

650,000

140,000

640,000

980,000

WEST

NORTH

SOUTH

San Francisco

Denver

Los Angeles
San Diego

Fort Worth

Dallas

Houston

Memphis

Mobile

Baton Rouge

Detroit

New York

Washington, D.C.

Average population increase of fast-growing cities, 1940–1950

Over 400,000

200,000–400,000

100,000–200,000

50,000–100,000

Africa and the Mediterranean were now secure, as was Britain's life line to India and the Far East through the Suez Canal. But the action in North Africa did not constitute a proper second front. On the continent of Europe, the Russians continued to absorb punishment on a colossal scale from the Germans, and redoubled their pleas for help in the west.

At Casablanca in Morocco, President Roosevelt met with Prime Minister Winston Churchill in January 1943 to discuss their next steps in the war. To reassure the Russians that they would conclude no separate peace with Germany (and to discourage the Russians from entertaining any such thoughts of their own, as they had done in World War I), the two leaders declared that they would accept only "unconditional surrender" from the Axis powers. But the western Allies were still of two minds about a second front. The Americans wanted to take the North African invasion force and use it for a cross-Channel attack as soon as possible; the British again counseled delay. As a compromise, Roosevelt and Churchill proposed to invade Italy.

9 World War II in Europe and North Africa, 1939–1945

Axis Powers and their allies

Axis-held, early November 1942

Allied Powers and their allies

Neutral nations

Allied advances

Major battles

Murmansk

Finland

Norway

Sweden

Leningrad besiegd
Sep 1941–19 Jan 1944

Estonia

Latvia

Moscow
Germans repulsed
Dec 1941

Lithuania   *Sep 1944*

Aug 1943

Great Britain

Northern Ireland

North Sea

Denmark

E. Prussia

Jul 1944

Apr 1945   **Berlin surrendered 2 May 1945**

London

Neth.

Dunkirk

Belg.

Germany

Warsaw

Ireland

Battle of the Bulge
16 Dec 1944–
31 Jan 1945

Poland

Stalingrad
21 Aug 1942–31 Jan 1943

Normandy D-day
6 Jun 1944

Slovakia

Apr 1945

Aug 1944

Paris liberated
25 Aug 1944

Switz.

Hungary

Dec 1944

Atlantic Ocean

France

Aug 1944

Italy

Romania

Yugoslavia

Yalta

Rome liberated
4 Jun 1944

Adriatic Sea

Bulgaria

Black Sea

Portugal

Spain

Monte
Cassino
Salerno

Albania

Greece

Turkey

Sardinia

Sicily

Nov 1942

Tunis

Jul 1943

Crete

Syria

Kasserine Pass
14–22 Feb 1943

Spanish
Morocco

Tunisia

Mediterranean Sea

Lebanon

Iraq

Casablanca

Palestine

Alexandria

Transjordan (U.K.)

Morocco

French North Africa
(Vichy France)

Libya
(Italy)

Nov 1942

El Alamein
23 Oct–5 Nov 1942
Egypt

Saudi Arabia

Limit of Axis advance

The Italian campaign was the longest American engagement in the European theater, but it was always something of a sideshow. It began with massive British and American landings in Sicily in August 1943. The defending German troops successfully escaped across the Straits of Messina to the Italian mainland, and though the Italian government capitulated in September the Germans remained in Italy. Under Field Marshal Albert Kesselring, they organized a brilliant defense of the mountainous peninsula, using only minimal reinforcements. The Allies landed troops at Salerno in southern Italy in early September 1943, but they were soon stopped by Kesselring's defenses at Monte Cassino, just north of Naples. To break the stalemate, the Allies landed a second force at Anzio, near Rome, in January 1944. It too was quickly contained, prompting Churchill to remark that he had expected to hurl a wildcat ashore, but instead got a stranded whale. At tremendous cost, the Allies finally broke the German line at Monte Cassino in May 1944 and entered Rome the next month. The Germans fell back northwards to a succession of new defensive positions. They were still entrenched just north of Florence when the European war ended in May 1945.

Neither side treated Italy as a major theater of operations. The Germans, making shrewd use of the terrain, defended the peninsula with minimal effort. The British and the Americans by early 1944 were already withdrawing part of their forces from the Mediterranean in preparation for the long-awaited invasion of France, which would constitute a genuine second front against the Germans.

Roosevelt and Churchill met in the Iranian capital of Teheran in November 1943 for the first time with their third partner in the "Grand Alliance," Soviet leader Joseph Stalin. The Russians agreed in principle to enter the war against Japan once Germany was defeated. In addition, vague agreements were sketched regarding the postwar settlement, including Soviet reparations from Germany and the recognition of paramount Soviet interests in eastern Europe. Most important, the leaders agreed to coordinate a Soviet spring offensive in 1944 with the opening, at long last, of a second front in the west.

In Britain, preparations for the cross-Channel invasion, code-named OVERLORD and under the direction of newly named Supreme Allied Commander Dwight Eisenhower, reflected the now-familiar American prodigiousness in warfare. Britain's fast-anchored isle groaned under the weight of 3 million troops, thousands of tanks, trucks, and aircraft, and countless millions of tons of other supplies. On D-day, 6 June 1944, this gargantuan force fell upon the French coast of Normandy. Hitler, duped by an elaborate Allied deception into thinking that a still larger force would soon land near Calais, refused to release armored reinforcements and hence missed his chance to check the invaders on the beaches. Aided by Hitler's confusion and by the secure possession of air supremacy over the landing areas, the Allies swiftly established a strong beachhead and began to penetrate inland.

The German defenders at first made excellent use of the Norman hedgerows—dense, tangled plantings, sometimes ten feet thick, marking the boundaries of fields—to stall the Allied advance. But by August the Allies had broken out of the hedgerow country, and the Germans beat a rapid retreat to the Rhine. A second Allied force landed in southern France on 15 August, and joined in the pursuit of the fleeing Germans. On 25 August, Paris was liberated. The Russians, meanwhile, were advancing relentlessly into Poland on Germany's east. Ever suspicious, Russian leaders remained skeptical that a second front had actually been opened in the west until they were shown films documenting the landings.

On 16 December 1944, Hitler made one last desperate throw of the dice. Catching the Americans off-guard in Belgium's snow-mantled Ardennes Forest, he launched a powerful attack that created a huge bulge in the Allied line. The German objective was to seize the port of Antwerp, fouling Allied supply operations and perhaps forcing a second Dunkirk-style evacuation. At a minimum Hitler apparently hoped to stall the war long enough to bring his new V-1 and V-2 rocket-bombs into play against Britain. The Battle of the Bulge ended when Russian forces stepped up their offensive in the east, and Hitler could no longer sustain his western assault. On 30 April 1945, the Führer committed suicide in his Berlin bunker. Just eighteen days earlier, Franklin Roosevelt had died of a cerebral hemorrhage.

Allied troops crossed the Rhine into Germany in March 1945. American GI's were horrified to discover reeking death camps where millions of Jews, gypsies, and political foes of the Nazis had been systematically exterminated. The Third Reich was crushed between the Anglo-American and Soviet armies the following month when the two forces joined hands at the River Elbe. On 7 May 1945, Germany surrendered.

THE WAR'S END, 1945

A final meeting of the Big Three Grand Alliance partners at the Crimean city of Yalta in February 1945 had produced agreement on a postwar United

President Harry S. Truman and General Dwight D. Eisenhower. NATIONAL ARCHIVES

Atomic bomb cloud over Nagasaki, Japan, 9 August 1945. ARCHIVE PHOTOS/AMERICAN STOCK

Nations organization. Other agreements at Yalta, though somewhat vague, concerned postwar arrangements for defeated Germany and for Eastern Europe, where the Soviet army was firmly entrenched. Dispute over exactly what had been agreed at Yalta, especially regarding Eastern Europe, clouded the postwar years, with each side accusing the other of breaking its solemn promises.

Most important, the Yalta negotiators had agreed that the Soviets should enter the war against Japan within three months of the German surrender. Thus the target date for a Russian declaration of war on Japan was 7 August 1945.

Harry S. Truman, who succeeded to the American presidency on Roosevelt's death, was scheduled to meet with his British and Soviet counterparts at Potsdam, near the bomb-gutted German capital of Berlin, as soon as practical after the German surrender. But Truman, at the urging of his advisers, postponed the meeting until late July. Truman delayed primarily to await word of the development of a new weapon, the atomic bomb, which British and American (but not Russian) scientists had been developing under top-secret conditions. On 16 July, while en route to Potsdam, Truman received word of the successful testing of the first atomic device at Alamagordo, New Mexico. Curiously, however, Truman made little use of this information to bend the still-suspicious and increasingly intransigent Soviets to his will. Instead, the Allies issued an ultimatum to Japan, calling for unconditional surrender.

The Japanese spurned the warning and, on 6 August 1945, a B-29 bomber took off from the Mariana island base of Tinian, dropping history's first atomic bomb on the Japanese city of Hiroshima. More than 70,000 people died instantly and that many again were left with ghastly radiation burns and other wounds. Three days later the Americans dropped a second bomb on Nagasaki, killing more tens of thousands of Japanese. Japan at last asked for peace on 10 August. A formal surrender was executed aboard the battleship *Missouri* in Tokyo Bay on 2 September 1945.

The war thus ended on a morally ambiguous note, as controversy has swirled ever since around the decision to inaugurate the age of atomic warfare when the Japanese appeared to be on the verge of collapse. Some historians have suggested that the atomic bombings of Japan should be understood not as the last shots fired in World War II, but the first

Table 3.   ESTIMATES OF TOTAL COSTS AND NUMBER OF BATTLE DEATHS
OF MAJOR U.S. WARS[a]

War	Total Costs[b] (Millions of Dollars)	Original Costs (Millions of Dollars)	Number of Battle Deaths
Vietnam Conflict	352,000	140,600	47,355[c]
Korean Conflict	164,000	54,000	33,629
World War II	664,000	288,000	291,557
World War I	112,000	26,000	53,402
Spanish-American War	6,460	400	385
Civil War { Union only	12,952	3,200	140,414
Civil War { Confederacy (est.)	n.a.	1,000	94,000
Mexican War	147	73	1,733
War of 1812	158	93	2,260
American Revolution	190	100	6,824

[a] Deaths from disease and other causes are not shown. In earlier wars especially, owing to poor medical and sanitary practices, nonbattle deaths substantially exceeded combat casualties.
[b] The difference between total costs and original costs is attributable to continuing postwar payments for such items as veterans' benefits, interest on war debts, and so on.
[c] 1957–1990.
SOURCES: *Historical Statistics of the United States, Colonial Times to 1970* (1975); *Statistical Abstract of the United States,* relevant years; *The World Almanac and Book of Facts, 1986.* Table reprinted from David M. Kennedy and Thomas A. Bailey, *The American Pageant* (1986), p. A34.

shots fired in the Cold War that was shaping up with the Soviet Union. The real purpose of those bombs, the argument runs, was to intimidate the Russians and end the war quickly, before the Soviet army could establish itself in Asia. Those considerations no doubt colored American thinking; but the decision to use the bomb as soon as it was available was in a fundamental sense implicit in the decision to build the bomb in the first place. Moreover, the awful casualty rates at Iwo Jima and especially Okinawa in early 1945 convinced American planners that a conventional invasion of the Japanese home islands—regarded as the principal alternative to the bombings—would have been horribly costly, in all likelihood claiming more American and Japanese lives than the atomic attacks themselves.

At war's end Americans had suffered 291,557 battle deaths and virtually no civilian casualties (see table 3). Almost every other combatant counted casualties in the millions, including large numbers of civilians. Also, alone among the combatants, the United States—with the single exception of Pearl Harbor—had been spared the ravages of modern warfare in its own heartland. Much of the rest of the world in 1945 was a smoking ruin. America, in contrast, had used the war to fire up its smokeless factories and invigorate its economy. Its experience in the war was unique; no other combatant paid so low a price or reaped such extravagant rewards. "America stands at this moment at the summit of the world," Winston Churchill declared in 1945. But how responsibly would the Americans use that privileged position, and how long could the United States maintain its lofty perch? Would the ancient preachments of isolationist doctrine again find a receptive audience among Americans? The answers to those questions lay in the lap of the uncertain future that dawned in 1945.

SEE ALSO Limited Wars; Pacifism and Arms Limitation; Foreign Policy (all in this volume).

BIBLIOGRAPHY

Howard K. Beale, *Theodore Roosevelt and the Rise of America to World Power* (1956), puts early-twentieth-century American diplomacy into a global context. Edward Coffmann, *The War to End All Wars: The American Military Experience in World War I* (1968), is a definitive history of America's military effort in 1917–1918. David M. Kennedy, *Over Here: The First World War and American Society* (1980), concentrates on the home front, and has substantial discussions of military history and international economic relations. Robert Ferrell, *Woodrow Wilson and World War I* (1985), is a thoroughly readable account of events both at home and abroad. Gerd Hardach, *The First World War: 1914–1918* (1977), gives an impressively cogent analysis of the economic context and consequences of the war. Thomas A. Bailey, *Woodrow Wilson and the Lost Peace* (1944) and *Woodrow Wilson and the Great Betrayal* (1945), provide lively accounts of Wilson's peacemaking efforts. George F. Kennan, *American Diplomacy, 1900–1950* (1950), reflects a "realist" critique of Wilson's diplomacy.

On the interwar period, see Kennedy, *Over Here,* as well as Manfred Jonas, *Isolationism in America: 1935–1941* (1966), an especially thoughtful discussion that ranges through cultural and intellectual history as well as the political events of the pre–World War II years. Robert Dallek, *Franklin D. Roosevelt and American Foreign Policy, 1932–1945* (1979), gives an exhaustive account of Roosevelt's struggle against isolationism in the 1930s, and his leadership in World War II. Herbert Feis, *The Road to Pearl Harbor* (1950), recounts in painstaking detail the events leading up to war between Japan and the United States. Gordon Prange, *At Dawn We Slept: The Untold Story of Pearl Harbor* (1981), is an exhaustively researched and colorfully written narrative; see also Prange's *Miracle at Midway* (1982). P. W. Schroeder, *The Axis Alliance and Japanese-American Relations, 1941* (1958), explores the thesis, sometimes associated with Ambassador Joseph Grew, that the Japanese-American war might have been avoided by more skillful diplomacy.

On the military history of World War II, John Keegan, *The Second World War* (1989), is the most useful single-volume study. Kent R. Greenfield, *American Strategy in World War II* (1963), is a masterly exposition of the evolution of American high strategy. Samuel Eliot Morison, *History of United States Naval Operations in World War II* (15 vols., 1947–1962), is the canonical account; a single-volume condensation appeared as *The Two-Ocean War* (1963).

Ronald Spector, *Eagle Against the Sun* (1985), provides a comprehensive history of the Pacific War. Richard B. Frank, *Guadalcanal* (1990), is the definitive study of that important battle. John W. Dower, *War Without Mercy: Race and Power in the Pacific War* (1986), is a fascinating essay on the cultural dimensions of the Japanese-American conflict. Akira Iriye, *Power and Culture: The Japanese-American War, 1941–1945* (1981), suggests that both adversaries in the Pacific War achieved their long-term goals by 1945. Christopher Thorne, *Allies of a Kind: The United States, Britain, and the War Against Japan, 1941–1945* (1978), presents a thorough discussion of interallied tensions in the Pacific theater of operations.

On the European theater, see David Eisenhower, *Eisenhower at War, 1943–45* (1986), which discusses the Supreme Allied Commander's wartime decisions in lavish detail. Eric Larabee, *Commander in Chief* (1987), shrewdly analyzes Roosevelt's relations with his principal military chiefs. Consult also Max Hastings, *Overlord: D-Day and the Battle for Normandy, 1944* (1984), which makes sense out of the sometimes bafflingly complex developments in the battle for northwest Europe.

Gabriel Kolko, *The Politics of War: The World and United States Foreign Policy, 1943–1945* (1968), gives a New Left revisionist analysis of wartime American diplomacy and, allegedly, the roots of the Cold War. Gar Alperovitz, *Atomic Diplomacy* (1965), raises provocative questions about the use of the atomic bombs at the end of World War II. See also Richard Rhodes, *The Making of the Atomic Bomb* (1986), a detailed and balanced account of the bomb's development and use, and the controversy surrounding it.

LIMITED WARS

George C. Herring

Limited war is a conflict in which at least one of the belligerents fights with less than total means for objectives short of the complete defeat and unconditional surrender of the enemy. The conflict may also be limited geographically, and the fighting restricted to primarily military targets. During the height of the Cold War, when total war threatened nuclear catastrophe, limited war attained a certain vogue among academicians and policymakers in the United States. In actuality, such wars proved very difficult for Americans to fight. In both the Korean "police action" and the conflict in Vietnam, America's two major twentieth-century limited wars, there was widespread public frustration with the government's unwillingness or inability to attain victory. There was also extended and often heated controversy between those political leaders who insisted on keeping the wars limited and some military and political leaders who poorly understood and deeply resented restraints on the conduct of the war.

LIMITED WAR AND THE AMERICAN MILITARY TRADITION

Limited war is not, of course, exclusively a twentieth-century phenomenon. After the carnage and destruction of the Thirty Years' War, European rulers in the late seventeenth and early eighteenth centuries deliberately set out to restrict the means and ends of combat. They had seen the dangers of unleashing the passions of their own people. They had made huge investments in their armies, needed them to maintain domestic order, and thus were loath to risk them in battle. Once involved in war, as a consequence, they sought to avoid major battles, employed professional armies in cautious strategies of attrition, used tactics emphasizing maneuver and fortification, and adopted unwritten rules protecting civilian lives and property. The aim was to sustain the balance of power rather than destroy the enemy. Wars were to be conducted with minimal intrusion into the lives of the people. Indeed, that master practitioner of limited war, Frederick the Great, once observed that a war was not a success if most people knew it was going on.

Although the United States came into being in the age of limited war, that type of conflict proved incompatible with the American experience and character. Native Americans were not familiar with the rules of "civilized" warfare applied in Europe, and the recurrent conflicts on the frontiers of the New World took a very different shape. Colonists' homes were often their fortresses and all men and women were soldiers. The wars were for survival, as Daniel Boorstin has written in *The Americans: The Colonial Experience,* "the urgent defense of the hearth by everybody against an omnipresent and merciless enemy." Vulnerable to external threats in the early years of their existence as a nation, Americans sought to relieve the chronic fear and insecurity through the total elimination of their enemies. To be sure, the United States, out of weakness, fought essentially defensive wars against Great Britain in 1776 and 1812, and wisely avoided the pursuit of total victory against Mexico in 1846. Still, in seeking the elimination of British power from much of North America, Revolutionary leaders foreshadowed what came to be a peculiarly American approach to warfare. The remarkable success of the United States in its early years also fostered a false optimism of what might be achieved from war and left an enduring perception of how conflicts should end. For Americans, the concept of security came to be expressed in absolute, not relative, terms.

Warfare underwent major changes in the nineteenth century. The genteel age of Frederick the Great gave way to the violent age of Napoleon. With the French Revolution, war was again harnessed to ideological and nationalistic goals, and popular passions, once aroused for such ends, could not easily be turned off. Nations again fought for survival, making the ends of war more difficult to attain.

Leaders therefore felt compelled to mobilize all available resources to defeat an enemy by breaking its will to resist. Napoleon sought to do this through the climactic battle in which he employed a strategy of annihilation, lavishly expending manpower and using new military technologies such as mobile artillery to inflict decisive defeat on the enemy's main forces.

That approach closely fit the American temperament and experience, and it became deeply entrenched as the nation's power grew. Indeed, in the American Civil War, Union Generals U. S. Grant and William Tecumseh Sherman carried Napoleonic concepts a step further. Using new rifled weaponry to inflict huge casualties, Grant developed the strategy of annihilation into a brutal art form, looking beyond the decisive battle to a prolonged and costly campaign that would exhaust and eventually destroy the enemy's army. Sherman went still further, carrying the terror and destruction of war to the enemy's people, depriving them of their resources and crippling their will to support the war. The Civil War thus established an American way of thinking in which the complete overthrow of the enemy, the destruction of his military power, became the object of war.

In the twentieth century, the American way of total war became the worldwide norm. To exploit the enormous military potential made possible by the industrial revolution, leaders had to mobilize their nations as never before, and the emergence of mass communications gave them new means to do so. Wars thus became all-encompassing in a way they had not before. In World War I, the size of the armies and advances in technology rendered obsolete the Napoleonic concept of the climactic battle. Engagements were continuous, rather than sporadic, and warfare degenerated into a series of assaults and counterassaults across deadly killing zones, bloody, exhausting, and indecisive. The further mobilization of technology in World War II offered a way around the slaughter of trench warfare, but required even greater totality of effort.

The United States found twentieth-century warfare compatible with its traditional way of doing things. Although it entered each of the world wars well after they had begun, in each case it fully mobilized its vast resources in pursuit of victory against demonized enemies. In each case, its intervention determined the outcome. Instead of opting for limited involvement in World War I, Woodrow Wilson decided on full-scale participation, in part perhaps to satisfy the passions he had aroused to secure a declaration of war against Germany. Although Wilson spoke eloquently of a peace without victory and the allies eventually accepted an armistice that left the German government intact, the United States mobilized its people and economy in unprecedented ways, committed a mass army to the western front, and in the Saint Mihiel and Meuse-Argonne offensives employed it decisively against German strong points.

The U.S. involvement in World War I was so brief and relatively painless that it confirmed rather than challenged traditional approaches to warfare. Learning from World War I, the Allies early committed themselves in World War II to the unconditional surrender of Germany and Japan. Mobilizing as never before, the United States by 1944 was producing close to 50 percent of the war materials being used in the entire war, and it employed its vast superiority of resources to isolate Japan, cripple it economically, and through airpower reduce its major cities to rubble. In Europe, in the best tradition of U. S. Grant, American strategists overrode British preference for a peripheral approach and in the Normandy landings applied a strategy of annihilation against German strong points. Thanks to Russian sacrifices on the eastern front, the western allies were able to achieve decisive victory in Europe at acceptable cost. In the eyes of civilians and military planners alike, World War II therefore became the archetype of the way wars were to be fought.

There were, of course, exceptions. Between 1899 and 1902, the United States Army fought and eventually defeated a rebellion of those Filipinos who refused to accept the imposition of American rule in the Philippines in a conflict that in some ways foreshadowed the later war in Vietnam. Between 1900 and 1934, the Marines fought a series of so-called "banana wars" to enlarge and protect American economic interests in the Caribbean and Central America and impose stability on the chronically unstable and strategically important nations in the new U.S. empire in that region.

Yet, in important ways, these exceptions proved the rule. The Philippine and banana wars were very difficult for Americans to fight. It took more than three years, $400 million, 125,000 men, 4,200 killed and 2,800 wounded (a casualty rate of 5.5 percent, one of the highest of any American war), for the United States Army to defeat relatively small, scattered, and poorly armed Filipino guerrilla forces. Most of the banana wars involved only sporadic, if sometimes brutal, fighting against local bandit groups. In the last of them, however, as many as 5,000 U.S. Marines in the period between 1927 and

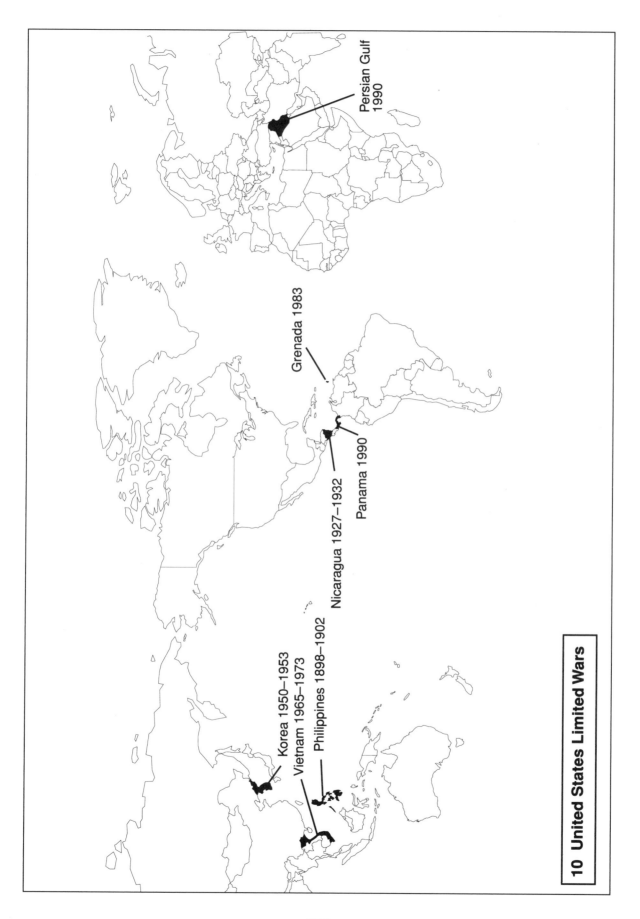

Persian Gulf
1990

Grenada 1983

Nicaragua 1927–1932

Panama 1990

Korea 1950–1953
Vietnam 1965–1973
Philippines 1898–1902

10 United States Limited Wars

1932 fought a savage and ultimately futile jungle war against elusive rebels under the skillful leadership of Nicaraguan folk hero Augusto Sandino. The inability of the Marines to catch Sandino and the financial pressures of the Great Depression eventually forced U.S. withdrawal from Nicaragua.

These counterinsurgency wars also provoked a special brand of anger and occasionally disillusionment among those Americans fighting them. Soldiers were frustrated by the guerrilla warfare of the Filipinos, denouncing them as cowardly and treacherous for refusing to fight in the open. The constant threat of ambushes, snipers, booby traps, and sabotage provoked fear and hatred among American soldiers and also aroused latent racial antagonisms against the "gugus" and "niggers," leading to the application and easy justification of brutal methods and sometimes to atrocities. The same was true in Central America and the Caribbean, especially during the conflict with blacks in Haiti, where U.S. Marines killed scores of Haitians in the process of pacifying the country. At least a few Americans came to find such warfare unpalatable and incompatible with their ideals. One officer labeled the Filipino war an "unholy war"; another conceded that the insurrection was "better justified than was our own Revolution of glorious memory." Some participants in the banana wars came to lament their work on behalf of such giant corporations as the United Fruit Company and National City Bank. Later recanting his role as the hero of U.S. interventions in Nicaragua and Haiti, Marine General Smedley Butler described himself as a "high-class muscle man for Big Business," a "racketeer for capitalism."

The wars also aroused opposition at home. In all instances, they were conducted without formal declarations and without public support. They were fought by small numbers of professional troops. The nation was therefore willing to tolerate them as long as they did not interfere with everyday life. In no case did the opposition reach proportions significant enough to exert a decisive influence on policy. Still, the Philippine war and Wilson's banana wars in Haiti and the Dominican Republic did become the objects of partisan political conflict. Especially in the Caribbean and Central America, intellectuals and liberal politicians heatedly condemned the narrow economic interests served by U.S. interventionism and the brutal methods employed. Senate investigations of both the Philippine war and the interventions in Hispaniola sharply criticized U.S. actions and helped to speed their end, and weariness with the frustrating chase after Sandino contributed to the eventual withdrawal of U.S. troops.

KOREA: LIMITED WAR BY NECESSITY

The war fought in Korea from 1950 to 1953 between United Nations forces under U.S. direction and North Korean and Chinese forces with Soviet support was America's first true limited war. It was characterized in its early stages by dramatic reversals of fortune, each change in momentum tempting one side or the other to seek victory. Ultimately, expediency required both the United States and China to accept a limited war, resulting in a prolonged and bloody stalemate. For the United States, this experiment with a new kind of warfare proved particularly frustrating. It was the first major conflict Americans had fought without using the full range of weapons available to them and without seeking victory. The U.S. armed forces were not prepared to fight in this way. In addition, this "sour little war," as W. Averell Harriman called it, was so sharply at variance with America's traditional manner of fighting that it caused great political and psychological trauma in the United States.

The Korean War stemmed from settlements made hastily and haphazardly at the end of World War II. Korea had been a colony of Japan through most of the twentieth century. The Allies agreed that, along with other Japanese colonies, it should be freed "in due course" after the war, and at the Cairo and Teheran conferences in 1943 they made formal pledges to that effect. President Franklin Roosevelt had envisioned a long-term trusteeship during which the Korean peoples would be prepared for independence. Characteristically, however, he had done little to implement his plan, and when the war against Japan ended suddenly in August 1945, no provisions had been made for Korea. By this time, the Cold War between the United States and the Soviet Union was already taking form. Fearful that the Soviets might fill the vacuum left by the Japanese surrender, giving them the upper hand in northeast Asia, State Department officials persuaded Roosevelt's successor, Harry S. Truman, to accept a joint, Soviet-American occupation of Korea with the 38th parallel the dividing line between their respective zones.

As the Cold War intensified between 1945 and 1950, Korea became one of its major battlegrounds. Although professing support for the independence and unification of Korea, the two great powers could not agree on the mechanism or form for accomplishing these goals, and Korea remained divided. Within their own zones, moreover, they supported political groups and shaped institutions compatible with their own ideologies. In southern Korea, the United States

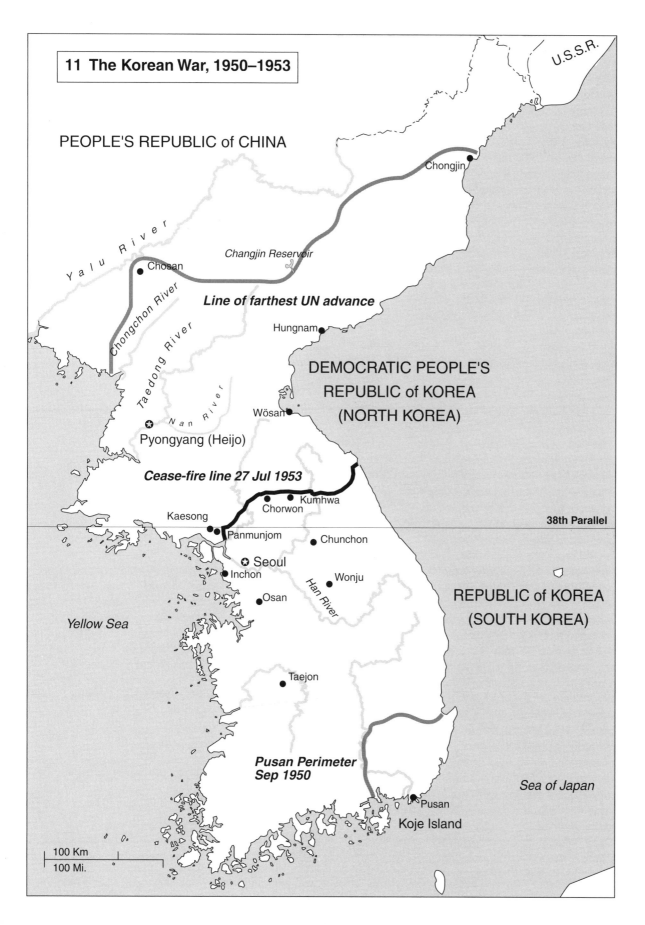

11 The Korean War, 1950–1953

PEOPLE'S REPUBLIC of CHINA

U.S.S.R.

Chongjin

Yalu River

Chosan

Changjin Reservoir

Chongchon River

Line of farthest UN advance

Taedong River

Hungnam

DEMOCRATIC PEOPLE'S
REPUBLIC of KOREA
(NORTH KOREA)

Nan River

Wösan

Pyongyang (Heijo)

Cease-fire line 27 Jul 1953

Kumhwa

Chorwon

Kaesong

38th Parallel

Panmunjom

Chunchon

Seoul

Wonju

Inchon

Han River

Osan

Yellow Sea

REPUBLIC of KOREA
(SOUTH KOREA)

Taejon

**Pusan Perimeter
Sep 1950**

Sea of Japan

Pusan

Koje Island

100 Km
100 Mi.

suppressed leftist agitators and favored the property owners, professional men, and bureaucrats (some of whom had collaborated with the Japanese) who rallied to the Korean Democratic party (KDP) and its venerable leader Syngman Rhee. In the north, the Soviet Union backed the Korean Communist party and its youthful leader, Kim Il-sung. As the years went on, without any agreement on unification, the temporary division of Korea assumed the form of permanency with two separate governments and armies.

In terms of its immediate origins, the Korean War had both indigenous and international causes. Despite the division of their country, Koreans of all political persuasions were still deeply committed to unification. Rhee's KDP and Kim's Communists were each determined to unify Korea under their own control and waged an intensive, if undeclared, civil war. Throughout much of 1948, South Korean police and North Korean border guards regularly attacked each other across the 38th parallel. During the entire period of the U.S. occupation, Rhee brutally suppressed leftist groups, made threatening noises against his enemies across the 38th parallel, and sought from the United States the offensive military capability to conquer North Korea. South Korean guerrillas roamed across the 38th parallel, and in 1949 South Korean army units penetrated several miles into North Korea and attacked isolated settlements. During the same time, as many as 3,000 guerrillas sponsored by Kim infiltrated South Korea and fomented rebellion against the U.S.-backed Rhee government. A particularly bloody uprising on Chejudo Island in 1948 took an estimated 30,000 lives. In all, some 100,000 Koreans were killed between 1948 and 1950 in the ongoing civil war. Finally, on 25 June 1950, under circumstances that remain obscure and controversial, North Korea launched a full-scale invasion of the south, sending 110,000 soldiers, more than 1,400 artillery pieces, and 126 tanks across the 38th parallel.

Why North Korea acted as and when it did remains something of a mystery. At the time, most Americans viewed Kim's government as a stooge of Moscow and attributed the attack to the larger global designs of the Soviet Union. It now seems clear that while Soviet leader Joseph Stalin probably knew of North Korea's plans and even gave them general endorsement, he may not have been aware of the timing. Otherwise, he would not have kept his representatives out of the United Nations Security Council in protest against its refusal to seat the new communist government of China. The invasion seems to have reflected Korean motives above everything else. Kim was deeply committed to unification of the country under his own control. He may have viewed the invasion as a preemptive strike to head off Rhee's threats before they assumed dangerous proportions. He was under enormous pressure from his communist rival, Pak Hon-yong, and he may have launched the attack to undercut Pak and rally support to his cause. Economic and political turmoil in the south during the first half of 1950 may further have encouraged him to believe that he would not meet effective resistance.

In a classic miscalculation, Kim also seems to have acted in the certainty that the United States would do nothing. Indeed, virtually every sign pointed in that direction. Most concerned at this time about Western Europe and Japan, American officials had dismissed Korea as strategically insignificant. They increasingly feared that Rhee's repressiveness would provoke an uprising in South Korea or that his aggressiveness against the north might trigger a war in which the United States would become involved. United States officials did regard South Korea as an important symbol of "democracy," but they hoped to preserve its independence through military and economic aid. Thus they gradually withdrew American forces from Korea, cut back military assistance, and refused Rhee's requests for offensive weapons. In a much-publicized speech to the National Press Club in January 1950, Secretary of State Dean Acheson implicitly excluded South Korea from an American defense perimeter that included Japan and the Philippines.

It must have come as a profound shock to North Korea therefore when the United States responded quickly and decisively to the invasion of South Korea. The Truman administration immediately took the matter to the United Nations. With the Soviet Union absent, the Security Council approved a resolution calling for the cessation of hostilities and the withdrawal of North Korean forces from South Korea. The United States also dispatched naval and air forces to assist in the evacuation of Americans from Seoul. When the North Korean onslaught threatened the South Korean capital, Truman authorized American naval and air forces to take part in the fighting. The president subsequently approved the dispatch of U.S. ground forces and freed air forces to take action against North Korea. In short, within several days of the North Korean invasion, the United States was committed to defend South Korea with its own military forces.

The reasons for America's action seem clear. Remarkably, despite its magnitude, the decision aroused virtually no debate, Truman and his advisers readily agreeing that they must respond. They perceived the North Korean invasion as part of the Soviet grand design for global conquest, and felt that it signaled a new willingness on the part of Moscow to use military force to advance its aims. They saw the invasion as a test of American willingness to resist communist expansion. Guided by the lessons of the 1930s, when the democracies had failed to react to similar aggression, they felt they must do something in order to support the United Nations, uphold the principle of collective security, and prevent World War III. In their view, the U.S. response would have a profound impact among both its allies and its communist adversaries, determining the shape and durability of the postwar world order.

They were also influenced by domestic political considerations. If Korea were to fall to communism so soon after the "loss" of China and in the wake of the administration's decisions to reduce military aid and withdraw U.S. forces, Truman's credibility at home would be further eroded and his enemies emboldened to even more vicious attacks. In the atmosphere of crisis and near hysteria in the United States following the fall of China, the testing of a Soviet atomic bomb, and revelations of Soviet spy activity in the United States, the administration also felt compelled to do something to reverse what many Americans perceived as a tide running against them. As Burton Kaufman has written, moreover, to the extent that it seemed to clarify Soviet intentions and provide a reason for American action, the North Korean invasion occasioned a sense of relief in Washington and indeed across the country. For Truman and his advisers, there was no question but that the United States must respond decisively and forcefully.

In its first six months, the Korean War went through wild and dramatic reversals of fortune. Splendidly prepared for war and well equipped by the Soviet Union, the North Korean invaders easily pushed back a South Korean foe that was poorly trained and had not been given planes, tanks, and other modern equipment. The South Korean capital of Seoul fell four days after the beginning of the invasion, and roughly one-half of the Republic of Korea (ROK) army was destroyed. The initial American reinforcements were garrison troops from Japan, also poorly equipped and not battle ready, and they too suffered huge losses and embarrassing defeats. By mid-July the onrushing North Koreans had advanced more than halfway through South Korea. By the beginning of August, thanks in part to U.S. airpower,

United Nations forces finally stabilized a perimeter around the port of Pusan on the southeast coast. Later that month they beat back a major North Korean assault, ending the first phase of the war.

General Douglas MacArthur's Inchon counteroffensive in September 1950 sharply reversed the fortunes of war. During World War II, MacArthur had utilized amphibious end-runs, and he had begun conceiving such an operation at the beginning of the war. By striking the enemy's rear on the west coast, he hoped to sever crucial supply lines and catch North Korean forces in a vise. Most military leaders in Washington opposed MacArthur, viewing a landing at Inchon as too risky and fearing yet another disastrous failure. Ultimately, lacking alternatives to propose and deferring to the imperious MacArthur, the Joint Chiefs of Staff gave in. The landing took place on 15 September.

The Inchon operation succeeded beyond even MacArthur's wildest expectations. Seventy thousand United Nations troops went ashore against a token force of only two thousand defenders, and within hours Inchon had been taken. Seoul was recaptured within two weeks. In the meantime, U.S. and South Korean forces had broken out of the Pusan perimeter. Caught in a gigantic pincer, the North Korean troops that had just won dazzling victories suffered huge losses, retreated in disarray, and began streaming back toward the 38th parallel.

MacArthur's brilliant victory at Inchon had profound consequences for the war. It increased the general's self-confidence, never small, making him impossible to deal with in the weeks to come. It enhanced his already considerable stature as a popular national hero and even gave him an aura of infallibility, making political and military figures less inclined than before to challenge him. It contributed to a significant change in national mood from the despair of the early weeks of the war to something approaching euphoria.

Most important, it brought about a fundamental change in United States–United Nations objectives. Even though, at the outset the Truman administration could think of little more than holding on in South Korea, administration officials had begun a vigorous debate over future goals. Thinking in altogether traditional terms, some State and Defense Department officials insisted that nothing short of victory in Korea would satisfy America's broader needs. Only by destroying North Korean military power and holding free elections to unify the entire country could the United Nations resolution calling for the restoration of international peace and security in Korea be upheld. Minimizing the risks of Soviet or Chinese intervention, these officials insisted that to settle for the status quo ante bellum would leave the fundamental problem unresolved. More cautious advocates of the restoration of the status quo warned, on the other hand, that an advance across the 38th parallel risked Soviet intervention and World War III.

By the time of the Inchon landing, the debate on future policy remained unresolved, but the tendency was toward crossing the 38th parallel. A National Security Council document affirmed that the UN goal in Korea was to achieve the "complete independence and unity" of the country. If this could be accomplished "without substantially increasing the risk of general war" with the Soviet Union and China, it should be done. Although deliberately vague, the policy statement opened the way to an advance into North Korea.

MacArthur's victory at Inchon settled the issue. The rout of the North Korean army permitted an advance across the 38th parallel and possibly the unification of Korea under United Nations aegis. Rhee had long been pressing for such a move. In the United States, there was broad support for it, and in the flush of victory at Inchon, Truman would have been taking serious political risks by settling for the status quo ante bellum. The possibility of a military and political victory, in any event, must have been appealing to the President and his advisers who had been savaged by political foes for the alleged "loss" of China. All Americans appear to have minimized the likelihood of Chinese or Soviet intervention, thereby removing what might have been a major constraint.

Thus in late September, Truman gave his commanding general broad and notably vague authorization to move across the 38th parallel. Bowing gently in the direction of caution, the order provided that MacArthur should not use U.S. troops in the areas near the Soviet and Chinese borders. In case of Soviet intervention, he was to assume a defensive position. Should China intervene, he was to maintain offensive operations as long as he saw a reasonable chance of success. Beyond these vague limits, MacArthur was free to move beyond the 38th parallel to destroy North Korean forces and he was even instructed to "feel unhampered tactically and strategically" in doing so. On 7 October, the General Assembly of the United Nations endorsed the change of objectives, authorizing UN forces to move into North Korea and remain there until the nation had been unified.

Predictably, MacArthur stretched the broad and vague authorization he had been given by the Truman administration and the United Nations. On the day after the passage of the UN resolution, U.S. troops began crossing the parallel. Meeting little resistance, they advanced as rapidly as the North Koreans had moved in the opposite direction, capturing the port of Wŏnsan on 10 October and the capital of Pyongyang on 19 October. While MacArthur noisily demanded the surrender of North Korean forces, South Koreans drove up the east coast toward the Chinese border. At Wake Island in late October, MacArthur reiterated earlier affirmations that China would not intervene. He assured Truman that formal resistance would end by Thanksgiving and expressed hope that some American troops might be withdrawn by Christmas.

By the time of MacArthur's bold and foolhardy statements, Chinese troops had already begun secretly entering the war, initiating the second reversal of fortune in less than six months. From the outset, the new communist government of China had seen in the war both opportunity and danger. North Korea's early success raised the possibility of extending the revolution in northeast Asia and eliminating American power from the mainland. At the same time, the placement of the U.S. Seventh Fleet in the Taiwan Straits temporarily thwarted China's plans to "liberate" Taiwan, and America's intervention in the Korean War posed at least an indirect threat to China's security. Thus the Chinese leader Mao Zedong had shifted large numbers of his best forces to the Korean border and initiated plans for possible intervention well before the American counteroffensive at Inchon.

China's decision to intervene was made in early October when South Korean forces crossed the 38th parallel and MacArthur issued his ultimatum. Mao saw intervention as necessary to defend the revolution in Asia and protect China's security, threatened by the advance of UN forces toward the Yalu River. He recognized America's technological superiority, but he was certain that China's superior manpower and moral strength, the product of revolutionary zeal, would prevail. He dismissed the atomic threat, doubting that the United States would employ the bomb and minimizing the impact if it did. Even when the Soviet Union reneged on its promise of air support, China proceeded, entering the war on 15 October to liberate Korea and eliminate U.S. power from the peninsula.

Chinese intervention had an immediate and profound impact. The first UN forces to cross the 38th parallel had advanced pell-mell toward the Yalu and were overextended and vulnerable. Using a defensive strategy to perfection, the Chinese lured the advancing forces into a trap, attacking them from the flanks and rear. On 25 October, Chinese units struck the advance guard of South Korean forces, driving them back from the Yalu and killing (by Chinese count) fifteen thousand.

Continuing to underestimate his new enemy and meeting no resistance from a complacent Washington, the arrogant and reckless MacArthur now initiated what he called an end-the-war offensive, plunging straight into a deadly Chinese trap. In late November, employing massive human wave assaults in frigid subzero temperatures, the Chinese mounted a huge counteroffensive against the advancing U.S.–UN forces, inflicting enormous casualties. The result was one of the most humiliating retreats in American military history, what the troops themselves unaffectionately labeled "Operation Bugout." By mid-December, the Chinese and revitalized North Korean forces had driven the enemy back across the 38th parallel and reoccupied most of North Korea. Like the Americans just two months earlier, Mao now expanded his objectives. Ignoring voices of caution among his own advisers, he ordered his troops to move across the 38th parallel and reverted to his original goal of unifying Korea under Communist control and eliminating American power from the peninsula. It was, MacArthur ruefully noted, an "entirely new war."

In the next six months, the war stabilized along a shifting front near the 38th parallel. North Korean and Chinese forces took Seoul on 4 January, and U.S. forces fell back to a line roughly along the 37th parallel, completing a retreat of some 300 miles, the longest in U.S. military history. By late January, however, under the leadership of their new commander, General Matthew Ridgway, U.S.–UN forces had regrouped and launched a major counteroffensive. The conflict then settled into what Ridgway called an "accordion war," a series of thrusts and counterthrusts with neither side able to gain a clear-cut advantage.

As the conflict devolved into a bloody stalemate, the United States and China scrapped their dreams of victory and acquiesced in the waging of a limited war with limited means for limited objectives, namely, restoration of the status quo ante bellum. As early as 28 November 1950, in the immediate aftermath of the Chinese counteroffensive, the Truman administration had all but abandoned its quest for victory in Korea. Shaken and angered by the new turn of events, and more concerned about Europe, which they accorded a higher priority, most top administration officials agreed that the United States must not be pulled into an all-out war with China. Some even advocated withdrawal from Korea. Whip-

sawed between its allies and the UN, which feared World War III, and domestic critics, who were not prepared to concede defeat, the administration delayed for weeks before defining its war aims. It did, however, decisively reject MacArthur's proposals for all-out war with China. By early 1951 administration officials had formally committed themselves to limiting the war in Korea and seeking a peace on the basis of the status quo ante bellum.

The administration's acceptance of limited war provoked an all-out war with MacArthur. Humiliated by his smashing defeat, eager for vindication for himself and retribution against his enemies, and persuaded that Asia was the critical battleground in the Cold War, the general pleaded with Washington for additional troops and authority to carry the war to China. When rebuffed, he blatantly violated the letter and spirit of the restrictions placed upon him. In a series of what Secretary of State Dean Acheson called "posterity papers," he warned Washington of a prolonged and costly military stalemate unless he could strike at China's war-making capacity. He issued several public statements denouncing the administration's decision to fight a limited war and suggesting that he could win if given the authority and resources. At precisely the moment when the administration was planning to propose a cease-fire, MacArthur issued a virtual ultimatum, warning the enemy to surrender or risk annihilation. In a March 1951 telegram to House Minority Leader Joseph Martin of Massachusetts, subsequently made public, he proclaimed that "we must win. There is no substitute for victory." MacArthur's open defiance of the administration's limited war policies left Truman no option but to recall him, a step the President later lamented he had not taken much earlier.

The public reaction to MacArthur's firing in April 1951, in historian Burton Kaufman's words, "stands as one of the singular events in modern American political history." Fearful of the harsh new realities of the Cold War and the atomic era, anxious in the face of external and internal threats, perplexed by a failure and defeat to which they were not accustomed and whose causes they did not understand, frustrated with the administration's unwillingness to fight in the usual manner, and lured by MacArthur's siren song of victory, Americans responded with an emotional outpouring of support for a national hero. State legislatures and prominent politicians praised the general and called for the President's impeachment. Flags were flown at half mast; Truman and his advisers were burned in effigy. MacArthur was given a hero's welcome in San Francisco and New York.

His eloquent address to a joint session of Congress, proclaiming that "once war is forced upon us, there is no other alternative than to apply every available means to bring it to a swift end," evoked wild applause.

Ultimately, while finding comfort in MacArthur's appeals, Americans rejected his proposals as too costly and risky. At a series of congressional hearings following his recall, the deposed general was given full opportunity to defend his plan for all-out war. He reiterated that Asia was the crucial theater of the Cold War and that victory must be the object of war.

At the same time, he conceded that as a theater commander he was not in a good position to evaluate the larger strategic picture. In addition, administration witnesses were able to get across the possible risks and costs of what MacArthur had proposed, raising the possibility of World War III or a larger stalemate at a higher cost. Most memorable and perhaps most telling was Joint Chiefs of Staff (JCS) chairman General Omar Bradley's observation that MacArthur's proposals would have resulted in "the wrong war, at the wrong place, at the wrong time and with the wrong enemy." Although it went against the grain, Americans grudgingly acquiesced in limited war and the lionization of MacArthur stopped. Yet while accepting the administration's policy, they took out their frustration on the President, and Truman's popularity plunged to 24 percent in the summer of 1951.

For Mao Zedong, acceptance of limited war in Korea was also difficult. Although he perceived that his forces were overextended, exhausted, and short of supplies, and that achieving his goal might take much longer than originally anticipated, Mao still hoped to drive the United States from the peninsula. The failure of a major Chinese offensive in the spring of 1951 changed his mind. Tactics that had worked earlier now ensnared Chinese forces in Ridgway's meatgrinder of firepower. Suffering huge casualties in this their greatest offensive of the war, the Chinese recognized that they now faced a reinvigorated enemy with vastly superior equipment, logistics, and air support. In June 1951, they also abandoned their hopes of victory and settled for a protracted limited war, the objective of which was a negotiated settlement on the basis of the status quo ante bellum.

Although both sides were committed to a settlement by June 1951, it would take more than two years to end the war. Peace talks began on 10 July 1951, and quickly broke down on procedural questions. When these issues were resolved, the conferees deadlocked over such substantive matters as a cease-fire line and the modalities of an armistice. The most intractable issue turned out to be repatriation of prisoners of war. Largely at Truman's insistence and in contradistinction to the Geneva Convention of 1949, the United States insisted that prisoners of war who did not wish to be repatriated could not be compelled to do so. The communist side took the more conventional position in favor of compulsory repatriation. It took two years and 575 of the most torturous and painful meetings of the Cold War to resolve these issues and end the Korean "police action."

The difficulty in ending the war reflected the stalemated military situation that prevailed between June 1951 and July 1953. In a limited war setting, where neither side had the upper hand and neither was willing to go all-out, military power could not be used to promote diplomatic objectives. While the negotiators droned on at Kaesong and Panmunjom, each side stabilized its position on the ground. The Chinese brought in huge reinforcements, constructed near-impregnable positions along the cease-fire line, and vastly improved their artillery and airpower. The United States did not increase the size of its own forces, but it significantly upgraded their equipment, and vastly enlarged and improved the training of Korean forces. It also used airpower extensively, dropping more bombs than in the first two years of World War II.

The strengthening of forces on each side merely hardened the military stalemate. Throughout the period of the peace talks, the adversaries engaged in position warfare, mounting probing actions and sporadic attacks against enemy positions. Conditions at the front came to resemble the trench warfare of World War I. The names given to the sites of major battles—Heartbreak Ridge, Bloody Ridge, No-Name Ridge—suggest the deadliness, cost, and general frustration of such efforts.

Only toward the end of the war did the fighting again assume major proportions. The Chinese launched a massive offensive in October 1952, presumably in hopes of pressuring the United States out of the war. The result was the heaviest fighting since 1950, both sides employing tanks and artillery on a massive scale. The Chinese lost an estimated 10,000 in the first days of the fight; the United States took casualties at the rate of about 1,000 per week. Again in the spring of 1953, when peace appeared at hand, the Chinese and North Koreans stepped up the action, producing heavy fighting at such places as Porkchop Hill. In all, during the period of the peace talks, the United States lost 44,700 killed and wounded in actions that had little discernible effect on the negotiations.

The Korean negotiations were difficult in other ways. The experience was sui generis for the United States, a nation that was accustomed to imposing peace terms on defeated enemies and had never before confronted a stalemated battlefield and the necessity of a compromise peace. It was especially difficult for Americans to deal on a position of equality with the Chinese and Koreans, people they considered inferior, in a situation where they were unable to use for military purposes all the power available to them. The Truman administration erred in entrusting to military officials the task of negotiating peace, a job they were not well prepared for by experience or temperament. The American negotiators had great difficulty dealing with their communist counterparts whom they considered savages and criminals.

The differing negotiating styles of the Americans and Chinese contributed to the problems. The Americans tended to be impatient negotiators, sticklers for details, while the Chinese had infinite patience and preferred to deal in the realm of general principles. At least on the cease-fire line and the handling of prisoners of war, U.S. negotiating positions came as a surprise to the Chinese, who had expected positions based on the 38th parallel and the 1949 Geneva Convention. The Chinese used the talks at Panmunjom as a propaganda forum, playing to the world galleries with charges that the United States was using germ warfare in Korea. The Chinese were also especially concerned with matters of status and form, adopting a tit-for-tat approach across the board that Americans found objectionable and difficult to cope with.

Each side's negotiating position derived from a cumbersome decision-making process that limited its flexibility and ability to compromise. Although the dominant power, the Chinese could not ignore the North Koreans, who on certain issues were disposed to be more intransigent, and both were beholden to the Soviet Union. The United States was caught between such allies as Britain, Canada, France, and Australia, who wanted to end the war quickly and urged concessions, and Syngman Rhee's South Korea. Rhee remained stubbornly and foolishly committed to unification on his terms, and he repeatedly threatened to withdraw his troops from the coalition and block any compromise at the peace talks. Indeed, Rhee posed such problems that at one point the United States developed contingency plans for a

coup to remove him. The Truman administration also had to be sensitive to domestic critics who resented the whole idea of negotiating with Communists and were prepared to label any concessions as appeasement. The United States had further difficulty in a large and often divided bureaucracy formulating and then sticking to a clear-cut negotiating position. Given these problems, it is not surprising that it took roughly two years to end the war.

The Korean War finally ended in July 1953. Threats by the new president, Dwight D. Eisenhower, to use nuclear weapons if the enemy did not settle may have contributed to the outcome. More likely, the death of the Soviet dictator Joseph Stalin and the launching of a peace offensive by his successors resulted in Soviet pressure on China and North Korea to end the war. In any event, the enormous drain on China's limited resources made ending the war desirable for its leaders. After months of haggling over the details, the belligerents agreed to an Indian-sponsored compromise on repatriation. All prisoners of war would be turned over to a Neutral Nations Repatriation Commission. Those who chose to go home would be repatriated within sixty days. Others would be released as civilians or turned over to the United Nations General Assembly. The major obstacle to peace now was Syngman Rhee, who continued to hold out for victory and threatened to disrupt any settlement. Through a combination of threats to leave Rhee on his own if the war continued and promises of increased military aid if he cooperated, the Eisenhower administration finally brought a disgruntled Rhee into line. On 27 July 1953, an armistice was signed at Panmunjom ending the Korea War after more than three years of fighting.

Because of the limited, stalemated, and yet costly nature of military operations, the difficulty of the negotiations, and the outcome, Korea was America's least popular war to that time. The nation went to war in June 1950 resignedly and without any hint of enthusiasm. Americans enjoyed a brief moment of euphoria in the fall of 1950 as U.S. troops drove toward the Yalu, promising an early and victorious end to the war. But they sank into deep frustration and despair with Chinese intervention and the devastating and humiliating retreat back into South Korea. Frustrated and angry at the new and unaccustomed circumstances in which they found themselves, some preferred outright withdrawal from Korea. Others fantasized about a preemptive nuclear strike against the presumed source of all problems, the Soviet Union. Clearly disheartened with this new kind of war and the president who had led them into it,

Americans empathized with the sentiments expressed by MacArthur and briefly rallied to him. They agreed, according to the wording of one poll, that Korea was "an utterly useless war." When pressed, however, they rejected MacArthur's traditional appeals for victory as too risky and too costly. Agreeing that intervention had been a mistake, they also reluctantly accepted the necessity of seeing the war through.

What is perhaps most remarkable is that this support persisted, however grudgingly, until July 1953. For the sake of a matter of principle and 50,000 enemy prisoners of war, the war continued for another fifteen months and the United Nations Command suffered another 125,000 casualties. This happened because the United States was able to shift an increasing burden of the fighting to the South Koreans. As U.S. casualties declined, the war got less attention in the press and assumed less importance in the public consciousness. In addition, the policy of rotating troops home after eighteen months made the war more tolerable, as did the high level of prosperity enjoyed by the nation during these years. Most important, perhaps, the fact that Americans generally agreed on the necessity of containing communism in Korea made possible their continuing support.

For the Truman administration and the Democratic party, the war turned out to be a political albatross. From the outset, right-wing Republicans had accused Truman and especially Acheson of bringing on what Senator Robert Taft (R-Oh.) called an "unnecessary war." Appealing to traditional American instincts, the Republican platform of 1952 attacked the administration for refusing to fight an honorable war and charged that its policies had "produced stalemate and ignominious bartering" and offered "no hope of victory." Republican candidate Eisenhower at first took a more restrained line, but as the campaign went on he too charged the administration with bringing on the war and then falling into a trap by agreeing to negotiate. If, as some scholars believe, the war did not decide the outcome of the election, it was still a major factor in the margin of Eisenhower's victory. The inconclusive, seemingly endless fighting contributed mightily to the public impatience and frustration that helped swell the Republican vote. Eisenhower's pledge to go to Korea personally, if elected, helped persuade Americans that the Republicans were better equipped to end the war.

The end of the war brought no sense of euphoria, merely gratification that it was over, no celebration, merely a collective sigh of relief. There was no more war, but neither was there peace. For the first time in its history, America could not claim victory. For the first time, the end of a war meant a cease-fire not a return to peace. Right-wing Republicans denounced the settlement as a "last tribute to appeasement." "You cannot go into a military campaign with any hope of success without victory as its objective," protested Representative Martin. "I cannot find it in me to exult in this hour," said General Mark Clark, commander of U.S. forces in Korea. Eisenhower agreed, warning that "we have won an armistice in a single battleground—not peace in the world. We may not now relax our guard nor cease our quest."

The Korean War left an especially bitter taste in the mouths of those touched directly by it. The harsh weather, rugged terrain, and inscrutable people gave to the war a peculiar and indelible stamp. American GIs called Korea "the land that God forgot" and complained that the peninsula was a "helluva place to fight a war." "If the best minds in the world had set out to find us the worst possible location in the world to fight this damnable war," Acheson agreed, "the unanimous choice would have been Korea." Yet it was primarily the indecisive and inconclusive nature of the war combined with the deadliness of the fighting that made it so unappealing to Americans. Enormously frustrated with a war that had cost him so dearly, the commander in chief, Harry S. Truman, never really accepted limited war and yearned to use all the weapons available to him to end it decisively and in his favor. "Failure to do all in our power to support our troops is a new development," Republican Henry Cabot Lodge, Jr., observed. "It shocks our sense of national decency."

The legacy of the war and the lessons learned from it were as ambiguous as the war itself. Most Americans were content to put it out of their minds, and a sort of collective amnesia quickly set in. The war did not produce a large or distinguished literature or classic films. Caught between World War II and Vietnam, wars that deeply touched the national psyche in diametrically opposite ways, Korea became, in the words of its later historians, an "unknown war," a "forgotten war," an uninspiring tale, Joseph Goulden has written, that Americans were "eager to permit to slip through the crevices of memory."

Among those who fought it, of course, forgetting was not so easy. Colonel Creighton Abrams, a hero of World War II and later commander of U.S. forces in Vietnam, denounced the Korean War as "a stalemate—a frustration of desires—a compromise with principle—an acceptance of that which is unacceptable." Some senior officers formed a "Never Again" club, vowing not to permit themselves to become drawn into a comparable situation where they were forced to fight with their hands tied behind their backs. Others, like Generals Matthew Ridgway and Maxwell Taylor, concluded that in the nuclear age this type of war, however unpleasant, was the only type of war that was feasible. Korea "taught us," Ridgway proclaimed, "that all warfare from this time forth must be limited. It could no longer be a question of *whether* to fight a limited war, but of how to avoid fighting any other kind."

From the longer perspective, what stands out most about the Korean War is the willingness of the belligerents (Koreans excluded, of course) to accept the limits imposed by the new international environment. Whatever its frustrations, the Truman administration refused to use nuclear weapons, rejected Mac-Arthur's proposals for drastic escalation, and carefully confined the fighting to the Korean peninsula. The Soviet Union stayed out, refusing even to inject its naval and ground forces directly into the struggle. The Chinese did not declare war and did not initiate diversionary actions in other areas such as Formosa. The "most remarkable phenomenon" of this "strange and ugly limited war," D. Clayton James has concluded, was the "inexplicable communication, neither oral nor written, between implacably hostile camps who signaled restraint to each other" and established an "intricate system of limits" that helped to prevent the outbreak of general war.

EXPERIENCE INTO THEORY: THE CULT OF LIMITED WAR

In the aftermath of Korea, among some academics, political figures, and even military officers, limited war acquired vogue status. The Eisenhower administration's emphasis on nuclear weaponry and massive retaliation in its New Look defense strategy seemed to some Americans a dangerous return to total war concepts. Once the Soviet Union had developed effective delivery systems for nuclear weapons, moreover, it was obvious to such theorists as the political scientist Robert Osgood that massive retaliation could not work. With nothing but nuclear weapons as a deterrent, the United States in responding to communist challenges in marginal areas would face the unthinkable choice of nuclear war or doing nothing.

To escape that dilemma and find a means of containing communist expansion while minimizing the risks of a nuclear holocaust, Osgood and other theorists promoted the alternative of limited war.

Such a strategy would harness the nation's military power more closely to the attainment of its political objectives. In the strategic concept that came to be called flexible response, a variety of military instruments, including conventional forces, would be readied to respond to different threats at different levels. The amount of force employed in any situation would be limited to that necessary to achieve political aims. The objective would be not to destroy an opponent but to persuade him to break off the conflict short of achieving his goals and without resorting to nuclear war.

Osgood's classic 1957 study, *Limited War: The Challenge to American Strategy,* provided a set of broad guidelines for the conduct of limited war. Statesmen must "scrupulously limit" the political objectives of war and clearly communicate those objectives to the enemy. They must make every effort to keep open diplomatic channels to terminate the war through negotiations on the basis of limited objectives. They must restrict to the area and the amount consistent with the attainment of the desired political objectives the geographic locality of the war and the instruments used. Limited war must be directed by the civilian leadership. The special needs of the military should not affect its conduct and indeed the military must be a controllable instrument of national policy.

Thomas Schelling and Herman Kahn subsequently refined limited war theory, focusing on the use of military power to persuade an adversary to act in the desired way by conveying threats of force. Military action was less important for the damage it did than for the message it sent. War became a sort of bargaining process through which force was employed to persuade an enemy that persisting in what he was doing would be too expensive to continue. "The object," Schelling wrote, "is to exact good behavior or to oblige discontinuance of mischief, not to destroy the subject altogether." The implicit assumption was that the use of force could be orchestrated in such a way as to communicate precise and specific signals and that an opponent would back down in the face of such threats of pressure.

Limited war theory had numerous flaws. It was primarily an academic, rather than a military, concept, and it drastically misunderstood the dynamics of war. Both Osgood and Schelling seemed to say that, since limited war was mainly about bargaining and diplomacy, it required no knowledge of military matters and indeed military considerations should not effect its conduct. Despite the popular frustrations caused by fighting a limited war in Korea, the theorists were also grandly indifferent to the domestic political problems it posed. Osgood conceded that this type of conflict ran counter to the American way of war and that Americans might not easily accept the "galling but indispensable restraints" required by it. But he neatly dodged the problem with platitudes, calling for candor and courage on the part of leaders, surmising that if Americans were treated as adults they would respond as such.

The limited war theorists also devoted more effort to explaining why their type of war should be fought than determining how it was to be fought. In terms of bargaining theory, moreover, they assumed a greater capacity than was warranted on the part of a gigantic bureaucracy like the United States government to send clear, precise signals, and they reduced the behavior of potential enemies to that of laboratory rats.

VIETNAM: LIMITED WAR BY DESIGN

Fought, at least in its initial stages, as limited war theory decreed wars should be fought, the conflict in Vietnam graphically exposed the flaws in that theory. Culminating fifteen years of gradually expanding U.S. involvement in Vietnam, the administration of Lyndon Johnson in July 1965 committed itself to wage limited war against the National Liberation Front (NLF) insurgency backed by North Vietnam. The administration reasoned that if the United States steadily increased the application of its military power against Hanoi, the North Vietnamese would stop supporting the insurgency and the South Vietnamese government would be saved.

The reality for the United States was quite different and disastrous. North Vietnam did not respond as limited war theory said it should, refusing to bend to Washington's pressure and matching its escalation. The American people in time tired of another stalemated, limited war, and Vietnam aroused far more opposition than Korea. The result for the United States was a war that lasted eight years and took 58,000 lives. It was the first war in which the United States failed to achieve its objectives, moreover, and it had a profound impact. It set the economy on a downward spiral. It crippled the military, at least temporarily, corroding military organizations, destroying discipline in the ranks, and undermining popular confidence in and esteem for military personnel and institutions. It left America's foreign policy in disarray, discrediting the postwar policy of containment and shattering the consensus that had supported it. It divided the American people as no

other event since their own Civil War a century earlier. It battered their collective soul.

By mid-1965, Johnson and his advisers perceived that the United States faced a major turning point in Vietnam. Following the overthrow and assassination of Ngo Dinh Diem in late 1963, the government of South Vietnam had gone through a prolonged period of chronic instability, governments replacing each other as though going in and out of revolving doors. In the meantime, the NLF insurgency gained momentum. Supported by a steadily growing flow of men and supplies from North Vietnam, the insurgents took advantage of the near-anarchy in the south. By early 1965, they had secured uncontested control of the vital Mekong Delta region south of Saigon and appeared capable of splitting the country in half. The corruption-ridden South Vietnamese army (ARVN) could not slow, much less stop, the enemy onslaught.

The Johnson administration saw little choice but to respond militarily. Since early 1950, the United States had been committed to containing communist expansion in Indochina. In that year, the Truman administration had begun providing economic and military assistance to support French efforts to suppress the communist-led Vietminh revolution in Vietnam. By 1954, the United States was paying close to 80 percent of the cost of the war. Defeated in the spring of 1954 at the climactic battle of Dien Bien Phu, the French, after the Geneva Conference of July 1954, prepared to withdraw from Indochina, and the United States filled the vacuum. Hoping to create an independent, noncommunist government in the south that could stand as a bulwark against further penetration of Southeast Asia, the Eisenhower administration supported the fledgling government of Ngo Dinh Diem and began to provide massive economic and military assistance.

The Kennedy and Johnson administrations steadily expanded the U.S. commitment. Frustrated by Diem's refusal to abide by the provisions of the Geneva Conference calling for elections to unify the country, former southern Vietminh in 1957 launched an insurgency against the government. North Vietnam provided support, and as the insurgency gained momentum, the United States responded. The Kennedy administration increased the number of U.S. military "advisers" to more than sixteen thousand. When the Diem government's repression of Buddhists and general ineptitude threatened prosecution of the war, the administration sanctioned its overthrow. Faced with a deteriorating situation in Vietnam after Diem's assassination, the Johnson adminis-

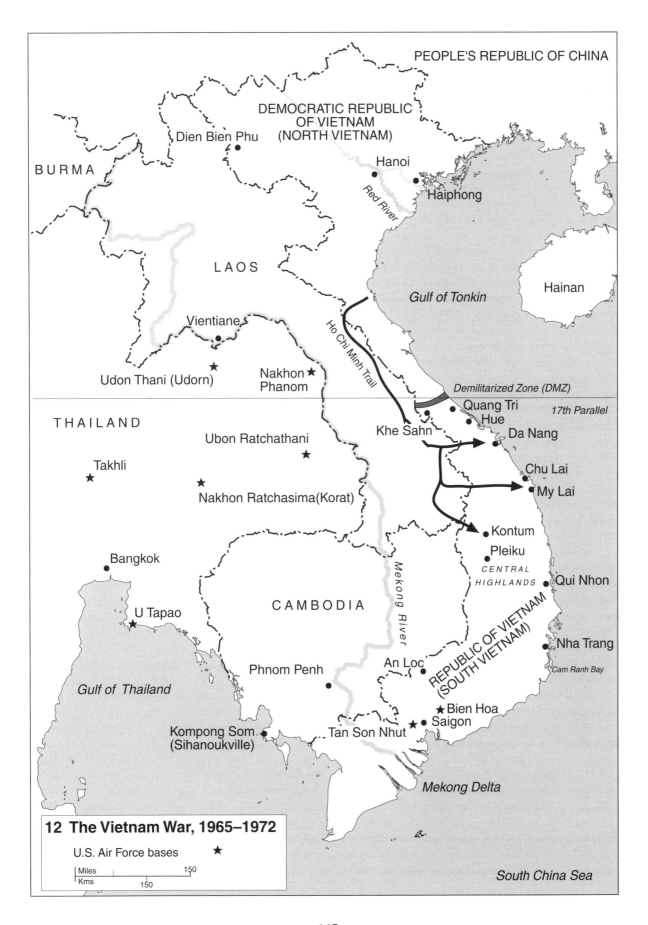

12 The Vietnam War, 1965–1972

U.S. Air Force bases   ★

Miles   150
Kms   150

tration continued to increase U.S. aid and began planning more drastic measures.

Administrations from Truman to Johnson viewed the containment of communism in Vietnam as a vital national interest. From the outset, American officials saw Ho Chi Minh's Vietminh as an instrument of the Soviet Union's drive for world domination and regarded the conflict in Vietnam as an integral part of their broader struggle with communism. From this flowed yet another key assumption, that the "loss" of Vietnam would threaten interests deemed vital. In the frantic milieu of early 1950, after the fall of China to Mao Zedong's Communists and the first Soviet nuclear test, American policymakers concluded that communist expansion must be stopped. "Any substantial further extension of the area under the control of the Kremlin," a National Security Council document warned, "would raise the possibility that no coalition adequate to confront the Kremlin with greater strength could be assembled." In this context of a world divided into two hostile power blocs, a fragile balance of power, a zero–sum game in which any gain for communism was automatically a loss for the United States, areas like Vietnam that had previously been of no more than marginal importance suddenly took on great significance.

There were other more specific reasons why U.S. policymakers attached such significance to Vietnam after 1950. The so-called domino theory held that the fall of Vietnam would cause the loss of all Indochina and then the rest of Southeast Asia, with implications extending far beyond. Because of its location on China's southern border and because it appeared in the most imminent danger, Vietnam was considered crucial. If it fell, all of Southeast Asia might be lost, denying the United States access to important raw materials and strategic waterways. Americans especially feared that the loss of Southeast Asia's raw materials and markets would undermine Japan's economic recovery and leave a vital ally no choice but to come to terms with communism.

In the Kennedy-Johnson era, the domino theory was supplanted by the notion of credibility, the idea that the United States must stand firm in Vietnam to demonstrate its determination to defend vital interests across the world. During this most intense and dangerous period of the Cold War, U.S. policymakers felt certain that if they showed firmness in one area it would deter the adversary elsewhere; if they showed weakness, that adversary might be tempted to take steps that would ultimately leave no option but nuclear war. The so-called Manchurian or Munich analogy, derived from events of the 1930s,

reinforced the idea of credibility, the obvious conclusion being that a firm stand must be taken against "aggression" at the outset. During the Kennedy-Johnson years, policymakers were also determined to prove that the United States could effectively combat communist- supported "wars of national liberation," presumably the greatest menace to U.S. security in the 1960s.

Administrations from Truman to Johnson also shared the assumption that the fall of Vietnam to communism would have disastrous political consequences at home. This too stemmed from perceived lessons of history, the rancorous and divisive debate following the "loss" of China in 1949, the frustrations of Korea, and Republican exploitation of these issues at the polls in 1952. The conclusion, again obvious, was that no administration, especially a Democratic administration, could survive the loss of Vietnam. Lyndon Johnson repeatedly affirmed that he would not be the president who saw Vietnam go the way of Cuba or China.

Acting on the basis of these assumptions, Johnson in 1965 launched a full-scale, although carefully limited, war in Vietnam. Responding to the urgent warnings of his advisers that South Vietnam was on the verge of collapse, the President in February 1965 mounted regular, sustained bombing raids against North Vietnam. The bombing had only a marginal impact on the war, however, and by the late spring General William Westmoreland, head of the U.S. military assistance program in Vietnam, requested a massive increase in American military forces and the commitment of U.S. combat units to reverse a rapidly deteriorating situation. After several weeks of intensive deliberations, the President committed himself to provide such forces as needed.

The Johnson administration's strategy in Vietnam was deeply influenced by limited war theory. Fearful that the actions they were taking to prevent a third world war might themselves provoke a dangerous confrontation with the Soviet Union and China, the President and his top civilian advisers put precise geographical limits on the war. They kept their military commanders on a tight rein, rejecting proposals to invade enemy sanctuaries in Laos, Cambodia, and North Vietnam, mine Haiphong harbor, and bomb near the Chinese border. Vividly recalling Korea, Johnson and his civilian advisers fretted about military recklessness and a MacArthur-like challenge to civilian authority. "General, I have a lot riding on you," Johnson told Westmoreland in February 1966, "I hope you don't pull a MacArthur on me."

The administration fought the war according to

the dictates of limited war theory. The theory of gradual escalation presumed that a steady increase in the level of military pressure would coerce an adversary into compliance. Thus the administration slowly increased the bombing and steadily expanded the number of U.S. troops and the intensity of ground operations. At no point did the President accede to the full requests of his military commanders. Yet, once underway, the process of escalation achieved a momentum of its own, the failure of one level of force providing justification for the next level. By 1967, the United States had concentrated close to 500,000 men, roughly one-half its tactical airpower, and 30 percent of its naval strength in Vietnam. It was spending more than $2 billion per month on the war.

The vast quantities of men, money, and material poured into Vietnam failed to achieve U.S. objectives. Military planners expanded the list of targets and intensified the bombing, and by 1967, the tonnage dropped on North Vietnam exceeded that dropped on Germany, Italy, and Japan during World War II.

America's heavy reliance on airpower seriously underestimated the commitment of the North Vietnamese and overestimated the capabilities of strategic bombing. The gradual escalation of the bombing permitted the North Vietnamese to protect vital resources, and losses were more than made up by expanded aid from the Soviet Union and China. The North Vietnamese showed a remarkable capacity for coping with the bombing, repairing bridges and railroads within hours after destruction. The daily pounding from the air seemed to stiffen their will, and they showed no sign of bending under the pressure. The rate of infiltration into the south increased after the bombing was started and continued to increase as it expanded. By late 1967, North Vietnamese forces were four times greater than in 1965.

The steady expansion of U.S. ground troops also failed to turn the war around. Westmoreland's so-called search and destroy strategy, a strategy of attrition, sought to inflict such heavy losses that the enemy would quit the fight. But the North Vietnamese had a cause in which they believed and virtually unlimited resources. Two hundred thousand northerners reached draft age every year, and Hanoi was able to match each U.S. escalation. The tough North Vietnamese infantry proved at least an equal to its American counterpart. Hanoi's tacticians quickly learned that they could neutralize American air support and artillery by drawing U.S. forces into close-quarters fighting. The North Vietnamese fought in

the rugged central highlands on territory favorable to them and usually dictated the time and place of battle. When losses reached unacceptable levels they retreated into sanctuaries in Laos, Cambodia, or across the demilitarized zone into North Vietnam. The United States inflicted huge losses, but it was not able to subdue a stubborn enemy.

As the war became the dominant factor in Vietnam and the Americans the dominant factor in the war, the fundamental problem, the Saigon government, remained unresolved. A coalition of generals headed by Nguyen Cao Ky and Nguyen Van Thieu finally emerged from the long series of coups and counter-coups, but it represented few of the multiplicity of political factions in the south. Neither the government nor the United States was capable of broadening South Vietnam's narrow political base. The United States paid lip-service to democracy, arranging for the drafting of a new South Vietnamese constitution and the holding of elections in late 1967. But the mammoth public relations effort that accompanied these changes did not obscure the reality. The election was carefully rigged. Even then, the Thieu-Ky group won a shockingly narrow victory and the government continued to owe its existence to the United States.

The huge influx of Americans after 1965 and expansion of the war created new problems that even the most responsible and effective government would have found difficult to handle. Relations between Americans and Vietnamese were tense from the outset. The newcomers expected gratitude for their sacrifices and became resentful when they encountered indifference or hostility. The massive bombing and artillery fire in the south drove thousands of sullen refugees into already overcrowded cities. The South Vietnamese economy was geared around providing services to the Americans and quickly reached the point where it could not absorb the ever-expanding volume of money and goods. In the cities, corruption, profiteering, and vice ran rampant.

As the war developed into a bloody stalemate in Vietnam, Johnson's support collapsed at home. Even more than Korea, Vietnam highlighted the difficulty in limited war of maintaining public support without arousing public emotion. The United States went to war in July 1965 in a manner uniquely quiet and underplayed. Despite Truman's experience with Korea, public opinion played a negligible role in the decisions for war. The President announced the major troop increase at a noon press conference rather than at prime time and lumped it in with a number of other announcements to obscure its significance.

With the exception of several hastily arranged, characteristically Johnsonian public relations blitzes, the administration persisted in this low-key approach until 1967.

Prevailing notions of how to fight limited wars explain better than anything else this approach. Johnson undoubtedly feared that a public debate on Vietnam would jeopardize major pieces of his cherished Great Society legislation then pending in Congress. He and his advisers also feared that mobilizing the nation for war would unleash irresistible pressures for escalation and victory that would demand a larger war with the Soviet Union and China, perhaps even the nuclear confrontation that the commitment in Vietnam had been designed to deter in the first place. The administration thus concluded, as Secretary of State Dean Rusk later put it, "that in a nuclear world it is just too dangerous for an entire people to get too angry and we deliberately . . . tried to do in cold blood what perhaps can only be done in hot blood." "I don't want to be dramatic and cause tension," the President told his National Security Council on July 27.

For Secretary of Defense Robert McNamara, the U.S. official who gave practical application to limited war theory, Vietnam was indeed the very prototype of the way wars must be fought in the nuclear age. "The greatest contribution Vietnam is making," he observed early in the war, "is developing an ability in the United States to fight a limited war . . . without arousing the public ire," almost a necessity, he added, "since this is the kind of war we'll likely be facing for the next fifty years." The United States therefore went to war in July 1965 in "cold blood." Johnson and his advisers gambled that without taking exceptional measures they could hold public support long enough to achieve their goals in Vietnam.

They badly miscalculated. By the end of 1967, the war had bogged down, and the American people had become polarized over Vietnam as over no other issue since their own Civil War a century earlier. On one side, those labeled "hawks" protested the restraints imposed on the military and demanded that the administration do what was necessary to win the war or get out of Vietnam. At the other extreme, the war generated a protest that by 1967 had reached formidable proportions. The New Left joined older left-wing protesters in denouncing the war as a classic example of the way the American ruling class exploited helpless people to sustain a decadent capitalism. Antiwar liberals increasingly questioned the war on practical as well as moral grounds, arguing that it was of no more than marginal significance to U.S.

security. Small-scale, generally civilized dissent mushroomed by 1967 into massive and sometimes angry street demonstrations and widespread individual and group acts of civil disobedience and war resistance. On 21 October 1967, an estimated 100,000 opponents of the war gathered in Washington for the largest antiwar protest to date, and 35,000 demonstrated at the entrance to the Pentagon, "the nerve center of American militarism."

The great majority of Americans rejected both the hawk and dove positions, but as the war dragged on and the debate became more divisive, public disillusionment increased markedly. Expansion of the war in 1965 had been followed by the usual rally-around-the-flag surge of popular support. But the failure of escalation to produce any discernible results and indications that more troops and higher taxes would be required to sustain a prolonged and perhaps inconclusive war combined to produce growing frustration and impatience. Public support for the war dropped sharply in 1967, and Johnson's public approval rating fell even further, dipping to a low of 28 percent in October. This "pinpoint on the globe [Vietnam]," presidential "adviser" David Lilienthal confided to his diary, was "like an infection, a 'culture' of some horrible disease, a cancer where the wildly growing cells multiply and multiply until the whole body is poisoned."

Faced with a stalemated war and declining support at home, Johnson's advisers pressed him to change course. The Joint Chiefs of Staff and General Westmoreland urged him to drastically escalate the war to break the stalemate, recommending intensified bombing of North Vietnam, mining of the major ports, a sharp increase in the number of ground troops, and expansion of the war into Laos, Cambodia, and North Vietnam. At the other extreme, a now thoroughly disenchanted McNamara, more than anyone else the architect of America's limited war strategy in Vietnam, urged stopping the bombing, putting a ceiling on the number of ground troops, and seeking a compromise political settlement. In between the two extremes, other Johnson advisers and some "doves" in Congress proposed to check dissent at home by cutting back the bombing and shifting from Westmoreland's costly search-and-destroy strategy to a "clear-and-hold" strategy that would stabilize the war at a "politically tolerable level" and perhaps save South Vietnam without surrender and without risk of a wider war.

Unmoved by the increasingly urgent appeals of his advisers, Johnson stubbornly continued down the middle-of-the-road path he had staked out in 1965.

He continued to fear the risks of an expanded war. Thus, while approving modest escalation he rebuffed repeated military proposals for drastic expansion of U.S. ground and air operations. He also doubted that McNamara's recommendations would bring results, and he flatly rejected his defense secretary's most radical proposals, a bombing halt and a compromise peace. Although increasingly concerned with Westmoreland's conduct of the war, the President would go no further than commit himself to review the ground strategy at some later unspecified date.

To salvage a rapidly deteriorating situation, Johnson in late 1967 launched a belated public relations campaign to shore up domestic support for the war. Believing that his major problem was a widespread perception that the war was a stalemate, he sought to persuade a skeptical public that the United States was in fact winning. He ordered the embassy and military command to provide "sound evidence of progress in Viet Nam." U.S. officials dutifully responded, producing reams of statistics to show a steady rise in enemy body counts and the number of villages pacified. As part of the public relations campaign, Westmoreland was brought home in November, ostensibly for top-level consultations, in reality to reassure a troubled nation, and in a series of public statements he affirmed that "we have reached an important point where the end begins to come into view."

The Communist Tet Offensive of 1968 cut the base from under the administration's public relations campaign and indeed its conduct of limited war in Vietnam. On 31 January 1968, the North Vietnamese launched a series of massive, closely coordinated attacks through the cities and towns of South Vietnam. As perhaps nothing else could have, the Tet Offensive put the lie to Johnson's year-end claims of progress. Polls taken in late 1967 had shown a slight upswing in popular support for the war and even in the president's public approval rating. But in the aftermath of Tet, support for the war and especially for the President plummeted, and popular convictions of a stalemate became even more deeply entrenched.

Tet also forced Johnson to confront the failure of his limited war strategies. After nearly two months of high-level deliberations, focusing for the first time on the crucial issue of how the war was being fought, he rejected new Joint Chiefs of Staff proposals for escalation and instituted some of the measures proposed by his civilian advisers in late 1967. He stopped the bombing above the 20th parallel and launched major new initiatives to open peace negotiations. He

placed a firm upper limit on the numbers of ground troops and removed Westmoreland from command in Vietnam. He and his top advisers agreed that to ease pressures at home responsibility for the war should be shifted as rapidly as possible to the South Vietnamese. In a bombshell announcement that shocked the nation, a beleaguered Johnson emphatically declared that he would neither seek nor accept his party's nomination in the upcoming presidential election. LBJ's belated intervention came too late, however, and did not go far enough to end the war. He thus passed on to his successor a far more complex and intractable problem than he had inherited.

Despite the grief visited on Johnson and the nation by the war, Richard Nixon and his national security adviser, Henry Kissinger, continued to entertain hopes of success in Vietnam. Kissinger, a former Harvard professor, insisted that every fourth-rate power—North Vietnam included—must have a breaking point. Nixon believed that Johnson had been too cautious and timid in waging the war, and gambled that his own reputation as a hard-line anticommunist might intimidate the North Vietnamese into accepting a settlement that permitted an independent, noncommunist South Vietnam. Thus at several crucial points between 1969 and 1973, Nixon and Kissinger sharply escalated the war, initiating the secret bombing of Cambodia in 1969, invading Cambodia in 1970 and Laos in 1971, mining Haiphong harbor and reinstituting a furious bombing of North Vietnam in 1972. Nixon on several occasions sent through intermediaries only slightly veiled threats that if the North Vietnamese did not agree to an "honorable" settlement they might be subjected to "cruel and punishing blows."

Despite their bold talk, threats, and escalation, Nixon and Kissinger carefully remained within the broad parameters of limited war. Although frustrated by North Vietnam's stubborn refusal to give in, like Johnson before them they hesitated to unleash the full range of American military power. Fearing the international and domestic reaction, perhaps recognizing that the destruction of North Vietnam would be counterproductive in terms of the balance of power in East Asia, they did not seek victory in the classical sense. In addition, growing popular disillusionment with the war, increasing congressional reaction against its persistence, and angry protest against the incursions into Cambodia and Laos, put further constraints on their use of American military power.

Unable to achieve their goals through intimidation, Nixon and Kissinger fell back on what became known as Vietnamization. This strategy combined the phased withdrawal of U.S. troops with a massive build-up of the South Vietnamese armed forces and a gradual shift of the burden of the fighting to South Vietnam. The theory was that by reducing U.S. involvement and casualties, domestic unrest with the war would ease, permitting the United States to preserve an independent South Vietnam and leaving Hanoi no option but to come to terms.

As with the strategy of graduated escalation, Vietnamization turned out to be fundamentally flawed. Despite massive U.S. aid, the ARVN did not improve significantly. Its incursion into Laos in 1971 resulted in a humiliating withdrawal, and when its sternest test came in 1972 with the North Vietnamese Easter Offensive, it was unable to function effectively without major U.S. assistance. The Thieu government remained corrupt, irresponsible, and ineffectual. Nixon's troop withdrawals undercut protest in the United States temporarily, but as the war dragged on inconclusively, a pervasive war-weariness set in. Vietnam war veterans joined the ranks of protesters, ceremoniously tossing their medals in front of the U.S. Capitol. In May 1971, another round of angry demonstrations rocked Washington, touching off the worst riots in the city's history. Popular disillusionment reached an all-time high in the summer of 1971, a whopping 71 percent agreeing that the United States had made a mistake and 58 percent viewing the war as immoral. Nixon's public approval rating plunged to a low of 31 percent. A majority of Americans approved removal of all troops from Vietnam within a year even if the result was a communist takeover of South Vietnam. Although it continued to stop short of decisive action, Congress reflected public uneasiness, on several occasions only narrowly defeating resolutions setting a specific deadline for the removal of all troops.

During the Nixon years, rampant demoralization set in among U.S. troops in Vietnam. From the outset, the war had posed difficult challenges for Americans. It was fought in a climate and on a terrain that were singularly inhospitable: thick jungles, foreboding swamps and paddies, rugged mountains, insufferable heat and humidity. In the beginning, at least, it was a peoples' war, where people rather than territory were the primary objective. Yet Americans as individuals and as a nation could never really bridge the vast cultural gap that separated them from all Vietnamese. Not knowing the language or culture, they had difficulty even distinguishing friend from foe.

More important, perhaps, was the formless yet lethal nature of warfare in Vietnam, a war without distinct battlelines or fixed objectives, where traditional concepts of victory and defeat were blurred. This type of warfare was particularly difficult for Americans schooled in the conventional warfare of World War II and Korea. And there was always the gnawing—but fundamental—question, first raised by President John F. Kennedy: how can we tell if we are winning? The only answer that could be devised was the notorious body count, as grim and corrupting as it was ultimately unreliable as a measure of success.

Fighting such a war caused enormous frustration for many Americans. "We fly a limited aircraft," one Navy pilot complained, "drop limited ordnance on rare targets in a severely limited amount of time. Worst of all we do this in a limited and highly unpopular war. . . . What I've got is personal pride pushing against a tangled web of frustration." Deeply entangled in a war they did not understand and could find no way to end, Johnson's advisers struggled merely to put a label on the conflict. "All-out limited war," one official called it, with no apparent sense of paradox, "a war that is not a war," some military officers complained. Johnson's speechwriter, Harry McPherson, phrased the problem in terms of a question. "What the hell do you say? How do you half-lead a country into war?"

After the initiation of Nixon's troop withdrawal policy, the purpose of the war became even more murky to those called upon to fight it, and many GIs became much more reluctant to put their lives on the line. Discipline broke down in some units, enlisted men simply refusing to obey their officers' orders. Attacks on officers in time of war were not unique to Vietnam, but "fragging" reached unprecedented proportions in the Vietnamization period, more than two thousand incidents being reported in 1970 alone. The availability and high quality of drugs in Southeast Asia meant that the drug culture that attracted growing numbers of young Americans at home was reflected in Vietnam. The U.S. command estimated in 1970 that as many as 65,000 American servicemen were using drugs. Nor were the armed services immune from the racial tensions that tore America apart in the Vietnam era, and numerous outbreaks of racial conflict in units in Vietnam and elsewhere drew growing attention to the breakdown of morale and discipline.

By late 1972, Nixon and Kissinger found compelling reasons to seek a compromise settlement in Vietnam. Through the massive application of airpower in South and North Vietnam, the United States had blunted the enemy's 1972 Easter Offensive, inflicting huge losses and saving South Vietnam from what had appeared near-certain collapse. But the United States was in no better position than before to achieve its original goals, and with an election rapidly approaching Nixon had to stem the rising tide of popular dissatisfaction with his Vietnam policies. The United States thus made major concessions in secret peace talks in Paris, permitting North Vietnamese troops to remain in the south and agreeing to a political arrangement that amounted to a thinly disguised coalition government. After more than six months of torturous, on-and-off negotiations, an agreement was signed in January 1973 providing for U.S. military extrication from Vietnam.

The Paris peace agreements did not bring an end to war in Vietnam. The Nixon administration still hoped to keep the Thieu government in power. The United States used various subterfuges to provide continued military assistance to the Saigon government, and civilian advisers assumed the role previously played by military officials. Both the Thieu government and North Vietnam jockeyed for position in South Vietnam militarily and politically and refused to cooperate in furthering the peace process. Finally, in early 1975, North Vietnam launched another massive offensive. Without U.S. support, South Vietnam could not withstand the onslaught. Nixon had been forced to resign the previous year because of the Watergate scandals, themselves in part a product of Vietnam. His successor, Gerald Ford, presiding over a nation paralyzed by war-weariness and growing economic recession, could do nothing. South Vietnam fell on 30 April 1975, ending a war that in its various phases had lasted nearly thirty years and resulting in the first clear-cut military defeat for the United States.

THE LEGACY OF VIETNAM AND THE FUTURE OF LIMITED WAR

Although the United States emerged physically unscathed, the Vietnam War was among the most debilitating in its history. The economic cost has been estimated at $167 billion, a raw statistic that does not begin to measure its overall impact. The war triggered an inflation that helped to undermine America's position in the world economy. It also had a high political cost, along with Nixon's Watergate scandals, increasing popular suspicions of government, leaders, and institutions. It crippled the military, at least for a time, and temporarily estranged the United States from much of the rest of the world.

Nowhere was the impact of Vietnam greater than on the nation's foreign policy. The war destroyed the consensus that had existed since the late 1940s, leaving Americans confused and deeply divided on the goals to be pursued and the methods used. From the Angolan crisis of the mid-1970s to Central America in the 1980s to the Persian Gulf in 1990, foreign policy issues were viewed largely through the prism of Vietnam and debated in its context. Popular division on the Persian Gulf crisis in 1990 derived to a large extent from the Vietnam experience, and the Gulf War was fought on the basis of its perceived lessons.

Much like World War I for the Europeans, Vietnam's greatest impact was in the realm of the spirit. As no other event in the nation's history, it challenged Americans' traditional beliefs about themselves, the notion that in their relations with other people they had generally assumed a benevolent role, the idea that nothing was beyond reach. It was a fundamental part of a much larger crisis of the spirit that began in the 1960s, raising profound questions about America's history and values. The war's deep wounds festered among some of its 2.7 million veterans, for whom victory in the Persian Gulf reinforced rather than erased bitter memories. The persisting popularity of Vietnam novels, television shows, and films suggests the extent to which the war remained etched in the nation's consciousness.

The legacy of Vietnam for limited war was as ambiguous and uncertain as the war itself. In the eyes of many Americans, the Vietnam experience totally discredited the limited war doctrines that had been popular in the 1950s and 1960s. Those liberals who had opposed the war while it was being waged concluded in its aftermath that to avoid similar trauma in the future the United States must refrain from intervening in any situation remotely similar to Vietnam. Conservatives, on the other hand, including many military leaders and theoreticians, concluded that limited war was unworkable and even immoral. The United States had failed in Vietnam, they insisted, because it had not sought victory and because timid civilian leaders had imposed crippling restrictions that prevented the military from using American military power effectively. The obvious lesson was that in any future war American power must be used decisively and without limit to achieve victory. So discredited was limited war theory that its father, Robert Osgood, would lament in 1979 that the "trauma of Vietnam had suspended creative thought" in that area. Vietnam raised the fundamental question of whether a democracy like the United States with a volatile electorate could successfully wage a limited war for limited objectives, leaving unanswered the fundamental question of how communist expansionism was to be resisted. Indeed, if nuclear war was unthinkable and limited war unwageable the military option seemed to have lost its utility entirely.

For Osgood, the lessons were not so clear. He conceded that some of the conditions that had made limited war seem so necessary no longer existed and also that the so-called "Vietnam syndrome" had made it far more difficult for the United States to intervene in crisis situations abroad. He even admitted that a greater U.S. tolerance for disorder in the Third World might reflect a realistic assessment of the limits of power. Most important, he agreed that "political and material impediments to the United States waging full-scale limited war as an instrument of policy in the Third World on the pattern of the Korean or Vietnam wars are immense, perhaps prohibitive."

Still, in his 1979 book, *Limited War Revisited,* Osgood continued to make a qualified case for the strategies he had pushed with such great vigor in the 1950s. The Soviet Union still posed a threat to the United States, he averred, and containment of Soviet expansion was still essential for the United States' security. Given the increasing destructiveness and sophistication of nuclear weapons, avoidance of all-out war was even more urgent than two decades before. The United States still had interests in some Third World areas that might require intervention on a smaller scale with aid, advisers, or highly trained and specialized strike forces that might carry out raids, "police actions," or other kinds of quick interventions for specific, limited purposes. The Middle East, an area of especially vital U.S. interests, might even require intervention on the scale of Korea or Vietnam. The key, Osgood concluded, was to determine when to resort to limited war. At a minimum, it must be in defense of a vital interest and must be in a political and military setting where U.S. power could be used effectively.

The Persian Gulf War of 1991 appeared on the surface to herald the end of the "Vietnam syndrome" and limited war and a return to more traditional American approaches to warfare. The end of the Cold War removed the restraints on the use of American military power that had applied during much of the post–World War II era. President George Bush declared upon going to war in January 1991 that "this will not be another Vietnam," vowing that American troops would not be required to fight with one hand tied behind their backs and that the United States would use its power without stint to attain victory. In the war that followed, the United States and its allies employed a panoply of new and sophisticated weapons in a stunning display of the military art in a brief war that drove Saddam Hussein's Iraqi forces from Kuwait. At first wary of intervention in the Middle East, Americans responded to the Gulf War with unalloyed enthusiasm and welcomed home the triumphant military forces with displays of "old-fashioned" patriotism. "By God, we've kicked the Vietnam syndrome once and for all!," President Bush exulted in a euphoric victory statement at the end of the war.

Appearances were deceptive, however, for while the Bush administration did not limit the means used, it carefully limited the objectives. The allied coalition could easily have driven to Baghdad and toppled Saddam Hussein's government in the final stages of the war, but it refused to do so. In part, it seems to have been deterred by still other lessons of Vietnam—the quagmire that awaits those who plunge recklessly into the internal politics of remote countries with alien political cultures. In part, also, the United States may have feared that other members of the coalition, especially the Arab nations, would not support such a move. And the United States and its Western allies appear also to have feared that the destruction of Iraq would leave a vacuum in a critical area that would have to be filled by their own occupying forces to prevent Syria and Iran from doing it. Thus, while the United States and its allies soundly defeated Saddam Hussein, they did not fight on in the classic manner to total victory even though it appeared within their grasp.

The future of limited war remains murky. The end of the Cold War has removed, at least for the moment, the geopolitical conditions that made limited war an essential instrument of U.S. strategy in the 1950s and 1960s. Classical limited war in the form prescribed by Osgood and other theorists and waged in Korea and Vietnam appears to be a thing of the past. The United States now enjoys such a vast preponderance of military power and technological superiority that in theory at least it could do anything it wished without fear of retaliation. At the same time, such is the complexity of the modern world that America's power, however vast, has limited utility. As nuclear capabilities proliferate, moreover, some of the old restraints may be reimposed. In addition, as far as the United States is concerned, the expenses of interventions past and the pressing economic burden of four decades of Cold War have placed constraints on the willingness to use power in any form.

The reluctance of the United States and its allies to intervene militarily in the Balkan crisis of 1991 suggests the extent of such constraints.

It thus seems likely that in the new world order the use of military power will remain limited in terms of ends and means. What remains unclear is for what purpose such wars should be fought. The end of the Cold War has unleashed hundreds of ethnic and nationalist conflicts across the globe, threatening international peace and stability. As of this point, at least, the United States lacks any doctrine for determining where or for what purpose it should intervene. Is it obligated, as with Operation Restore Hope in Somalia, to take action when the magnitude of human suffering becomes intolerable to the international community? If so, is it not also required to intervene in war-torn Bosnia, or should it only undertake missions that seem militarily "doable" and stay out of situations where the results appear more costly and less certain? Should the United States go in when other countries do not invite it? Should it attempt to run countries that seem incapable of running themselves? Must the burden of such interventions fall on the United States? If so, how many interventions will the international community tolerate? In the light of Korea and Vietnam, how long will the American public willingly accept such a role? As the world heads into a new and uncertain era, there are more questions than answers about the future of limited war and the uses of American power.

SEE ALSO The World Wars; Pacifism and Arms Limitation; Foreign Policy; The National-Security State; Cultural Interactions (all in this volume).

BIBLIOGRAPHY

The background for a peculiarly American approach to war is skillfully traced in Russell F. Weigley, *The American Way of War* (1977), a readable survey by one of the nation's foremost military historians. America's early twentieth century "limited" wars are chronicled in Stuart C. Miller, *"Benevolent Assimilation": The American Conquest of the Philippines, 1899–1903* (1982), a sharply critical account of America's little known turn-of-the-century war; Brian M. Linn, *The U.S. Army and Counterinsurgency in the Philippine War, 1899–1902* (1989), a recent, careful study; and Lester Langley, *The Banana Wars: An Inner History of American Empire, 1900–1934* (1983).

For the limited war in Korea, James I. Matray, ed., *Historical Dictionary of the Korean War* (1991), is an excellent, up-to-date reference work. Joseph C. Goulden, *Korea: The Untold Story* (1983), is a dramatic general history emphasizing the American perspective and the first six months of the war. Burton I. Kaufman, *The Korean War: Challenges in Crisis, Credibility, and Command* (1986), is broader, stresses U.S. politics, and gives good coverage to the years after 1951. Although dated in some respects, David Rees, *Korea: The Limited War* (1964), remains useful.

For the causes of the Korean conflict, Peter Lowe, *The Origins of the Korean War* (1986), is a good recent survey that emphasizes the crucial part played by internal Korean conflicts. Bruce Comings, *The Origins of the Korean War*, vol. 1, *Liberation and the Emergence of Separate Regimes* (1981), and vol. 2, *The Roaring of the Cataract, 1947–1950* (1991), provide magisterial treatment of the subject, drawing heavily on Korean sources and sharply criticizing U.S. policies.

Rosemary Foot, *The Wrong War: American Policy and the Dimensions of the Korean Conflict* (1985), and *A Substitute for Victory: The Politics of Peacemaking at the Korean Armistice Talk* (1990), are up-to-date, scholarly accounts of the war. The latter is especially valuable since it deals with a topic often given short shrift in general histories. Jian Chen, "China's Changing Aims during the Korean War, 1950–1951," *The Journal of American–East Asian Relations* 1 (Spring 1992): 8–41, is based on Chinese archival material. An impressive new multiarchival analysis is Sergei N. Goncharov, John W. Lewis, and Xue Litai, *Uncertain Partners: Stalin, Mao, and the Korean War* (1993). John Edward Wilz, "The Korean War and American Society," in Frances H. Heller, ed., *The Korean War: A 25-Year Perspective* (1977), remains the best account of an important but virtually neglected dimension of the Korean War.

The Korean War spawned a great deal of theorizing and philosophizing among Americans about limited war as a concept and instrument of policy. Robert Endicott Osgood's two books, *Limited War: The Challenge to U.S. Policy* (1957), and *Limited War Revisited* (1979), remain the classic accounts by one of the foremost theorists. Thomas Schelling, *Arms and Influence* (1966), sets forth a theory of coercion, and Herman Kahn, *On Escalation* (1965), proposes escalation strategies that were actually applied by the Johnson administration. Stephen Peter Rosen, "Vietnam and the American Theory of Limited War," *International Security* 7 (Fall 1982), demonstrates the role of limited war theory in the conduct of the U.S. war in Vietnam and analyzes its flaws as a strategy.

There are numerous general accounts of American involvement in Vietnam. William J. Duiker, *The Communist Road to Power in Vietnam* (1981), is an excellent survey of the war from the perspective of the North Vietnamese and the National Liberation Front of South Vietnam. George C. Herring, *America's Longest War: The United States and Vietnam, 1950–1975* (1986), emphasizes U.S. policies and strategies, while Stanley Karnow's *Vietnam: A History* (1983), stresses the early years of U.S. involvement. George McT. Kahin, *Intervention: How America Became Involved in Vietnam* (1986), is a splendid, critical account of American escalation of the war to 1966. Gabriel Kolko, *Anatomy of a War: Vietnam, the United States, and the Modern Historical Experience* (1985) is a sweeping radical indictment of U.S. involvement that is

particularly good in analyzing South Vietnamese society.

For Vietnam as a limited war, the following can be usefully consulted. George C. Herring, *"Cold Blood": LBJ's Conduct of Limited War in Vietnam* (1990), stresses the role played by limited war theory in President Lyndon Johnson's management of the war and the frustrations resulting therefrom. Wallace J. Thies, *When Governments Collide: Coercion and Diplomacy in the Vietnam Conflict* (1980), expertly analyzes the Johnson administration's difficulties in implementing limited war and coercion theories. Earl Tilford, *Setup* (1991), is a superb critique of the way the air war was fought. Douglas Kinnard, *The War Managers* (1977), reports and analyzes the results of surveys of senior U.S. officers who fought in Vietnam, making clear the frustrations caused by limited war strategies. Samuel Lubell, *The Hidden Crisis in American Politics* (1971), a contemporary account, remains one of the most astute analyses of growing popular frustration in the United States with the Vietnam War. David W. Levy, *The Debate over Vietnam* (1991), is an excellent analysis of the domestic debate over America's most divisive war.

WORLD REGIONS

Akira Iriye

The globalization of the United States, strategically, politically, economically, and culturally, constitutes a major theme of twentieth-century American history. From the 1890s to the 1990s, the nation was increasingly involved in the affairs of Latin America, Europe, Africa, the Middle East, South and East Asia, and the Pacific. Although this often led to conflict and war, it also contributed to political and economic transformations of other countries. Even more important, the whole process has had such a profound impact on U.S. domestic developments that the destiny and direction of the American people have become increasingly bound up with those of other peoples.

Yet this process of globalization has been neither continuous nor consistent. At one time the nation identified its interests most closely with countries in Central America and the Caribbean that were closer to home, while in other periods it defined the Atlantic, or Southeast Asia, as the area on whose stability and well-being America's own survival and welfare seemed to depend. Moreover, U.S. involvement in global affairs has taken different forms over the years, from mostly commercial relations to military presence, from cultural endeavors by private individuals and groups to state-backed business enterprises and intelligence activities. This essay will fit these approaches into an overall framework of foreign relations over the span of a century.

The story begins with the 1890s, for before that decade the United States had not defined a special approach to foreign affairs except in the Western Hemisphere. To be sure, the nation was a principal trading country in the world, and the government had stressed the importance of promoting and protecting American commercial interests abroad. But the bulk of these activities was in Europe, and so long as the European powers—which dominated the international political and economic system throughout the nineteenth century—observed the basic rules of the game in commercial matters, as they did except in times of war, there was little need for Washington to devise a special strategy in this regard. Fully three-fourths of American trade was with Europe, and the latter also provided capital needed for the nation's economic modernization. Until the last decade of the century, no foreign policy initiatives on the part of the United States appeared necessary to safeguard such connections with Europe.

Compared with Europe, other parts of the world were much less important for American economic interests. But in the Western Hemisphere, the Monroe Doctrine of 1823 had been reiterated by officials and publicists frequently to enunciate the idea of hemispheric identity. The inference was that the United States regarded this region as distinct from all other parts of the globe. Neither strategically nor economically, however, could it be said that American policy here differed markedly from its approaches elsewhere. Indeed, it may even be questioned whether there was a well-defined policy toward any region of the world prior to the 1890s. To have a foreign policy, a nation must develop an idea of what it seeks to preserve and protect in its dealings with other nations. But one would be hard put to find such ideas before the end of the nineteenth century, or to disagree with James Bryce's famous statement in *The American Commonwealth* (1888) that the American people showed little inclination to understand foreign affairs. It was not simply that America's security was not threatened throughout most of the century, or that the American people were too preoccupied with domestic problems, especially the slavery question of mid-century, to develop a sustained interest in external affairs. More fundamentally, there was the lack of an ideology that would enable Americans to establish a connection between domestic and international affairs. Earlier in the nation's history, it may be argued, there had been ideologies—notably republicanism at the beginning of the nineteenth century and manifest destiny in the 1840s—that defined certain approaches to international as well as national issues; after the Civil War, however, Americans did not develop a comparable, clearly articulated vision that would serve as the basis for their foreign relations. Even the idea of a distinctive hemispheric policy was more an extension of the domestic preoccupations than a coherent principle; it was believed important to prevent European encroachment on the hemisphere while the American people were busily conquering nature and establishing communities in North America. Little, however, was done prior to the turn of the century to entrench U.S. power or influence in the region.

ACTIVISM IN THE THIRD WORLD, 1890s TO 1914

Toward the end of the nineteenth century, two developments combined to induce the United States to define a more cohesive approach to Central America and, to a lesser extent, Asia and the Pacific. One development was domestic: the emergence of political forces that coalesced in the Progressive movement, with its emphasis on order, discipline, leadership, and sense of direction in national life. The other was external: the accelerated tempo of arms buildup and colonial acquisition on the part of the European powers. These two were not necessarily connected, but their coincidence meant that when the American people became aware of what was happening in the world, they, or at least their leaders, had an ideology with which to comprehend international affairs. Conversely, those who embraced the Progressive ideology were ready to turn their attention outward and establish a connection between world affairs and domestic politics. (This is not the place to discuss the Progressive movement in detail, but it may be noted that its grounding on Social Darwinism and its emphasis on nationalism implied the superiority of Anglo-Saxons over other races as well as their obligation to "civilize," or "control" as was often said, the latter.)

In some such fashion, the United States government came to define a systematic approach to Central America and the Caribbean. This amounted to establishing a sphere of special interest in the region in which the United States would assert its prerogatives as well as carry out certain obligations befitting its power. Interventionism best sums up American policy in the region from the 1890s through the era of the First World War. First, the United States intervened in the civil war in Cuba, a Spanish colony, eventually driving out Spanish forces and substituting American troops. Although these troops were withdrawn, and the United States supported the independence of Cuba, it retained "residual sovereignty" over the island republic until 1933, enabling it to intervene in Cuban affairs to maintain law and order. The war with Spain also resulted in the American acquisition of Puerto Rico, and, indirectly, in the building of an isthmian canal. The war, which had been fought in the southwestern Pacific as well as in the Caribbean, demonstrated the critical importance of building a canal so that American warships could move more easily between the Atlantic and the Pacific, rather than going around Cape Horn. The canal, begun in Panama in 1904 and completed in 1914, would have to be protected, so American forces occupied areas on both sides of the waterway, although the "canal district" was technically part of Panama, an independent country after it broke itself off from Colombia in 1903 with considerable U.S. support.

To defend these interests, the United States developed a new Caribbean and Central American policy, best expressed in President Theodore Roosevelt's "corollary" to the Monroe Doctrine which he enunciated in 1904. It asserted that the United States had the right to intervene in the domestic economic and political affairs of the countries in this region in order to maintain their "independence" and prevent European encroachment. The Progressive ideology of discipline and order sustained such a policy; to the extent that the people and leaders in such countries as Cuba and Santo Domingo appeared incapable of controlling their own affairs and opened themselves to European intervention, it was incumbent upon the United States to step in and assume responsibility for their welfare.

Exactly the same reasoning was behind the decision to acquire the Philippines, following the war with Spain. To leave the islands to the indigenous population seemed tantamount to condoning chaos or, worse, the establishment of control by Germany, Japan, or another power. It was thought that the United States had the duty to help the Filipinos develop in an orderly fashion so as not to disturb the regional peace or to engage in fratricide. The American colonial administration would concentrate on the building of roads and schools, in the meantime initiating the Filipinos into the art of democratic self-government at the local level. But the islands needed defense, and the United States had to develop a Pacific strategy as a result. Hawaii, annexed in 1898 during the Spanish-American War, would provide the key naval base, but it would be supplemented by the fortification of Manila and its environs.

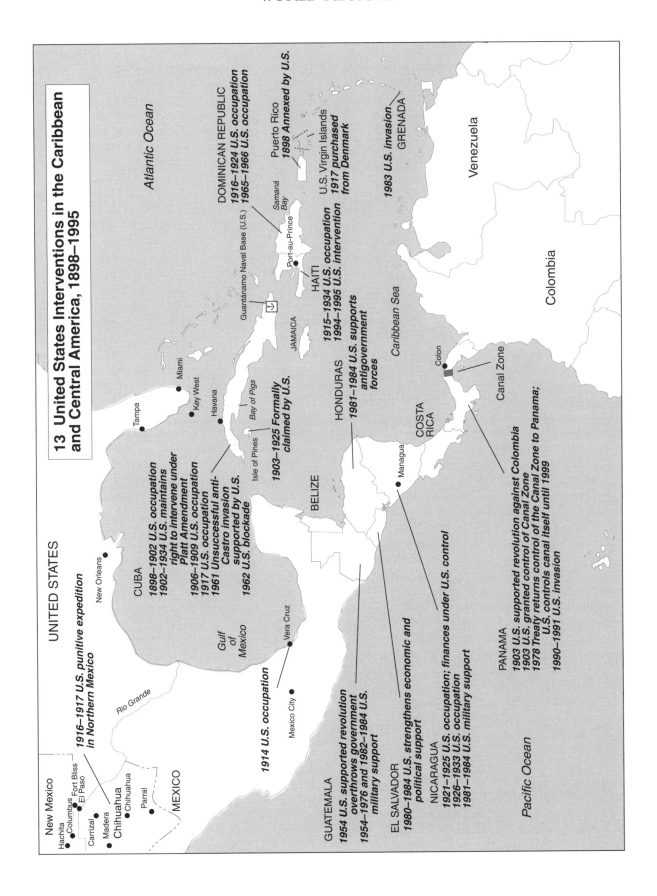

13 United States Interventions in the Caribbean and Central America, 1898–1995

UNITED STATES

1916–1917 U.S. punitive expedition in Northern Mexico

New Mexico
Hachita
Columbus · Fort Bliss · El Paso
Carrizal
Madera
Chihuahua
Chihuahua
Parral

MEXICO

Rio Grande

New Orleans

Gulf of Mexico

Vera Cruz

Mexico City

1914 U.S. occupation

Tampa

Miami

Key West

Havana

CUBA
*1898–1902 U.S. occupation
1902–1934 U.S. maintains right to intervene under Platt Amendment
1906–1909 U.S. occupation
1917 U.S. occupation
1961 Unsuccessful anti-Castro invasion supported by U.S.
1962 U.S. blockade*

Isle of Pines

Bay of Pigs

1903–1925 Formally claimed by U.S.

Atlantic Ocean

DOMINICAN REPUBLIC
*1916–1924 U.S. occupation
1965–1966 U.S. occupation*

Puerto Rico
1898 Annexed by U.S.

Samaná Bay

Guantánamo Naval Base (U.S.)

Port-au-Prince

HAITI
*1915–1934 U.S. occupation
1994–1995 U.S. intervention*

JAMAICA

U.S. Virgin Islands
1917 purchased from Denmark

GRENADA
1983 U.S. invasion

Caribbean Sea

Venezuela

Colombia

BELIZE

GUATEMALA
*1954 U.S. supported revolution overthrows government
1954–1976 and 1982–1984 U.S. military support*

EL SALVADOR
1980–1984 U.S. strengthens economic and political support

NICARAGUA
*1921–1925 U.S. occupation; finances under U.S. control
1926–1933 U.S. occupation
1981–1984 U.S. military support*

Managua

HONDURAS
1981–1984 U.S. supports antigovernment forces

COSTA RICA

Colon

Canal Zone

PANAMA
*1903 U.S. supported revolution against Colombia
1903 U.S. granted control of Canal Zone
1978 Treaty returns control of the Canal Zone to Panama; U.S. controls canal itself until 1999
1990–1991 U.S. invasion*

Pacific Ocean

In the rest of the Asia-Pacific region, in the meantime, the United States also began to define an approach. Next to Central America and the Caribbean, the area held special interest to the nation because of the acquisition of the Philippines and because China, a vast potential market where the European powers were fast establishing their spheres of influence, appeared in disarray. The American approach was to seek to maintain some regional stability through the assertion of the Open Door policy (or the principle of equal treatment for American commerce and investment abroad) and through balancing the rising power of Japan. A China dominated by European commerce, or a Japan with a strong armed force, would be a potential threat to American interests. The open door policy did not envisage the use of force by the United States, but it did imply America's interest in preserving the status quo. As Japan appeared more and more bent on challenging the status quo, especially after its victory over Russia in 1905 (the Treaty of Portsmouth, negotiated through Roosevelt's good offices, resulted in Russian territorial cessions to Japan), the United States sought to restrain that nation by augmenting its own naval presence in the Pacific and by encouraging China to orient its foreign policy toward Washington. No formal entente was indicated, but the United States was intent on playing a role in the regional order.

Although the United States was not as deeply involved in the Middle East or Africa, its initiatives in the Caribbean, East Asia, and the Pacific signaled the nation's emergence as a world power. It would be more correct to say that the United States now joined the European countries as one of the great powers. Japan, too, was developing as one, so that the globe was coming under the domination of what today are called the G-3 powers: Europe, the United States, and Japan. Hitherto, the great powers of Europe had determined the shape of international affairs in all parts of the world; henceforth, they would share the role with the United States and Japan. The rest of the world—the Third World—would be considered less powerful and, therefore, less "civilized," incapable of managing their own affairs without the guidance of the "civilized." The United States would "take up the white man's burden," a phrase made popular by the English poet Rudyard Kipling, to maintain order in the Third World.

It is important to note that America's emergence as a world power took the form of active involvement in Third World areas, not in Europe, where the United States retained its emphasis on commercial affairs and refrained from playing any political role. In such internal European affairs as the French-German dispute over Alsace and Lorraine or the Balkan crisis involving the various nationalities' assertiveness against Austrian and Ottoman rule, the United States remained uninterested. Europe's road to war, which came in August 1914, was constructed without American involvement. There was, in other words, a sharp contrast between America's economic interests, which were largely tied to Europe, and its military and political initiatives in the Third World.

WILSONIANISM, FROM 1914 TO THE END OF THE GREAT WAR

All this was to change when war broke out in Europe. Although the origins of the war had little or nothing to do with the United States, once war came, Washington was forced to define an approach to Europe, regardless of whether or not the nation was going to become involved in the conflict. If it was to abstain from intervention, that, too, would call for a rationale, to explain why it was that such an unprecedentedly large-scale war did not concern the United States. Presented by pacifists and anti-interventionists, this position asserted that the European powers were hopelessly short-sighted, that the United States would not help them to put an end to their folly, and that in the meantime commercial and other links with the belligerents would be preserved.

Because the United States was expected to expand its trade during the war, such noninterventionism was tantamount to arguing that after the war American influence and interests in Europe would grow. Going a step beyond this position, those, like President Woodrow Wilson, who were interested in mediating the European conflict assumed that since the Europeans appeared incapable of managing their own affairs, America would have to step in, not as a combatant but as a disinterested intermediary. Wilson's call for a "peace without victory" was important as it indicated America's readiness to visualize such a peace; henceforth the United States would have to become engaged in European affairs. Thus, even if the United States had not become involved in the war, it would have defined a role for itself in Europe. What role it would have taken is difficult to say, but at least President Wilson would have tried to ensure that America would shape the peace following the war.

After 1917, with the United States actually entering the war on Britain's and its allies' side, this became a certainty. To the extent that American entry made the difference in the war, the nation would be expected to play a major role in shaping the peace. For the first time in recent history, the United States was now forced to define an approach to European affairs. There were two basic assumptions. First, the growth of German military power had been the root cause of the war, and the United States would destroy that power, in cooperation with the Allies. The implication was that after the war, too, it would be incumbent on America to keep Germany from developing offensive capabilities. Second, not just Germany, but the entire system of European power politics had somehow to be transformed. The prewar military buildups, colonial acquisitions, and secret alliances and agreements had produced a situation where war became more or less inevitable. If a more stable situation were to develop, therefore, it would be necessary to restructure the European state system. The United States would take the lead in this direction.

Thus wartime American policy, as well as Wilsonian diplomacy at the end of the war, clearly envisaged a new American approach to Europe. On one hand, the United States would help restore regional balance by defeating Germany and its allies. On the other, it would promote the creation of a new European order. The best example of this latter approach was Wilson's Fourteen Points, enunciated in January 1918. It envisaged a new European order through the application of the principle of nationality or national self-determination, as it came to be popularly known. Europe would be reconstituted in such a way that nations would consist of well-defined nationalities or ethnic entities. The Poles, for instance, would have their own nation, and Turkey would be expelled from Europe and its geographical boundaries restricted to areas inhabited by ethnic Turks. A new state, Czechoslovakia, would be established in central Europe not, it is true, in terms of a single ethnicity but consisting of several. The idea here was that the Czechs, Slovaks, and others who constituted the new entity wanted it that way. In any event, with these states and with Hungary, Austria, Germany, Yugoslavia (another multiethnic nation), Italy, and others, Europe would look very different from how it had prior to 1914. What is important is that this was a Europe to whose creation the United States contributed much. Whether it would also play a role in its preservation was not yet clear, however.

Wilsonian policy had implications for U.S. relations with other parts of the world. Here, however, there was no sharp break from the past. The nation had already staked out an approach to the Third World, and President Wilson essentially carried out his predecessors' policies in the Western Hemisphere and in the Asia-Pacific region. In the former area, the United States would continue to stress its special duties and responsibilities as the hegemon of Central America. Wilson paid particular attention to Mexico, the Dominican Republic, and Haiti to ensure not only their financial solvency and economic stability but also their "good government." In Asia and the Pacific, the open door policy would be reaffirmed, but Wilson was also eager to promote China's economic and political development after the overthrow of the Ch'ing (Qing) dynasty in 1912. China was the biggest challenge confronting the United States in developing a Third World strategy, and Wilson wanted to make sure that the "sister republic's" successful transformation would not be jeopardized by an ambitious Japan eager to take advantage of the European war to entrench itself on the continent of Asia.

No less significant was Wilson's interest in the Middle East. By applying the self-determination principle to Turkey, the United States in effect involved itself in Middle Eastern affairs. Under Wilson's initiative, the victorious powers agreed to turn over most of what had constituted the Ottoman empire to the League of Nations which, in turn, would ask some nations to govern portions of the former empire as "mandates." Thus Palestine, Transjordan, Syria, Lebanon, and Iraq became mandates, to be administered by Britain or France. There was some possibility that the United States might establish its own mandate in Armenia, but the ethnically Armenian areas north of Turkey remained within Russia. Still, by calling for this new form of administration, the United States established a Middle Eastern policy for the first time in its history. Moreover, there was much interest in the petroleum resources of the region. Washington was determined that these resources be opened to American as well as to European exploitation.

United States policies toward Europe and toward the Third World were conceptually unified through Wilsonian internationalism, a framework for promoting American interests and visions in all parts of the world. Although by no means consistently or uniformly applied, this framework included the principles of collective security, the open door, self-determination, and democratization. A world of peace, reform, and development was visualized, with the United States playing a central role in promoting them.

POSTWAR INTERNATIONALISM, 1919–1929

That role was to have been expressed through America's leading participation in League of Nations affairs. When the U.S. Senate rejected the Versailles peace

14 Europe after World War I

treaty, the incipient globalism of American foreign policy was set back. This did not mean, however, that the nation abandoned its commitment to involving itself in international affairs. On the contrary, the United States remained active both in G-3 and Third World relations, although the Republican administrations of the 1920s did not usually couch them in the internationalist rhetoric of Wilsonianism.

First of all, it should be noted that the nation continued to have a European policy. To be sure, it was somewhat different from what Wilson had envisaged and did not involve a military or political

presence in the region. (U.S. troops that occupied the Rhineland as part of the armistice arrangement were withdrawn by 1925.) The key framework for postwar European stability, the Locarno treaties of 1925, which froze Germany's frontiers with France and Belgium, were worked out without American participation. At the same time, however, the United States was deeply involved in Europe's financial and economic affairs. American bankers, with the encouragement of Washington officials, cooperated with their European counterparts to devise a scheme for restabilizing the European currency system, an essential condition for regional stability. At bottom was the need to restore a framework for multilateral exchanges of goods, services, and capital. That necessitated a system of currency convertibility, since without the unrestricted conversion of one currency into another, no financial transactions across national boundaries could take place. Trade, shipping, and investment would be at the mercy of exchange control and arbitrary currency policies. In order to ensure the smooth functioning of these transactions, more-

over, it would be desirable to develop stable rates of exchange among different currencies. This could best be done by reestablishing the gold standard that had existed prior to the Great War. Major currencies would be linked to each other through the medium of gold, and the United States, holding one-half of the world's gold reserve, would serve as the ultimate guarantor of the system. Moreover, because the questions of Germany's reparations to its former enemies, and the latter's wartime and postarmistice debts to the

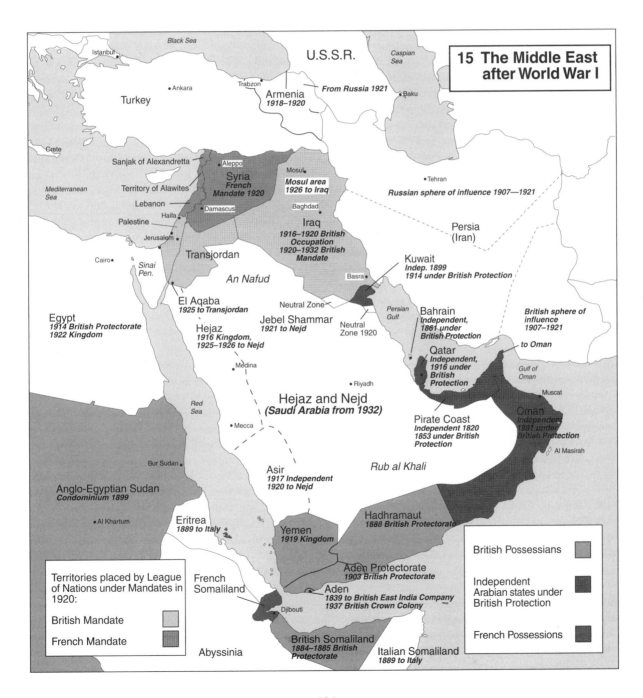

United States, posed a threat to European economic stability, American bankers helped resolve these questions through working out, in 1925 and again in 1929, revised plans for reparations and debt payments.

It is obvious that the United States not only had a stake in the economic recovery of Europe but also had to sustain it constantly through shipments of capital in the form of loans, portfolio (indirect) investments, and direct investments. These amounted to over $10 billion a year in the late 1920s. At least economically, therefore, the United States could be said to function as a key participant in European affairs. America's European policy, in other words, assumed that the infusion of the nation's capital would create a stable regional order which, combined with the European countries' security arrangements such as Locarno, should help maintain the peace.

In Asia and the Pacific, in the meantime, the United States was even more willing to play a role. In fact, it was the key player in redefining both G-3 and Third World affairs. Regarding big-power relations, the primary emphasis was on disarmament. The United States took the initiative in limiting the navies of the leading naval powers, America, Britain, and Japan. The assumption was that their naval building programs had created a dangerous situation in the region and that only their agreement on limiting armaments would restore stability. At the naval disarmament conferences in Washington (1921–1922) and London (1930), the United States took the lead in persuading Britain and Japan to limit the tonnage of each navy so that the three navies would never be a threat to each other. Coupled with a nonfortification agreement (i.e., the three powers would not further fortify their Pacific possessions except in Singapore and Pearl Harbor) and the abrogation of the Anglo-Japanese alliance (first signed in 1902), the arms limitation agreements defined a new status quo in the Pacific.

On the Asian continent, in the meantime, China's future continued to preoccupy Americans. The development of a Third World country along liberal lines was considered a cardinal objective of U.S. policy at a time when much of the Third World was coming under the influence of Bolshevism. The Third International, or the Comintern, organized in 1919, opposed the League of Nations, the Locarno treaties, and other instruments of liberal capitalist ("bourgeois") internationalism, and the United States saw China as a test case for the struggle between these two visions of a future international order. Here the G-3 powers, under the initiative of the United States, managed to enter into several agreements to

respect China's territorial integrity and to cooperate with each other for the latter's economic development. Although the Chinese did not at first accept the "Washington system," considering it did not go far enough to meet their national aspirations, by the end of the decade their leadership incorporated their country into the regional scheme, a major achievement for the United States.

Postwar American policy in the Western Hemisphere may also be fitted into such a framework. Superficially, the United States gave the impression of retreating from the region as the Republican administrations departed from the overtly interventionist policies of Wilson, Taft, and Theodore Roosevelt. Not only were U.S. troops withdrawn from the Dominican Republic and Nicaragua, American officials also expressed a willingness to modify the earlier, more assertive interpretation of the Monroe Doctrine. As best represented by a memorandum written by Under Secretary of State Reuben Clark in 1928, the new approach would look to the doctrine as a symbol of special ties between the United States and its southern neighbors, not as something that justified unilateral U.S. interventions. Stability in this region would be promoted through establishing mutually more agreeable relations, taking into consideration the interests and sentiments of people elsewhere in the hemisphere. This policy was sustained by massive American investment in and trade with Latin American countries which came close in scale to those with Europe. Here again, the United States sought to promote a well-defined approach to Third World countries.

Likewise, the search for a Middle Eastern policy, begun under the Wilson administration, continued in the 1920s. The United States participated in the Lausanne conference (1923), convened primarily for concluding a peace treaty with Turkey, which had sided with Germany during the war. American participation is notable since the United States had never been in a state of war with Turkey. Nevertheless, Washington sent its representatives to help define the postwar order in the Middle East. One major objective was the demilitarization of the Dardanelles straits. The United States and its former European allies succeeded in obtaining Turkey's agreement on this point so that henceforth the straits would not be patrolled by its warships. Another, equally important, aim was to ensure that the region's rich oil resources would be made available to American firms on equal footing to European. With the use of automobiles expected to spread throughout the country, and indeed throughout the world, it was imperative to procure an adequate supply of petroleum, but British, French, and Dutch companies controlled the oil fields with concessions going back to the prewar years. The United States broke this monopoly in 1928, concluding with the European governments a "red line agreement," which specified that henceforth European and American companies would cooperate in the oil-producing areas of the Middle East (excepting Kuwait and Iran). This, too, was part of the postwar American strategy toward the Third World.

One area of the world where the United States did not pursue an active foreign policy was eastern Europe. It refused to recognize the Bolshevik regime in Moscow, nor did it involve itself in the security question of eastern Europe. Although President Wilson had had much to do with the creation of the states of Poland and Czechoslovakia, the Republican administrations did little to ensure their independence, assuming that the area would somehow benefit from the economic and political stabilization in western Europe. Trade with and private investments in these countries and the Soviet Union were encouraged, but there was no overall approach to this part of the world. It may be said, then, that while the United States was fully involved in G-3 and Third World relations, it remained aloof from the Soviet world even as the latter isolated itself from international affairs. Nevertheless, there is little doubt that American foreign relations were now far more globalized than before. In the story of the development of the United States as a world power, the 1920s were significant not, as is so often asserted, as indicating a temporary setback, but as a confirmation of the trend.

DEPRESSION DIPLOMACY, 1929–1939

The decade of the 1930s is usually described with such terms as "isolationism," "neutrality," and "appeasement." While not incorrect, these words do not help explain what happened to the postwar American strategies in G-3 and Third World relations, and why. Nor do they tell much about specific approaches to different regions. Was the United States "isolationist" everywhere? Obviously not, since it was quite active in promoting a new definition of its relations with Latin American countries. Nor was the United States "neutral" in the Chinese-Japanese war. As for "appeasement," the term covers a multitude of sins and conceals from view some important developments in the economic sphere.

It would be best to start with the economic dimension, which had been so important in postwar U.S. foreign affairs. It cannot be denied that the Great Depression at home and abroad severely challenged international economic relations. Virtually overnight, American funds became unavailable to finance foreign (especially German, Japanese, and Latin American) industrialization as well as huge trade deficits vis-à-vis the United States. With the nation's own national income as well as output cut in half in four years (1928–1932), and with unemployment increasing from 1.5 million to 12 million in the same period, American purchasing power was drastically curtailed, with the result that its trade, which had accounted for at least 16 percent of the world's total, also sharply declined. America's economic resources that had sustained the international order of the 1920s could no longer do so. With the linchpin of American economic power gone, the international economic system threatened to disintegrate, with each country and each region looking after its own interests without regard to the stability of the whole. There was a real danger of the world economy becoming split into regional subunits, if not into national fortresses.

The administration of Herbert Hoover (1929–1933) tried to stem the tide and restore global economic activities through emergency measures such as a moratorium on reparations and debt payments, and through international conferences to work out long-term solutions. The key assumption was that the system of multilateral trade and investments within the framework of the gold standard (which in turn was based on the principle of stable rates of exchange among different currencies) had to be maintained in order to provide stability in international economic affairs, a condition believed to be intimately linked to domestic recovery. Before anything came of his efforts, however, Hoover left office, defeated for reelection by Franklin D. Roosevelt.

President Roosevelt's initial reaction to the economic crisis was not to force an internationalist solution to the global crisis, such as the restoration of exchange stability, but to focus on unilateral domestic measures like public works and increases in money supply. In thus abandoning, however temporarily, the commitment to economic internationalism, the United States joined other powers in undermining the foundation of the postwar world order. Japan in Asia and Germany in Europe were attempting to establish their own regional autarkies, while the British Empire was turning itself into a huge trade bloc of "imperial preferences." There was a danger then that the globe would be split into separate economic (and political) units.

683

After 1934, however, the Roosevelt administration began an attempt to prevent such an outcome and reintegrate the world economy. It would do so not, as had happened under Hoover, through international conferences, but primarily through bilateral negotiations. Altogether twenty trade agreements were signed by the end of the decade, all designed to lower mutual trade barriers in the spirit of "reciprocity." (Congress authorized the government to conduct such negotiations through the enactment of the Reciprocal Trade Agreements Act of 1934.) By 1939 the American economy had sufficiently recovered that there was a good chance that these negotiations could become the basis for an even more ambitious attempt at reestablishing a global economic order. Such an objective, of course, would have had to be preceded by agreements with three key powers that stood outside the reciprocity trade agreements: Germany, Japan, and the Soviet Union. Even so, one should note Washington's serious interest until the very end in pressuring these countries to give up their autarkic and otherwise restrictive trade policies. It is in this sense that there is some justification for terming U.S. diplomacy in the 1930s an "appeasement." The policy did not necessarily mean acquiescing in the aggressive behavior of some powers; rather, it entailed efforts at persuading them, as well as others, to cooperate with the United States and with one another to restore a semblance of order in international economic transactions.

Outside the economic sphere, however, the United States did not involve itself in world affairs as actively as it had in the 1920s. This was the key to the nation's "isolationism." We can best see this in America's response, or rather lack of response, to increased armaments in various parts of the world. Germany, Japan, and the Soviet Union began spending enormous sums of money on armament, thus clearly destabilizing the power balance in Europe and Asia. The United States could have responded either by strengthening its arms to match their programs, or by initiating a serious effort at an international arms control agreement, as in 1921–1922. This time, however, Washington hesitated to act assertively. To be sure, in 1930 it promoted a naval disarmament agreement among the United States, Britain, and Japan to cover "auxiliary craft" (not covered by the 1922 agreement). But that was more a continuation of the earlier initiative than a response to the world in depression. During the 1930s the United States did little to stem the tide of armament increases. It watched powerlessly, even with a measure of indifference, as Germany used its newly strengthened army

to reoccupy the Rhineland (1936) and annex Austria (1938), or as Japan likewise employed its superior military force against China in conquering Manchuria (1931–1933) and trying to subdue the rest of that country (1937 onward). It was only after 1938, and especially after 1939, that the United States began to undertake a serious program of building up its military power and, at the same time, to ship some of its arms to Britain, France, and China to balance the might of Germany and Japan. Clearly, the nation had a late start, but perhaps this was inevitable, given the public's hostility toward the armament industry (which was often blamed for having involved the nation in the Great War) and toward militarism in general. The neutrality laws of the 1930s, forbidding Americans from selling arms or lending money to belligerents, reflected this same sentiment. Others might arm themselves and engage in military action; the United States would not do so but would concentrate on domestic issues, isolating itself from international affairs.

In the context of our discussion, these trends in the 1930s amounted to America's diminished role in shaping G-3 relations. Until near the end of the decade, the nation would not use military force to influence the course of events in Europe or Asia. The European powers, Japan, and the Soviet Union would be left to work out their own regional arrangements without any input from the United States. This can be seen in the way the Soviet Union reentered the world arena, starting with its admission into the League of Nations in 1934 and ending with its non-aggression pact with Germany, signed on the eve of the outbreak of World War II. Had the United States been more active in G-3 affairs, for example in checking German designs, the Soviet Union might have remained longer isolated from European politics. In effect the Soviet Union was now joining the G-3 powers to make a major difference in the global balance of power. Unfortunately, however, this took the form of the Nazi-Soviet pact, to which Japan also sought to attach itself.

The United States was, at the same time, more willing to pursue an activist foreign policy toward the Third World. Continuing the already well-defined approach to Third World countries, the nation, despite the Depression, sought to promote their economic and political transformation. In Asia and the Pacific, the United States was quick to respond to Japan's aggression in northeast China, seeing in it a clear violation of the various agreements signed at the Washington Conference to promote Chinese modernization. The Hoover administration was so concerned over the fate of China that it sent a representative to participate in League of Nations deliberations on the crisis. Although little came of it, as Japan persisted in defying the League's mediation efforts and its eventual warning (in 1932) that it should restore the status quo in northeast Asia, Washington's message to Japan was unambiguous. Even though the United States did little specific to aid China during the mid-1930s, public opinion grew strongly in favor of doing so. When renewed war broke out between China and Japan in 1937—a war that would last for eight years—President Roosevelt refused to invoke American neutrality by not calling the conflict a war, with a view to providing China with the arms it needed. While Japan could, and did initially, benefit from this decision and purchase weapons and other items such as iron, steel, and petroleum, these would in time be embargoed so that China, not Japan, would augment its military force. When, in late 1938, the Japanese government proclaimed a "new order in Eastern Asia," a zone of Asian resources, markets, and people under Japanese control, Washington quickly denounced it. Japan was seeking to turn the whole of Asia into its sphere of influence, and the two powers were engaged in a struggle for the future of this Third World region.

Likewise in the Western Hemisphere, both the Hoover and the Roosevelt administrations aimed at building a sphere of mutual accommodation and cooperation under the principle of "the good neighbor," a policy that had political, economic, and cultural connotations. During the world economic crisis, it seemed to make good sense to solidify ties to the other American republics, and the U.S. government time and again emphasized "hemispheric solidarity." Secretary of State Cordell Hull attended a meeting of American states in Montevideo in 1933, and President Roosevelt went to a similar gathering in Buenos Aires in 1936, both to stress the commitment of the United States to maintain the sphere as an interdependent region free from the turmoil of G-3 politics. It is interesting to note that at Buenos Aires a series of agreements was signed between the United States and Latin American nations for an exchange of students and scholars, the first officially sponsored exchange program (outside the "Boxer indemnity" program for bringing Chinese students to the United States). One logical outcome of these developments was the Lima conference of 1938, at which the American states all pledged cooperation against a threat to the security of any of them from the outside. The hemispheric order thus being constructed in a sense went back to the spirit of the original Monroe Doctrine in its self-promoted isolation from Old World complications, but at the same time it was much more specific and envisaged more even-handed cooperation between the United States and the rest of the hemisphere. Here, too, was evidence that American strategy in the Third World had not changed despite the Depression.

GLOBAL WARFARE, 1939–1945

The coming of the European war in 1939 did not immediately bestir the United States to reformulate its G-3 strategy; President Roosevelt's principal efforts were confined to the sending of Undersecretary of State Sumner Welles to the European capitals to ascertain chances for peace. He found them rather dim, and the Roosevelt administration began searching for a more activist foreign policy in Europe when Germany's spring offensive of 1940 was launched against Scandinavia, the Low Countries, and France. Germany's European victories encouraged Japan to extend its power to Southeast Asia, a region filled with British, French, and Dutch colonies. The Axis alliance of September 1940, combining Germany and Japan, and later Italy and fascist Spain, was a worldwide coalition of antidemocratic countries, and in late 1940, when Soviet Foreign Minister Vyacheslav Molotov went to Berlin to see Hitler, the former expressed the Soviet leadership's interest in joining the Axis with a view to dividing up the British Empire into the new partners' respective spheres of influence. Had that occurred, the United States, alone or with only Britain and the Latin American countries on its side, would have had to confront a formidable global combination of power. That did not come about, as Hitler deceived Stalin and marched into Soviet territory in June 1941, but for the United States these momentous developments clearly necessitated the adoption of a global strategy encompassing all parts of the globe, G-3 as well as Third World.

Rainbow plans, a series of war plans hypothesizing U.S. involvement in a worldwide conflict, best exemplified the global perspective. Like a rainbow, representing different colors, the nation would work out a strategy of war against a plurality of enemies in all parts of the world. To be sure, one or two areas of the world would be stressed as priority items, for instance the defense of the Western Hemisphere and the British Isles. Only after their security was ensured would the United States undertake major military operations elsewhere, such as Asia or the Pacific. Nevertheless, by 1941 it was clear that no separate regional approach would do. Policies toward various regions of the world had become closely intertwined. For example, the defense of Britain would entail measures to ensure the survival of its Asian empire. After the fall of France to Germany in June 1940 and the establishment of a wartime French government in Vichy, Washington devised a policy of preventing the French colonial empire in North Africa and Southeast Asia from falling into hostile (German or Japanese) hands. Policy toward the Soviet Union, too, had to be global; the United States would extend its military assistance, under the Lend-Lease Act of March 1941, to that country so that it would withstand the German onslaught, while at the same time pressure would be brought to bear upon Japan to discourage the latter's possible attack on Siberia. Aid to China, too, had now more global significance than earlier; the country was turning to the United States as the principal supporter now that neither Britain nor the Soviet Union could provide much help. America's increasingly stiff stance toward Japan in the fall of 1941, besides obviously aiming at preventing China's collapse, was also intended as a sign of encouragement to Britain and all other European countries, whether occupied by German forces or not, to persist in their resistance. In such a global strategy, there was to be no distinction between the G-3 world, the Third World, or the Soviet world. They were all involved in a struggle for power between Axis and anti-Axis forces, a struggle the outcome of which would depend to a large extent on the manpower, economic resources, and visions that the United States could provide.

Japan's attack on Pearl Harbor ensured that the United States would indeed employ all the resources at its disposal in the worldwide conflict of nations and peoples. Global strategy and coalition warfare were the terms used by American officials as they devised ways of fighting the Axis powers. There was no part of the world not covered by U.S. military plans and operations. To begin with, the Western Hemisphere developed a system of joint defense under which U.S. forces were stationed in various parts of South America, especially Brazil where airfields were constructed as bases of attack on German forces in the Atlantic and North Africa. In 1942 and 1943, U.S.-British strategy focused on North Africa and the Mediterranean, as their troops first landed in Morocco and occupied it as well as Algeria and Tunisia, French protectorates under the Vichy regime's control. After driving out German troops, American and British forces attacked Sicily and Italy. In the meantime, a Middle East supply center was estab-

lished to ship military and other provisions to the Soviet Union through Iran. Further east, the Anglo-American allies established a China-Burma-India theater to engage Japanese forces in Southeast Asia so as to prevent their conquest of Burma and northern India. In China itself, an American general, Joseph W. Stilwell, was put in charge of administering Lend-Lease shipments as well as of U.S. forces fighting alongside Chinese. In the Pacific, the U.S. army under General Douglas MacArthur and the navy under Admiral Chester Nimitz planned and executed a counteroffensive as early as 1942, trying to keep Japanese forces from extending their sway into New Guinea and Australia in the south and Midway and the Hawaiian islands in the east. It can be seen, therefore, that World War II was quickly establishing the United States as a key global power whose military operations and arms and other shipments had a major impact on the course of the war.

The war also involved postwar planning, that is, preparing for the end of the war and the treatment of enemy nations after their defeat, and here it is to be noted that the United States saw its role after the war in terms of a world order that continued to embrace G-3 and Third World countries, as well as the Soviet Union. President Roosevelt, his successor, Harry S. Truman, and their aides assumed that the victorious Allies, in particular the United States, Britain, the Soviet Union, and China would maintain their cooperation as "four big policemen," in Roosevelt's words. It was not always clear how the four would act—by pooling their resources to deter and combat aggression, or through a division of labor so that each would take care of the security of a particular part of the world. The latter was easier to visualize and probably to implement as well. It is not surprising that throughout the war thinking in Washington often envisaged some system of postwar collective security in which the United States would retain its power and responsibilities in the Western Hemisphere and the Pacific Ocean, Britain in Western Europe and the Middle East, the Soviet Union in Eastern Europe and parts of northeast Asia, and China in the rest of Asia. There were some gray areas such as central Europe, where Germany and Austria would be divided into zones of occupation by Allied forces (American, British, and Soviet, to which French forces were later added). Much of Africa also was conceptually murky. Nevertheless, here was a globalist approach which, combined with the new world organization, the United Nations, seemed a certain way to define the peace. Because some, if not all, of these various schemes for future security were discussed and agreed to, at least tacitly, among Roosevelt, Churchill, and Stalin at their meeting in Yalta in February 1945, this conception of the postwar international order is sometimes called the Yalta system. It envisaged an interconnected world after the war in which representatives of the G-3, the Third World, and the Soviet world—the United States, Britain, France, China, and the Soviet Union—would work together to ensure the peace. They, as well as other members of the international community, would be beneficiaries of new mechanisms, such as the International Monetary Fund and the World Bank, both established at the Bretton Woods conference of 1944, which were designed to restore world trade and investment activities without the rigidities that had been inherent in the gold standard system of the 1920s.

THE G-3 VERSUS THE SOVIET UNION, 1945–1949

Why such a vision of the new international order did not materialize and was replaced by a definition of international affairs known as the Cold War is the key question as one traces the development of American foreign affairs after World War II. If the Yalta system had continued, the United States would have shared power with the Soviet Union and China, as well as with Britain and other European powers, for the preservation of the postwar peace. At the same time, economically and culturally various parts of the world would have become more closely integrated than before, and the United States would have been at the forefront of this movement. The Cold War, in contrast, pitted most of the G-3 world against the Soviet world, both forming their respective military alliances, and it ultimately also divided the Third World into two camps. International economic and cultural affairs likewise tended to be fractured, instead of promoting global interconnectedness. In both the wartime and Cold War definitions, the United States was the principal actor, and its globalist orientation did not change. But there were fundamental differences in the nature of this orientation, one standing for the promotion of an integrated world order, the other for the containment and ostracization of one part of the world.

The breakdown of the power-sharing approach defined at Yalta was in part a consequence of the strategic realities defined by the new atomic weapon. Air power obliterated geographical boundaries. High-speed aircraft and nuclear weapons could be deployed anywhere, and by the same token America's own security was now that much more vulnerable. Unless efforts were made to control the bomb through international cooperation, the entire world would be threatened with a nuclear war, and America's own security, already vulnerable through the Pearl Harbor experience, would be compromised. The fear of, and preparation for, nuclear war, became a decisive factor in American conceptions of international affairs in the immediate aftermath of the war, the more so when the United States and the Soviet Union found it impossible to agree on a mutually acceptable arrangement for sharing nuclear technology and weapons through the United Nations.

Nuclear fears were exacerbated by fears of communist machinations throughout the world. They were fueled no doubt by Soviet political control over Eastern European governments through the local communist parties but also by the growing tide of radicalism in Western Europe, now freed from wartime constraints, and by nationalistic movements in Asia, the Middle East, and elsewhere. Although these were disparate phenomena, it was easy to make a connection among them and to link them to Moscow, where a successor to the Communist International that had been disbanded in 1943 was established in 1947 (the Cominform, or the Communist Information Bureau). It was all too easy to view the world as being threatened with another totalitarian menace, just when it had defeated the Axis aggressors. Instead of cooperation, confrontation became the theme in U.S.-Soviet relations, and thus Cold War rather than internationalism came to provide the framework for formulating American globalism.

Cold War globalism was all-embracing in the domestic context as well. The establishment of the National Security Council, the unification of the armed services under the roof of the new Defense Department, the creation of the Central Intelligence Agency—all indicated a conscious decision on the part of American leaders to define the challenge facing the nation as total, requiring a concerted effort to mobilize national resources to struggle against "the ideological foe."

National leadership, in the process, broadened. One could term it a new corporatism, to distinguish it from the prewar arrangement in which government and business leaders (and, in the New Deal, labor leaders as well) had cooperated. Now the corporatist structure included the academic community, particularly scientists, teachers' unions, the religious establishment, and mass media. Of course, this was not exactly the same thing as the corporatism of fascist Italy or Spain, and disagreement among the new leaders as well as dissident voices outside the leadership structure were often aired in the open. Still, far more individuals and groups than ever before in peacetime were now dedicated to working together in "the national interest," another concept establishing its legitimacy.

The concept was more than geopolitical, although fundamentally it stressed geopolitics, that is, balance of power, armament, military strategy, and national security. But national security could be, and was often, defined broadly to include the preservation of "the American way of life" such as the nuclear family, the neighborhood, and religious worship. Nationalism, in other words, was at the core of the postwar globalism. Even such obviously internationalist activities of the United States as the Marshall Plan, Point Four (for technical assistance to developing countries), or the Fulbright exchange programs could be integrated into the new Cold War strategy. They could be justified as a means for expanding American influence abroad, for maintaining the "pro-American orientation" of other peoples, and for combating communist conspiracies everywhere. In other words, economic and cultural internationalism which, as noted earlier, had been well formulated by 1945, could, in the new situation, be adapted to buttress Cold War globalism.

During its initial phase (1945–1949), the Cold War policy, despite its unmistakably globalist character, was primarily implemented in G-3 relations. As formulated by George F. Kennan, the State Department's chief architect of the containment strategy, it was of cardinal importance for the United States to prevent the Western European countries and Japan, that is, the principal G-3 powers, from falling to Soviet domination. Despite wartime devastation, these countries were, besides the United States, still the most advanced parts of the world, and their addition to the Soviet world would be a catastrophe. For this reason, the United States allocated major portions of its military power and economic resources to the defense of Britain, France, Germany, Italy, and other countries in the immediate postwar period. The founding of the North Atlantic Treaty Organization aimed at establishing America's strategic presence there, while the Marshall Plan sought to help these nations recover from the devastations of the war so as to frustrate radical political movements that might destabilize domestic order. Although the emphasis on Western Europe was in a sense a throwback to the 1920s, we should note that, unlike the earlier period, the United States was willing to commit its military power to defend the status quo. Peace-time strategic coordination in the framework of NATO indicated the degree to which Washington was willing to part from tradition in developing an Atlantic policy.

Next to the Atlantic and Western Europe in importance was Japan. The country was occupied by U.S. troops to ensure its demilitarization and democratization. From around 1948, however, its future came to be seen in the context of the global Cold War. The civil war in China in which communist forces appeared to be winning added urgency to restoring Japan's potential usefulness as a military base and as an economic resource in the struggle against the Soviet Union. Just as in Europe, where West Germany was being steadily reintegrated into a Western alliance system, Japan, too, was encouraged by the United States to consider its future as an indirect participant in that system. China, in contrast, would lose the status visualized at Yalta as one of America's major partners in world affairs.

MILITARIZATION OF THE COLD WAR, 1949–1969

The Cold War became truly globalized after 1949, the year of the first Soviet testing of atomic weapons and the communist victory in China. These momentous developments, inevitably interpreted in Washington as threatening to tip the scale in the global balance of power, called for a more concerted effort than before in containing the communist bloc. In the spring of 1950, the National Security Council drafted a memorandum (NSC-68) which called for massive military spending and peacetime preparedness to cope with the crisis. Before the new globalist approach was fully developed and incorporated into official policy, however, the Korean War broke out, causing an immediate shift of national attention and strategy toward East Asia. But the North Korean attack on the South was interpreted in Washington as part of the Soviet-led global expansionism, and President Truman quickly approved NSC-68 as the basic policy statement of the U.S. government, although the document itself was not to be declassified till the 1970s. In any event, the Cold War had come to Asia, and the doctrine of containment was applied to the Korean peninsula and the Taiwan straits. A peace treaty with Japan was hastily drawn up, and the San Francisco peace conference of 1951 served to formalize the new regional approach to the Pacific, the San Francisco system, that would complement the Cold War strategy in Europe and the Middle East. As in these regions, a series of mutual defense

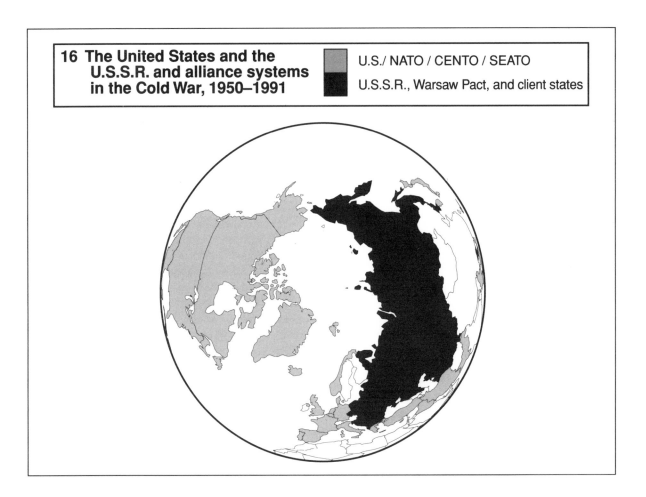

16 The United States and the U.S.S.R. and alliance systems in the Cold War, 1950–1991

U.S./ NATO / CENTO / SEATO

U.S.S.R., Warsaw Pact, and client states

agreements was signed with Asian countries, including the Philippines, Australia, and New Zealand. The People's Republic of China was now viewed as the primary threat in the Asia-Pacific region. It was not surprising that the same strategy would be applied to southeast Asia. Whereas earlier, for instance, American policy had been rather vague toward Indochina, in the wake of the Korean War and after the French defeat by Vietnamese forces in 1954, the United States developed a much more definitive stand, determined to preserve the status quo on the peninsula. That involved the arming and training of South Vietnamese forces against the northern communist regime, steps that inexorably led to U.S. military intervention in the country. The United States also entered into a regional security alliance, the Southeast Asian Treaty Organization (SEATO), corresponding, at least superficially, to NATO.

Elsewhere, Cold War globalism similarly tended to obliterate regional differences and to place all areas of the world in the framework of a unitary, geopolitically defined, strategy. Thus in South Asia, the United States focused on military assistance to Pakistan, choosing this country as its strategic partner against China and the Soviet Union. At the same time, while Washington looked with disfavor upon the Indian government's espousal of neutralism, it did not hesitate to provide New Delhi with arms when India became involved in a border conflict with China (1962), or when it threatened to turn to the Soviet Union for support against Pakistan. It was of fundamental importance to prevent the extension of Soviet or Chinese power to the subcontinent.

Pakistan was also important in the Middle East, as it was linked to Britain, Turkey, Iran, and Iraq in the Central Treaty Organization (CENTO), the Middle Eastern equivalent of NATO. Although the United States was not a member, its Middle Eastern policy, already defined in the context of the Cold War before 1949, became confirmed in the 1950s. Washington intervened in Iran's domestic affairs to help restore the Shah's rule in 1953, as he was considered more pro-Western than the existing government; the United States similarly sought, though unsuccessfully, to prevent the radicalization of some countries in the area such as Egypt and Iraq; and it enunciated a doctrine, the so-called Eisenhower Doctrine (1958), expressing a determination to prevent the spread of Soviet influence in the region even through the dispatching of American forces, if necessary. In the meantime, Washington gave political, economic, and military support to Israel, established in Palestine in 1948, viewing the Jewish state as one constant factor, a key to stability in the region.

Africa, too, became an object of U.S. foreign policy for the first time in the aftermath of the Korean War. The 1950s and 1960s saw the creation of many independent states on the continent. Fears of Soviet infiltration here were much less limited than elsewhere, and there would be few instances of the overt use of force by the United States to preserve the status quo. But Washington, especially in the 1960s, became concerned with domestic instability in African countries that could invite a radical takeover with a pro-Soviet orientation. To prevent such a situation, the administration of John F. Kennedy undertook a strategy of promoting economic development of underdeveloped areas of the world. Buttressed by the economist Walt W. Rostow's theory of "stages of economic development," the policy aimed at combating radical and communist influences in these areas through helping them undertake economic modernization. That would require a massive infusion of foreign, especially American, aid in the form of capital and technology, as well as the launching of such projects as the building of roads and improving the level of education. These were precisely projects that the United States had promoted in the Philippines before the latter gained independence (1946); the Truman administration had initiated a modest project of foreign aid, the so-called Point Four program. It was during the Eisenhower and Kennedy administrations that policies toward the Third World came to be defined as an integral part of the United States' Cold War strategy. Thus in Latin America, too, in the late 1950s and early 1960s, Washington formulated a systematic approach, one that came to be known as the Alliance for Progress, an ambitious program for overcoming poverty and enhancing the standard of living of the American states. If President Kennedy had stayed in power longer than he actually did (1961–1963), this strategy might in time have developed its own momentum, apart from the vicissitudes of the Cold War. President Lyndon B. Johnson (1963–1968), however, tended to view the program in the framework of Cold War geopolitics, and so, throughout most of the 1960s, the Latin American

policy of the United States differed little in essence from the approaches to other parts of the world.

The fact remains that during the 1950s and 1960s the Third World became incorporated into U.S. strategy in the framework of the Cold War. The irony was that the Cold War itself, in the sense of U.S.-Soviet confrontation, became more and more stabilized, while conflicts and tensions in Third World countries created ever newer challenges and difficulties for U.S. foreign policy. It may well be that the nuclear confrontation served to produce what some have called a long peace, that is, the state of military preparedness without an actual war. By the late 1950s, both Washington and Moscow came to recognize that a nuclear war between the superpowers would end up devastating the entire globe. Such realization did not stop them from continuing to build up their respective arsenals, but, starting with the 1963 partial test-ban treaty, the two powers began taking steps to ensure that a nuclear holocaust would not take place. One important by-product of this "balance of terror," which led to a nuclear stalemate and then to a détente, was the stabilization of G-3 affairs. The European powers and Japan were able to concentrate their energies on economic growth, and throughout the decade of the 1960s they achieved spectacular successes in this regard. In Europe a forceful movement for an integrated community developed, whether in terms of what Charles de Gaulle characterized as a Europe "from the Urals to the Atlantic" or of a European economic community. Japan, too, emerged by the end of the decade as a formidable industrial and trading nation. The Cold War, then, by establishing a balance between the two superpowers, brought about the general stability and economic growth of the G-3 nations.

The United States' relations with the Third World were, in contrast, more volatile. The developmental strategy that underlay policies toward Asia, Africa, the Middle East, and Latin America ran into a growing self-consciousness on the part of people in these countries that responded with their "dependency" theories, according to which imperialism and foreign control had created a situation of economic and political dependence on the part of the local elites on the "metropoles" (colonial powers). America's developmental programs did not alter the situation, as they came to be seen in many parts of the Third World as an attempt at perpetuating such dependency relations. The war in Vietnam in many ways symbolized the clash of developmental and dependency theories; whereas the United States saw in the war a genuine attempt at helping South Vietnam's nation-building efforts, the Vietcong and North Vietnamese argued that American policy was only aiding the elites in the south and making the task of establishing a Vietnamese nation that much more difficult. To add further complications, the People's Republic of China defined itself as the spokesman for Third World aspirations, calling on all people in the global "countryside" to rise up against "the cities" dominated not just by the G-3 powers but also by the Soviet Union. Such revolutionary rhetoric did not always appeal to Third World countries, but all the same created profound uncertainties in international relations. Neither America's Cold War strategy nor its developmentalism was adequate to meet the challenge.

TOWARD A NEW ERA, 1969–1993

United States foreign relations in the last quarter-century have entered a new phase. The position and role of the United States as a world power have been redefined in response to two trends that, while by no means new phenomena, have increasingly asserted themselves and affected the shape of the international order: trends toward transnational moves on one hand, and toward subnational (religious, ethnic, individual) diversity on the other. Both these developments have challenged the traditional patterns of international relations which have, since the seventeenth century, been built on the concept of the sovereign national state. In the context of this essay, it may be said that both G-3 and Third World affairs have had to accommodate these new trends, sometimes called postmodern forces, that have emerged in the wake of the Cold War confrontation and of modernization programs to assist underdeveloped countries. It may also be said that, just as American foreign policy appeared to have reached an impasse in the late 1960s in various parts of the world, so the new forces provided the United States with an opportunity to reformulate its global strategies.

The United States made its own contribution to the reformulation of world affairs by taking steps to end its long war in Southeast Asia as well as its ostracization of the People's Republic of China. Both steps amounted to recognizing the failure of a globalist approach to Asia and the acceptance of regional forces and initiatives as part of the international system. As early as 1969, Richard M. Nixon, replacing President Johnson, was determined to end the war in Vietnam by developing an alternative strategy toward Asia. His "Guam Doctrine," announced shortly after he became president, said in effect that henceforth the United States would not involve itself in another costly land war in Asia and that for the security of the region the Asians themselves would shoulder the burden. The United States would still maintain its military presence there, but it would not be the sole police force. This doctrine was followed by secret steps to effect a rapprochement with the People's Republic of China. A complete reversal of the strategy aimed at containing that country, the policy reflected the conclusion on the part of Nixon and Henry Kissinger, his national security adviser, that global stability could better be ensured by accepting, not fighting, China's power in Asia. The new policy toward China meant the United States would no longer consider the latter the enemy to contain in Vietnam and elsewhere in Asia. In other words, the rationale for the Vietnam War was undermined, and it became easier to disengage from the Indochina peninsula. Thus the road that ended in 1975, when the last U.S. troops (embassy guards) left Saigon, went through Beijing.

As U.S.-Chinese relations were undergoing transformation, America's position in the Pacific, in particular its relations with Japan, was also changing. Japan was fast becoming an economic power, emerging as a net trade exporter for the first time since World War II. In 1971 it showed trade surpluses vis-à-vis the United States, and the trend, once set, would not be easily reversed. The two countries began to view each other as trade rivals even as they renewed their security alliance—and the security alliance was becoming more and more an anomaly in a world where familiar Cold War frameworks were rapidly undergoing change and where transnational economic and cultural forces were increasingly asserting themselves.

The global economic transformation became noticeable in the 1970s when the United States lost its hegemonic position in the world economy. This is another way of saying that other countries and other parts of the globe were improving their positions vis-à-vis the United States. At the beginning of the decade, the United States found itself no longer capable of maintaining the postwar global economic order, the Bretton Woods system, which had been based on the predominance of American financial power and economic resources, in particular the strong dollar and its convertibility into gold. Because of increasing balance of payment deficits and inflation—both traceable to Vietnam War expenditures—and because the European and Japanese currencies had in the meantime increased in value, it became impossible to sustain the existing rates of exchange between the dollar and these others. This led to the "Nixon shock" in the summer of 1971, putting an end to dollar convertibility into gold and thus to the Bretton Woods system itself. In a few years, the system of floating exchange rates came to be adopted by the trading nations, and the value of the dollar steadily eroded. American economic power, in other words, could no longer support a globalist strategy, and instead trade competition with its Cold War partners became more and more serious.

Simultaneously with the Nixon shock, there occurred "oil shocks," first in 1973 and then in 1979: curtailment of oil production and steep increases in the price of crude oil produced by the countries belonging to the Organization of Petroleum Exporting Countries. These developments forced the industrial countries to pay much more than they had for energy resources and brought about an abrupt halt to their economic expansion. Some Western economies recorded negative growth rates, which, coupled with double-digit inflation, threatened to undermine the fabric of Western civilization, as an American official remarked. The importance of the oil shocks underscored the growing assertiveness on the part of raw-material producing areas of the Third World in world politics just at a time when the Cold War was losing its centrality. In the Middle East, specifically, the petroleum question necessitated an approach that would ensure a stable supply of petroleum to the United States and its allies, while at the same time upholding the nation's commitment to the independent existence of Israel. That objective was extremely hard to attain, given the hostility existing between Arabs and Israelis, but Washington nevertheless tried to mediate between the two. Henry Kissinger's shuttle diplomacy to bring both sides together, and President Jimmy Carter's successful Camp David accord between Egypt and Israel (1977) were significant if only because they went much beyond the general Cold War strategy in the region.

In Europe, in the meantime, forces for transnationalism could be seen in the further steps being taken toward economic integration, with Britain joining the European Community, and toward the coming together, however tentatively, of NATO and Warsaw Pact countries. The SALT (strategic arms limitation talks) treaties worked out by the Nixon and Carter administrations suggested that for the first time since the war—indeed, for the first time since 1930—the world's great powers were willing to limit their arms. There was even talk of the ending of the Cold War. This proved premature, and it would take

another decade before the East-West division of world affairs would be replaced by the newer concerns of universalism and diversity. Yet signs pointing in this direction were everywhere. The establishment, in 1972, of the CSCE (Conference on Security and Cooperation in Europe) was particularly symbolic, as it brought together the members of NATO and the Warsaw Pact, in other words, all nonneutral European states plus Canada and the United States, to explore the further lessening of tensions. The 1975 meeting of the CSCE in Helsinki adopted a resolution on human rights and religious freedom, something that was more rhetoric than substance then, but a major development all the same. It indicated that the United States, the Soviet Union, and their allies—by implication, indeed, all nations of the world—would now increasingly have to turn their attention to nonmilitary, even noneconomic, questions and consider the implications of the rising demand for freedom and human rights for international affairs. The Third World, for its part, forced itself on the consciousness of the G-3 powers by working, primarily through the United Nations, for a "new economic order," for a better distribution of the world's wealth, and protection of its resources. In the meantime, the Iranian revolution of 1979, resulting in the triumph of Islamic fundamentalism and its assault on Westernization—the seizure of the U.S. embassy in Teheran and the incarceration of its personnel for over a year were among the dramatic examples—demonstrated the challenge of self-conscious religious and ethnic forces to the G-3 powers.

All these trends continued into the 1980s and beyond, creating both cohesiveness and confusion in U.S. foreign affairs. For a while during the first term of President Ronald Reagan (1981–1985), to be sure, it seemed as though the Cold War had returned as the key framework for policy. The Soviet invasion and occupation of Afghanistan, Cuba's support for revolutionary regimes in Angola, Mozambique, and elsewhere, and the coming to power of a leftist Sandinista regime in Nicaragua tended to reintroduce Cold War themes into American foreign affairs. The Reagan administration returned to the rhetoric of the Cold War, castigating the Soviet Union as an "evil empire" seeking world domination.

In the long run, however, these proved to be temporary phenomena, not sufficient to reverse the trend toward redefinition of international affairs. After the mid-1980s, the United States and the Soviet Union effected an amazing series of steps to reconcile themselves, first through strategic arms limitation agreements and then through the encouragement of democratic changes within the Soviet-bloc countries. Between 1988 and 1991, reflecting—to a large extent, initiating—the worldwide movement for democratization (in itself part of the transnational and subnational forces undermining sovereign state authority almost everywhere), one Eastern European country after another repudiated a communist dictatorship for a more open form of government. The Berlin Wall fell, Germany was unified, and the Soviet Union was dissolved. The Cold War truly came to an end, and with it Europe resumed its march toward transnational integration—toward a new Europe that included both Western democracies and the former allies and members of the Soviet Union. Forces were afoot not only further to integrate the former countries, but also to open their markets to the latter. Movements of people from Eastern to Western European countries gained momentum, and through all these phenomena one Europe, however filled with local diversities, was emerging. The United States began dealing with Europe, not, as earlier, in the framework of a struggle for influence in a zero-sum game with the Soviet Union, but in terms of European needs and ambitions as a whole.

In the Middle East, efforts resumed to bring the Arab states and Israel together for a peace conference. The region was no longer a scene of Cold War confrontation, so the United States was in a position to devise a new strategy. One good example of this was its response to the Iraqi invasion of Kuwait in 1990. Earlier, such an event would have been put in the context of the struggle for power with the Soviet bloc or of the Arab-Israeli conflict, but here was one Arab nation attacking another, both rich in petroleum resources. The administration of President George Bush took the matter to the United Nations and succeeded in persuading all the major powers, including the Soviet Union and the People's Republic of China, to declare Iraq an aggressor and impose economic sanctions against it. The United States and its United Nations partners forged a military combination to restore the prewar status quo, and henceforth a United Nations Peace-Keeping Operations (PKO) would become an important aspect of American policy in the Third World. As if to demonstrate that newer forces were affecting even the deep-rooted animosity between Israelis and Arabs, Prime Minister Yitzak Rabin and PLO Chairman Yasir Arafat performed a famous handshake in the presence of President Bill Clinton in Washington in September 1993.

In the meantime, America's ties to Asian countries were also undergoing major redefinition. The 1980s witnessed spectacularly successful economic performances in many parts of Asia. Earlier, only Japan had attained the rank of an economic power, but now such countries as South Korea, Taiwan (whether one viewed it as an independent nation or as a province of China), Hong Kong, and Singapore were registering even faster rates of growth than Japan, and per capita incomes of some of them even exceeded those of European countries such as Greece and Portugal. Soon Indonesia, Thailand, and Malaysia followed in their footsteps, and even mainland China, one of the poorest in the region in terms of per capita income, definitely entered a period of high growth. All these countries adopted an export-oriented strategy, earning income through aggressive trade expansion in North America and Europe. American trade with the Asian and Pacific countries began to exceed that with Europe in 1982. Observers started talking of the coming of the age of the Pacific Basin, or the Pacific Rim, comprising the countries of Asia and the Pacific, including the west coasts of Canada and the United States. Clearly, the latter was compelled to approach the region in a different fashion from the way it had earlier. With the waning of the Cold War, the importance of Asia and the Pacific was more and more economic, with the area's expanding economies providing America not only with goods and markets but also with surplus capital to finance part of its growing fiscal deficits.

In the Western Hemisphere, too, economic growth was no less notable, if less conspicuous. Here, too, Washington shifted its focus from strategic to economic issues and encouraged closer interconnections such as those among the Andean states in South America and among Canada, Mexico, and the United States. The North American Free Trade Agreement, negotiated in the early 1990s, was but one aspect of the global trend toward international cooperation. Of course, traditional, nationalistic forces resisted such a trend, in the Western Hemisphere, Europe, and Asia, no less than in the United States itself. The weakening of the sovereign state in all parts of the world may or may not facilitate the formation of integrated economic communities, but it will be hard to turn the clock back.

Fundamental to the contemporary world are the twin themes of universalism and diversity. Both challenge the traditional powers of the state, and both contribute equally to broadening the scope of international affairs. Religious fundamentalism, not only of Islam but also of Judaism and Catholic and Protestant Christianity; the search for greater freedom, human rights, and democracy; the concern with the protection of the natural environment and the preservation of endangered species; and ethnic self-consciousness—these are the forces that confront the United States, and other nations as well, as they grope for a new international order. The ending of the Cold War has coincided with the emergence of these movements and at once enhanced a sense of shared concerns globally and also threatened international stability. On their surface, these are two diametrically opposite forces, one bringing all peoples together in terms of their common objectives and aspirations, the other pulling them apart through an emphasis on their differences. But they need not be. There is no justification for the fatalism that we must either have universalism or diversity, the traditional international system or a wholly novel world order. The world is likely to have all these things in different proportions for many years and decades to come.

The challenge faced by the United States at such a historic juncture is to do its part to encourage more universalistic forces while at the same time developing a sensitive awareness of human diversity. The question is no longer one of globalism versus regionalism; rather, it is one of universalism *and* particularism, shared values *and* cultural diversity. It remains to be seen whether the United States will undertake the leadership, as it did throughout most of the twentieth century, in defining a new international order built upon this twin commitment.

BIBLIOGRAPHY

For a systematic survey of the history of U.S. foreign relations, the most recent synthesis is the four-volume *Cambridge History of American Foreign Relations* (1993): Bradford Perkins, *The Creation of a Republican Empire;* Walter LaFeber, *The Search for Opportunity;* Akira Iriye, *The Globalizing of America;* and Warren Cohen, *America in the Age of Soviet Power.* To trace some underlying ideologies and assumptions in the evolving patterns of U.S. foreign policy, the most suggestive titles include Felix Gilbert, *To the Farewell Address* (1961); Michael Hogan, *Ideology and American Foreign Policy* (1985); and Alexander DeConde, *Ethnicity and American Foreign Policy* (1992).

To cite a few leading works for each period covered in this essay, Ernest R. May, *American Imperialism* (1968), and Robert Beisner, *Twelve against Empire* (1968) offer penetrating analyses of imperialism and anti-imperialism in the 1890s. For Wilsonianism, consult John Milton Cooper, *The Warrior and the Priest* (1984); and Frederick Calhoun, *Power and Principle* (1988). For the 1920s, see Melvin Leffler, *The Elusive Quest* (1979), and Frank Costigliola, *Awkward Dominion* (1984), both examining in detail U.S.-European economic, political, and cultural relations. The Depression years and the isolationism of the 1930s are treated by such standard works as Robert N. Ferrell, *American Diplomacy and the Great Depression* (1963); Arnold A. Offner, *American Appeasement* (1968); and Manfred Jonas, *Isolationism in America* (1963). For Franklin D. Roosevelt and World War II, see Robert Dallek, *Franklin D. Roosevelt and American Foreign Policy* (1979); and Waldo Heinrichs, *Threshold of War* (1987). Finally, among the numerous works on the Cold War, the best book to start with is John Lewis Gaddis, *The United States and the Origins of the Cold War* (1972). The most up-to-date and succinct summary of the Vietnam War is offered in Gary Hess, *Vietnam and the United States* (1990).

CULTURAL INTERACTIONS

Emily S. Rosenberg

During the early conquest of the New World, a scientist in Europe prophesied that "The New World, which you have conquered, will now conquer you." The United States in the twentieth century, having become the most powerful of the states created in the New World, did indeed launch what many Europeans considered a reverse conquest. What Englishman W. T. Stead in 1901 called the "Americanization of the World," however, came less through armaments, armadas, and mass movements of population than through the exportation of cultural products. In recent years, scholars of American foreign relations, taking cues from social and cultural history, have given increased attention to this history of cultural expansion.

Two themes emerge from this growing body of scholarship. First, mass commercial culture, encompassing both mass-mediated entertainment and mass-consumption lifestyles, provided the most dynamic engine of U.S. expansion. In fact, over the past century, American mass culture came to provide the very definition of what was "modern": assembly-line production for a broad market, consumerism fed by advertising, and media packaging of identity, lifestyle, and taste. *America* came to signify the future, affluence, modernity, and freedom. Such power over meanings and expectations about the future should not be taken lightly; it may be a power more important than the kinds measured in throw-weights or megatons.

Second, throughout the twentieth century, the U.S. government played a significant role in promoting the expansion of cultural industries and activities. Domestic discussions about international cultural exchange have often assumed that, because the United States had a privately owned media, its cultural expansion was divorced from government policy. But the lack of public ownership over media certainly has not meant an absence of governmental involvement. Especially during times of war, the government energetically promoted U.S. cultural and informational enterprises as the advance agents of "freedom."

Analyzing American cultural expansion presents interpretive challenges. Modernization theories of the 1950s simply assumed that America's cultural influence was both "free" and benevolent. Repelled by the state-manipulated informational systems of Hitler's Germany and Stalin's USSR, intellectuals in the early Cold War era claimed that the growth of American-style, privately owned media would promote both democracy and prosperity in countries around the globe. Advocating an international open door for information and culture seemed a nearly uncontestable counterpart to the Cold War goal of advancing freedom and democracy.

During the 1960s and 1970s, more critical scholars challenged modernization theories by adapting the concept of "imperialism" to the cultural realm. Studies of America's "cultural imperialism" tended to link cultural expansion, especially by U.S.-based media, to global exploitation by American capitalism. Scholarship in this tradition raised important questions about the process of international cultural exportation and helped stimulate critical study of a subject that, too long, had been guided by unexamined faiths.

This essay departs from both the modernization and the cultural imperialism paradigms. It neither portrays America's growing cultural dominance as inexorably uplifting nor implies that cultural implantation has destroyed the world's rich cultural diversity and turned everyone into passive recipients of American capitalism. Influenced by poststructuralist theory, this essay assumes that cultural exchanges are contextually negotiated, vary considerably according to time and place, and are marked by both acceptance and resistance. It also suggests that U.S. cultural products have been important purveyors of trends that now ironically seem "international." In the late twentieth century it may be that Americanization and internationalization have actually become blended phenomena, both characterized by the simultaneous globalization and cultural fragmentation associated with postmodernity.

AMERICAN CULTURAL EXPANSION AT THE TURN OF THE CENTURY: MISSIONARIES, REFORMERS, ENTERTAINERS

From the 1880s until World War I, a burgeoning Protestant missionary movement attempted to spread American culture to other parts of the world. Missionaries drew inspiration from evangelical impulses, notions of racial destiny, and new convictions that altering environmental influences could transform degraded and heathen human beings into uplifted Christians. The Student Volunteer Movement of the YMCA, perhaps the most dynamic of the missionary organizations, pledged its members to accomplish the "evangelization of the world in one generation."

The mission movement had an ambiguous relationship to economic imperialism. Missionaries often expressed scorn for the materialistic values of American entrepreneurs operating in foreign lands and criticized practices of imperialist exploitation. Living closer to another culture over a long period, some missionaries and YMCA workers gradually became advocates of grassroots empowerment and anti-imperial resistance. Still, missionaries were also the handmaidens of empire: as converts adopted Americanized Christianity, they often accepted associated cultural tastes and products. Outposts of Americans abroad, for whatever reason, introduced new values and new goods.

The American Protestant lifestyle that missionaries hoped to spread included strong ideas related to gender roles. Women made up a large portion of the American missionary presence abroad (60 percent in China, the largest mission field). Overseas missionary work provided women, particularly single women, with respectable alternatives to the limited career opportunities they found at home. But at the same time that women missionaries often transgressed the boundaries of domestic gender roles by remaining single and working outside the home, they also diligently upheld and spread their own culture's norms about female domesticity. Most turn-of-the-century Americans believed that there were vast natural differences between the sexes and sought to spread what they considered to be a proper, Christian gender order, one that elevated women to positions of respect and gentility while assigning arduous mental or physical labor to men. Mission groups often concentrated attention on women's domestic education and centered their crusades around gender issues—footbinding in China and sati (or suttee, the self-immolation of widows) in India, for example. In a

"proper" gender order, women would be placed in charge of the domestic sphere, facilitating development of moral homes in which male vices were kept in check.

Race, like gender, usually figured significantly in missionary work. For the most part, missionaries were white, and racial difference helped cast the hierarchy of cultural differences into even sharper relief. But when race did not reenforce the boundaries of cultural difference, imperialist governments often got nervous. When a few American churches sent middle-class African Americans as missionaries to Africa in the early twentieth century, whites in Africa became afraid that the missionaries might develop grassroots affections and stir anticolonial unrest. Some complained that the example of African Americans acting as missionary leaders in Africa might upset racial hierarchies and pose a danger to the colonial order. After about 1920, European governments began to exclude African American missionaries from their colonies in Africa.

The fervor associated with American international missionary work declined almost as fast as it had arisen. Even before World War I, enthusiasm waned as conversion rates proved slower and intercultural negotiation more difficult than early recruits had imagined. World War I further disrupted the mission movement, and after the war American congregations affected by the postwar popular backlash against international involvements provided diminished economic support. Ironically, hard times may have strengthened impact in some respects. Declining revenue from home meant that overseas mission efforts really needed a grassroots base to survive. Many seasoned veterans of foreign mission fields in the 1920s developed greater intercultural sophistication and empathy toward those with whom they worked. Improving social conditions increasingly became a more significant goal than conversion; social reform seemed more important to human uplift than formal rituals of salvation. Growing numbers within the mission community began to concentrate on this-worldly service: raising living standards and improving agriculture. But clashes with fundamentalist approaches that emphasized salvation alone remained, and in the 1930s a backlash against social activist missionary work intensified.

In the 1920s and 1930s, broader social reform movements of all kinds, secular as well as religious, spread American values. A wide variety of domestic reform impulses traveled overseas, particularly after the world war. Charles Beard advised the Japanese on urban planning and reform after Tokyo's destruction in the devastating earthquake of 1923. Americans such as Lossing Buck, Pearl Buck's husband, helped establish agricultural schools in China. Rotary clubs, YMCA affiliates, Boy Scouts and other organizations internationalized their memberships. John Dewey attempted to revamp China's educational system. The economist Edwin Kemmerer established American-style reserve banks and currency systems in many countries in Latin America. Samuel Gompers's American Federation of Labor sought to globalize its version of moderate unionism through the Pan American Federation of Labor in the Western Hemisphere and the Alliance for Labor and Democracy in Europe. Jane Addams and Emily Balch expanded prewar global networks of peace activists and established a Woman's International League for Peace and Freedom. Elizabeth Washburn Wright crusaded internationally against narcotics trafficking. Political reformers, particularly in the Caribbean and in Japan, encouraged the spread of American baseball as a presumed bulwark against social instability. Ida B. Wells took her antilynching campaign to Europe to raise international pressure against white oppression

in the United States. The Rockefeller Foundation formed the China Medical Board, its first philanthropic program in China, and followed with establishment of women's colleges in Asia. These individuals, organizations, and campaigns certainly projected no single set of cultural messages or values. But they did represent an associational and organizational style characteristic of Americans, who have often seemed convinced that change directed by them meant improvement.

Despite the impressive number of missionaries and reformers who built international organizations, American influence in the early twentieth century probably spread far faster through new networks of mass entertainment and information. The emerging mass culture, which was binding many Americans together into a national community during this period, extended into the world.

As the student volunteer missionaries worked toward global conversion, Buffalo Bill Cody's Wild West show introduced a variant vision of salvation. Buffalo Bill's elaborate outdoor pageants portrayed "civilization" triumphing over "barbarism" to en-

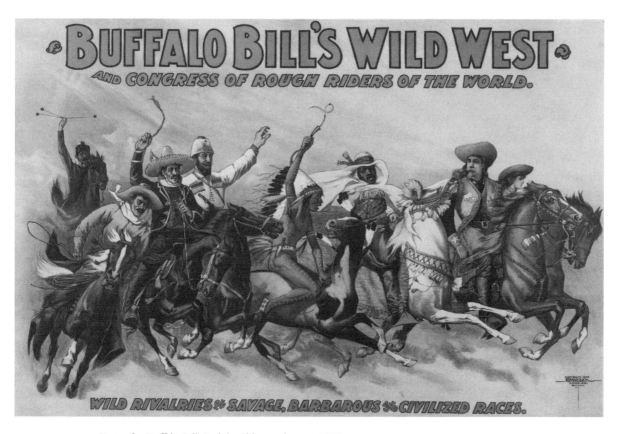

Poster for Buffalo Bill Cody's wild west show, c. 1898. PRINTS AND PHOTOGRAPHS DIVISION, LIBRARY OF CONGRESS

thusiastic crowds all over the globe. The show's pageantry featured jingoistic displays of national power: soldiers defeated Indians in the American West and replayed the Rough Riders' ascension at San Juan Hill. Although the Wild West shows lacked official government sponsorship, presidents and other high officials were often featured viewers.

By World War I the United States had not only built the military, economic, and administrative infrastructure to exercise global power, but Buffalo Bill's popularity foreshadowed an emerging entertainment industry with a semiotic formula of unparalleled global appeal. The carefully crafted shows fused symbols for "America," "freedom," "individualism," and "strength," and dramatized all in struggle against their opposites. The international travels of the Wild West Show skillfully packaged the popular images upon which a string of future American products, from Western B-movies to Marlboro cigarettes to Ronald Reagan, would build later success in foreign markets. The genius of the Wild West shows involved endowing a geographically specific region with symbolic meanings about progress that transcended geography.

WORLD WAR I AND AFTER: GOVERNMENTAL PROMOTION OF CULTURAL EXPANSION

Exportation of mass cultural products predated the Great War, but the national emergency enlarged governmental promotion of America's entertainment and informational industries. The war, and governmental assistance, formed the basis for rapid international expansion of American mass culture in the 1920s.

President Woodrow Wilson appointed George Creel, a journalist and progressive reformer, as head of the Committee on Public Information (CPI), charged with selling the war at home and abroad. Creel did not see these promotional activities as propaganda or manipulation. Rather, he insisted that he was purveying truth, information, and education. Firmly believing in what he termed the Gospel of Americanism, Creel shared Wilson's conviction that the United States had a special mission in the world to promote international harmony and peace, even if the means involved war. Creel did not try to sell the war so much as he tried to sell America as a symbol of progress and of social and industrial fairness.

Undertaking a broad range of activities, the CPI not only censored war reporting but also created and disseminated news. It sponsored distribution of pamphlets, posters, and lecture tours; established in many countries reading rooms that offered U.S. publications and free instruction in the English language; and created a newspaper wire service providing free U.S.-originated news to foreign newspapers, most of which had previously been served by the large European wire services. U.S. news stories and cultural products, for the first time, reached Latin America and Asia on a regular basis. As the war ended, American newspaper syndicates took advantage of wartime gains in international news markets to consolidate their positions. The Associated Press (AP), which until the mid-1920s maintained cartel agreements with the large European services, finally broke away and established direct, independent ties to newspapers around the world. During the 1920s both United Press (UP) and the Associated Press rapidly enrolled subscribers.

Creel appreciated the persuasive power of the printed word, but his true genius lay in marshaling moving images to serve the national cause. America's motion pictures were already fairly popular exports. Developed in the United States by an immigrant-influenced film industry for a largely immigrant audience, Hollywood's films of the silent era easily crossed boundaries of language and culture. Pamphlets, Creel realized, required both translation by authors and literacy by readers; films required neither. Moreover, audiences suspicious of overtly political messages took more readily to "entertainment," or at least tolerated political films when they played along with entertainment features. The CPI thus created a Division of Films to display America's virtues.

Wartime trade controls enacted by Congress put muscle behind Creel's film program. The CPI denied export licenses to American films that it considered insufficiently celebratory; it blacklisted foreign movie houses that screened German film products; and it insisted that CPI-made "educational" films be shown along with Hollywood's more entertaining products. The CPI also encouraged development of film distribution networks in countries where motion pictures had not yet been introduced. A representative of the CPI's Division of Films commented, "It may be true to say that the Government has gone into partnership with the moving-picture industry."

Governmental promotion, of course, was not solely responsible for the breakthrough in markets for American movies. During the war, competition tilted decidedly in America's favor. The film industries of Britain, France, and Germany collapsed under the pressures of financially strapped governments, shortages of material such as film, and disruption of export trade. Creel, meanwhile, made sure that Hollywood producers received allotments of carefully controlled nitrate, a scarce component vital to both the film and munitions industries. Moreover, the technical and stylistic innovations of American filmmakers attracted audiences. Unlike their European counterparts, American films owed more to the streetwise influences of vaudeville and the lavish extravaganzas of nineteenth-century popular pageants (including Wild West shows) than to elite art and culture. With or without governmental assistance, Hollywood had laid the basis for a global entertainment empire.

D. W. Griffith's epics, *Birth of a Nation* and *Intolerance,* were the singularly most important films in breaking the hold of the European film industry in Latin American and other markets. Affected by the smashing popularity of these films, many theaters broke London's block-booking system and began negotiating directly with representatives from U.S. film companies. Under the prewar system, all American films had to be booked into foreign markets through London agents; during the war, Hollywood pushed toward a system of direct distribution. As the United States captured the key film markets of Australia and South America, the chances that the European film industry could revive itself after the war by tapping international profits became dimmer and dimmer.

Why was *Birth of a Nation* (1915), a film structured by themes of race and gender, so popular among foreign audiences? Domestically, its popularity suggested widespread acceptance of the idea that race, like gender, constituted an immutable line of distinction, marking not just physical features but capacity for intelligence, rational thought, self-control, self-reliance, and governance. The film may have touched a similar nerve in other multiracial societies as well; it clearly built on types of racial coding (civilization versus barbarism) that had become prominent in the writings of many Latin American intellectuals of the period and was also a standard formula in the Wild West show's popular global spectacles.

Still, scholars have given little attention to assessing the popularity or the impacts of this and other American films in multiracial countries, particularly in the Western Hemisphere. Among what classes and groups did films receive acclaim and upon what grounds? How did Hollywood's unique styles and lavish production techniques interact with the discursive traditions in the films to reenforce their popularity? Response theory, difficult but not impossible to apply historically, could illuminate much about cultural interactions between societies with different systems of race and class. But these kinds of questions about the 1920s have not yet been addressed by scholars.

Whatever the reasons for their popularity, American film exports boomed throughout the 1920s and came to dominate world markets: American films constituted 95 percent of those shown in Britain and Canada, 70 percent of those in France, 80 percent of those in South America. Even the advent of talkies, which many people had predicted would bring the death of film exports, had little effect. After a short period of experimentation, subtitles and dubbing began to work satisfactorily, adding little additional production cost.

Governmental assistance for the American film industry continued, even after the Creel committee was disbanded. In 1926 Will Hays, head of the Motion Picture Producers and Distributors Association and a former Republican politician, successfully lobbied Congress to create a Motion Picture Section in the Bureau of Foreign and Domestic Commerce that would survey world markets and promote American film exports. The government was especially active in attempting to counteract nationalistic backlashes against the avalanche of Hollywood films. Hays and the U.S. Department of State argued that unregulated trade in films, by eroding nationalistic barriers, would promote international peace. But foreign governments with small film industries saw such liberal rhetoric as a formula for entrenching Hollywood's already substantial monopoly.

A Film Europe movement coalesced in a congress in Paris sponsored by the League of Nations in 1926. Organizers of the congress invited U.S. participation, but Hollywood and representatives of Hays's office refused to attend and charged the gathering with being anti–American. The film congress passed strictures against film portrayals of militarism and racism, thinly veiled critiques of American film fare. Meanwhile, some European governments, acting individually, attempted to enact quotas and other means of protecting their undercapitalized film industries from competition. Pressure from the U.S. State Department and evasive action by the powerful American film industry, however, were fairly successful in blocking or dodging protectionist barriers. Outside of Europe, underdevelopment made nationalistic resistance even more difficult. Restrictions advocated by the Film Europe movement and individual governments never succeeded in seriously rolling back Hollywood's onslaught.

In the interwar period, audiences around the

world avoided low-budget European products and flocked to American films, with their lavish sets and narrative styles. And to ambitious international directors and stars, it often seemed better to join Hollywood than to fight it. Hollywood became the mecca of the international film industry. Many German directors and artists, such as Fritz Lang and Marlene Dietrich, left Berlin for Hollywood during the 1920s and the Nazi-dominated 1930s.

Like the motion picture industry, America's radio industry also received a jump-start from government during World War I and then expanded during the 1920s. Before World War I, Britain dominated international cable lines, the chief form of international communications, and could easily invade the confidentiality of both commercial and strategic cables originating in the United States. For the U.S. government, promoting a new network of point-to-point wireless communications became a priority. During the war, the government nationalized the radio industry, rapidly enlarged its capacities, and worked with business leaders to forge a global communications network. When broadcasting (as distinguished from point-to-point transmissions) of radio messages emerged as a major medium of entertainment and information after the war, American technology was in the forefront.

The United States government did not go as far in radio promotion as some people wanted. The secretary of the Navy and others advocated retaining radio as a government-owned monopoly, but advocates of a British-style, nationally owned broadcasting system did not prevail in the United States. The industry was privatized after the war when a new company, Radio Corporation of America (RCA), was created by Owen Young of General Electric at President Wilson's personal urging.

Although during the 1920s some critics still bemoaned the lack of a concerted national policy to push radio networks faster in directions private companies could not afford to go, RCA continued its role as a chosen instrument of American policy and rapidly extended its global empire. By 1930, American broadcasters reached steadily into Latin America and developed markets in Africa and along the Pacific rim. Radio manufacturers also experienced booming sales, especially in the Western Hemisphere. In 1924 the Bureau of Foreign and Domestic Commerce instituted a regular series of reports on potential markets for the radio industry. And underscoring America's leadership over radio issues, Washington sponsored a major international radio conference during the 1920s to draw up regulatory rules.

Exports of information, film, and radio were part of a much broader outflow of products associated with American mass culture. American specialty products in the post–World War I era—electrical goods, automobiles, oil—were strong carriers of cultural values. America's giant electrical companies, for example, sold the hardware for the growth of radio broadcasting, made illumination more widespread, and pushed home consumer items such as refrigerators. The American automobile, oil, and rubber industries all reenforced each other in promoting internationally a car culture that was also developing at home. And modern advertising, given a boost by the example of Creel's wartime success in salesmanship and by new studies on the psychology of selling, introduced these lifestyle-transforming products to international markets in more compelling ways than ever before. In Brazil in the mid-1930s, for example, 64 percent of all advertising space in major media was purchased by North American exporters. The export wave of American products in the post–World War I era began to create in the world what Daniel Boorstin described at home as new "communities of consumption"—affinities created not by place or productive activity but by shared consumer tastes.

International ads for American-made cars, appliances, and a host of other consumer marvels set up what semioticians have called "codes"—that is, new discourses established by the relationships between images, in which (as in language) some things stand for other things. Through the international marketing of U.S. consumer products, America itself became a code for modernity and consumer lifestyles. Increasingly losing its geographical specificity, it came to signal affluence, consumerism, middle-class status, individual freedom for both men and women, and technological progress. American chain stores, pioneers in mass retailing, reinforced such codes. Woolworth, A&P and Safeway grocers, and Montgomery Ward opened stores worldwide in the 1920s; Coca-Cola expanded its global bottling operations. Two of America's dominant cultural symbols of the period were the skyscraper and Charles Lindbergh, the international hero of the first solo flight across the Atlantic. In their own ways, both helped associate America with the harnessing of technology that set the standards for what was "modern."

Films also helped project America as the future and the future as America. American movies were quasi-advertisements themselves. In fact, one of Will Hays's major arguments advocating governmental promotion of the film industry was that Hollywood stimulated demand for American products. Hays

Charles Lindbergh and *The Spirit of Saint Louis*. PRINTS AND PHOTOGRAPHS DIVISION, LIBRARY OF CONGRESS

and consumer products in various ways, one cultural export boomed without official encouragement: jazz. Jazz was one of the most controversial of cultural exports. Evolving from African American rhythms, jazz music and dance projected a sensuality that alarmed many middle-class, white Americans. The custodians of culture, who would have liked America represented abroad by "high" art and literature, hardly considered it an asset to America's international image. America's greatest jazz dancer of the interwar period, Josephine Baker, received little attention in her own country. But jazz enthralled audiences in Paris, Berlin, and elsewhere. In France, Baker became a sensation and eventually even received an award from the French government for her work in the Resistance movement during World War II. In Germany in the 1930s, a large youth counterculture grew up around "Swing Clubs." In the Soviet Union, the tremendous popularity of jazz, despite official disapproval, produced a great debate

liked to quote a Department of Commerce report claiming that each foot of film sent abroad generated one dollar of export revenue.

American tourists and intellectuals of the 1920s (even those who often denounced America for its materialism) also spread consumer values. The age of mass tourism was just dawning. By the late 1920s, many middle-class Americans could afford foreign travel. Numbers of tourists to Europe—the favored destination—rose from 15,000 in 1912 to more than a quarter of a million in 1929. American intellectuals also had a growing impact, especially in Europe. The American writers and artists who migrated to Paris in the interwar period contributed to what Jean-Paul Sartre described as France's greatest literary experience. American Studies developed respectability, as the Sorbonne, inspired by the World War I alliance between France and the United States, became the first European university to establish a permanent teaching position in American Civilization (in 1917). Universities in England, Germany, Austria, the Soviet Union, and elsewhere also instituted American Studies.

Although the U.S. government promoted the expansion of American newspapers, movies, radio,

Josephine Baker. Photograph by Carl Van Vechten. PRINTS AND PHOTOGRAPHS DIVISION, LIBRARY OF CONGRESS

over whether jazz (or which kinds of jazz) constituted "proletarian" music or bourgeois decadence. To those in the European jazz scene in the 1920s, not only was jazz the best thing in American culture, it *was* American culture. As at home, however, jazz alarmed cultural conservatives. In Europe, disputes over jazz, like those over Hollywood films, showed that American cultural products generated resistance as well as acceptance.

The American cultural invasion of the interwar years brought a backlash of cultural nationalism. Influential, sensational books in many countries around the world assailed the rising cultural power of the United States. Adolf Halfeld's *Amerika und der Amerikanismus* (1927) fueled anti-Americanism in Germany; W. T. Colyer's *Americanism: A World Menace* (1922) was published in London; Manuel Ugarte, an Argentine who became a cultural adviser to the Mexican government during the 1920s, published *Destiny of a Continent* (1923), probably the most widely read of the interwar Yankeephobic works in Latin America. Critiques such as these leveled an array of charges, from German disgruntlement at a country that would enforce a constitutional ban against beer drinking to broader jabs against America's alleged crass materialism, soulless individualism, and worship of technology. A board of concerned British citizens, including the novelist Thomas Hardy, warned that the tasteless melodramatics of American films imperiled the Empire by portraying whites as fools who worshiped money and fashion and had no stable home life.

French intellectuals during the 1920s were especially critical. Many charged that America's mass culture, with its prominent role for advertising, standardized the individual in order to standardize and sell commodities. They portrayed American movies, usually designated as the most pernicious purveyor of mass values, as escapist pastimes for the ignorant and illiterate. In attacking mechanization, puritanism, and materialism, French intellectuals' critiques paralleled those of many American writers, some of whom were actually émigrés in Paris during the same period. In France during the 1920s there were more references to Sinclair Lewis's *Babbitt* than to any other American book.

The discourses of anti-Americanism that accumulated as American cultural influence grew, however, need to be treated cautiously. In the countries of Europe, and also of Asia and Latin America, the "meaning" of America came to be encoded within cultural and political debates that often had little to do with the United States itself. The European avant-garde, for example, greeted American jazz and some consumer goods as democratic impulses that could help sweep away class pretensions in a new Europe. (Many of the most fervent admirers of America, however, had never visited the country; and many others did not like it when they did.) Similarly, anti-Americanism created a foil against which presumed national virtues or characteristics could be reinforced and applauded. Anti-American critics stressed U.S. crime and violence (frequently mentioning Al Capone), materialism, and licentiousness to argue for cultural preservation at home.

Establishing oppositional categories was one way of employing a rhetoric of nationalism in the defense of European cultural elites. The French writer André Siegried's statement that "there exists a European spirit of which the American spirit is often the perfect antithesis" expresses more about the author's attempt to formulate his version of "a European spirit" than it does about America. Those who favored state-owned, public broadcasting in Britain, for example, strengthened their own arguments for political support by consistently portraying American broadcasting (and America itself) as an antithesis, rather than just a variant, of British patterns. The BBC played up an identification of Britain with public service/high cultural standards/public uplift by associating the U.S. broadcasting system with private interest/economic profit/degradation of public tastes and education. America became the dangerous Other against which cultural conservatives and antimodernists could promote their own programs.

The economic depression of the 1930s fueled even greater cultural, along with economic, nationalism. The National Socialists in Germany, of course, carried the cultural critique against America the farthest, intensifying the long-smoldering German backlash associated with stab-in-the-back theories of the previous war. The Third Reich, charging that Hollywood was dominated by Jews, completely banned American films in August of 1940 and attacked jazz, dominated by African American and also Jewish artists, as degenerate art that was inappropriate for the Aryan master race. As Benny Goodman performed in Carnegie Hall in 1938, marking jazz's greater acceptance by America's cultural elite, Hitler banned his records. Gradually the ban tightened to cover all American music.

In Japan a similar upsurge of cultural protectionism developed. The Japanese government instituted restrictions on American movie imports in 1937. The Japanese news agency broke its cooperative ties with the AP and moved aggressively to drive the

American news service out of Japan and to expand its own independent network in China.

In Latin America, defenses of national culture and distrust of U.S. influence emerged within the context of U.S. imperialism and gunboat diplomacy. Throughout the 1920s many Latin Americans complained that U.S. movies tended to portray Latin Americans, especially Mexicans and Central Americans, as traitors and cowards. The Mexican government, during the nationalistic, anti-Yankee revolutionary period from 1910 to 1920, banned films that portrayed Mexicans in a derogatory fashion. Under such pressure, Hollywood's producers became a little more mindful of offensive stereotypes. In mid-1927 the Mexican government again embargoed offensive films. During the 1930s, as cultural nationalism deepened everywhere, the Mexican government began to build its own domestic film industry that, by the mid-1940s, had captured the majority share of the Mexican market and also cut substantially into U.S.-dominated film markets in other Latin American countries.

WORLD WAR II AND THE POSTWAR CULTURAL OFFENSIVE

If economic hard times and cultural nationalism during the 1930s challenged American expansiveness, World War II brought new and unparalleled opportunities for extending U.S. influence. New wartime propaganda agencies, the presence of U.S. army troops around the globe, the Americanization associated with postwar occupations, postwar aid and informational programs, and the anticommunist cultural offensive launched in the early 1950s all helped the United States attain preeminent cultural, as well as military, power in the post–World War II era.

The cultural offensive began well before America's entry into the war. In 1939 President Franklin Roosevelt asked Nelson Rockefeller to head a new agency to counter Nazi influence in Latin America. This agency, the Office of Inter-American Affairs (OIAA), developed technical assistance programs and emphasized the extension of mass communications—film, radio, and newspaper wire services. Elaborating the "good neighbor" theme, the OIAA produced Spanish-language newsreels and documentaries and also made effective use of entertainment film. Walt Disney Studios, for example, created *Saludos Amigos,* a feature-length cartoon using Disney's famous characters in Latin American settings, as a contribution to good neighborliness. The OIAA's radio division broadcast twenty-four hours a day to Latin America by 1941, compared to twelve hours a week in 1939. The OIAA supplied newspaper clients throughout the hemisphere with news and photos.

The OIAA's activities set a pattern for the Office of War Information (OWI), established after the United States entered the war. At first Roosevelt had resisted creation of a propaganda office, arguing that dissemination of "truth" by an Office of Facts and Figures would be enough. In the spring of 1942, however, the President ordered creation of the OWI to centralize and better coordinate the promulgation of war aims and news of the war's progress. The OWI worked with *Collier's* magazine to publish a slick magazine called *Victory,* established twenty-eight information libraries abroad, and distributed cheap "overseas editions" of American books. American broadcasters had only limited international transmission capabilities before the war; in 1942 the government leased all shortwave facilities, rapidly added a network of new transmitters, established Voice of America for its worldwide broadcasts, and developed around-the-clock programming in more than forty languages.

The OWI's Bureau of Motion Pictures developed a generally cooperative relationship with Hollywood's movie moguls. Even before December 1941, Hollywood's products reflected a highly interventionist stance. But after the United States declared war, messages of support for the war, together with brutal portrayals of Germans and Japanese, became even more overt. The OWI helped shape Hollywood's products, exercising prior review over Hollywood scripts and refusing export licenses to films with "negative" portrayals of American life—gangsters, slums, Okies, labor discontent. Moreover, the OWI actively assisted filmmakers in North African and European war zones, providing army commissions to some one hundred Hollywood artists and directors. The government hired Frank Capra, producer of such smash hits as *Mr. Deeds Comes to Town* and *Mr. Smith Goes to Washington,* to produce a series explaining the purposes of the war. The resulting *Why We Fight* series used harrowing footage from the enemy's own propaganda films interspersed with nostalgic homefront images. Cartoons, as well as feature films and documentaries, rallied people to war: Warner Brothers' Looney Tunes brought audiences titles such as "Plan Daffy," "Draftee Daffy," and "Bugs Bunny Nips the Nips."

Americans dispatched around the globe in armed fighting units were perhaps as important as the OWI in spreading American cultural influence. American GIs carried fashions and tastes: chewing gum, blue jeans, T-shirts, cigarettes made from U.S. tobacco. The Armed Forces Network beamed American popular music, especially jazz. Coca-Cola bottling plants, financed by the government, advanced along with American troops to supply the army's needs. (Coke's advertising manager left to take a key post in graphic design at the OWI.) In even more direct cultural legacies, 90,000 German American children were born in the American zone of occupied Germany during the year after the war; there were 70,000 marriages between Americans and Englishwomen. In areas where U.S. troops were stationed long after the war, of course, the influence of GIs was the most intense and long lasting.

In postwar zones of occupation in Germany and Austria, U.S. government agencies developed an extensive cultural offensive. Informational bureaucracies, promising to instill democracy while wiping out legacies of fascism and militarism, undertook nothing less than the "reeducation" of the whole society. Information officers financed the translation and publication of American fiction and nonfiction books and made them available through new information centers called America Houses. They reorganized and financed major newspapers and radio stations, updating and professionalizing operations to correspond more to American practices. Newspapers began to employ more commercial advertising, and journalism became more independent from specific political parties. Newspapers and radio both eventually shed their American-directed image by employing nationals of the country itself, but U.S. officials long maintained ultimate control over these media. Occupation officials also shaped programs of educational reform, fearing that political conservatives identified with the old fascist orders might lead an antidemocratic backlash. Reaching the children took on special urgency because of the very literal "generation gap" in defeated countries, where so many fathers had been killed in war. The number of classes offering instruction in English language and American Studies expanded greatly; revised curricula emphasized the teaching of democracy.

In Japan, General Douglas MacArthur, who directed the American occupation, thoroughly revamped the governing structure, personally overseeing the drafting of a new Japanese constitution that had democratization and antimilitarism as its basic principles. As elsewhere, Americans reformed educational systems, brought citizenship rights to women, helped reconfigure economic institutions, and, while ensuring greater rights for organized labor, clamped down on labor radicalism, especially after 1947.

Broad controls over the Japanese press shaped the kinds of news allowed in postwar Japan; American censors, for example, limited information about the effects of the atomic bombing, apparently for fear of accentuating dislike of the United States.

Americans also exercised tight control over the Japanese film industry. Censors prohibited themes that might encourage militarism, nationalism, antiforeign sentiment, degradation of women, or suicide. Explicit guidelines for films promoted sexual expression, women's rights, the new constitution, and baseball. Kissing, never before seen in Japanese film, was encouraged on screen as a way of fostering displays of public emotion and thereby supposedly discouraging the kind of duplicity that American officials held responsible for the attack on Pearl Harbor. One Japanese film director recalled that democratizing Japan was based on three S's: "screen, sports, sex."

Gradually, anticommunism, rather than antifascism, emerged as the central goal of informational policy in occupation governments. By the late 1940s, America Houses began distributing anticommunist brochures and screening their libraries for allegedly "un-American" content. As the United States organized a new "cultural offensive" against communism, the activities of occupation agencies became directed from Washington rather than shaped within particular occupied countries. Older occupation officials often resented the new heavy-handed approach, believing that a hard sell of America's virtues, with no self-criticism allowed, actually backfired as a strategy for selling America as a land of diversity and tolerance. But informational officials in Washington were understandably worried about congressional outrage if taxpayers' money funded criticism of the United States. Germany, Austria, and Japan increasingly became staging bases for informational campaigns targeted at fomenting discontent within the Soviet and Chinese blocs.

The global anticommunist cultural offensive of the 1950s arose together with the economic, political, and military mobilization recommended in the important 1950 National Security Council document NSC-68. Immediately after World War II, the OWI had been disbanded and the State Department, settling into peacetime, emphasized "cultural" rather than "informational" (i.e., propaganda) initiatives. Congress provided direct funding for educational exchanges under the Smith-Mundt Act of 1948, which created the Fulbright program. As Soviet-American antagonism grew, however, those advocating more aggressive promotion of Americanism attacked expenditures for slow, elite-based cultural exchanges.

In 1950 President Truman, responding to the recommendations of NSC-68 and to the Korean War, initiated a "Campaign of Truth." The State Department consequently revived the wartime techniques of the OWI. The new initiative expanded Fulbright exchanges but also laid the foundations for more targeted propaganda by placing information offices, libraries, and mass media products in countries around the world. Nearly 300 centers were established by the late 1950s, offering English and stressing the value of American-style democracy, labor unions, and technological accomplishments.

One creation of the Campaign of Truth was the Congress for Cultural Freedom (CCF). The CCF, secretly funded by the CIA and formed to counter various international "peace conferences" sponsored by the Soviet Union, held conferences of noncommunist intellectuals and artists. The first met in Berlin in 1950. In the late 1950s the CCF also began courting intellectuals from the Third World, and it convened in New Delhi and Rio de Janeiro in the early 1960s. In 1967, however, revelations about CIA funding embarrassed many of CCF's members, and the organization dissolved. There was heavy irony about an organization that gathered together to denounce state manipulation of culture—at CIA expense.

Another initiative involved promotion of a "democratic" international labor movement to counter the influence of the socialist-leaning World Federation of Trade Unions (WFTU) and the Latin American Confederation of Labor (CTAL). The American Federation of Labor (AFL) built on its World War I collaboration with the Wilson administration and its work with government information agencies during World War II to organize and finance "free" (i.e., nongovernmentally linked) labor unions. Working with the CIA, after its creation in 1947, the AFL was especially active in Latin America, where in 1948 its major organizer formed a new regional union to counter CTAL, and in Italy, where the AFL supported noncommunist unions and tried to sway workers away from voting for the communist party in the 1948 election. The CIO, America's more radical labor union, also split with the WFTU in 1949, took a sharp turn toward demonstrating its fervent anticommunism, and joined in supporting the AFL's international efforts in the 1950s.

Architects of the Campaign of Truth saw radio as the most promising anticommunist tool because it could easily cross borders. The funding and mission of the Voice of America (VOA) greatly expanded from 1950 on, as more and more transmitters and watts successfully parried the Soviet Union's attempts to jam the airwaves. VOA developed broadcasts in almost every language in the world, including twenty of the languages spoken in the Soviet Union.

Meanwhile, the European Recovery Program (ERP or the Marshall Plan) provided an excellent opportunity for the anticommunist propaganda effort. ERP agencies used "counterpart funds" to convince Europeans that an alliance with the United States would dramatically improve living standards and usher in a mass consumption lifestyle. Displays of life in America featured personal automobiles and electrically powered kitchen appliances and washers. Paul Hoffman, the ERP administrator, wrote that Italians learned from the ERP's informational program that the United States "is the land of full shelves and bulging shops, made possible by high productivity and good wages, and that its prosperity may be emulated elsewhere by those who will work towards it." The ERP helped shape the mass production processes at Fiat, making automobiles a central feature of Italy's postwar modernization. What the historian Charles Maier has called the "politics of productivity"—the promise that consumer abundance and high wages would wipe away the current deprivation and physical destruction in Europe—constituted the most powerful cultural weapon in the Cold War. Marshall Plan Freedom Trains carried the slogan "Prosperity Makes You Free."

This selling of abundance worked on another level as well. Because the ERP was one of the major purchasers of advertising time and space, European media developed an enhanced reliance on U.S. advertising firms, public-opinion polling companies, and revenues related to both. Moreover, Marshall Plan funds helped revamp many European businesses, which then developed U.S.-style commercials and pushed for advertiser-sponsored media systems—the kind that U.S. officials called "free" media because they were tied to business, not government, funding.

The new activism in informational diplomacy gathered even greater momentum during the Korean War. President Dwight Eisenhower, taking an aggressive stand, decided to institutionalize the Campaign of Truth in a new agency, the United States Information Agency (USIA), formed in 1953. The USIA built on the earlier informational policies of the OWI, the occupation governments, and the Campaign of Truth to design its programs. It undertook the dissemination of American books, art, music, and films. It instituted and expanded programs to encourage educational exchange, American Studies curricula, educational reform, magazine publication, lectures, and exhibitions. USIA news services devised ways of getting American-slanted news into local newspapers and magazines under the by-lines of local journalists. In Brazil, for example, articles such as "Watch Out for Spies" or "100 Things You Should Know about Communism" were written by the U.S. Press Section Chief but appeared as front page news without attribution. In view of such practices, it was ironic that official U.S. policy denounced government-originated news and publicly championed the cause of "free flow." The idea that news generated by governments was harmful applied, apparently, only to other governments. Meanwhile, U.S. officials also encouraged the aggressive market expansion undertaken by U.S. press agencies, AP and UP, on the grounds that their domination of markets would also promote press freedom.

USIA officials similarly designed radio and television programming to appeal to mass audiences and appear to be domestically produced. For example, a popular news program in Brazil, secretly written and controlled entirely by the U.S. embassy's radio editor, was carried by three-fourths of all Brazilian stations and elevated its Brazilian announcer to the status of a media celebrity.

The USIA book distribution program helped make the United States the global leader in book markets. During the 1950s U.S. book exports increased almost tenfold. Large new audiences became acquainted with prewar novelists such as William Faulkner and Ernest Hemingway, probably America's most influential writers, and also with newer authors such as Norman Mailer. Charges by McCarthyite anticommunists that the USIA was promoting communist propaganda by allowing "un-American" works, however, substantially shaped the book program's offerings. A few months after it came into existence, the USIA instituted a policy of removing books that could be construed as critical of the United States and those by authors with leftist affiliations. At the end of the war, the U.S. Army had distributed in Europe millions of copies of Stephen Vincent Benet's *America* to promote "reeducation"; in the 1950s, Benet's same ode to democratic diversity and free expression appeared on the list of dangerous authors banned from American informational centers abroad.

Despite the growing international reputations of some American authors, however, attempts to promote American "high culture" met with only selective success. Neither Europe's cultural elite nor popular audiences applauded American playwrights and composers. American Studies courses became more common in universities in the postwar period, and in 1954 the European Association for American Studies was formed. But informational agencies quickly realized that avant-garde and popular culture were America's best weapons in the cultural cold war.

In the 1920s, one of America's most attractive cultural exports had been jazz, and the propaganda officials of the 1950s understood its value. In 1954 the Voice of America hired Willis Conover, whose "Music USA" program would run for thirty-eight years and build a larger audience than any other internationally broadcast program. The Voice of America brilliantly turned Conover's once-controversial insight that "jazz is America's classical music" to political purpose. Conover became a legend, especially in communist-bloc countries where his program provided musicians an exciting, if politically dangerous, link to American musical trends. In 1967, after jazz had become "respectable" almost everywhere in the world, the VOA instituted a program of rock and soul music, again appealing to youthful dissenters in communist societies. Jazz and then rock became the music of "freedom."

The American cultural offensive also incorporated another previously controversial trend: abstract expressionist painting. Shortly after the war, government sponsorship of a controversial exhibition of America's new modernist art was denounced by both Congress and the White House as degenerate, possibly communist-inspired. In the late 1940s, however, New York's art establishment elevated abstract expressionism into the exemplification of free, individualistic expression, hence the antithesis of socialist-realist art. Abstract expressionism suggested rebellion from artistic canons and a challenge to the conformity of modern life, but it also rejected left-wing social commentary and "people's art" that had been popular in the 1930s and championed in the Soviet Union. Museums could safely invest in an art with politically obscure meanings that could be celebrated as freedom. In the early 1950s, the CIA's supervisor of cultural activities and former head of the Museum of Modern Art, Thomas Braden, turned abstract expression into an overt weapon of the cultural cold war. Exhibitions toured the world, promoting New York as the successor to Paris, the center of the world's art scene and avant-garde culture. Abstract expressionism became not only an icon of "freedom" but, as the historian Serge Guilbaut suggests, "the avant-garde wedge used to pierce the European suspicion that Americans were only capable of producing kitsch."

The postwar cultural offensive, of course, also

involved film. Although Americans had dominated international film markets from the 1920s, Hollywood's international profits were relatively small and therefore had little effect on overall production decisions. After World War II, however, motion picture moguls warned that their industry's survival would depend on open access to international markets, and they lobbied extensively for governmental assistance in resisting international trends toward cultural protectionism. The Motion Picture Export Association (MPEA), a cartel representing the American film industry, formed in 1945. In the red-baiting climate of the 1950s, major film studios extended the wartime practice of screening each film for content that might be objectionable to either the U.S. government or a friendly foreign nation. Industry leaders such as Ronald Reagan and Walt Disney regularly reported to the FBI concerning left-wing activity in Hollywood. In return for this self-regulation and demonstrated anticommunism, the American government used its economic and political muscle on behalf of "free flow" for the film trade.

In the postwar period, the U.S. government maneuvered to beat back foreign restrictions designed to protect national film industries from Hollywood's dominance. European governments wanted protection not only for cultural but also economic reasons. They stressed that the backlog of Hollywood films flooding their markets sapped hard currency that was desperately needed for postwar reconstruction. When Britain instituted a 75 percent customs duty on imported films in 1947, the MPEA began a boycott, and negotiations over film markets ensued. In 1948, film agreements with Britain, France, and Italy were reached: France and Italy maintained a weak quota system and remittance of profits to the United States was generally prohibited. But these measures only made American film companies hire more of their production work overseas, thus accelerating the globalization of Hollywood's control. The West German government also requested film import quotas, but the MPEA successfully argued that it was illogical for the U.S. government to fund Voice of America and then accede to restrictions on private communications media. Hollywood retained market dominance in West Germany, and the German film industry remained weak for decades. (Unable to come to settlements with Spain and Denmark, the MPEA sustained a lengthy boycott of these countries, ironically damaging their long-range market position in an attempt to secure it.)

Mexico had built the leading film industry in Latin America, helped by the strong cultural and economic nationalism of Mexican governments during the 1930s and 1940s and also by U.S. "good neighbor" assistance during the war. In the postwar era, however, Hollywood and the U.S. government threatened to retaliate with quotas on Mexican access to the U.S. Spanish-speaking market if Mexico enforced protectionist measures against Hollywood films. Needing the U.S. market to ensure profitability, the once strong and nationalistic Mexican film industry bowed to "free flow" principles and had to accept Hollywood's growing dominance over both Mexican and other Latin American markets.

The various international film agreements of the late 1940s and early 1950s, though not always everything Hollywood desired, certainly strengthened the global position of the U.S. industry. American movies retained hegemony over international markets not just because of their popularity but also because of savvy political maneuvering. The American government made satisfactory settlements of issues over film markets a condition of desperately needed economic agreements. Marshall Plan aid, for example, leveraged advantageous treatment for American films. MPEA persuasively argued that it made no sense to devote Marshall Plan funds to propagandizing American values and then allow restrictions to keep out the most successful anticommunist propaganda of all—Hollywood movies. Hollywood's usefulness in combating communism was especially evident before the critical 1948 elections in Italy. The largest distributors of U.S. films carefully programmed their offerings so that pro-United States propaganda films and documentaries played in tandem with the most popular entertainment films.

During the 1960s, even mildly protectionist film quotas were generally eliminated in Europe, and Hollywood solidified its control over production and distribution worldwide. The MPEA then worked to cultivate new markets: the association was especially concerned, for example, that nations gaining independence in Africa should embrace open access rather than erecting protectionist barriers or establishing state control over film industries.

Nearly all European countries developed another form of resistance to the postwar Hollywood invasion: public-sector assistance for their struggling film industries in the form of loans, credits, prizes, and subsidies. Fostering national film industries became important in the state-building programs of many non-European nations as well, particularly Japan, Brazil, and India. As production became more global and cooperative, however, the specific nationality of a film became less easy to identify. Many films with heavy U.S. participation through international subsidiaries or dummy companies ironically proved able to attract state-sponsored financing. Even these statist policies, then, hardly weakened Hollywood's international position.

Historians have tended to focus on nuclear shields, alliance systems, and joint military maneuvers as the substance of "free world" alignments during the Cold War. The strength of these political/military arrangements, however, emerged within the context of another mighty force: the semiotic power that equated America with an inevitable and desirable future that was "modern." Just as anticommunism helped reinforce symbolic associations between "freedom" and American cultural products, the semiotics of America's consumer-driven, mass-mediated products also helped bind the anticommunist coalition together. Policy and business elites of the postwar era clearly understood that a "cultural offensive" powerfully served larger geopolitical and economic interests.

THE AMERICAN CENTURY AND INTERNATIONAL BACKLASH

Creation of a permanent peacetime propaganda apparatus to spread American culture marked a significant departure for U.S. policy, but America's cultural influence abroad did not come solely from governmental design. America's mass culture seemed to have almost boundless appeal, especially to youth. Although USIA officials sometimes complained about movies that portrayed Americans as gangsters, racists, foolish millionaires, and corrupt materialists, Hollywood's America packed box offices and fed the fascination with American life. Like movies, privately sponsored radio programs, such as *Hit Parade* and *The Jack Benny Show*, attracted audiences and won friends. U.S. television networks, fearing saturation in domestic markets, aggressively invested in foreign stations and arranged syndication. By 1962, television revenues from syndication overseas came to equal those from domestic sales. Comic strips similarly became popular abroad, so disturbing the cultural elite in Germany and Austria that, as in the United States during the 1950s, a control committee was established to watch for deleterious influences.

As in the 1920s, U.S. consumer products continued to be successful missionaries for the American Way. American-style self-service grocery stores, chain-store retailing, and installment buying developed in Europe as well as in parts of Latin America and Asia in the 1950s. America's mass-marketed mag- azines, especially Henry Luce's *Life,* fed the identification between America and consumer abundance, between "freedom" and purchasing power. *Life's* 1946 feature entitled "Dreams of 1946," for example, pictured a dishwasher, radio, power lawnmower, and other household technologies. Magazines featured women with leisure time provided by electric kitchens and new prepackaged foods. Glamorous housewives with the time to dote on their husbands became another icon for "freedom" during the Cold War.

Supermarkets and department stores around the globe became monuments to the "American Century" that Henry Luce of the Time-Life magazine empire had proclaimed in 1941. So did large, modernist-style American hotel chains. West Berlin, the symbolic outpost of freedom in the Cold War, featured both. The huge Kaufthaus des Westes boasted the greatest array of consumer items imaginable. In 1958 a bevy of American celebrities flew in to help open the new Berlin Hilton. In 1950, the founder of the Hilton chain commented that "no new nation has got it going until it has a seat in the United Nations, a national airline, and a Hilton Hotel." American tourism surged under the influence of a strong dollar that made nearly everywhere in the world seem a bargain to middle-class Americans.

Postwar Americanization, of course, was no simplistic process by which a dominant economic power arm-twisted or deceived poorer nations into accepting its cultural products. Responses to the American century's cultural side ranged from eager acceptance to adaptation to many forms of resistance.

Some people eagerly embraced American models. Around the world, commentators remarked about the special appeal of American culture to youth. If older generations had seen Britain or France as preeminent cultural centers, the generation born during World War II increasingly looked to the United States. The lingua franca of this global youth culture emanated from the United States in words such as "bar," "DJ," "rock 'n' roll," "sex appeal," "teenager," "be-bop," "glamour girls," "minibar."

Even when Americanization seemed most blatant, however, it almost always had a syncretic twist. Historian Alan Milward has emphasized that the Marshall Plan's impetus and money may have come from the United States but its result was to strengthen the apparatus of individual European nation-states. This state-building had cultural consequences by enhancing governmental support for national traditions: active national arts boards in Britain and France dwarfed American state support for cultural activities.

Although the BBC made some concessions to the American model of broadcasting after the war, for example, public broadcasting in Britain survived for decades as the special custodian of British culture. ERP monies helped establish Fiat, but the company's tiny, inexpensive cars served Italy and in no way resembled their huge and powerful American counterparts. As David Ellwood writes in *Rebuilding Europe,* "Every European society and social group constructed its own filtering mechanisms for taking what it wanted from the American model and rejecting the rest."

Brazilian television provided another example of adaptation rather than implantation. Television in Brazil during the 1950s and under the military government after 1964 initially developed as a reflection of the North American model, stressing advertiser-based funding, mass (rather than elite) appeal, and American-style programming formats. But TV Globo's programs were nevertheless locally produced and distinctively Brazilian. The network refined the *telenovela* into such a popular format that U.S. shows, so prevalent in many other TV markets, became peripheral and were used largely as filler. Thus, many

postwar policies designed to spread American cultural influence actually contributed simultaneously both to American cultural expansion and to the kinds of distinctive national hybrids that could resist it.

Overt resistance to Americanization also grew dialectically along with American influence. The conservative British magazine the *Economist* in 1944 complained about the ways in which American journalistic competitors wrapped competitive strategies in high-minded principle: "Democracy does not necessarily mean making the whole world safe for the AP," grumbled an editorial. Francis Williams's *The American Invasion,* published in London in 1961, warned of the danger of Europe becoming a "bastard imitation" of American society, which he charged with being label-driven and consuming to gross excess. Williams especially targeted for criticism suburban houses, credit buying, advertising, and teenage culture.

In France the idea again surfaced that American and French cultures were antithetical, a proposition upon which intellectuals from both the Left and the Right could agree, though for different reasons. Claude Julien, for example, decried the control over

Opening of EuroDisney, 1992. ARCHIVE PHOTOS/IMAPRESS

America by a monied oligarchy who showed little concern for the general well-being of common people. Street riots in France in 1949 greeted the introduction of Coca-Cola; the opening of EuroDisney outside of Paris in 1992 prompted massive labor strikes and cultural opposition. When McDonald's in 1992 inadvertently used the picture of France's most famous chef, Paul Bocuse, in an ad without realizing who he was, French outrage soared nearly to the level of an international incident.

In Latin America, dependency theorists and popular folk-oriented movements combined to develop intellectual critiques and grassroots resistance against Americanization. Armand Mattelart and Ariel Dorfman's *How to Read Donald Duck* (1975) charged Disney and other forms of American commercial culture with "cultural imperialism" that assisted the spread of North American, capitalist economic dominance. Jamaican reggae turned resistance against American cultural influence into a popular art. In many new nations in Africa and Asia, state ownership of mass media predominated, partly due to the colonial influence of British and French statist patterns and partly in order to foster cohesive national policies that could resist the western media's cultural intrusions.

The fear that U.S. "cultural imperialism" would facilitate its political and economic domination became even more widespread during and after the generally unpopular Vietnam War. In the 1970s, the global dominance of the American media and the formation of a "nonaligned movement" in Cold War politics prompted some international politicians to try to redefine "free flow" as having to do with the balance of information sources rather than simply with private ownership. Urho Kekkonen, the president of Finland, for example, noted in a 1973 speech that the global flow of information is "one-way, unbalanced traffic, and in no way possesses the depth and range which the principles of freedom of speech require."

The new technology of space-based communication satellites increased fears of imbalance. The U.S. government's National Aeronautics and Space Administration (NASA), after all, spent more per year on research and development than some nations produced in their entire GNP. The capacity to develop and maintain satellite systems, in addition to the need to allocate frequencies and spaces in orbit, raised the prospect that only a few major countries might control systems. Satellite technology seemed another giant step toward the economic and cultural subordination of have-not nations.

An organized backlash against American cultural power began to develop during the 1970s within the United Nations Economic and Social Council (UNESCO). In its early years, U.S. dominance in the UN had led UNESCO to endorse private media ownership and unrestricted access, America's definition of "free" media and "free flow." But in the late 1970s, after the influx of new African states into the UN, UNESCO began to refocus attention on the issue of balance, examining the interrelated problems of both who owned media companies and what was being represented within the content of news and entertainment. UNESCO proposed a "New World Information Order" that would help developing nations break the monopolization of information by giant Western media companies.

Most of the critical analysis associated with the UNESCO proposals emerged within the discourse of "cultural imperialism," a theoretical framework of growing popularity during the 1970s and 1980s. Some proposals suggested licensing journalists and putting overt restrictions on the entry of cultural products.

Reminiscent of interwar resistance movements against American motion pictures, however, these efforts were similarly unsuccessful. U.S. government and media representatives invoked traditional arguments equating "freedom" with unregulated, private marketplaces and dismissed concerns over U.S. monopolization as being simply unenlightened, selfserving, or communist-inspired. The United States continued to advocate both deregulation and privatization, moves that would presumably strengthen the position of U.S. media conglomerates even further. President Reagan took a more direct approach than simple argumentation: he withdrew U.S. funding from UNESCO, weakening both the organization and its demands.

Paralleling the movement on behalf of a new world information order, controversies also emerged over assigning radio frequency bands and space positions for satellite systems. Some Third World countries argued that the international associations in charge of allocation should reserve some space for the future use of currently underdeveloped nations. Otherwise, they warned, radio and satellite-based systems would lock the present high-tech powers into their dominant positions far into the future.

In addition to concerns over balance in the present and future informational order, another complicated backlash against American cultural power emerged. Controversies over CIA sponsorship of cultural activities developed, initially centering around a Kennedy-era program, Project Camelot. The Kennedy administration, alarmed by Fidel Castro's regime in Cuba and its apparent sponsorship of revolutionary movements in Latin America, began funding "counterinsurgency" programs designed to prevent revolution. In 1964 the Department of the Army sponsored Project Camelot, which was to be a multimillion dollar study of insurgent behavior developed by scholars at American University and headed by the chair of the Sociology-Anthropology Department at Brooklyn College. The goal of the project was to "wage peacefare"—that is, to study how revolutionary grievances developed in Latin America and to recommend policies to head off insurgent movements. As anthropologists paid by the project began to do extensive field work in Chile, however, the Chilean press disclosed their governmental backing and political purposes. The revelations grew into a major international incident because secret work for government agencies seemed to compromise the ideal of independent scholarship. Augmenting the controversy over compromised professionalism, the former head of the American Anthropology Association also reported that CIA agents often used scholarly credentials as their "cover." With these revelations, suspicions rose about the independence of all American scholars abroad and, indeed, about the purposes of cultural exchange generally. How could countries know when scholarship was only a veneer for spying and imperial manipulation?

The uproar over Project Camelot preceded new revelations of connections between the CIA and supposedly independent cultural entities. The CIA, it now came out, had secretly funded the Congress for Cultural Freedom and had covertly subsidized the publication of many books supportive of U.S. Cold War policy. As in the case of Project Camelot, this funding was often unknown to participants or beneficiaries and undermined their scholarly credibility. Worse still, American academics and intellectuals found that American private organizations and research were suspect in many parts of the world: who could tell which people, organizations, and projects were, in fact, CIA covers?

Doors to cultural exchange, which had been so assiduously opened to provide Cold War advantages, began to close. The critics who had warned of the dangers of heavy-handed cultural manipulation seemed vindicated. In the late 1960s and early 1970s, several countries expelled Peace Corps volunteers, technical advisers, and others because of the backlash against such revelations. The irony was that, in many instances, CIA support for anticommunist intellectuals had probably been unnecessary. After the Congress

Peace Corps volunteer Loral Patchen working with local campesinos in Honduras, 1992. Photograph by Sandee Radtke. COURTESY THE PEACE CORPS.

for Cultural Freedom was disbanded, for example, the Ford Foundation changed the group's name and picked up its funding for a time.

The backlash against American "cultural imperialism" seemed to peak in the 1970s and early 1980s. Resistance to American power, however, often had a twist. Just as young protestors in the United States used rock 'n' roll songs as their protest anthems, so did youth abroad. Crowds who might one day throw stones at U.S. embassies might, the next day, gather to listen to American rock music. The worldwide student unrest of 1968 seemed interwoven in a kind of global youth culture, often with origins in the United States itself. Ironically, even when America's international policies failed to bring goodwill, its popular culture often gained converts for the future.

Rock music in the Soviet Union, like jazz of an earlier era, became the music of dissent and of free expression. In the late 1960s, accompanying a general crackdown on dissent, Soviet authorities began to restrict jazz and banned rock altogether, thereby helping to create an underground youth culture devoted to both. Rock groups sprang up throughout the Soviet Union, often punctuating their protest by composing their lyrics in English. Shadowy rock entrepreneurs staged Woodstock-like festivals, and an underground market for Western recordings spread. Through rock, Western popular culture came to an entire generation of Soviet youth who would increasingly demand more and more access to Western lifestyles.

In China, similarly, Americanization became linked to youthful protests. In the mid-1980s the Chinese government began a program to attract tourist money by developing historical sites, golf courses, theme parks, and resorts. In 1984 the luxurious Zhongshan Hot Springs Golf Club opened in Guangdong province, featuring a golf course designed by Arnold Palmer. As more recreation facilities spread, attracting foreigners who displayed Western concepts of leisure time, new segments of Chinese society became affected—particularly the young. Along with displays of leisure came fashion. New designs in clothing and shoes, Chinese disco, and a burgeoning presence of advertisements by international companies showed the new influence of westernized, consumer-oriented tastes. These trends also accompanied outspokenness against Chinese officials and dissatisfaction with the structure of China's political economy.

The westernization that was cautiously encouraged by the government early in the decade took an abrupt and brutal turn with the government's massacre of student protesters in Tiananmen Square in 1989, but cultural change continued to spread. The popularity of rock music, kept out of China until the mid-1980s, continued to grow, and Chinese rock stars emerged in the major cities. Thousands of Chinese youth jammed rock concerts while traditional Beijing opera played to half-full houses. Though not enthusiastic about the westernized youth culture, the Chinese government nevertheless removed its most conservative cultural ministers in the early 1990s, gesturing toward a cultural "open door." American exporters, noting the double-digit growth of China's economy, enthusiastically embroidered century-old dreams of a fabled China market and introduced more and more American products. The largest McDonald's in the world opened in Shanghai in the early 1990s; huge billboards sprang up advertising Mastercard.

Not everywhere, of course, was Western popular culture embraced as liberating. Under westernizing regimes in the Islamic world, such as Shah Reza Pahlevi's in Iran, dissenters often focused on the evils of Western mass culture in order to call for a return to Islamic fundamentalism. In 1979, when Iran's shah was overthrown by Islamic fundamentalist clergy, the action took the form of a cultural as well as political revolution. Women, who under the westernized regime had forsaken the veil, were obliged or chose to put it on again. The new politicians proclaimed rock music and Hollywood movies as agents of the "Great Satan"—the United States. Islamic fundamentalist movements that gained strength in various parts of the world throughout the 1980s identified U.S.-style mass culture not with an inevitable and desirable future but with a past marked by Western colonialist domination.

Resistance to U.S. "cultural imperialism," which waxed so strong in the late sixties, seventies, and early eighties, seemed to atrophy somewhat in the late 1980s. The United States scored two major victories for its cultural policies: the decline of state-owned broadcasting systems in Western Europe and the fall of communist governments in the Soviet Union and Eastern Europe. Both were part of a larger trend, championed by President Ronald Reagan in the 1980s, toward "privatization" of government-run enterprises—the fulfillment of America's postwar "free flow" agenda.

In Europe before the mid-1970s, radio broadcasting and television in most countries were public monopolies financed by licensing fees and regulated by governing boards to provide the quality and balance that were presumed to be in the public good. In the 1970s, however, European nations began a general trend toward economic privatization, a rollback of the doctrine of state ownership over key industries, which had dominated Europe's political economy since World War II. As part of this trend, Italy and France began to allow private companies to compete with state-owned systems, and new radio and television stations proliferated. In the mid-1980s, West Germany and England also began adding new commercial stations. The advent of new technologies such as cable television and direct-broadcast satellite systems fueled the trend toward privatization. Because financially strapped governments wished to avoid the expense of going into satellite broadcasting, the new space-based technologies enlarged the private sector of the communications industry and eroded the government-directed component.

Outside of Europe, privatization also became the dominant trend. By the late 1980s, financial pressures emanating from large government debts and the budgetary stringency enforced by the International Monetary Fund helped reverse the trend toward media nationalism that had been so evident in the 1970s. State-directed communications networks fell into general disfavor. In a sign of the times, Kenya and Mexico, two countries with strong traditions of state-sponsored, nationalist communications systems, privatized their television networks.

Privatization, proliferation of channels, the advent of VCRs, and greater competition in the communications industry all benefited American television producers. U.S. production companies churned out the greatest volume of material at the lowest cost because their huge domestic market conferred economies of scale. As growing numbers of new channels sought inexpensive ways to fill air time and still attract audiences, they turned to U.S. producers. During the 1980s, the amount of American television programming shown internationally increased exponentially. And Hollywood also benefited. In just the two years from 1986 to 1988, for example, total spending on American feature films for foreign television grew by nearly two-thirds. Some discussion within the European Economic Community of placing restrictive quotas on U.S.-produced television material floundered on definitions and on ideological differences. International trends toward what French minister of culture Jack Lang called "wall-to-wall 'Dallas'" continued apace.

The domino-like fall of communist governments in Eastern Europe during 1989 and 1990 opened even more opportunities for U.S. cultural expansion. As Pepsi developed ads that associated their cola with images of the crumbling Berlin Wall, McDonald's gloated over the taste that Eastern Europeans were developing for American cuisine. Billboards in Prague carried the message "I am a billboard, I sell your products." *Playboy,* in a full-page ad in the *New York Times* (15 December 1989) proclaimed itself to be in the forefront of "EXPORTING THE AMERICAN DREAM."

> On November 29th, Hungarians came one step closer to something they've been fighting for since 1956. Freedom. Not just political freedom but freedom of the press. And the first American consumer magazine published in Hungarian was PLAYBOY. No surprise, since we're the magazine that led a social revolution in America by standing for personal, political, and economic freedom. That's the power of PLAYBOY.

Playboy's ad summed up the central article of faith of American cultural expansion: American products =

American lifestyle = freedom. It also exemplified the ever-ambiguous gender messages often encoded in American products. The new freedom to buy Barbie dolls, reportedly one of the most coveted purchases among young girls in Eastern Europe, suggested how American marketers skillfully create and package a consumer audience by the same process through which they then fulfill its demand. Some Western feminists doubted whether the reconstruction of women's images by primarily male Western designers and advertisers clearly advanced personal "freedom" for women, but the semiotics of gender and "modernity" could surely not be captured within any single formulation.

The dramatic fall of both cultural and economic barriers in the late 1980s and early 1990s seemed to confirm the major characteristics of American cultural expansion throughout the twentieth century. First, mass, commercial culture was central to America's overseas expansion and came to cement an identification between America and notions of progress. America, the country, reaped national advantage from its semiotic associations. Second, overt governmental involvement in cultural expansion grew as policymakers increasingly saw their mass-consumer-based culture as a vehicle to serve larger geopolitical interests. Cultural influence existed within, not in a different realm from, national interest.

Although victory in the Cold War seemed to advance America's global reach, however, trends in mass culture during the 1980s and 1990s also began to point toward a new epoch, away from the nation-state and into an era characterized by both transnationality and subnationality. A growing number of scholars have noted an emerging and unstable set of arrangements called postmodernity—a decentered condition in which "Americanization" and "internationalization" are probably becoming indistinguishable.

AMERICAN CULTURAL EXPANSION IN A POSTMODERN AGE: GLOBALIZATION AND FRAGMENTATION IN THE LATE TWENTIETH CENTURY

In the late twentieth century, international flows of finance, information, and entertainment—managed by computers, digitalized information networks, and satellites—are rendering national boundaries less important. Whereas major media industries in the past were clearly anchored within the nation-state system, the information revolution that will extend into the twenty-first century transcends state boundaries.

Theorists of postmodernity suggest that media revolutions transform social situations, producing a culture of multiplicity and a collapse of unifying, totalizing discourses. Under the influence of the explosion in computer and media images, floating signifiers proliferate, less attached to specific representations than before. Culture becomes fragmented and de-centered; communities and selves need to be continually reconstituted. From the level of individual psyches to the level of nation-states, culture is not stable in this new world.

As new modes of information simultaneously globalize and fragment identities and cultures, distinctions between "American" and "international" cultures blur and become less important. Marshall Blonsky's *American Mythologies* explores the notion that "America" is simply a metonym, the name for technical modernity—a process that accelerated faster in North America because of the lack of deep-seated, resistant traditions. "Americanization" stands for a way of living that both erases and then reconstitutes pasts and distinctive cultures with astonishing speed. Indeed, America was the perfect place from which postmodern society could emanate. United States culture was never a melting pot of shared pasts or shared traditions. It was a quilt of disparate patches stitched (sometimes barely so) together, each representing a reconstitutive process of group self-identification and expression. The film industry had clear immigrant origins; jazz and rock had African American roots; exiles from European fascism contributed much of the World War II–era scientific and critical thought. Just as the United States tried to Americanize the world, it must also be stressed that a variety of world cultures had always provided America with its special characteristics. The United States, the first thoroughly mass-mediated and globalized society, pioneered postmodernity.

During the 1980s and 1990s, the rapid blurring and blending of national cultures became increasingly evident. A scare-cover on *Newsweek* magazine on 9 October 1989 warned "JAPAN INVADES HOLLYWOOD" and depicted the familiar female logo of Columbia Pictures as a Japanese woman. The picture fit (in reverse) the familiar mode of concern with "cultural imperialism," suggesting that foreign ownership of cultural industries was a threat to national power. But despite what the image suggested, it emblemized no simple tale of nation-state rivalry, of U.S. decline and Japanese rise. Japanese conglomerates acquired American entertainment companies not to alter or obliterate their cultural messages but to cash in on them. Japanese bicycle makers were unsuccess-

ful selling in Europe until they shaped their advertising campaign around an image of the bicycle as horse in the American West. Ironically, Japanese businesses continue to "export America" as a semiotic structure.

As advertisers look for themes that will sell throughout Europe, and as European nations lurch toward the kind of economic unity once envisioned by the American architects of the Marshall Plan, American cultural references grow increasingly useful as common currency. Whereas nationalistic resentments might rise against German programs or advertising references in Italy or against British ones in France, U.S. programs and references raise fewer problems for international marketers. The French television commentator Christine Ockrent wrote that "The only truly pan-European culture is the American culture." In a similar vein, French Minister of Culture Lang stirred controversy in 1992 by allowing rock 'n' roll and other cultural trends once imported from America to be subsidized by the French government's arts grants. In the ensuing ferocious political debate over what was truly French, Lang, a socialist critic of Americanization, took the position that rock music was no longer country-specific but simply "culture" in an international sense. As cultural production becomes more and more internationalized, nation-state policies become increasingly problematic in their ability to control or regulate.

The very consumer-oriented specialty commodities upon which America built both economic and cultural power in the 1920s now comprise the sectors that best exemplify the new transnational, globalized economy and culture: automobiles, electrical appliances, food processing. During the 1980s, most giant American manufacturing firms substantially cut jobs in the United States and added to their labor forces abroad. Ford now builds a "world car" from parts manufactured and assembled on four continents. Even America's signature specialty product, the Hollywood film, is now a globalized phenomenon.

The so-called "global film" developed during the 1980s and 1990s. Production companies, with nearly half of their profits coming from international markets, increasingly make decisions based on the potential of global appeal. Films with clever, hard-to-translate language or culturally specific themes have hard going compared to barely-verbal action films. Mayhem and carnage, after all, do not need subtitles. Like the old Wild West shows, such films probably have special appeal because of the flexibility of their meanings and discursive structures. One study, for example, reports that Dominican audiences viewing *Robocop* and *Platoon* cheered at opposite times from those that the filmmakers said they intended. Another shows how Tongans interpreted *Rambo,* through their own cultural experience, to be a fighter against imperialism.

Not only has Hollywood been shaped increasingly by the buying power of international markets, but its companies no longer automatically equate with "American owned." In 1990 half of Hollywood's eight largest movie companies were in foreign hands: Columbia and MCA-Universal owned by Japanese conglomerates; MGM (United Artists) in receivership with Credit Lyonnais, the giant French bank, and losing (in 1993) one million dollars a day; Twentieth Century Fox held by the Australian newspaper tycoon Rupert Murdoch. Globalized production, distribution, and even ownership have all contributed to shaping new types of films whose meanings cross cultural and national boundaries.

Throughout much of the twentieth century, Americans exported, often with significant assistance from government, a distinctive mass culture that identified America with the future and served the country's geopolitical interests. As technologies of information and entertainment have spread in the late twentieth century, however, cultural interactions are less and less amenable to an analytical frame focused on the nation state. In this postmodern era, marked by simultaneous globalization and fragmentation, Americanization and internationalization increasingly overlap, and sites of cultural interaction multiply with less and less relationship to national boundaries. One might paraphrase the older prophecy that opened this essay and direct it to the United States itself: "The world, which you have conquered, will now conquer you."

SEE ALSO Nontraditional Religions (volume IV); The National-Security State (in this volume).

BIBLIOGRAPHY

On the missionary movement of the turn of the century and after, see William Hutchison, *Errand to the World: American Protestant Thought and Foreign Missions* (1987); Jane Hunter, *The Gospel of Gentility* (1984); Sylvia Jacobs, "Give a Thought to Africa: Black Women Missionaries in Southern Africa," in Nupur Chaudhuri and Margaret Strobel, eds., *Western Women and Imperialism: Complicity and Resistance* (1992), pp. 207–230.

An excellent book on gender and cultural expansion in the late nineteenth century is Ian Tyrrell, *Woman's World/Woman's Empire: The Women's Christian Temperance Union in International Perspective* (1991).

The standard work on the Wilson administration's propaganda efforts during World War I is Stephen Vaughn, *Holding Fast the Inner Lines: Democracy, Nationalism, and the Committee on Public Information* (1980).

Works that broadly synthesize trends in the interwar period include Frank Costigliola, *Awkward Dominion: American Political, Economic, and Cultural Relations with Europe, 1919–1933* (1984); and Emily S. Rosenberg, *Spreading the American Dream: American Economic and Cultural Expansion, 1890–1945* (1982).

On specific cultural trends during the 1920s and 1930s, see Merle Curti, *American Philanthropy Abroad* (1963); Barry Kennan, *The Dewey Experiment in China: Educational Reform and Political Power in the Early Republic* (1977); Phyllis Rose, *Jazz Cleopatra: Josephine Baker in Her Time* (1989); Alan M. Klein, *Sugarball: The American Game, the Dominican Dream* (1991); Helen Delpar, *The Enormous Vogue of Things Mexican: Cultural Relations between the United States and Mexico, 1921–1935* (1992); Sigmund Skard, *The American Myth and the European Mind: American Studies in Europe, 1776–1960* (1961); S. Frederick Starr, *Red and Hot: The Fate of Jazz in the Soviet Union, 1917–1980* (1983); Randall E. Stross, *The Stubborn Earth: American Agriculturalists on Chinese Soil, 1898–1937* (1986).

Kristin Thompson, *Exporting Entertainment: America in the World Film Market, 1907–34* (1985), is the best book on global film markets before World War II; Ian Jarvie, *Hollywood's Overseas Campaign: The North Atlantic Movie Trade, 1920–1950* (1992), is also a fine book and extends the treatment into World War II and the early Cold War. More specialized, regional studies include Gaizka S. De Usabel, *The High Noon of American Films in Latin America*

(1982); Peter Morris, *Embattled Shadows: A History of Canadian Cinema, 1895–1939* (1978).

The expansion of radio in the 1920s and 1930s is covered in Fred Fejes, *Imperialism, Media, and the Good Neighbor: New Deal Foreign Policy and United States Shortwave Broadcasting to Latin America* (1986); James Schwoch, *The American Radio Industry and its Latin American Activities, 1900–1939* (1990); and Valeria Camporesi, " 'We Talk a Different Language': The Impact of U.S. Broadcasting in Britain, 1922–1927," in *Historical Journal of Film, Radio and Television* 10 (1990): 257–274.

Works treating issues of Americanization in U.S.-French relations, both before and after World War II, include David Strauss, *Menace in the West: The Rise of French Anti-Americanism in Modern Times* (1978); Richard Kuisel, *Seducing the French: The Dilemma of Americanization* (1993); Jacques Portes, *Une fascination réticente: Les États-Unis dans l'opinion française* (1990).

On the impact of American soldiers in Britain during World War II, see Juliet Gardiner, *"Over Here": The GIs in Wartime Britain* (1992); and Norman Longmate, *The GIs: The Americans in Britain, 1942–1945* (1975).

For informational policies during the period of World War II and the early Cold War, see Alan M. Winkler, *The Politics of Propaganda: The Office of War Information, 1942–1945* (1978); and Frank Ninkovich, *The Diplomacy of Ideas: U.S. Foreign Policy and Cultural Relations, 1938–1950* (1981). On film, see Clayton R. Koppes and Gregory D. Black, *Hollywood Goes to War: How Politics, Profits, and Propaganda Shaped World War II Movies* (1987); and Richard Shale, *Donald Duck Joins Up: The Walt Disney Studio during World War II* (1982). On radio, see Holly Cowan Shulman, *The Voice of America: Propaganda and Democracy, 1941–1945* (1990).

The acceleration of the cultural offensive during the Cold War is examined in several books. On the press, specifically, see Margaret Blanchard, *Exporting the First Amendment: The Press-Government Crusade of 1945–1952* (1985). On a variety of other aspects of the offensive, see Robert E. Elder, *The Information Machine: The United States Information Agency and American Foreign Policy* (1968); Lawrence C. Soley, *Radio Warfare: OSS and CIA Subversive Propaganda* (1987); Peter Coleman, *The Liberal Conspiracy: The Congress for Cultural Freedom and the Struggle for the Mind of Postwar Europe* (1989); James F. Tent, *The Free University of Berlin: A Political History* (1988); Hans Tuch, *Communicating with the World: U.S. Public Diplomacy Overseas* (1990); Serge Guilbaut, *How New York Stole the Idea of Modern Art: Abstract Expressionism,*

Freedom, and the Cold War, Arthur Goldhammer, translator, (1983); Thomas Guback, *The International Film Industry: Western Europe and America since 1945* (1989).

On the relationship between labor and Cold War cultural expansion, see Ronald Radosh, *American Labor and United States Foreign Policy* (1969); and Ronald Filippelli, *American Labor and Postwar Italy, 1943–1953: A Study of Cold War Politics* (1989).

Many excellent studies examine the impact of American Cold War cultural policies on specific areas of the world. See, for example, Gerald K. Haines, *The Americanization of Brazil: A Study of U.S. Cold War Diplomacy in the Third World* (1989); David Ellwood, *Rebuilding Europe: Western Europe, America and Postwar Reconstruction* (1992); Nicholas Prosnay and Keith Wilson, ed., *The Political Re-Education of Germany and Her Allies after World War II* (1985); Hermann Glaser, *The Rubble Years: The Cultural Roots of Postwar Germany* (1986); Ralph Willett, *The Americanization of Germany, 1945–49* (1989); Reinhold Wagnleitner, *Coca-Colonisation und Kälter Krieg: Die Kulturmission der USA in Österreich nach dem Zweiten Weltkrieg* (1991). On France, see citations given above. On Asia, see Akira Iriye, *China and Japan in the Global Setting* (1992); Akira Iriye and Warren I. Cohen, eds., *The United States and Japan in the Postwar World* (1989); Kyoko Hirano, *Mr. Smith Goes to Tokyo under the American Occupation, 1945–1952* (1992); and Orville Schell, *Discos and Democracy: China in the Throes of Reform* (1988).

Resistance to American cultural expansion is expressed in works such as Francis Williams, *The American Invasion* (1962); Ariel Dorfman and Armand Mattelart, *How to Read Donald Duck: Imperialist Ideology in the Disney Comic* (1975); and Ariel Dorfman, *The Empire's Old Clothes: What the Lone Ranger, Babar, and Other Innocent Heroes Do to Our Minds* (1983). For discussions of the UNESCO debate and other issues related to North/South communications, see George Gerbner et al., eds., *The Global Media Debate: Its Rise, Fall, and Renewal* (1993); Kaarle Nordenstreng, *The Mass Media Declaration of Unesco* (1984); and Geoffrey Reeves, *Communications and the 'Third World'* (1993).

Recent trends relating to deregulation are covered in Edward Buscombe, "Coca-Cola Satellites? Hollywood and the Deregulation of European Television," in Tino Balio, ed., *Hollywood in the Age of Television* (1990).

John Tomlinson's *Cultural Imperialism* (1991) provides a fine introduction to the theoretical issues and literature on recent global cultural interconnections.

A few works that develop specific interpretive perspectives are Herbert I. Schiller, *Communication and Cultural Domination* (1976); Jeremy Tunstall, *The Media Are American: Anglo-American Media in the World* (1977); Jean Baudrillard, *Selected Writings,* Mark Poster, ed. (1988); Douglas Kellner, *Jean Baudrillard: From Marxism to Postmodernism and Beyond* (1989); Marshall Blonsky, *American Mythologies* (1992); Dean MacCannell, *The Tourist: A New Theory of the Leisure Class* (1989); Mark Poster, *The Mode of Information: Poststructuralism and Social Context* (1990). Christine Gailey's "Rambo in Tonga: Video Film and Cultural Resistance in Tonga," in *Culture* 9 (1990): 20–33, provides one example of "resistant readings."

AMERICA AND THE WORLD ECONOMY

Jeffry A. Frieden

The United States, like all countries, is part of a world economy fraught with danger and rich in potential. Foreign competition can drive wages down, force factories to close, push companies out of business. Foreign markets and investments can create jobs, raise incomes, and boost profits. The contradiction between the attractions of international markets and the threat of international competition is central to most debates over international economic policy. In the United States, this contradiction has often given rise to bitter battles. Americans who have little direct or indirect contact with the world economy are indifferent to it, and therefore want to see political energies put into domestic policy; those with links to world trade and payments are passionate about its significance for our own economy.

The characteristics of supporters and opponents of greater integration of the United States into the world economy have changed over the centuries. Those drawn toward overseas markets, sources of supply or capital, or investment opportunities have advocated greater economic openness—whether they were cotton plantation owners, multinational corporations, or international banks. Those faced by foreign competition have favored relative closure—whether they were domestic manufacturers, affected workers, or dairy farmers.

The issues, too, have changed. When the United States was an underdeveloped debtor country, most debate was over whether and how the country should honor its debts to foreigners. As it became the world's leading creditor, the debate shifted to how the country should treat its debtors. As it regained its position as the world's largest debtor, controversy erupted over the causes and implications of the renewed reliance on foreign capital. Attachment to the gold or silver standard, free trade or protection, international economic engagement or isolation, have all motivated great conflict at one time or another. Battles over the country's position within the world economy have run like a red thread through the development of the American political economy. The twentieth century is no exception.

HISTORICAL BACKGROUND

For nearly the first century of its existence, the United States exported raw materials to Europe, especially cotton to England, and imported manufactured goods from Europe. In the years before the Civil War, the principal political division over foreign economic policy was between the export-led cotton South, on the one hand, and the industrializing Northeast, on the other. Southern agriculturalists wanted access to foreign markets and foreign goods; northern manufacturers wanted protection from foreign products. The tariff pendulum swung back and forth for decades.

From the first days of the Civil War until well into the twentieth century, the United States imposed high tariffs on a wide range of manufactured imports. As industry grew up behind high tariff walls, however, agriculture and mining were unprotected and indeed relied heavily on exports. Even after the Civil War, political battles over the tariff tended to pit the agrarian and mining South and West against the industrial Northeast and Midwest.

A second great divide of the era, known then as the Money Question, also had major international components. In the nineteenth century, America's leading commercial and financial interests were tightly tied to world trade and payments. The import-export business was central to America's ports and to the shipping, insurance, and trade they managed. The country's leading financiers were heavily involved in attracting foreign capital for investment in the United States, which was the world's leading borrower throughout the century. As international trade and investment were organized around the gold standard, all those involved in managing the nation's foreign commerce and finance supported American adherence to gold.

However, businessmen and farmers in the interior had little use for the gold standard. They were primarily concerned with the declining prices of their products and the high cost of borrowing, both of which were in some measure a result of the dollar's tie to gold. Farm prices, set on world markets, were falling; interest rates, set in London, were high. To use today's terms, farmers wanted a devaluation of the dollar to raise the dollar price of the wheat and cotton they produced; borrowers wanted a floating dollar that would unlink American from British interest rates. Whether as greenbackers, silverites, or Populists, farmers and others resented economic conditions they believed were imposed from abroad.

Both tariffs and gold were at the center of American politics from the Civil War until the 1896 presidential election decided the matter. In that year, a coalition of pro tariff Midwesterners and pro gold Northeasterners led by Republican William McKinley squared off against anti tariff, anti gold farmers and miners in the South and West enthused by the populism of Democrat William Jennings Bryan. McKinley's victory marked the triumph of a combination of protectionism and financial conservatism.

EXPANSION AND EMPIRE

With gold and protection firmly ensconced, America's business leaders turned their attention to other problems. Foremost among these was the need to secure export markets for the country's burgeoning industrial output. By the 1890s, indeed, the United States was far and away the world's leading manufacturing nation, and despite continued demands for protection many American industries were internationally competitive. Satisfaction was tempered, however, by the experience of depressed business conditions between 1893 and 1897. In its wake many business and political leaders regarded future prosperity as at least in part dependent upon overseas sales of American manufactures and importation of inexpensive foreign raw materials to fuel American industry.

Heightened business interest in the rest of the world coincided with the rise of the "Power School" of American diplomatic thinkers, led by Elihu Root, Henry Cabot Lodge, and Theodore Roosevelt. For them, with the frontier closed and the country industrialized, the next step for the United States was to establish itself as a major diplomatic power. This required a larger military, especially a navy, and the definition and protection of spheres of military and economic influence. Economic and diplomatic concerns came together in the last years of the nineteenth century.

As in other industrial countries at the time, U.S. manufacturers of certain products were obsessed with the prospects of opening new markets, or getting into existing ones, abroad. In the American context, most attention turned to Asia and Latin America because European markets were primarily satisfied by European production, especially as trade protection in Europe increased. Much of the rest of the world was divided into colonial empires, which tended to have explicit or implicit preferential trading and investment ties with their mother countries. The race for China, however, was still in progress, and American businessmen stood a chance of procuring a share of the world's most populous market. In an attempt to secure America's place, Secretary of State John Hay issued a series of open door notes in 1899 and 1900, asserting the right of all nations to Chinese trade and investment opportunities. For a decade thereafter, until the Chinese empire collapsed into revolution, American businessmen and policymakers tried to force their way into railroad projects, financial consortia, and other commercial endeavors, with mixed success. But the United States had established its economic position in Asia, and its Philippine colony helped reinforce its claim to status as both a diplomatic and an economic power.

The Spanish-American War of 1898 projected American military might into areas of economic interest to American businesses. The peace treaty gave the Philippines, Puerto Rico, and Guam to the United States; Cuba became a de facto American protectorate; and Hawaii was annexed during the war. The new Asian possessions helped establish the nation's claim to be one among the many imperial players there. The Caribbean outposts served as beachheads in making the region an American sphere of influence.

Even as American diplomats and financiers argued for an open door in China, they had plans to reserve the Caribbean basin for the United States. The nations surrounding the Caribbean, and the islands in it, had long attracted the intrigue of European powers. With some exceptions, their intrinsic economic importance was slight, but they could affect strategic control of shipping in the area—especially if a transisthmian canal, under discussion for decades, were built.

As soon as the Spanish-American War ended, the McKinley administration began plans for an American canal in Central America. Diplomatic obstacles from the British were overcome, and the reticence of the Colombian government was sidestepped by the American-encouraged secession of the Colombian province of Panama. By 1904 the Panama Canal was being built. At the end of the year, the American president enunciated the Roosevelt Corollary to the Monroe Doctrine, asserting American rights to intervene in the Western Hemisphere in the event of "chronic wrongdoing, or an impotence which results in a general loosening of the ties of civilized society."

American concern to secure the Caribbean was only indirectly economic in motivation. Certainly Mexico was commercially significant, and Cuba and Venezuela had potential, but the region as a whole was no financial prize. However, constant European intervention in an area close to the United States was threatening—especially in 1914 with the Canal in place—and the Caribbean basin might be a stepping stone to the economically much more important South American republics. The principal American goal, then, was to supplant the Europeans in the area surrounding the Caribbean.

Although the chronologies and details varied, the typical Caribbean application of what was called Dollar Diplomacy used a combination of financial and military means. Typically, American investors bought out European financial and commercial interests, while the U.S. government encouraged new American investments and trade, especially government loans. The threat or reality of American military force helped stabilize local politics. By the 1920s, the United States owned Puerto Rico, the Virgin Islands, and the Canal Zone, exercised significant rights over Cuba, and had intervened militarily in the Dominican Republic, Haiti, Honduras, and Nicaragua. The Caribbean was an American lake (see map 13 in the article "World Regions" in this volume).

The era of frequent American military intervention in Central America and the Caribbean lasted until the early 1930s. It is almost certainly the case that the proximate causes of intervention were primarily military and political rather than economic. Nonetheless, American resident investors in the region did sometimes encourage their home country to send troops. More generally, strategic concerns about the Caribbean basin had economic dimensions: most policymakers and businessmen believed that American economic interests were linked to American diplomatic influence. They saw hegemony in the Caribbean as crucial to a broader role in the world.

American involvement in the Caribbean and Asia was not universally supported. Some Americans found cause for moral indignation in America's pursuit of quasi-colonial goals. Others simply felt that attention paid to foreign matters detracted from resolving problems at home. Foremost among the latter were many former supporters of the populist movement, whose anti-imperialism was more isolationist than internationalist. Nonetheless, it was difficult even for those who opposed intervention in principle to avoid it in practice, as Woodrow Wilson and the Democrats—including Secretary of State William Jennings Bryan—found when they took office in 1913. Conditions in the Caribbean area were so unsettled that the temptation to try, as Wilson put it, to "teach the South American Republics to elect good men" was sometimes irresistible, and Wilson oversaw a real upsurge in "gunboat diplomacy" during his two terms.

Other economic policies also evolved in the years before World War I. Exports, especially to Latin America, grew in importance, and the government paid increasing attention to helping American firms supplant European ones in competition for third markets. As the nation's trade expanded, interest in reducing American tariffs grew: exporters worried about retaliation, and more domestic producers wanted access to inexpensive imports.

The movement for "tariff reform," principally a reduction in import barriers, gathered support in the early years of the century. The 1909 Payne-Aldrich Tariff, enacted by the traditionally high-tariff Republicans, undertook a modest reduction in duties. After the Democrats swept the 1912 elections, they implemented their low-tariff ideas in the form of the 1913 Underwood tariff, which brought trade barriers down to their lowest levels since the Civil War.

By the eve of World War I, the country's economic growth had brought about important changes in its international economic relations. Manufactured and semimanufactured products went from only one-fifth of total exports in 1890 to one-half in 1914, while non-European markets similarly increased their importance from one-fifth to one-half of American exports in the same time period. From a major international borrower, the United States had become an overseas lender and investor. By 1914, American corporations had about $2.5 billion in foreign direct investments ranging from plantations and oil fields to manufacturing plants. Americans had also lent a billion dollars to foreigners, a turnaround from the country's longstanding reliance on foreign borrowing of its own. While total American foreign investments of about $3.5 billion in 1914 were small by European standards—the United Kingdom's overseas assets were approximately six times this size—they demonstrated the ability of American firms to compete in the international economy.

WORLD WAR I AND ITS AFTERMATH

The Great War drew the United States into the world economy with a vengeance. The country emerged from the war in a position of unchallenged international economic leadership, both because of the devastation of Europe and because of the extraordinary growth of the U.S. economy in wartime. However, America's politics and policies lagged behind its economic evolution, as resistance to international involvement persisted.

Almost as soon as the war broke out, American farms and factories began supplying the Allies (the Central Powers were effectively blockaded by the British Navy). Armaments exports went from $40 million in 1914 to $1.3 billion in 1916, while total exports went from $2.4 billion to $5.5 billion. Initially, the Europeans paid for their purchases by selling off their investments in the United States, but soon funds ran out. At that point, after some wavering about the implications of lending to only one side (and the resignation of Secretary of State William Jennings Bryan in protest), the government allowed private bankers to advance the Allies the money necessary to buy what they needed in the United States. By the time of U.S. entry, Americans had lent $2.6 billion, primarily to the French and British. J. P. Morgan and Company was the principal manager of the credits and served as purchasing agent for the Allies. After the United States declared war on the Central Powers, private investors were replaced by $9.6 billion in government-to-government loans from America to Europe.

As American economic ties with Europe grew, so too did trade and investment interests in Latin America and other developing regions. European competitors were retired from the scene, preoccupied with events at home. In many instances, they were forced to sell off investments in developing countries to pay for raw materials, food, and war matériel. American businesses stepped quickly into the vacuum, supplanting European manufacturers, lenders, and investors throughout the developing world—even in some European colonies.

By about 1924, wartime conditions were over, and the United States was firmly ensconced as the world's principal trader, lender, and investor. However, American political commitment to the rest of the world was far less substantial than its economic interests. Almost as soon as American troops arrived home, public sentiment retreated from overseas affairs, and those with foreign economic concerns lost political influence. American signature of the Versailles Treaty and participation in the League of Nations, based on Woodrow Wilson's hopes and ideals, were defeated by domestic political resistance to overseas involvement.

With the war over, the American body politic separated into "internationalists," "isolationists," and a large number who were apathetic toward the whole subject. The former wanted the nation to play a leading role in world political and economic affairs: to sign the Treaty, join the League, reduce trade barriers, and cooperate with other economic powers. Support for internationalism was especially strong among those heavily involved in the world economy, such as northeastern banks and corporations and southern producers of export crops. Isolationism was particularly powerful in the more insular Midwest, where many industrial and agricultural producers depended primarily on the domestic market and feared foreign competition. They preferred diplomatic disengagement and trade protection, in order to resolve domestic economic problems.

Wilson and his internationalist allies lost the battle for the League of Nations, and the mostly isolationist Republicans swept the 1920 election. With isolationism ascendant, official participation in international economic organizations was largely ruled out. Congress would not agree to any substantial American involvement in the sorts of cooperative agreements that Wilson and his supporters had envisioned.

In trade policy, too, the movement toward commercial liberalization undertaken before World War I was reversed after the war. With Republicans back in control of the White House and Congress, American tariffs were raised in 1921 and 1922. Many business and political leaders expressed a desire to restrict American lending and investment abroad. Even as American producers, traders, and investors came to dominate the world economy, U.S. government involvement in international economic affairs was strictly limited.

THE INTERWAR YEARS

The conflict between America's central position in the world economy and its reluctance to play a corresponding diplomatic role defined much of the interwar period. The ambivalence of American policy contributed to instability of the world economy in the 1920s, and exacerbated the impact of the Great Depression in the 1930s.

However, the American private sector remained central to the world economy in the 1920s. American foreign direct investment reached $7.9 billion in 1929, while foreign loans outstanding topped $8.1 billion. The European economies, along with those of many developing countries, were fueled by American capital and access to the enormous American market.

Private American bankers and businessmen themselves were heavily involved in designing and implementing a series of stabilization programs in Europe. The most famous of these were the Dawes and Young plans in Germany, put in place in 1924 and 1929 respectively, but similar schemes were developed elsewhere. The general pattern involved a loan from American private bankers, typically led by Morgan and Company, as well as from central bankers in Britain and France. The loans normally carried with them promises from borrowing governments to implement a series of economic reforms, such as reducing budget deficits and inflation. In some instances, foreign supervisors were appointed to monitor compliance with the terms of the loans. Although such foreign control grated on nationalist sensibilities, in return for good behavior countries could expect access to the capital and lucrative markets of North America and Western Europe.

As important as American private businesses may have been to European reconstruction, their support was often undermined by the indifference or hostility of the United States government. To be sure, some in the government were sympathetic to demands that the United States become more active. Officials from the State Department, the Treasury, and the Federal Reserve sometimes assisted behind the scenes as American bankers or businessmen worked out stabilization loans.

However, American economic policy was often at cross-purposes with the activities of American businesses abroad. Perhaps the thorniest issue of the era was the war debts and reparations tangle. The U.S. government was owed about $10 billion by the Allies, lent during and right after the war. The Allies (principally France, Britain, and Belgium) were in turn owed billions in reparations by the defeated Germans. Both sets of debts tended to dampen economic recovery and to fuel nationalist resentments. Internationalists on both sides of the Atlantic felt the logical solution was for the U.S. to cancel or substantially reduce the war debts, thus allowing the Allies to cancel or substantially reduce reparations

demands. But American isolationists would not hear of forgiving debts owed to American taxpayers simply to placate the passions of unreasonable Europeans, and so the issue festered.

Refusal by the United States to contemplate war-debt reduction exacerbated conflict in Europe. High American tariffs impeded exports to the United States, making it more difficult for Europeans to earn the dollars to service their debts. American unwillingness to join the League and other international organizations weakened attempts to forge cooperative monetary, trade, and investment relationships.

American economic policymakers found themselves torn. On the one hand, they recognized that U.S. policies had a profound impact on the world economy and that world economic trends could in turn affect the American economy. This gave them ample reason to take into account the international impact of what was done within America's borders. On the other hand, most Americans were indifferent or hostile to anything that smacked of subordinating American economic interests to global considerations. This made it difficult for policymakers to balance the demands of the world's largest economy with domestic concerns.

In monetary policy, for example, the new Federal Reserve System (Fed) was continually torn between foreign and domestic pressures. Low interest rates in the United States might stimulate the U.S. economy, but they also led foreigners to sell dollars, which endangered the dollar's position at the center of the international monetary system. Higher American interest rates stabilized the dollar, but dampened American economic growth. Throughout the 1920s, the Fed was driven back and forth between demands for a tight monetary policy to maintain the dollar as the anchor of the international economy and demands for a looser monetary policy to encourage American growth.

The inconstancy of American economic policy almost certainly exacerbated the Great Depression. Between 1928 and 1933, the Fed was buffeted by conflicting demands. When it lowered interest rates to stimulate the U.S. economy, the dollar came under attack. When it raised interest rates to defend the dollar (or to stanch speculation on Wall Street) it dampened recovery at home, and drained funds from foreigners in desperate need of new loans.

On another front, as the Depression hit, the United States substantially raised trade barriers. The Smoot-Hawley tariff of 1930 raised the average tariff on dutiable imports to its highest level in American history. Increased American protectionism may have contributed to retaliation from other countries and to a world trade war that brought international commerce, too, nearly to a standstill.

When the Roosevelt administration took office in March 1933 both the world and the American economies were in dire straits. Britain had gone off the gold standard to devalue the pound sterling and was refocusing its international economic activities on its Empire. Trade wars were breaking out among the world's commercial leaders, exacerbated by rounds of competitive currency devaluations. Most of the countries to which American bankers had extended loans had defaulted on their payments. All over the world, the global crisis was helping bring to power nationalists who blamed foreigners for their peoples' tribulations.

The situation in the United States was as bad as, or worse than, that abroad. In his first few months in office, Roosevelt chose to downplay international initiatives and concentrate on the domestic economy. In July 1933, despite his traditional association with internationalism, Roosevelt broke up an international economic conference in London, arguing for the primacy of national policies. A few months later, the new administration began devaluing the dollar to make American goods more competitive on world markets. Whatever hopes the internationalists may have had were dashed.

But Roosevelt soon began showing interest in additional international cooperation. Secretary of State Cordell Hull was indeed a strong free trader, and in June 1934 Congress responded to Hull's demands to pass a Reciprocal Trade Agreements Act that allowed the president to negotiate tariff reductions with other countries. While the actual impact of the Act is controversial, it took trade policy one step away from Congress, and may have imparted a less protectionist orientation to it. Meanwhile, the dollar had stabilized and the administration began working with the British and French on international monetary cooperation. These negotiations culminated in the Tripartite Agreement of 1936, which brought the dollar, the pound, and the franc back onto a gold exchange standard.

While most attention centered on relations with other industrial countries, American interests in the developing world, especially Latin America, grew apace. Originally, defaults by Latin American debtors were the cause of considerable tension. However, the era of gunboat diplomacy was over, and a new age, dubbed by Roosevelt that of the Good Neighbor, had begun. By the late 1920s, indeed, the experience of the Mexican Revolution and the maturation of American economic interests in Latin America had led to a rethinking of traditional U.S. policy. Intervention appeared far less effective in such large, relatively advanced countries as Mexico or Brazil than it had been in Haiti or the Dominican Republic. The typical American economic interest in the region was no longer a banana plantation but an automobile plant or a private loan, and these were much harder to protect with the Marines. Meanwhile, European competition had diminished greatly.

When Latin American governments, and those of a few other developing countries, defaulted on their debts in the 1930s, the U.S. government essentially stepped aside. It did try to facilitate renegotiations, and to ensure that markets were opened to American exporters and investors. When the Mexican government nationalized American oil properties in 1938, the United States protested vigorously. But military intervention in the Third World was no longer considered a routine option.

By the late 1930s, halting moves toward renewed international economic cooperation were overtaken by diplomatic crises in Europe and Asia. Even before the shooting began, American planners began thinking about the sort of world they might like to build after the war. In leading circles, internationalism appeared vindicated by the disasters of the 1930s. Internationalist businessmen and policymakers resolved not to repeat the mistakes of American retrenchment after World War I.

BRETTON WOODS AND EUROPEAN RECONSTRUCTION

Even before the United States entered World War II, it made clear to its eventual allies that it had war goals with important international economic components. The Atlantic Charter of August 1941 committed the United States and Great Britain to some form of freer trade after the war, much to the chagrin of British supporters of the Imperial Preference System, a series of trade barriers around the British empire. Pressures on the Allies to abandon barriers to American trade and investment continued with the Lend-Lease agreements.

The implementation of postwar plans began in earnest at an Allied conference in Bretton Woods, New Hampshire, in July 1944. The negotiations were dominated by Harry Dexter White, of the U.S. Treasury, and John Maynard Keynes, of the British Treasury. They proposed two new organizations. The

International Bank for Reconstruction and Development (World Bank) would make long-term loans to encourage the growth of war-ravaged regions and developing countries. The International Monetary Fund (IMF) would supervise a reconstituted and modified gold exchange standard. Parallel negotiations produced a plan for an International Trade Organization (ITO) that would lead members toward reduced trade barriers and freer trade.

None of the three organizations evolved exactly as anticipated. The ITO ran into opposition within the United States, from both sides of the trade issue. Protectionists feared it would force more trade liberalization than they wanted; free traders believed it would be more forgiving of trade barriers than they wanted. By 1950 the ITO was dead, and a provisional organization arose in its stead, the General Agreement on Tariffs and Trade (GATT).

The IMF was supposed to oversee a quick return to a functioning international monetary order of relatively fixed exchange rates. Instead, most European governments kept their currencies inconvertible—restricting their use in international trade and payments—until 1958. In the interim, the world moved onto a modified dollar standard. The American currency was tied to gold at $35 per ounce; other currencies could tie to the dollar. But in the unsettled conditions of postwar Europe, the IMF had little to do.

Nor did the World Bank play its expected role in financing European reconstruction. The needs were too great for World Bank resources, and the organization soon turned toward the developing world, where it began to act as a large-scale development bank. It was to lend to countries in the Third World so that they could build infrastructural and other projects that the private sector might not otherwise be willing to finance; in return it would demand both a general respect for the property of foreign investors, and specific economic policies deemed appropriate.

Important as they later became, the three Bretton Woods organizations—GATT, IMF, and the World Bank—were practically dormant for a decade after World War II. Postwar reconstruction was dominated, not by the careful plans of the Bretton Woods negotiators, but by the geopolitical turmoil of the new Cold War.

Inside the United States, despite the turn toward more international engagement in the Roosevelt administration, the end of the war raised the possibility of a return to traditional isolationism. The Republicans swept the 1946 midterm elections, controlled the House and Senate, and were widely expected to take the presidency in 1948. And the Republican party continued to have a large isolationist wing, led by Ohio senator Robert Taft, that was wary of global economic and political commitments.

The Truman administration needed the support of the Republicans for its postwar policies, but appeals to Wilsonian globalism were ineffectual. In a series of debates between 1946 and 1949, Truman and his foreign policymakers were able to win over enough Republicans to create a centrist consensus that dominated American foreign policy for decades thereafter.

The masterstroke was to tie the administration's international economic proposals together with its attempts to oppose the spread of communism in Europe and Asia. While many Republicans had little use for freer trade or the IMF, they were militant in their concern about an expansion of the Soviet sphere of influence. Truman, Secretary of State George Marshall, and his assistant Dean Acheson convinced Republican Arthur Vandenberg, chair of the Senate Foreign Relations Committee, that American international economic engagement was inseparable from the fight against communism. On this basis, reworked versions of the American postwar plans were acceptable to a Republican Congress.

In 1946, the United States loaned $3.75 billion to the United Kingdom in return for a series of British commitments to move toward opening its empire to foreign (including American) economic interests. In 1947, the Truman Doctrine and the Marshall Plan committed the United States to billions more dollars in aid to its European allies in return for their standing fast against the Soviet Union.

In addition to the strategic alliance formalized with the creation of NATO in 1949, American assistance in postwar reconstruction also carried economic strings. The United States insisted on a liberalization of international economic ties, and on a cooperative relationship among its European allies. It encouraged the formation of the European Coal and Steel Community in 1950, and its evolution into the European Economic Community (Common Market). These initiatives were almost certainly good for the countries involved, but American support was motivated less by this than by the hope that greater economic openness would benefit U.S. interests, and that prosperity in Europe would strengthen pro-American, anti-Soviet governments.

The melding of economic internationalism and geopolitical goals was not without difficulties. At times the two worked at cross-purposes, as with

American attitudes toward the trade policies of its European and Japanese allies. On economic grounds, the United States wanted the Europeans and Japanese to open their markets to American products. But America's allies argued that too rapid a liberalization of trade would cause economic dislocation that might lead to social and political unrest, and that this unrest could feed into pro-Soviet or neutralist political movements. Faced with a choice between freer trade and more unstable allies, American economic policymakers often had to content themselves with an uneasy compromise.

The Common Market itself was aimed in part at restricting the access of American goods to the markets of its member states. American support for the EEC was predicated on the calculation that, even on purely economic grounds, a stable pro-American Europe partly closed to American exports was better than an unstable anti-American Europe forced open to trade. And in any event, while trade barriers could keep out American goods, they did not keep out American corporations. In fact, European protection tended to suck American firms into European operations, as they jumped trade barriers to gain access to the continent's markets.

A similar conflict between economic principles and geopolitical concerns affected American colonial policy in the 1950s. On the one hand, the United States had long demanded access to the markets and resources of the colonial empires and, if possible, independence for the colonies. This dovetailed with concerns that colonialism played into the hands of the Soviet Union, by setting colonial populations against the leading capitalist powers in independence movements that the Soviets supported. On the other hand, America's colonialist allies argued that their empires were crucial economic assets, and that rapid decolonization would weaken socioeconomic and political structures in metropolitan Europe. Again, American policymakers found themselves torn between one set of desires, to encourage a breakup of the European empires, and another, not to weaken unduly its European allies.

Contradictory or not, the American-led international regime that emerged from the early postwar years had some clearly defined characteristics. It was organized around the so-called Bretton Woods institutions: IMF, the World Bank, and GATT. These three symbolized the contours of the Bretton Woods system: trade liberalization, international monetary relations centered around a gold-backed dollar, and multilateral lending to the developing world. While none of these three was truly in place until about 1958, they were the goal toward which U.S. (and Western) policy was striving.

THE HEYDAY OF BRETTON WOODS

The year 1958 is usually regarded as the start of the full-fledged Bretton Woods system. In December of that year, the currencies of most European countries returned to convertibility, making them available for international trade and investment. The gold dollar-based international monetary system, monitored by the IMF, was in place. Five GATT negotiating rounds had reduced tariffs substantially among Western industrialized nations. In 1957, six European countries had signed the Treaty of Rome establishing the EEC, and trade barriers were dropping rapidly among the Common Market Six. The World Bank's lending programs were beginning to direct substantial amounts of money to Latin America and the newly independent countries of Asia and Africa.

The fifteen years from 1958 to 1973 were the high point of the postwar international economic order. With European and Japanese reconstruction complete, the world economy grew more rapidly than ever. World trade grew even more than world production, as economies became increasingly open to foreign products. International investment expanded, especially in the form of foreign direct investment (FDI) by multinational corporations. And, after thirty years of dormancy, international lending picked up as well; by 1973 global financial markets held over $160 billion.

The United States was the centerpiece of the Bretton Woods system. In fact, a major source of the global prosperity of the era was the world's access to American markets, American capital, and the American dollar. All of these in turn relied on U.S. commitments to international economic openness.

American support for trade liberalization remained strong, for American industry dominated most markets. Under U.S. leadership, the most ambitious round of GATT negotiations began in 1962 and ran until 1967. The Kennedy Round, as it came to be called, brought about a reduction in nonagricultural tariffs among the industrial nations of over 35 percent in weighted average terms.

American firms also led the charge toward the era of the multinational corporation (MNC). In one sense, such international investment was not new, for European companies had often looked for overseas opportunities in the nineteenth century. But the MNC as it emerged in the 1950s and 1960s, largely as an American phenomenon, was different. First, most new MNCs were in manufacturing rather than plantation agriculture or mining. Second, most MNCs had integrated global management: they operated simultaneously in many regions and countries, and were capable of shifting funds and operations from one part of the world to another with great ease. And finally, MNCs tended to provide fierce and often unwanted competition for local companies.

Direct investment became, in fact, a more important way than trade for U.S. firms to tap into markets abroad. American corporations were able to take advantage of their substantial edge in technology, marketing, and management expertise in many industries, not to speak of the spread of American consumption patterns to much of the rest of the world.

Expansion into Europe was the first step for most American multinationals. The creation of the EEC gave U.S. firms great incentives to locate production facilities in Europe. The process of bringing many European nations together made the Common Market an essential target for American producers. Since this was associated with maintaining moderate barriers to imports from outside the EEC, U.S. firms often found themselves faced with the choice between losing a lucrative market and locating branch factories inside the Common Market. The result was a rush of American companies to get inside the EEC.

Foreign lending by U.S. banks followed soon after the upsurge in foreign direct investment. American bankers, scared off international operations by the defaults and other upheavals of the 1930s, concentrated on domestic business until the mid-1960s. But as the corporate customers of American banks went abroad in ever increasing numbers, major banks were drawn after them. By the 1960s, many U.S. banks had built branch networks in Europe and were lending large amounts there. Even the Third World was looking more attractive, especially as the World Bank had showed that some developing countries might be creditworthy. Cautiously at first, but with growing enthusiasm, American bankers looked to make loans to the apparently more reliable of the less-developed countries, especially in Latin America.

Despite the general prosperity of the Bretton Woods era, there were plenty of sources of friction, even within the United States. Trade liberalization was relatively easy at the outset, as American firms faced little foreign competition. But over time new competitors grew up, especially in Europe and Japan, and U.S. producers began to lose markets to imports. The result was a gradual increase in protectionist sentiment. This was most striking in the labor movement. In the postwar period, American labor had

been largely supportive of free trade, which appeared to bring about the creation of jobs in the country's export industries. As imports chipped away at domestic manufacturing, though, the AFL-CIO rethought its position. In the late 1960s, most labor unions came to feel that trade protection was necessary to preserve high-wage jobs in U.S. industry, and by 1970 the AFL-CIO was consistently protectionist.

Foreign direct investment (FDI) by multinational corporations, lucrative as it may have been for many American firms, was also a source of controversy. Many workers resented the increasingly common pattern in which an American company would reduce production in the United States, only to open a new factory in Europe or Latin America. Labor unions, and regions losing industrial employment, complained about "runaway shops" and called for government measures to keep companies at home.

American FDI was far more controversial abroad than inside the United States. The first wave of concern was in Europe, where fear of an invasion of the continent by American MNCs reached a peak in the late 1960s. The rapid spread of American corporations inside the EEC gave rise to protests that American MNCs were taking Europeans' own markets away from them.

Concern about MNCs was also increasingly common in the developing world. Here the general irritation at the competition represented by foreign, especially American, multinationals was compounded by the sense that MNCs were large and experienced enough to evade developing-country regulations. Some also feared the political influence of foreign corporations that could be extremely large as compared to the size of the national economy. When developing countries attempted to control or even nationalize foreign corporations, they resented the support given by home governments, especially the United States, to their firms.

Developing-country apprehension about MNCs was part of a rising tide of political and economic nationalism throughout the Third World. By the late 1960s, decolonization had run its course, and the former colonies—along with long-independent developing nations—turned their attention to economic independence. The Cuban Revolution of 1959 crystallized many of developing countries' hopes, and America's fears. In its aftermath, the United States tried a combination of positive and negative incentives to shore up its supporters in the developing world.

Foremost among attempts by the United States to counter the rise of anti-American sentiment in the Third World was the Kennedy administration's Alliance for Progress, originally touted as a sort of Marshall Plan for Latin America. But these plans were soon frustrated by realities in the United States and Latin America itself. The tens of billions of dollars originally envisioned for the Alliance to channel to Latin American development never materialized. There was entrenched opposition within the region to the sort of reformist policies the United States proposed, especially land reform.

More generally, U.S. policy in the Third World was often frustrated by contradictions among modern capitalism, strivings for democracy, and solid anti-communism. Democrats were frequently lacking in firm anti-Soviet credentials, while local anti-Soviets were generally either undemocratic, or hostile to economic modernization, or both. Over the course of the 1960s and early 1970s, Alliance for Progress or not, a wave of authoritarianism swept Latin America, and American policymakers were generally resigned to supporting dictatorial regimes so long as they were anti-Cuban. The American record in the South, then, was mixed. The United States continued to be admired for its living standards, and the economic impact of trade and investment ties with the United States was welcome. However, in much of Africa, Asia, and Latin America, corporations based in the United States and the American government tended to be associated with tolerance for authoritarianism and maintenance of an economic order widely seen as inequitable.

Economic problems among the industrialized countries were less ideological, but more important in the long run. While trade relations and FDI remained somewhat controversial in the 1960s, the focus of most concern was macroeconomic. American domestic policies were increasingly at odds with the central role of the United States dollar in the international monetary system, and American unwillingness to adjust its policies to accommodate its European and Japanese partners was the source of great conflict.

The core of the problem was the contradiction between the dollar's international role and its status as the currency of a country overwhelmingly concerned with its domestic economic affairs. This issue had not arisen with the international monetary system that prevailed before World War I, based as it was on the pound sterling, for the British economy relied heavily on world trade and investment. Nineteenth-century Britain was typically willing to sacrifice some domestic economic goals in the interest of stability on international markets for goods and

capital, for its domestic prosperity depended on its international ties. This was not the case for the United States, which could—and did—often ignore the international impact of its domestic economic policies.

The problem was dormant until about 1966. At that point, the Johnson administration undertook a combination of increased outlays for the Vietnam War abroad, and increased social spending on the War on Poverty at home, and was loath to finance both wars by increasing taxes. The result was a rise in inflation inside the United States from an average of 1.2 percent a year between 1960 and 1964 to 3.8 percent between 1965 and 1969, reaching 6.1 percent in 1969. This level of inflation was modest by standards of the 1970s, but it exceeded that of many of the country's trading partners; between 1965 and 1969, American prices rose 23 percent while German prices rose 12 percent.

American inflation created international monetary problems because it meant that world trade and payments were denominated in a currency, the U.S. dollar, that was losing real value. Traders and investors were willing to hold dollars, and to use them internationally, inasmuch as they had faith in their value. But as the dollar's real value declined, firms and individuals had less reason to accept or hold on to the American currency. This left the international economy with a less stable key currency at its center. As faith in the dollar declined, wary investors redeemed the American currency for more reliable gold. The United States soon faced a drain on its gold reserves that could not continue indefinitely.

Two simple resolutions of the problem were available. The United States could have changed its domestic economic policies to strengthen confidence in the dollar. This, however, would have implied tax increases, government spending reductions, and other politically unpopular austerity measures. Especially given the concern of the Johnson and Nixon administrations about the weakness of popular support for their domestic and foreign policies, this was an unappealing choice. Alternately, the United States could devalue the dollar so that its nominal value would more accurately reflect its true worth. But this would have called into question the very structure of the Bretton Woods system, based as it was on a dollar whose value was supposed to be fixed in terms of gold. And undermining the role of the dollar might contribute to a broader erosion of Western confidence in American international leadership, already at a low point due to the Vietnam War.

Faced with one alternative with major domestic

political costs, and another alternative with major international political costs, successive American administrations temporized. Because foreign investment and lending by American corporations and banks increased the world supply of dollars and put downward pressure on the value of the dollar, starting in 1963 the U.S. government restricted the degree to which American firms could directly export capital. These capital controls were meant, among other things, to partially segregate American monetary conditions from international confidence in the dollar, and vice versa—thereby postponing attempts to bring the two into line.

At the same time as it tried domestic measures to prop up the dollar, the United States pursued parallel international initiatives. American monetary authorities cajoled other governments into restricting opportunities for foreigners to exchange dollars for gold. A separate private market for gold was established, in which the precious metal's price was allowed to rise, while governments agreed to continue to pay the Bretton Woods price of $35 an ounce. Central banks committed themselves to lend each other money in case of pressure on one of their currencies, thus staving off devaluations. In this way, the immediate pressures on the dollar, and on the international monetary system, were mitigated.

The years from 1958 to 1973 were in many ways a golden age of modern economic growth. World output and trade grew at extremely rapid rates, and the American economy led the way. International markets became ever more linked in an environment of generalized and increasing prosperity, and again the United States was in the forefront of attempts to reduce barriers to trade, investment, and financial flows. Prices were relatively stable, and the dollar-based monetary order seemed reliable. Despite the strains on the system, the world economy did remarkably well until the early 1970s.

THE COLLAPSE OF BRETTON WOODS AND THE OIL SHOCKS

During the 1970s, the world economy encountered serious difficulties. The United States was both an important source of international economic tension and significantly affected by broader trends. Some of the problems were the outgrowth of cross-cutting pressures on the Bretton Woods system that had built up over the previous fifteen years; others represented the rise of new economic issues.

The international monetary difficulties that accumulated over the course of the 1960s came to a head in 1971. At the root of the problem was the erosion of confidence in the dollar caused by relatively high rates of inflation in the United States. Despite stop-gap measures, it was increasingly clear that the United States would either have to undertake serious domestic austerity measures, or devalue the dollar.

This longstanding dilemma was joined by two further developments that complicated America's international economic role. The first was the rise of Europe and Japan as economic powers more or less on a par with the United States. The American economy had so dominated the world economy after World War II that many in the United States came to regard this as the normal course of things. But European integration had, by the early 1970s, created a unit roughly equivalent to the United States in economic importance. And while the Japanese economy remained substantially smaller than the American, its products, banks, and corporations were increasingly able to compete with American products, banks, and corporations. As Europe and Japan grew in economic influence, the ability of the United States to manage the world economy single-handedly eroded noticeably.

A second development whose significance became clear only in the 1970s was the growing level of international economic integration, and especially the growing importance of the global economy for the American economy. This interdependence offered great gains to many Americans, but it also imposed some new constraints on American economic and political activities. From the 1930s until the 1970s, despite gradual trade liberalization and increasing international investment, most economies remained relatively closed to the rest of the world. Even the United States remained nearly oblivious to external economic trends.

By the 1970s, national economies were increasingly tied together. Trade had grown enormously, even for the United States: manufactured imports went from just 4 percent of total American manufacturing output in 1960 to 16 percent by 1974. Investment links were massive and growing, too, as the multinational corporation became a global phenomenon. Even the United States saw a major influx of European and Japanese MNCs. And the principal national financial markets were ever more closely drawn together, so that financial conditions in the United States directly and immediately reflected conditions elsewhere. Higher levels of international economic integration generally, and of the United States into the international economy specifically, heightened the contradictions of American economic policy.

The first pillar of the Bretton Woods system to give way was the gold dollar-based international monetary regime. As world financial markets grew in size and sophistication, massive capital flows in response to uncertainty about the U.S. economy made it impossible for the Nixon administration to ignore pressures on the dollar. Unwilling to subject the American electorate to economic austerity in the year before a presidential election, on 15 August 1971 Nixon took the dollar off gold and devalued it. For a couple of years, the leading economic powers attempted to hold together some semblance of the Bretton Woods system of fixed exchange rates, but by the middle of 1973 most such efforts were abandoned. From that point on, the world's major currencies fluctuated in value against each other according to the dictates of currency markets.

In the United States, the collapse of Bretton Woods meant, among other things, that the strictures of the gold-dollar standard were loosened. This opened the way for higher rates of inflation, as successive administrations attempted to deal with mounting domestic and international economic problems. In 1974 consumer prices rose by more than 12 percent.

To make matters more complex, the unraveling of the postwar order was accompanied by attempts on the part of developing countries to secure a better deal for their products. A series of commodity cartels were formed, mostly by Third World nations, to try to raise world prices for everything from bauxite to bananas. The most spectacularly successful of these cartels was the Organization of Petroleum Exporting Countries (OPEC), which was able to quadruple the world price of oil in 1973–1974 and triple it again in 1979.

At the same time, another group of developing nations was industrializing very rapidly. These newly industrializing countries (NICs), largely in Latin America and East Asia, were manufacturing products that had previously been the private preserve of the developed North: steel, automobiles, pharmaceuticals, even airplanes. Many of them were developing sophisticated industries with money they had borrowed from American, European, and Japanese banks. The NICs' economic dynamism might otherwise have been welcomed by the developed countries, and indeed it was by many, but it also meant an upsurge in competition from regions with low wages and the ability to undercut many American producers.

The combination of rising inflation, the oil-price

shocks, increased competition, and general economic uncertainty was exacerbated by a recession that affected all major countries in 1974–1975. Unemployment rose to levels not seen since the 1930s, and it appeared that the postwar golden age had ended. Unsettled economic conditions tended to inflame conflict both among developed countries and between the developed and developing world.

Inside the United States, the "stagflation" of the 1970s gave rise to increased concern about foreign products. Imported steel, clothing, footwear, and other items confronted American industries with ever stiffer competition. By 1980 manufactured imports were equal to 22 percent of total domestic manufacturing output, one-third higher than 1974 levels. Not surprisingly, protectionist sentiment grew. Some of it met with success as the Carter administration used a variety of tools, from antidumping findings to a steel "trigger price mechanism," to restrict imports.

To some extent, protectionist pressures were reduced by the continued depreciation of the dollar during the late 1970s. The Carter administration regarded a decline in the value of the dollar favorably, as it would make American products more competitive both at home and abroad. Between 1976 and 1980, the dollar dropped by 28 percent against the deutsche mark and 24 percent against the yen. By making German and Japanese goods more expensive in the United States, this dollar depreciation reduced the force of protectionist demands.

However, the dollar depreciation, and the Carter administration's other attempts to stimulate the American economy, led to yet another round of inflation. In 1979 inflation went above 13 percent and continued to rise, exacerbated by the second round of oil price increases.

Surprisingly, in these inauspicious circumstances the seventh, or Tokyo, round of GATT negotiations was relatively successful. Between 1973 and 1979, members of GATT agreed to further tariff reductions, and especially to try to limit the use of nontariff barriers to trade. Such barriers, ranging from quantitative quotas and export restraints to health and safety regulations, had come to replace tariffs as favorite protectionist tools. The United States led the way in trying to rein in the use of nontariff barriers, and the Tokyo Round was a modest success in achieving these and several other goals.

But in essence the 1970s were a period of generalized economic unrest. Consumer prices more than doubled over the decade, and wages did not keep up with prices. Productivity stagnated, growth slowed, and unemployment rose. Traditional American ambivalence about the international economy grew as domestic problems were exacerbated by growing foreign competition.

REAGANOMICS AND THE TWIN DEFICITS

The 1980 election of Ronald Reagan to the presidency was in large part due to dissatisfaction with the country's economic performance during the 1970s, and especially under the Carter administration. Reagan undertook a drastic reorientation of American economic policy. Although most of the changes were domestic in focus, they also had important international components.

One of the more prominent economic developments of the 1980s in fact began under Carter with a major shift in monetary policy to attempt to bring inflation under control. In October 1979, Federal Reserve Board chairman Paul Volcker announced a change in central bank operating policy that presaged serious inflation fighting. In the space of a few months, American interest rates began to soar: the prime lending rate went above 20 percent for the first time. One immediate result was two deep recessions between 1980 and 1982. From under 6 percent in 1979, unemployment reached 11 percent by the end of 1982, while capacity utilization in American factories dropped to its lowest levels since the Depression. Inflation, however, fell dramatically from its 1979 peak of over 13 percent to below 4 percent in 1982.

After Reagan took office, the Fed's tight monetary policy was joined by an extremely loose fiscal policy. A combination of tax cuts and increased defense spending led to a budget deficit that passed $200 billion in 1983. The deficits, despite the expectations of Reagan administration policymakers, persisted throughout the 1980s and into the 1990s. As deficits were financed by borrowing, federal debt more than doubled in inflation-adjusted terms between 1980 and 1992, passing $4 trillion as George Bush left the White House.

The combination of tight monetary policy and loose fiscal policy led inexorably to a massive inflow of foreign capital into the United States. As American interest rates skyrocketed, foreigners were eager to buy dollar investments. This also reflected the need, on the part of the federal government, to finance its budget deficit: foreigners were willing purchasers of U.S. Treasury securities in a period in which many

other countries seemed less than fully reliable. The flood of capital toward the United States and the dollar bid the price of the dollar up steadily through the early 1980s. From 1980 to 1985 the dollar rose by 50 percent against other currencies.

The strong dollar had mixed effects on the U.S. economy. On the one hand, it allowed Americans to buy foreign products—and to travel—more cheaply. For some, the strength of the dollar was simply a reflection of the strength of the United States, and of faith in its economy. On the other hand, the higher the dollar went the cheaper foreign goods became relative to American products. Beneficial as this might have been to the consumer, it put tremendous pressure on firms in the United States that competed with imports, and those that were trying to export to other markets.

As a result, along with the budget deficit came a growing trade deficit. By the middle 1980s the United States was importing over $150 billion more than it was exporting. This import surge was perhaps the most prominent public indication of the country's changed international economic position. American consumers who had barely gotten used to Japanese products now found, mostly for the first time, that large portions of what they bought came from such countries as Korea, Taiwan, Brazil, and Mexico. Many American producers who were already having trouble keeping pace with foreign competition in any event were driven to the wall by the rush of imports the strong dollar brought into the American market.

The nation's altered international position was in part an inevitable result of its heavy foreign borrowing. The United States had been a lending nation since the early part of the century, and indeed had been the world's leading lender since the beginning of World War I. But as foreigners rushed to buy high-interest American investments, the tables turned. By 1987 the United States was a net debtor to the rest of the world, and by the end of the Bush presidency the country owed half a trillion dollars more to foreigners than it was owed by them.

A predictable result of these economic trends was a resurgent nationalistic reaction to real or perceived international economic threats. A flurry of protective bills were introduced into Congress, and industries dramatically increased their filing of "antidumping" complaints against foreign competitors.

The most prominent trade barrier of the decade came with the imposition of a "voluntary" restraint agreement on Japanese automobile imports. Under the terms of the 1981 agreement, Japanese producers agreed to limit exports to the United States to about

1.8 million cars and trucks a year. The effect was to raise the price of Japanese (and thus all) cars in the American market. This form of protection was politically viable because its benefits were divided between the American and Japanese automobile industries. As the price of cars in the United States was driven up by supply restrictions, both American and Japanese producers made more per vehicle. This blunted whatever complaints the Japanese might otherwise have raised about American trade protection, and indeed similar "voluntary" restraint agreements proliferated during the 1980s.

The upsurge of protectionism was muted by the economic recovery that began in 1983 and by the decline in the value of the dollar that began in 1985. Both of these reduced the immediacy of protectionist demands, although the size of the nation's trade deficit and tough competition from foreigners continued to inflame the passions of American manufacturers.

By the late 1980s, much of the concern had shifted away from specific competitive pressures toward a broader worry that the country's ability to sustain industrial jobs more generally was being eroded. The ready availability of inexpensive manufactured products from developing countries and Japan appeared to have made obsolete many of the well-paying factory jobs that had been the hallmark of much of the middle-American dream.

Developments in the American economy, especially in the face of the Volcker-Reagan era economic policies, had important effects on the rest of the world. The developing countries that had borrowed heavily in the 1970s were hard hit in the early 1980s by interest-rate increases and recession in the developed world. With their debt at floating interest rates, debtor countries found debt-service payments soaring. Meanwhile, a combination of stagnant demand and protectionism in Europe and North America dampened their ability to sell their products. The result was a wrenching debt crisis in which dozens of developing countries were forced to undertake massive austerity programs to rebuild their shattered finances.

Europe, too, chafed at American policies. High American interest rates drew capital out of Europe, and confronted European governments with the choice either of standing by as money flowed out of their economies at an ever-increasing pace, or of matching American interest rates with similarly high interest rates of their own. Most eventually chose the latter course, thereby imposing recessions on their own economies. In much of the world, complaints multiplied about the unilateralism of the Reagan administration, its apparent unconcern for the global effects of its domestic policies.

The administration began reassessing its unilateral stance as the problems associated with the strong dollar, import competition, and the debt crisis multiplied. In a major shift in policy, in September 1985 the United States agreed to cooperate with the other major economic powers to encourage a decline in the value of the dollar. This agreement, which did in fact reinforce the dollar's decline back to 1980 levels, marked a tentative step toward more cooperative arrangements between the United States and other leading industrial countries.

In this context, the United States also encouraged the opening of a new round of GATT negotiations. The Uruguay Round, which began in 1987, focused on several thorny issues that had been left unresolved in previous GATT agreements. First was a reduction in barriers to agricultural trade, which had been exempted from earlier GATT rounds. Second was further restrictions on the imaginative nontariff trade barriers many countries had become expert in developing. Third were attempts to elaborate rules on the protection of intellectual property (patents, royalties, and licenses, for example), and on such new arenas as trade in services.

Despite the newfound interest in international cooperation on the part of the Reagan and Bush administrations after 1985, the experience of the late 1970s and early 1980s had driven other industrial countries to look for alternative ways of dealing with their economic problems. Most prominent was the renewed push toward European integration. By 1987 the twelve members of what was now called simply the European Community (EC), and later (1993) the European Union (EU), had resolved to remove all barriers to the movement of goods, people, and capital among themselves by the end of 1992, and to begin a process of monetary integration whose goal was a single currency for the EC.

In parts of East Asia, there were some indications that a Japanese sphere of economic influence was developing. The yen was ever more widely used in regional trade and payments, as many of the region's countries were doing most of their trade with Japan. Japanese investors came to dominate the region, as did Japanese financial institutions. Observers differed on whether this was simply a natural process associated with Japan's economic growth, or reflected purposive Japanese policies that required an American response.

The United States, too, appeared willing to contemplate a renewed regional focus for its economic activities. The Bush administration negotiated agreements with Canada and Mexico to remove trade barriers within North America. Complementary agreements with other Latin American countries were also discussed, and the prospects of a Western Hemisphere trade and investment area seemed appealing to many Americans.

This apparent tendency toward further regional integration, whether in Europe, Asia, or North America, was complicated by the collapse of the Soviet Union and Eastern Europe between 1989 and 1991. The emergence of more than a score of new countries eager to build market economies introduced a new element of economic and political uncertainty both in Europe and elsewhere. These formerly centrally planned economies, from Vietnam to Slovenia, were desperate to trade with the West and attract Western investors. Whether their needs can be accommodated by a world economy already strained by the tensions caused by economic integration, heightened competition, and fear of stagnation, remains to be seen.

INTO THE TWENTY-FIRST CENTURY

As the United States heads toward the next century, it faces daunting economic problems, almost all of which have at least some international dimensions. At the most basic level, the choices open to the United States are analogous to those it has faced throughout its history. At one extreme, Americans can choose to engage themselves fully in a closely integrated world economy. This would mean subjecting the nation to ever greater international competition, but also opening up new economic opportunities for American producers, traders, and investors.

At the other extreme, Americans might react to the international economic threats by turning more resolutely inward, protecting themselves from external competition. This would mean forgoing the benefits of global markets and goods, but also avoiding the costs of foreign competitive pressures that threaten many American industries.

Neither extreme is particularly likely. Too much would be sacrificed if the country moved either toward the world federation feared by nationalists in the United States or toward the Fortress America feared by internationalists on both sides of the Atlantic and Pacific. The most serious issue will probably be the relative significance, and desirability, of regional economic blocs. For some, "blocification" is desirable. A rough division of the world into European, Japanese, and American spheres of economic influence is superior both to globalized disorder and to provincial country-based nationalism. Each regional power will be able to keep order in its camp, and to cooperate (if warily) with leaders of other camps.

For others, the division of the world into economic blocs is more sinister. Apart from raising the specter of commercial and investment conflict leading to shooting wars, it reduces the scope for economic cooperation among the world's great centers of economic activity. For the United States, the choice may be between secure opportunities in all or parts of the Western Hemisphere, and uncertain opportunities in a much larger world economy. These choices are of varying attractiveness to different economic actors in the United States, of course. Globe-straddling multinational banks and corporations are loath to give up their access to the global economy; uncompetitive manufacturers and farmers shudder at the thought of being exposed to truly global competition.

At a less abstract level, the United States faces economic issues that strongly implicate the rest of the world. The interrelated budget and trade deficits are inherently international. Inasmuch as the nation has financed its spending by borrowing, at some point it will have to generate the resources to service its debt. This will require, among other things, turning the trade deficit into a surplus to use the increased export earnings to pay off the country's foreign debt.

This in turn raises the question of how the international competitiveness of the United States economy can be sustained and enhanced. There are myriad contending positions on this issue. Some analysts focus on the government taking an aggressive stance to force open markets in Japan, Europe, and the developing world. Others want more protection of American producers from imports, or support for American exporters. Still others believe that the answer lies not abroad but at home.

Among those whose attention centers on domestic actions to respond to the global challenge, some want the government to let the market take its course, and to encourage a flourishing of entrepreneurial activity. Many of them believe that excessive government intervention has dampened saving and investment, and that getting the government out of the economy is a prerequisite to getting the United States back to the head of the global economic race. For others, purposive but primarily domestic government policies are key—from a redoubled emphasis on education and innovation to methodical targeting of crucial American industries.

Whatever the direction taken by the American political economy as it heads into the twenty-first century, two things are certain. First, whatever choices the country makes must perforce respond to trends in the global economy. The United States is indeed more closely tied to international markets for goods and capital than it has been at any time in this century; it could not ignore the rest of the world economy even if it wanted to. Second, American choices will themselves exert a powerful influence over global economic growth and development. While the United States is not quite the economic titan it was for much of the twentieth century, it is still an economic superpower. It remains the world's largest market and its largest producer. What happens inside the United States is as important for the world economy as the world economy is for the future of the United States.

SEE ALSO Foreign Policy (in this volume); Economic Thought; Economic Performance; Economic Policy (all in volume III).

BIBLIOGRAPHY

Two books provide excellent surveys of American foreign economic policy in a general setting. William Becker and Samuel Wells, Jr., eds., *Economics and World Power: An Assessment of American Diplomacy since 1789* (1984), contains essays that survey crucial periods in the history of American international economic relations. Walter LaFeber, *The American Age: United States Foreign Policy at Home and Abroad since 1750* (1989), covers economic aspects of American foreign policy very well. More recent topics are covered in Joan Edelman Spero, *The Politics of International Economic Relations,* 4th ed. (1990), which also contains an outstanding overview of trends in the world economy since World War II.

Particular historical trends and eras are the topic of several other excellent studies. David Lake, *Power, Protection, and Free Trade: International Sources of U.S. Commercial Strategy, 1887–1939* (1988), analyzes America's commercial relations with the rest of the world in the early part of the century from a theoretically sophisticated standpoint. Richard Gardner, *Sterling-Dollar Diplomacy in Current Perspective* (1980), is a detailed analysis of the origins of the Bretton Woods system.

Other works treat particular economic issue areas in more detail. Robert Baldwin, *The Political Economy of U.S. Import Policy* (1986), analyzes the politics and economics of American trade policy since World War II. Jeffry A. Frieden, *Banking on the World: The Politics of American International Finance* (1987), discusses the rise of American international banking and its implications for the American political economy. Benjamin J. Cohen, *In Whose Interest? International Banking and American Foreign Policy* (1986), looks at the relationship between American banking interests and broader issues in American foreign policy. I. M. Destler and C. Randall Henning, *Dollar Politics* (1989), is a thorough survey of the making of American international monetary policy, with applications to the stormy 1980s. John Odell, *U.S. International Monetary Policy* (1982), explores the domestic and international politics of the dollar in the 1960s and 1970s.

Part 4

SCIENCE, TECHNOLOGY, AND MEDICINE

INTRODUCTION

David A. Hollinger

Science, technology and medicine are more international in character than are most of the historical phenomenon taken up in this Encyclopedia. The principles of physics, engineering, surgery, and psychology are founded on observation and experimentation in a variety of human settings. The claim of these principles to validity is decidedly transnational. Scientific truth does not change when it crosses the border from Canada to the United States, nor from India to Pakistan. Recognition of the international character of the history of science, technology, and medicine long led historians to ignore, or to slight, the role of specific nations in this history, and to overlook the role played by science, technology, and medicine in the development of nations. Traditionally, reference works on "American history," like college courses on this subject, gave only passing attention to these topics.

At the end of the century, however, historians of the United States have reversed this neglect. They have acted on the insight that science, technology, and medicine constitute a substantial segment of the life of all industrialized nations, especially this one. Historians have also come to recognize that national circumstances can affect the particular shape of many specific features of certain sciences and technologies, and of both the theory and practice of medicine. National and international history thus intersect intimately, and constantly, in the topics included in part 4, now pursued by specialists in American history with the same commitment and rigor long brought to the study of more traditional fields, such as political and social history.

In no nation is "big science" bigger than in the United States. This term of art has come to refer to the vast, capital-intensive research enterprises developed the most dramatically in the wake of World War Two and in relation to the Cold War but fully in evidence even earlier in the century. Part 4 opens with Robert W. Smith's article on these projects of enormous scale and cost, prominent among which have been observatories, cyclotrons, accelerators, and the Human Genome Project.

As these specific examples of "big science" immediately suggest, natural science in the twentieth century has been closely connected with technology. This relationship is a theme of the articles "Aerospace Technology" (Roger E. Bilstein), "Computer and Communications Technology" (Steven W. Usselman), and "Industrial Research and Manufacturing Technology" (David Hounshell) that follow quickly upon "Large-Scale Scientific Enterprise." Yet these essays do not attempt to chronicle and explain the overall advance of scientific knowledge in physics, astronomy, chemistry, biology, geology, and other natural scientific disciplines. The intellectual history of these fields, like mathematics, is nested within international communities that extend well beyond the United States. This history is best obtained through reference works on the history of science as such.

The same might be said of the social scientific and biomedical disciplines. But there is a difference. In many of these fields, the interaction between intellectual development and the national setting in which it takes place is more intense, and the international history of ideas is harder to separate out from the national history of ideas. This is most often the case when the object of inquiry is the human species itself, and when the evidence and reasoning invoked are accessible to an educated public that feels a stake in the results of these branches of science. Hence part 4 includes a series of four essays addressed to the development of scientific ideas about human beings and their social existence.

The first of these, by Gregg Mitman and Ronald L. Numbers, concerns ideas about the place of human life in the universe as a whole. "Creation and Evolution" traces the controversy over evolutionary theories in the context of the widespread American predilection for creationist accounts of the origins of human life. Here, as so often in the history of science, religion has influenced both public and professional discussion of what counts as a convincing, "scientific" idea.

Theories about the human psyche have also engaged wide segments of the public. The article "The Human Mind and Personality," by Jon H. Roberts, addresses psychological theories put forth in the name of science in the American cultural context. The nature and significance of the distinction between male and female is another area of scientific work that has attracted extensive public attention, to which the article by Jill Morawski, "Gender Theories," is devoted. Theories of society are among the most contested of enterprises carried out in the name of science, taken up here in an essay on "Society" by Howard Brick.

Ideas about economic behavior, politics, race, ethnicity, and the family have also been advanced in

the name of science. This Encyclopedia does include treatments of the development of ideas about these facets of human life, which could easily have been placed within this section. But in the organization of this Encyclopedia the history of these ideas is dealt with in articles in other sections in order to connect more closely with other topics.

Part 4 concludes with a set of three articles on medicine. Richard A. Meckel's "Health and Disease" provides a demographic overview of the struggle between people and a multitude of ailments throughout the century. In this context, Susan E. Lederer's "Medical Science and Technology" addresses the efforts of the medical profession to take advantage of the opportunities presented by modern science, and Vanessa Northington Gamble's "Health Care Delivery" details the development and functioning of social systems by which people receive, or fail to receive, medical care.

LARGE-SCALE SCIENTIFIC ENTERPRISE

Robert W. Smith

In 1953, the provost of the Massachusetts Institute of Technology wrote that there "was a time when scientific investigation was largely a matter of individual enterprise but [World War II] taught scientists to work together in groups; they learned to think in terms of a common project, they were impressed by the progress to be made through unified action. A notable degree of this spirit has been transfused into the life of our larger universities. . . . The scale of research and the complexity of techniques have grown beyond anything imagined a few decades ago. . . . It was the war that contributed to a major revolution in the method and spirit and scale of laboratory investigations." By the early 1960s, a new term was widely used to describe the phenomenon the MIT provost described: Big Science, generally taken to imply the sort of science associated with multidisciplinary teams of scientists and engineers whose work centers on big, costly machines.

One type of large-scale science has certainly entailed the construction of major research facilities and so has meant big, sometimes very big, investments in expensive plant and equipment. For paradigmatic examples of this sort of Big Science, analysts have pointed to the particle accelerators employed in high-energy physics that engage armies of physicists, engineers, and technicians for their building and use. As in the case of the MIT provost, it has been argued that the birth of Big Science lies in the crash programs to develop new technologies to fight World War II, including, for example, the atomic bomb. But large-scale scientific enterprises, often driven by scientists with the desire to collect various sorts of data over vast geographical areas were pursued well before the twentieth century, involved disciplines other than physics, and emphasized various kinds of coordinated research.

Expeditions have often had important scientific components in their research programs, even if not always pursued solely for scientific ends. An example of a huge coordinated project that will cost billions of dollars is the Human Genome Project (which will examine human genetic material) in which the research is spread among a number of work sites. Science on such a grand scale helps to underline that the usual equation of Big Science—Big Bucks plus a Big Machine equals Big Science—is too limiting. Mission to Planet Earth, a multibillion-dollar project intended to combine ground-based and space-based activities (using expensive and relatively complex satellites) exploits facilities as well as large-scale, coordinated, multidisciplinary research directed at wide-ranging problems and issues. Incorporating both the machine-centered and coordinated approaches to Big Science noted above, it might be termed "mixed" Big Science. Although it encompasses a broad range of activities and experiences, it is nevertheless useful to keep in mind this simple fourfold breakdown of Big Science: machine centered, expedition driven, coordinated, and mixed.

Another central point is that cost and scale in themselves are not only indicators of shifts in science and technology, but of deep-seated social forces, too. Among the most important of these shifts has been the changed political economy of science since the 1930s. One result is that Big Science has been shaped by, and itself helped to shape, what some historians have called the national-security state. In the 1950s, America's science policymakers decided, for example, that the Cold War dictated that the United States be the leading nation in high energy physics, which in turn meant the construction of ever more powerful particle accelerators.

In telling the story of Big Science, the focus here is on large-scale projects in which the principal goal was to secure novel scientific results. This means that projects such as, for example, the Space Shuttle or the Strategic Defense Initiative (Star Wars), in which science obviously plays a crucial part but where the goal is the construction of a new technology or system of technologies, are not considered. Accounting for the history of each Big Science project or even examining each scientific discipline in which Big Science methods have been adopted, would entail vastly more space than is available here. Instead, the emphasis is on those enterprises and institutions that are particularly revealing of the principal themes in the history of Big Science in the United States.

LARGE-SCALE SCIENCE IN THE NINETEENTH CENTURY

By the middle of the nineteenth century, a time when, as the historian David Knight has put it, physics was essentially an individual affair, perhaps supplemented with an assistant or two, and relying on relatively cheap tabletop equipment, expeditions having a more or less scientific character represented one sort of large-scale scientific enterprise. The Wilkes Expedition, named after Charles Wilkes, its commander, was initiated when in 1836 the Democratic administration and Congress—in an effusion of nationalism, to occupy naval officers in peacetime, and with various diplomatic aims in mind—appropriated $300,000 for the navy to explore Antarctica as well as a section of the Pacific Ocean that had already drawn commercial interest. After much bickering about where responsibility should lie for the scientific work, seven civilian scientists joined the expedition, together with two artists to record scenes and specimens (crucial in the days before photography had come of age) and two technicians. Naval officers were themselves to tackle hydrography, mapping, astronomy, and terrestrial magnetism, while the entire expedition also encompassed a range of other subjects including zoology, geology, and botany.

Six ships set sail from Hampton Roads in 1838. And in 1842, after voyages of about 85,000 miles, four returned (one ship was lost off Cape Horn, another at the mouth of the Columbia River). Among the treasures were hundreds of examples of new species, together with very large collections in various sciences. The execution of the expedition had been in many respects a scientific, diplomatic, and navigational triumph. But from the time the expedition docked, matters began to go awry. Wilkes, who had expected to be welcomed as a hero, was stunned to be met by an indifferent President John Tyler as well as a court-martial charge. The expedition, which had sailed under a Democratic president, returned to a Whig administration, and much different political circumstances from four years earlier.

At a time when the relationship between science and the federal government was unclear, the collec-tion of specimens and data was one thing, their publication quite another. Although Congress appropriated hundreds of thousands of dollars for the task, not all the completed reports were printed. Some reports were never finished. Due to a congressional decision, only one hundred copies were printed of each volume, an action that greatly limited the reports' usefulness as relatively few scientists were able to read them. There were numerous other problems too. In 1874, the Congress, some thirty-eight years after the expedition had started, decided finally to bring down the curtain and to cut off funds to finish the reports. Nevertheless, despite difficulties, the Wilkes Expedition stands as an example of a government-sponsored expedition in which science took its place alongside a mix of technological, commercial, navigational, and diplomatic goals. As we shall see, science for the sake of science has never been sufficient to draw the interest and support of the federal government.

Another type of large-scale scientific enterprise undertaken in the nineteenth century was the coordinated project embarked on, for example, by Matthew Maury, superintendent of the Navy's Depot of Charts and Instruments and head of the newly founded Naval Observatory from 1842 to 1861. Maury emphasized the synthesis of large amounts of data gathered by a wide-ranging network of observers. Perhaps his most spectacular success was assembling information on the winds and currents of the oceans from private as well as naval ships' logs. As Maury put it, "Never before has such a corps of observers been enlisted in the cause of physical science . . . and never before have men felt such an interest with regard to this knowledge." By 1851, Maury was receiving reports from one thousand ships. With these data, Maury prepared ocean charts that aided ships in reducing their passage times between ports; for instance, some clipper ships covering the 15,000 miles from New York to California cut up to a month from their sailing time.

But despite his successes, Maury too obviously exhibited what many of his fellow scientists judged to be amateurish and wrong with science in the United States. As the historian Robert Bruce has described, "Maury's inability to accept and accommodate to valid criticism, his flowery prose, his airy theorizing, his lack of mathematical and logical rigor, his inadequate training, and his overblown scientific pretensions all marked him as part of a passing era. Buoyed up by popular acclaim, Maury never understood the scorn of the professionals." Maury therefore faced stiff opposition at home to some of his initiatives. When, for example, he tried to persuade Joseph Henry, secretary of the Smithsonian Institution, to participate in a meteorological network, Henry, who eagerly sought chances to cooperate with others because by doing so he could stretch his meager funds, resisted Maury's attempts to extend his system of observations inland.

Henry did, nevertheless, cooperate with, among others, the states of Maine, Massachusetts, and New York, as well as the Canadian government, the Coast Survey, the Army Topographical Engineers, and the Patent Office in assembling a meteorological network. As James Espy, one of the leading figures in American meteorology in the nineteenth century, told the secretary of the navy in 1851, "The astronomer is, in some measure, independent of his fellow astronomers; he can wait in his observatory till the star he wishes to observe comes to his meridian; but the meteorologist has his observations bounded by a very limited horizon, and can do little without the aid of numerous observers furnishing him contemporaneous observations over a wide-extended area." Scientists such as Espy and Henry judged that collections of observations from a range of sites were essential. The observations, however, had to be carefully converted from their raw or unreduced form if they were to be useful. Since the size of Henry's network generated a great many observations, he contracted out for the raw material to be reduced and tabulated. In 1856, for example, James Coffin of Lafayette College analyzed, with the aid of around a dozen part-time human computers, more than 500,000 separate observations.

In the late nineteenth century, large-scale data collection was also one of the goals of the Harvard College Observatory under the direction of E. C. Pickering. Trained as a physicist, Pickering had taken over the directorship of the observatory in 1877, beginning a forty-two-year reign in which he transformed the observatory's astronomical prospects. One of Pickering's principal goals was to undertake "large pieces of routine work," especially the measurements of the brightnesses and spectral properties of stars. This sort of labor meant the "employment of numbers of inexpensive assistants whose work is in large measure mechanical, such as copying and routine computing. . . . In each important investigation . . . this involves a repetition of the work many hundreds, or even thousands of times, and renders it necessary that the observers and computers shall continue for years upon work of the same character." Through these large-scale coordinated projects requiring the collection and reduction of vast quantities of data, Pickering set his stamp not only on Harvard, but also the new discipline of astrophysics.

These enterprises would nevertheless have been stillborn without Pickering's success as a fund-raiser. To take one example: between 1886 and 1914, Pickering persuaded Mrs. Henry Draper, widow of one of the pioneers of astrophysics, to part with $237,000 for the observatory. Through her will, in 1914 she bequeathed an additional $150,000. With the aid of these monies, Pickering established a fund to "photograph, measure and classify the spectra of all stars visible from Cambridge as a memorial to her late husband." The first results of this project were published in 1890, and made up a catalog of over 28,000 spectra of more than 10,000 stars (even bigger catalogs were to come later). In an arrangement typical of the Harvard College Observatory under Pickering, the taking of the photographs was the charge of a male astronomer, but their reduction, measurement, and classification were performed by a team of women who sat at the bottom of a hierarchy of management and control and who were not generally allowed access to the observatory's telescopes. By 1886, the two workrooms set aside for the women assistants usually held more than fifteen occupants, an operation that was expanded by Pickering early in the twentieth century. With his clarity of vision, abilities to mobilize funds, innovative instruments, and growing staff, Pickering fostered a new and bigger scale of activity in astrophysics at Harvard. These abilities would also be crucial to the success of other "entrepreneurs" of large-scale science, as we shall see.

THE TURN OF THE CENTURY AND THE CARNEGIE INSTITUTION OF WASHINGTON

By 1900, the United States was a rising scientific power, and, as already noted, no stranger to large-scale scientific projects. "America," a writer in the *Atlantic Monthly* opined in 1898, "has become a nation of science," one testimony to the point that science and scientists had gained enormously in cultural authority in the second half of the nineteenth century. The sort of amateurism represented by Maury was now largely a thing of the past. While the United States still lagged a long way behind Germany and Great Britain, it was already comparable to some much older scientific communities. Also, in the last quarter of the nineteenth century, the United States had made striking advances in graduate training for its scientists. Starting with the establishment in 1876 of the Johns Hopkins University, which itself was inspired by the research-oriented universities of Germany, graduate education began to be put on a solid footing and to be more highly regarded at a growing number of colleges and universities. It had almost always been the case that Americans who wanted an advanced training in science traveled abroad, especially to Germany. Now there were opportunities in the United States too. Much of the funding that made advanced training in this country possible was a consequence of industrialists who set aside part of their fortunes to endow universities or establish philanthropic foundations.

At the turn of the century, however, the future dominant roles of foundations and universities in scientific research were far from obvious. One widely held belief—based on the growing role of the federal government in science in the last quarter of the nineteenth century—was that scientific research would be centered in government bureaus. In 1884, a federal commission had even been assembled to decide whether or not it was appropriate to establish a department of science. But private support for science was also increasing. By 1900, as, for instance, in the case of the Harvard College Observatory, private money was already a potent force in shaping American science. With the advent of the Carnegie Institution of Washington (CIW) private philanthropy became still more important.

The Carnegie was the leading research foundation for American science in the early years of the twentieth century in terms of both influence and money. Founded in 1901 with $10 million in United States Steel Corporation bonds, a board of trustees was swiftly assembled. The trustees in turn established committees of experts to help them convert into concrete proposals the Institution's general aim to "conduct, endow, and assist investigation in any department of science, literature, or art, and to this end to cooperate with governments, universities, colleges, technical schools, learned societies, and individuals."

But what were the appropriate ways to use the Carnegie funds? In particular, was it better to support a few large-scale projects or a much bigger number of smaller-scale efforts? The Harvard chemist and later Nobel Prize winner Theodore W. Richards pressed his views in a letter to the Carnegie's president in 1905:

> The other point of which you spoke was concerning the possible cooperation of scientific men in America. It seems to me that such cooperation might in some cases bring very valuable results and in other cases be almost equally destructive. In astronomy particularly I should think that cooperation might be effective and almost necessary because of the enormous difference of opportunity and range of vision afforded by different latitudes and because of the frequent desirability of having simultaneous observations made from very different stations. . . . On the other hand it seems to me that the making of a great original discovery in science is not unlike the writing of a great poem or the painting of a great picture. The thought and its execution must be hammered out by genius alone and without the multitude of administrative duties which cooperation would be likely to bring upon its professor. . . . In short it seems to me that cooperation may be highly productive of routine work and of a general rounding off of already acquired knowledge; but might be equally destructive of great advance in an entirely new direction.

In the very early years of the Carnegie, one emphasis, in Andrew Carnegie's own phrase, was on finding and supporting "exceptional men," the aim being to free such men from other duties so they could pursue research in an untroubled way. This led to a program of minor grants and fellowships to individuals. But when Robert S. Woodward assumed the Carnegie presidency in 1904, he worked to shift the Institution away from this policy. In the end, Woodward won over the trustees to a new policy of supporting proven investigators through long-term research associateships, together with the already established aim of forming and building up the Carnegie's own research laboratories and bureaus. For Woodward, the Carnegie was to be a "university in which there are no students."

Many of the Carnegie's operations placed it within the well-established tradition of large-scale data collection through coordinated enterprises or expeditions. For example, the study of the earth's magnetic field and its changes had spawned a number of nineteenth-century research enterprises, including internationally coordinated efforts in which American scientists and institutions had played a variety of parts. In fact, the Carnegie Institution quickly established both a Geophysical Laboratory and Department of Terrestrial Magnetism (DTM). The latter was headed by Louis Agricola Bauer. In 1896, he had founded the international journal *Terrestrial Magnetism,* and in 1899 he became the first head of the Coast and Geodetic Survey's Division of Terrestrial Magnetism before leading the Carnegie's own Department of Terrestrial Magnetism.

Bauer's great goal was, as he put it, to establish the links between "terrestrial magnetism and other sciences, such as meteorology, geology, and astronomy." To do so, he wanted to measure the earth's magnetic and electrical fields, not only on its surface, but also in its oceans and atmosphere. The Carnegie gave Bauer the resources and an institutional home through which he could pursue this goal on a world-wide scale through coordinated projects or expeditions. His first aim was to survey the magnetic fields of those parts of the earth not currently being investigated in order to produce a comprehensive map of the earth's field. As Bauer was to explain in 1923: "since we can not bring the body—the Earth—which is the chief object of our investigation into the laboratory and experiment upon it . . . we must depend for steady increases in our knowledge as to causes for magnetization, or electrification, of the Earth upon careful and intelligent observance of the phenomena disclosed when Nature herself performs some striking experiment upon our Earth-magnet, or upon our electrically charged Earth." Bauer wanted to establish magnetic observatories as well as for the DTM to be an international coordinating bureau. Bauer also supported other researchers. For example, he directed Carnegie funds for many years to a German magnetic observatory at Apia in Western Samoa. In this manner, Bauer's DTM, although a part of a private institution, could press for the study of geomagnetic variations to be made uniform across the globe, and for the data to be collected and reduced by intercomparable methods.

A key part in the DTM's early years was played by the *Galilee*, a wooden sailing vessel that contained relatively little magnetic material to disturb the instruments it carried to plot magnetic fields. But despite the precautions taken to reduce the amount of magnetic material, the ship's remaining iron nevertheless caused significant difficulties. Bauer decided on a radical solution: build a ship that was totally nonmagnetic. The result was the *Carnegie,* "a sailing vessel as had not been seen before. It was made of white oak, yellow pine, Oregon pine, and teak, held together by locust tree nails, copper and bronze bolts, and composition spikes. Its four anchors were each 5500 pounds of bronze, and in place of anchor chains it had 11-inch diameter hemp cable." The *Carnegie,* launched in 1907, cost $115,000. In effect, it was a traveling observatory. Its battery of instruments was operated by a scientific staff of seven, giving a crew of twenty-one in all. With a mixed team of scientists and technicians (the sailors), large and costly apparatus (the *Carnegie* and the instruments), and a mission-oriented approach, the voyages of the *Carnegie* meant a form of scientific practice that resembles what would later be termed Big Science.

COOPERATIVE RESEARCH

By the time of Bauer's death in 1929, the new Carnegie president, John C. Merriam, had already sought to reorient the DTM. Merriam wanted DTM to move from what he judged to be an overemphasis on data gathering toward the analysis of the data, together with closer cooperation with other Carnegie departments working in seismology, solar-terrestrial relations, and other geophysical problems. Indeed, the move toward what was called cooperative research—what might now be termed interdisciplinary research—was one of the key developments in American science in the early twentieth century.

One of the most devoted and successful preachers and exponents of the gospel of cooperative research was George Ellery Hale. A key moment in the young Hale's life was when he first encountered the spectroscope, a device for splitting the spectrum of light into its component colors. Swept off his feet by "the possibilities of this extraordinary instrument" for linking astronomy with physics and chemistry, Hale was driven to fashion institutions and mobilize resources to bring such cooperative research into being. An accomplished astrophysicist in his own right, Hale was also a brilliant and innovative promoter of scientific institutions. As one colleague put it after a talk with Hale in 1916, "Hale is the most *restless* flea on the American continent—more things *eating* him than I could tell you about in an hour."

Son of a wealthy industrialist, Hale had entered MIT in 1886. While there, he showed his talent for the tools of science when he conceived of the idea, and then proved the success, of a new sort of instrument for studies of the sun. In 1892, Hale became an associate professor at the newly founded University of Chicago, as well as director of its observatory. Later that year he learned of a lens forty inches in diameter that when mounted in an appropriate tube would form the most powerful refracting telescope in the world. When the University of Southern California could not raise the money to pay for it, Hale, eagerly aided by the president of the University of Chicago, seized the opportunity to persuade the Chicago traction magnate C. T. Yerkes to donate $200,000 plus for the lens, mounting, and building so that Chicago could acquire the world's biggest refracting telescope. Once this was accomplished, however, Hale became frustrated with the lack of support at his university and was soon fretting for a new means by which to enact his vision of how astrophysics should be practiced.

He would later recall that in 1902 he had seen

a newspaper report that Andrew Carnegie had provided $10 million for the purpose of research. To Hale it "seemed almost too good to be true." Soon he was a member of the Carnegie Institution's Advisory Committee on Astronomy. He swiftly allied himself with the Institution's executive secretary, C. D. Walcott, who shared his views on the potential of cooperative research. As Walcott told Carnegie himself in 1903, they "might as well try to make a great research institution of the [Carnegie Institution] by pure individualism as to expect success in great industrial enterprises by the individualism of 1850–1870." Although the advisory committee on astronomy judged Hale's plans for astrophysics to be important, they were far from the only ones under consideration. But Hale, delighted by the clear skies atop Mount Wilson in California and drawn by the prospect of observations from such a site, decided to gamble. He took his family, together with a solar telescope, to the mountain. There he began building an observatory. Hale's optimism was borne out when in 1904 the Carnegie's Executive Committee voted $300,000 to establish the Mount Wilson Solar Observatory and named Hale its first director. Under Hale's directorship, Mount Wilson became in many ways a concrete manifestation of the cooperative research in which he believed. He brought physicists into the observatory by establishing a physical laboratory, as well as machine shops, in nearby Pasadena.

With access to relatively ample funding, Hale worked hard to secure ever better equipment to serve the institution's research goals. But Hale, through the Carnegie, had created more than a set of telescopes on Mount Wilson. As the historian Albert Van Helden has stressed,

> [the] problems that had traditionally plagued astronomers in obtaining funds for new instruments and, perhaps even more importantly, for maintaining them and staffing the observatory were substantially eliminated in the case of Mt. Wilson. . . . Informed budgetary decisions on staffing and maintenance provided for continuity and full use of the facilities. Ambitious expansion projects, when properly justified, were funded whenever possible with intelligent allowances for concomitant increases in staff. The initial appropriation of $300,000 was spent in two years, after which funding was maintained at about $100,000 per year until 1911, when it was more than doubled. By 1915 the Observatory had received about $1,500,000, of which about $1,000,000 had been for permanent installations, the remainder being for operating expenses.

Mount Wilson represented astrophysics on an unprecedentedly big scale. But, typically, even before the construction of a 60-inch reflecting telescope had been completed in 1908 (making it the most powerful in the world), Hale had begun to think about, and scheme for, one with a primary mirror 100 inches in diameter. J. D. Hooker, a wealthy Los Angeles merchant, was persuaded by Hale to donate $45,000, and the St.-Gobain glassworks in France set about casting a 100-inch disc. Fraught with difficulties, the mirror's production took eight years, and seeking further funds sapped Hale's health. But in 1910, Andrew Carnegie, always a strong supporter of Hale and his observatory, donated a further $10 million to the Carnegie Institution, expressing the hope that the work of Mount Wilson would be vigorously supported; the Institution soon agreed to find the rest of the funds for the 100-inch telescope.

By 1919, the Hooker telescope, as it was called, was in regular use. The $45,000 from Hooker and over $600,000 from the Carnegie Institution enabled Mount Wilson astronomers to produce a string of very important and sometimes spectacular researches. Perhaps most notably, in the hands of Edwin P. Hubble and Milton Humason, it played a crucial role in the debates of the 1920s and the 1930s on the nature and evolution of the universe. In 1923 and 1924, for example, Hubble exploited the 100-inch to convince astronomers that the problematic spiral nebulae were in fact other galaxies of stars and that the universe is full of such galaxies. While these particular findings did not absolutely depend on the power of the 100-inch, its prodigious light grasp made Hubble's task easier than it might otherwise have been, and when Hubble and Humason turned the 100-inch to examining the light of very faint galaxies, it proved indispensable.

Hale's ambitions, however, did not stop at the 100-inch telescope. Even after bouts of ill-health forced him to resign as director of Mount Wilson in 1923, he embarked on another hunt for funds for a monster telescope. Extolling the possibilities of such an instrument in the April 1928 issue of *Harper's Magazine,* he underscored that "each expedition into remoter space has made new discoveries and brought back permanent additions to our knowledge of the heavens," and that "the opportunity remains for some other donor to advance knowledge and to satisfy his own curiosity regarding the nature of the universe and the problems of its unexplored depths." Before the article was published, Hale arranged for a copy to be sent to Wickliffe Rose at the Rockefeller Foundation so he might consider awarding a grant to conduct tests that would determine how big a mirror might be cast. Rose was enthusiastic about the proposition and after some hard and sometimes stormy bargaining, the Rockefeller and Carnegie Institutions agreed that the huge instrument was to be run by the California Institute of Technology (of which Hale was in many ways the chief architect), but the Mount Wilson staff was to cooperate fully in the planning. With this agreement, in 1928, the International Education Board awarded $6 million for the project, a sum that dwarfed the spending for even the biggest projects in physics.

A 200-inch telescope was settled upon. But the novel designs and technical innovations, as well as the very wide range of engineering, management, and scientific expertise needed, confronted the builders of the 200-inch with enormous problems, and to help tackle them a series of interlocking committees was put into place. In overall charge was the Observatory Committee, a group of four headed by Hale. As well as a general advisory committee, there were other committees on, for example, the mirror. Nor was the job within the reach of academic scientists alone. To turn Hale's dream into reality, a number of industrial firms were engaged. Teamwork and the involvement of industry would indeed become characteristic of many large-scale scientific projects in the making.

Due to a variety of problems (mainly concerning casting and mounting the 200-inch mirror), as well as delays caused by the diversion of observatory staff and machinery to war work, the 200-inch did not start its scientific life until 1948. When it did, it was by far the most powerful optical telescope in the world. However, it is important to stress that this huge machine was used in practice by individuals or small groups, not big teams in the manner of, say, physics accelerators in the 1980s (as we shall see later). Although Hale had died in 1938, the 200-inch was operated very much in the spirit in which he had run Mount Wilson.

When the term *Big Science* came into widespread usage in the 1960s, it was usually taken to be characterized by very costly apparatus and teams of scientists and engineers. But a crucial point here is that although Hubble and his Mount Wilson colleagues often employed large and expensive telescopes, and drew on substantial support from the rest of the observatory and its mix of astronomers, physicists, engineers, technicians, and human computers, their scientific practice was essentially individual. Reflecting in 1977 on the use of big telescopes before World War II, Albert Whitford, one of the leading astronomers of his generation, emphasized its indi-

vidual character. Whitford recalled how it had been a matter of taking one's own photographic plate out of the deep freeze, "warming it up and mixing it with your own developer, and coaxing the telescope into good mirror shape somehow, by opening and closing the domes at the right time, and then exposing a plate with high artistry: 'doing it yourself.' Real mastery of a beautiful and sometimes cantankerous instrument, a big telescope." The astrophysics pursued at Mount Wilson in the 1910s, 1920s, and 1930s, then, was in its spirit small-scale science conducted with big instruments; researchers essentially chose their own problems and generally worked alone or in a very small group, and usually wrote scientific papers alone.

For Hale, the new gospel of cooperative research was mixed with a legacy of nineteenth-century American individualism. He was also a social and political conservative. As one prominent fellow scientist told Hale in 1920: "You believe that aristocracy and patronage are favorable to science." Hale and his fellow conservatives, who led American science during World War I and between the two world wars, recoiled from accepting federal dollars for scientific research in peacetime; to do so was to risk interference in their work from lawmakers, a prospect they dreaded. For Hale and his close colleagues, their natural patrons were the leaders of industry and commerce, as well as those in charge of great fortunes, such as the Carnegie and Rockefeller foundations. Much of Hale's success in fundraising was due to the fact that, as the historian Robert Kargon has put it, he "moved easily among prominent financiers and industrialists, spoke their language and shared their assumptions about the world and its future. Scientific patronage depended on the willingness of the patron to see the importance of research, which in turn depended on the conviction that science was central to the wealth and proper functioning of a modern nation."

THE RAD LAB

Hale's grand vision was of cooperative research fueled by private support. Cooperative research of a different and in some ways more intense kind than that envisaged by Hale began to be pursued in the early 1930s at what became the Radiation Laboratory (often shortened to Rad Lab) at the University of California at Berkeley. There, under the brash and dynamic leadership of Ernest Lawrence, a distinct style of doing physics developed that was to be replicated in many other places, and that exhibited some characteristics that would later be regarded by many as typical of Big Science itself (in the simple classification scheme we have adopted it would be machine-centered Big Science): multidisciplinary teams, large and costly machines, committees, social hierarchies, and autocratic leaders. How, then, did this form of physics arise?

Much was due to Lawrence's lust to build ever more powerful "atom smashers." In 1919, Ernest Rutherford, director of the famous Cavendish Laboratory of Cambridge University, England, had artificially converted one element into another by firing alpha particles from a radioactive source at nitrogen and producing oxygen. But radioactive sources were often prodigiously expensive, nor, it seemed, could heavier elements be disintegrated by the particles emitted by radioactive sources. The key to atom smashing, then, was judged by physicists to lie in producing the bombarding particles by artificial means. As Rutherford was to put it in 1927: "This advance of science depends to a large extent on the development of new technical methods and their application to scientific problems." Thus one of the central aims of many physicists during the 1920s and 1930s was to develop machines to accelerate subatomic particles to higher and higher energies, aim them at targets, and to analyze the results of these collisions. A direct method was to subject charged particles to enormous voltages inside vacuum tubes so as to push them to high energies, but this raised all sorts of technical difficulties. How, for example, were the particles to be prevented from banging into the walls of the tubes? Another tack was to increase the particles' energies in a series of steps, rather than in one big jump as was the case with vacuum tubes. The idea of such an incremental accelerator was being discussed in the physics journals at the time and Lawrence's own novel design was sparked by reading about one possible machine. In 1931, Lawrence's graduate student, M. S. Livingston, fashioned a small but working incremental accelerator of this type, a type that became known as a cyclotron. The first device cost about $1,000, easily sat on a tabletop, but, as the historians John Heilbron and Robert Seidel have explained, it was around successively larger, heavier, and more powerful versions of the cyclotron that the Rad Lab was structured during the 1930s.

Building bigger cyclotrons confronted Lawrence with a range of problems: scientific, technical, organizational, and economic. The technical demands of large cyclotrons, like the building of large telescopes, far outstripped what could be done without the aid of a variety of industrial concerns. Indeed, the Rad

Lab's position in Southern California was a crucial factor. In an area lacking in coal and water supplies, there was a very strong dependence on the skills of electrical and civil engineers to transport water and electrical power over long distances, which meant that high voltage technology was crucial for the Californian economy. The application of such high voltage technology was also essential to Lawrence's atom smashing. In addition, constructing cyclotrons meant exploiting the techniques of radio engineering and mechanical engineering; again, local resources were very important. For example, for one of his big cyclotrons, as Seidel tells us, an "84-ton relic of radio engineering, the massive magnet used in the larger Poulsen arc generators developed by the Federal Telegraph Company of Palo Alto, California, to generate intercontinental radio waves, was reconfigured for Lawrence by a mechanical engineering firm, the Pelton Waterwheel Company of San Francisco, which had come into existence to supply the power needs of the California mining industry." The increasing reliance on engineers would later become central to Big Science.

A common picture of experimental science is of scientists fashioning apparatus to test particular hypotheses and theories. Experiment, however, often takes on a life of its own. Certainly Lawrence was driven not so much by the phenomena expected of nuclear reactions of certain energies, but by the resources he judged were available to him in building ever larger and more powerful cyclotrons. His style was to spend the money at hand. Like Hale and his big telescopes, Lawrence did not wait for a cyclotron to be completed before planning its more powerful successor. But as the historian Michael Dennis has emphasized, unlike, say, atomic researchers at the Department of Terrestrial Magnetism of the Carnegie Institution, Lawrence operated in a market where the need to find external patrons was a continual battle. Lawrence's success owed much to his legendary charm, energy, demonstrated ability to deliver, as well as a lack of squeamishness in overselling the products that might emerge from the use of the cyclotrons. The key that opened the door to much of the money spent at the Rad Lab in the 1930s was the use of cyclotrons for medical studies and treatment, especially cancer research and therapy. Lawrence's biggest coup came in 1940 with the commitment of $1.15 million from the Rockefeller Foundation, with the state of California bringing the total to $2 million, toward what would be much the biggest cyclotron to date, Whereas Hale had regarded the taking of federal money in peacetime as pernicious, Lawrence eagerly seized on federal funds. The federal government in fact provided a reasonable fraction of the capital and operating expenses for the development of the Berkeley cyclotrons before 1940, with even more sizable amounts from the state of California and philanthropic foundations. Thus, even before World War II, the federal government was an important patron of Lawrence's endeavors, most importantly through the National Advisory Cancer Council.

Lawrence's sponsors, moreover, expected a return on their investments. Their needs helped to shape not only the specific research programs pursued at the Rad Lab, but also the manner in which they were carried out. The drive to build ever more powerful machines as well as the need to satisfy the demands of patrons worked against meticulous research efforts, as did the intense time pressure on researchers' use of the cyclotron. These various pressures led to a method of operation that used small crews of people. Crews were arranged by shifts, and labored not only to construct the cyclotrons but also to maintain them so that they worked dependably. As one visiting scientist recalled: "I was particularly impressed in Berkeley with the method of operating the cyclotron. The experiments were divided into shifts: maintenance shifts and experimenters. When a leak or fault developed in the cyclotron the maintenance crew rushed forward to plug the leaks by melting the numerous wax joints and fixed the fault when the operating shifts rushed in again."

The crews, however, were only one part of the complex social structure that had evolved at the Rad Lab by the late 1930s to build and operate the cyclotrons. At the top was Lawrence. Below him was a directing committee. Other committees, each with its own leader, were responsible for building specific pieces of apparatus. The directing committee was itself composed of Lawrence, committee leaders and supervisors, and others who might be required on particular points. Such a structure, of course, would have been impossible without a relatively large number of people, and at the end of the 1930s, the staff totaled around sixty. In addition to many doctoral students and postdoctoral fellows on extramural fellowships, some people, including some physicists hit by the Depression who hoped the experience would aid their chances of finding a job, worked at the lab without pay.

The cyclotron became a work site for interdisciplinary research, bringing together not just physicists and engineers, but also chemists, biologists, and physicians. One product of this mix was nuclear science combining radiochemistry, radiobiology, nuclear physics, and nuclear medicine. Although during the 1930s, many of the leading discoveries in nuclear physics came from researchers using sources of natural radioactivity, not accelerators, in 1939, Lawrence won the Nobel Prize in physics for "having invented and developed the cyclotron and especially for the results attained by means of this device in the production of artificial radioactive elements." Lawrence's cyclotrons undoubtedly boosted the prestige of American physics as groups throughout the world, as well as the United States, sought to build their own cyclotrons.

The first cyclotron had been built by a graduate student for about $1,000 and could be used on a tabletop; a decade later a machine about 100 times more powerful was under construction that cost 2,000 times as much, engaged around one hundred physicists, engineers, and managers, and weighed over 4,000 tons. But more than a machine had been invented at Berkeley. A new way of organizing work in physics in an academic setting had also been fashioned. Both Hale and Lawrence demonstrated the skills to move easily to new scales of enterprise. They swiftly mastered the ability to bring together, in Charles C. Gillispie's words, "large masses of men, money, and equipment together over great distances to achieve a result. Indeed, throughout all of American history, one of the leitmotifs has ever been the enlargement of scale."

In discussing the novelty of activities at Berkeley, it is important to note that by the end of the 1930s, the Rad Lab had developed a form of what has been termed corporate physics. In fact, by 1931, there were over 1,600 companies in the United States supporting research laboratories employing around 33,000 people; within a decade, despite the Depression, over 2,000 companies employed almost 70,000 people in their laboratories. Although many were merely laboratories in which routine tests were conducted, in the others, scientists and engineers pursued research to gain a better knowledge of science and technology that related to their companies' activities, even if the relevance was only long-term. As the historian Leonard S. Reich summarized it, "Industrial research scientists and engineers often worked on group projects, to which they contributed specified types of results under the direction of a group leader. Their leeway for digression was often quite small, and they sometimes faced schedules for the completion of their work. Because research directors had to be certain that a large portion of results coming from their laboratories would be commercially applicable, they frequently supervised projects themselves or placed them under the control of a senior staff member." Thus in some respects, the form of life for a scientist at the Rad Lab matched that in an industrial laboratory.

The Rad Lab greatly expanded its activities in the lead-up to and during World War II, but this was not a simple scaling up of operations. The war-related activities were centered very largely on the development of technologies. This development work called for large numbers of technicians and engineers who would come to far outnumber the scientists. In fact, numbers at the lab grew during the war to around a thousand, a very big jump over the approximately sixty employed in the late 1930s. The lab designed modified cyclotrons—calutrons—to be used in the production of uranium for weapons. Even the colossal magnet for the cyclotron under construction at the start of the war was put into the shade by the combined magnets for the calutrons, which weighed about one hundred times more. The calutrons were themselves only one unit in the hugely complex enterprise to build atomic bombs.

Lawrence's influence was felt in other wartime laboratories. Most importantly, he helped fashion the deliberately misleadingly named Radiation Laboratory at MIT where radar work was carried out, as well as the special weapons laboratory at Los Alamos headed by J. Robert Oppenheimer that designed atomic bombs. Methods of research at the Radiation Laboratory and Los Alamos were significant in their own right, but were important too because, when at war's end the scientists—the majority of whom were physicists—dispersed, they carried these methods back to their laboratories, most of which were in academic institutions. Research at Los Alamos, for example, was directed rigorously toward a definite mission—building atomic bombs. In an environment where funds were plentiful, time short, and a successful outcome was judged vital, there was, as in the early days of cyclotron building, an emphasis on speed and systematic trial-and-error methods, not detailed theoretical analyses. This did not mean that the researchers were not interested in, or did not sometimes need to secure, new scientific knowledge, but, rather, that they were interested in it only insofar as it contributed toward bomb building. In other words, they pursued a way of working in which, as the historian Lillian Hoddeson has aptly expressed it, the emphasis was squarely on use, not understanding.

There was also an elaborate structure of committees at Los Alamos, including committees of outside experts to review the work being performed. The basic research unit was the group, usually an interdisciplinary group of scientists and engineers. Oppenheimer, and the leaders under him, ran matters in a quasi-military fashion. Researchers, for instance, could find themselves transferred at very short notice to projects with a higher priority.

In its aims, Los Alamos represented Big Technology, not Big Science. But it gave to many of the staff at Los Alamos an enormous sense of confidence in what could be achieved by large-scale methods and a crash program. Such beliefs, of course, were not the product of the war alone. As David Lilienthal, head of the Tennessee Valley Authority and later the Atomic Energy Commission, put it in 1944 in *TVA: Democracy on the March,* "There is almost nothing, however fantastic, that (given competent organization) a team of engineers, scientists, and administrators cannot do today." But the war amplified this message. As one Los Alamos veteran claimed, "Los Alamos is an example of how a scientific-technological miracle can be performed." This sense of accomplishment was not confined to Los Alamos veterans, but was shared by many of those scientists who had learned by participating in war work how to think big, deal with the military, work in teams, and devise innovative and often big technologies and technological systems, skills that would prove to be crucial for much postwar science.

THE POSTWAR WORLD AND PERMANENT MOBILIZATION

The waging of war across the globe had even brought about a consensus between liberals and conservatives on Capitol Hill and in policy-making circles that the federal government had a far wider role to play in supporting the nation's scientific enterprise than had been the case before 1941. United States policy was now directed toward continuing supremacy in scientific and military matters, not just in certain areas, but in all areas. During World War I, science and industry had been mobilized to serve the nation, in large part through the National Academy of Sciences and the War Industries Board. But when the fighting ended in 1918 it had been generally agreed that there would be a rapid return to normality. However, in 1945, with the lesson of Pearl Harbor ever in mind and the judgment that the pace of technological development meant that for the next war the United States would have very little, if any, time to mobilize its military forces and put the economy onto a war footing, the conventional wisdom was that the U.S.

must be in a constant state of readiness. National survival, it seemed, depended on the swift extension of scientific knowledge. As the historian Daniel Kevles has explained,

> Physicists won World War II with radar and ended it with the atomic bomb, decisively eliminating the need to risk ground troops in an invasion of the Japanese Home Islands—so the history of the war was instantly understood by physicists and policy makers in the United States. The consequences seemed clear: National security would depend, henceforth, upon technological superiority; nuclear weapons and other military technologies could offset the Soviet manpower advantage in postwar Europe. Technological superiority, in turn, needed state programs and facilities of scientific research, and state efforts to enlarge the nation's pool of people trained in relevant technical disciplines, especially physics, the practitioners of which had been in notably short supply during the war.

Therefore military support flowed not only toward the military's own laboratories—for example, the Naval Research Laboratory in Washington, D.C.—but, through the use of contracts, to laboratories that had come into being during the war and that had been officially the charge of universities, as well as to industrial laboratories and the universities themselves. The new institutions included the Applied Physics Laboratory of the Johns Hopkins University and MIT's Radiation Laboratory.

At war's end, national policymakers faced the issue of what was to be the fate of the laboratories of the Manhattan Engineer District funded by the War Department—such as, for example, Los Alamos. In fact, very extensive resources continued to be directed to them. When the Atomic Energy Commission (AEC), a civilian agency, came into being on 1 January 1947, it was essentially the Manhattan Engineer District reborn, although the AEC was charged with fostering research and development on civilian as well as military uses of atomic power. While the constituent AEC labs were far from homogeneous in the sorts of things they did and the aims toward which they were directed, the labs' chief mission was military, and a similar style of research characterized by teams and elaborate and costly sorts of apparatus pervaded all of them. As at the Rad Lab, this was not simply a larger-scale version of what had happened before the war. In many ways it was instead a continuation of wartime, mission-oriented research that often led to classified meetings, reports, and journals so that much of the research conducted at the AEC labs could not be published in the open

literature. It was also, as AEC Commissioner and physicist Henry Smyth suggested, research by "big groups of scientists who will take orders."

One of the AEC labs, however, pursued a more open approach in which visiting scientists were positively encouraged to use its facilities. At Brookhaven National Laboratory, the activities centered on fundamental nuclear science. As the historian Allan Needell has argued,

> Brookhaven National Laboratory was created in 1946 at the initiative and largely under the direction of scientists who were then returning from wartime assignments to academic positions at universities in the northeastern United States. Those scientists, primarily physicists who had been associated with the development of radar at the MIT Radiation Laboratory or with the atomic bomb project, pressed for a federally financed laboratory for research in the "nuclear sciences." The laboratory they had in mind was one that would provide the organization and the administrative and support services needed to manage and facilitate large scale, technologically innovative projects that for reasons of expense, potential hazards, or national security could not be carried out at a university. Nuclear reactors were the devices they had in mind. Like their government benefactors, they believed that recent experience had demonstrated the importance of science to the nation, and that the way to encourage science was to supply the best scientists with the newest of tools and the support they needed to pursue the most promising areas of research.

The reactor, moreover, could be exploited by other scientists besides physicists: biologists, chemists, and metallurgists. Hence the reactor was a means to again bring into being the teams that had proved so potent during the war, as well as to provide scientists in the Northeast with a state-of-the-art facility.

Brookhaven's leaders also pressed for a powerful accelerator to give the laboratory an advantage over Lawrence at Berkeley. Instead of seeing this as a wasteful duplication of effort, the AEC encouraged the pursuit of multiple approaches. As one of its commissioners remarked in 1949, "When we set out to discover new continents over uncharted oceans, the chances of arrival at a distant beach-head are greatly enhanced if the voyage is undertaken by more than one ship's company." The result was the Brookhaven "cosmotron," completed in 1952 at a cost of about $20 million and the "bevatron" at Berkeley, which began operations in 1954. At the time of their completion, both were the most powerful accelerators of their type in the world. Both were types of a machine known as a proton synchrotron in which protons were accelerated to unprecedented energies by use of a ring-shaped magnet. As M. Stanley Livingston, builder of the first cyclotron, and John P. Blewett were to put it in 1962, the proton synchrotron "represents the ultimate development of the accelerator art, involving such complicated techniques that all the skills of mechanical and electrical engineering are taxed to provide the wide variety of complex components and to assure that they function as a unit. Advanced techniques of theoretical computation are required in design, and the electronic computer has become an essential tool." These machines were employed for pathbreaking research. With the aid of the bevatron at Berkeley, Emilio Segrè and Owen Chamberlain converted energy into protons and antiprotons, winning the 1959 Nobel Prize in physics for their discovery of the antiproton.

By acting in this "leapfrog" fashion, the AEC and its client physicists were acting very like Hale and Lawrence before the war in driving for ever more powerful machines even before their predecessor had been built. But the private philanthropies that had made possible many of Hale and Lawrence's earlier enterprises were now hugely outspent by the military and the AEC, and, in the physical sciences at least, lost nearly all of their original influence. The sponsors' motives for building big physics machines in the late 1940s and early 1950s were also very different from the justifications earlier offered up by Hale and Lawrence. The particle accelerators funded by the Manhattan Engineer District and the AEC in the years just after World War II were supported for largely military reasons, even if the pay-offs were judged to be years away. After all, modified cyclotrons had been used in the processes of isotope separation that had refined the uranium for the bomb dropped on Hiroshima and nuclear reactors had produced plutonium for the Nagasaki weapon. At war's end, then, the clear historical message drawn by the military and policymakers was that nuclear science was crucial to military preparedness. The rediscovery at Brookhaven in 1952 of a concept known as "strong-focusing" also led to an AEC–Defense Department program to investigate the possibility of using a beam of charged particles as a defense against atomic bombs. As the AEC's director of research noted in 1953, "the military usefulness of particle accelerators should be included as an additional justification in further defense of ultrahigh energy particle accelerator construction items before the Bureau of the Budget and the Congress."

The so-called Materials Testing Accelerator (MTA) was also designed specifically to produce materials for nuclear weapons. Once the Soviets had exploded their first fission bomb, the debate in U.S. policy-making circles over whether or not to pursue the hydrogen bomb came to an abrupt end with President Truman's approval of a crash program to build the new weapon. And with what appeared as a looming shortage of fissionable material, as well as the need for tritium for the hydrogen bomb, Lawrence and his colleague Luis Alvarez at Berkeley proposed an ambitious scheme: meet the shortfalls by constructing a gigantic linear accelerator to fashion the materials artificially. Pressed hard by Lawrence and the AEC's director of research, the AEC funded the building of a prototype of the MTA at Livermore, California, work that was aided by accelerator experts who had been transferred for the task from Brookhaven. But although the prototype was a technical success and $20 million was spent on the program, plans for the full-size MTA—estimated to cost around $5 billion, more than twice the amount spent on the Manhattan Project—were dropped when new supplies of uranium ore were mined in the West and the Savannah River Reactors provided a cheaper supply of tritium than that offered by the MTA.

While the AEC put most of its research funds into its own labs, it also provided some funds to university researchers during the 1950s. The Office of Naval Research (ONR), however, was the chief patron of academic science in the years immediately after World War II, and on the eve of the Korean War the ONR was directing funds to over a thousand research projects in nearly two hundred universities. ONR funded civilian science liberally and the scientists it supported moved easily between problems of, say, nuclear physics or cosmic rays, and weapons building. Among its projects were the building and operation of on-campus accelerators for various kinds of unclassified research. In fact, by 1949 the Department of Defense and the AEC provided some 96 percent of all of the federal monies spent on U.S. campuses for research in the physical sciences. Just before the outbreak of the Korean War, the U.S. federal government was spending some $1 billion on research and development, but the war itself drove this figure permanently higher, and in late 1951, as a result of the emergency, some two-thirds of the nation's scientists and engineers were at work on defense projects. In the late 1940s, military spending (in constant dollars) on research and development had held at some thirty times its prewar level, but by the late 1950s had climbed even above the levels reached in World War II, and during the 1950s, the Department of Defense provided about 80 per cent of the entire federal budget for research and development.

The experience of World War II, mounting Cold War tensions due to (among other things) the "loss of China," the Berlin crisis, the Soviet success in 1949 in exploding an atomic bomb, as well as the scientific mobilization of the Korean War and internal anxieties about Communists in high places, led to what was, in Daniel Kevles's phrase, "a pervasive psychology of permanent mobilization, a commitment to expansive military preparedness." James B. Conant, the president of Harvard and one of the architects of science policy during the war, even told the National War College in 1952 that "the military, if anything, have become vastly too much impressed with the abilities of research and development. They are no longer the conservatives . . . at times they seem to be fanatics in their belief of what the scientists and the technologists can do."

In this atmosphere, the modern pattern of patronage of high-energy physics entailed, as Robert Seidel has described, a trade-off between scholarly and state purposes that contained three chief elements. First, those trained for high-energy physics could also apply their expertise to other, perhaps more directly military, enterprises. Second, high-energy physicists could act in times of national emergency as a kind of "bull pen" and be brought in to strengthen the staff of the weapons laboratories. And third, the tools of the physicists, the particle accelerators and associated detectors of radiation and particles, were also tools of international prestige and could be turned into instruments of national security. In return for the tight ties to the federal government, physicists had access to resources of which their pre–World War II colleagues, including Lawrence, could only have dreamed. While U.S. physicists had become closely linked to the military, and policymakers had decided that Cold War demands dictated that the United States be the leading nation in high-energy physics, at the same time physicists were relatively free of direct control.

It was this new political economy, which itself was founded on the consensus on the enormous importance of science to the nation's security and well-being, that made possible the rise and rapid spread of Big Science. During World War II, many physicists had been given a crash course in mission-directed, team-oriented and executed research in which engineers and industry played very important roles; research was conducted with clear divisions of labor and often autocratic team leaders. The war had therefore taught academic physicists to think about their research on new sorts of scales and to establish new—at least for the great majority of them—

organizational models. In the AEC-funded labs, as in the war, there was a tight linking of science and engineering, often to the place where the two were indistinguishable, together with the crucial involvement of industry. Scientists, engineers, and technicians clustered around the capital-intensive reactors and accelerators of the AEC labs in a collective process to generate knowledge for a variety of purposes. The laboratories of the AEC became the chief home of Big Science enterprises in the first decade or so after the war, and thus modern Big Science was in large part constituted by, and itself in part constitutive of, what some historians have termed the national-security state. The federal government drove a permanent mobilization so that the nation was continually prepared to wage warfare of great destruction by, as Walter McDougall has expressed it, "folding the intelligence agencies, the armed forces, corporations, research institutions and universities into a national complex for the provision of ever more sophisticated weapons." The Cold War had consolidated the demands for new groups of professional scientists, who also played key roles in creating for themselves an organizational infrastructure in terms of federal agencies such as the Atomic Energy Commission, and this new state bureaucracy subsequently became self-reinforcing.

CRITICS OF BIG SCIENCE

The spread and development of Big Science techniques and working methods provoked controversy. For some academic scientists, the change in the form of scientific life—with the increased emphasis on teamwork which carried in its wake a diminution of autonomy, for instance—brought undesirable consequences. One criticism leveled at large-scale research was that it was essentially a form of industrialized research in which the spark of individual creativity was smothered. As the brilliant maverick mathematician Norbert Wiener wrote in 1948, reflecting on judgments he had made two years earlier, "It is clear that the degradation of the position of the scientist as an independent worker and thinker to that of a morally irresponsible stooge in a science-factory has proceeded even more rapidly and devastatingly than I had expected. This subordination of those who ought to think to those who have the administrative power is ruinous for the morale of the scientist, and quite to the same extent it is ruinous to the quality of the objective scientific output of the country." For him, the U.S. "big science-factories" were producing a new generation of scientists who would spurn any scientific project "which does not have millions of dollars invested in it."

Another scientist who vehemently criticized the new form of scientific practice was Merle Tuve, a boyhood friend of Ernest Lawrence and, like Lawrence, a pioneer in the 1930s of the construction and use of atom smashers. But Tuve had been based in the Carnegie Institution's Department of Terrestrial Magnetism (DTM), a very different environment from Lawrence's Rad Lab and one in which, through relatively lavish Carnegie funding, the need to continually drum-up outside funds was absent. During World War II, Tuve had led Section T of the Office of Scientific Research and Development, which developed proximity fuses. He had then become director of the Applied Physics Laboratory (which was the institutionalization of Section T) of the John Hopkins University before returning after the war to the Carnegie's DTM. There Tuve established a number of relatively small-scale projects, including one on radio astronomy. And, as Allan Needell has explained, Tuve's engagements in the battles over the nature and direction of radio astronomy in the United States, and the recently founded National Science Foundation's possible role in supporting the new discipline, provides an important window onto opposing values and beliefs in the 1950s about Big Science.

The battle began in 1954 when AUI (the consortium of universities that managed the Brookhaven National Laboratory) indicated that it might like to manage a facility devoted to radio astronomy conducted with big facilities. In fact, the president of AUI, Lloyd V. Berkner, had been hired shortly before to assure AUI expanded. Trained in electrical engineering, Berkner had joined the DTM early in his career, worked on radar in the war, and afterward became a major player in various positions that mediated between the military and scientific leaders. Unlike Tuve, Berkner reveled in matters of organization. He had thought hard about the relationships among science, politics, economics, and military matters, and he positively embraced links between science and the military. And it was Berkner, the one-time electrical engineer, who led AUI's drive toward radio astronomy. In so doing he built on a sentiment among astronomers for guiding radio astronomy along the lines followed by the nuclear sciences after World War II in terms of highlighting costly equipment and interdisciplinary research.

Another crucial factor in the negotiations between AUI and leading astronomers was the National Science Foundation's attitude toward providing the funds for a large radio astronomy facility. One argu-

ment Berkner and AUI made to NSF was in terms of "spin-offs," including those for military applications:

> Most radio astronomy signals are very weak by normal communication engineering standards, and the demands of the astronomers have forced advances in electronic techniques, the benefits of which in other fields cannot be estimated. To mention only a few, material improvements have been made in the noise factors of receivers, in the precision of constructing and controlling various types of antennas, in discrimination and integration techniques, in broad-banding radio-frequency components, and in data display devices. The value of such advances as these to our military security is very great.

Berkner's argument underscores the fact that Big Science projects were justified not only for advancing military security or because of the scientific results they promised, but for a number of reasons depending on the intended audience.

Tuve, however, mounted a strong attack on Berkner's advocacy of a big radio telescope on the basis of a number of issues: (1) Was there a proven need for such a radio astronomy facility with large instruments? (2) Who should manage such a facility? (3) Large expenditures on radio astronomy might damage small projects in, or research on, other areas of astronomy by siphoning off resources (in the mid-1950s, the NSF budget was only of the order of $50 million, with little room to absorb big and expensive projects). Tuve wanted radio astronomy to develop in a step-by-step manner, rather than be pulled in certain directions by the magnet of massive federal expenditures, to be shaped by creative individual researchers, not government administrators. Tuve wanted to back "men and ideas," not huge facilities.

Despite Tuve's arguments, the NSF's governing body, the National Science Board, decided in 1955 to provide resources for large, basic-science facilities "when the need is clear and it is in the national interest, when the merit is endorsed by panels of experts, and when funds are not readily available from other sources." The astronomers also sided with Berkner. Astronomy, one of the least immediately utilitarian of the sciences had became the mostly richly endowed of all the sciences in the United States early in the twentieth century. Despite this relative wealth, by the mid-1930s, as one observer has put it, there were fewer than two hundred active astronomers in this country, "only a handful of whom were privileged to observe with the three 'modern' reflecting telescopes, then located in favorable climates on the West Coast, the newest of these instruments being more than fifteen years old." For the NSF and leading astronomers, the availability of powerful new research tools was greatly advanced by big government-funded projects.

One important result of the battle over the future of radio astronomy was that the NSF had cast its lot with the support of large facilities. After the NSF contracted in 1956 with AUI to build and operate the National Radio Astronomy Observatory, astronomers were alerted to the value of creating a university consortium. The Kitt Peak National Observatory, an observatory for optical astronomy composed of telescopes, workshops, and laboratories, was founded shortly afterward. It was the responsibility of the Association of Universities for Research in Astronomy (AURA), a newly created consortium. In the words of Merton England, the foundation's most recent historian, Kitt Peak's establishment "was in the main a successful example" of the National Science Foundation behaving as the foundation's director said it should, as leading astronomers "largely controlled events with [the foundation's] blessing." However, while the construction of the big telescopes and their associated apparatus at Kitt Peak and the National Radio Astronomy Observatory engaged large and interlocking multidisciplinary teams, optical and radio astronomers generally used these telescopes as individuals or small groups. Although large sums of money and substantial groups of astronomers, engineers, and technicians were needed to maintain and update the apparatus, the individual scientist, despite the size of the facilities, could often operate in ways like those Tuve had urged. It is also important in discussing machine-centered Big Science to distinguish the science in the making, that is, the building of the technologies to make the Big Science possible, from the actual operation of those technologies to produce scientific data. Even in the case, for instance, of the *International Ultraviolet Explorer,* an astronomical satellite launched in 1977 that cost well over $100 million to build and involved large international teams of scientists, engineers, and technicians in its construction, the users to a large degree have followed the methods of small-scale science. Research time on the telescopes of both Kitt Peak and Green Bank was also available to any astronomer whose proposal survived review by a committee of peers. For the majority of astronomers, then, these facilities were a boon and gave them unprecedented access to state-of-the-art research tools. The giant telescopes that had been financed by private philanthropy on Mount Wilson, for example, were all but closed to researchers from outside the Carnegie Institution.

In a way, Big Science had helped to democratize the discipline.

Tuve lost the battle over the National Radio Astronomy Laboratory, but he was not alone in his criticisms of large-scale scientific enterprises supported by huge amounts of federal dollars. Such criticisms became more widespread when, in the wake of the launching of the Soviet Union's *Sputnik I* satellite in 1957, vast new expenditures were directed toward space endeavors. One of the most influential commentators on the new form of scientific practice was the director of the Oak Ridge National Laboratory, Alvin Weinberg. In 1961, in "The Impact of Large Scale Research on the United States," he contended that the monuments of what he termed Big Science—and these he regarded as the high energy accelerators, the high flux nuclear reactors, and so on—were the symbols of our time, just as surely as we find in the cathedral of Notre Dame a striking symbol of the Middle Ages. Weinberg not only brought the term *Big Science* into wide currency, but he also crystallized the anxieties of many people, both within and outside of the scientific community. Of course, by the early 1960s, Big Science was hardly novel. Rather, the issue, to put it bluntly, was that there was a great deal more Big Science than there had ever been before. Weinberg warned that if Big Science's growth was not checked, it would lead to the decline of science itself, for, among other evils, it tends to turn scientists into journalists to win funding for their projects, and it produces far too many science administrators. He also charged that the style of science was changing. Scientists were spending money instead of thought. In an environment where money was plentiful and thought scarce, there was a natural rush to spend dollars. Weinberg was also deeply concerned by what he regarded as Big Science's bad effects on the universities, particularly in turning some university scientists into what he termed "Big Operators." To sum up then, for Weinberg, Big Science was a kind of pathology and carried the germs of three diseases: journalitis, moneyitis, and administrativitis.

Weinberg nevertheless conceded that for better or worse, Big Science was here to stay, and that scientists had secured impressive results through the access provided by Big Science tools to previously inaccessible phenomena. The central challenge facing policymakers and scientists was to let Big Science flourish without at the same time allowing it to trample smaller-scale efforts. With these concerns in mind, Weinberg's proposed solution was that Big Science be kept in what he saw as its proper place:

in the national laboratories funded by the federal government.

In part this solution perhaps has to be read as Weinberg's concern as the director of the Oak Ridge National Laboratory to maintain his institution at a time when the AEC laboratory system had been criticized and its future debated. But other commentators were making similar points too. Writing a few years later, Ralph E. Lapp, one-time assistant director of the Argonne National Laboratory and head of the nuclear physics branch of the ONR, argued, "Big Science has become an institution in the United States; this is taken for granted, but many scientists are concerned because Big Science is not necessarily great science. . . . Scientists are worried that massive science, bloated on federal funds, may not turn out excellent science." Philip Abelson, director of the Carnegie's Geophysical Laboratory, had decided that "Government money has been the Frankenstein of big science, and in many instances the monster has invaded the universities."

THE U.S. RESPONSE TO SPUTNIK

In his famous farewell address to the American people on 17 January 1961, President Eisenhower had sounded a warning not just against unwarranted influence by the military-industrial complex, but also against the rise of federally funded research. As Eisenhower argued:

> Today, the solitary inventor, tinkering in his shop, has been overshadowed by task forces of scientists in laboratories and testing fields. In the same fashion, the free university, historically the fountainhead of free ideas and scientific discovery, has experienced a revolution in the conduct of research. Partly because of the huge costs involved, a government contract becomes virtually a substitute for intellectual curiosity. For every old blackboard there are now hundreds of new electronic computers.
>
> The prospect of domination of the nation's scholars by Federal employment, project allocations, and the power of money is ever present—and is gravely to be regarded.
>
> Yet, in holding scientific research and discovery in respect, as we should, we must also be alert to the equal and opposite danger that public policy could itself become captive of a scientific-technological elite.

But Eisenhower himself, especially in the aftermath of the launch of *Sputnik I* in 1957, had played a major, even if reluctant, part in directing vast funds toward those members of this "scientific-technologi-cal elite" concerned with various Big Science endeavors as well as space activities. The 184-pound Russian satellite orbited the earth every ninety minutes, emitting persistent "beep, beep" radio signals that mocked the United States, as Secretary of State John Foster Dulles put it. But perhaps the most far-reaching repercussion of *Sputnik I* was the wave of near hysteria it provoked in the United States.

To a nation with a profound distrust of Soviet intentions, the unexpected demonstration of Russian technological prowess, with its warning that the United States was apparently slipping badly in the battle for international supremacy, was startling and deeply disturbing. Underlying this response was the realization that a Soviet missile powerful enough to launch a satellite into space could also be used to carry atomic weapons from Russia to obliterate American cities. Science and technology figured centrally in America's dreams of abundance and world leadership, but now they appeared in America's nightmares of a dangerous world with uncertain prospects of security. *Sputnik I* was nine times heavier than the first planned U.S. satellite, implying a big Russian lead in large rockets (a point reinforced when the even more massive *Sputnik II* was launched soon after *Sputnik I*). To make matters worse, on 6 December 1957, in full view of the nation's television cameras, the first attempt to launch a U.S. satellite ended in disaster. The Vanguard rocket rose a few feet from its launch pad and faltered; as it fell back, the fuel tanks ruptured, and the rocket folded and crashed back to the ground surrounded by flames and a sea of billowing smoke.

The reactions to *Sputnik* were to a large degree genuine expressions of shock and apprehension. They were also to a significant extent controlled, guided, and fashioned by certain politicians and a section of the news media anxious to use *Sputnik* as a stick with which to beat the Eisenhower administration. As Senate leader Lyndon Johnson exclaimed when Vanguard exploded, "How long, how long, oh God, how long will it take us to catch up with the Russians' two satellites?"

Eisenhower's previous approach to missiles and satellites had been, according to one of his biographers, to let each military service "develop its own program and hope one of them would score a breakthrough. The result had been failure. The generals and admirals squabbled with one another, made slighting remarks about their fellow services' efforts, and ignored the Secretary of Defense." Given the buffeting he had to endure from the political storm whipped up by *Sputnik*, Eisenhower could not hold his ground. Facing the overwhelming political pressure of nearly all Democrats, most Republicans, and a majority of columnists and scientists, on 2 April 1958, the president requested that Congress establish a civilian space agency, the National Aeronautics and Space Administration (NASA). The bill establishing the agency was swiftly passed through the Congress in the spring and summer of 1958, and NASA came into being on 1 October 1958.

Not only did *Sputnik* help to bring NASA into being, it also reshaped the thinking of politicians to such an extent that many old assumptions about the federal funding of space activities were promptly swept away. The usual rules on Capitol Hill lapsed for a time as the legislators could hardly dispense money to NASA fast enough. As NASA's first administrator was to recall, "The Congressional attitude was: Why can't we do this tomorrow? . . . I don't remember in those first years ever going up on the Hill where I wasn't asked: What did you ask for? Don't you need more money?" "Only a blundering fool" could have come back from Capitol Hill with a result detrimental to the space agency.

The political pressure to counter, and surpass, the achievements of the Soviets meant that the American riposte to *Sputnik* led to a space race—in effect, another front in the battle to win the Cold War. Science would play a significant part in the chase, and budgets for space science would reach levels undreamed of in pre-*Sputnik* days, when monies had come very largely from the military, with small amounts from the AEC and NSF. The military had fostered both new research practices with rockets as well as new practitioners of space science. Some of these scientists had also given the initial push to the International Geophysical Year (IGY) of 1957–1958, an international effort to study and collect data on the lands, seas, and atmosphere of the earth, an effort very much in the tradition of the large-data collecting expeditions and networks of the nineteenth century.

The catalyst for the International Geophysical Year (IGY) was provided by a dinner meeting in April 1950 of six U.S. geophysicists and a British colleague. They proposed a third International Polar Year, an international science effort to be modeled after the earlier polar years of 1882–1883 and 1932–1933. The goal, however, soon shifted to a coordinated international enterprise to study large-scale geophysical processes. In the end it engaged over sixty countries and thousands of observing stations. However, the central emphasis was on the physics of the ionosphere (a region of the earth's atmosphere reaching from around 60 km above the earth's surface to 10,000 km) and the physical interactions between

the earth and the sun. But in discussing the U.S. efforts in the IGY it is important to recognize that the IGY was not a scientific venture alone. Permeating scientific goals were foreign policy and national security goals. For example, the Science Advisory Committee of the White House Office of Defense Mobilization argued in 1954 that a "relatively small U.S. investment in the IGY could add immeasurably to the effectiveness of civilian and military activities costing hundreds of millions of dollars. The urgency of carrying out the IGY is apparent when one reflects on the important implications of the IGY program on the well-being and security of our country." To take one example: in 1952, three meridians were chosen for particularly detailed ionospheric observations in the IGY (75 degrees west; 10 degrees east; and 140 degrees east). It is certainly no coincidence that in 1950, a committee of the Department of Defense's Research and Development Board had stressed the importance of establishing observing stations near the 75-degrees-west meridian.

One large part of the U.S. effort for the IGY was the Vanguard project to launch a series of satellites, which ended up costing around $120 million. After the first attempt at a launch ended in a disaster as the rocket exploded on the launch pad, an alternative program was mounted on a crash basis to use the Army's Juno I rocket to put a satellite into orbit about the earth. Although the scientists, the disciplines, and the institutions that were carried into the space age had been shaped by their postwar and Cold War contexts, the vast infusion of resources and new people radically transformed the institutional structure, as well as expanded the scientific and technological possibilities, of space science. In short order, satellites made possible in 1958 the discovery of what became known as the Van Allen radiation belts, that is, that the earth is surrounded by two bands of ionizing radiation composed of protons and electrons contained by the earth's magnetic field, a spectacular find that had far-reaching implications for a range of geophysical phenomena, as well as for any future spacecraft that would have to cross the radiation belts. The discovery was the product of a large-scale enterprise that engaged costly apparatus (the rockets and launch complexes) and teams of scientists, engineers, and technicians to make the launch possible, then secure and analyze the data.

Issues of national prestige also permeated space science endeavors. For example, following *Sputnik* some astronomers were quick to take advantage of the new political economy for space science and were pushing for a series of astronomical observatories to be put into space so as to obtain data unobtainable from the surface of the earth. When President Eisenhower's science adviser told him "about the potential gains in national prestige if we establish the first astro-observatory on a satellite [the] President was very much interested and said he would certainly be in favor of proceeding vigorously." This jump into space astronomy meant that a range of scientific, technical, and institutional issues had to be thrashed out as the teams of scientists and engineers went along. The astronomers wanted to build steadily toward the orbiting observatories via less sophisticated spacecraft but, as one of the NASA managers involved in this decision making later wrote, "exposed directly to the outside pressures to match or surpass the Soviet achievement in space, NASA moved more rapidly with the development of observatory-class satellites and the larger deep-space probes than the scientists would have required. . . . Some of the most intense conflicts between NASA and the scientific community arose later over the issue of the small and less costly projects versus the large and expensive ones— conflict that NASA's vigorous development of manned space flight exacerbated."

With the White House and Congress clamoring for NASA to demonstrate the United States was ahead in the space race, NASA managers and administrators often responded by eschewing small missions that were incremental advances on earlier efforts. Instead, they preferred big enterprises, even if these required much larger technological steps and entailed more risk. Given the urgent competition with the Soviets, the voices of the astronomers calling for a more conservative program of space observatories, were drowned out.

Perhaps not surprisingly, the first Orbiting Astronomical Observatory (OAO) took longer to complete than was anticipated. The launch, originally planned for 1963, had to be postponed. The 3,900-pound OAO-I (containing more than 440,000 parts and over thirty miles of electrical wire) also underwent rigorous qualification and testing procedures that had not originally been included in the project plans. Despite the delays, by early 1966, OAO-I was at Cape Kennedy ready for launch. The observatory was deposited perfectly in space. However, when the system used to point the satellite to its target stars was turned on by ground controllers, the batteries overheated. Soon contact was lost with the satellite. When tracking radar picked up several pieces of the observatory, it seemed likely that the batteries had exploded.

In fact, of the four OAO spacecraft, two ended as complete failures, but the other two sent back to earth high-quality science data for periods longer than planned, one for four years, and the other for nine years. These data, for the most part the record of ultraviolet radiation from astronomical sources, could not have been secured from the earth's surface using conventional telescopes, and were only available to instruments lofted above the obscuring layers of the atmosphere. But these data had come at a cost of over $200 million for the entire program, a staggering sum for those astronomers who protested that many ground-based telescopes of the size of the 200-inch Hale Telescope at Palomar Mountain could be secured for this much money. Some ground-based astronomers, particularly those with ready access to large and powerful telescopes at good sites in the West, objected to what they saw as an extremely extravagant sort of Big Science, and were fearful that space astronomy might pull funds away from their own researches.

NASA also pursued a vigorous program of planetary exploration. When the agency was formed in 1958, there were relatively few planetary scientists. The space agency therefore set out to create such a community through support for various educational opportunities, institutions, and apparatus, including telescopes to be used on the ground to examine the planets. One billion–dollar–plus project to result from the efforts of NASA and its client planetary science community was *Viking,* which sent two robot spacecraft to Mars. Each was a kind of double spacecraft and carried both an orbiter and a lander, the lander to touch down on the Martian surface, and the orbiter to circle the planet returning data. The first lander descended to Mars's Chryse plain on 20 July 1976. As well as returning 4,500 images from the planet's surface, each lander carried a retractable boom. Controlled from the earth, the boom could be extended to scoop up and collect samples of Martian material. These samples were then carried by the boom to a number of experimental packages aboard the lander so that they could be analyzed using a variety of techniques. In this fashion, the robotic spacecraft searched, among other things, for signs of life among the Martian soil. Although the results were somewhat ambiguous, the consensus among the *Viking* scientists was that they had not found evidence of life on the red planet.

BIG SCIENCE AND DISCIPLINE BUILDING

Big Science projects were attractive to proponents not just because of their scientific potential, but also because they offered the hope of drawing people, funds, and prestige to a discipline. One such project, Mohole, arose in early 1957 from discussions among a group of leading earth scientists on an NSF panel to review various proposals for earth science projects. To that date, the earth sciences—a hybrid discipline drawing on a range of other sciences such as geology, physics, chemistry, biology, astronomy, and oceanography—had received only relatively small sums from the federal government, and certainly nothing of the scale of, say, physics accelerators. As Harry H. Hess, then chairman of the Princeton geology department, recalled, Walter Munk, an oceanographer at the Scripps Institution of Oceanography at the University of California, pointed out that none of the proposals was "really fundamental to an understanding of the earth." Munk also complained of a shortage of geophysicists and oceanographers. To draw people into these fields Munk wanted "projects in earth science—geology, geophysics, geochemistry— which would arouse the imagination of the public, and which would attract more young men into our science. . . . It is necessary at times to have a really exciting project . . . Walter Munk suggested that we drill a hole through the crust of the earth. I took him up and said let's do it." Such an idea had been floated before. In 1956, for example, a letter in *Science* magazine referred to drilling such a deep hole, together with the confident claim that "massive financial backing can with increasing ease be obtained for organized group attacks on basic problems." The key to Mohole, in fact, was that it be big. Even a small and exciting project would not do for those advocates who sought wider discipline-building goals and not just scientific results.

To drill through the crust of the earth, which meant drilling beyond the Mohorovicic Discontinuity (named after a Yugoslav geologist, and hence the origin of the name Mohole) at the border of the crust and the mantle, offered the scientifically exciting prospect of investigating directly the composition of the earth's interior to an unprecedented depth. But drilling through to the mantle posed obvious and enormous technical challenges. If the project were to be pursued on land, a hole of at least 50,000 feet would have to be drilled. Boring through an ocean bed would mean going down some 18,000 feet at least, and this at a time when the deepest hole ever drilled on land was one 22,570 feet beneath a Louisiana bayou, and the deepest through the ocean bed only a few hundred feet deep.

As the earth's crust is thinnest beneath the oceans, Mohole's advocates easily decided on an ocean drilling site. This meant some sort of drilling ship would be needed. A 1961 description of what such a ship might be like indicates the expected scale of the effort:

> It must be an exceptionally well-built ship, able to stand the endless bending and racking imposed by passing waves and rugged enough to stay on station for a year or more in all except the most severe storms. It must be large enough to carry several thousand tons of equipment and have living space for at least a hundred men. It must be completely self-sufficient, able to operate for a month or more when the ocean is too rough to permit transfer of drilling and living supplies from other ships. It must be equipped with the best navigational and propulsion devices for remaining on station. It must have power plants and repair facilities and scientific laboratories. In short, it must be not only a ship but a completely self-contained drilling laboratory.

In the minds of its advocates, Mohole "would generate so much scientific excitement that deep-sea drilling will never stop . . . [drilling ships] will become necessary scientific tools to be operated on a routine basis, like radio telescopes, nuclear-particle accelerators, and satellites."

The obvious and massive engineering problems were not the only issues faced by the project's supporters. Also central was the question of how the project was to be managed. Reflecting its origins outside of the usual institutional structures, Mohole initially was housed in the National Academy of Sciences, a very odd arrangement. A range of institutions and individuals nevertheless backed the project, including the International Union of Geodesy and Geophysics, the International Association of Physical Oceanography, and the International Association of Seismology and Physics of the Earth's Interior. To add Cold War spice to the situation, advocates seized on reports that the Soviet Union was working on a similar project, and this in the late 1950s when to play the "Russian card" was often a relatively easy way to win backing. Just as there was a space race between the United States and the Soviet Union, there were even speculations on a "race to the mantle." Shortly after the flight of *Sputnik I,* for example, Alan Waterman, the director of the NSF, told an official of the secret "Operations Coordinating Board" of the National Security Council that he rated Mohole above other candidates in terms of a race with the Soviets for scientific and technological prestige. Along with this judgment, Waterman sent a CIA assessment that "should it become desirable on a crash basis, the U.S. could probably drill through the crust before the Soviets could."

The first stage of Mohole, which entailed a series of test drillings from a converted Navy barge went extremely well and led, in water two miles deep, to the drilling of a hole to a depth of just over 600 feet. The results were even written up in a report that included a message of warm congratulation from President Kennedy. But from this point, the project became beset by a growing number of problems. An issue never clearly resolved, for example, was how many holes would penetrate the earth's crust or be drilled in the deep ocean bed. Mohole's scientific objectives proved slippery at best, even some years after the project had started. Costs seemed to keep rising. Also, the National Science Foundation awarded the prime contract for building the platform that would be used as the site from which to drill the Mohole to a giant engineering firm, Brown and Root, of Texas. Brown and Root had a long and extensive construction record, but no experience with scientific projects. The firm had also placed well out of first place in the initial evaluation of the bids the NSF had received. It so happened, however, that Brown and Root was sited very close to the congressional district of Congressman Albert Thomas, who oversaw NSF's budget in the House of Representatives. In addition, the firm's president, George Brown, was well known as a crony of President Lyndon Johnson. Although NSF leaders protested no political deals had been struck, many outside of the NSF looked suspiciously at the award to Brown and Root.

The lack of a clearly defined program, ever increasing cost estimates (from an early estimate of $5 million to ones of at least $125 million by 1966), the odor of a possibly questionable political deal, the slow pace of technical progress, and the death of Congressman Thomas in 1966, spelled disaster for Mohole. Thomas's old committee had seen enough and denied any further funds. For a time it seemed a compromise might be patched-up because of Senate support of Mohole. But in August 1966, a Republican representative disclosed that over $20,000 had been directed by George Brown and family members to a Democratic fundraising group. President Johnson had asked only a few days earlier for the Senate to back Mohole and reverse the House's action. "This revelation," the leading historian of the Mohole Project tells us, "irrelevant as [it was] to the question of whether Mohole should be permitted to proceed, added a weight that brought the entire venture crashing down." The Senate now agreed with the House. Mohole was dead. But the demise of Mohole did not spell the end of projects in deep-sea drilling. In fact, with the lessons of Mohole's failure in mind, geophysicists went on to a string of less ambitious, but far more scientifically fruitful, projects.

The National Science Foundation was very active too in promoting various sorts of "Big Biology" projects in the 1960s. NSF administrators concerned with biology supported these projects in part because of the, to them, enormous imbalance between the funds directed toward the Foundation's Division of Mathematical, Physical, and Engineering Sciences and the Division of Biological and Medical Sciences. Big Biology projects, they hoped, would not only produce good research, but also help offset this disparity by attracting funds to biology. Increasing biology's visibility at the NSF would, in turn, act to justify further resources.

The NSF modeled its Big Biology initiatives on efforts such as, for example, the Kitt Peak National Observatory, and concentrated in the areas of environmental biology and plant and animal physiology. One such institution was the University of Wisconsin's Biotron, which received a $1.5 million grant from the NSF in 1959. The Biotron was in effect a means to provide a large controlled environment that allowed researchers to vary parameters such as the hours of light and dark, as well as weather conditions. Experiments began in 1967, but the Biotron never drew the level of interest from researchers that the NSF had hoped. After a further $1.2 million had gone toward operating costs, the NSF withdrew its support in 1976. In fact, the Big Biology projects failed as national facilities, in considerable part because the projects were conceived in a "top down," fashion, and were as much a product of internal NSF politics as scientific demands. As the historian Toby Appel has explained, "Biologists at NSF did not simply shepherd unsolicited large-scale proposals through the system, but they interacted with academic biologists at all stages to shape the projects according to their own ideal images of big science. They deliberately encouraged the rhetoric of national biological laboratory, multidisciplinary collaboration, multiuniversity cooperation, complexity of the research to be done, and teamwork. Their role was essential in the process of organizing the projects and obtaining funds for them." But the NSF seriously misjudged the interest among biologists in national facilities. Most preferred to avoid large-scale national facilities and cooperative research programs and pursue the smaller scale efforts with which they were familiar and more at ease. Big Biology in the 1960s was therefore, at best, a very modest success.

If biologists were wary of Big Science methods, the same was hardly so for high-energy physicists. By the late 1950s, however, the costs of the biggest accelerators had grown so large that they were giving pause to both AEC administrators and Congress. In the late 1940s and for most of the 1950s, state-of-the-art accelerators had been approved by the AEC with little dispute. But advocates of the proposed two-mile-long Stanford Linear Accelerator (SLAC)—intended to build on Stanford's experience of constructing a series of smaller linear accelerators, and designed to produce an electron beam with the highest energy in the world—faced serious objections both within the AEC and on Capitol Hill. The new accelerator's electron beams could be used as probes of elementary particles, as well as to perhaps create new sorts of particles. These capabilities, however, came at a price. In 1958, the accelerators's cost was estimated to be around $100 million. High-energy physics had received $12.5 million from the federal government in 1950, but this figure had risen steeply in the 1950s. As a result of the concern surrounding these costs, in the summer of 1958 a panel was chartered to report to the recently formed President's Science Advisory Committee. As the official AEC historians inform us, however, the "panel urged sharp increases in federal support for high-energy physics from an annual rate of $59 million in 1959 to $125 million by 1963, without taking away funds from other areas of basic science." The panel's top priority was SLAC.

President Eisenhower met with his science adviser and the panel in April 1959 to give his backing to SLAC as well as to the growth of high-energy physics. While Eisenhower was concerned about the cost implications, he decided that the importance of the science to be pursued and the prestige it would accrue warranted approval. Still the head of the AEC balked. The panel was convened once more and reaffirmed the recommendations it had already made. The President's science adviser, George Kistiakowsky, told the AEC head that "the Federal Government [had] committed itself to support of science in order to further national welfare, health, security, and prestige." In Kistiakowsky's opinion, space endeavors could win support on prestige alone. But in high-energy physics, "the selection [could] be based more on scientific grounds: the promise of the most fundamental contributions to human knowledge and therefore the anticipation of the most far-reaching effects on human future."

SLAC's cost meant that it drew strong interest from lawmakers. In fact, SLAC, despite its solid White House support, confronted stern opposition in Congress from the Democrat-controlled Joint Committee on Atomic Energy. Only when the Kennedy administration entered office did relations be-

tween the JCAE and the White House warm to the point where SLAC could be approved.

The origin of the next really big accelerator was even more convoluted and difficult than SLAC's. By now, too many ideas were chasing too little money. The birth of what would become Fermilab saw high-energy physicists from the established accelerator sites at Brookhaven and the Lawrence Berkeley Laboratory battle each other for the right to build the new machine. Another strong pressure came from physicists who were not staff members at Brookhaven or Berkeley and who believed themselves to be discriminated against in terms of access to the biggest machines and their ancillary equipment. As the number of accelerators was falling, these "outsiders" wanted what one physicist called a "Truly National Laboratory." In such a laboratory, the director would be responsible to a committee composed of representatives from across the nation. The users would also be accorded equal status with the in-house research staff in terms, for example, of office and laboratory space and representation on the committee deciding which experiments were to be run.

Powerful regional forces were also in play. Whether or not federal research funds should be awarded in part on a regional basis had formed a major issue of contention in the debates that swirled around the proper relationship of the state to the scientific community in the mid and late 1940s. For example, Sen. Harley M. Kilgore of West Virginia, a staunch New Dealer, championed the use of research funds on a geographical basis to meet social goals, not just scientific ones. But the leaders of American science strongly opposed such an idea. They wanted federal dollars to go to the best investigators, without heed to their location or the social purpose of the research. In the lengthy battle over what became in 1950 the National Science Foundation, for example, the advocates of a "best science approach" won out.

Strong echoes of the clamor of this fight were soon heard in the dealings over high-energy physics. In 1954, a group of high energy physicists from a number of universities in the Midwest had helped to found a university consortium, the Midwestern Universities Research Association (MURA). For around a decade, MURA, with AEC funding, worked on designs for an accelerator. But in 1964, MURA's planned machine was deleted from the AEC budget because it had not won broad support from other high-energy physicists. Faced with the extinction of its schemes if it did nothing, MURA and its supporters decided to bypass the scientific community and mount a lobbying campaign aimed directly at the White House and Congress. MURA found eager advocates in midwestern lawmakers who saw in a new accelerator for the Midwest a means to balance out what they judged as an unfair distribution of high-energy research facilities across the country. For them, there were too many facilities on the East and West coasts and too few in the Midwest. Also, a new Midwest accelerator could act, in their view, as a means to draw new industry to the region. Although MURA lost the battle to revive its own accelerator, it in effect won the war when the next big machine was sited in the Midwest.

Since 1959, U.S. physicists had been drawing up plans for a new accelerator facility that would be priced in the multihundred-million-dollar range and so cost substantially more than SLAC. When completed, it was named Fermi National Accelerator Laboratory (Fermilab for short and in honor of the eminent physicist Enrico Fermi), but its road to completion was tortuous. The site for what would become Fermilab went out for bids and drew intense interest and 125 proposals from across the nation. This scale of science was also very big business and attractive to many communities. To no one's great surprise, the AEC and the Universities Research Association—URA, a newly formed consortium of universities that would oversee the management of Fermilab—chose a site in the Midwest, at Weston, Illinois. Not only had there been earlier pressure from MURA and its supporters for a Midwest site, but the Johnson administration pursued a policy in which geographical considerations did count in the allocation of research monies. As Johnson himself noted in a speech in 1965: "At present, one-half of the Federal expenditures for research go to 20 major institutions, most of which were strong before the advent of Federal research funds. During the period of increasing Federal support since World War II, the number of institutions carrying out research and providing advanced education has grown impressively. Strong centers have developed in areas which were previously not well served. It is a particular purpose of this policy to accelerate this beneficial trend since the funds are still concentrated in too few institutions in too few areas of the country." The location of Fermilab was in line with, if not directed by, this policy.

Berkeley had completed a design study in 1965 in which the proposed new accelerator was estimated to cost $340 million. The AEC and some physicists judged this figure to be too high to defend before the White House and Congress, and so the AEC announced a cost ceiling of $240 million (a figure, as it turned out, comparable to the cost of the four Orbiting Astronomical Observatories). Reflecting a new mood of skepticism about the relationship of science to society, even this figure drew robust public criticism. The bill containing funding for the accelerator reached the Senate in April 1967, at a time when as an editorial in the *New York Times* put it, "The nation is engaged in a bloody war in Vietnam; the streets of its cities are swept by riots born of anger over racial and economic inequities. . . . It is a distortion of national priorities to commit many millions now to this interesting but unnecessary scientific luxury." In the face of these criticisms, as the historian Catherine Westfall has described, the AEC and its client physicists sought to sell the achievements of their field and underline its prestige among other scientific disciplines. Also, the "project benefited from URA efforts to quell site and design disagreements within the physics community, efforts that relied heavily on the often repeated admonition that without unanimous support the [physics] community would not get the machine, an admonition that only worked because large numbers of physicists strongly wanted the new research tool." After a bruising fight, the project's advocates garnered enough votes to win congressional approval and in July 1967 President Johnson signed the funding bill into law.

Some physicists thought it would be impossible to construct the giant accelerator (in fact a combination of accelerators that would step-up the energies of particles) for the $243 million allotted by the White House and Congress. But under the very strong and at times markedly autocratic leadership of Robert Wilson, who had worked on cyclotrons under Lawrence at Berkeley in the 1930s, the project was completed within budget. Wilson's approach to accelerator-building was distinctly American and followed what he saw as Lawrence's own: to build the best accelerator within the available money by caring more for quick and clever technical fixes to problems than for reliability and methodical engineering. In so doing, Wilson took big risks, which for a period seemed to have put the project in jeopardy. But by late 1971, matters were back on track and the accelerator was in operation in 1972. It had been finished ahead of schedule and $20 million below budget.

MEGAPROJECTS 1970s–1990s

As the histories of the approval of SLAC and Fermilab emphasize, by the late 1950s and through the 1960s, the biggest sorts of machine-centered Big Science projects were reviewed skeptically by their potential patrons in the White House and Congress. This skepticism continued into the 1970s and 1980s. One example of what came to be called a megaproject is the Space Telescope (better known as the Hubble Space Telescope). Even in the 1960s when what became the Space Telescope program was first seriously discussed, the cost estimates for orbiting a large optical telescope above the obscuring layers of the earth's atmosphere were around $1 billion, a price that everyone agreed put it well beyond the reach of private patronage. The telescope's advocates accepted that if it was to come into being, the telescope would, like nearly all the U.S. Big Science facilities constructed since the war, have to be built with money from the federal government. Despite the technical, political, and economic obstacles, the telescope was an extremely attractive project to many astronomers who judged that, if all went well, it would provide a spaceborne observatory of exceptional power. The telescope would, for instance, provide images of unprecedented clarity of distant objects in the universe.

The story of how political approval was won for the telescope is essentially one of coalition building, bargaining, and compromise. The battle to win White House and congressional support lasted from 1974 to 1977. The selling campaigns for the Space Telescope were much different in character from those conducted by, say, George Ellery Hale and other leaders of the astronomical community of his time. In fact, the essence of the campaigns launched by the leading astronomy advocates of the Space Telescope was the large number of their colleagues who participated and who, within two or three years, had been mobilized into an energetic lobbying group. But the astronomers were far from alone in their efforts. By the time it was over, the coalition that had been assembled in its favor included not just astronomers, but NASA officials (NASA was the federal agency that would be charged with managing the construction of the telescope), various members of the White House and the Office of Management and Budget, representatives, senators, congressional staffers, firms with an economic interest in seeing the telescope go ahead, other interested scientists, the Department of Defense, sympathetic journalists, and the European Space Agency (which had agreed to build part of the telescope and provide 15 percent of the costs). Policy making on the telescope was hammered out in a variety of arenas according to ever shifting rules and players; it was a process in which no one ever had a complete grasp of what was happening. The fundamental question of whether or not to approve the Space Telescope was constantly being reframed as the issues bearing on the decisions were themselves reshuffled and repackaged, often because of the needs of coalition building. Moreover, the telescope's design and the associated program to build it were central elements in these changes. Issues of, say, congressional politics, which one perhaps might expect would not have any significant influence on the telescope's design and associated program, proved to be crucial. The approval process therefore played a central role in shaping the telescope. Hence the Space Telescope and the program to construct it were the products of a great range of forces: scientific, technical, social, institutional, economic, and political.

But the telescope as approved was both oversold and underfunded, points that contributed to an environment in which the telescope's main mirror was ground to the wrong shape, thereby drastically limiting its usefulness for its first years in orbit. This blunder, only discovered in 1990 when the telescope was in orbit, drew strong criticism from Capitol Hill and the media for the telescope and its builders, as well as Big Science enterprises in general (in late 1993, the project was to be largely redeemed in the eyes of Congress and the media through the spectacular repairs of the telescope conducted by space shuttle astronauts). In so doing, the telescope's problems became elements in an animated public debate on the merits of "Big" versus "Little" Science. This debate aired again the sorts of arguments advanced by, for example, Alvin Weinberg in the 1960s and even Theodore W. Richards in his letter of 1905 on the advantages and disadvantages of large-scale science, including, for example, the danger of drawing money away from smaller-scale efforts.

A project of an even larger scale than the Hubble Space Telescope and one that raised even more public questions was the so-called Superconducting Supercollider (SSC), a huge physics accelerator in an elliptical tunnel about fifty-four miles in circumference. The plans for this gigantic machine underlined the growth of the size of the teams engaged in high-energy physics. In the mid-1960s, a collaboration to devise and use a particular experiment was typically composed of five to ten members. In the planning for the SSC, it was reckoned that teams of around a thousand from many different institutions would work on a single experiment for periods of over a decade. Even for a 1992 Fermilab paper, the names of over three hundred people were listed as authors.

First proposed by U.S. high-energy physicists in 1983, the SSC—designed to accelerate protons to unprecedentedly high energies—did not win presidential approval until 1987. Then, priced at some $4 billion in an era of growing worries about federal budget deficits, the SSC ran into a great deal of opposition before it was approved by President Reagan and the Congress, including opposition from physicists engaged in areas other than high-energy physics who judged it wasteful and who worried it would strip their own favored endeavors of funds. This opposition only hardened when a few months after the project finally got underway, the official cost estimate roughly doubled. In fact, a number of lawmakers mounted very determined campaigns to kill the SSC in 1992 and 1993, campaigns that led in turn to intense lobbying from proponents seeking to justify the proposed accelerator. But with Cold War pressures dissolved by the disintegration of the Soviet Union, the old standby argument used by many Big Science advocates of increasing national prestige at a time of competition with the Soviets had been undercut. The claims about the possible spin-offs that would result from this most esoteric kind of physics research proved unpersuasive to many lawmakers. Direct military justifications of accelerators had also fallen from the kind of favor in which they were held in, say, the late 1940s. Congress had pressed hard for some of the SSC's costs to be borne by international partners. When substantial funds from outside the United States were not forthcoming, this failure, together with what congressional opponents portrayed as management failures, intense political pressure to reduce the federal budget deficit, and a relative decline in the political influence of Texas (the accelerator was being built in the state), put the project in severe jeopardy. Although the Senate still backed the SSC, its support in the House of Representatives had collapsed. In late 1993, the House insisted that the giant accelerator be canceled.

Thus while Big Science methods became commonplace in a number of disciplines, two of its biggest manifestations—the Hubble Space Telescope and the Superconducting Supercollider—have encountered severe public criticism. Yet at the same time, these huge machines and technological systems became for some lawmakers and many Americans symbols of cutting-edge American technology, surrogates for national technical prowess and spearheads of a drive to increase the United States' economic competitiveness. In 1989, during the House floor debate on the Superconducting Supercollider, one representative termed it an "investment in the new wealth of tomorrow." Another, anxious about Japanese gains in high technology, called the Supercol-

lider "an opportunity to gain that technology back," while a colleague urged, "Vote yes for America's future."

In the early 1960s, not all leading physical scientists had felt it necessary to make direct claims to Congress about the technological spin-offs of Big Science research. Arguing for increased funding for the Stanford Linear Accelerator in 1964, its director had stated that, "I am not of the school who tries to defend this kind of work through its byproducts. I believe if you want the byproduct, you should develop the byproduct. I think you would do it more economically and do it more effectively. If you want to push high powered radio tubes, then the best way to do so is to push high powered radio tubes and not to build accelerators which require high powered radio tubes." When Robert Wilson had been pressed by congressional questioners to offer up military justifications of Fermilab, he bent over backward to avoid doing so, and pointed instead to the wider cultural significance of high-energy physics. But Big Science for the sake of Big Science was hardly enough to sell really large-scale scientific projects in the 1970s or 1980s.

Unlike, say, the high energy physics of the SSC or the astronomy of the Hubble Space Telescope, the multibillion-dollar Human Genome Project has been widely agreed to offer long-term medical and commercial benefits. The human genome comprises all the genetic material in the human cell; the Human Genome Project is designed to map and sequence this genetic material. In the words of one Nobel laureate, this task is the "grail of human genetics." Promoters of the project have pointed to a variety of benefits to be spun-off from mapping the genome: technological advances in manipulating genetic material, new diagnoses for genetic defects, new therapies, and commercial applications. Indeed, it won some early support on Capitol Hill because it was seen as a boon to the U.S. biotechnology industry, both for the information it was expected to generate as well as for the technologies and skills that will be developed to complete it. The advocates of the Human Genome Project have therefore been able to rally lawmakers around the flag of improving economic competitiveness for the nation.

Some molecular biologists, however, have not expressed the same enthusiasm and have regarded the money directed toward the Human Genome Project—expected to be around $200 million per year for fifteen years—as a diversion of funds that could be much better spent on smaller-scale, less mission-directed efforts. To these biologists, the Human Genome Project represents the unwanted invasion of their discipline by Big Science methods and techniques with its, to them, associated drawbacks of politicization and bureaucratization, and a relative loss of autonomy. Echoing Tuve's 1950s criticisms when he wanted money spent on "men and ideas," not machines, some biologists have also rejected the technological emphasis of the Human Genome Project. The often pejorative overtones carried by the term *Big Science* by the early 1990s led to a debate on whether or not the Human Genome Project is even Big Science. In April 1990, project director James Watson likened the Human Genome Project to the $26 billion Apollo program to land astronauts on the moon. Months later he was backtracking: "The project is nothing like the Big Science research and development initiatives with which it is continually compared." Other advocates and analysts have argued that although it might be Big Science, it is Big Science of a decentralized, coordinated sort that essentially eschews the kinds of hierarchies in evidence in, say, the work sites of physics accelerators. These advocates concede that substantial sums of money have gone to improve the technologies of mapping and sequencing the genome, but the actual work of mapping and sequencing has been and will be performed largely by relatively small groups of scientists who have selected their own problems relevant to the Project's overall objectives. In the opinion of Daniel Kevles and Leroy Hood, "what characterizes the human genome project is not central direction, hierarchy, and concentration but loose coordination, local freedom, and programmatic as well as institutional pluralism." It is much closer to what we earlier termed coordinated Big Science than the machine-centered Big Science attacked by the Human Genome Project's critics. By the early 1990s, the mapping of the genome was underway in many different institutions in the United States—including industrial laboratories, universities, national laboratories, and clinical laboratories—as well as in other countries.

The debate on the Human Genome Project has reached well beyond its potential patrons and the scientific community that engage it. The project also carries far-reaching medical, social, ethical, and economic implications. Not only does the genetic knowledge it will generate offer the promise of breakthroughs in medical treatments of many diseases, but it has also raised for some critics the specter of the potential misuse of genetic knowledge, as occurred with eugenics earlier in the century in the United States. One response to such concerns was the decision in 1988 by Watson to devote about 3 percent of the federal budget for the Project to examine its ethical implications, a first in the history of the federal funding for major scientific projects. As Watson was to put it: "We have to be aware of the really terrible past of eugenics, when incomplete knowledge was used in a very cavalier way. . . . We have to reassure people that their own DNA is private and that no one else can get at it." But mapping and sequencing the human genome has underscored issues, for example, of employment discrimination based on genetic factors. If, for instance, it is found that an employee carries a gene that makes him or her likely to show the symptoms of a disease in a few years, will the employer fire the employee in order to avoid facing the health care costs of the disease?

Modern Big Science has placed enormous demands on the scientific and technical communities that engage it. A big scientific instrument or large-scale cooperative program placed at the frontiers of knowledge also represents a political and managerial achievement every bit as significant as the technical feat. While the United States still has the undisputed lead over the rest of the world in terms of the number of Big Science projects, the benefits this lead brings to the scientific community, as well as the nation as a whole, have recently been questioned as never before. By the late 1980s, an era of enormous federal budget deficits, a widely asked question was, "Has Big Science, when it reaches the cost levels of such 'megaprojects' as the Hubble Space Telescope and the SSC reached the limits of what society can afford, no matter how great the potential scientific rewards?" Big Science's patrons in the White House and Congress have also grown increasingly concerned over rising costs and the possible distortions of research priorities, as well as the contested contributions of Big Science to national security and well-being. The future of the biggest sorts of Big Science therefore probably lies in international enterprises. Big Science is surely here to stay, but as throughout its history, new forms will develop that will be shaped by, as well as help to shape, scientific and technical demands, as well as changing political, social, economic, and institutional forces.

SEE ALSO Industrial Research and Manufacturing Technology; Computer and Communications Technology; Aerospace Technology; Medical Science and Technology (all in this volume).

BIBLIOGRAPHY

In preparing this entry, I have drawn heavily on the research and insights contained in the writings of many people. What follows lists those works I found particularly helpful. On the Wilkes Expedition, see William Stanton's *The Great United States Exploring Expedition of 1838–1842* (1975). For a fine short account of the expedition see Robert V. Bruce's *The Launching of Modern American Science 1846–1876* (1987). On expeditions and science in the eighteenth and nineteenth centuries, David Knight's *The Nature of Science: The History of Science in Western Culture since 1600* (1976), makes some telling points. On Henry's meteorological network, see James Rodger Fleming's *Meteorology in America, 1800–1870* (1990). On E. C. Pickering, see Bessie Zaban Jones and Lyle Gifford Boyd, *The Harvard College Observatory: The First Four Directorships, 1839–1919* (1971), and Howard Plotkin, "Edward Charles Pickering," *Journal for the History of Astronomy* 21 (1990): 47–58, and Plotkin's other papers on Pickering cited therein. On the early Carnegie Institution of Washington, see Michael A. Dennis, *A Change of State: The Political Cultures of Technical Practice at the MIT Instrumentation Laboratory and the Johns Hopkins University Applied Physics Laboratory, 1930–1945* (Ph.D. dissertation, the Johns Hopkins University, 1990), ch. 2; Gregory Good's "Vision of a Global Physics: The Carnegie Institution and the First World Magnetic Survey," paper presented in 1992 at a conference, "The Earth, the Heavens and the Carnegie Institution of Washington: Historical Perspectives"; Robert E. Kohler, *Partners in Science: Foundations and Natural Scientists 1900–1945* (1991); and Nathan Reingold, "National Science Policy in a Private Foundation: The Carnegie Institution of Washington," in *The Organization of Knowledge in America, 1860–1920,* ed. Alexandra Olesson and John Voss (1979). Helen Wright's *Explorer of the Universe: A Biography of George Ellery Hale* (1966) is a fine biography of Hale. Wright has also written an account of the genesis of the 200-inch telescope, *Palomar: The World's Largest Telescope* (1952). There are important insights on Hale and cooperative science in Robert Kargon's *The Rise of Robert Millikan: Portrait of a Life in American Science* (1982) and "Temple to Science: Cooperative Research and the Birth of the California Institute of Technology," *Historical Studies in the Physical Sciences* 8 (1977): 3–31. On Hale, see also Daniel J. Kevles, "George Ellery Hale, the First World War, and the Advancement of Science in America," *Isis* 59 (1968):

427–437. On Hale and the transformation of astronomy and astrophysics, see Albert Van Helden, "Building Large Telescopes, 1900–1950," in *The General History of Astronomy,* vol. 4, part A, ed. Owen Gingerich (1984). The early history of the Rad Lab has been treated superbly in John Heilbron and Robert Seidel's *Lawrence and his Laboratory: A History of the Lawrence Berkeley Laboratory,* vol.1 (1990). Robert Seidel also provides a relatively short and thematic account in "The Origins of the Lawrence Berkeley Laboratory," *Big Science,* ed. Peter Galison and Bruce Hevly (1992); the same volume also contains an important essay by Lillian Hoddeson, "Mission Change in the Large Laboratory: The Los Alamos Implosion Program, 1943–45." On the rise of industrial research in the United States see David A. Hounshell and John Kenly Smith, Jr., *Science and Corporate Strategy: Du Pont R & D 1902–1980* (1988); Thomas P. Hughes, *American Genesis: A Century of Invention and Technological Enthusiasm 1870–1970* (1990); and Leonard S. Reich, *The Making of American Industrial Research: Science and Business at GE and Bell, 1876–1926* (1985).

On the AEC laboratories and Big Science, see Robert Seidel's very important paper "A Home for Big Science: The Atomic Energy Commission's Laboratory System," *Historical Studies in the Physical Sciences* 16 (1986): 135–175. Seidel also provides an important account of "The Postwar Political Economy of High-Energy Physics," in *Pions to Quarks: Particle Physics in the 1950s,* ed. Laurie M. Brown, Max Dresden, and Lillian Hoddeson (1989). On the early history of the Brookhaven National Laboratory, see Allan A. Needell, "Nuclear Reactors and the Founding of Brookhaven National Laboratory," *Historical Studies in the Physical Sciences* 14 (1983): 93–122. The notion of the national-security state is discussed in Clayton Koppes, *JPL and the American Space Program: A History of the Jet Propulsion Laboratory* (1982). The figures on ONR programs and defense spending in the late 1940s and 1950s are taken from Daniel J. Kevles, "Cold War and Hot Physics: Reflections on Science, Security and the American State," in *The Restructuring of Physical Science in Europe and the United States 1945–1960,* ed. Michelangelo De Maria, Mario Grilli, Fabio Sebastiani, (1989); and Paul Forman, "Behind Quantum Electronics: National Security as Basis for Physical Research in the United States" *Historical Studies in the Physical and Biological Sciences* 18 (1987): 149–229. On the disputes over the future of radio astronomy, see Allan A Needell, "Lloyd Berkner, Merle Tuve, and the Federal Role in Radio Astronomy," *Osiris* 3 (1987): 261–288. The early years of the National Science Foundation and the establishment of the Kitt Peak National Observatory are examined in Merton England's *A Patron for Pure Science: The National Science Foundation's Formative Years, 1945–1957* (1982). Rip Bulkeley's *The Sputniks Crisis and the Early United States Space Policy: A Critique of the Historiography of Space* (1991) contains important new material on the International Geophysical Year and the Sputnik crisis. The establishment of SLAC is examined in Stuart W. Leslie, *The Cold War and American Science: The Military-Industrial-Academic Complex at MIT and Stanford* (1993); while the genesis of Fermilab is reviewed in Catherine Westfall's "Fermilab: Founding the First US 'Truly National Laboratory,'" in *The Development of the Laboratory: Essays on the Place of Experiment in Industrial Civilization*, ed. Frank A. J. L. James (1989). A fuller account of Fermilab's origin is contained in Westfall's 1988 University of Michigan Ph.D. dissertation, "The First 'Truly National Laboratory': The Birth of Fermilab." For an anthropologist's view of high energy physics, see Sharon Traweek, *Beamtimes and Lifetimes: The World of High Energy Physics* (1988). The early days of space science are described in David H. DeVorkin, *Science with a Vengeance: How the Military Created the U.S. Space Sciences after World War II* (1992). On space astronomy with the Orbiting Astronomical Observatories and the Space Telescope, see Robert W. Smith, *The Space Telescope: A Study of NASA, Science, Technology, and Politics* (1989). On NASA and planetary science see J. N. Tatarewicz, *Space Technology and Planetary Astronomy* (1990). The best history of Mohole is still by far that contained in Daniel S. Greenberg's *The Politics of Pure Science* (1967); Greenberg's book also contains much on MURA. Toby A. Appel has opened important new ground on Big Biology in her manuscript "Biotrons, Boats, and Biomes: NSF and Managing Big Biology," a version of which was presented to the 1992 History of Science Society's annual meeting. An excellent account of some of the history and the scientific and ethical issues raised by the Human Genome Project is presented in Daniel J. Kevles and Leroy Hood, *The Code of Codes: Scientific and Social Issues in the Human Genome Project* (1992). Also important is John Heilbron and Daniel Kevles, "Finding a Policy for Mapping and Sequencing the Human Genome," *Minerva* 26 (1988): 299–314. A number of essays on Big Science are included in *Big Science*, ed. Peter Galison and Bruce Hevly (1992); the thematic essays by Galison and Hevly are especially noteworthy. On the history of high energy physics, see also Peter Galison *How Experiments End* (1987). A very important work that discusses many of the topics treated here is Daniel Kevles, *The Physicists: The History of a Scientific Community in Modern America* (1979).

A useful compilation of data on big science facilities is contained in U.S. Congress, House of Representatives, Committee on Science and Technology's *World Inventory of "Big Science" Research Instruments and Facilities* (1986).

AEROSPACE TECHNOLOGY

Roger E. Bilstein

Although the Wright brothers' historic flight in 1903 fixed America's role in aviation history, other nations rapidly pulled ahead. When World War I began in 1914, the United States was already far behind the Europeans in planes, pilots, and policy, and the gap was wider still when America declared war on the Central Powers in 1917. Yet America's aviation business became an aerospace industry of worldwide dominance during the next half century.

Aviation and aerospace technology evolved as essential elements of national security. Civil aviation employed thousands of aircraft in such tasks as crop treatment, aerial surveying, business trips, and emergency rescue. Commercially scheduled airlines not only replaced railroads as America's prime long-distance transport system but also revolutionized intercontinental travel.

EARLY FLIGHT TO 1918

The Wright brothers developed their powered airplane with information that had accumulated during half a century of experiments involving winged aircraft. Hundreds of short flights in gliders had followed pioneering work by Sir George Cayley in England during the 1850s. In Germany, Otto Lilienthal made over two thousand gliding flights during the 1890s, photos of which appeared all over the world. Because Cayley and Lilienthal were professional scientists, their activities were reported and discussed at various scientific conferences, giving researchers in the United States a chance to keep abreast of progress overseas.

Samuel Pierpont Langley, a distinguished astronomer and secretary of the Smithsonian Institution in Washington, D. C., was determined to be the first to perfect a powered airplane piloted by a human. A number of glider flights and a small propeller-driven model appeared to verify his design concept. Built by Langley's associate, Charles M. Manly, the engine for the full-sized plane was a notable piece of machinery for its day. In the autumn of 1903, Manly twice tried to fly Langley's plane, catapulted from a houseboat in the Potomac River. The problem was not the engine (its basic design was similar to the modern radial engine), but Langley's catapult system, the plane's structural faults, and controls. The highly public fiasco convinced many skeptics that human flight in a powered airplane would never happen. Just nine days after Langley's second failure, Orville Wright became the first person to fly a powered airplane.

The Wright brothers, Orville and Wilbur, had eagerly followed news about Lilienthal's glider flights and had corresponded with the Smithsonian Institution to receive available literature on aviation. The sons of a widely known minister in Dayton, Ohio, the Wrights lacked professional training but fortunately had the intellectual stimulation of a well-read, inquisitive family. The brothers operated a successful bicycle shop and became skilled, intuitive designers and builders of bikes and other machines. They exchanged aeronautical insights with the well-known engineer Octave Chanute. Born in France, Chanute settled in the United States, and his international contacts in the aeronautical community often provided useful perspectives on contemporary developments. Through correspondence and animated discussions, the Wrights sharpened their minds on the prevailing trends, adapting them to the line of development already suggested by their own experiments. Using their own small wind tunnel (six feet long and sixteen inches square), they compiled new data on the relationship of various wing shapes and lift and corrected the errors of their predecessors, including Lilienthal.

Working methodically, the Wrights analyzed results from their ingenious experiments and began to build full-size gliders designed to carry a human. Realizing that repeated test flights needed a location characterized by reasonably consistent winds, a study of weather patterns led them to the remote, wind-swept sand dunes along the Atlantic Ocean at Kitty Hawk, North Carolina.

At Kitty Hawk, each brother gained a wealth of experience in mastering successively advanced designs in the air. The Wright gliders boasted significant new features, including controls for warping (or twisting) the wings slightly so that the glider would bank in flight. They linked the wing-warping controls to a movable rudder in order to make controlled turns in either direction and installed forward elevators to control the gliders' ability to climb or descend. By 1902, the problem of control was solved, and both brothers had become skilled glider pilots. Returning to Ohio, they tackled the problem of a powerplant to keep them aloft for longer periods of time. Knowledgeable mechanics, the Wright brothers designed their own twelve-horsepower engine because they could not find a suitable lightweight unit to buy. Based on additional data from their wind tunnel, they built their own aerodynamically efficient propellers rather than rely on outmoded theories taken from marine designs.

In the autumn of 1903, the Wrights crated up the new plane and returned to Kitty Hawk. A series of frustrating mechanical problems, bad weather, and other difficulties delayed the inaugural flight until mid-December. The brothers flipped a coin to decide who would try the new plane first, but Wilbur's initial attempt on 14 December ended in a low-altitude stall and a damaged plane.

Three days later, after minor repairs, it was Orville's turn. Like the previous attempt, the plane was positioned on a small trolley that ran along a wooden track laid across the soft sand. Orville clambered in, the plane's engine warmed up, then Wilbur helped steady the wing tips as the plane rolled down the track, gathered speed, and lifted into the air under its own power. On the morning of 17 December 1903, the Wright brothers achieved the first controlled flight made by humans in a powered airplane: a distance of 120 feet and a duration of twelve seconds. Exhilarated, they made three more flights, and Wilbur kept the plane up for almost a full minute to cover 852 feet. The brothers sent their father a telegram proclaiming their success and assured him they would be home for Christmas.

When the Wrights tried to demonstrate the Wright "Flyer" to newsmen near their home in Dayton, various problems delayed or frustrated each flight, until skeptical reporters refused to believe that the Wrights could actually do what they promised—fly. Since the Wrights had a number of improvements

Wright brothers' first flight, 17 December 1903. Orville is in the plane; Wilbur is at the right. Photograph by John T. Daniels. PRINTS AND PHOTOGRAPHS DIVISION, LIBRARY OF CONGRESS

they wanted to perfect, they decided to forsake publicity, preferring to labor on in almost total obscurity. Activity in Europe culminated in a wavering flight near Paris by an energetic Brazilian expatriate, Alberto Santos-Dumont in 1906. He and most of the world were certain that he was the first man in history to make a powered flight. Continued European success, and the publicity won in America by Glenn Curtiss and his associates in 1907–1908, finally convinced the Wrights to prove their leadership.

The year 1908 began a period of unprecedented flying activity that lasted until the outbreak of World War I six years later. While Orville amazed spectators at home during flights for the U.S. Army, Wilbur demonstrated a second Wright biplane in France and took Europe by storm. Contemporary European planes were clumsy and difficult to maneuver. With Wilbur at the controls, the Wright biplane easily performed climbs and dives, graceful banks in any direction, and generally made a shambles of vaunted European expertise. The dazzled Europeans graciously acknowledged the Wrights' preeminence in aviation, and the Wright biplane style became a dominant design for many years on both sides of the Atlantic.

But the airplane remained a fragile machine, and the Wrights wound up spending the better part of 1908–1910 refining their handiwork. Moreover, they wanted to file patents that would provide as much legal protection as possible for their designs. In the meantime, they pondered several potential markets. Considering the fragility of planes at the time, the Wrights concluded that military application was most likely—in the form of aerial surveillance. This capability, plus the possible development of destructive fighting machines, might actually serve as a deterrent to warfare. Following military development, the Wrights proposed aerial exploration (a logical follow-up to surveillance), then commercial development for passengers and freight.

The U.S. Army took formal delivery of its first plane (for $25,000) in 1909. During the same period, American investors began to take an interest in airplane manufacturing. The organization of Wright interests in Britain, France, and Germany caught the eye of such financiers as Cornelius Vanderbilt, Howard Gould, and August Belmont. With their backing, the Wright Company was incorporated with a capitalization of $1 million on 22 November 1909. The Wrights received $100,000 outright, 40 percent of the stock, and a 10 percent royalty on every plane sold.

There were other competitors, all hoping to cash in on the anticipated boom in the airplane business. From about 1907 on, dozens of airplane companies sprang up, including aspirants such as the Swivel Buggy and Wagon Company. Obviously, most of these hopefuls had little chance for survival. One of the few to emerge with any likelihood of success was the Aerial Experiment Association, which boasted Alexander Graham Bell as one of its principals, along with Glenn Curtiss, one of the most successful pilots and promoters of the era. The G. H. Curtiss Manufacturing Company sold some planes to the U.S. Navy and a handful to the small but enthusiastic private market, where prices averaged about $7,500. Curtiss persisted in producing planes despite a bitter patent dispute with the Wrights concerning control systems. Most early builders simply ignored the controversy, but the implications of volume production required resolution. In 1917, when the United States entered World War I, a cross-licensing agreement was put into effect under pressure from the government, and the patent controversy finally ended.

Corporate changes and mergers were inevitable. Saddened by the death of his brother from typhoid fever in 1912, Orville Wright sold the Dayton factory and patents two years later to an eastern bankers' syndicate. In 1916, with the promise of military business, this group merged with the Glen L. Martin Company. The same syndicate also controlled the Simplex Automobile Company, and Wright-Martin intended to be one of the first to adopt the production techniques of the auto industry. By 1917, prospective war contracts had led to a consolidation of most of the smaller companies, and the early plethora of airplane firms had slimmed down to seven major groups, including Curtiss and Wright-Martin.

Manufacturers of aircraft during the prewar era realized that military sales alone were not going to make a profit. For that reason, the Wrights, Curtiss, and others organized aerial exhibition companies and paid a daring band of "birdmen" to fly in them. The Wright Exhibition Company, formed in 1910, grossed up to $1 million per year, and pilots could earn $6,000 or more. These early aerial shows played at county fairs, circuses, carnivals, or any other local gathering that attracted a crowd and gate receipts. At first gawking crowds were satisfied just to see a human being clatter overhead in a flying machine. Before long, such prosaic events began to grow stale, leading promoters to arrange contests with autos, conduct mock aerial bombing, stage endurance flights, and encourage various styles of fancy flying, including loops. Racing meets featuring international competitors became the rage, with several planes in the air at once, careening around a specified course to the cheers of tens of thousands of spectators. News headlines reported impressive speeds of 65 to 70 mph attained by aerial racing machines.

As a technological symbol, airplanes generated several different responses within the American public. To many, flying manifested an incredible leap in mechanization and the annals of civilization. To conquer the air—to achieve the age-old goal of human flight—symbolized a sublime achievement of technology, a metaphor reflecting the twentieth century's prospects for unprecedented progress. Others pointed fingers at the mounting death toll of aviators in search of wealth and fame. Aviation was merely another avenue in the service of greed. In fact, much of aviation's popularity seems to have grown from a ghoulish fascination with the consistent fatality rate characteristic of so many aerial meets. Henry H. "Hap" Arnold, who eventually commanded the American air forces in World War II, remembered one such event he attended as a young lieutenant in 1910. "The crowd . . . gaped at the wonders, the exhibits of planes from home and abroad, secure in the knowledge that nowhere on earth, between now and suppertime, was there such a good chance of seeing somebody break his neck," he wrote.

A growing roster of female fliers shared these dangers. Harriet Quimby, a journalist, claimed to be the first American aviatrix after her solo flight in 1911, and gained international fame a year later as the first woman to fly the English Channel. Katherine Stinson performed loops and other stunts, as did Ruth Law, who worked as an exhibition pilot and also established several long-distance solo records.

In the carnival atmosphere of the prewar period, aviation all too often was equated with daredevil antics and fatal crashes, an image that dogged its progress for decades. Nonetheless, the carnival years included many events that illustrated aviation's potential in transportation and communication. In 1909, Louis Bleriot's flight across the English Channel dramatically underscored the impact aviation would have on traditional notions about geographic barriers. In 1911, the cigar-chomping Cal Rodgers flew 3,220 miles from New York to Pasadena—in forty-nine days of flying over a period of three months. The tribulations of Rodgers revealed the problems of early fliers in dealing with balky engines, fragile planes, absence of navigational equipment, and lack of airfields. But progress was rapid; in 1916, Ruth Oliver set a new U.S. long-distance mark of 512 miles nonstop. This sort of record presaged the impending role of aviation in rapid long-distance transportation.

The prewar years also included the first experimental air mail flights in England, India, and the United States, and the first attempt to fly bulk cargo by air, from Dayton to Columbus, Ohio, in 1910. In Florida, a commercial passenger service equipped with small flying boats enjoyed some popularity early in 1914, carrying one passenger each way across the bay between St. Petersburg and Tampa. But such peaceful pursuits were short-lived. In Europe, intense national rivalries flared into open hostilities in the summer of 1914, and airplanes soon became highly publicized weapons of combat.

At the start of the war, Germany had about 300 airplanes, or roughly the number commanded by its major opponents in the air, Britain and France. Both sides used unarmed planes for reconnaissance and artillery observation, and early military pilots on both sides frequently waved to each other as they passed en route to their battle stations. As warfare grew more intense, it seemed pointless to allow the enemy unrestricted access into the airspace above one's own military operations, and single-seat "scouts" took to the air to drive off the intruders with pistol and rifle fire, and eventually with machine guns. The sedate sporting plane of the prewar era became a deadly fighting machine, with opposing pilots locked in bitter duels thousands of feet above the trenches. The glamour and exhilaration of flight gave way to the grim realities of numbing cold, the psychological strain of combat fatigue, and the fear of death in a flaming dive—there were no adequate provisions for parachutes.

The struggle for air superiority was a seesaw battle throughout the war, as first one side and then the other introduced improved combat planes to win control of the air. Volume production of military aircraft became a national priority on both sides. By the end of the war, the British alone had an air force of 290,000 men and 22,000 aircraft.

The United States did not enter the conflict until April 1917, and the war ended approximately eighteen months later, in November 1918. The United States supplied manpower but few planes. American "aces" like Eddie Rickenbacker (a pilot qualified as an ace by shooting down five or more enemy planes) flew English and French machines. Because the United States had so confidently promised its allies thousands of fighting airplanes, and its mass production reputation had been invoked so often as a guarantee, the aircraft industry's glaring failure resulted in a series of hostile government hearings that began as the war ended. True, there was a sordid trail of graft and corruption, but most of the failure involved simply a naive grandiosity. Most aviation companies had close ties to the auto industry, whose executives proved to be grossly overconfident about the ease of manufacturing flying machines. Even though special efforts allowed American firms to build about 400 planes in 1916, plans for 20,000 aircraft in twelve months were absurd.

Some pride could be taken in the remarkably swift conception and manufacture of the Liberty engine, with early production versions coming off the line in about six weeks. The de Havilland DH-4 biplane scout bomber, copied from British designs, also reached production numbers of 1,213 before the war ended, but only a handful ever flew in combat over Europe.

Although many of the thousands of pilots, mechanics, and technicians trained in the hectic years 1917 and 1918 failed to gain postwar aviation jobs, scores of highly skilled aviation workers gave a huge boost to future aeronautical development. Surplus equipment represented a useful as well as negative legacy. A huge postwar inventory of engines and airplanes provided the impetus for dozens of peacetime aviation enterprises. Available to private buyers at bargain prices, surplus military stocks often depressed the market for newer designs more suitable for commercial purposes. Still, wartime cast-offs formed the basis for innumerable aviation enterprises that otherwise would have never begun and which became the market for new equipment when military surpluses began to disappear.

PROGRESS IN AVIATION, 1918–1941

In the postwar era, a series of pioneering flights kept aviation in the forefront as a major news item for American newspapers, newsreels, and radio broadcasts. In the spring of 1919, the U.S. Navy dispatched a trio of flying boats, the NC-1, -3, and -4, on the first flight across the Atlantic ocean. Departing Newfoundland for the Azores, their difficulties underscored the challenges faced by aerial explorers of the period. After experiencing mechanical problems, two planes made forced landings in the Atlantic. One sank; the crew of the second managed to rig a crude sail and steer a course for the Azores. The NC-4 stayed in the air long enough to reach the Azores, then flew on to Portugal and England. Later in the spring, two British pilots managed the first nonstop flight across the Atlantic from Newfoundland to Ireland. During 1924, the U.S. Army launched the first

flight around the globe, supported by the U.S. Navy and the British Royal Air Force, who stationed ships, engines, and other equipment along the planned route. Four planes departed Seattle on a northwest course to Alaska and across the Pacific to the Orient. Eventually, after 175 days, two of the battered planes and their exhausted two-man crews made it back to Seattle. There were numerous other flights during the decade, establishing nonstop records across the U.S., crossing the North and South Poles, and conducting goodwill visits to Latin America. The era also included the first successful dirigible flights across the Atlantic by British and German airships. Lindbergh's epic flight from New York to Paris in 1927 generated monumental attention because he had flown solo and relied on a small, single-engine monoplane, as compared to the larger, crewed aircraft and elaborate support organization used by others.

Such aerial adventures also reflected the increasing sophistication of aircraft design, navigational and meteorological knowledge, and remarkable progress in the reliability of powerplants. These advances rested on an amalgam of research and development achieved by individual companies, military projects, federally sponsored investigations, and private support. The contributions of two organizations proved especially valuable: the National Advisory Committee for Aeronautics for federal research, and the Daniel Guggenheim Fund for the Promotion of Aeronautics, for private support.

The programs of the National Advisory Committee for Aeronautics (NACA) generated results with a signal impact on both military and civil aviation. Established in 1915, NACA represented a somewhat belated response following several years of discussion about the need for a national center of aeronautical study. Aware of impressive European aviation progress and concerned about even more lethal advances following the outbreak of war in Europe in 1914, Congress finally took action. The legislation provided only an advisory committee, "to supervise and direct the scientific study of the problems of flight, with a view to their practical solutions." With twelve members chosen from military, federal, and private organizations, NACA's charge was to narrow down a field of investigation, then find some government or university agency willing to conduct specified research on a shoestring budget. The agency's most notable wartime success involved its assistance in settling the patent dispute that cleared the way for volume production of planes during and after the war.

Wartime experiences led NACA to lobby suc-

The *Spirit of St. Louis.* Charles Lindbergh's plane is wheeled onto the flying field at Le Bourget airport near Paris after repairs. Lindbergh flew the 3,600 miles from Long Island to Paris in 33½ hours on 20–21 May 1927. The crowd that welcomed him at Le Bourget damaged the fuselage. ARCHIVE PHOTOS

cessfully for its own research facilities, which were dedicated in 1920 at an Army installation—Langley Field, Virginia. With a growing array of increasingly sophisticated equipment, NACA pursued a variety of research programs that translated into vastly improved aerodynamic knowledge. Disseminated in numerous published papers and formal reports, NACA's research contributed to significant improvements in military as well as commercial aviation. By the end of the 1930s, "Langley" had become a catchword for NACA's reputation as one of the most successful aeronautical research establishments in the world.

In the process, NACA often borrowed successfully from European sources. The United States lacked expertise in theoretical aerodynamics. Through prewar contacts with the renowned German research university at Göttingen, NACA re-

cruited Dr. Max Munk, a brilliant theoretical aerodynamicist. At Langley, Munk supervised design and construction of an advanced high-density wind tunnel, allowing engineers to develop highly accurate aerodynamic designs through the use of scale model test shapes. By 1927, NACA also had a mammoth wind tunnel, measuring twenty feet at the throat, that allowed detail testing of full-size components and contributed to the development of retractable landing gear and improved efficiency of wing-mounted engines. The NACA design for a cowling to cover radial engines, reducing drag, had an immense impact in producing speedier military planes and more economical airliners.

During the 1920s, the Daniel Guggenheim Fund sponsored competition for safe aircraft design and conducted basic research in meteorology for weather

772

forecasting as related to aviation and the location of airports. Tests in 1928 led to successful technique and practical instrumentation for "blind flying" at night and in bad weather. Money from the Guggenheim program also helped establish centers of professional college and university training in aeronautics at such schools as the Massachusetts Institute of Technology, the Georgia Institute of Technology, and the California Institute of Technology, graduating dozens of skilled young aeroengineers.

In contrast to the United States, Europeans quickly developed an extensive passenger airline system. Cramped single-engine planes gave way to multi-engine transports, and European air passenger routes extended for thousands of miles to their dependencies and spheres of influence in Africa, the Middle East, and the Far East. By the end of the 1930s, European airlines were carrying passengers and mail across the South Atlantic from the west coast of Africa to airports in Brazil.

In the United States, an efficient railway system and expanding road network for cars and trucks proved too competitive for extensive air travel in the early postwar era. The origins of the American airway service can be traced to the government-operated air mail, begun in 1918. By 1925, the air mail routes were supported by a string of beacon lights that permitted day and night air mail runs from coast to coast. In open cockpit DH-4 planes (from war surplus), air mail averaged thirty-two hours on transcontinental routes, about three days faster than train service. It was one of the marvels of its day and government air mail routes developed the market for the private enterprise operations that followed.

With the passage of the Air Mail Act in 1925 (otherwise known as the Kelly Bill) the Post Office Department contracted for air mail service operated by privately owned lines. Over a period of years, many of these early routes were consolidated under the control of such larger companies as United, American, TWA, Delta, Eastern, Northwest, and others. Additional legislation encouraged the carriage of passengers, and new airplanes like the Boeing and Ford trimotors were designed and built to do the job.

Banks soon depended heavily on the new airway service, air-mailing checks, interest-bearing securities, and other documents when saving time meant making money. Air express became a routine method of business for companies needing emergency parts, for sending pharmaceuticals, and for shipping commodities such as fresh-cut flowers. Many companies saved money by reducing inventories, since air express could quickly meet unexpected requirements.

The prospect of saving time while making out-of-town business trips drew increasing numbers of passengers. The trend toward decentralization of business activities during the 1920s and 1930s meant that factories and subsidiaries were cropping up all over America, and airline service won rising numbers of intercity travelers.

Fierce competition among the new passenger airlines encouraged airplane manufacturing companies to produce improved aircraft. The modern airliner was born in 1933, when the Boeing 247 and the Douglas DC-1, forerunner of the DC-3, took to the air. Both planes shared essential features that set them apart from their predecessors: all-metal monoplanes, improved aerodynamic design, modern radial engines, engine cowlings to enhance cooling and reduce drag, retractable landing gear, and improved navigational aids and radio equipment. Quickly developed from the DC-1 and DC-2, the 190-mile-per-hour DC-3 became one of the most successful airplanes ever built. With these planes, airline companies advertised coast-to-coast trips of only eighteen hours, compared to journeys of two-and-a-half days by passenger train. By 1939, the twenty-one passenger DC-3 carried over 75 percent of all domestic air traffic in the United States and, as late as 1966, comprised one-third of all the transport planes in the world. Including the military versions manufactured in World War II, over ten thousand of these classic airplanes were produced.

The phenomenal success of the DC-3 helped give the United States an important lead in the design and production of modern air transports. Before World War II, a new generation of four-engine airliners began to evolve, featuring long-range capability and cruising speeds of well over 200 miles per hour. Boeing introduced the first pressurized air transport, the 307-B Stratoliner. With pressurization, the capability to operate at higher altitudes meant the opportunity to fly above bad weather, thereby increasing passenger comfort and promoting better schedules for passenger flying. Douglas also built a four-engine transport, the DC-4, which was pressed into military service as the C-54 and was developed after World War II into the pressurized DC-6 and DC-7.

Long-range transports such as these held the promise of regular transoceanic passenger flights. Since the first models did not have quite the range necessary for safety, big four-engine flying boats flew the first pioneering routes. The American leader in such international service was Pan American Airways. Beginning with over-water routes throughout the Caribbean in the late 1920s and early 1930s, Pan

Douglas DC-3. ARCHIVE PHOTOS/ENELL

Am cooperated with Igor Sikorsky in the design and development of several flying boats. By 1936, Pan Am also used newer multi-engine Martin Clipper flying boats to fly to the Philippines by way of Hawaii and other Pacific islands. In 1937, Pan Am flying boats began service between the Philippines and Hong Kong, completing a series of aerial bridges between the Asian mainland and the United States, more than 8,500 miles across the Pacific.

Regular air mail and passenger service across the Atlantic began just before the outbreak of World War II. Multi-engine Boeing 314 flying boats, larger than the Martin Clippers, began flying in 1938 and continued special priority flights during the war. High fares on transoceanic flights limited the clientele. Nonetheless, combined domestic and international statistics attested to the rising popularity of air travel.

Passenger traffic recorded 475,000 fares in 1932 and grew to a record 4 million by 1941.

The era between the two world wars is probably best remembered for its heroic long-distance flights, colorful air races, and the introduction of modern airliners like the DC-3. At the same time, however, a special aviation phenomenon was already gaining momentum—general aviation and the light-plane industry. General aviation (or utility aviation, as many liked to call it) is typically defined as all flying that is neither military nor part of scheduled airline operation. It is a phenomenon that puts aircraft to work in a variety of ways. After World War I, many former military pilots purchased cheap, military surplus planes in the hope of making a living by commercial flying activities. Many of these fliers became known as "barnstormers," haphazardly flying across the country from one town to another, earning a few dollars by taking passengers for a pleasure flight, stunting, and maybe advertising a parachute jump by another pilot. As barnstorming and air shows began to fade in popularity, many of these pilots tried other pursuits—photography, surveying, air express, and so on—until their old planes finally wore out or proved to be unsuitable for the task at hand.

With the cooperation of the Army Air Service, crop-dusting experiments began in Ohio in 1921 and began to focus on cotton dusting in Louisiana in 1923. These early trials led to more effective application techniques by commercial firms with special planes for crop-dusting operations, as well as aerial dusting to kill destructive insects in forests. Aerial dusting was faster than other methods, often more economical and efficient, and indispensable in the treatment of otherwise inaccessible woodland areas.

Planes were also used for aerial seeding and for crop surveys, as well as forest fire patrol. The Army Air Service also cooperated in the early 1920s during several early experiments to apply aerial photography in mapping and surveying. Difficult terrain, such as the Mississippi delta, was easily mapped from the air, and remote wilderness areas, like Alaska, were thoroughly surveyed for timber and natural resources for the first time. In the United States, the rapid and flexible transport of key personnel by means of aircraft began to develop more rapidly than any other sector of general aviation. Small companies and independent business people, as well as large corporations, found that private business flying was a sensible and profitable option. By the late 1920s, the number of business aircraft numbered well into the hundreds, ranging in types from three-place biplanes with open cockpits to Stinson monoplanes with closed cabins

Martin Clipper flying boat. PRINTS AND PHOTOGRAPHS DIVISION, LIBRARY OF CONGRESS

to Ford trimotors with comfortable wicker seats, dictaphones, and bars for "bootleg" refreshments.

As the supply of military castoffs dwindled, new companies began to build and sell original designs, and during the 1920s a distinctive light-plane industry began to take shape. The famous Piper Cub served as a primary trainer for hundreds of new pilots, with all models sharing the same basic features: a high-winged monoplane with wing struts, a simple, tandem seat cabin, and Continental or Lycoming engines of 45 to 65 horsepower. With a cruising speed of about 75 mph, the docile Cub was an ideal instructional plane for the increasing numbers of new pilots entering general aviation, as well as the airlines and the military.

The low-speed Cub left something to be desired in terms of performance and comfort required for executive aircraft and business flying. During the 1930s, the light-plane industry perfected several new types of planes with the performance and comfort that made them useful, even in the midst of the severe Depression era. The Cessna Airmaster was one such design. Equipped with a 165-horsepower engine, the Airmaster could carry four to five passengers at 140–150 mph. It was introduced in the late 1930s, when improved radio communications and navigational aids were available, and the plane's good performance made instrument flying feasible, even for the business people who flew their own planes.

In the meantime, Beechcraft had a striking corporate airplane on the drawing boards. The design itself was not radical, but the concept of a twin-engine, multipassenger business plane, with a speed, range, and operational capabilities comparable to airliners then in service made the design unique. Like an airliner, the "Twin Beech" required a pilot and copilot to handle flying duties, so that corporate owners usually needed to develop their own flight department. When introduced in 1937, the Beechcraft Model 18 cost $33,000. In 1939, Beechcraft sold only nine of its twin-engined gamble, but the company sold thirty-four the next year, and the multi-engine corporate aircraft became an accepted design within the general aviation sector and the light-plane industry.

Other designers and manufacturers were active during the 1920s and 1930s, but Piper, Cessna, and Beechcraft became major producers and survived into the postwar era. Their products typified the models that evolved during the years between the wars, when general aviation and the light-plane industry became a universal feature of aviation in the twentieth century.

General Billy Mitchell with Discovery, 1923. Photographic print made from a glass negative. PRINTS AND PHOTOGRAPHS DIVISION, LIBRARY OF CONGRESS

MILITARY AVIATION, 1919–1991

The last thing Americans wanted to think about after World War I was preparing for another war, and the American military establishment fell into a state of disrepair. The U.S. air forces were arguably the most neglected of the military services at the same time that other nations were developing their air forces into potent instruments of international relations and war.

Officers like William (Billy) Mitchell had realized the potential of combat aviation for long-range strategic bombing against transport systems and production centers as well as other key military targets during World War I. Promoted to the rank of general, Mitchell became a passionate advocate of American air power. In 1921, he shattered many myths about the inadequacies of the aerial weapon by bombing and sinking several major vessels, including a presumably invulnerable captured German battleship. Mitchell wanted an independent air force and promoted several dramatic long-distance flights to show the military capability of war planes, demonstrate the vulnerability of cities to air attack, and expose the weakness of the Army and Navy air arms. After a series of bureaucratic skirmishes, the belligerent and flamboyant Mitchell was court-martialed for "insubordination and conduct unbecoming to an officer" in 1926, without achieving the independent U.S. air force he wanted.

Although the Air Corps Act of 1926 created an assistant secretary of war for aeronautics and changed the title of the Air Service to the Army Air Corps, the new organization still lacked independent status. Nevertheless, a series of military appropriations allowed the Army Air Corps to place orders for a variety of new military aircraft, permitting the Army Air Corps to start replacing its obsolete equipment,

which still included many biplanes, with up-to-date fighter and bombardment aircraft.

In the two decades before the outbreak of World War II, the growth of naval aviation became significant. The U.S. Navy acquired several huge dirigibles built as rigid airships, but they proved awkward to operate—all of them crashed. Trial flights with smaller, nonrigid airships (blimps) for long-range ocean patrol proved more promising and led to successful deployment during World War II. Many world powers planned development of the aircraft carrier as a new class of warship, but the two dominant nations in the evolution of ship-borne aviation were the United States and Japan. The Pacific Ocean region, with its vast open seas and small scattered islands, made it difficult to maintain conventional air bases. Thus, the flexibility and versatility of aircraft carriers became a paramount factor of tactics and strategy in the Pacific. The nature of carrier opera-

Military airships. The 785-foot-long rigid airship *ZRS-4*, christened the *Akron*, was built in 1928; it crashed in the Atlantic in 1933. The 658-foot-long rigid airship USS *Los Angeles* was built in Germany in 1924 as part of war reparations after World War I. The semirigid *RS-1* was built in 1925 and was decommissioned in 1928. The small nonrigid airship (blimp) at lower left is unidentified. PRINTS AND PHOTOGRAPHS DIVISION, LIBRARY OF CONGRESS

tions put a premium on reliability and ease of maintenance of carrier-borne aircraft, and particularly their engines, and this influenced the wide application of comparatively uncomplicated radial engines in naval planes as opposed to the Army's liquid-cooled engines. In cooperation with NACA, the Navy took the lead in encouraging the design and production of high-power radials in the United States during the 1920s.

During 1939 and 1940, the tactics of the German *Blitzkrieg* (lightning war) successfully coordinated armored and infantry units with overwhelming air superiority in the conquest of Poland, France, and other European countries. As victors in the Battle of Britain (1940–1941), the British Royal Air Force (RAF) finally ended the myth of the invincibility of the German *Luftwaffe*. Outnumbered, valiant RAF pilots took advantage of British radar to catch the German bomber squadrons at the most opportune point of attack over British territory. While the highly maneuverable British Spitfires engaged the German fighter cover, older Hurricane fighters ferociously pressed their attacks against the weakly defended German bombers. After disastrous losses, the battered *Luftwaffe* finally withdrew. The survival of Britain assured the Anglo-American allies of military facilities and air bases crucial to the invasion of Europe. Hitler became more vulnerable after opening up a second front against Russia in the spring of 1941. Operating on two European fronts throughout the war, as well as in Africa, Germany's air forces were stretched beyond their limits and began to wear down.

The scope of World War II widened further in December 1941, when Japanese carrier-based planes attacked the U.S. naval base at Pearl Harbor in Hawaii. Fortunately, the U.S. fleet of aircraft carriers escaped destruction, and their survival helped the Allies in the Far East to prevent Japanese military forces from attaining a decisive advantage. The Japanese attack on Pearl Harbor brought the U.S. into the conflict, but the Allies decided to concentrate first on the defeat of Hitler in Europe, where England and Russia already held strong positions.

With Allied air superiority a decisive factor in forcing the German retreat in Africa and the Mediterranean theaters in 1942–1943, American and British bomber offensives against Germany increased in intensity, operating from airfields in England. Heavy bombers such as the Boeing B-17 and Consolidated B-24 acquired additional defensive armament as the result of high losses from German fighters like the Messerschmitt Bf-109. Allied bomber losses contin-

ued to be costly until fast (400 mph) fighters such as the P-47 Thunderbolt decisively contributed to air superiority over Europe. Long-range fighter escorts like the P-51 Mustang also became operational. Additional harassment from the skies came from twin-engine light bombers like the North American B-25 and Martin B-26 aircraft, along with Mustangs and Thunderbolts operating as fighter bombers. Armed with heavy machine guns, rockets, and light bombs, they provided close tactical air support for the ground troops while continuing to protect them from enemy air attacks.

In a desperate attempt to halt the destructive Allied air offensives, the *Luftwaffe* pressed the development of advanced planes, including the jet-powered Me-262. Fortunately, Hitler decreed that the Me-262 be used as a high-speed, low-level bomber, rather than a fighter-interceptor, and chronic shortages of fuel and experienced pilots further reduced its effective use against the Allies. Germany also developed the V-1 "flying bomb" (powered by a small ram-jet engine) and the awesome V-2, a rocket-powered ballistic missile. The V-1 could be shot down by fighters or antiaircraft fire, but there was no defense against the V-2 rocket, which attained speeds of 3,600 mph before dropping on its target from an altitude of 60 miles. Allied capture of European rocket launching sites choked off the V-1 and V-2 attacks. The relentless bombing of German production facilities, destruction of oil refineries, and disruption of the German transport network all attested to the impact of air power in contributing to Allied victory in Europe.

There is no doubt that combat air operations were costly in terms of planes and personnel. The principal long-range bombers flown by U.S. air forces in Europe, the Boeing B-17 and Consolidated B-24, each carried a crew of ten men. In Mediterranean operations during one week in July 1944, the 15th Air Force lost 318 bombers and fighters, leaving huge gaps in the ranks of bomber squadrons. Casualties of air crews in the Italian campaign often exceeded the weekly losses of American and British soldiers in ground offensives. Operations of the 8th and 9th Air Forces alone over western Europe took the lives of 48,847 airmen in the last three years of the war. By 1945, air combat in the European and Mediterranean theaters had killed 79,265 American fliers; the RAF lost 79,281. According to some estimates, Allied air raids resulted in the deaths of over 300,000 German civilians.

Meanwhile, the Allies had increased the tempo of the air war in the Pacific. In May and June 1942, the effectiveness of carrier operations had been demonstrated in the Battle of the Coral Sea and the Battle of Midway, when aircraft carrier squadrons engaged in bitter air fights and attacks against opposing surface ships. Neither the American nor Japanese fleets came within sight or gun range of each other: the conflict was fought entirely in the skies by carrier planes. The American victories in both battles gave offensive momentum to the United States, whose new Grumman F6F Hellcat fighters proved to be a match for the Japanese Zero fighters.

With air superiority, carrier-supported amphibious landings on heavily defended Pacific islands became feasible. Once ashore, engineers prepared rough air strips to support operations by air force and Marine fighters and fighter bombers. The latter proved especially effective in attacking fortified strong points with rockets and napalm bombs. As air strips improved, cargo planes arrived with supplies and reinforcements; heavy bombers flew off to pound targets deep in Japanese-held territory. By 1944, American troops had captured several key islands in order to provide support and air bases for Boeing B-29 Superfortress bombers. These huge bombers carried tons of incendiary bombs dropped over dozens of cities during devastating raids on the Japanese home islands. As in the case of Germany toward the end of the war, early intentions to rely on pinpoint bombing gave way to comprehensive destruction of major urban centers, along with their civilian population. In August 1945, B-29 planes dropped atomic bombs on Hiroshima and Nagasaki, finally compelling the Japanese government to surrender. Debate over the use of these atomic weapons, when so much destruction had already occurred, became punctuated by ethical, diplomatic, and strategic controversy.

The role of aviation was expanded in many areas during the war, including escort duties for ocean convoys, as well as antisubmarine patrols. For antisub work, the Navy resurrected the nonrigid airship, since its slow speed and long endurance permitted airship crews to spend extended time on patrol duty. The general aviation industry made a substantial contribution in the production of flight trainers and small twin-engine planes as transition trainers for pilots and crews of larger transports and bombers. Painted in a new uniform of olive drab, various types of light planes were also pressed into military service for special transportation of officers and important wartime personnel. Known as "Grasshoppers," versatile and maneuverable light planes like the Piper Cub J-3 performed vital front-line service in liaison work, observation and artillery spotting, and evacuation of

the wounded. Nearly 6,000 Piper Cubs served in the wartime Grasshopper fleet.

Women played a key role in the American war effort, particularly in aviation training and production. They served as instructors for ground school as well as for flight training. An organization known as the WASPs (Women Airforce Service Pilots) accounted for countless hours of flight instruction, transport flying, and an aerial ferry service that took hundreds of planes to shipment points for delivery to overseas combat zones. Thousands more women went to work in aircraft factories, where production records seemed to increase week by week. During the war, the aircraft industry delivered 300,000 airplanes. In dollar value of output, the industry ranked 44th in the nation for 1939 but by 1944 claimed the number one spot. Even with the inevitable peacetime contraction, aviation manufacturing emerged as one of the nation's premier industries in the postwar era.

The effectiveness of strategic bombing in World War II continues to be analyzed, but there can be little doubt that air power was immensely important in the Allied offensives. Aircraft carriers exerted a profound influence on naval strategy, replacing battleships as the center of fleet operations. Air superiority helped assure the capture of Pacific island strongholds, as well as the successful Normandy invasion in 1944. The value of close tactical air support and the deployment of reinforcements and supplies, in addition to paratroops, was demonstrated many times in all theaters of the conflict.

COLD WAR TRENDS

In the postwar decades, global tensions of the Cold War, rapidly changing technology, and the advent of space flight all created profound changes in the aviation community. By the late 1950s, the term *aerospace* had come into wide usage to describe the changing character of aeronautical and astronautical activities.

Although naval and marine aviation units remained under the umbrella of the U.S. Navy, the striking advances in wartime air power dictated a major change in the postwar military establishment. The National Security Act, passed in 1947, created a unified Department of Defense and recognized the new status of air power by establishing a secretary of the Air Force on a level equal to that of the secretaries of the Army and Navy.

With its new bureaucratic independence, the Air Force reorganized itself into several new commands, including the Strategic Air Command (SAC), which had primary responsibility for a postwar generation

B-29 bombers dropping incendiary bombs over Japan, June 1945. PRINTS AND PHOTO-GRAPHS DIVISION, LIBRARY OF CONGRESS

of big bombers intended to carry nuclear weapons to potential Cold War targets. Along with the medium-range Boeing B-47 jet bomber, the principal SAC bombers included the mammoth Convair B-36, with six piston engines bolstered by an additional pair of jets under each wing, and the Boeing B-52, a later development with swept wings and eight jet engines of advanced design. Although these big jets were designed as intercontinental bombers, with the B-52 equipped for air-to-air refueling, the Air Force nonetheless needed a global network of air bases for their support. Growing numbers of bombers, tankers,

fighters, and a plethora of other types including transports were based in the United States and overseas, representing high-tech hardware generated by the military-industrial complex of the Cold War decades. Over the years, these military assets played key roles in projecting American national interests in trouble spots around the world.

Similarly, the U.S. Navy's aircraft carriers usurped the role previously held by battleships in "showing the flag" internationally. Aircraft carriers also became mobile air bases equipped with specialized planes and equipment to counter Soviet submarine forces anywhere in the vastness of the world's oceans. Aircraft carriers of necessity became larger and more complex; the first nuclear-powered carrier, *Enterprise*, was commissioned in 1961. These and other postwar supercarriers weighed over 85,000 tons, required a crew of some 6,000, and handled 55 to 100 planes, depending on mission assignments. But the immense cost of such carriers and their escorts, the construction of sprawling Air Force bases, increasingly expensive aircraft, and continuing maintenance expenses touched off sharp debates in Congress and newspaper editorials about budgetary priorities for military projects as opposed to domestic needs.

As the stockpiles of American and Soviet atomic weapons increased, a rash of cautionary novels and such films as *Fail-Safe* and *Dr. Strangelove* reflected the nervous mood of the American public facing a possible nuclear catastrophe. Indeed, the concern about atomic weapons and hostile actions from the Soviet Union during the 1950s led to aerial surveillance missions flown by modified American warplanes. When Soviet units shot down several aircraft over their territory, the Pentagon funded development of the Lockheed U-2 spy plane, capable of flying above the range of Soviet air defenses. With improved weapons, the Soviets shot down a U-2 in May 1960, triggering a diplomatic confrontation that cancelled a scheduled international summit meeting of President Eisenhower and Soviet Premier Khrushchev. The United States built more advanced spy planes, such as the Lockheed SR-71, but these were replaced in the late 1980s by extremely sophisticated spy satellites.

Two major trends of the early postwar era—jet engines and swept-back wings—represented European technology adapted by the United States and then pushed to new levels of record performance. Gas turbine powerplants had been considered by NACA before World War II, but early test devices devoured so much fuel and generated such high pressures and temperatures that further experimentation seemed pointless. The British experience was similar, but Frank Whittle, an RAF officer, simply refused to give up on the idea. He raised money through a private investment bank, found a report that helped solve combustion problems, incorporated some advanced metallurgical components, and ran a successful bench test of the first (centrifugal flow) jet engine in 1937. In 1941, just before the first successful test flight of the Whittle engine, the visiting commander of the U.S. Army air forces, H. H. "Hap" Arnold, learned about some ground trials of the new British jet plane. He was amazed; the United States had

absolutely nothing like it. The British, still concerned about a possible German victory in Europe, sent an engine and complete blueprints to the United States as a safeguard. Soon after, Whittle himself made a wartime trip to the United States, staying several weeks to explain the peculiarities of jet engines. From this generous gesture, American development of jet engines began to grow. The Germans, led by aerodynamicist and physicist Hans von Ohain, had already flown the world's first jet plane in 1939. Their successful development of the axial flow jet engine became standard in the postwar era. After the war, von Ohain and several dozen other German experts settled in the United States as government scientists for the Air Force.

The application of swept wings on postwar airplanes had similar origins in European expertise. The first formal analysis of swept wings for high speed flight was delivered in 1935 by a German, Hans Busemann, during an aerodynamics conference in Italy. In his paper, he discussed the use of swept wings to delay the effects of shock waves at very high speeds. Propeller-driven planes of the era could not approach such speeds (500–600 mph), so that little was done— until the advent of jet-powered aircraft. By the end of World War II, the Germans had a swept-wing rocket fighter in action (the Me-163), as well as several types of swept-wing jet combat planes in limited production or under test. These examples of advanced aerodynamics, and documents acquired by the Allies, prepared the way for such advanced postwar American swept-wing combat jets as the Boeing B-47 bomber and North American F-86 fighter.

Even before the advanced types of swept-wing jets took to the air, American engineers and technicians were setting new records in high-speed flight. The higher speeds of jets quickly brought aerodynamicists to the edge of the sound barrier, about 760 mph at sea level, or Mach 1 (after the Austrian physicist, Ernst Mach, who quantified the characteristics of the speed of sound). A combined effort led by NACA and Air Force researchers settled on a relatively conservative design for a supersonic plane: rocket engines for maximum thrust, and straight wings with a short span and narrow cross-section to minimize high speed shock waves. Dropped at high altitude from a modified B-29 bomber on 14 October 1947, the Bell X-1, in the hands of test pilot Chuck Yeager, became the first plane to fly faster than the speed of sound. This flight and others occurred over Muroc Air Base, sited in the California desert northwest of Los Angeles. Over the years, the term *Muroc* symbolized the center of exotic flight

781

tests in an era of rapid advances in high speed aerodynamics leading to fighters like the F-86 and its successors. A succession of experimental jet aircraft and rocket-powered planes, like the X-15 and others, probed the challenges of sonic and supersonic operations, aerodynamic heating, control at extreme altitudes, and related problems in the arcane world of flight testing. Known collectively as the "X-Series" of experimental planes, their test data formed the basics for design and development of improved military types as well as advanced designs for jet airliners and other civil aircraft.

Although the F-86 finally made its mark during the Korean conflict, it was ironic that the first active use of air power in the Cold War relied on lumbering, piston-engined air transports rather than agile exotic fighters. In the spring of 1948, Soviet forces blocked surface routes into West Berlin, located inside the Soviet zone of occupation. Air transport was the only viable means of carrying cargo and passengers into the beleaguered city, short on fuel, food, medicine, and other supplies. With winter approaching, bringing abominable flying weather, the survival of West Berlin—occupied by British, French, and American forces—seemed problematic. The western Allies held on by organizing the remarkable Berlin Airlift of 1948–1949. Most of the transports were American, called in from outposts across the United States and the Far East, although additional planes from Britain and cooperation from France contributed heavily to a successful operation. Recent strides in radar allowed ground controllers to pace the streams of Douglas C-47 and C-54 transports across Soviet-occupied Germany, then guide them down through foggy approaches to West Berlin airfields. At times, planes landed in intervals as frequent as three minutes around the clock. By the time the blockade ended a year later, largely because of the success of the airlift, a new dimension of air power had been demonstrated as a forceful instrument of foreign policy.

In June 1950, only a year after the successful conclusion of the Berlin Airlift, a new crisis broke in the Far East when North Korean forces struck across the 38th parallel into South Korea. The United Nations quickly condemned this violation of diplomatic agreements made at the close of World War II and sponsored armed resistance, although the vast majority of UN forces and equipment came from the United States. After an initial retreat, UN armies counterattacked back across the 38th parallel, a decision that drew massive Chinese forces across the Yalu River into North Korea. American and UN strategists realized that air attacks against communist military targets inside China were likely to trigger a third world war and the possibility of nuclear strikes by Soviet forces. Thus the conflict in Korea proceeded under the stricture of limited warfare—a new and often frustrating concept for many Americans.

The U.S. Air Force, primed for a war in which long-range bombers carried nuclear weapons and high-flying fighter jets contested for air superiority, found itself unprepared for the Korean arena. Flight crews in B-29 strategic bombers had to relearn the art of dropping conventional bombs on smaller targets like bridges and storage dumps. Jet pilots had to relearn the tactics of low-level close air support within confined—and often confusing—combat zones. Quickly assimilating strategic and tactical lessons, American and other UN fliers soon made air power an effective battlefield weapon. Postwar analysis acknowledged UN air power for its extensive destruction of bridges, railways, and other vital transport targets as well as the obliteration of innumerable enemy bunkers and strong points. When MiG-15 fighters of the Chinese air force finally ventured out, F-86 fighters of the USAF shot them down at a ratio estimated at ten or twelve to one. Such air superiority also allowed methodical low-level raids against several North Korean dams, so that flooding severely hampered enemy ground offensives and deprived rice farmers of the controlled irrigation essential to crop production. Some postwar analysts felt such attacks played a strong role leading to armistice negotiations in 1953. They also credited aircraft carriers that launched effective air strikes up and down the North Korean coastline. In addition, helicopters became integral elements of combat operations. Used primarily for battlefield evacuation of wounded troops, they saved countless lives. But helicopters proved indispensable in freighting in reinforcements, weapons, light artillery, and emergency supplies. As deployed by the U.S. Army and the Marines, helicopters were essential to ground combat offensives, as demonstrated only a few years later in Vietnam.

During the early 1960s, an insurgent movement in South Vietnam drew in U.S. troops as advisers, then as full combatants, in a conflict the American government identified as a communist effort to defeat the South Vietnamese regime. It was generally a guerilla-style war, with no clear-cut front line in a dense jungle environment. As the American presence mushroomed, U.S. Air Force and Navy air power eventually sought industrial, military, and even civilian targets in North Vietnam and carried out attacks in Cambodia as well. There was a paradox in using the striking power of planes like the B-52, designed

B-52 Stratofortress dropping 750-pound bombs in South Vietnam. NATIONAL ARCHIVES

for devastating attacks with conventional bombs and atomic weapons, in huge formations against rural and agricultural regions in Southeast Asia. Despite heavy American air offensives with the B-52s, supplies and combat personnel continued to reach units fighting against United States and South Vietnamese armed forces.

American air power remained constantly engaged in the Vietnam air war until the cease-fire agreements that led to American withdrawal in 1973. The conflict became an intensive proving ground for aircraft, electronic gadgetry, and tactics that defined military aviation over several future decades. Nearly every military aircraft in the American inventory saw action at one time or another, from Douglas B-26 bombers of World War II vintage through the most modern combat jets available to Air Force, Navy, and Marine pilots. Transport planes like the venerable C-47 and the big C-130 Lockheed Hercules were modified to carry batteries of rapid-firing automatic weapons. These low-flying gun platforms could deliver devastating streams of bullets against enemy positions; searchlights, radar, and electronic sensors were carried to locate the elusive enemy in darkness.

Helicopters experienced rapid development after

the Korean War, and improved models carried large numbers of combat troops to the patchwork of hot spots that seemed to characterize the frustrating nature of war in Vietnam. The "choppers" provided logistical support to isolated units and proved unusually effective in rapid evacuation of wounded soldiers, reducing battle deaths. As a means of providing close-in fire support for harrowing jungle engagements, new designs brought the helicopter gunship into operation. Armed with automatic weapons and air-to-ground rockets, gunships like the Bell UH-1 "Huey Cobra" represented a significant element of battlefield air power.

Electronic warfare reflected a new facet of combat in the skies over Vietnam. Air-to-air missiles proved to be deadly against enemy jet fighters. For American pilots, the heavy concentration of surface-to-air-missiles (SAM) encountered on bombing missions over North Vietnam represented a fearsome barrier. Consequently, increasing research went into electronic countermeasure (ECM) technology during the long Vietnam War. Additional research was given over to increasingly sophisticated electronic reconnaissance equipment to pinpoint SAM radars and launch sites for attack. The United States also pushed development of guided weapons that permitted war planes to launch bombs and rockets from a longer, safer range. Such "smart" munitions were aimed at enemy radar and other highly defended targets.

As the conflict dragged on, the intensity of aerial warfare accelerated and the air campaign drew heavy criticism. Active bombing of targets in North Vietnam began after the controversial Gulf of Tonkin incident (an alleged attack on American military vessels) in August 1964 and spread into Cambodia during 1969. The air war included planes from USAF bases in South Vietnam, Thailand, and the Pacific islands, as well as planes launched from U.S. Navy carriers that ranged up and down the Vietnamese coast. The U.S. Army also deployed hundreds of helicopters in daily operations, losing about 2,000 in combat and 2,500 in other assignments. The high rate of attrition resulted, in part, from the inherent complexity of the rotor machinery and the extremely high sortie rate compiled during military actions. The helicopters' frequent combat missions were also conducted at low level and in close proximity to hostile forces, exposing them to intense enemy fire that resulted in numerous losses. Over 3,400 pilots and aircrew died. In addition to attacks on conventional military targets, U.S. forces also began a program of spraying herbicides from the air. This defoliation strategy, known as Operation Ranch Hand, was intended to reveal enemy camps and supply trails hidden by the jungle canopy, and to curtail food production, particularly rice. An estimated 6 million acres were sprayed, largely with Agent Orange, a herbicide with chemicals that not only killed vegetation but also created long-term health problems for the native population and for military personnel who handled it.

During 1969, when air operations were at their highest level, about 6,400 Air Force, Navy, and Army aircraft were deployed in Southeast Asia. By the war's conclusion in January 1973, an estimated 6,162,000 tons of munitions had been delivered by aircraft, compared to 2,150,000 tons dropped in World War II. Although half the tonnage dropped in Vietnam was delivered by jet fighter-bombers such as the Republic F-105, television images of B-52 bombers unloading dozens of bombs in broad, saturation attacks galvanized strong antiwar sentiments. North Vietnamese SAM batteries took a heavy toll of low level attackers as well as high altitude bombers. Over 300 F-105 jets were lost; about 100 B-52 bombers were deployed at one time or another, and 31 were shot down or written off. The U.S. Air Force and

Navy lost over 3,700 fixed-wing aircraft to hostile action and operational accidents, resulting in over 2,000 casualties.

Despite the scope of the effort and the high costs in aircraft and crew, the air campaigns never achieved the degree of success that planners desired. Environmental problems created by actions such as Operation Ranch Hand added to the bitterness that persisted as a legacy of the war in Southeast Asia. However, professionals in the military community concluded that many specialized operations had often achieved tactical success. Consequently, the Vietnam experience generated advanced designs for combat helicopters and resulted in extensive research involving guided weapons and computerized combat systems.

During the 1980s electronics played an increasingly central role in computer-aided design systems, navigation and communication systems, cockpit displays, and in other applications for civil and military aircraft alike. But the most dramatic demonstration of electronic sophistication occurred in January–February 1991, when Operation Desert Storm sent the Iraqi military into disarray and defeat in the Persian Gulf War. Coalition units seized the initiative in the opening hours of the air offensive, when night-flying helicopters used laser-guided munitions to wipe out key radar installations inside Iraq. Over the next few weeks, intensive air attacks seemed to paralyze Iraqi forces. United States Air Force F-117 Stealth aircraft flew repeated sorties, and television news broadcasts showed electronically directed weapons making pinpoint strikes through vulnerable doorways or down chimneys of reinforced structures. Cruise missiles scooted through enemy warning systems to obliterate highly defended targets while America's Patriot air-defense missile batteries engaged hostile Scud missiles. Postwar reassessments suggested that the accuracy of many high-tech weapons fell short of early reports and the success of Patriot antimissile batteries was debatable. Still, the Patriots played an important political role to reassure Israel, as well as Saudi Arabia, and many military observers remained impressed by the destructive threat of weapon systems deployed during the Gulf War.

ROCKETRY AND SPACE FLIGHT

Germany's dramatic use of V-2 ballistic missiles in World War II gave momentum to rocket technology and unquestionably riveted public attention on military and peaceful uses in the years after 1945. The invention of rockets propelled by volatile powder mixtures is usually traced back to tenth-century

F-117A Stealth aircraft. ARCHIVE PHOTOS/IMAPRESS

China. As fireworks for entertainment or as combat weapons, vignettes of rockets in human history have a long tradition. During the War of 1812, rockets used by the British to bombard Fort McHenry in Baltimore prompted Francis Scott Key to write a poem that eventually was set to music as the U.S. national anthem. Later in the nineteenth century, powder rockets propelled deadly harpoons used in the hunt for whales; rescue rockets trailing lifelines to stricken ships saved the lives of thousands of crew and passengers. Although some early dreamers wrote about using powder rockets to reach the moon and other galactic destinations, solid-fuel rockets had inherent limitations in terms of weight and propellant efficiency. High energy, liquid chemical rockets held far more promise but awaited progress in metallurgy, electronics, and liquefaction of gases that finally became available in the late nineteenth and early twentieth centuries.

The American experience in space research, as in many other areas of the history of flight, owed much to a European heritage. Nearly every significant individual involved in modern space flight acknowledged as a source of inspiration the science-fiction novels of the French writer Jules Verne. Around the turn of the century, the Russian theorist and mathematician Konstantin Tsiolkowsky first calculated the energy and process required for liquid-propellant vehicles to launch payloads into space. Soviet politics, plus language barriers, meant that his contributions were long unrecognized by American researchers. Meanwhile, Robert Goddard, a physics professor at Clark University, offered his students what they regarded as fanciful descriptions of how to design and build small liquid propellant rockets that could streak into space. Goddard even wrote a concise treatise on the subject, *A Method of Attaining Extreme Altitudes* (1920), but the shy professor was disturbed by some of the skeptical press and sensationalized accounts that followed and thereafter preferred to carry out his engineering tests in anonymity.

By the mid-1920s, advances in cryogenic engineering yielded enough affordable liquid oxygen to enable Goddard to use it as an oxidizer in combination with kerosene as rocket fuel. An awkward looking arrangement of tubes and sheet metal provided the architecture for a fuel tank connected to a small rocket engine; a blowtorch lashed to the end of a long pole sufficed to ignite the contraption. On 16 March 1926, the first liquid-propellant rocket flashed upwards from the apple orchard owned by Goddard's Aunt Effie near Worcester, Massachusetts. Goddard's

Robert H. Goddard. PRINTS AND PHOTOGRAPHS DIVISION, LIBRARY OF CONGRESS

coast at Peenemünde, Wernher von Braun supervised development of the V–2 missile—the largest and most awesome rocket weapon of World War II. Nearly fifty feet in height, its range of about 200 miles allowed Hitler's forces to hit British targets across the Channel. Part of the logic of the Allied invasion of Normandy in 1944 hinged on occupying V–2 launch sites, forcing such weapons out of range of England. Operation Paperclip, organized as the European war ended in 1945, gave the highest priority to the capture of Wernher von Braun, his principal engineers, and German rocket technology.

After arriving in the United States, the von Braun team became Army employees at White Sands, New Mexico, where they used captured V-2 rockets in an extensive series of test flights. In 1950 the Germans transferred to the Army Ballistic Missile Agency (ABMA) in Huntsville, Alabama. Working with various American corporations, ABMA developed a family of battlefield missiles based on the Redstone rocket. Engines, for example, were supplied by Rocketdyne, a subsidiary of North American (later, Rockwell International). The Air Force inaugurated its own missile program under a congressional mandate that kept Army weapons within limited ranges while giving the rival Air Force freedom to deploy intermediate range ballistic missiles as well as intercontinental ballistic missiles (IRBMs and ICBMs). Although McDonnell Douglas, Martin Marietta, and General Dynamics held contracts for separate missile programs, Rocketdyne dominated the engine market, along with Pratt and Whitney.

The Navy sustained a separate line of development, building a new class of submarines to launch ballistic missiles and focusing on solid propellant boosters, since liquid propellants were too volatile and tricky to handle in the confined space of a submarine. In the late 1950s, the Navy's new Polaris class of nuclear-powered submarines entered service, armed with a battery of Polaris missiles to be launched under water.

The relatively sudden arrival of sophisticated missile systems during the 1950s, the ramifications of intercontinental rockets following stratospheric trajectories above the earth, the arcane world of electronic control systems and radar tracking, and the phalanxes of space contractors both large and small boasting increasingly complex specialties—all conspired to make the conventual term "aviation industry" seem hopelessly inadequate. Instead, "aerospace," joining aeronautics and astronautics, exemplified the new etymology.

Significantly, the acceptance of aerospace into

rocket climbed to forty-one feet in a flight of only 2.5 seconds—a very small step toward an eventual manned lunar landing, perhaps, but a step in the right direction.

Although amateur rocket societies were active in America, Britain, the Soviet Union, and elsewhere prior to World War II, effective military support in Germany led to accelerated development there. German developments were substantially enhanced by the pioneering contributions of the Verein für Raumschiffart (Society for Spaceflight) or Vf R, established in 1927. One of the Vf R members, Wernher von Braun, completed his doctorate degree on rocket propulsion and became a principal figure in a research and development group that came under military control during the 1930s. At a sprawling and well-equipped test center located on the Baltic

the national lexicon coincided with humanity's first historic ventures beyond the gravity of Earth. The catalyst for these new journeys into space was the International Geophysical Year, 1957–1958. Boldly, the United States declared its intention to orbit the world's first satellite, to be carried aloft by the Vanguard, a rocket launch vehicle put together by a consortium of public agencies. But Vanguard kept exploding on the launch pad. Already embarrassed, U.S. government officials listened in even greater mortification to the mocking beeps of *Sputnik,* the satellite dramatically launched into orbit by the Soviet Union on 4 October 1957.

For a nation that prided itself on technological leadership, particularly in the realm of aerospace activity, *Sputnik* triggered a national catharsis, since *Sputnik*'s triumph also seemed to throw a shadow over American competition with the Soviet Union in the context of the Cold War rivalry for global preeminence. Further, if the Soviets could orbit heavy satellites, then it stood to reason that their burly boosters could hurl nuclear warheads toward American cities. In the Cold War sweepstakes, national security, as well as national pride, appeared to be trailing the Soviets in a cloud of cosmic dust. It became national policy to "catch up with the Russians."

With public support, Congress passed the National Defense Education Act, designed to overhaul the American educational curriculum from kindergarten through graduate school with an eye to turning out more scientists and engineers. A crash program reorganized an ABMA research project on the Redstone rocket, which became the launch vehicle for Explorer I, America's first satellite placed in orbit on 31 January 1958. Its 31-pound payload paled in comparison to the 184 pounds of *Sputnik I* and the 1,100 of *Sputnik II* (launched in November 1957, it also carried a dog into space) but still accounted for a scientific "first" by confirming the presence of a dense radiation zone—the van Allen belts—several hundred miles above the earth.

The Soviet *Sputnik* also triggered national debate over the merits of an aggressive, unified national space program. Following twelve months of intense committee work, the Eisenhower administration finally settled on a new scheme, in which the Department of Defense pursued relevant projects for national security. At the same time, there would be a new initiative run by a civilian agency committed to the peaceful exploration of space, although aspects of research and development would be pursued cooperatively. In fact, the new agency turned out to

be one that had followed a similar pattern in the past. On 1 October 1958, NACA became NASA—the National Aeronautics and Space Administration.

Space programs directed by the Department of Defense often demonstrated technical brilliance (as well as astronomical budgets) but were just as often shielded from public view. Progressively improved versions of IRBMs were deployed in selected countries of the North Atlantic Treaty Organization (NATO), although the presence of nuclear-tipped missiles triggered increasingly vocal opposition from citizens and politicians within NATO itself. Within the United States, progressively improved versions of ICBMs were housed in underground missile silos, in order to survive a possible Soviet strike. The ability to survive and to retaliate with hydrogen bomb warheads against Soviet targets, it was argued, would discourage an enemy attack in the first place. Appropriately, the profusion of these missile systems and the prospects of a nuclear Armageddon became known as Mutually Assured Destruction—MAD. During the 1980s, the administration of Ronald Reagan initiated a costly and controversial Strategic Defense Initiative (dubbed "Star Wars" by skeptics) to intercept and destroy incoming enemy missiles and warheads. By the early 1990s, the collapse of the Soviet Union and reduced U.S. military budgets left the SDI program in limbo.

In addition to missiles, the Department of Defense administered an array of extraordinarily sophisticated satellites. Some were components of elaborate communications and navigational systems of global coverage. Other satellites eavesdropped on electronic signals and radio messages of different nations, took high-resolution photos over astounding distances while in orbit, or used a variety of sensory equipment to acquire revealing data. After the demise of the Soviet Union in the early 1990s, much of this same equipment was used to verify the dismantling of nuclear missile sites by both sides. In any case, the security surrounding Department of Defense space programs meant that NASA became the center of attention in space exploration. During his presidential campaign, John F. Kennedy had warned of a "missile gap" that gave the Soviet Union a military advantage. Although this factor proved to be problematic, the presumed gap helped sustain ambitious U.S. programs in rocketry and space exploration.

Over the first three years of its existence, NASA began to make some progress in the arcane world of satellites for communication and for weather forecasting. Then, on 12 April 1961, Soviet cosmonaut Yuri Gagarin roared into earth orbit aboard *Vostok*—

the first human in space. To recently elected President John F. Kennedy, the United States again appeared to be trailing in Cold War prestige. The President was already pressing his advisers for a more aggressive space program when failure to topple Fidel Castro through an abortive landing at Cuba's Bay of Pigs gave added incentive for projects to refurbish the nation's tarnished image. On 25 May 1961, Kennedy addressed a joint session of Congress: "Now it is time to take longer strides—time for a great new American enterprise—time for this nation to take a clearly leading role in space achievement, which in many ways may hold the key to our future on earth." Before the end of the decade, the President declared, the United States should send an American to the moon and back. "No single space project in this period will be more impressive to mankind," he said. And so, the United States set out to beat the Soviets to a manned lunar landing.

All of this meant radical changes for the old NACA as the new NASA. NASA's aeronautical research continued, much as before. But the demands of satellite development, space probes, and the awesome challenges of manned space exploration dictated fundamental alteration of inherited management styles. NASA not only conducted research but also became an operational agency, directly responsible for the development and management of hardware and missions. Moreover, most of its work was done by contractors, rather than in-house efforts. The agency also acquired new centers responsible for scientific payloads and tracking, launch vehicle development, astronaut training, and launch operations.

During the 1960s, the nation's manned space program claimed the attention of a fascinated public. The Apollo lunar landing effort embodied a step-by-step approach: the Mercury program put the first Americans into earth orbit; the Gemini program orbited two-place space craft and worked out crucial rendezvous techniques in space. Launch vehicles adapted from military missiles (Atlas and Titan) gave way to Saturn rockets developed solely for manned lunar missions. The early launches by powerful Saturn rocket boosters put a three-place Apollo Command Module into orbit and tested the Lunar Module in a space environment. In each case, bigger and more powerful boosters raised confidence about the safety and reliability of hardware required for the lunar voyage.

On 16 July 1969, *Apollo 11* rocketed into space aboard a Saturn V vehicle on its journey to the moon. Four days later, Neil Armstrong became the first human to set foot on lunar soil, followed by Edwin

Aldrin. Fellow astronaut Michael Collins kept station in the Command Module, orbiting the moon as Armstrong and Aldrin spent the night aboard the Lunar Module on the moon's surface. The next day, the pair of astronauts blasted into lunar orbit for a rendezvous with Collins; the trio then steered a course for earth. A triumphal tour to cities around the globe underscored America's leadership in space, but also celebrated human achievement in opening new vistas for exploration of the cosmos.

For some observers, the issue of space ventures to come hinged on the debate over manned versus unmanned projects. Partisans of the latter argued that manned missions were unnecessarily complex and costly. Advanced satellites and automated systems permitted greater diversity and boldness. In any case, NASA's space program embraced both initiatives. A series of earth satellites revolutionized communications, including live TV coverage anywhere on earth. Other satellites provided advance weather alerts, located natural resources, diagnosed agricultural problems, spotted environmental dangers, and became indispensable—if unseen—factors in human civilization. The sophistication and imagery of such satellites inevitably led to heavy reliance on military space surveillance systems by the United States, the Soviet Union, and other nations.

Various unmanned lunar probes and assorted space probes amassed amazing quantities of information. In 1976, the Viking program sent two pairs of orbiters and landers to Mars, yielding a wealth of detail about the planet but no evidence of life forms. Among a distinguished list of deep space probes, the odysseys of *Pioneer 10* and *Voyager 2* captured intense public interest in the United States as well as abroad. Launched in 1972, Pioneer 10 flashed away from earth at a record velocity of 32,000 mph, steering a course for Jupiter that required a year and a half to reach. After transmitting historic photos and data about its Jovian encounter, Pioneer 10 ventured onward through space, the first human object from earth to leave our solar system on a journey through infinity.

In 1977, the aptly named *Voyager 1* and *Voyager 2* space craft also began flights to Jupiter, although *Voyager 2* followed the most spectacular route because its program sent it on a "Grand Tour" of the solar system by flying past the outermost planets. Both craft were vastly improved over the *Pioneer 10*, transmitting stunning details of Jupiter and Saturn. Planetary scientists received reams of challenging data to analyze and interpret; a wealth of scientific information that continued when *Voyager 2* traveled

Apollo 11 astronaut Edwin E. Aldrin, Jr., walks on the moon, 20 July 1969. Photograph by Neil A. Armstrong.

past Uranus in 1986. Some 1.8 billion miles away on earth, scientists successfully pulled off a tricky maneuver to send *Voyager 2* on its way to a 1989 rendezvous with Neptune, twelve years after its launch.

Such space spectaculars became increasingly expensive, and NASA was not averse to cooperative efforts with other countries. Following several ad hoc arrangements during the 1960s, more formalized agreements developed during the early 1970s. One

Voyager 1 photograph of Jupiter and three of its satellites, 5 February 1979. The Great Red Spot is at the lower left on the planet's surface. The satellite Io can be seen against Jupiter's disk, to the right. At the far right is the satellite Europa (white spot). Callisto is barely visible at the bottom left of the photograph. NASA

related facilities available, NASA looked for ways to use these assets while maintaining skills of astronauts and launch crews until space shuttle missions began. A series of three Skylab missions in 1973—twenty-eight, sixty, and eighty-four days long—made use of a converted Saturn V upper stage, and each three-man crew completed productive scientific experiments while compiling instructive data on long-term human activities in space. It was something of a paradox that such equipment developed to compete with the Soviets found use in 1975 for the Apollo-Soyuz Test Project, or ASTP. A successful link-up of Soviet and American space capsules, including an exchange of astronaut/cosmonaut crew members, symbolized a thaw in superpower tensions and demonstrated potential rescue operations in space.

Although large rocket boosters had become very reliable, they were completely expended on a single launch. The idea of a reusable Space Shuttle, good for 100 trips, seemed compelling. During the late 1970s, with a fleet of four craft in production, the Shuttle program commanded the biggest share of NASA's budget and its management. Shuttles were needed to deliver components for the Space Station and for its maintenance. Also, the Shuttle's cargo bay could carry a mixed payload of satellites into orbit, repair and retrieve satellites already in orbit, lift scientific instruments for specialized experiments, and carry a reusable Spacelab module large enough for scientists to carry out complex experiments in a shirt-sleeve environment. The Spacelab and certain instrument pallets were supplied by ESA, representing an investment of several hundred million dollars. Canada supplied the Shuttle's robotic arm. These commitments reflected the continuing, international collaboration in NASA's post-Apollo space research and underscored the need for foreign investment to sustain many programs.

Beginning in 1981 and through 1982, four missions qualified the Shuttle for regular operations. During 1983, ESA's Spacelab made its debut, and NASA recorded flights with its first foreign astronaut (Ulf Merbold from Germany), the first American woman in space (Sally Ride), and the first African American (Guion Bluford). As all four vehicles became operational and completed one mission after another, human space flights seemed to be routine. They were not. On 28 January 1986, *Challenger* exploded about seventy-three seconds after liftoff; all seven crew members died.

Officials immediately grounded the three remaining shuttles while investigative panels searched

example was Helios, in partnership with the Federal Republic of Germany. The Helios project (launched in 1976) studied solar phenomena, and the Germans supplied not only funding but major scientific payload work as well. Further international collaboration attended the organization of the European Space Agency (ESA) in 1975. Moving into the 1990s, principal space projects like the Hubble Space Telescope, the Galileo mission to Jupiter, and the Ulysses solar polar mission all included significant funding and hardware contributions from German and ESA sources. In developing plans for a large space station to begin operating in the 1990s, NASA actively enlisted support from Japan, Canada, and ESA, all of which agreed to supply considerable investment and provide such major components as laboratory modules for scientific experiments and the robotic arms needed to construct and operate the space station in orbit.

International cooperation also characterized many manned activities in the post-Apollo era. With unused Apollo components, Saturn boosters, and

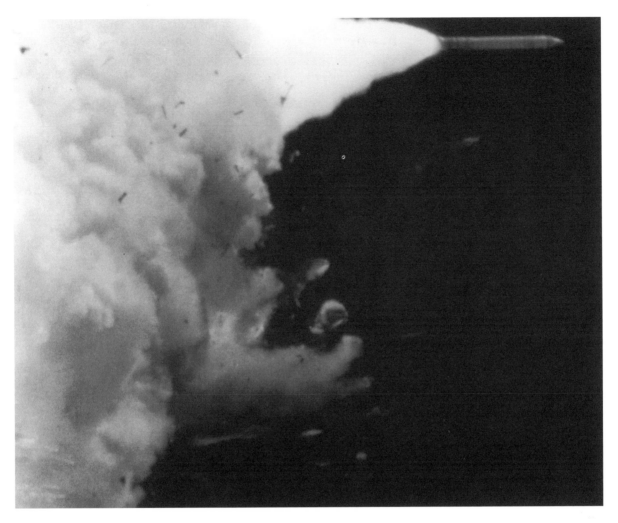

Explosion of the space shuttle *Challenger*, 28 January 1986. NASA

for the explosion's cause. Eventually, analysis pinpointed a defective joint on one of the two solid boosters, where O-rings were used as seals to control volatile gases during combustion of the solid propellants. NASA revised procedures for installation of the O-rings and corrected a variety of additional technical problems criticized by investigators. During the two-year hiatus until Shuttle flights resumed in 1988, NASA overhauled its management structure and made a host of other changes in Shuttle operations. But many missions dependent on scientifically requisite "launch windows" had to be scratched; many more were compromised in scientific value. NASA's image suffered, and foreign launch operations, especially from ESA, became far more competitive in the following years. Reliance on the Shuttle system alone left the agency with no back-up hardware. Military customers revitalized their expendable launch vehicle programs and other alternatives to NASA launches appeared. The Reagan administration authorized launch programs by private companies that became commercially successful.

By 1990, NACA/NASA's seventy-fifth anniversary, the agency had obviously changed. A technology transfer program was in place as a determined effort to take the agency's advances in materials, medicine, electronics, and other areas and to apply them in the down-to-earth marketplace. NASA carried on a variety of projects related to environmental issues such as windmills to generate electricity and better insulation for houses. Its powerful computer programs were available to architects, business forecasters, civil engineers, and others. NASA's aeronautical heritage was now paralleled by ambitious plans for space exploration. And many of these programs, specifically focused on national interests in the past, were now conceived and conducted with foreign partners. Internationalism had become an integral facet of American aerospace programs.

AEROSPACE TRENDS SINCE WORLD WAR II

Compared to the radical advances in military aviation, changes in commercial air transport technology happened more slowly. Nonetheless, improvements in speed, comfort, and range revolutionized travel patterns in regard to volume and demographics.

In the immediate postwar era, designers generally agreed that jet-powered transports were not feasible because jet engines had short lifetimes and consumed too much fuel. Propeller-driven piston engines powered the ubiquitous Douglas DC-3 and larger, four-motored types like the DC-7, the Lockheed Constellation, and Boeing Stratocruiser. With improved engines and aerodynamics, these big transports typically carried as many as fifty to sixty passengers at over 300 mph. Stretched versions might have seventy-five to one hundred seats. Additionally, they were pressurized, permitting them to fly at 20,000 to 30,000 feet, altitudes that usually left turbulent weather (and passenger discomfort) far below and also improved the speed and fuel efficiency of the airliner. Such planes had the range for non-stop flights across the United States, as well as for long-distance routes across the Atlantic and Pacific oceans. Because of an American technological lead in transport design dating back to the 1930s, foreign operators also acquired U.S. aircraft, giving the United States a near-monopoly in the manufacture and sale of postwar airliners.

The British moved to take the lead through development of the first successful turboprop (in which the propeller is driven by a geared, gas turbine engine) airliner in 1950 and the world's first operational jet airliner, the de Havilland Comet, which began operations in 1952. A series of tragic crashes grounded the Comet until 1958, by which time a new generation of U.S. jet airliners had surpassed the Comet's performance.

Entering service in 1958, the Boeing 707 was followed by the Douglas DC-8, a year later. Borrowing heavily from its experience in building swept-wing jet bombers and jet tankers, Boeing's new design also incorporated newer, reliable jet engines having greater fuel efficiency. Because the new American jet carried 110 passengers at 600 mph

(compared to the Comet's 40 passengers at 500 mph), its operating costs were compelling. Various models of the DC-8 offered similar performance. The resounding popularity of jet travel spawned other types of transports during the 1960s. Fascination with high speeds in airline travel, plus advanced aeronautical technology, prompted serious proposals for a supersonic transport (SST). Studies began in Europe and in the United States during the 1960s, but Congress cancelled the American program in 1971 in the face of environmental worries (including the effects of sonic shock waves) and predictions of excessively high passenger fares. The Anglo-French Concorde SST began scheduled flights in 1976, although its supersonic routes were limited. Less radical designs proved far more successful. The ponderous Boeing 747, boasting some 450 seats, gave rise to the term *jumbo-jet* or *wide-body* airliner, emulated by somewhat smaller (around 350 passengers) trijets such as the Lockheed L-1011 TriStar and Douglas DC-10. For shorter routes, the Boeing 727 or Douglas DC-9 types carried 100 to 150 passengers in and out of less-populated regions.

By the early 1970s, the speed and comfort of jet-powered travel was available to cities large and small throughout the country and around the world. Statistics for intercity travel in America portrayed the impact of airline service. Already in 1957, airline passenger miles (25 billion) exceed those of rail travel. The introduction of jets spurred dizzying growth, reaching 110 billion passenger miles by 1970. The same revolution occurred in transoceanic travel. In 1958, over one million passengers crossing the Atlantic went by airlines, outnumbering ocean liner passengers for the first time; by 1970, of 5 million foreign travelers annually, only 3 percent went by sea. The jet age had truly arrived.

After World War II, many people in aviation anticipated a big boom in general aviation and the light-plane industry. Instead, a sluggish postwar economy resulted in very difficult times for the general aviation sector, and the availability of many cheap war-surplus utility aircraft cut into the potential sales of new light planes. Nevertheless, there existed a steady, if somewhat diminished, demand for general aviation services, and business flying continued to increase steadily in volume.

The style of general aviation activities in the post–World War II era reflected prewar developments. Aerial crop treatment, seeding, photography, and surveying continued, with the introduction of modern techniques and improved equipment. Crop dusting of the prewar days expanded to include new

Boeing 707 Stratoliner. ARCHIVE PHOTOS

kinds of chemical sprays, and older biplanes like the war-surplus Stearman and others gave way to special monoplane designs from Piper, Cessna, and other manufacturers. With larger carrying capacity for either dry or liquid chemicals, interchangeable equipment to dispense various kinds of these two basic materials, and special design features for safety, maneuverability, and pilot visibility, the new breed of "ag-planes" helped make this sector of general aviation into a rapidly growing enterprise. In similar ways, advanced light-plane designs and improved accessories expanded the activities of general aviation aircraft in aerial photography and survey work.

In contrast to the years before World War II, postwar general aviation included an increasing number of helicopters. The highly maneuverable choppers won enthusiastic acceptance in agricultural roles,

police and rescue work, a wide variety of industrial and utility jobs, and business/executive flying. With their unique ability to land and maneuver in restrictive areas, helicopters were used to deliver personnel, parts, and repairs to the tops of skyscrapers, isolated construction work sites, off-shore oil well derricks, and polar research camps.

Other aspects of general aviation grew in the post–World War II era, including flight training and pleasure flying. But the most rapidly developing segment of general aviation was business flying, sustained by an expanding fleet of many different kinds of general aviation aircraft. At one end of the scale, there were the high-winged single-engine designs with fixed landing gear. In the early postwar years, designs such as the four-place Piper Pacer and Cessna 170 were popular. Their handling characteristics and performance (130–150 mph) appealed to farmers and ranchers, who flew them from rough fields and pastures, as well as to increasing numbers of business people on short trips. By the early 1950s, low-wing, high-performance light planes like the Beechcraft Bonanza were available. Bigger engines, controllable pitch propellers, and retractable gear gave planes like these a cruising speed of 180 mph, along with a range of up to 1,000 miles, which made them highly versatile business planes. In the late 1950s, the introduction of the Piper Comanche and similar high-performance single-engine planes with sophisticated electronic equipment for flying on instruments gave the business pilot a wide choice of aircraft.

The improving business climate of the 1950s encouraged manufacturers to broaden their product line to include twin-engine designs featuring greater room, comfort, and seating potential. A number of light-plane manufacturers developed a range of light, medium, and heavy twins to accommodate anywhere from four to ten passengers or more. In spite of the growing network of scheduled airline routes, individual business pilots and corporations alike appreciated the flexibility that such planes afforded. They were released from the sometimes inconvenient rigidity of airline schedules, and with the decline of rail passenger trains, many smaller communities without airline service were difficult to reach. The designs produced by Aero Commander, which became operational in the early 1950s, exemplified the new kind of high-performance twins that enlivened business flying after the war. Advanced models in 1955 made it the fastest executive twin of its time, carrying five to seven passengers for 1,600 miles at speeds up to 200 mph. Many types like the Commander were updated in the 1960s and 1970s to include turboprop engines and pressurized cabins to fly above bad weather.

The top performers of the multiengine corporate fleets were the jets. The first entry on the market was the Lockheed JetStar in 1961, a four-engine model that carried up to twelve executives to their appointments at 500 mph. But the market for corporate jets was soon dominated by maverick entrepreneur William Lear, whose compact, racy Learjet entered service in 1964. Early models seated only six to eight passengers, although the Learjet's speed of over 500 mph, efficient operating costs, and sleek lines made it a corporate status symbol, leading to sales that soared. Lear's surprising success prompted others to enter the market, so that a number of American as well as foreign manufacturers produced a range of business jets to meet the require-

ments of small corporations or international conglomerates.

Production and sales in the general aviation–light plane business reached full stride in the mid-1960s. The lively market for general aviation rested on rising prosperity, corporate profits, and especially on the decentralization of American industry. In the late 1970s, for example, of over 14,000 airports, only 425 offered scheduled airline services. With a third of new factories in smaller towns, corporate aviation was often the only way for busy executives, sales personnel, and other business travelers to maintain a schedule requiring personal visits. When deregulation of scheduled airlines in 1978 prompted many airlines to eliminate routes to smaller, less profitable destinations, general aviation sales surged again. In 1980, commercial airlines listed about 2,300 transports in service. The general aviation fleet numbered about 200,000 planes, with production running close to 13,000 units per year.

During the 1980s, the general aviation scene radically changed. Conglomerates snapped up stalwarts like Piper, Cessna, and Beechcraft. A swollen market of surplus planes, increased fuel costs, and product liability suits caused drastic curtailment in production of single-engine planes. Cessna and Beech concentrated on profitable corporate aircraft, leaving the lower end of the market to smaller manufacturers and used plane dealers. By the 1990s, Piper struggled to stay alive.

Still, general aviation persisted as an integral part of American aviation. Helicopters became commonplace in off-shore oil operations, police work, and emergency ambulance roles. Agricultural uses (and specialized manufacturers) continued as a stable market. The continuing decentralized style of the nation's businesses meant that business flying occupied a recognized niche in corporate and individual enterprises.

The decades after 1970 also brought significant changes to the airlines and to the aerospace manufacturers. Deregulation sparked a definite boost to airline traffic as the initial round of fare cuts and new services on major routes attracted passengers. Domestic and international airline travel rose from 275 million in 1978, to 295 million by 1980. Rising fuel prices and a sluggish economy, plus a strike called by aircraft controllers in 1981, accelerated a decline in revenues and profits. Although an improving economy stimulated air travel again, serious problems persisted in the airline travel industry. Several operators had invested heavily in new routes and new equipment, so that high interest payments became a burden. A wave of mergers added to the debt structure, while fuel costs continued to eat into profits. By 1991, earlier bankruptcy victims like Braniff International (bankrupt in 1982) were joined by honored airline pioneers like Eastern and the legendary Pan Am. Other airlines struggled to survive bankruptcy proceedings while continuing to operate. Industry leaders American, Delta, and United snapped up various international segments, transforming themselves from U.S. domestic airlines into major global operators. Air travel remained very popular, increasing more than 50 percent since 1980 to 465 million passengers in 1990 and continuing to rise.

Some analysts still endorsed deregulation because it sharpened competition and generated lower fares. Others warned that the few surviving airlines would emerge as monopolistic giants capable of manipulating higher fares at public expense. In any case, the airlines had contributed to striking changes in American travel habits and cultural life. Before World War II, foreign travelers typically went by steamship; a round trip to Europe took two weeks, plus a healthy bank balance. After the war, midwesterners who had traditionally vacationed in the Black Hills now jetted off to London, Tahiti, or the Seychelles. Travel at jet-age speeds made ten-day vacations feasible, and coach/charter fares made them affordable. By the same token, business and leisure travel within the United States experienced an astonishing process of democratization. Professional sports, with schedules geared to train and bus timetables, had traditionally operated up and down the Atlantic seaboard and east of the Mississippi River. Airliners, especially jets, opened up coast-to-coast schedules and the organization of expansion teams all over the country. Likewise, college teams regularly flew to distant encounters too remote to schedule in the prewar years.

Beginning with early postwar piston airliners and accelerating with jet routes, the performing arts became a much more globalized phenomenon. In music, for example, European musicians and conductors appeared not only in traditional venues on America's East and West Coasts, with occasional forays to Chicago; artists from overseas also headlined in Dubuque, Salt Lake City, Houston, and elsewhere. Similarly, Americans and other nationals arranged concerts across every continent, wherever the airlines went.

Success of a plane in airline sales or for military service did not guarantee easy survival for its manufacturer in the postwar era. Political and economic turbulence during the 1970s and 1980s brought the demise of several familiar aircraft firms, even though some found temporary sanctuary as divisions of larger

conglomerates. Republic had disappeared, along with Vought; Fairchild survived only as a supplier of aerospace specialty items; while Martin's rocket and missile business effectively displaced its pioneering role as aircraft manufacturer. Nor were the giants in aerospace manufacturing immune to the politics of change. As early as 1967, North American perceived the need for financial stability beyond its then-current resources and found a partner with Rockwell, a manufacturer of machine tools and heavy duty transport equipment. The initial entity of North American Rockwell eventually emerged as Rockwell International. Also, in 1967, Douglas Aircraft became a division of McDonnell Douglas Corporation after cash flow problems, among other things, prompted Douglas to accept an offer made by the profitable defense manufacturer from Saint Louis. Lockheed corporation went through a traumatic phase in the early 1970s, when Rolls-Royce engine development problems stalled progress on the L-1011 TriStar and Lockheed's new C-5 military transport ran huge deficits. Lockheed survived, but only after a controversial loan of $250 million passed by Congress in 1971. The TriStar's late entry into the airline market hampered sales, and production ended in 1984.

A variety of causes lay behind these and other horror stories that beset the aerospace industry. The cost of research and development had escalated dramatically, driven by increased reliance on electronic warfare systems that became standard practice during the Vietnam conflict. Combat planes and civil aircraft alike utilized exotic metallurgy in construction; designs for higher speeds and greater size added to fabrication costs. Advanced, electronic navigation systems and flight systems for all aircraft were more expensive. Burgeoning costs for tooling, manufacture, and testing of innovative products like these represented more investment risk than most companies could afford.

When the Air Force conducted competition for a new lightweight fighter in the 1970s, various American and European contenders (the plane was also for NATO air forces) stressed coproduction agreements. This was partly for political reasons, although manufacturers also needed to spread the financial liabilities. In what was called the "deal of the century," General Dynamics took the estimated $15 billion contract award for its F-16. A complex production scheme gave four European partners coproduction rights, in which they not only built major sections of their own planes, but also shared in sales to the USAF and other foreign customers.

Although later combat designs for the USAF did

not include such heavy overseas involvement, the expense of developing new combat planes led to collaboration by American firms on one project while competing with each other on others. These "teaming" arrangements characterized competition for the new USAF fighter early in the 1990s. The losing team included Northrop and McDonnell Douglas for the F-23 model, while the winning F-22 team featured Lockheed, Boeing, and General Dynamics. NASA used similar teaming arrangements on contracts for its Space Station, and the same approach characterized research and development on the National Aero-Space Plane (NASP) concept in which several government agencies themselves supplied joint funding to design a Mach 25 transport capable of orbiting the Earth.

Despite these significant changes, aerospace manufacturing enjoyed an impressive growth after World War II. Nobody expected to continue the production rate of 1945, a record of 110,000 planes for the year, and wartime plans eased the industry into peacetime conversion. During the 1950s, production of all planes averaged about 11,000 annually, with civil planes accounting for 80 percent of the total by 1960. The work force reached 1.5 million in 1968, but usually numbered about 1.2 million through the early 1990s. Production of aircraft swelled to 20,000 in 1966, with over 15,000 general aviation planes delivered that year. By 1991, production of general aviation types numbered 1,000; airliners at 593, helicopters at 596, and military aircraft at 907. Aerospace sales, including space hardware, came to $3 billion in 1950, passed $25 billion in 1974, and totaled $140 billion in 1991. Except for agriculture, aerospace exports represented one of the few areas in which the United States enjoyed a favorable balance of trade,

a consistent record since 1968. Nonetheless, the early 1990s marked an uncertain future. The fragmentation of the former Soviet Union and reduction of Cold War tensions brought major cuts in defense budgets, sending waves of layoffs through the military departments of aerospace contractors. A series of mergers and realignments occurred, including a decision by General Dynamics to sell its famous aircraft manufacturing division to Lockheed. Grumman was bought out by Northrop. A continuing slump in the world economy led airlines to cancel orders and defer deliveries of new aircraft, putting additional pressure on aerospace manufacturers. Adequate funding for current and projected programs was a constant challenge.

The future was bound to be colored by international financing arrangements. For example, Boeing and McDonnell Douglas signed risk-sharing agreements with Asian and European firms in order to develop new jet airliner designs in the 1980s and 1990s. Development of Boeing's 777 transport in the early 1990s included a substantial stake from foreign sources, including the Japanese, who contracted to build 20 percent of the airframe. Such multinational arrangements became the norm during the 1980s and 1990s, and Europeans marketed their own Airbus transport series under the umbrella of Airbus Industrie, heavily funded by member governments including France, Germany, and Britain. The impressive success of the Airbus designs gave them the number two position in worldwide sales of airliners, behind Boeing but ahead of McDonnell Douglas. In a market dominated so long by American technology, the success of Airbus symbolized continuing change in the aerospace community and the theme of international competitiveness.

See Also Large-scale Scientific Enterprise; Industrial Research and Technology; Computer and Communications Technology; Medical Science and Technology (all in this volume).

BIBLIOGRAPHY

The author wishes to thank the University of Illinois Institute of Aviation and the Johns Hopkins University Press, respectively, for permission to utilize materials from Roger Bilstein, ed., *Fundamentals of Aviation and Space Technology* (1974), and Bilstein, *Flight in America: From the Wrights to the Astronauts* (1991).

Dominick Pisano and Cathleen Lewis, eds., *Air and Space History: An Annotated Bibliography* (1988), organizes a startling variety of sources in aeronautics and astronautics that encompass economic, political, technical, and cultural implications. Two books offer informative surveys: Joseph Corn, *The Winged Gospel: America's Romance with Aviation, 1900–1950*

(1983), provides many insights on aviation and popular culture, women, and minorities; Roger Bilstein, *Flight in America: From the Wrights to the Astronauts*, rev. ed. (1994), considers major trends in both aviation and astronautics and comments on socioeconomic implications.

For the early years of aviation, see Tom Crouch, *The Bishop's Boys: A Life of Wilbur and Orville Wright* (1989), the premier study of the fascinating brothers, their technological achievements, and the formative era of the aviation business. On the subject of air travel, R. E. G. Davies, *Airlines of the United States since 1914* (1972), is an indispensable survey with encyclopedic coverage. William Leary, ed., *Aviation's Golden Age: Portraits from the 1920s and 1930s* (1989), contains original essays on pivotal but little-known figures who shaped the institutional and political dimensions of aviation. Henry Ladd Smith, *Airways: The History of Commercial Aviation in the United States* (1942), continues to be a useful starting point on pioneer airlines; Carl Solberg, *Conquest of the Skies: A History of Commercial Aviation in America* (1979), summarizes airline developments with special attention to the post–World War II years. John Newhouse, *The Sporty Game* (1983), represents an unusually well-informed discussion of the challenges and pitfalls inherent in designing, building, and marketing modern jet airliners on a global basis.

Regarding aviation manufacturers, John B. Rae, *Climb to Greatness: The American Aircraft Industry, 1920–1960* (1968), covers finances and contributions of the major producers of civil and military planes. Jacob Vander Meulen, *The Politics of Aircraft: Building an American Military Industry* (1991), is a fascinating and detailed analysis of the aviation industry in the 1920s and 1930s. Ronald Miller and David Sawers, *The Technical Development of Modern Aviation* (1970), explains the essential technologies that gave rise to successful air transportation, from the piston engine era through the impact of jets and swept-back wings. James Hansen, *Engineer in Charge: A History of the Langley Aeronautical Laboratory, 1917–1958* (1987), summarizes institutional evolution of NACA and offers a deft study of a government research center, set in the context of sweeping changes in aviation engineering.

As for military aviation, Robin Higham, *Air Power: A Concise History* (1988), continues to stand out as a cogent, magisterial analysis with an impressively rich bibliography. James Hudson, *Hostile Skies: A Combat History of the American Air Service* (1968), chronicles the realities of American experience during World War I. Lee Kennett, *The First Air War, 1914–1918* (1991), provides an unusually informative summary of popular opinion, weapons, and strategic trends, with coverage of friend and foe alike. Stephen McFarland and Wesley Newton, *To Command the Sky: The Battle for Air Superiority over Germany, 1942–44* (1991), represents an important interpretation of American fighter power in the aerial conflict over Western Europe. Michael Sherry, *The Rise of American Air Power: The Creation of Armageddon* (1987), offers a perceptive history of long-range strategic bombing, culminating with World War II, as a cohesive policy of mass destruction, including atomic weapons. David Anderton, *The History of the U.S. Air Force* (1981), is thoroughly illustrated, and the informative text analyzes Korea and Vietnam, as well as post-Vietnam trends. Richard Hallion, *Storm over Iraq: Air Power and the Gulf War* (1992), not only presents a knowledgeable analysis of the Gulf War but also discusses the evolution of Air Force doctrine and technology during the 1970s and 1980s.

The role of military forces in space, such as the Strategic Defense Initiative, is assessed by Donald R. Baucom, *The Origins of SDI, 1944–83* (1993), which also comments on the evolution of ballistic missiles and related security issues. On the origins of NASA, see Lloyd Swenson, James Grimwood, and Charles Alexander, *This New Ocean: A History of Project Mercury* (1966), a study that considers the relevant historical background of space technology while presenting a comprehensive study of the early years of America's space program. Michael Collins, *Liftoff: The Story of America's Adventures in Space* (1988), is a splendidly written memoir covering the Apollo Program and post-Apollo initiatives by NASA. Walter McDougal, *The Heavens and The Earth: A Political History of the Space Age* (1985), a Pulitzer Prize winner in history, delivers an engrossing analysis of Soviet and American pursuit of space exploration as a vehicle for global recognition in the context of the Cold War.

COMPUTER AND COMMUNICATIONS TECHNOLOGY

Steven W. Usselman

In a century that has lent itself to revolutionary changes, perhaps no aspect of life has spawned more epithets than the business of gathering, manipulating, and transmitting information. Twentieth-century Americans have experienced an Electronic Revolution, lived in an Information Age, entered the Computer Era, formed an Information Society, and undergone a Control Revolution. As the century draws to a close, the prominence of communications and computing technologies shows no signs of abating. During the presidential election of 1992, the victorious Bill Clinton stressed the need for Americans to prepare for a new information-centered world. Nothing evoked the coming era more vividly than Clinton's oft-stated commitment to build an "electronic superhighway," a network of optic cables, wireless hook-ups, and personal computers that would link all citizens, enabling them to summon and send information and images at will.

For those familiar with the history of communications in the twentieth century, the notion of an electronic superhighway evokes conflicting emotions. On the one hand, the emerging network marks an exhilarating culmination of a century of extraordinary technical change. The highway promises to bring together in a single integrated system all of the major technologies of communications and information processing. Telephones, radio and television, and computing, each with their own distinct histories for the first three-quarters of the century, have converged on the common technical base of solid-state electronics and digitized data. Instruments of mass communications—radio and television—have become entangled with private means of exchanging and processing information. Ideas long considered fantastic suddenly seem commonplace realities. Giant telecommunications companies, entertainment producers, and cable television operators, scrambling to capitalize on new opportunities, stand poised to execute some of the most momentous mergers in the history of American enterprise. Regulatory agencies and congressional committees struggle to maintain their bearings. And baffled consumers, drifting in a sea of metaphors invoking the new technology, await the promised bonanza. No area of life appears likely to go untouched.

Yet many experienced observers view these developments with a healthy dose of jaded complacency as well—for in a sense, they have seen and heard it all before. Like the telephone and broadcasting systems in the bloom of their own youth, the information superhighway seems at once to open vast new opportunities for individual communications while potentially giving birth to a powerful natural monopoly. It thus raises the central challenge that changes in communications have persistently posed in American public life: the attempt to balance a desire for access against a potential for control in the face of rapidly changing technology. As in previous cases of innovation, Americans will attempt at every turn to establish the degree of standardization essential for unleashing the full potential of the technology while creating an entrenched bureaucracy unresponsive to the needs of individuals and incapable of incorporating the continuing fruits of innovation. This balancing act will be, as it always has been, an intensely political process. Technology alone will not dictate the shape of the new communications system.

If history proves an accurate guide, the politics of the superhighway will likely reflect a distinctly American mix of ideology and interests. The sustained commitment of Americans to democratic principles has consistently infused discussion of communications with a special urgency. Nothing is more central to the maintenance of democratic culture than fair and equal access to information. Champions of democracy from Thomas Paine forward have placed extraordinary faith in the potential of technology to advance their cause. Often innovations have been accompanied by grandiose, visionary claims for their potential to realize democratic ideals. Communications technologies consequently have sparked unusually impassioned public debate and have fueled regulation on the federal level much more readily than even other utilities such as electric power and ground transportation. Despite the intensity of feeling, however, Americans have been much more reluctant than their European counterparts to nationalize their communications technologies. They have relied instead on a mixture of private initiative and public regulation, using a combination of legislation, agency supervision, and antitrust proceedings. In choosing this course, Americans have opened the political process to powerful vested interests. Such interests have been especially prominent in the case of communications because existing technologies have tended to converge with one another and to give birth to their own successors. AT&T, for instance, was a vibrant force in the emergence of radio. Later, RCA played the central role in the creation of television. The superhighway represents merely the latest and most conspicuous example of a recurrent process; and the jockeying among cable television operators, telephone companies, and regulatory agencies fits squarely within the tradition of communications policy in the United States.

Consumers, too, have exerted a strong influence in the struggles to shape communications technologies. Innovation in communications and information processing has consistently been stimulated primarily by two groups: business organizations that handle large volumes of information pertaining to costs and financial accounts; and the military and others concerned with national security. In particular, large financial institutions and highly capitalized corporations have provided the sustaining motivation for innovation. By processing their accounts more quickly, such organizations can save vast interest charges. No firm can long forego innovation that promises such savings. Those responsible for national defense have found themselves in a similar competition, only with lives and secrets rather than money hanging in the balance. In each realm, technology has often pressed steadily forward in increments against well-defined objectives, without entering the public consciousness or stimulating utopian visions. In this respect, too, the information superhighway exhibits characteristic features of American communications. For while public discussion of the network often evokes images of universal access and individual liberation, the network itself has taken shape in re-

sponse to more mundane considerations. The superhighway is already a commonplace reality for many within the financial community and the military-university research establishment. Others are left to catch up. One of Bill Clinton's first acts as president was to replace the antiquated White House switchboard with a new electronic communications system, replete with electronic mail addresses for himself and Vice President Al Gore.

In the realm of mass communications, firms seeking to reach national markets have provided a similar impetus for innovation and have exerted a powerful influence over public policy. They, too, have felt the irresistible pull of technology. Few manufacturers would run the risk of not advertising their products via the new media of radio and television. Entertainment companies have likewise sought to influence the technologies of mass communication. Meanwhile, the television networks and other purveyors of mass communication have taken a strong role in shaping telecommunications and other transmission technologies on which they depend to distribute their programming. Again the information highway merely echoes longstanding issues in the history of communications.

For these reasons, a brief history of communications and computing cannot venture far from tales of corporate maneuverings in the private and public arenas. Operating within the framework of American political traditions, firms with established expertise and interests have attempted to ride the perpetually shifting winds of technological change and to give shape to the prevalent methods of communicating and processing information. Yet in tracing these efforts, we must not lose sight of the dynamic force provided by individuals who stood outside those institutions. Successful business institutions reflect social desires more than they dictate them; they succeed by devising strategies and assuming forms that meet pressures from outside. Throughout the history of communications, some of the strongest pressure has come from independent innovators and consumers who have made of the technology what they wanted. Time and again, groups such as amateur radio operators and computer hackers have led communications and computing technology in directions that no organized lobby or established corporation anticipated. Similarly, audience desire has perpetually shaped mass communications, usually to the chagrin of those who have hoped the new media would "uplift" the masses and advance the democratic ideal of neutral, accessible communications open to all. The people, not the interests, have made radio and television instruments of popular entertainment, just as they are currently turning the superhighway toward such functions as home shopping and movies-on-demand.

Because business institutions and regulatory arrangements are the products of broad social inputs, their histories reveal a great deal about the ways in which communications technologies have affected life in twentieth-century America. Business strategies evolved and political debates proceeded in response to the demands of countless individuals whose lives were being reshaped by those technologies. Rather than trace those changes through individual examples, the survey that follows relies on the aggregated results evident in market behaviors and political outcomes. The extraordinary profits earned by communications firms pursuing certain strategies and the continual regulatory ferment associated with them testify to the nature and extent of the changes.

Yet for all the obvious importance of communications and computing, we should be cautions about overestimating their effects. The pervasiveness of these technologies in our ordinary routines makes it difficult to imagine life without them and to assess clearly just what changes they have wrought. These technologies have often generated expectations and rhetoric that had little connection to the more mundane considerations that actually shaped them. Some measure of the difficulty can be gleaned from the realm of politics, an arena in which many observers have been quick to assert the centrality of communications technology. During the presidential campaign of 1992, analysts repeatedly praised the Clinton organization's skillful use of communications technologies, especially its network of fax machines that produced and distributed prompt responses to attacks from the press and the opposition. Mastery of communications technology, many said, yielded victory. Yet nearly a century before, during the momentous election of 1896, William McKinley responded to the public utterances of William Jennings Bryan in virtually identical fashion by using the telegraph network, then a fifty-year-old innovation. A century of change in communications technology has generated less change than we think. But throughout, communications has remained a vital force in the most precious affairs of Americans.

THE EMERGENCE OF TELEPHONY AND RADIO, 1894–1925

At the moment William McKinley and his handlers orchestrated their successful strategy, the United States stood on the brink of a new age in communications. Two technologies, the telephone and radio, would over the next quarter-century make communication by spoken word as common and widespread as communication via print media had been for previous generations of Americans. Few could ignore these novelties, with their startling potential to transmit the human voice through space and across distance and bring it instantaneously into intimate private spaces. The two technologies changed daily routines at home and at work and ultimately altered the very ways in which people perceived the world and their place within it. Such sweeping innovations opened vast commercial possibilities and stimulated extensive public discussion. Within a generation, twentieth-century Americans had placed both the telephone system and radio in a framework of regulated private enterprise that would survive for nearly another half-century.

The Audio Age dawned in 1894, when the original telephone patents expired. The Bell Company, one of the most notorious monopolists of the Gilded Age, suddenly faced stiff competition from lower-cost suppliers. Consumers responded enthusiastically. Between 1894 and 1908, the total number of phones increased from 291,000 to nearly 6.5 million, an annual rate of increase (21 percent) never approached before or since. By 1914, Americans owned more than 10 million phones, fully 70 percent of all those in the world. They had invested nine dollars per capita in telephony, making the telephone industry the fourth largest in the country after steel, lumber and timber, and illuminating and heating gas.

While the sudden emergence of telephone service no doubt altered routines in myriad ways for millions of Americans, its potential for change was far greater than that initially exerted in actual practice. In theory, a network of telephones would link everyone together, enabling them to speak instantaneously and interactively with everyone else, all in the privacy of home or office. This was the image proffered after 1907 by the giant American Telephone and Telegraph Company. AT&T rushed forward under the dynamic leadership of Theodore N. Vail beneath the banner of "One System, Universal Service." Vail hoped to persuade Americans that by concentrating resources in a single system operated by AT&T, they could obtain quality telephone service for everyone and ready connections between all users. In just five years, he promised in 1909, AT&T would even provide long distance service from coast-to-coast.

In time Vail's vision would become reality, but in 1907 his slogan expressed merely a strategy. AT&T was actually a collection of local companies—

the legacy of the Bell interests—held together by their access to a common pool of capital and equipment. Only through a crash program of research did its engineers manage to complete a telephone connection between New York and San Francisco for the Pan-Pacific Exhibition of 1914, just in time to fulfill Vail's pledge. Long after that demonstration, such long-distance service remained a luxurious alternative to the established telegraph system, well out of reach of most Americans. In 1920, a three-minute call between New York and San Francisco cost $16.50. Only those with especially valuable information to send, such as newsmongers and financiers, could afford to pay the premium. George W. Perkins, a partner with the investment banking house of J. P. Morgan, boasted that through "rapid transit telephony" he could in under an hour line up a chain of ten to thirty investors in cities stretching from New York to Chicago and raise $10 million. But few traveled in such circles, and even those who did often still preferred the telegraph, with its professional operators and printed messages. The giant Pennsylvania Railroad, with its obvious long-distance communication requirements, persisted in using the telegraph almost exclusively in its operations. Only rising labor costs and fear of operator strikes prompted it to shift to the telephone during the teens.

Telephones held their broadest appeal among those without ready access to telegraphs who wished to communicate with others in their local exchange or with friends and associates in exchanges immediately adjacent to their own. Such users existed throughout America. The greatest concentrations could be found in growing urban centers and their surrounding areas, especially among the swelling ranks of suburban professionals. At work, phones kept these professionals connected to colleagues and customers even as they relocated to new manufacturing districts or towering skyscrapers. At home, wives could stay within easy reach of friends and merchants despite having set up house in an outlying area. The phone was thus a perfect suburban tool, especially suited to a culture that lacked abundant servants and other ready messengers.

Residents of these new, affluent urban areas were the real targets of Vail's strategy. To provide universal service, AT&T relied on young female operators it recruited overwhelmingly from the ranks of the educated middle class. This work force put AT&T's professional clientele at ease and helped the firm establish a reputation for quality, which it enhanced by installing expensive equipment that performed with unusual clarity and reliability. Such investments could

only be justified in urban areas, where dense settlement ensured that the switchboard and other common components of the system would be used intensively.

The urban strategy proved extraordinarily successful for AT&T during the first quarter of the twentieth century. By 1911, the AT&T affiliates in New York City could connect suburban callers to a phone in the central city or in a neighboring community in under ninety seconds; in London, it took over half an hour to make a similar connection. Suburban residents soon came to see the company's services as being as indispensable to their daily routines as the trolleys that carried them to and from work. In many locales, AT&T affiliates began to operate much like transport companies, electricity suppliers, and other utilities. By agreeing to have their rates regulated by local governing boards, these "baby Bells" were granted monopolies. As they grew and encroached on one another's territories, such companies frequently merged, and the scope of monopoly and regulation expanded from local to regional or state levels. Since the local and regional phone companies obtained financing and technology from AT&T and used its facilities to make long-distance connections, Vail's goal of one system, universal service grew ever closer to reality.

Yet for all its ability to generate profits and infiltrate the urban scene, the telephone can hardly be said to have revolutionized communications and reshaped the city during this period, as some have claimed. European cities assumed much the same form as their American counterparts without acquiring phones in anything like the numbers found in the United States. European residents coped with congestion and sprawl by relying on servants, messengers, and enhanced local mail delivery. Phones presented urbanites in labor-scarce America with a convenient alternative, which they seized energetically but without great fanfare. Most used phones in a perfunctory manner. Studies of Boston-area exchanges during the early decades of the twentieth century reveal a preponderance of brief, local calls. The typical call involved the placing of an order with a merchant. Subsequent surveys have consistently shown that most people employ telephones simply to convey brief factual information, usually to someone with whom they have frequent personal contact. Few use the telephone to persuade or to resolve conflicts. Even the affable Franklin Roosevelt spoke on the phone only about five times daily. We have no reason to suspect that callers acted differently during the opening decades of the century, when services were not only more expensive, but far less private. With exchanges requiring an operator and most residential customers sharing lines with other parties, wise conversationalists presumed others were eavesdropping. The phone system was still a long way from the secure, private communications medium later generations would come to expect.

Ironically, the group of Americans whose lives were perhaps most meaningfully affected by the coming of telephones was one that AT&T largely passed by. Farmers and other residents of rural areas hungered after phones, which, for far less cost than a Model T, could break down the isolation that plagued their lives. Since sparsely settled areas could not initially support service of AT&T's caliber, into the breach rushed innumerable smaller companies, offering more limited services of lesser quality. Local exchanges sprang up in one community after another, usually for no purpose other than connecting residents with a network of their nearest neighbors, and public pay phones became a standard feature at country stores. The agricultural Midwest consistently had more phones per capita than any other region of the country. Even with the poor rural South lagging well behind all other regions, in 1920 farmers nationwide accounted for nearly half of the approximately 13 million phones in the United States.

Instead of using the phone simply to relay matter-of-fact messages, rural Americans frequently employed the local exchanges in ways that mixed the later practices of the telephone conference call and talk radio. Any evening, farmers could pick up the phone and join in conversation with several of their neighbors, as if they had gathered around a kitchen table. In addition to this social function, rural exchanges provided farmers with a communications lifeline. In the event of a fire or dangerous storm, operators would alert all subscribers with a sustained ring or other prearranged alarm signal. Surveys later revealed that people born before 1920 were far more likely to respond to the ring of a telephone with dread rather than enthusiasm, because in their youth a phone call had often brought bad news. Such usage appears to have been an essential feature of phone service in rural areas, for with the coming of radio broadcasting, the number of phones in the countryside actually declined.

Radio broadcasting burst upon the American scene during the 1920s with exhilarating, disorienting suddenness. Radio itself, however, was not new during the twenties. For nearly three decades, a number of prominent inventors and countless "amateur operators" had been pushing forward the art of wire-

less communication. Among those who sought to earn profits from their endeavors, the Italian Guillermo Marconi took the lead. During the 1890s Marconi secured a contract to supply wireless telegraphs to the British Royal Navy, which wished to use the devices for ship-to-shore communication. Within a decade Marconi had set up companies in several European countries and the United States, and ship-to-shore communications had become a common feature of ocean transport. Although Marconi essentially cornered the commercial market for wireless telegraphy, thousands of amateurs patched together primitive wireless sets of their own, using crystals and a "cat's whisker" antenna to tune in the signals, and headphones or a speaker (often stolen from a public telephone) to amplify the faint dots and dashes. Many amateurs also built crude transmitters and sent messages of their own. When the *Titanic* sank in 1912, so many amateurs clogged the airwaves with extraneous and unreliable messages that official distress signals failed to get through in timely fashion. In the wake of the disaster Congress created a Radio Board and required all operators to obtain licenses. These measures established the public nature of radio and laid precedents for subsequent regulation that would shape the course of its development.

In 1912, however, government could not yet bring order to what was still an emerging field with a rapidly changing, small-scale technology and few barriers to entry. Amateurs and aspiring entrepreneurs still reigned. A few, such as Americans Reginald Fessenden and Lee DeForest, had made substantial inroads toward the elusive and tantalizing goal of transmitting the human voice without wires. This task required that inventors establish a continuous connection between transmitter and receiver via a radio wave, rather than just the intermittent contact necessary to send and detect Morse code. Fessenden developed devices that could reliably generate regular waves and transmit them over long distances. Working independently, DeForest focused his efforts on the difficult tasks of tuning in such waves and amplifying the weak signals they carried. In 1911 he developed a novel device, the audion tube, which dramatically enhanced the quality of reception. This tube, when modified and evacuated of air, would prove essential to virtually all subsequent radio equipment and many other electronic devices.

With the emergence of vacuum tube technology, the world of radio crossed with that of the emergent giants of the electrical industries, AT&T and General Electric. AT&T recognized DeForest's tube as a potential means of boosting signals over long distances, the most pressing technical problem in AT&T's pursuit of universal long-distance service. The company obtained patent rights to the tube for its first transcontinental hook-up. Scientists and engineers in the firm's laboratories analyzed the tubes and found ways to enhance their performance and production. Meanwhile, their counterparts at GE acquired extensive knowledge of tubes as well. In an effort to improve the light bulb, researchers at GE had for many years studied the behavior of electric currents as they passed through metals and gases. They readily turned this expertise toward tubes. After analyzing tube performance under various conditions, one GE engineer patented the high-pressure vacuum tube, a variant that offered significantly enhanced amplification and superior quality control in a much smaller package.

The emergence of vacuum tube electronics brought corporate America to the threshold of radio, but it was World War I that pushed the established firms across it. Before the war, AT&T had monitored developments in wireless but had taken pains to portray the technology as supplemental to its wired networks. Managers at GE had viewed radio as an uncertain field cluttered with conflicting patent claims and an established competitor in Marconi. The outbreak of war changed the situation dramatically. The Wilson administration wanted U.S. ships and forces equipped with radio, and it did not wish to entrust the task to a group of amateurs or to a foreign-owned corporation. Antitrust officials at the Justice Department let managers at GE know that they would not oppose a purchase of American Marconi. The subsequent deal led to the creation of the Radio Corporation of America (RCA), a wholly owned subsidiary of GE dedicated exclusively to the development of radio. At the same time, the federal government assumed responsibility for all patent liabilities that might arise in the pursuit of radio for the duration of the war.

Radio emerged from World War I in a much heightened state of development. Voice transmission via continuous wave, accomplished by transmitters and receivers employing vacuum tube circuitry, had become a proven technique. RCA, AT&T, and Westinghouse—firms with well established capabilities in design, production, and sales—stood poised to exploit it commercially. With the patent system again in force, the three negotiated a pooling agreement that segmented the market. AT&T would produce long-distance transmitters and assume responsibility for radio technology used in conjunction with existing wired communications. RCA and Westinghouse would sell radio receivers and small transmitters to amateurs, who would presumably replace their homemade sets with mass-produced ones in order to gain the superior performance made possible by tube technology and other patented componentry.

None of the parties to this agreement anticipated what happened next. Each still envisioned radio as a means of point-to-point communication between individuals. The growing flock of amateurs knew otherwise. Many amateurs had derived endless pleasure and fascination from simply tuning in and listening to powerful transmissions from distant sources, such as those sent out by the attention-seeking pioneers Fessenden and DeForest. The iconoclastic DeForest had become widely known among radio operators as a prophet of such "broadcasting." David Sarnoff, an amateur operator employed by American Marconi, wrote a memo to his bosses in 1916 that essentially described broadcasting and home reception as the wave of the future. Within a decade Sarnoff would become the driving force at RCA as it came to dominate the industry. Appeals such as his continued to fall on deaf ears, however, until an engineer and amateur operator employed by Westinghouse convinced his employer in 1920 to transmit programs on a regular basis from its Pittsburgh facilities. He thought the transmissions might boost interest in radio and generate sales of receivers.

This experiment proved wildly successful. Broadcasts of election returns and college football games over KDKA generated tremendous enthusiasm throughout the Pittsburgh area. Listeners appreciated being able to turn to the same spot on the dial at specific times and hear programs that had been listed in the newspaper. Within a year, Westinghouse had opened stations in Chicago (KYW) and Newark (WJZ). RCA soon followed suit with a number of its own powerful stations. The success of these corporate-owned broadcasting facilities spawned numerous imitators. In 1922 alone, over 500 broadcasters received licenses from the Radio Board, and by the end of the year a total of 576 stations were in operation. Millions of new listeners rushed to acquire sets. Between 1924 and 1928, consumers annually spent over $500 million on radio equipment, with the lion's share going toward home receivers. Many purchased inexpensive sets built by unlicensed manufacturers. By inserting the patented tubes into these receivers, listeners could obtain quality reception for considerably less than the cost of an RCA or Westinghouse machine.

The broadcasting craze that swept through the United States during the mid-1920s was fueled above all by the simple pursuit of pleasure. Radio was fun. For a modest investment, a receiver brought countless surprises into kitchens and parlors across the land.

With hundreds of small stations trying out the new medium, one never knew what to expect. Only a few powerful stations, such as those operated by Westinghouse and RCA, offered regularly scheduled programming. Most broadcasters sent out weak signals on an irregular basis. Some did not even consistently use the same portion of the radio band. Changes in the weather and other atmospheric conditions played havoc with the primitive receivers. Many listeners initially derived their greatest pleasure just from scanning the spectrum and adding to the list of stations they had heard. In most large cities, broadcasters voluntarily observed what were known as silent nights, an evening each week during which they sent no messages so that those with receivers could tune in distant stations without interference.

The nature of radio programming during these early years added to the sense of adventure. Few stations sought to earn money by attracting a large audience and selling airtime to advertisers. Instead, most licensees looked upon radio as a useful publicity tool that might benefit their established endeavors. Together they offered an extraordinary variety of programming that shared little other than low production costs and an unpolished, spontaneous character. Newspapers were some of the most common operators; typically an announcer read early editions over the air while newsstands offered the latest news in traditional print format. In industrial cities such as Chicago, ethnic fraternal organizations usually operated several stations. Their primary purpose was to provide information in the native languages of immigrants. Universities, which accounted for nearly 20 percent of all licenses issued before 1924, generally offered a mix of lectures, readings, and announcements. In addition to attracting new readers and students, many academics hoped these stations would establish universities as the most appropriate stewards of the miraculous new medium. Few other early broadcasters held such elevated aspirations. Department store owners, another common licensee, used broadcasts from sales floors and display windows to lure curious listeners to their showrooms. Several hotels set up stations in their lobbies for similar effect. For these broadcasters, as for many a dial-turning listener, the point was not so much to convey particular information as to attach themselves to the excitement generated by the medium itself.

MASS COMMUNICATIONS AND THE NETWORKS, 1922–1940

There was more to broadcasting, however, than a playful experiment conducted by countless amateur participants and a simple extension of previous forums of communication. Broadcasting also made possible an entirely new phenomenon. For the first time, millions of people could hear an account of events as they happened, and they could do so in the privacy of their own homes and neighborhoods. Right from the start, this feature held enormous appeal among listeners. Nothing attracted a larger audience to pioneering stations such as KDKA than live reports of sporting events and elections. When broadcasts such as these came on the air, the people of Pittsburgh forgot their search for new or distant stations and tuned in en masse. Radio had given them an entirely new way to participate in a common culture. While in complete privacy, they were also part of the crowd. Indeed, they were sharing an identical experience with far more people than at any previous moment in their lives.

The unprecedented ability of broadcast radio to command the attention of a mass audience assumed heightened importance in 1922, when AT&T began to operate a network of powerful stations. Programs broadcast over WEAF in New York City were transmitted simultaneously via long-distance telephone lines to a dozen cities across the nation, where affiliated stations with powerful radio transmitters sent them out over the airwaves. Soon live broadcasts over WEAF were available to virtually everyone in America. The crowd was now the entire population. All could hear a single voice. Network coverage of the 1925 Scopes trial in Tennessee captivated the nation in large measure because people wanted to hear the voice of William Jennings Bryan, whose Cross of Gold speech from the 1896 campaign had long been the stuff of legends.

The extraordinary power of the network placed AT&T in a tenuous position. With its capacity to engage so many people at once, the network seemed to possess enormous commercial potential. Having missed out on the booming market for receivers, which it had agreed not to sell, AT&T saw the network as its primary means of salvaging something from the thriving radio business. Because the firm controlled long-distance telephony, no one else could create a network without its assistance. When RCA's and Westinghouse's increasingly powerful stations broadcast live reports phoned in by reporters, AT&T accused them of violating their pooling agreement. AT&T threatened to withhold essential transmission equipment from them and to begin manufacturing receivers that would compete with theirs.

In pursuing these strategies, however, AT&T had to take care not to alienate the public. Radio was widely perceived as a populist technology in which listeners could freely participate without dependence on a giant intermediary. In some locales, independent stations and amateurs tried to crowd out the network affiliate by broadcasting at the same frequency. Secretary of Commerce Herbert Hoover, who subscribed to a doctrine of voluntary associationalism, tried to forge a compromise that would allow local and network broadcasting to coexist. He held a series of conferences at which stations agreed to restrict their broadcasts to certain segments of the radio band. But Hoover's efforts were grounded on questionable authority, and in the end they failed to resolve the tensions. Commentators began to call the network chain radio, thus branding it with a pejorative label fresh in the public's mind from the recent disputes over chain store merchandising. More ominously for AT&T, antitrust investigators at the Federal Trade Commission let it be known that they were beginning preparations for hearings on the radio industry, slated to take place in October 1925.

AT&T was quite sensitive to charges of monopoly. Over the course of many years, it had negotiated an agreement with government under which it effectively monopolized telephone service but in exchange subjected its operations to rate regulation. Complaints about the radio network might place that agreement in jeopardy. The company tried to avoid this by portraying the radio network as a public-service endeavor. It limited access to producers who projected an upright image and who promised programming that would "uplift" the population. Initially AT&T hoped various voluntary associations would fill the airtime with announcements and educational programming. When it found few takers, the company accepted programming sponsored by commercial enterprises. But in order to avoid the appearance of crass commercialism it prohibited sponsors from discussing particular products or mentioning prices. Such restrictions alienated many potential sponsors, of course, and dampened the price of airtime. Network broadcasting thus left AT&T facing a conundrum: in control of a powerful new communications medium but unable to generate sufficient revenue to cover the costs of programming and transmission.

A way around this impasse emerged during 1926 and 1927. As the Justice Department pursued its investigations, the parties to the radio patent pool secretly entered into arbitration proceedings. When the arbitrator chastised AT&T for trying to control broadcasting and warned it sternly to stay out of the receiver business, the firm threatened to reveal the pooling agreement and expose the complicity between RCA and Westinghouse. David Sarnoff, now chief executive at RCA, hastily orchestrated a compromise. A new RCA subsidiary, the National Broadcasting Company (NBC), would take over AT&T's stations and rechristen them the Red Network. In return, Sarnoff guaranteed AT&T substantial revenue over the next decade for providing the necessary long-distance telephone linkages.

RCA's new approach to radio hinged on Sarnoff's conviction that the real potential for profits came from the sale of airtime on national networks rather than from the sale of equipment. This feeling stemmed in part from frustration and disappointment. The patent pool had not secured RCA the three-fifths share of the market for receivers it had anticipated. In 1922, the company had garnered just $11 million of the $60 million spent on radio equipment. Although its annual sales had soared to $50 million by 1924, its share of the market had actually fallen to less than one-seventh. In response, RCA had launched a vigorous campaign of lawsuits against alleged infringers and had threatened to withhold tubes from the market, moves that drew intense criticism and fueled the antitrust fires.

Sarnoff perceived tremendous economic opportunities in network broadcasting, which he felt RCA and NBC would be able to exploit much more fully than AT&T. His thinking hinged in large measure on anticipated changes in public policy. With the telephone company operating as a common carrier, offering its services to anyone who might wish to organize a network, Sarnoff believed the cloud of monopoly would lift and government would relax its vigilance. To help ease public concern, he pledged to retain most of AT&T's standards regarding advertising and created a programming advisory council consisting of distinguished educators, artists, and public servants. RCA also agreed to drop most of its patent suits against rival manufacturers. As Sarnoff had hoped, the Justice Department soon stopped its investigation. In 1927, moreover, Congress empowered a new Federal Radio Commission with authority to divvy up space on the radio band and to stipulate the power levels at which stations could operate. These measures promised to bring an unprecedented degree of order to the airwaves and put a stop to the sabotage that had plagued network broadcasts. The commission immediately displayed a strong preference for network broadcasting; twenty-one of the twenty-four stations it authorized to operate at high power were affiliated with networks.

With the political path clearer than ever before,

Sarnoff drew network broadcasting steadily toward entertainment of broader appeal and more explicit salesmanship. RCA formed its own orchestra and purchased the Victor recording company, which had many of the most popular artists of the day under exclusive contract. Sarnoff insisted that programs follow detailed scripts performed by accomplished actors and narrators. This emphasis on polished entertainment gave network broadcasts a quality few independent stations could match. The new approach immediately paid handsome dividends. Whereas AT&T in 1925 had charged just $2,600 for an hour of transmission over its thirteen principal network stations, RCA earned $10,000 per hour for its network broadcasts. Others rushed to cash in on the bonanza. NBC itself launched a second venture, the Blue Network; Westinghouse linked its stations through the Mutual Broadcasting System; and a new group of investors started what soon became known as the Columbia Broadcasting System, or CBS. The Era of the Networks had arrived.

No one valued these networks more than the purveyors of inexpensive, brand-name products. Network broadcasts gave manufacturers of soaps, cigarettes, medicines, packaged foods, and other personal and household products a means of reaching millions. Such merchandisers bought the lion's share of broadcast time during the prime evening hours. Audiences soon grew accustomed to hearing weekly programs sponsored by a particular firm. Often the name of the sponsor and title of the program ran together seamlessly, so that listeners would hear a brand name mentioned dozens of times during an hour broadcast. Because these announcements reached so many potential consumers, marketers could afford to spend vastly greater sums than before in an effort to establish brand-name identities. A spate of glossy new national magazines had recently provided advertisers with similar opportunities; now the networks presented them with another medium of even broader and more pervasive reach.

Radio, moreover, equipped advertisers with a powerful tool that printed material could not match. It gave them a chance to link their brands to the celebrity personalities that broadcasting seemed inherently to create. The tendency of radio to foster celebrity had been apparent from the start of the broadcast era. When a station interviewed former President Woodrow Wilson on the eve of the 1924 election, the next day 20,000 people gathered spontaneously in front of his home. AT&T, anxious to maintain an aura of dispassionate public service, had tried to suppress the creation of personalities by re-

quiring its announcers at WEAF to identify themselves only by their initials. Soon the public grew attached to particular voices, however, and stations learned to promote their announcers as stars. Later, correspondents such as H. V. Kaltenborn and Edward R. Murrow developed extensive followings. Their extemporaneous accounts of live events provided engaging relief from the ordinary diet of carefully scripted broadcasts.

Radio generated such strong personal attachments in large part because it engaged listeners in the intimacy of their own private spaces. Virtually all successful radio personalities cultivated a sense of intimacy with the listening audience. Perhaps nothing demonstrated this more strikingly than the contrasting experiences of Herbert Hoover and Franklin Roosevelt broadcasting as president. Hoover, an early enthusiast of radio, failed to grasp the important distinction between speaking to an assembled throng and broadcasting to millions listening in the privacy of their homes. His radio addresses bellowed with a weightiness appropriate for a nominating convention, but lacked the gestures and punctuations of applause that help bind public speakers to their audiences. The effect reinforced Hoover's image of callousness in the face of gross human tragedy. Roosevelt spoke as if he were talking with someone across his desk. His fireside chats, which were at first reserved for special occasions (he gave only five during his first year in office), projected a reassuring, comforting tone. Much to Roosevelt's consternation, his populist rivals Huey Long and Father Charles E. Coughlin exhibited a similar aptitude for the new medium. Coughlin, known popularly as the Radio Priest, proved so effective in generating contributions via radio that he built his own Sunday afternoon network.

But commerce, not politics or religion, drove American radio broadcasting between the wars, and it was in the hands of the emerging advertising agencies of the era that the powerful combination of mass audience and personal intimacy was used to its fullest potential. As ad men grew more familiar with the new medium, they steadily refined and enhanced their techniques for fixing listener attention on their clients' products. During the early years of the networks, when RCA insisted that sponsors purchase blocks of time and refrain from promoting specific products directly by name or price, much of their efforts involved programming rather than advertising itself. By developing novel methods of evaluating listener response to various programs, advertising experts assumed influential roles in script preparation and direction. As they discovered that much of a program's appeal hinged on the force of personality, advertising firms increasingly came to resemble talent agencies. They identified emerging performers and signed them to contracts, then marketed the stars to potential sponsors and to the networks. Agencies also learned to hire spokespersons with distinctive voices that listeners would come to associate with particular brands. The essence of network advertising was to package personalities in appealing fashion and link them in the public memory to a particular brand or product.

As advertising experts mastered the new medium, they steadily pressed the boundaries of propriety by promoting specific products ever more explicitly. Networks resisted but gradually relaxed their standards. Fearing a drop in revenue with the onset of the Depression, they even began selling "spots" of time expressly for product promotion. Ad men then turned their energies toward developing clever slogans and other devices that would quickly grab listeners' attention. Broadcast repeatedly, such spots supported carefully planned campaigns, which soon emerged as the new stock-in-trade of the advertising agencies. In one famous campaign, advertisers for the Pepsi-Cola company devised a clever musical jingle to promote its slogan. The jingle helped Pepsi capture a substantial share of a market once considered the exclusive domain of Coca-Cola. As other alert merchandisers realized that advertising could be used to counter the effects of depression, network revenues resumed their phenomenal ascendance.

The increasingly commercial character of radio raised cries of protest in some quarters. Critics had long complained that if left in private hands network radio would inherently favor corporations and other large interests who sought a mass market. The growing prevalence of explicit advertising and sensational entertainment confirmed their fears. There seemed little room left on the national airwaves for perspectives that fell outside the mainstream. One recurrent crusade called for a clearer separation of advertising from programming. Promoted as a first step in stemming the power of advertising agencies and raising the standards of programming, this movement inadvertently facilitated the trends toward spot advertising and more overt salesmanship. Not for the last time, reformers pushed mass media precisely where they hoped it would not go.

Barring wholesale censorship or widespread rejection of mass consumption, such critics stood little chance of reforming network radio. "The broadcasters really had nothing to sell except access to a mass audience," historian David Potter later pointed out, "and the only parties who had reason to pay for such access were advertisers." As instruments of mass communications, the networks and their clients necessarily appealed to emotions rather than to intellects. The search for a broad audience compelled this approach, for as Potter wryly observed, "the minds of men vary more than their emotions." In attempting to forge a general desire out of a multiplicity of individual wishes, programmers and advertisers needed to employ what Walter Lippmann termed "the use of symbols which assemble emotions after they have been detached from their ideas." "The process by which general opinions are brought to cooperations," Lippmann explained, "consists of an intensification of feeling and degradation of significance." As the experience of Europe's totalitarian regimes of the period suggests, government ownership would not in and of itself have altered these basic characteristics of mass communication.

The specter of Hitler and Mussolini and their propaganda machines, together with the continuing commercial success of the networks, had by the end of the Depression emboldened supporters of the American system of radio. Testifying before Congress in 1939, Sarnoff confidently explained the rationale for private network broadcasting and explicitly contrasted it with the more statist European approach to the medium:

> Network broadcasting provided greatly improved programs by tapping the talent centers of the nation and syndicating these programs over telephone lines to local independent stations. Not only did the network system appeal to the independent station owners, but it also attracted business interests of the nation to use the radio broadcasting as an advertising medium. The economic support thus developed to meet the needs of the three parties whose interests were at stake: the public, the station owner, and the advertiser.

As Americans mobilized to rid the world of dictators, few questioned the wisdom of Sarnoff's benign vision. A year later, when President Roosevelt's address to Congress was broadcast following the attack on Pearl Harbor, an estimated 79 percent of the population tuned in.

Radio reached its pinnacle of prominence in American life during World War II. Mass communications proved the ideal complement to mass warfare. People tuned to network broadcasts for news of distant hostilities and for relief from the ordeals they created. Leaders such as Roosevelt and Winston Churchill masterfully used the medium to shape the common will. Meanwhile, the needs of the armed forces propelled a new surge of research into techniques such as radar and long-distance transmission via short wave. The Radiation Laboratory, home to the radar research effort, took over virtually the entire campus of the Massachusetts Institute of Technology. There, and at countless centers operated by the Army Signal Corps, a generation of college engineers received intensive training in the most advanced radio electronics.

When peace returned, however, many of these experts turned their attention not to radio, but to new technologies. One was television. An experimental venture on the eve of the war, it would within a few years of the peace completely displace the radio networks in American life. Another was the stored program electronic computer. Brought forth by the war and spurred onward by both civilian and military requirements during the early Cold War, electronic computing would by the late 1960s attain a prominence rivaling that of telephones and television.

COMPUTERS AND INFORMATION-PROCESSING TO 1968

Although the immediate technical origins of electronic computing were directly related to the wartime experience, its development drew upon foundations that had been laid over the previous half century. During that period corporate bureaucracies and their counterparts in government had learned to process unprecedented quantities of data. This quiet revolution in data-processing initially depended more on organizational innovations and statistical techniques than on changes in equipment, but over time drew increasingly upon new technology as well. The massive processing of routine data by hand created powerful inducements and some obvious opportunities to reduce labor inputs. Incentives were amplified when the data pertained to billing statements and other financial transactions. The faster a firm processed such information, the quicker it could convert liabilities into assets. For institutions that processed enormous volumes of transactions, even a small savings in processing time could generate substantial savings.

Numerous inventors and manufacturers responded to these opportunities. Revenue at the Burroughs Corporation, which built a variety of adding machines, increased from $323,000 in 1900 to nearly $40 million in 1916. During this same period the National Cash Register Company turned out well over a million machines for recording transactions at

An IBM 026 printing card punch machine, 1949. COURTESY IBM

the point of sale. Other companies, such as Remington Rand and Underwood, manufactured an array of accounting devices. By 1920, the office equipment industry annually generated about $200 million in revenue, a level it sustained for the next two decades.

The most elaborate machines—and those which would have the most substantial impact on the development of computing—were the punched-card accounting devices supplied by the International Business Machines Company (IBM). Developed initially by the independent inventor Herman Hollerith for use in processing the 1890 federal census, these machines employed complex arrangements of gears, ratchets, and electrical relays in order to sort, manipulate, and print information stored on punched cards. The cards contained numerous columns of numbered circles or slots that could be punched out or left intact. By assigning labels to the different columns and developing codes based on which holes were punched, all sorts of information could be encoded on the cards. (Such binary codes remain the basis of all digitized information today.) The alphabet could be encoded almost as easily as the decimal system of numbers, so that customer names and other labels could be stored and printed along with numerical data. Operators entered the information simply by striking a standard typewriter keyboard on a machine known as a card punch, which automatically punched holes in the appropriate rows and columns.

Information stored on these cards could be totaled in a variety of ways, depending on the particular arrangement of gears and ratchets in the calculating machine. The capabilities of a given piece of equipment were largely embedded in the machine by the skilled shopworkers at IBM's production facility in Endicott, New York. Working in consultation with IBM representatives in the field, they learned to build equipment tailored to the particular needs of each customer. By removing or temporarily disengaging sections of the calculators, however, customers and service representatives could to some extent "program" their machines on-site to perform different tasks. Such programming grew steadily easier as IBM substituted electrical components for mechanical ones. Electrical devices also increased the speed of processing, thus freeing the machine to perform a wider variety of calculations. Additional flexibility came from sorting machines, which enabled operators to identify and separate cards containing particular characteristics. A variety of complex printers could generate statements and summaries of encoded information in various formats. These also underwent continual refinement.

Even with its enhanced capacity and flexibility, IBM's Hollerith equipment remained best suited for repeated routine processing of large banks of standard numerical data, such as the issuing of regular financial statements. Banks, insurance companies, and other large institutions with regular billing requirements were IBM's largest customers. Such firms could store account information on cards in files and update it easily by utilizing additional columns or cards. (In some years, up to three-quarters of IBM's revenue came from sales of cards, and in 1936 the Justice Department forced the firm to open the card business to other suppliers.) IBM thus found its fortunes tied closely to the rise of finance capitalism. Not surprisingly, it flourished during the corporate expansion of the teens and twenties. By the end of World War I, over 650 customers used Hollerith equipment. Annual revenues at IBM already exceeded $10 million, and during the subsequent decade they more than doubled. By 1930, its profits had reached $10.9 million. Remington Rand, which offered a competitive line of punched-card equipment as well as numerous other devices, earned another $9.7 million. Like broadcasting, moreover, data-processing proved quite resistant to depression. Routine accounting diminished slightly, but emergent government bureaucracies provided an important new boost. In 1936, IBM won a lucrative contract from the new Social Security Administration. Other New Deal agencies such as the Federal Housing Administration not only generated substantial data-processing requirements of their own, they burdened private organizations with many reporting requirements as well. IBM revenues,

which in 1933 had fallen to just $17.6 million, had by 1937 reached $31.7 million. In 1940 the company earned profits of $21.7 million on revenues of $45.3 million. Rival Remington Rand, which failed to garner much business from government, now lagged well behind, with profits of under $5 million.

The coming of World War II triggered an explosion in demand that would forever transform the world of data processing. Military procurement programs pumped public funds to thousands of suppliers, many of whom needed to meet stringent specifications and timetables. Such programs required massive efforts at coordination and called for unprecedented levels of accountability. As more and more segments of the American economy were drawn into the wartime effort, knowledge of advanced data-processing permeated virtually every corner, and demand exploded. Punched-card techniques attracted particular interest, in part because all draftees and other government personnel had their names and vital information entered on cards. IBM saw its revenues more than triple, and Remington Rand did nearly as well.

In addition to stimulating demand for existing equipment, the war helped spur development of a new, more powerful data-processing tool—the electronic computer. Wartime urgency prompted officials in a variety of programs to contemplate calculations that would have been deemed impossibly time-consuming under peacetime conditions. Scientists associated with the Manhattan Project, for instance, set about calculating rates of nuclear reactions and strengths of alloy containers. At the Aberdeen Proving Ground south of Philadelphia, scientists and engineers from the University of Pennsylvania supervised teams of women as they prepared ballistics firing tables that accompanied new weapons into the field. Calculations such as these were not conceptually difficult; they just required massive repetitive analysis of simultaneous differential equations under various parameters. Scientists and engineers had frequently arrived at similar crossroads in their peacetime research, but had lacked the means to carry out the calculations. Now, given access to talented conscripted labor and motivated by war, they plowed ahead.

These labor-intensive wartime projects gave the engineers and scientists associated with them an opportunity to pursue novel approaches to the problem of rapid repetitive calculation. One avenue, pursued most successfully during the war by Howard Aiken of Harvard University, was to design an electromechanical machine specifically suited for scientific

The ENIAC Computer, 1946, COURTESY IBM

calculation. Building upon the existing differential analyzer, a machine designed by wartime presidential science adviser Vannevar Bush while a young engineer at MIT, Aiken created the Mark I computer. Others deemed mechanical components too slow and sought to build entirely electronic machines. The sequence of calculations would be temporarily wired into an array of vacuum tubes rather than built into a chain of gears, and intermediate results would be stored in electronic memories rather than tallied by mechanical counters. Two University of Pennsylvania engineers associated with the Aberdeen project, John Presper Eckert, Jr., and John William Mauchly, achieved the greatest wartime success in this endeavor. Their Electronic Numerical Integrator and Computer (ENIAC) was the first electronic stored-program computer.

As world war gave way to cold war, scientific computing grew in importance. Defense considera-

tions gave birth to a number of institutions with significant budgets and numerous complex problems to solve. The laboratories of the Atomic Energy Commission at Livermore, California, and Los Alamos, New Mexico, supported many efforts to build electronic computers of ever greater speed. Scientists at Los Alamos worked closely with the mathematician John von Neumann of Princeton's Institute for Advanced Study. Von Neumann used Boolean algebra to suggest how the circuits of such machines should be organized logically to best facilitate rapid calculation. His pioneering papers provided a critical foundation for early computer designers. Additional support for computer design came from the various branches of the armed services. The Air Force was concerned about pilot training and guidance for its own planes and also sought ways of detecting and targeting enemy aircraft as rapidly as possible. Its Project Whirlwind, headed by the MIT

811

engineer Jay Forrester, proved especially influential in spurring development of "real-time" applications, in which computers immediately processed information as they received it from radar. Many of the largest defense contractors, such as the aerospace firm Northrup Aviation, also assumed an active role in computer design. Meanwhile, numerous scientists and engineers who had been drawn into wartime research programs returned to universities and civilian employers with a desire to pursue the novel efforts at calculation. In effect, the war had created a market for sophisticated calculating devices and a cadre of interested experts ready to pursue design alternatives.

As this new field of scientific computing took shape, a second technical frontier opened. This was solid-state componentry. The most famous example, the transistor, was announced in 1947 by Bell Laboratories. Invented by three of its engineers, William B. Shockley, John Bardeen, and Walter Brattain, the transistor provided a seemingly ideal substitute for the vacuum tube. It was smaller and more reliable, used less power, and could be manufactured at lower cost. By agreement with the federal government, AT&T was required to make innovations such as the transistor available to anyone who paid a small fee. It even held classes to help educate others in the new technology. The transistor, moreover, was really just the tip of a gigantic iceberg. Drawing on an extraordinary base of knowledge about the electrical, magnetic, and photochemical properties of materials, experts in electronic componentry generated continual innovation that amounted to a "revolution in miniature." An important watershed occurred in 1961, when a research team at the Fairchild Semiconductor Company headed by Robert Noyce produced an entire integrated circuit on a chip of silicon. Over the next quarter-century, through a sustained effort at manufacturing engineering, integrated circuits would come to hold staggering amounts of circuitry. By 1969, Marcian "Ted" Hoff, an employee of Noyce's recently-created Intel Corporation, had already placed an entire computer on a single chip.

In addition to yielding processors of faster speeds and lower cost, solid-state technology supported the development of computer memories that could hold massive amounts of encoded information. Prior to the 1970s, these memories usually involved magnetic media applied to tape, disks, and drums, or a grid of small ferrous cores that could be polarized in one of two directions. Later, silicon chips served as memory. Larger memories with rapid entry and retrieval capabilities enabled computers to store and process much larger sets of data. These might consist of enormous volumes of statistical information, or they could involve written language and other more complex forms of information that had been translated into binary code. (Today, the desire to transmit and process detailed graphic information and audio drives the pursuit of increased computer memory.) In addition to increasing the pool of information being processed, larger memories gave designers a means of programming computers to perform various tasks without having to rewire circuits. Users could "instruct" a computer by entering a program into its memory. Improved memories thus made each successive generation of computers much more flexible. Designers could concentrate on building fast basic processors and leave users to devise all sorts of applications for their machines.

The dynamic interplay between solid-state technology, computer design, and programming, together with the expanded market for data-processing, generated a remarkable series of technical developments. During the first twenty-five years of the Cold War, Americans refined and adopted computer technology at rates that dwarfed all other countries' efforts.

This rapidly expanding market was dominated by IBM. From the early fifties onward, it accounted for over 80 percent of computer industry revenues. IBM gained a foothold in the emerging field of scientific and defense computing by capitalizing on its reputation for assembling complex equipment and working closely with customers to maintain and update it in the field. These traits prompted the Air Force during the mid-fifties to award IBM a contract to build the Semi-Automatic Ground Environment (SAGE) anti-aircraft defense system; an outgrowth of Project Whirlwind, it called for twenty-three pairs of massive computers operating in real time. This and subsequent government contracts helped IBM keep abreast of the most sophisticated logical designs and componentry. Meanwhile, the company introduced electronic computing into its established business markets. Using modified designs of its scientific computers, IBM marketed sophisticated computers to large customers such as insurance companies. It achieved even greater success by adding stored-program capabilities and electronics to equipment designed for firms with more modest accounting needs. During the late fifties and early sixties, its 650 and 1401 computers became familiar sights in American businesses and universities. In all of these commercial markets, IBM benefited from its experience in working closely with customers to adapt machinery to address specific problems and from its knowledge of printers, card-punches, and other "peripheral devices" that worked in conjunction with the processing unit.

IBM drew considerable criticism during these early decades of computing. Detractors complained that the company unduly influenced the course of technical development by tying consumers to its comprehensive series of data processing equipment. IBM, which leased rather than sold all of its machines, would not allow customers to attach devices built by another firm to their computer installations. The Justice Department, which had shadowed the company since the dispute over card sales during the thirties, pressured IBM to unbundle its equipment and allow consumers to purchase parts of their systems from competitors. In a 1956 consent decree, IBM agreed to sell as well as lease its equipment and to take steps that would allow competition in the markets for printers and other peripheral devices.

These negotiations between IBM and the Justice Department closely paralleled those that had occurred at the start of the century in the audio industries. IBM played a role in computing much like that AT&T had in telephony and network radio during their infancies. The computer giant functioned as an intermediary between a rapidly changing technology and a market of consumers who were anxious to put that technology to a variety of uses. As with voice communications, this role involved ongoing compromises between the seemingly unlimited potential of the new technology and the need to attain a degree of standardization. By controlling such a large share of the market for central processors and peripherals, IBM instilled a measure of stability into an industry that very well could have foundered in a sea of conflicting, incompatible approaches. It provided the emerging semiconductor industry with demand for standardized componentry, and it enabled programmers to develop a few basic languages and then allocate their energies toward developing specific applications. Through its consent decree, the Justice Department hoped to put manufacturers of cards and peripherals on a similar basis, much as government pressure in the case of radio had encouraged AT&T to become a common carrier for the networks.

For the most part, IBM provided the desired stability without prematurely freezing computer technology. The company's history during the fifties and sixties was marked by recurrent cycles of innovation and standardization. The ongoing process of regeneration reached its climax in 1964, with the announcement of System/360, a complete family of computers built from identical components. Spanning the gamut of computer users, these machines employed interchangeable peripheral devices and ran common programs. System/360 established new standards, incorporated the benefits of volume production, drove down prices, and brought computing into far more realms than it had ever reached before. Much to IBM's consternation, it also opened huge opportunities for competitive manufacturers to concentrate on building lower-cost versions of its many peripheral devices.

As with the telephone system and radio, stability and uniformity may have come at some cost to diversity and performance. Computer technology in the hands of IBM perhaps assumed a more limited form than it otherwise would have. Banks and insurance companies remained IBM's best customers. These institutions usually employed computers much as they had used the older electromechanical equipment, to monitor financial assets and issue account statements. Some industry observers complained that their influence kept IBM from aggressively pursuing other applications and from devising approaches to computing that would have suited more creative customers. By the early sixties, sophisticated scientific users had begun to look elsewhere for computers. A small team of designers at Control Data Corporation, led by the maverick Seymour Cray, put together machines that outperformed IBM's most sophisticated processors. Meanwhile, the technical press roundly criticized IBM for not utilizing the new integrated circuitry in its System/360 computers.

Whatever the merits of such critiques, no one could deny that IBM computers had worked profound changes in many quarters. Even within the traditional business market, computers did more than merely lower the costs of calculation and bookkeeping. The added flexibility of easy programming gave institutions the ability to analyze their financial status in novel ways. Computers were tools of study rather than just labor-saving devices. Because computers could easily handle a much greater variety of information, moreover, businesses could use them to monitor all sorts of assets. By the end of the 1960s, firms in all sectors of the economy routinely employed them to keep track of inventory and materials-in-process.

As business institutions collected more and more information in computer memories, impetus mounted to devise means of entering and retrieving data more readily. Following the introduction of System/360, IBM found itself swamped by orders for "terminals"—keyboards with electronic display

813

The IBM System/360 Computer. COURTESY IBM

screens—as its customers sought to link scores of operators directly to banks of data stored on a massive central computer. Employees equipped with terminals could gain access to the latest centralized information and automatically update that information as they performed their tasks. In a dramatic early demonstration of the potential of such networks, American Airlines and IBM developed SABRE during the mid-sixties. This system enabled the carrier to keep track of reservations issued by agents around the country and to assign appropriate aircraft and personnel in response. SABRE thus offered a potent combination of benefits—new levels of customer convenience and enhanced utilization of resources. Similar arrangements soon became commonplace throughout the service and distribution sectors of the economy. Bank tellers and insurance account representatives increasingly worked at terminals, and retail clerks conducted transactions at registers that kept running inventories, eventually with the aid of electronically read bar codes. Many of the dramatic national marketing successes of the sixties and seventies, such as the giant toy distribution chain Toys "R" Us, attained their competitive advantage by quickly seizing the potential of electronic inventory control.

Yet for all its capacity to alter the realms of business, science and engineering, and the military, electronic computing at the close of the 1960s remained outside the immediate experience of most Americans. Computing was still a highly centralized endeavor involving large installations monitored by experts. Even those with access to terminals were restricted to entering and retrieving routine information. They could not program the system to perform novel functions. A new generation of college students was beginning to learn programming languages, but most students still gained access to the computer by handing stacks of punched cards to central operators and returning later to pick up the printed results. In this respect, computing shared many essential attributes with the centralized technologies of the Bell System and network broadcasting. Computers had by no means acquired the commonplace status of telephones and radios.

TELEVISION DURING THE NETWORK ERA

While the stored-program computer remained a device for experts, remote from the daily lives of most

814

Americans, a second electronic marvel of the postwar era rapidly became a fixture in living rooms across the land. Television—video broadcasting—swept over the United States with an explosiveness that rivaled the birth of radio a quarter-century before. Almost immediately, it displaced the radio networks in public life. Although the addition of pictures obviously introduced a new dimension to mass communications, this transition from radio to television occurred with remarkable ease and continuity. Popular culture, social criticism, and government regulation readily shifted from the old medium to the new, often with little perceptible change. Networks, not pictures, remained the primary focus of attention.

The technical roots of television can be traced back at least to the early twenties. By then groups of engineers on both sides of the Atlantic were engaged in efforts to transmit images by wave or wire. In 1924, AT&T began offering a radio facsimile service between Europe and America. Newspapers used this service to transmit photographs, and by the end of World War II it had become so routine that several publishers tried selling facsimile editions of their papers, transmitted directly to the rooms of elite hotels. Meanwhile other electrical innovators tackled the stickier problem of transmitting moving images on a sustained basis. Here the challenge was to encode an optical image electrically, transmit the encoded signals, then use the signals to reproduce the image. One approach employed a revolving disk perforated with small holes to scan a picture and generate a grid of electrical impulses. Developed most fully by Englishman John Logie Baird, it was pursued as well by Americans John Fleming and Ernst Alexanderson, an employee of General Electric. Other inventors and engineers tried avenues that would eliminate all mechanical components and employ electrical scanners. Their efforts complemented technical endeavors underway in the recording industry, where electrical techniques were rapidly driving acoustical recordings from the market. Pioneers in electrical television could also draw on expertise developed in the course of attempting to synchronize sound with motion pictures. AT&T, for example, was working on a system that would store both sound and images on the same electrical medium.

David Sarnoff of RCA closely monitored developments pertaining to television. In 1923, he lent support to a research group at Westinghouse headed by the Russian immigrant Vladimir Zworykin. This team hinged its efforts on an electronic tube, the iconoscope, which could scan an image electrically and act as a receiver as well. Eventually Zworykin

joined RCA, and in 1930 he took charge of the recently consolidated television research programs of GE, RCA, and Westinghouse. Two years later RCA began experimental broadcasts from the Empire State Building, using a mechanical scanner, and three years after that Sarnoff announced his intention to invest $10 million in a five-year effort to make television a commercially viable communications medium. With the help of techniques obtained from the independent inventor Philo T. Farnsworth, RCA refined an electronic system, and in 1937 it began broadcasting from mobile units in the New York metropolitan area. Meanwhile, Sarnoff carried the fight for television to Washington. He won a commitment from the Federal Communications Commission (FCC), successor to the Federal Radio Commission, to devote the very high frequency (VHF) area of the band to television rather than to frequency modulated (FM) radio, a refined radio system developed and championed by Sarnoff's friend and former employee, Edwin Armstrong. By summer 1939, RCA was ready to begin regularly scheduled television broadcasts, using a mixture of programming from its studios and its mobile units. Sarnoff made the announcement at the New York World's Fair, with President Roosevelt in attendance.

The outbreak of war in Europe abruptly halted Sarnoff's plans to build a television network. Crucial electronic components began being diverted toward military projects well before Pearl Harbor, and in 1942 the FCC stopped issuing station licenses. RCA turned its research and development efforts toward military contracts for the duration of the conflict. In the end, however, these wartime interruptions may have aided the emergence of television, for they enabled the new industry to take advantage of the many improvements in electronic componentry the war induced. New production techniques, for instance, dramatically lowered the cost of tubes, which accounted for much of the cost of a television. Sets priced at nearly $1,000 before the war sold for $500 after it. RCA replaced the iconoscope with the more sensitive orthicon tube, dramatically improving picture quality. Wartime programs also spurred the development of better relays and improved microwave technology, both of which were essential for network transmissions.

Once these technologies became available for commercial purposes, television took off with an explosiveness that paralleled the introduction of broadcast radio twenty-five years earlier. Between 1948 and 1954, the number of sets increased from 1 million to more than 20 million. The number of stations during this period grew from 106 to 377, despite a two-year moratorium on new licenses during the Korean War. By 1958, television broadcasts were available to 90 percent of America's homes, and 80 percent of American households owned at least one of the 50 million televisions in use. Advertising revenues for the three television networks soared from $2.5 million in 1948 to $172 million in 1953.

As these last figures suggest, the rapid introduction of television owed a great deal to the foundations laid by network radio. In contrast to the extended shake-out period that characterized the early decades of radio, commercial networks dominated television virtually from the start. RCA and CBS, operators of the largest radio broadcasting systems, provided the major driving force behind television. Along with the upstart American Broadcasting Company (ABC), which was created in 1941 when government regulators forced RCA and NBC to divest themselves of the Blue Network, they funded much of the technical research and ran by far the most important television networks. Much of the early programming came directly from radio, often accompanied by the same stars and sponsors. As with radio, most shows were performed live but followed detailed scripts. Critics of television raised virtually the same set of concerns that had swirled around radio ever since the rise of the networks. Regulation focused almost exclusively on the familiar issues of access and crassness. In all of these respects, the coming of television was not nearly so convulsive a change as the rise of radio had been. The radio networks had created mass communications; television merely became its new principal instrument.

What television did bring, of course, was the compelling, arresting power of visual images. Even today, nearly half a century after the introduction of television, most people believe visual images speak more accurately and honestly than printed or spoken words. Surveys suggest that readers are much more likely to approach books and articles with jaded suspicion and dismiss their contents as mere opinion than they are to question the accuracy and validity of even the most highly produced and edited television programs.

During its infancy, several factors heightened this inherent verisimilitude of television. The preponderance of live broadcasts, including frequent reports from remote locations and extensive coverage of sporting events, emphasized the spontaneous, unfiltered dimensions of the new medium. Telecasts of the Army-McCarthy hearings, which captured the attention of the nation during the early fifties, gave viewers the opportunity to stand in judgment as they watched the faces of accuser and accused. Programs produced in the studio held much the same appeal. Broadcast live and without sophisticated production techniques, most simply gave viewers an opportunity to see characters they had grown accustomed to hearing on radio. These shows reinforced the notion that television merely added a level of authenticity to existing media. Frequent technical glitches and poor reception imparted an extemporaneous quality to even the most carefully scripted programs, one which stood in sharp contrast to the increasingly polished character of radio, movies, and newsreels. People watched television in part to see what might happen, and announcers such as Edward R. Murrow openly appealed to viewers to share in an experiment, to join him in seeing what they could make of the new medium. Much like radio during the twenties, television basked in an aura of disinterested public service. Here was an incomprehensible miracle of science that honestly conveyed information in a form accessible to all.

As with radio, however, this image competed with emerging realities. For television during the fifties was rapidly becoming primarily an instrument of popular entertainment and volume marketing, with the most frequently watched programming funneled through just three networks. As the new medium took hold, the emphasis turned from spontaneity and immediacy to high-quality production. The advent of magnetic videotape recording, commercialized successfully by the Ampex Corporation in 1956, rapidly accelerated a movement from live to recorded programs. New transmitters and receivers dramatically improved picture quality, and RCA embarked on an intensive effort to introduce color broadcasts. Television's fundamental contribution to mass communications—its ability to convey visual images—was increasingly being used not simply to inform, but to dazzle. No longer was television merely radio with pictures; it was Hollywood brought home.

The quiz show scandals of the late fifties stirred such passionate controversy precisely because they shattered the illusion of truthfulness and highlighted the inherent disjuncture between information and entertainment. When the public learned that contestants on such enormously popular shows as "The $64,000 Question" and "Twenty-One" had been fed questions and answers in advance as part of a calculated effort by sponsors to promote interest and build loyalty to contestants who generated increased sales, many viewers felt betrayed. The resultant outcry prompted Congress to hold a series of widely publicized investigations. Eventually it passed legislation forcing advertisers to remove themselves from direct involvement with the production and programming process. Such regulation did little to restore the image of television as public servant, however, and in certain respects the new laws may have hastened its evolution as an entertainment medium. Corporate-sponsored programs such as General Electric Theater, which had relieved creative teams of financial constraints and given them considerable editorial freedom, faded from the scene, not to be resurrected until Congress created the Public Broadcasting System in 1969. The networks increasingly acted as brokers between producers of popular entertainment and advertisers looking to reach a mass audience.

Throughout much of the history of television, the FCC embraced this conception of the television industry. Concerned about the inherent power of the networks but unwilling to nationalize the industry and stifle the advertising that sustained them, the agency focused its energies on maintaining as much competition and access as possible within the network-as-broker framework. In 1952, the FCC instituted a rule that prevented any group of investors from owning more than seven television stations or seven AM or FM radio stations. This rule kept a network from acquiring ownership in so many local affiliates that it effectively reached a majority of the viewing audience. (A 1982 revision increased the number of permissible stations to twelve but stipulated that no group could reach more than 25 percent of the national audience.) Together with a variety of regulations pertaining to affiliate relations and airtime, the rule enabled the FCC to maintain a degree of separation that was designed to curb network power and retain a measure of vitality among local stations. Affiliates would provide a forum for new, experimental programming, and together they would constitute a market of consumers for network offerings.

These efforts to promote a degree of competition and market input in the face of network hegemony ran up against several countervailing forces. Due to the narrow width of the VHF spectrum and the broad bands necessary for television transmission, the number of stations remained restricted in even the largest cities. Most people, moreover, concentrated their viewing in the evening hours. Inevitably, then, most of the money invested in television flowed toward a limited number of programs and advertising slots. In such a competition, networks enjoyed an overwhelming advantage. Only they could afford to hire the personalities that have always been a primary attraction of mass media. In the case of quiz shows, which relied on lesser talent and were cheaply produced, networks bid up the expenses of programming by offering prizes no local station could afford. Networks also funded expensive improvements in production techniques, which became an ever more important asset in the battle for ratings. Locally produced programs stood little chance of drawing viewers away from the slickly produced series sent out over the networks. Color television, which was funded almost entirely by the networks and RCA, opened an entirely new dimension to this production competition once it took hold during the early sixties. Design became an ever more important component of programming, and the gap between television and movies rapidly closed. The FCC, recognizing the growing importance of production, eventually forced the networks to get out of the business of producing programs. After 1970, all shows would come from independent production companies, which would compete for network airtime. The evolution of networks as brokers was complete.

Throughout this period of network control, critics and commentators mirrored the concerns of regulators. They focused their attentions overwhelmingly on the content of programming. Television shows inevitably catered to the same universal emotionalism that had proven so successful with radio during the network era. The addition of pictures and the growing importance of Hollywood-style production hardly reversed the trend toward sensationalism. Critics also complained that the networks, as inheritors of an oligopoly, had little incentive to take risks in their programming decisions. Rather than introduce novel entertainment, they mimicked one another, hoping not to jeopardize their share of a captive market. Criticisms such as these were a persistent feature of television during the network era, as they had been with radio. They dominated discussion, for example, at a 1966 conference jointly sponsored by Stanford University and the University of Texas, which brought together academics, advertisers, programmers, and, for the first time in seven years, the chief executives of the three networks. Participants for the most part agreed with David Potter, who explained that mass communications was inherently sensationalistic. Significant change in program content would not occur, he predicted, until new technologies such as UHF transmission opened the airwaves to more alternatives.

Amid the ceaseless hand-wringing about programming, only a few voices could be heard discussing the cognitive dimensions of television. The loudest and most persistent was that of the media critic Marshall McLuhan, who insisted in a famous aphorism that "the medium is the message." McLuhan hoped to direct attention away from the mere content of programming and focus it instead on the inherent differences in the ways humans engage print, aural, and visual communications. At root, the interaction involved basic neurological processes that occurred outside conscious control. Changes in communications technology thus inevitably and irresistibly altered the very ways humans perceived and processed information. At the Stanford conference, McLuhan argued that even the recent addition of color to television marked a fundamental departure in communications, because color images could arrest attention in ways black-and-white ones could not.

Although ridiculed and misunderstood by industry insiders and many media commentators at the time, arguments such as McLuhan's would gradually attain a greater place in public discussion of television. The proliferation of communications studies programs on college and university campuses during the seventies and after attested to their growing prominence. Educators, concerned with the time television occupied in children's lives, came to focus much of their critique on the medium's cognitive effects. They blamed television for eroding attention spans and fostering passivity. By the 1990s, an emphasis on reading rather than watching television had come to be widely perceived as a critical determinant in educational success. In a world in which social distinctions and economic rewards hinged increasingly upon educational achievement, television viewing thus loomed as a basic denominator of class relations.

Trends in television programming during the past three decades have also lent considerable credence to McLuhan's adage. Vast amounts of financial and creative resources have been directed toward the production of images, while comparatively little has gone toward the writing of screenplays. New series have increasingly sought to attract viewers by presenting a novel "look" or "feel." Rapid editing, intriguing lighting, and eye-catching graphics have become ever more important components in the struggles among news and sports departments to attract and retain viewers. Perhaps most telling, television advertisements have become the most lavishly produced bits of video in existence. Film directors of international reputation have lent their virtuosity to productions that last no more than a minute. As with programming itself, these ads rely increasingly on spectacular images and rapid editing—as many as a hundred images may flash across the screen in a single minute. Since such techniques impart motion and energy to even the most static product, they effectively expand the scope of television advertising.

If critics of television during the fifties and sixties perhaps underestimated the impact of the new medium by failing to appreciate its cognitive dimensions, they may very well have exaggerated concerns about access and control by overlooking the significant transformation of radio broadcasting during the period. Radio stations proliferated in the immediate postwar years, following the lifting of a wartime moratorium on new licenses, then were left suddenly to scramble for an audience when listeners abandoned them for television. Although devastating for the radio networks, competition with the new medium infused the market for local broadcasts with new energy. At the same time, several technical developments opened new opportunities for local stations. The spread of car radios and introduction of reliable and affordable portable receivers built from transistors gave stations access to a new audience that television could not yet reach. Frequency modulated (FM) transmission technology, freed by technical refinements from its competition with television for airspace, enabled stations to broadcast sound of a quality that captured the improved, high-fidelity recording techniques of the era. This volatile mix of crisis and opportunity remade radio into a vast proving ground for the mushrooming supply of recorded music and for other forms of audio entertainment. Colleges and universities, which had once accounted for a significant share of radio licenses but had dropped out under competition from the networks, began again to operate small stations, most of which offered "alternative" programming. Disc jockeys, ministers, and commentators on these and other small stations experimented with different formats and styles.

One important offshoot of this creative competition was that the listening audience became increasingly segmented along lines of race, ethnicity, age, and class. Rather than pursue a mass market of listeners, stations and performers cultivated niches of loyal devotees by developing distinct identities. Most communities had stations aimed primarily at an African American audience, and Spanish-language broadcasts grew common in northeastern cities and throughout the Southwest. Classical stations sought an older, affluent audience, while rock stations pursued the emerging youth market of baby boomers. Although much of this dynamic restructuring occurred at the local level, it eventually exerted a profound influence on the shape of national culture as well. In place of the networks rose loosely coupled groups of stations with access to common subgroups of the population in communities across the nation. Through recording and syndication, successful entertainers and program hosts could build a national following among a particular segment of the population.

These new organizational arrangements did not completely eliminate concerns about freedom and access. Recording companies sometimes tried to influence programming by threatening to deny stations their biggest stars, and individuals who owned groups of stations could withhold airtime from certain performers. But when compared to television and to radio during the era of the networks, radio now possessed an openness, variety, and unpredictability that was staggering. Listeners could tune in a cornucopia of offerings, and individuals and groups that had never gained access to the networks could now achieve national prominence, at least among particular subsets of the population. Radio in the immediate postwar decades thus foreshadowed developments that would, in time, sweep across all aspects of communications and computing.

BREAKING UP THE BELL SYSTEM

At the start of the 1960s, communications technologies were more tightly controlled than at any other time during the twentieth century. Three networks dominated television, with programming that differed only superficially from one another. AT&T, which had monopolized telephone service for over half a century, was rapidly replacing the postal service as the primary conveyer of personal communications in the United States. Its telex services promised to give it a comparable position in overseas communications. The dynamic industry spawned by the powerful new tool of data-processing, the computer, was dominated by a single firm: IBM controlled 85 percent of the market. Its giant central processors, accessible only through a center staffed by specialists or through terminals tailored for particular uses, served as a paradigm for the new technology. In each case—computing, telephony, and television broadcasting—these giant enterprises provided Americans with incomparable services and dominated the international market. Communications seemed inextricably linked to these organizations and the large systems they operated.

As the tumultuous decade drew to a close, however, seeds were sown that would ultimately reverse this trend toward consolidation and produce communications of much greater scope and diversity. During the subsequent quarter-century, the twin forces of technical change and political reform, exploited by individual entrepreneurs and consumers, would steadily erode the hegemony of AT&T, IBM, and the networks. Communications and computing entered a new phase characterized above all by increased availability and access. In the process, they came to resemble the more chaotic conditions that had prevailed at the start of the century. The amateur operators and independent telephone companies of that earlier day now found their modern counterparts in the computer hackers and "start-up" companies of the seventies and eighties. The ongoing balancing act between centralized order and creative individualism slipped decidedly in favor of the latter.

This shift occurred most cleanly and dramatically in the case of telephony. In 1982, the Justice Department ended AT&T's longstanding monopoly of long-distance service and forced the firm to divest itself of the regional phone companies. These moves, which seemingly heralded a far-reaching reorganization of the country's basic communications system, came as a surprise to most Americans. But the roots of the break-up actually stretched back several decades. They could be traced ultimately to the historical pricing mechanisms the Bell Companies had worked out with their regulators. Shifting demands for telephone services, stimulated in large measure by political motives and by new technologies, had long strained those pricing mechanisms. The Justice Department ruling capped an extended effort to reconcile these often conflicting forces.

When the Bell System took shape in the 1920s, it came to consist of seven regional companies, each with its own subscribers, exchanges, and central switchboard. AT&T linked these switchboards together via its Long Lines Division. When callers wished to reach someone in another region, they first gained access to the switchboard in their region. An AT&T operator then connected them to the appropriate switchboard in the receiving region, and a local operator put them through. Such callers were billed only for the board-to-board connection. In effect, then, the regional companies subsidized the long-distance service by providing free local connections.

In the 1930 case of *Smith* v. *Illinois Bell,* the Supreme Court ruled this pricing policy discriminatory. A dozen years later, after wartime demand had doubled the volume of long-distance business, the FCC responded with regulations stipulating that Bell charge on a station-to-station (or phone-to-phone) basis. This scheme compelled regulators to work out a mechanism, known eventually as the separations process, through which they could allocate expenses and revenues between the regional carriers and the Long Lines Division. Although this complex procedure defies easy analysis, it is widely perceived to have reversed the subsidy. Under pressure from a Congress that consistently taxed corporations in order to support social programs and defense, the separations process skimmed income earned from long-distance services, for which business provided the bulk of demand, and used it to hold down fees for local services. Because rates for long-distance were set on a strict per-mile basis, moreover, the pricing mechanism effectively subsidized callers in remote locations, where the actual expenses per call were greater than along more densely used corridors.

These cross-subsidies mattered little to the Bell System as long as it retained its monopoly, but they left the system vulnerable to a practice known as "cream-skimming" should its environment grow more competitive. Rivals could offer services to the high-volume long-distance customers who paid rates well in excess of AT&T's actual costs. Such competitors need not provide superior services or operate at lower costs in order to win customers away from Bell. They need only offer basic services at prices lower than AT&T's artificially inflated ones.

AT&T felt the first ripplings of such competition during the 1950s, as the development of microwave transmission techniques gave potential usurpers a ready means of creating alternatives to Bell's wired, common-carrier system. High-volume users such as the television networks expressed a strong interest in acquiring private microwave transmission networks, and leading developers of the techniques such as Motorola joined in support. These interests pressured the FCC and AT&T to clarify and formalize the separations process. In 1959, the FCC agreed to let private microwave networks function so long as they did not sell their services on the open market. AT&T responded by offering its customers TELPAK, an AT&T-installed private service with rates that reflected only the additional costs necessary to provide the service, rather than existing long-distance billing schedules with their cost-sharing subsidies. The FCC deemed this response predatory, however, and prohibited it.

As private microwave services flourished during the 1960s, a small company named Microwave Communications Incorporated (MCI) began pressuring the FCC to allow it to operate a microwave service on a slightly different basis. MCI proposed to organize users who could not afford their own private

service into groups who together would support a microwave connection between two points. AT&T saw this proposal as a clear case of cream-skimming and as a threatening encroachment on its monopoly as a common carrier. Over its protests, however, the FCC in 1968 permitted MCI to operate between Chicago and St. Louis. This decision opened a wedge that MCI exploited brilliantly. Under the leadership of William McGowan, a venture capitalist who joined the firm in 1968, MCI rapidly formed user groups in community after community and began knitting together a long-distance network. As it did so, MCI repeatedly ran up against resistance from the regional phone companies. Without their cooperation, customers could not gain access to MCI's microwave transmitters. McGowan and a team of lawyers launched a series of lawsuits in the state courts, which typically had jurisdiction over the local phone companies. Meanwhile McGowan continued to lobby Congress and the FCC in an effort to obtain greater freedom for his operations.

As MCI mounted this multifaceted assault on AT&T, it often found itself on surprisingly friendly terrain. Within the regulatory apparatus and the courts, and in the halls of academia that stocked them with personnel, a nascent movement toward deregulation had begun to coalesce. Old antitrusters and others within government, goaded by leftists and disillusioned liberals in the academy, grew persuaded that government agencies protected large corporations as much as they regulated them. At the same time, a growing body of neoclassical economists, enamored with the power of market mechanisms to allocate resources and encourage efficiency, sought to substitute competition for regulation and bureaucracy. These impulses would eventually find expression on both sides of the political spectrum. Richard Nixon drew on them in putting forth his initiative to return federal revenue back to the states, and Jimmy Carter embraced them when he authorized a guru of the deregulation movement, Albert Kahn, to remove the blanket of Civil Aeronautics Board protection from the airline industry.

By 1968, such sentiments had already begun to reach the telecommunications industry. That year, for instance, the FCC's Bernard Strassburg had with little provocation taken steps to ensure that AT&T keep its network open to "entry technologies" such as mobile telephones and computers, which might someday feed signals and data into the phone system. Strassburg wanted to make sure AT&T did not use its control of transmission technology to dictate developments in computing and telephony. One did not require a brilliant conceptual mind to see that MCI's request to use Bell's regional phone systems to gain access to its own microwave transmitters represented the inverse of the same principal.

The rising tide of competitive alternatives, private legal action, and deregulatory ideology eventually resulted in the filing of a federal antitrust suit against AT&T in November 1974. Over the next seven years, the company suffered a virtually continuous series of setbacks. In a 1977 ruling that went against both AT&T and the FCC, a federal judge permitted MCI to offer toll services. Private lawsuits filed by MCI and Litton Industries, a manufacturer of microwave equipment, also went against AT&T. An investigation begun by the FCC in 1976 applied additional pressure on the firm to further open its network to data transmission. Meanwhile, firms such as RCA and Satellite Business Systems appeared ready to capitalize on the rapid development of satellite communications to offer still other alternatives to Bell's wired network. Surveying the mounting chaos, Congress mobilized for extensive investigations in anticipation of comprehensive new telecommunications legislation.

All the while, the Justice Department suit rushed forward. President Carter sent the case to the court of Judge Harold Greene, an activist who gave every indication of moving it to a rapid conclusion. Then, with the ascent of Ronald Reagan to the presidency, the neoclassical economist William Baxter took responsibility for prosecuting the case. Over the objections of the Departments of Defense and Commerce and even of Reagan himself, Baxter negotiated his way past Congress and orchestrated a settlement. It called for Bell to cut loose its regional affiliates by the beginning of 1984 and to compete in long distance. Without any massing of public support, Americans had broken up their phone system.

COMPETITIVE ALTERNATIVES IN COMPUTING

On the very day the Justice Department disclosed this momentous settlement, it also announced that it would drop its thirteen-year-old lawsuit against IBM. Accusations that the computer giant had unfairly stifled competition were deemed to be "without merit." Since at the time IBM still controlled more than three-quarters of the market for computing, this judgment was at once extolled by the firm's admirers as evidence of its extraordinary performance and derided by its critics as a travesty of justice. Whatever the merits of the respective positions, however, no one could argue that the computer industry had lacked dynamic forces of change during the years the lawsuit had been contested. Technological innovation had continued to reshape information-processing at an extraordinary pace. Computing was in perpetual flux, and though IBM tenuously maintained its position, the forces of change would eventually prove overwhelming. Technology-based competition would accomplish for computing what Justice Department lawyers had done for telephony.

The fundamental source of change in computing during the seventies and eighties remained the same as before. Continual refinement of solid-state production technology made available processors of much higher speed and also dramatically increased the memory and storage capacities of computing systems. Increased capacities gave programmers much greater latitude. Instead of devoting the lion's share of their energies to conserving processor time, programmers increasingly could focus their efforts on making computers receive data in different forms, manipulate it in various ways, and present the results in more comprehensible fashion. Data-processing continued its metamorphosis into information-processing.

In addition to expanding the capabilities of central computing facilities, improved componentry also opened paths to alternative, less centralized approaches to computing. As costs plummeted and components shrank in size, computers could be made available to small groups of users who could program them to perform specific tasks. During the 1970s, so-called mini-computers (machines with less capability than the fastest and most expensive computers but with far more power than the earliest electronic calculators) represented the fastest-growing segment of the industry. Dynamic new firms led the way. By tailoring their machines to serve particular types of users, start-up companies carved out niches in the steadily expanding market for computing. Digital Equipment Corporation, led by maverick engineer and businessman Kenneth Olsen, marketed a series of Personal Data Processors that proved especially attractive to scientists and to educators in university computing programs. Wang Industries, formed by a Harvard University professor, An Wang, focused on office applications. Touting the image of a paperless office, Wang emphasized network installations, in which numerous small computers would be interconnected through a larger one. Workers attached to the network would be able to tap into vast data sets, perform their own unique operations (something those connected to a central computer by a simple terminal could not do), and communicate the results to colleagues throughout a facility or institution. The phenomenal success of firms such as DEC and Wang, which together helped fuel a widely publicized economic boom along Boston's Route 128, prompted IBM to respond with an array of new computers targeted for particular markets.

The ongoing transformation of computing in American institutions was complemented by a revolution in copying that had begun to occur during the 1960s. According to government estimates, during the mid-fifties Americans made approximately 20 million copies annually; a decade later, the total had soared to nearly 10 billion; and by 1966 it had reached 14 billion, with no end in sight. (In 1985, 700 billion copies were made worldwide.) This remarkable spurt was triggered by the introduction of the first reliable photocopier, the Xerox 914, in 1959. The brainchild of Chester Carlson, a patent examiner and law student who came up with the basic idea of photocopying during the 1930s after reading extensively in the scientific and technical collections of the New York Public Library, the photocopier gave anyone the means to produce facsimiles quickly and cleanly, without special training. Previous copying methods, such as Kodak's Verifax, 3M's Thermofax, and A. B. Dick's Ditto Master, had required users to make negatives of the original, pass them through caustic activator solutions, and in some cases peel apart special papers. Although one could obtain these machines for only about $350, individual copies cost nearly a dime apiece, not including the clerical time required to make them. The 914, by contrast, cost several thousand dollars to build—so much that Xerox decided to rent the machine—but made copies much cheaper. Xerox charged $95 per month, including 2,000 free copies, and 4 cents for each additional copy.

This pricing policy and the copier's inherent ease of use proved an explosive combination, one that has confounded office managers and corporate security officers ever since. While early machines could make just 7 copies per minute, renters used them so intensively that many turned out well over 100,000 copies annually. Much of this use, to be sure, reflected the substitution of photocopying for printing. Reports that had once been sent to a print shop now flowed directly from photocopiers that spewed out duplicates of ever greater clarity at speeds that by the mid-seventies had reached seventy copies per minute. Xerox found that its revenue came increasingly from such giant machines. But photocopying was also exerting a strong decentralizing influence on the diffusion of information. Since one of the principal advantages of the machines was that they required no special training, most copiers sat unattended, accessible to all without supervision. People in institutions with photocopiers could now immediately obtain a copy of any document that came into their hands. Suddenly, nothing written down was as secret as it had been before. Although this posed profound concerns about privacy for those with information to protect, the effect was extraordinarily liberating for anyone who desired greater access to written information.

The development of affordable, easy-to-use facsimile machines further contributed to these trends. Newspapers and other information services had sent copies by wire since the twenties, but the techniques had remained cumbersome and costly: in 1970, the best machine still took between four and six minutes to scan a letter-sized page. Gradual improvements in fax equipment and falling long-distance rates helped make the machines far more common during the next decade, so that by 1980 perhaps a quarter of a million were in use. Salespeople began sending daily reports to warehouses and offices by fax, and teams of engineers working at remote locations found them useful for exchanging diagrams and other graphic information. Still, most people wishing to send documents rapidly across distances turned to the overnight courier services that sprang up in the late seventies and early eighties. Faxing remained exceptional until several Japanese firms introduced digital machines that not only scanned very rapidly, thus dropping the cost of transmission, but eliminated offensive odors and awkward procedures as well. The number of fax machines grew from half a million in 1985 to over 6 million in 1991, while the number of transmitted pages soared from 1.5 billion to over 17 billion.

As photocopiers and fax machines transformed immediate access to written information from a privilege into a common expectation, they inevitably affected the ways people perceived other communications technologies. The telephone attained new prominence as a private, secure means of communication (though the Watergate scandal, with its notorious tapes, demonstrated that in an age of magnetic recording telephones were not so secure as one might imagine). The effect on computing may have been still more profound. The growing volume of printed materials spurred development of programs for document preparation and word-processing, which by the eighties had become the most common computer applications. Networks assumed added emphasis as well. As employees received copies routinely made available to everyone on a distribution list, they intuitively came to perceive themselves as parts of networks. An Wang's vision of the paperless office would have made little sense in a pre-copier world. The spread of fax technology, though it did not eliminate paper, contributed further to the idea of an electronic network.

As computers and other communications technology penetrated ever more deeply into the fabric of America's institutions during the 1970s, less organized elements of society pressed forward with a far different image of computing. Anonymous individual enthusiasts, known collectively as "hackers," began to patch together one-of-a-kind computers of limited capacity. They combined small processors made possible by continual improvements in integrated circuit technology with keyboards and monitors scavenged from terminals or obtained from parts suppliers. Hackers formed clubs, wrote newsletters, and pored over catalogs in search of the latest components and programs. Infused with a strong anti-institutional ideology and renegade spirit, they brought the vision of a "home computer" into reality, much as the amateur radio operators of an earlier day had demonstrated the potential of voice transmission and home reception.

As in the case of those earlier hobbyists, the era of the unshackled amateurs did not last for long. Apple Computer, the creation of hackers Stephen Wozniak and Steven Jobs, soon imposed a degree of order on the personal computer market when it introduced the Apple II in 1976. Rather than offer a stripped-down, expandable kit that customers would assemble and refine themselves, Apple sold a standard machine that included its own monitor, disk drive, and keyboard. The company also provided several basic software packages. Compared to virtually any other supplier of home computers, Apple projected an image of stability, enticing large numbers of less technically minded customers into the domain of the hackers. Apple's revenues soared from three-quarters of a million dollars in 1977 to just under a billion dollars in 1983. Not surprisingly, several other firms soon mimicked Apple, with considerable success. By far the most important imitator was IBM itself, which launched a crash program to develop a microcomputer of its own. This effort resulted in the personal computer. Introduced in 1981, it immediately captured 26 percent of the market. The impact of the PC went well beyond IBM's own sales, moreover, because the product's modular design and extensive use of licensed components left other manufacturers free to produce clones that accounted for another 50 percent or more of the market.

Within a remarkably short time of its birth, the booming microcomputer industry achieved an astounding degree of stability. The market quickly split between Macintosh machines built by Apple and PCs produced by IBM and its many competitors. Within each realm, responsibility for two fundamental issues—the design of the microprocessor and the basic operating language—had been largely resolved. With Apple, both were proprietary; in the case of the PC, they were shaped respectively by Intel and Microsoft, the firms IBM had chosen as its original suppliers. Like IBM in the early mainframe computer industry, these firms established a degree of uniformity in the essentials of computing without stifling further development. They themselves continued to introduce new generations of operating systems and processors that placed greater computing power at the hands of individual consumers. Their influence and market power gave suppliers of memory, printers, and monitors confidence to pursue techniques of mass production. Most importantly, software writers proceeded with some assurance that their work would find a broad market and not be rendered obsolete by subsequent changes in basic hardware or in the basic operating system. As a result, the microcomputer industry sustained a vibrant competition to develop new applications, and computers came to perform a much broader array of functions.

The rise of this dynamic microcomputer industry, together with the emergence of minicomputers and the continual improvements in semiconductor technology, gradually moved computing away from the centralized paradigm that had long sustained IBM. That company's products and services took on the character of commodities available to individuals or small groups and supplied by a vast array of competitive firms. Computers would soon penetrate into schoolrooms and households throughout the United States, with effects we cannot yet discern. For computing in the closing decades of the twentieth century had only just entered a watershed not unlike that experienced by transportation at the century's outset as it passed the from the railroad network of J. P. Morgan to the Model T of Henry Ford. A highly efficient, centrally managed system of limited flexibility stood poised to give way to one of vastly greater potential diversity that would be shaped by innumerable decisions made by countless individual operators. Perhaps not even Marshall McLuhan would have dared anticipate the consequences.

PROLIFERATING CHOICES IN VIDEO

Much the same could be said of television, the third cornerstone of modern communications. During the 1970s, two innovations—cable transmission and the home videorecorder—began transforming the television industry from an oligopolistic fiefdom into a competitive cornucopia of choice. By the end of the eighties, so many outlets existed that the primary question confronting the industry was how it could possibly fill the available airspace. Amid jokes about "five hundred stations and still nothing worth watching," Americans tuned in more often than ever.

Cable television itself was not new in the seventies. Remote areas had been served by cable since the inception of television. Communities with poor reception had licensed firms to set up large central antennas and distribute the signals to subscribers through coaxial cable. By 1975, 4.2 million homes (about 6 percent of American homes) had access to cable, and 1.9 million actually subscribed. That year, the Home Box Office Corporation (HBO) launched an experiment that would transform cable into a source of alternative entertainment rather than just an extension of the standard broadcast networks. Using space rented on a new RCA communications satellite, HBO transmitted programming to a local cable service in upstate Pennsylvania, which picked up the shows in a dish receiver and offered them to customers for an additional monthly fee. With the backing of Time, Inc., HBO rapidly took hold. Soon imitators such as the Cable News Network (CNN) and the Entertainment and Sports Programming Network (ESPN) began offering round-the-clock coverage of events from all over the world, while local stations such as WGN in Chicago and WTBS in Atlanta began sending their broadcasts out via satellite for cable distribution. Households with cable suddenly had access to a much wider range of programming. Communities without it rushed to grant licenses to local operators who would install a cable distribution system as rapidly as possible. By 1987, 71.8 million homes had access (80 percent of total American households), and 42.3 million subscribed to at least a basic service.

The rapid proliferation of cable television unleashed forces of change that a generation of FCC regulators and social critics could hardly have imagined. Within a decade of the HBO experiment, programming available only via cable already accounted for about a third of the sixty hours an average American household viewed television each week. The three major networks could now claim barely half of audience viewing time, and their share during the lucrative prime time was falling most rapidly of all. In 1988, advertising revenue among cable networks surpassed $1.4 billion, more than a threefold increase since five years before. Subscription fees totaled about $7 billion, with the largest operator, TCI, collecting

nearly $2 billion from its 8 million subscribers. Such revenues put TCI on a scale with the major broadcasting networks, which each collected approximately $3 billion in revenues annually. TCI thus could compete with the networks for programs, and the market for entertainment moved closer to the competitive ideal the FCC had long pursued.

In addition to enlivening competition for the entertainment market, the rise of cable opened the airwaves to alternative types of programming. Some of these, such as C-SPAN's live broadcasts of congressional proceedings, fulfilled long-sought desires that television function as a public-service medium and tool of democracy. Others brought to television activities that had previously taken place in other venues. Several networks, for instance, featured home shopping services, which displayed merchandise and encouraged viewers to order by phone. By 1988, these services sold more than $2 billion worth of merchandise. The largest, Home Shopping Network (HSN), reached over 45 million households. Religious broadcasting also thrived on cable. Between 1982 and 1987, the number of stations offering exclusively religious programming grew from 62 to 221. The giant Christian Broadcasting Network (CBN) reached over 30 million homes. The star of its 700 Club, Pat Robertson, made a run for the presidency in 1988 and appeared on the podium of the Republican National Convention four years later. Another religious network, the PTL Club, raised more donations than the 40,000 churches of the Southern Baptist Convention combined, until a sex scandal and charges of tax fraud brought down its leaders, Jim and Tammy Bakker. All told, religious broadcasters on television collected over a billion dollars in contributions during 1988, an amount equal to the budget of the Public Broadcasting System.

With the proliferation of stations, programmers and advertisers further refined their capacity to target particular audiences. The fastest-growing area of television during the late eighties, for example, was Spanish-language broadcasting. By 1988, the 130 stations transmitting in Spanish already accounted for more than half a billion dollars of advertising annually. Revenues were expected to quadruple by the early nineties. Other stations, including some licensed under federally mandated minority set-aside programs, aimed primarily at an African American audience. Ever more sophisticated survey data enabled programmers and advertisers to track viewing patterns and responses by race, age, and gender. When several advertising agencies announced their intention to redress the historical underrepresentation of African

Americans in their industry, one could reasonably wonder whether they planned to integrate the perspectives of their new employees into a common culture or assign them to campaigns aimed at African American viewers.

The potential to expand the possibilities of television while subdividing its audience was also characteristic of the second major innovation of recent decades, the home videorecorder. Introduced during the late seventies by two Japanese firms, Sony and JVC, VCRs suitable for home use rapidly penetrated markets around the world. In the United States, 22 percent of homes had a VCR by 1984. Four years later, the number had jumped to 46 percent. (In 1993, fewer than a third of American homes were without a VCR.) The number of blank and prerecorded video tapes sold annually grew from about 22 million in 1980 to nearly 400 million in 1987.

VCRs offered consumers a new level of discretion in their television viewing. Initially, marketers believed their greatest appeal would come from the ability to record programs for viewing at a later time. No longer would viewers have to conform to the dictates of network scheduling. But such time-shifting actually constituted a fairly small percentage of VCR use. Instead, consumers used their VCRs primarily to play prerecorded entertainment either purchased or rented from a vendor. With the average owner renting four movies per month, the number of prerecorded videos distributed annually had reached 66 million by 1988. Sales and rentals of videos for home viewing that year brought in more than $2 billion, 20 percent more than movie box office receipts. Rather than extending the reach of existing programming, VCRs had brought the movie industry directly into competition with broadcasters and cable operators.

The effects of this competition were not immediately clear. Surveys indicated that adults watched videotapes an average of just two hours per week, compared with the over four hours per day they watched television. Children watched more recorded programming—3.4 hours per week—but this difference was proportional to that in their overall viewing habits. The number of hours spent watching broadcasts and cable programming continued to rise, moreover, suggesting that VCRs added a new dimension to television rather than cutting into established behaviors. Since the number of television sets grew as well, with 195 million receivers in use during 1988 in the 90 million homes that had television, one can readily imagine how VCR use could develop as an ancillary to broadcast television and cable, rather than as an alternative to them. While some members of a household tuned in a telecast in one room, others could watch a prerecorded film elsewhere in the home.

Perhaps the most important result of the coming of cable television and the VCR, then, was simply their contribution to the ever-increasing pervasiveness of visual images in the homes and in the lives of Americans. Television screens occupied not just dens, but kitchens and bedrooms; not just taverns, but classrooms and waiting rooms. Each of these screens could be filled with an ever-increasing variety of images, as viewers with remote controls flashed through the array of cable offerings or inserted a movie of their choice into the VCR. An army of entertainers, sports figures, producers, and programmers scrambled to occupy the available space, each hoping to tap the $25 billion a year expended on television advertising (a quarter of all advertising, including $6 billion from automobile manufacturers alone) and the $10 billion Americans spent annually to gain access to cable programming and provide movies for their VCRs.

Although this pool of revenue represented an average of over $400 from each of America's 90 million households, it did not keep up with the explosion in available airtime. Consequently, viewers were presented with a diversity of offerings not unlike that which had flowered on radio during the early twenties and again in the postwar era. For the first time since television's inception, the production quality of much programming slipped, as broadcasters sought to fill airtime as cheaply as possible. In perhaps the clearest and certainly the most ironic expression of this trend, during the 1990s each of the networks aired programs featuring videotapes filmed by viewers. Many local news broadcasters also actively solicited home videotapes. In 1992, an amateur video showing fleeing black suspect Rodney King being beaten by Los Angeles police officers galvanized the nation and the verdict in the subsequent trial sparked the most serious race riots in a generation. Anything and anyone, it seemed, might be on television, and everyone was a potential producer.

PROSPECTS AND REFLECTIONS

As the twentieth century entered its final decade, the United States was awash with communications technologies and computing. Not since the dawn of the Audio Age, when telephones and radios first emerged on the scene in significant numbers and AT&T and the networks had not yet asserted their centralizing influence, had consumers faced so much new technology available from so many providers. This unprecedented variety of electronic media penetrated ever more deeply into the fabric of American life. School libraries became media centers, family rooms were replaced by home theaters, and quiet studies were transformed into buzzing home offices.

Yet, paradoxically, the realm of communications and computing seemed in the eyes of many informed observers and anxious financiers to be poised on the brink of a new epic consolidation. For beneath the numbing proliferation of options, there rested the potential for a grand convergence in the common underpinnings of digital technology. Virtually all forms of information—music, film, numerical data, voice, books and documents—were now translated into electronic code that could be entered into computers, retained in electronic memories, manipulated in countless ways, and transmitted virtually anywhere via any of several media. Individuals could gain access to this vast pool of digitized information through terminals or workstations that combined computers, telephones, fax machines, and televisions into a single instrument. Might not some shrewd entrepreneur or organization seize the apparent opportunities for convergence and attain a position comparable to those of the networks and AT&T during the middle decades of the century?

The history of communications during the twentieth century suggests otherwise. AT&T and the networks achieved their influential positions primarily because they controlled the limited transmission techniques of the day. Before mid-century, those wishing to transmit audio or printed information across long distances simply had no alternatives to the telephone lines. Microwave technology and satellites introduced a measure of competition following World War II, but for many years the costs of transmission remained high. Those expenses, together with the limited space available on the broadcasting spectrum, kept networks in a powerful position well into the age of television. By the end of the century, however, several techniques had been firmly established as alternatives to Bell's long lines. Indeed, following the telephone breakup AT&T itself largely replaced its own system with new fiber optic cables capable of carrying vastly more data than its previous coaxial ones. While some feared this new technology might give AT&T a means of again dominating long distance, the emergence of fiber optics provided further evidence that vibrant technical change would keep the transmission business in a state of perpetual

flux, with numerous viable alternatives contending for a share of the market.

Even if a single new technique should prove overwhelmingly superior, history indicates that Americans would through political action limit the authority of those who provide transmission services. Throughout its long period of monopoly AT&T operated in a highly regulated environment. Government took a large hand in determining its rate structure and insisted that the firm not block access to the communications system. Under pressure from federal regulators and antitrust officials, AT&T backed down from its attempt to monopolize network broadcasting and later agreed to open its lines to data transmission. Regulatory agreements also compelled AT&T to share critical technical breakthroughs such as the transistor with companies that would later provide its stiffest competition. Americans thus gained the efficiencies of a single system while ensuring that the monopolist would neither stifle innovation nor deny access. The same was true of their approach to the broadcasting networks. Americans attempted through regulation to place the operators of such networks in the position of brokers who offered services to anyone willing to pay. Statutes eventually prohibited broadcasters from controlling the programs they aired. Like AT&T, the networks would function as "common carriers." By the 1990s, this common carrier approach had secured an enduring place in the American political tradition. Regulators employed it almost instinctively as they observed the proposed mergers of entertainment companies with communications firms. They would undoubtedly move swiftly to stifle any blatant attempts to turn communications back toward the more limited access of the network era.

A similar combination of vibrant technological change and threatened regulation would also likely prevent anyone from asserting undue control over either the crucial electronic components or the fundamental operating systems upon which modern communications depend. In the early nineties, Apple and the PC continued to present consumers with two entirely distinct alternatives to computing. Within the much larger PC domain the Intel Corporation did manage to attain a surprising preeminence among designers and makers of microprocessors, but it still faced intense competition from numerous domestic and foreign firms. In the realm of software, giant Microsoft posed something of a more serious threat to openness. Owner of the MS-DOS and Windows programs through which most users gained access to their personal computers, Microsoft had by the nineties grown larger than IBM. But like IBM during its heyday, Microsoft did not go unchallenged. Critics sought antitrust action that would have forced the company to sever all connections with hardware suppliers and banned it from the applications business, in effect leaving the firm to operate as a common carrier for specialized software programs written by others. A settlement announced in the summer of 1994 stopped short of either action. As it had in the case of IBM, the Justice Department determined that Microsoft managed to provide a healthy stability without stifling development. Although this ruling left the industry largely unaltered, the investigation left no doubt that all aspects of communications and computing would continue to operate under the watchful eye of government regulators. Competition, innovation, and access seemed likely to remain the hallmarks of American communications even in the era of interconnectedness.

What precisely Americans would make of their revamped communications system, however, remained far less clear. As before, considerable speculation swirled around the possibility that the new techniques would dramatically alter the prevailing sense of community. Some envisioned the computer network as the fulfillment of direct democracy on a national scale. All individuals would gain access to any information they desired and have the ability to respond interactively. Others observed a growing fragmentation, as people retreated from public settings to private spaces, from which they engaged via machine only those who shared their narrow, idiosyncratic interests. Still others saw the network as merely a revised technique of mass communication, offering entertainment on demand. They cited polls showing that most Americans anticipated using the network almost exclusively to receive movies, games, and other prepackaged amusements.

Contrary to the dogmatic assertions that often accompanied such forecasts, none of these scenarios necessarily excluded the others. Indeed, the experience of the twentieth century suggests that the network will probably assume several roles, and that even then older media will likely persist. The century has grown increasingly cluttered with options piled one on top of the other. Not even the telegraph has disappeared entirely. During the early decades of the century, Americans made myriad use of tele-

phones and radios. They tolerated consolidation in the Bell System and the networks not because these systems choked off options, but because they opened new possibilities and extended them to greater numbers of people. The radio networks, as vehicles of instantaneous mass communication, did permanently alter the ways humans connected to one another. Surely no modern society would willingly forego them or their video successors. It is true as well that Americans have exhibited a seemingly endless capacity to wallow in the offerings of mass communications. They now spend on average a third of their waking hours watching television. But one must also note that those offerings have grown steadily more diverse. The realm of mass communications has itself come to be characterized by extraordinary choice.

Perhaps the most profound effects of the computer network will again involve matters of individual cognition rather than collective social behavior. As communications technology entered an exclusively digital age, it came increasingly to resemble the very neurological processes that underlay human perception and cognition. Designers sought to incorporate lessons learned from neurophysiology into their machines and to provide ever more responsive sensory interfaces between computers and their users. These efforts yielded practical benefits such as computers that responded to simple voice commands, but they also involved more grandiose visions. The Air Force, for instance, investigated computer guidance systems that would respond directly to a pilot's perceptions rather than to the physical movements those perceptions prompted. Run in reverse, such systems could perhaps induce a vivid feeling of flying. Experiments such as these inspired designers of theaters and amusement rides to contemplate entertainments that would launch sedentary individuals into various states of virtual reality. Meanwhile, lesser forms of deception took hold. Moviegoers watched computer-enhanced films that deftly melded contemporary actors into historical footage, leaving some to ponder how in a digitized world one could ever again trust the veracity of an image. Electronic communications, which at the start of the century had been thought of simply as tools to inform, appeared destined at century's end to obliterate all meaningful distinction between perception and reality.

SEE ALSO Large-Scale Scientific Enterprise; Industrial Research and Technology; Aerospace Technology; Medical Science and Technology (all in this volume).

BIBLIOGRAPHY

The diffusion and social impact of telephony is examined creatively in two works by Ithiel de Sola Pool, *The Social Impact of the Telephone* (1977), which he edited, and *Forecasting the Telephone: A Retrospective Technology Assessment of the Telephone* (1983). For a more recent synthetic treatment, see Claude Fischer, *America Calling: A Social History of the Telephone to 1940* (1992). Louis Galambos, "Theodore N. Vail and the Role of Innovation in the Modern Bell System," *Business History Review* (1992), discusses the strategies of AT&T and their principal architect.

On early technical developments in radio, see Susan Douglass, *Inventing American Broadcasting, 1899–1922* (1987); and Leonard S. Reich, *The Making of American Industrial Research: Science and Business at GE and Bell, 1876–1926* (1985). Two works by Eric Barnouw, *A Tower in Babel: A History of Broadcasting in the United States to 1933* (1966), and *The Golden Web: A History of Broadcasting in the United States, 1933–1953* (1968), remain the starting points for an understanding of the emergence and evolution of networks. Walter B. Emery, *Broadcasting and Government: Responsibilities and Regulations* (1971), contains a useful compendium of regulatory measures. A more recent work, Tom Lewis, *Empire of the Air: The Men Who Made Radio* (1991), engagingly tells the story of radio through biographies of DeForest, Sarnoff, and Armstrong.

For an overview of data-processing in the pre-computer era, consult James W. Cortada, *Before the Computer: IBM, NCR, Burroughs, and Remington Rand and the Industry They Created, 1865–1956* (1993). More detailed treatment of important aspects of the industry will be found in Arthur L. Norberg, "High-Technology Calculation in the Early 20th Century: Punched Card Machinery in Business and Government," *Technology and Culture* (1990); JoAnne Yates, "Co-evolution of Information-Processing Technology and Use: Interaction between the Life Insurance and Tabulating Industries," *Business History Review* (1993); and Geoffrey Austrian, *Herman Hollerith: Forgotten Giant of Information Processing* (1982). The transition to electronic computing must still be traced through specialized studies of particular projects and individuals. Two of the more useful are Herman Goldstine, *The Computer: From Pascal to Von Neumann* (1972); and Emerson Pugh, *Memories That Shaped an Industry:*

Decisions Leading to IBM System/360 (1984). Technical developments at IBM have received extensive treatment in Charles Bashe et al., *IBM's Early Computers* (1986); and Emerson Pugh et al., *IBM's 360 and Early 370 Systems* (1991). For a more interpretative treatment focusing on corporate strategy, see Steven W. Usselman, "IBM and Its Imitators: Organizational Capabilities and the Emergence of the International Computer Industry," *Business and Economic History* (1993). An essential overview stressing the role of government is Kenneth Flamm, *Creating the Computer: Government, Industry, and High Technology* (1988). Ernest Braun, *Revolution in Miniature: The History and Impact of Semiconductor Electronics* (1978), traces the evolution of the fundamental engine of change in modern computing and communications.

Early technical developments in television have received nothing like the attention devoted to those in radio and computing. Albert Abramson, *The History of Television, 1880 to 1941* (1987), contains a wealth of detail but is dense and idiosyncratic. A more accessible overview can be found in the introductory chapters of Margaret B. W. Graham, *RCA and the VideoDisc: The Business of Research* (1986). The account presented here is derived from a variety of sources. The works of Barnouw and Emery cited above carry forward the story of broadcasting into the television era, though these can be supplemented by a vast literature on specific areas of programming. Peter Fornatale and Joshua E. Mills, *Radio in the Television Age* (1980), considers a neglected dimension of that story.

For the period since 1968, one must rely more on a vibrant journalistic literature and numerous policy-oriented studies than on traditional historical treatments. Two outstanding exceptions are Peter Temin, with Louis Galambos, *The Fall of the Bell System: A Study in Prices and Politics* (1987); and Richard N. Langlois, "External Economies and Economic Progress: The Case of the Microcomputer Industry," *Business History Review* (1992). Each provides a comprehensive narrative built around the critical issue of the relationship between market structures, public policy, and innovation. For lively accounts of two indispensable tools of modern office communications, turn to Gary Jacobson and John Hillkirk, *Xerox: American Samurai* (1986); and Jonathan Coopersmith, "Facsimile's False Starts," *IEEE Perspectives* (1993). Peter

Dunnett, *The World Television Industry: An Economic Analysis* (1990), assembles a wealth of interesting data on recent viewing habits. It can be supplemented by Mark R. Levy, ed., *The VCR Age: Home Video and Mass Communication* (1989); and Loy A. Singleton, *Telecommunications in the Information Age: A Nontechnical Primer on the New Technologies* (1986), which is especially useful on cable television and satellite transmission.

INDUSTRIAL RESEARCH AND MANUFACTURING TECHNOLOGY

David A. Hounshell

Industrial research in the United States is largely a twentieth-century phenomenon. This article maps out the principal factors that gave rise to industrial research, analyzes various forces that mediated its spread, identifies some of the major actors in its history, and suggests its significance. Although shaped by many factors both internal and external to industry, industrial research itself has been an important shaper of the twentieth century.

"Like poetry," wrote one mid-century manager, industrial research "cannot be defined in a manner that is universally acceptable." Yet it is almost invariably linked to the laboratories or organizations in which industry carries out scientific and technological research. As the historian Leonard S. Reich writes, "Industrial research can thus be characterized as follows: industrial laboratories set apart from production facilities, staffed by people trained in science and advanced engineering who work toward deeper understandings of corporate-related science and technology, and who are organized and administered to keep them somewhat insulated from immediate demands yet responsive to long-term company needs."

The National Science Foundation reported that in 1993 the United States spent roughly $161 billion on research and development (R&D), or about 2.6 percent of the country's total gross domestic product (GDP). Of these expenditures in the production and application of scientific and technical knowledge, industry provided about 52 percent of the funds, while the federal government supplied 42 percent. Colleges and universities, state and local governments, and nonprofit institutions such as private foundations funded the remaining 6 percent. The federal government spent 46 percent of its share of the national R&D budget in industry and affiliated federally funded research and development centers (as opposed to in-house governmental laboratories,

colleges and universities, and nonprofit organizations). Thus in 1993 industry conducted slightly more that 68 percent of the nation's R&D (on a dollar basis), or 1.77 percent of total GDP. The majority—almost two million in 1992—of all formally educated scientists and engineers in the United States worked in industry. Of these, a smaller number (950,000 in 1989) worked on a full-time-equivalent basis in R&D—almost 75 percent in industry, approximately 18 percent in colleges and universities, and roughly 6 percent in federal agencies.

Although R and D are usually linked with an ampersand to form the all-embracing, singular term R&D, this essay will focus mostly on the R of industrial R&D. Typically, research represents the most problematic aspect of R&D despite its being the minority partner when evaluated in terms of dollar expenditures. In 1991, almost 28 percent of all industrial R&D expenditures were devoted to "basic" and "applied" research (formal categories used by the National Science Foundation). The remaining 72 percent went to development. Although these percentages vary from year to year, they are typical for much of the post–World War II era. Development looms so large budgetarily because it entails the cost of making prototype products or the design, construction, and operation of production equipment larger in scale than that typically used in the laboratory but smaller in scale than commercial manufacturing equipment. This specialized hardware is employed to perfect manufacturing processes for a new product or to test new processes for making an existing product. Development also often entails testing potential products to gauge how well they will perform under conditions of use. This work is expensive compared to the cost of discovery and advancement of new knowledge, which is the central concern of research. Yet research is perceived to be riskier, with outcomes that are harder to measure and predict than those of development. In the absence of research, most people believe, there would be no development. Or at least development would be very different.

Industrial R&D constitutes one of the prime factors in technological change and economic growth, although economists have had difficulty measuring its magnitude. The conditions that obtain in industrial research toward the close of the twentieth century have not always prevailed, and they will unquestionably change markedly once the full logic of the end of the Cold War is realized. At the beginning of the twentieth century, industrial R&D barely existed.

THE PREHISTORY OF INDUSTRIAL R&D IN THE UNITED STATES

Historians seeking the roots of twentieth-century industrial research have found numerous instances in the nineteenth century in which professional scientists (individuals whose principal occupation is devoted to the generation of new knowledge about the physical and biological worlds) contributed to the development of new technologies and industries. These instances are scattered throughout the 1800s, but until the 1870s their pattern is largely undiscernible. Although interesting, the individual instances do not add up to much. Indeed, there is little evidence to suggest that either scientists or industrialists before the 1870s recognized that the systematic application or pursuit of knowledge for and within industry could be beneficial.

The increasing application of science in American industry was accompanied by the professionalization of American science, a process that gained momentum in the second quarter of the nineteenth century. Ironically, this professionalization was matched by ever more strident calls for the "independence" of science. Pleas poured forth to support "pure science" and "pure scientists" as opposed to what the more vocal professional scientists called "prostituted" science—science pursued for profit rather than for its own sake. The shrill tone and bitterness of the distinguished Johns Hopkins University physicist Henry A. Rowland as he addressed the American Association for the Advancement of Science in 1883 is indicative of this pure-science idealism:

> The proper course of one in my position is to consider what must be done to create a science of physics in this country, rather than to call telegraphs, electric lights, and such conveniences, by the name of science. . . . When the average tone of the [scientific]

society is low, when the highest honors are given to the mediocre, when third-class men are held up as examples, and when trifling inventions are magnified into scientific discoveries, then the influence of such societies is prejudicial.

Rowland's widely circulated address echoed earlier calls made by other major figures in the emerging scientific community and foreshadowed later and more strident calls for pure science. The pursuit by professional scientists in the United States of pure science—or "best" science—forms one of the most important motifs in the history of American science. More than a motif, however, the pursuit of pure science shaped, and continues to shape, American science and the course of industrial research in the United States in a fundamental way. The strength of the ideology of pure science must be taken into account to comprehend fully the dynamics of industrial research and development in the United States.

Rowland and other scientists (many with Ph.D.s from German universities), who were beginning to populate what would later be termed "research universities" were annoyed that the American public confused inventions such as the telegraph and the electric light bulb with science and mistook the inventors of those devices for true scientists. Even more galling was how successful independent inventors were at garnering resources from that period's equivalent of venture capitalists, while struggling scientists were forced to beg for support from an American public that did not appreciate the beauty of pure science. While confusing science with invention, the American public also believed that the true wellspring of invention and innovation was the heroic individual inventor. For a long time, even many of the leaders of technologically based industries and firms—including the Pennsylvania Railroad, one of the nation's largest firms—believed this to be true.

When the managers of the Pennsylvania Railroad in 1876 hired Charles B. Dudley to establish a chemical laboratory in Altoona, Pennsylvania—perhaps the first corporate laboratory in the United States—they were not intending fundamentally to shift the locus or nature of technological innovation and competition in the railroad industry. By the 1870s, patterns of innovation and competition in the railroad industry were well entrenched. For example, the Pennsylvania, although a recognized leader in locomotive development and overall system efficiency through the adoption of the latest innovations in rails, switching, and signaling, had never sought to develop proprietary technologies that could be turned to competitive advantage. Instead, the railroads used patents only to protect themselves from outsiders to the industry—independent inventors who might attempt to extract high rents through proprietary inventions. The Pennsylvania Railroad's imperative, and that of most of the trunkline railroads, was to increase the system's throughput, which required stronger rails, bigger and faster locomotives, bigger cars, and longer trains. Innovations by any large railroad quickly diffused to the others through a wide array of networks ranging from locomotive manufacturers (which followed, rather than led, the railroads in innovation) to visiting delegations of engineers, to industrywide standard-setting committees, to patent pools and industry publications.

Dudley's laboratory therefore focused on the standardization and testing of supplies required by the railroad: steel rails, lubricating oils, and so on. Dudley devoted his entire professional life to the establishment of standards for industrial materials. His work at the Pennsylvania developed into a national movement that was institutionalized as the American Society for Testing Materials, with Dudley as its longtime president.

Given the expense and complexity of railroad operations, technological innovation within the Pennsylvania Railroad was largely incremental, centered in the locomotive and car shops in Altoona. More radical change came from outside the system, from independent inventors and engineers such as George Westinghouse. His invention of the air brake and, later, of important new switching and signaling devices and his shrewd patent management gave him a proprietary position that even the powerful industry could not break. Westinghouse enjoyed enormous success in maintaining a strong, proprietary, and independent position in the railroad industry, but few, if any, inventors and entrepreneurs in the industry duplicated his performance. The hordes of independent inventors who worked on improving railroad technology mostly sold their patented improvements to the powerful (and associated) railroads and then moved on to other things.

The telegraph industry, which like railroads was system-driven, mirrored the railroad's pattern of innovation through most of the nineteenth century. This is unsurprising given that the telegraph and railroad industries grew hand-in-hand and were, as the historian Alfred D. Chandler has argued, highly dependent on one another. Established by Samuel F. B. Morse and his associates in the late 1840s, the telegraph industry faced many of the same imperatives as the railroad, with the difference that the telegraph moved information rather than freight and passengers. Developing instruments to transmit and receive messages faster, simultaneously, and with greater reliability became the order of the day. In his study of technological innovation in the American telegraph industry, *From Machine Shop to Industrial Laboratory* (1992), Paul Israel argues that the machine shop, rather than the laboratory, was the locus of technological change in the telegraph industry for most of the nineteenth century. These shops were owned and staffed by mechanic-inventors who had begun their careers as telegraph operators and who often made inventions in response to specific requests by telegraph system superintendents. These mechanic-inventors brought their practical skills and intimate knowledge of the industry's technology rather than theoretical scientific training to the process of invention. Their work was almost entirely void of theoretical development. The dominant firm in the industry, Western Union, eventually developed an organizationally distinct group of operator-inventors to integrate new technologies into Western Union's system. For a long time, however, the company relied on individual inventors, including Thomas A. Edison, for technological innovation.

Schooled in the telegraph office, Edison worked at inventing for the telegraph industry in various machine shops in Boston, New York, and Newark, New Jersey. He was a partner in several of these shops, and in some of them he equipped a separate area he called his "laboratory." In 1876, however, he broke away from the crowd in Newark and established his own laboratory–machine shop in the rural hamlet of Menlo Park, New Jersey, which he referred to as his "invention factory," or, more often, his laboratory. Some have seen Edison's Menlo Park laboratory as the forerunner of the organized industrial research and development laboratories of the twentieth century. The philosopher Albert North Whitehead, for example, once said that Edison's greatest invention was his method of invention, that is, industrial R&D. But Edison founded his laboratory to invent for a distinct market: the telegraph industry. Inventors like Edison—and there were several like him—clearly found a market for their inventions and could sell their patented improvements to the highest bidder. And in the 1870s there were many parties hoping to break Western Union's virtual monopoly in the telegraph industry by finding an alternative to the Morse-based technology it employed. And these parties pinned their hopes on a set of independent inventors to create this new technology.

Edison's Menlo Park operation seems similar to

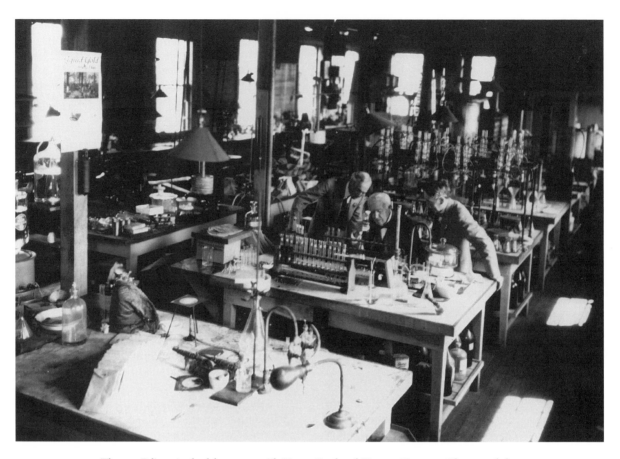

Thomas Edison in the laboratory, with Henry Ford and Harvey Firestone. Photograph by
Gravelle. PRINTS AND PHOTOGRAPHS DIVISION, LIBRARY OF CONGRESS

later industrial research laboratories principally because it was there that Edison and his growing band of
what he called "muckers" (machinists, glassblowers,
instrument makers, chemists, and even a physicist or
two) gave birth to the nation's first commercial system
of incandescent lighting. Edison and his muckers,
however, might also be viewed as one of the nation's
first high-technology start-up companies, because
after 1878 Edison abandoned the idea of inventing
for a market and focused on building a new industry.
Succeeding in this, Edison closed the Menlo Park
complex in 1882 and became an industrialist. As an
industrialist in electric lighting, Edison never developed the idea of building a research function geared
to the generation and application of new scientific
and technological knowledge. Only later, in 1887,
did he realize that invention, not capitalism, was
his forte. He then built a much larger and more
thoroughly equipped laboratory in West Orange,
New Jersey, and returned to mucking around.

By this time the name Edison was a household
word. And the attention accorded him and his new

laboratory was deeply disturbing to professionally
conscious scientists such as Rowland. The public continued to confuse invention with science and inventors
with scientists, and this confusion strengthened the resolve of research-oriented professionals to impart the
highest scientific ideals to the growing ranks of graduate students. For such scientists, the German system
offered a far better model of how knowledge should
be pursued, supported, and applied.

THE GERMAN MODEL OF SCIENTIFIC INDUSTRIAL R&D

During the last third of the nineteenth century and
the first decade and a half of the twentieth, a preponderance of U.S. physicists and chemists earned their
graduate (M.S. and Ph.D.) degrees in Germany.
These scientists not only observed a different system
of graduate education in German universities, but
also witnessed the large, nationwide system of scientific research and industrial-academic relations that
had evolved after German unification in 1871.

834

By the beginning of World War I, Germany possessed the world's most complex and advanced research system, comprising university research programs, government- and industry-sponsored research institutes, and industrial R&D programs. These components were linked by research scientists committed to advancing science and, as necessary to this goal, technology and industry. A key element of the German system was industrial sponsorship of research in the universities, largely through the vehicle of supporting, sometimes on an exclusive basis, individual professors and their cadres of graduate students. The directors of German firms, especially in the chemical and electrical industries, believed that their firms' interests and those of the professors were mutual. For their investment, firms gained privileged access to new scientific knowledge and were able to recruit high-caliber new graduates for the product-development and testing laboratories that they were organizing and expanding. For their part, professors gained access to otherwise expensive or impossible-to-get industrial materials, chemicals, and instruments as well as a window on evolving industrial practice. Created through both private philanthropy and state action and supported in part by industrial funds, the German research institutes generated basic knowledge important to university professor and industrial scientist alike.

In the two decades before the turn of the century, firms in the newly created electrical and chemical industries built up in-house R&D organizations that eventually became the dominant model for all science-based industries. These research organizations did not emerge full-blown but rather evolved in their form, function, and operation. In the chemical industry, the experience of the firm Friedrich Bayer, A.G. (i.e., Inc.), is representative. The firm tried several methods for harnessing science and scientists to its commercial objectives. By 1891 the major patterns and forms of Bayer's R&D programs had crystallized under the leadership of research director Carl Duisberg, who would later become a board member, then president of Bayer, and eventually the creator of the huge chemical combine, I. G. Farben. Bayer built a central research laboratory furnished with the latest scientific instruments and supplied with a scientific and patent library and a seminar room. It also established specialized applications laboratories and other facilities dedicated to improving in production processes. All these facilities were staffed by scientists, most of whom had earned doctorates from German research universities.

American scientists such as Henry Rowland admired Germany because of the high level of scientific research in the universities and institutes that drove its system of graduate education. American managers of technologically advanced firms admired Germany because of the evident success of the emergent industrial R&D programs in the German chemical and electrical industries. At the turn of the century research-based graduate education was only beginning to develop in the United States. Until 1900, no U.S. firm had founded an R&D organization comparable to those of such German firms as Bayer, BASF, and Hoechst in the chemical industry and Siemens in the electrical industry. Despite the hopes and plans of many American scientists, nothing comparable to the research system of imperial Germany existed in the United States at the turn of the century.

R&D PIONEERS IN THE UNITED STATES

Eventually, a research system comparable to but not identical with the German research system did evolve in the United States. This system took root in the first two decades of the twentieth century and was conditioned by many forces, some similar to those at work in Germany but others unique to the United States. The handful of firms that pioneered in establishing industrial research programs in the United States included General Electric (GE), American Telephone & Telegraph Co. (AT&T), E. I. du Pont de Nemours & Co. (Du Pont), and Eastman Kodak (Kodak), as well as a select number of other companies whose programs were either not as extensive or quite as influential. These other firms included General Chemical (laboratory founded in 1900), Dow (1900), Standard Oil of Indiana (1906), Goodyear (1909), and American Cyanamid (1912). Among these, only Standard Oil's research exerted considerable influence on national patterns of R&D in the period before World War I. Fortunately, we know quite a bit about the history of these firms' pioneering R&D programs, including the circumstances that brought them into being, their role vis-à-vis corporate strategies, their management and staffing, their scientific and technical achievements, and their not uncommon failures.

The founding of formal R&D programs by these manufacturers stemmed in part from competitive threats to their businesses or core technologies. General Electric, for example, which was organized from the 1892 merger of Edison General Electric and the Thomson-Houston Company, established its General Electric Research Laboratory (GERL) in 1900 in large part because its managers feared that the firm's incandescent lamp business would be rendered obsolete by new lighting technologies. These included radical improvements to gas lighting, new gas-filled electric lights that German academic and industrial scientists were developing, and a promising electric light under development by the New York inventor Peter Cooper. Even without these technological threats, GE faced entry into the highly profitable electric lamp business by new players owing to the rapid expiration of Edison's basic patents. Charles Steinmetz, GE's brilliant chief consulting engineer, feared that the company might be overwhelmed by these events in spite of its strength in electrical engineering. Believing that GE was ill-equipped to deal with chemical matters, Steinmetz finally convinced his superiors to establish a laboratory that would gather, advance, and apply the kind of chemical and electrochemical knowledge that seemed necessary to check or outdo the competition.

Hence Steinmetz, the GE consultant Elihu Thomson (cofounder of the predecessor Thomson-Houston Company and a significant independent inventor of the late nineteenth century), and company vice president Edwin Rice (who was responsible for GE's engineering and manufacturing) recruited the physical chemist Willis R. Whitney from the Massachusetts Institute of Technology to be founding director of GERL. From the very beginning of GERL, the institution was shaped by the pure-science ideology espoused by so many American scientists. Initially, Whitney, who had done his Ph.D. work in Leipzig under the famous Wilhelm Ostwald, would not consider leaving the academy completely. Rice, however, worked out an agreement with Whitney whereby the chemist would commute from Boston to Schenectady two days a week to direct research at GERL. Whitney was by no means opposed to the use of science for industrial or commercial purposes; like Henry Rowland, he had derived industrial income from his intellectual labors. But working full-time for an industrial company was another matter. Arthur D. Little once reported that in the 1890s Whitney had spurned his offer of a position with Little's consulting business at twice his MIT salary, telling Little he would rather be an academic "than be president." Indeed, although Whitney would soon recognize that the GE job offered intellectual challenges every bit as exciting as those of his MIT position, he obviously worried about his status within the profession. Many of the decisions he would make during his career at GE were driven as much by these professional concerns as they were by the company's business concerns. Consequently, even the brilliant, fiercely opinionated Steinmetz, who had helped to hire Whitney, soon began to criticize the scientist's approach to industrial research, and Steinmetz set up his own "creative engineering" organization within General Electric to do the things he thought Whitney should have been doing.

Whitney had to deal with the ideology of pure science every time he wanted to recruit a new physicist or chemist. Therefore, he had the difficult dual task of proving to his bosses that investment in science could pay off and to his academic peers and his recruits that GE's research program could compete with those of the new research universities. This burden was carried by all the research directors of the R&D pioneers, but Whitney succeeded far better than most of his counterparts in other companies. The General Electric Research Laboratory distinguished itself through its development of ductile tungsten filaments (1910) and then the gas-filled light bulb (1913), which possessed far greater efficiency than Edison's carbon-filament lamps and which outclassed the metal filament lamps developed in Europe. These lamps gave the company a highly rewarding proprietary position in the electric lamp industry and an important leg up in development of radio vacuum tubes. GERL's work on gas-filled lamps also yielded the lab's first Nobel Prize (1932) in recognition of Irving Langmuir's surface chemistry research. But for Whitney, the price was high. He suffered nervous breakdowns three times during his long tenure at GE, the first one six years after he had joined GE full-time and before the lab had begun to produce either scientifically outstanding or financially rewarding work. Whitney's last breakdown occurred when the Great Depression forced him to fire a large number of scientists, tarnishing his laboratory's and his own reputation and ending his career.

One Nobel Prize did not dramatically lessen the effects of the pure science ideal on industrial research at GE or in any firm. Suspicion about the quality of science pursued in industrial research persisted. Throughout most of the twentieth century, research directors like Whitney have had to find ways to give industrial researchers the semblance of an academic research environment. They did this by adopting liberal (though seldom unrestricted) publication policies and by giving their best researchers more latitude in choosing problems they would work on. Nevertheless, research directors always had to keep their policies within the general bounds of company management practices and consistent with the technical needs of their firms. For most of this century, industrial research has been seen by academic elitists as a poorer career option than that offered by the university or the private basic research institute.

The views of James B. Conant (1893–1978), a well-known organic chemist, head of Harvard University's department of chemistry, president of Harvard, then major shaper of World War II research policy, suggest how leading academicians and many of their students appraised industrial research in the 1920s and 1930s. In 1927, Conant's student Louis Fieser wrote to his mentor about the Du Pont Company's offer of an academic-style fundamental research position, saying, "I never expected to go into industrial work but the thing which makes a decision so difficult in this case is that I don't have to sell my soul at all; they even said that I could bring my quinones [a class of organic chemicals] along and continue my present work." Later, after he had turned down the Du Pont offer in order to stay at Bryn Mawr College, Fieser would write Conant of the excellent work being done by Du Pont chemists: "The industrialists [i.e., the Du Pont chemists] are really a keen lot, though I don't think that they compare with us academics. . . . They impress me particularly as lacking in the fine critical judgment of the best teachers, and I wonder whether this is the cause or effect of their industrial relations." After giving a seminar at Du Pont's Experimental Station, Conant would write to Fieser that "the crowd at du Pont's were the first people I met who seemed to have read my papers intelligently." Nevertheless, Conant almost turned down a simple consulting arrangement with Du Pont because he worried about being tainted, despite assurances by the important organic chemist Roger Adams that Du Pont science was as good as any in the world and would not injure the Harvard chemist's reputation. Although Conant displayed great concern that his own and his best students' reputations would suffer by being associated with Du Pont, he was not averse to recommending "a much less able man" to fill one of Du Pont's positions because he hated to see a better chemist leave the academic world. Conant's actions indicate that industrial R&D programs provided outlets for the growing numbers of scientists turned out by graduate programs at U.S. universities.

Competition drove the establishment of formal R&D programs in other pioneering firms in the United States. AT&T had initially followed the telegraph industry's practice of relying on the market for technological innovation. Over time, however, it began developing technical talent in both its tele-

phone division and its manufacturing arm, Western Electric. The expiration of the major Bell patents and growth of its network pushed innovative activity in the Bell system in the 1890s. Late in the first decade of this century the company faced another serious competitive threat, radio, which if not controlled might render its investment in wires obsolete. In response, AT&T launched a major research program in 1909, staffed by physicists (most of whom were trained in European graduate programs and some of whom did brilliant science) and theoretically inclined engineers. These researchers conducted work in electronics and communications and circuit theory with the goal of controlling radio. At the same time, AT&T's research was also driven by the adoption of an aggressive company strategy to build what company president Theodore Vail called "universal service," which ultimately translated into developing coast-to-coast telecommunications capabilities from anywhere in the system. Supported by Vail, chief engineer and research director J. J. Carty committed the company to coast-to-coast long-distance service by 1915. The technical problems of controlling radio and coast-to-coast telephone transmission were intimately related. As the historian Leonard Reich has shown, the R&D efforts coordinated by Carty and his assistant, physicist Frank B. Jewett, gave large-scale industrial R&D a permanent place in the Bell organization. By 1925, when Bell Laboratories was formally incorporated as a subsidiary of the company, AT&T labs would employ more than thirty-six hundred staff members and operate on a budget in excess of $12 million—by far the largest R&D program in the United States. (In 1925 Du Pont spent slightly less than $2 million, and GE spent about $1.4 million.)

Du Pont also faced competitive challenges, but its potential competitor was the U.S. government. During the 1890s, the navy had encouraged Du Pont to develop manufacturing capabilities and capacity in the new military propellant known as guncotton or smokeless powder (nitrocellulose). Du Pont had long supplied the slower and far smokier black powder to the navy and army. But after developing these new capabilities, and especially after a new generation of Du Pont family members began in 1903 to consolidate roughly two-thirds of the American explosives industry, some members of the military and Congress determined that the government should not be dependent on a "trust" for powder or for innovation in explosives.

Du Pont established the forerunner to its Experimental Station—what it called the General Experimental Laboratory—in 1903 to develop, among other things, improved products and processes for smokeless powder and deeper understanding of nitrocellulose chemistry. The company had already opened a highly successful R&D laboratory associated with its high-explosives division in 1902. That lab was created mostly to gain better control over manufacturing processes, to develop safer high explosives that would meet anticipated regulations for "permissible" explosives, and to lower manufacturing costs. Du Pont's R&D on smokeless powder yielded staggeringly successful results. It proved to be the means by which the company retained all its smokeless powder capacity (that is, *all* the smokeless powder capacity in the United States) after Du Pont was found guilty of violating the Sherman Antitrust Act in 1912. Through the intercession of the military, which recognized that Du Pont had devoted considerable sums to innovation in smokeless powder, the antitrust consent decree left this segment of Du Pont's explosives business intact, just in time for the outbreak of World War I in Europe. (Du Pont was, however, forced to divest two-thirds of each of its other two divisions, high explosives and black powder.) Thanks to its position in smokeless powder, money poured into Du Pont's coffers.

Competition and fear of government antitrust action also drove George Eastman to found his highly productive laboratory at Kodak Park in Rochester, New York, in 1912. As the German synthetic dye industry matured, many German firms put their researchers to the task of developing other fine chemicals, including pharmaceutical products and photographic chemicals as well as film. Eastman had long been committed to innovation; keeping ahead of the competition by continual product innovation had been official strategy since at least 1896. As Kodak's business continued to expand, however, it came to rely more and more heavily on the German chemical industry for its intermediates and photographic chemicals. Such reliance on firms that were aggressively building a strong international presence in Kodak's product lines posed a real threat to the firm's long-term health. While at a dinner on a business trip to Europe in late 1911 or early 1912, Eastman sat next to Carl Duisberg, the head of Friedrich Bayer, A.G., who had been the founding director of Bayer's research laboratory two decades earlier. Duisberg casually told Eastman that several hundred Ph.D. chemists were employed in Bayer's research laboratory, and he wondered how this figure compared to Kodak's research organization. Eastman was apparently too embarrassed to tell Duisberg that he

had no research laboratory and employed only a few chemists in development. At the same time, Eastman had grown alarmed about reports that Kodak was a subject of investigations of monopolies by the Justice Department's beefed-up antitrust division. In April 1912, the antitrust advocate (and later Supreme Court justice) Louis Brandeis, an outspoken critic of big business, addressed the City Club in Rochester, saying that large companies "wouldn't do any research because they were self-satisfied with their positions and didn't need any technical advice." Within a few months, Eastman had established a research laboratory.

One can speculate whether Eastman took this step merely to bring his company into vogue; unquestionably, fads have occasionally characterized twentieth-century U.S. business practices, including the management of R&D. Or perhaps Eastman resolved to build a world-class research laboratory because he realized how the growing antitrust climate in the United States as well as threats of international competition made rationalization, including organized R&D, imperative. Whatever his reason or motivation, his research laboratory at Kodak Park, directed by the brilliant English chemist C. E. Kenneth Mees, was highly successful and provided the company with the basis for successful innovation for a long time. Mees wrote the first textbook on managing industrial research published in the United States, if not the world, *The Organization of Industrial Scientific Research* (1920). Under Mees's guidance, Kodak's R&D program played a major role in Eastman's change of strategy away from horizontal combination toward vertical integration. This shift served not only to move the company away from increasingly suspect business practices but also to lessen Kodak's dependence on German intermediates and photographic chemicals and other products.

Several patterns, consistent with those elaborated by Alfred D. Chandler in his book, *Scale and Scope: The Dynamics of Industrial Capitalism* (1990), emerge from this survey of the R&D pioneers. The leading firms in science-based industries created formal R&D programs at roughly the same time and for many of the same reasons. First, competition and the threat of core technologies being undermined led executives, often in response to the urging of technically and scientifically gifted managers, to establish research and development programs independent of manufacturing and sales functions. These new R&D units were charged with the goal of providing for the long-term security of the firms' technology—"industrial life insurance," as GE's Whitney liked to call it. Second, the pioneering industrial R&D programs were frequently created in the context of federal antitrust action; they were part of a movement to rationalize and vertically integrate companies that corporate leaders believed would overcome the objections to large-scale industry that had surfaced at the end of the nineteenth century. Third, these pioneer firms invested in R&D for the same reason that they invested in manufacturing and marketing; investment in R&D was part of the development of managerial hierarchies in large-scale American enterprise, a development in which the R&D function (the generation and application of knowledge) was internalized within the firm rather than being left solely to "the market." Finally, industrial R&D played an important role in the diversification and long-run success of those firms in the twentieth century.

INDUSTRIAL RESEARCH BY PRIVATE RESEARCH INSTITUTES

The rise of the R&D pioneers in the early part of the twentieth century was accompanied by the significant development of private, contract research laboratories. This development reflected both the growing enthusiasm for industrial research in the United States and signs of maturation in the American research system. In 1896 Arthur D. Little, an important advocate of industrial research, established a firm that carried out chemical analyses for various companies that did not have their own analytical capabilities. Little's company then began to conduct larger studies for corporate clients of what today would be called the strategic possibilities of new technologies, and it actually got involved in some development projects for clients. Arthur D. Little, Inc., was not widely imitated at first, but as it expanded it eventually met with competition from both private for-profit organizations and private nonprofit research institutes.

The Mellon Institute in Pittsburgh represented yet another development in the American system of industrial research. The Pittsburgh-based bankers and venture capitalists (and brothers) Andrew and Richard Mellon brought sometime-chemist, sometime-prophet Robert Kennedy Duncan to the University of Pittsburgh in 1910 with the idea of replicating and expanding what Duncan had done at the University of Kansas. There, Duncan had created and promoted (with much less success than the Mellons were led to believe) a program of "industrial fellowships."

Firms would support advanced graduate students, who would in turn conduct project research for those supporting firms as part of their graduate studies. With the generous financial support of its benefactors, the Mellon Institute was established in 1913 to do contract research and operate a program of industrial fellowships. Together, these two sources of revenue were supposed to make the new institution self-sustaining. In fact, despite impressive early growth of contracts and industrial fellowships, the Mellon Institute always lost money; the Mellon brothers and their heirs poured enormous sums into the institute to keep it afloat. Yet the Mellon Institute won high praise and attracted imitators, and such private contract research firms have played an important role in the American system of industrial research.

The economist David Mowery has given us a precise—and ironic—picture of exactly what that role has been. The Mellon Institute and its imitators were created in large part with the idea of providing R&D capabilities to smaller firms that could not establish, say, a General Electric Research Laboratory, a Kodak Park, or a Du Pont Experimental Station. In practice, however, these contract research institutes were more used by those firms with strong in-house research capabilities (Du Pont, Kodak, etc.) to supplement their own research than by firms without internal research capabilities. Those firms with their own R&D organizations typically employed private research institutes such as Mellon to handle what they deemed routine types of research.

By the time the Mellon Institute was created in 1913, Arthur Little had become president of the American Chemical Society (ACS). He had also become a major, vocal proponent of organized industrial research in the United States, and invariably he held up as a model the German chemical industry, which then totally dominated the world markets in dyestuffs and pharmaceutical products. In a widely reprinted ACS presidential address, Little celebrated how U.S. industry had taken up industrial research. He detailed instance after instance of American triumphs in industrial research and implicitly compared them to those of Germany, which was on the verge of war. Little estimated that, in addition to a small number of private institutes and trade associations, about fifty U.S. firms had formal R&D organizations. A close reading of Little's 1913 speech suggests that American industrial research was then in its early adolescence. But the needs and opportunities posed by World War I allowed the American system of industrial research to mature rapidly.

WORLD WAR I

The outbreak of war in Europe in 1914 and the eventual entry of the United States into the conflict in 1917 proved critical catalysts for the rapid growth of industrial research and development in the United States. The British embargo of Germany threatened—and eventually choked off—the supply of dyestuffs and pharmaceuticals to the United States. At the time, the United States was almost wholly dependent on Germany for these and many other chemical products. Consequently, the United States government developed and implemented a program to promote domestic industries capable of producing dyestuffs, pharmaceuticals, and other synthetic organic chemicals during the war and of competing with Germany after the war. (There is nothing like confiscating manufacturing plants, patents, and trademarks and then implementing a large tariff to help an industry get started.) Firms that already had research capabilities, such as Du Pont and Kodak, used the wartime circumstances to diversify their businesses. They and other R&D pioneers also provided models for other firms to follow in establishing their own R&D programs. The chemical industry also got a boost from the research conducted by and for the Chemical Warfare Service and from the industry's manufacture of several types of poison gas. The pharmaceutical industry also benefited from some of the work done within the Chemical Warfare Service and from the need to produce drugs deemed vital for the nation's defense, such as the German-made, proprietary antisyphilis drug Salvarsan.

Although one or two American pharmaceutical companies had established some type of R&D program before the war (most notably Parke-Davis in 1902), the United States had only meager drug-synthesis and development capabilities compared to those of Germany. The threat of a cut-off of supplies of German pharmaceutical products led to significant new initiatives in the U.S. pharmaceutical industry and in American pharmacology, many initiated by the federal government. Like the nascent American dyestuffs industry, the pharmaceutical industry benefited from the confiscation of German drug patents by the Alien Property Custodian and their open licensing through the Chemical Foundation. After the war, most large American drug firms built extensive R&D laboratories and began major programs of collaboration with universities, which soon led to some very important drug developments. Interestingly, the academics in the American Society for Pharmacology, sharing a pure-science idealism with physicists like Henry Rowland, banned industrial scientists from being members of the society until the 1940s.

The American chemical and pharmaceutical industries were by no means the only ones affected by the war. World War I has been interpreted as being both the last old-style war and the first modern one. Submarines, airplanes, and wireless communications were used with varying degrees of effectiveness. The United States needed to develop these instruments of war and methods to counter them. The profound impact produced by these wartime needs on developments in industrial R&D can be seen in several areas.

First, as historian Daniel Kevles wrote in *The Physicists* (1978), scientists in the American research universities seized on the war in Europe and the perceived total lack of American preparedness as the opportunity to build world-class science in America. "I really believe this is the greatest chance we ever had to advance research in America," exclaimed George Ellery Hale, the astrophysicist and creator of Caltech, after the National Academy of Sciences (NAS) voted in 1916 to place the nation's scientific elite at the disposal of the federal government. Assisted by the chemist A. A. Noyes and the physicist Robert A. Millikan, two other outstanding scientists whom he would later attract to Caltech, Hale became the leader of this movement. Until then, NAS had largely been an honorific society, but Hale hoped to transform it into the central body conducting and directing scientific research in the United States on a scale and at a level of quality that would rival that of any nation in the world. Because they deemed NAS moribund, Hale and his cohort maneuvered to create the National Research Council (NRC) as the research arm of NAS but under the cohort's control. Their success in creating the NRC in 1916 stemmed from their theory—and its acceptance by the Wilson administration—that science and scientists could contribute to the war effort. To help their cause—indeed to legitimate it—Hale, Millikan, and Noyes enlisted the support of GE's Whitney, who had been Hale's classmate and Noyes's student and later colleague at MIT.

Throughout the entire period of war preparations and much of the war, the NRC's principal goal was to build the kind of scientific establishments that Henry Rowland had alluded to in 1883 and that Germany already had in its universities, the Kaiser Wilhelm institutes, the Physikalisch-Technische Reichsanstalt, and other research institutions. This was a case of pure opportunism on the part of Hale, Millikan, Noyes, and their followers. Indeed, Whitney's biographer George Wise stresses that during that critical year of 1916, Whitney and Hale spent as much or more time discussing how to get the government permanently committed to supporting science than they spent considering how to find submarines or fix nitrogen. . . . [Their] efforts [to promote research] distracted American scientists from the job of mobilizing science for defense in 1916. . . . Whitney and his contemporaries put the job of promoting science first with nearly fatal consequences to the defense technology effort.

This is not to say that Hale, Millikan, and Noyes and the university scientists who temporarily left their academic posts to serve the nation did not succeed in bringing science to bear on such difficult technical problems as chemical warfare and submarine detection. Certainly they did. Their success convinced them that professional scientists could contribute more to weapons development than could organizations such as the Naval Consulting Board (NCB). In collaboration with Thomas Edison, Secretary of the Navy Josephus Daniels created the NCB in 1915 and assembled its members under the leadership of the famous but aging inventor. The NCB was made up of leading inventors and representatives from most of the professional engineering societies, but it lacked representation from the National Academy of Sciences and some of the nation's other leading scientific societies, such as the American Physical Society. The NCB screened ideas for weapons submitted by American citizens in response to Daniels's and Edison's appeal to the nation for the ideas of its best and brightest inventors. Americans submitted some 100,000 ideas for weapons great and small, but the Naval Consulting Board found only one or two of these ideas worthy of further consideration. Most of them were tallied in the "crackpot" column. The age of the heroic inventor, if that age had ever existed, was over.

But the Naval Consulting Board debacle did have one long-lasting outcome. Backed by the other members of the board, Edison convinced Daniels and Congress to create a research laboratory within the navy (although Edison and the NCB members split over where the laboratory should be built). Today's Naval Research Laboratory traces its origins to World War I and the NCB. The construction and staffing of the laboratory shortly after the war was really something of a miracle considering that so many schemes and plans that had been hatched during the war were quickly abandoned after the armistice. The Naval Research Laboratory would carry out important research in the interwar period, including some pioneering work on radar.

One other World War I–era creation also survived the war, and it had an important impact on the development of both civil and military aviation. This was the research program and facilities of the National Advisory Committee on Aeronautics (NACA). At its research facilities, which included large wind tunnels and other equipment, NACA generated an enormous amount of fundamental knowledge in aerodynamics, airframe design, aircraft testing, and many other areas. NACA served its patrons and clients so well that it was transformed into the National Aeronautics and Space Administration (NASA) when the space race began in the late 1950s.

Finally, the war brought widespread attention within industry to the existence, organization, management, and achievement of the research laboratories of the R&D pioneers. The founding research directors at GE, Du Pont, Kodak, and AT&T—Willis Whitney, Charles Reese, Kenneth Mees, and J. J. Carty and Frank Jewett, respectively—moved into the limelight as they advised military, government, and industry figures on how scientific research could be harnessed for technological development.

Whitney and his counterparts at AT&T brought together their firm's best researchers at government facilities, called experimental stations, at Nahant, Massachusetts, and slightly later at New London, Connecticut, to work on the problem of submarine detection. (The creation of two separate facilities reflected a dispute over submarine detection between the Naval Consulting Board and the National Research Council that caught Whitney in the middle because he was a member of both organizations. Despite turf battles, however, the industrial researchers and the academics carried through.) Whitney assigned Irving Langmuir, who had already done the work for which he later won the Nobel Prize, and Charles Eveleth, who would later take charge of all of GE's manufacturing, to work on the problem. Two future presidents of Bell Laboratories, Harold D. Arnold and Oliver E. Buckley, were part of the AT&T contingent. Millikan himself, who had said that submarine detection was a "problem of physics pure and simple," worked with these industrial researchers and learned firsthand about the strengths and limitations of project research undertaken by first-rate scientists and electrical engineers. As head of the NRC's subcommittee on submarine detection, Millikan monitored the work at the New London Experimental Station, which at the time of the Armistice in November 1918 was staffed by thirty-two university professors and seven hundred enlisted men. More important, the teams at the two installations actually succeeded in developing successful submarine detection equipment, which helped solve a major problem of prosecuting the war in Europe and eased public fears of the German U-boat menace.

The wartime emergency brought industrial research programs under the purview of the National Research Council. The NRC established the Advisory Committee on Industrial Research, which in turn initiated the nation's first efforts to compile statistics and other information on industrial R&D programs. Reese, Whitney, and the other pioneering R&D directors published pieces on the benefits and management of industrial research and worked under the NRC's banner to promote industrial R&D. Kodak's Mees, for example, published an influential article in *Science* that became the basis of his textbook on the management of industrial R&D. In the article, he stressed that firms and industries "must earnestly devote time and money to the investigation of the fundamental theory underlying the subject in which they are interested." These efforts led to the establishment by several firms of research programs modeled on Kodak's, GE's, and other R&D pioneers' programs. For example, Westinghouse Electric founded a basic research program as prescribed by Mees and went so far as to recruit a Kodak scientist to manage the program. This program resulted in extensive scientific publication by the research staff recruited by Mees's protégé, including papers by the future Nobel Prize–winner Arthur H. Compton. But the program was essentially disbanded in 1920 by Westinghouse managers who did not share the enthusiasm for basic research.

Significantly, the NRC's efforts during World War I led Whitney, Reese, Mees, and others after the war to form a new organization, the Directors of Industrial Research (DIR), still very much alive today. Not affiliated with NAS, NRC, or any government agency, the DIR provided a critical forum in which research directors could informally share information on such topics as starting salaries for scientists with doctoral degrees, publication policies, and coordination of research in a diversified firm. In addition, members of the DIR hosted one- and two-day tours of their firms' research facilities for the entire organization. These sometimes elaborate events not only served as a means of seeing what kind of R&D facilities other corporations had built, but they also gave less-fortunate research managers considerable ammunition to use in convincing their firms' top management to expand their research facilities and programs.

Without question, therefore, World War I led to widespread quickening of interest in and enthusiasm for industrial R&D in the United States. The research programs of the R&D pioneers became exemplars for other corporations, and their founding directors became national leaders in the field. The war also gave the inheritors of Henry Rowland's pure-science idealism the wedge with which they hoped to open up institutional, governmental, industrial, and public support for pure science, which academic scientists had so desperately sought since the mid-nineteenth century.

THE INTERWAR PERIOD

Although most Americans sought what President Warren G. Harding called a "return to normalcy" following the war, many academic scientists did not. Mobilization for war had barely begun, it seemed, when the armistice was declared. The research infrastructure that Hale, Millikan, and others had started to put in place was by no means complete and was threatened by any return to normalcy. With some avenues closed, these scientists pledged themselves to exploiting existing channels for achieving "best science" as well as opening up new ones. They won a permanent charter for the National Research Council as a government-sanctioned (but not government-financed or -controlled) body acting on behalf of American science. They also found support from the Rockefeller Foundation for doctoral and postdoctoral research fellowships governed by the NRC.

Industry began to do its part vis-à-vis science education. Du Pont was among the first companies to offer "no strings attached" fellowships. In 1918, at research director Charles Reese's urging, Du Pont gave eighteen fellowships and thirty-three scholarships to particular institutions with strong programs in chemistry and chemical engineering. By 1940 some two hundred companies were offering more than seven hundred fellowships. These fellowships were fundamentally different from those advocated in the first decade of the twentieth century by Robert Kennedy Duncan and that had led to the creation of the Mellon Institute.

Hale, Millikan, and others then moved to create a German-style research institute, a national scientific laboratory devoted to basic research that would be managed and controlled by the scientists themselves. In 1919 the Carnegie Corporation gave Hale $5 million, a third of which was to be used to build a new home for the NAS and the remainder of which was to be used for NRC activities. Hale tried to supplement the Carnegie endowment with federal monies for NRC research programs, but it soon became clear that neither Congress nor the administration wanted to support basic science without political and programmatic controls. The NRC positioned itself to address issues deemed vital to the nation, but it met with limited success.

Failing in Washington, Hale, Millikan, and Noyes shifted their focus to a sleepy technical institute in Pasadena, California, and soon transformed it into a major scientific and technological research university: the California Institute of Technology, or Caltech for short. Hale's warning in 1916 that after the shooting stopped Germany would conduct an "industrial war" with the Allies resonated with Millikan's postwar analysis that "the War has taught the manufacturer that he can not hope to keep in the lead of his industry save through the brains of a research group, which alone can keep him in the forefront of progress." In a 1920 book called *The New World of Science,* Hale and Millikan exploited the gains made during the war to seek substantial private and private-foundation support for science and scientific research at Caltech. By pursuing "best science" at Caltech, they and their colleagues would serve the nation in peace as they had in war. Millikan declared, "As a result of all this [i.e., the war], there is indeed a new opportunity in every phase and branch of science." Hale and Millikan succeeded with their objectives at Caltech, and other scientists succeeded at their own research universities. But the advocates of "best science," including Hale and Millikan, fell short in winning permanent, unfettered, and unquestioning support for pure science, either from the government or from industry.

This failure is best illustrated by the mid-1920s effort to build a National Research Endowment led by the "Great Engineer" Herbert Hoover. Secretary of commerce at the time and a hero for his coordination of war relief in Europe following the armistice, Hoover led a campaign conceived by Hale, Millikan, and other NRC members to raise an endowment of $20 million, principally from industry. Hoover became a champion of pure science, arguing that both industrial and social progress depended on it. But only a few corporate donors contributed to the campaign despite appeals by Hoover and other members of the fund's board, which included Andrew Mellon, AT&T's J. J. Carty, GE's Owen D. Young, and Sears's Julius Rosenwald, among others. By 1932, the effort was declared stillborn. Hoover's message about pure science, however, served as a catalyst, pushing several corporate R&D programs either

to build fundamental research into their ongoing R&D programs or to increase spending for pure research. And the general enthusiasm for research led hundreds of corporations that had never performed any R&D to found laboratories in the interwar period.

Using data initially gathered by the National Research Council, the economist David Mowery has assembled and published figures that document this trend (in *Technology and the Pursuit of Economic Growth,* 1989). Between 1919 and 1936 some 1,150 industrial research laboratories were established by U.S. manufacturing firms, or roughly 54 percent of all industrial R&D laboratories founded from the beginning of industrial research until 1946. In 1921, 2,775 research professionals (scientists and research engineers) worked in industrial research establishments. This figure grew to 6,320 in 1927, 10,927 in 1933, and 27,777 in 1940. Even in the Great Depression, industrial research grew rapidly.

Research leaders such as Whitney and Mees declared that enormous dividends were available to any industrial company that would found a scientific research laboratory. These statements, coupled with the national campaign for efficiency engineered by Herbert Hoover when he was secretary of commerce and Hoover's statements about the commercial benefits of science, created a national frenzy for industrial R&D. By 1925, the General Electric Research Laboratory was known nationwide as the "House of Magic" in which scientists carried out modern miracles. The National Research Council launched a campaign run by the director of its division of engineering, Maurice Holland, to sell industrial R&D as the "royal road to riches." Holland and the NRC would go on to establish in 1938 the Industrial Research Institute (IRI), an association of industrial research programs and managers, which in 1945 incorporated as an organization independent of the NRC. The IRI continues to engage in both research on industrial research and lobbying on behalf of its members.

Given the campaigns to promote industrial research and the widespread public attention they generated during the 1920s and 1930s, leaders of those technologically based corporations that did not have any formally designated research and development organization felt out of step; such was the case at United States Steel. From the time of its formation in 1901 as a result of the largest, most famous, and most expensive merger in U.S. history, U.S. Steel had carried out all its developmental work in technical organizations located throughout the company's various divisions—divisions that corresponded closely to the formerly separate companies that had merged. These divisions did virtually no scientific research, and no research was done at the corporate level. Unlike Du Pont and dozens of other companies that had grown or been created through mergers, U.S. Steel had not rationalized its operations by closing down inefficient plants; it did not coordinate manufacturing across the former companies until long after the merger. And unlike many of these firms that had built R&D organizations as part of the process of rationalization, U.S. Steel created its research organization in 1926–1927 because industrial R&D was then in fashion.

As the historian Paul Tiffany has documented, U.S. Steel's top managers and directors knew almost nothing about scientific research either inside or outside the universities or about industrial R&D in general, even though the company operated a large number of product development and control laboratories spread throughout its many divisions and plants. In the mid-1920s the board of directors decided that, given all the attention Hoover had called to scientific industrial research, U.S. Steel ought to have a central R&D organization that would do scientific research. They appointed one of their own, George Crawford, the president of U.S. Steel's Tennessee Coal, Iron, and Railroad Company, to search for a suitable candidate to head the laboratory. Crawford visited Frank Jewett, president of Bell Labs, the largest industrial R&D organization in the world. Coincidentally, Robert Millikan was also visiting Jewett, and together, the two men recommended four possible candidates. Millikan also agreed to advise Crawford and the steel company on how to set up a research laboratory.

Subsequently, Crawford interviewed the four people recommended by Jewett and Millikan, plus seventeen other scientists. By March 1927, after receiving a four-page report from Millikan about how to organize the projected lab, Crawford and his committee had decided whom to hire. They came into a board meeting with a unanimous recommendation that the new research director should be none other that Millikan himself! At this time Millikan was president of Caltech, had recently received the Nobel Prize in physics, and was a major proponent of "best science" in the United States. Minutes of the board meeting make clear that the steel men knew little about Millikan; some were more concerned that he play golf than that his credentials included a Nobel Prize. Judge Elbert Gary, chairman of the board, then proceeded to telegraph Millikan and, without

telling him why, asked him to come east to talk to the board. Incredible as it sounds, these steel men assumed that, once they had assured themselves that Millikan was an "all-right fellow," if they asked him to become the founding director of U.S. Steel research, he would immediately accept the honor. They understood neither Millikan nor the politics of pure science in the United States. A gentleman and a diplomat, Millikan refrained from laughing in the board members' faces and politely refused. The board then offered the job to Jewett, who also declined (he was already president of one of the greatest research organizations of the twentieth century).

Millikan and Jewett again kindly offered the U.S. Steel board their help in recruiting a good scientist to establish and direct U.S. Steel's new department of technology and research. Soon, with Millikan's and Jewett's urging, the Yale University chemist John Johnston, one of the four they had originally recommended, signed on with U.S. Steel. Poor Johnston was not aware until later how little the company's board knew or cared about research and how little support he would receive. His research division was consigned to an old industrial building in Kearney, New Jersey, and received far less research money than Johnston had been promised.

How many of the hundreds of firms that established R&D programs in the 1920s did so for the same reasons as U.S. Steel? How many did so because they saw real immediate short- or long-term benefits from industrial R&D? In the absence of reliable histories of each individual case, the answers to these questions are uncertain. But as Mowery's figures make clear, the number of R&D programs and researchers in those programs rose markedly in the 1920s and, despite some very large layoffs in the early years of the Depression, for the decade of the 1930s as well.

The interwar period is also noteworthy because of the significant science that came out of some of the industrial R&D programs in the United States. Of course, GE's Irving Langmuir had already done the research that led to his Nobel Prize in 1932, but he continued to turn out excellent science, which in turn helped GE recruit other outstanding scientists. In 1927, only two years after AT&T had created Bell Labs to conduct the majority of its research, the physicist Clinton J. Davisson began his work on electron diffraction that led to his 1937 Nobel Prize in physics, the first of many Nobel Prizes that have been won by Bell Labs researchers. Davisson's science did not lead to any revolutionary new products, nor did it dramatically transform Bell's technology, but it furthered Bell Labs' understanding of electron behavior by confirming that electrons were diffracted by a target (such as an element in a vacuum tube) in the way predicted by wave mechanics. Moreover, Davisson and Germer's publication on electron diffraction in the *Physical Review* in 1927 served as a clear sign of the quality of science done at Bell Labs.

Outstanding fundamental research performed in industrial R&D laboratories occasionally produced some rather different outcomes, as is shown by Du Pont's experiences in the late 1920s and early 1930s. In 1928, a young organic chemist named Wallace H. Carothers left an instructorship at Harvard to join a Du Pont program devoted exclusively to fundamental research. The company had recently established the program within its central research department, in part as a response to Hoover's call for more basic research. Carothers had been hired to head a group in organic chemistry, and he had been especially encouraged to focus his research on polymers. Although he had never worked in this area, Carothers was well aware that chemists were intensely debating the nature of polymers. One school of thought believed that polymers were aggregates of colloidal particles held together by special forces that did not operate like ordinary covalent chemical bonds. Another school, led by the German chemist Hermann Staudinger, believed that polymers were "macromolecules" made up of ordinary molecules bound together by ordinary bonds, but nobody had been able to prove this. In a little over two years, however, Carothers and his team of young Ph.D. organic chemists built a massively documented case in favor of the Staudinger view. Carothers published two landmark papers, one of which developed the general theory of polymers, or macromolecules, and the other of which described and gave lasting names to the basic processes of polymerization.

Carothers's work was disseminated rapidly owing to the initially unrestricted publications policy of Du Pont's fundamental research program. Both the work and the freedom to publish brought critical acclaim to Du Pont's research community. But in 1930, things changed. New leadership in Du Pont's central research division, increased pressure stemming from the nation's worsening economic situation, and (most importantly) two very important discoveries by Carothers's group hastened the change. The first discovery was a polymer Carothers named chloroprene, which had a chemical formula directly analogous to that of isoprene (natural rubber). Chloroprene possessed rubberlike properties and could be processed in the same way as rubber. More importantly,

unlike rubber, it was highly resistant to degradation by gasoline and oil, which suggested that it had important marketable properties. Carothers and his group had synthesized the world's first wholly synthetic rubber, later known as neoprene.

That same month (March 1930), owing to some creative laboratory techniques, Carothers's group polymerized a high-molecular-weight aliphatic polyester and discovered that it could be spun into a filament and then "cold drawn" (stretched, which aligned the polymeric chains, thus yielding much finer and stronger filaments). This was the world's first wholly synthetic fiber, and the research that produced it would lead in 1934 to Carothers's synthesis of nylon.

These two discoveries transformed Carothers's research program from one devoted to pure research to one focused on "pioneering" research. Instead of seeking deeper knowledge about polymers or polymerization, Carothers and his group were now dedicated to finding commercially viable products. On chloroprene, Carothers and his group published twenty-three papers, which he said were "abundant in quantity but a little disappointing in quality." They also worked to synthesize a polymer that could be spun and drawn into a fiber having properties qualitatively similar to natural fibers but possessing a high melting point and stability in water (unlike the first group of synthetic fibers they had polymerized and spun in March 1930). Ironically, discoveries in Carothers's lab and his group's unmatched capabilities in polymer synthesis and manipulation proved to be the group's undoing.

Although the group's work on neoprene was turned over to Du Pont's organic chemicals department, which had its own significant research capabilities in organic synthesis and rubber chemistry, the pursuit of a synthetic fiber remained with Carothers's lab. After working intensely to find a polymer with all the right properties and failing in that effort, Carothers returned to more fundamental research work. He did some very interesting work on large-ring compounds (as opposed to simple linear polymers), which, as with all his work, he published in the leading chemical journals. But when this work was finished and Carothers seemed uncertain where to go next, his research director—who had once been opposed to Du Pont's undertaking any fundamental research—encouraged him to return to the synthetic fiber problem, which he did. In a matter of a few weeks, Carothers's team, pursuing a synthesis route laid out by Carothers, discovered a class of polymers known as polyamids; the product that emerged from this work—nylon—gave Du Pont its first commercial blockbuster. Put on the market in 1940, nylon had by the 1990s earned the company as much as twenty to twenty-five billion dollars.

By 1940, a formula seemed to be emerging, at least at Du Pont and soon in other quarters. The formula seemed quite simple: Do world-class fundamental scientific research, and you will find important new products. You can then commercialize and profit from these products enormously because they will be completely proprietary. World War II, which had already broken out in Europe by the time nylon hit the market, served to confirm and ratify this formula a dozen times over. The war years would be a decisive watershed in the history of industrial R&D in the United States.

WORLD WAR II

The atom bomb, radar, the proximity fuse, antibiotics, the digital electronic computer, and numerous new materials, theories, and analytical techniques all emerged from the concentrated efforts of university scientists brought together to address the emergency caused by World War II. The scientific community in the United States had been looking for such an opportunity since the return to normalcy following World War I. Science and scientists came out of the war as heros, not as revered as Eisenhower or MacArthur but nonetheless held in awe.

World War II produced the Age of Big Science. The shibboleth of this new age was that basic science and well-funded scientists produced dramatic new technologies and that scientists knew better than generals, engineers, or industrialists what new science to pursue, which new technologies to develop, and how best to deploy those new technologies. Seldom have the lessons of war been more fundamentally misunderstood. Seldom have such misunderstandings been more important: they governed the course of national policy and the direction of American industrial R&D until the 1960s.

What contemporaries, including those who should have known better, overlooked was that none of these new technologies and products could have emerged without the enormous engineering and manufacturing know-how and capabilities of the nation's corporations. The Manhattan Project—which built the atomic bomb—itself depended on the advanced engineering, construction, and operational capabilities of numerous firms, from the engineering firm of Stone & Webster to manufacturing companies such as General Electric, Westinghouse, Union Carbide, M. W. Kellogg, and Du Pont. Even more

overlooked was the degree to which the nation's capabilities in mass production, rather than the absorbing and ultimately earth-shattering actions of a group of brilliant physicists on a mountaintop in New Mexico or in a laboratory in Chicago, actually determined the course of the war.

Yet the corporations that geared up to mass-produce war matériel, the engineers who designed products and production processes, the toolmakers who built the production equipment, and the workers who did the work failed to capture the public's imagination in the same way the scientists did. In numerous newspaper and magazine articles and in uncritical books such as James P. Baxter's Pulitzer Prize–winning *Scientists against Time* (1946), scientists were portrayed as the saviors of the nation. This misreading was further compounded by the carefully orchestrated actions of the nation's scientific elite, who sought above all else to achieve the permanent support for science that the profession had tried to garner since the mid-nineteenth century and that had particularly eluded them after World War I.

Vannevar Bush, an electrical engineer by training, had, with the assistance of the chemist James B. Conant, directed the nation's wartime efforts in science and technology. Bush manipulated the Roosevelt White House to request a study on postwar science policy. To carry out this work Bush assembled a team of scientists who shared a pure-science ideology. Together, Bush and his team issued a document that established the new catechism. Bush played on two generations of Americans who had been taught, thanks to the historian Frederick Jackson Turner, that the frontier had shaped the destiny, character, and institutions of the United States. He titled the report *Science—The Endless Frontier.* Whereas the American frontier had been officially closed in 1890 (a fact that troubled Turner and all who believed in the transforming power of the frontier), Bush promised Americans an endless frontier through science. By building and supporting institutions committed to "best science" and governed by scientists, Americans would reap an endless bounty of new technologies that would ease their burdens and bring wealth to the United States and stability to the world. Without these institutions, Americans faced dim prospects because the war had seriously harmed many of the scientific institutions in Europe on which American science had long depended.

Daniel Kevles and other historians have described and analyzed how Bush's agenda was actually played out in Washington after the report was issued in July 1945. The details need not detain us, except to note that the creation of the National Science Foundation (NSF) in 1950 was a pyrrhic victory for Bush. He had promoted the creation of the NSF to support basic research in universities. But he had then done battle for five years with President Harry S. Truman, who sought democratic control of government-sponsored science rather than supporting science and scientists without providing for their accountability. As Kevles and others show, by 1950 the military, once critical of "wild-haired scientists," had become the largest funder of basic research in the United States.

Although Bush and Truman and their respective followers battled over democratic controls of science, no one ever questioned Bush's linear model of new science as the principal source of new technology. American industry firmly embraced the Bush model, with the exception of Bush's belief that all basic research should be done in the universities. In the postwar period, increasing numbers of companies that previously had no R&D programs created them in response to wartime developments. For example, in 1945 Thomas J. Watson, Sr., the founder and president of International Business Machines (IBM), created a new department of pure science within his company and hired the astronomer Wallace Eckert to direct it. In 1949, Ernest Breech, a former manager of General Motors's Bendix Division who had been hired by the young Henry Ford II to help him rebuild the ailing Ford Motor Company, wrote to his boss, "I am convinced that Ford will not have many 'firsts' unless we get a few good thinkers and have a real research department." By "real research," Breech clearly meant scientific research. In mid-1951 Ford established within its Dearborn Engineering Laboratory a new "scientific laboratory" dedicated, according to its founding director, to "fundamental research and development in fields broadly related to the basic character of Ford Motor Company— transportation." Soon basic research in physics and chemistry was being pursued at Ford, a marked departure for a company that had been built around the homespun practicality of the first Henry Ford.

Firms that already had R&D programs dramatically expanded them near war's end and in the immediate postwar years, and they especially directed their expansions at fundamental research. Du Pont provides a good example of the new paradigm's power. Even before Pearl Harbor, Du Pont had begun to plan for the postwar era. The thinking of its executives was conditioned by several developments. First, they saw the dramatic expansion of the Antitrust Division of the Department of Justice and the continued anti–big

business sentiment in critical circles of Congress and the Roosevelt administration during the war. Second, they observed the tremendous success of nylon. The validity of the formula derived from the company's experience with nylon grew more certain as they learned more and more about wartime science projects. And because the company had been selected by General Leslie Groves to design, build, and operate the Hanford Engineer Works in Washington State, which produced plutonium for the Manhattan Project, they knew quite a bit about wartime science projects. After the Department of Justice brought suit in 1944 against Du Pont and Britain's Imperial Chemical Industries for violation of the Sherman Act and after it charged the company with several other antitrust violations, executives arrived at the company's postwar strategy for growth: increase the company's basic research and watch "new nylons" (blockbuster products) emerge. In their discussions and memoranda written between July 1945 and early 1946 the company's executives employed language that suggests that they had carefully read Vannevar Bush's *Science—The Endless Frontier* and accepted its call for more science.

In October 1945, the director of Du Pont's central research department, who commanded enormous respect throughout the company and in the Directors of Industrial Research group, reported to the president of the company that "the country is about to enter a period of unparalleled scientific activity." Research would be expanded in the universities. Industry was poised to "undertake a very substantial expansion of personnel and of research facilities" (indeed, a Du Pont study had indicated that more than fifty new industrial R&D laboratories had recently been built and far more were being planned). Moreover, the government's actions, through the army, the navy, and the National Science Foundation proposed in Bush's report, meant that research would be conducted "on an enormous scale." There would be no return to the "normalcy" that had followed World War I because now most people believed science to be the endless frontier. Most people believed in the linear model in which all new technology derived from basic research.

The strength of Du Pont's commitment to this model is perhaps best gauged by looking at how the company implemented its plan. At the time, Du Pont was a decentralized, multidivisional firm. It had eleven operating (manufacturing) departments, each working in its own segment of the chemical industry under relatively autonomous leadership. Each department possessed its own manufacturing, marketing, and R&D divisions. In addition, the company had a central research department (the one that had discovered and done much of the development on nylon). Its central engineering department also had its own fundamental research program in chemical engineering. Over the objection of the vice president for research, who in 1927 had created central research's fundamental research program, the company's executives decided to expand each of the operating departments' research programs dramatically and to commit a sizable portion of those expansions to fundamental research. Each department, they believed, would generate a stream of "new nylons" in its respective business. The vice president who objected to this strategy argued that the R&D units of the operating departments had their hands full with their existing businesses and would not be able to run effective programs of long-term fundamental research. Moreover, he maintained that because many of the departments manufactured products that possessed a common scientific basis (for example, paints, fibers, plastics, and films were all polymeric in nature), a given departmental research unit would be likely to duplicate the others' research as well as that of the central research unit. He asserted that Du Pont should definitely expand its fundamental research but that it should be done only by the central research unit. Shortly after losing this battle, this vice president reached the mandatory retirement age of sixty-five and left the company's employ.

Under the leadership of a new chief executive officer, Crawford Greenewalt, Du Pont proceeded to expand all its research dramatically—especially its fundamental research—with the faith that "new nylons" would soon flow forth. Trained in chemical engineering at MIT, Greenewalt had been a member of Du Pont's central research department for most of his career. He had also been one of the critical leaders in the nylon development project and had then served as the liaison between Du Pont and the Metallurgical Laboratory at the University of Chicago, where the basic research in the physics of plutonium and nuclear reactors was done for the Manhattan Project. Greenewalt himself had mastered nuclear physics and had proved so capable in this new field that both Enrico Fermi and Arthur Compton had asked him to join their newly created postwar research institutes.

Building basic research programs in all Du Pont's departments had a rather profound, if unexpected, impact on the company's central research unit. To avoid duplicating the work now being done by the operating departments, the central research unit undertook work that was very far out on the horizon and in areas in which the company had little or no technical capabilities or business interests. Two decades of such programs would eventually make the central research unit vulnerable to the charge that its research, although impressive by academic standards, was simply irrelevant to the company. Indeed, some would charge that central research had become an ivory tower.

The Du Pont experience in the postwar period was by no means unique. In examining the histories of the other major R&D pioneers—General Electric, Kodak, and AT&T—one sees virtually all of them committing themselves to the same type of research program expansion and pledging more resources to fundamental research. The leaders of the other R&D pioneers made their decisions for the same reason as Du Pont: they believed in the linear model. The wartime science projects, especially the Manhattan Project, and the widespread knowledge of nylon's origins and incredible success were too big and real to be gainsaid. The faith in the linear model and in its power to yield blockbuster products grew even stronger in the 1950s after the commercial importance of the transistor became apparent to a wider audience than Bell Labs' personnel; the history of the transistor's discovery, constructed in an age of faith in the linear model, revealed the device to be a product of pure research in an enlightened laboratory. Bell Labs' reputation and the basic research of the other R&D pioneers led IBM to expand its research enormously as well. In 1956 IBM established a research division devoted to building a world-class basic research program. By 1960 the company had opened its Thomas J. Watson Research Center, a massive laboratory designed by the Finnish-American modernist architect Eero Saarinen on a 240-acre site in the Westchester County countryside outside New York City. General Motors Corporation reoriented its research programs toward more basic research after Charles Kettering, its "professional amateur" research and engineering director, retired in 1947. In May 1956 it dedicated the new General Motors Technical Center, a Saarinen-designed complex that in turn inspired IBM's Watson. RCA also shifted toward fundamental research. The company expanded the RCA Laboratories that had been built in 1941 near Princeton University, and in the decade after 1945 RCA hired more theoretical scientists, who by 1955 represented 50 percent of the lab's staff. Similar commitments to the linear model were also made in the pharmaceutical industry. Merck & Co., which already possessed extensive research capabilities, expanded its basic research while also putting Vannevar Bush on its board of directors in 1949.

One other factor pushed corporations in the same direction as Du Pont: antitrust policy. With the Justice Department seeking stronger provisions against mergers and acquisitions, many other firms, including RCA and Alcoa, concluded that research offered one legally defensible way to grow.

THE MILITARY AGENDA FOR RESEARCH AND THE COLD WAR

While Vannevar Bush feuded with Harry Truman over the design of the National Science Foundation, the U.S. Navy became the major government funder of basic science in the United States after 1946. Even before the end of the war, one of the navy's admirals had decided that his branch of the service would have a leadership position in directing research for military purposes. Bush had run roughshod over the navy during the war, pushing it out of participation in the Manhattan Project and keeping many other critical projects out of its purview. In response, the navy created the Office of Naval Research (ONR) at the end of the war and then began a program of funding basic research in universities, which its leaders thought critical to the long-term development of a nuclear navy—a navy on the cutting edge of all military technologies. As Daniel Kevles points out, university scientists who had worked on military projects during the war were at first fearful of the red tape, compartmentalization, and strictures against publication that had characterized wartime research. But to their delight, they soon learned that the navy was offering them big research contracts largely free of these impediments. Moreover, much of the research funded by ONR seemed so far from any military application that it truly could be seen as "pure." Soon the army and the newly created air force were following the ONR's lead, offering civilians research contracts for pure research while establishing their own in-house research and development departments.

War's end did not spell the end of the special weapons research laboratories that had been established during the war. Initially these laboratories experienced declines in funding and personnel as projects wound down. General Groves became alarmed by the exodus of scientists from the Manhattan Project laboratories. He realized that the federal government would have to initiate new relationships with university scientists to support their pure research in order to further the development of nuclear weapons.

World events—what came to be known as the Cold War—made Groves's job much easier and put Big Science on a far more secure foundation. In conjunction with the linear model, the Cold War played a fundamental role in shaping the course of industrial R&D in the postwar era. The Cold War outlasted the linear model, and only after the Cold War ended were scholars and policymakers in a position to understand fully how deeply it had shaped industrial R&D in the United States.

Any idea of scientific demobilization was dashed when the Soviet Union began to give the United States and the other Allies problems on the eastern frontier, leading to the Truman Doctrine in 1947 and the confrontation over Berlin in 1948. The detonation of an atomic bomb by the Soviet Union in 1949 and the outbreak of the Korean War in 1950 brought about a scientifically and technically driven arms race that rivaled the big R&D projects of World War II. The facilities that had been created as temporary measures in World War II became National Laboratories in 1946 and 1947, and entirely new laboratories were created for weapons development and production. Work on the hydrogen bomb was done at the rapidly expanding Los Alamos complex in New Mexico, and in 1952 the Livermore Laboratory was established near San Francisco as the nation's second nuclear weapons laboratory to supplement work at Los Alamos. As a historian of Big Science, Robert Seidel, has argued, even those national laboratories whose mission was to pursue "pure science," such as Brookhaven National Laboratory on Long Island, New York, were authorized and sustained because of overriding concerns about national security brought about by the Cold War.

Early in the Cold War new generations of nuclear materials reactors were developed and built by General Electric, which had taken over operation of Hanford Engineer Works from Du Pont in 1946, and also by Du Pont, which in 1950 reluctantly agreed to assume responsibility for a whole new plant in South Carolina intended to produce nuclear materials for hydrogen bombs. Under the entrepreneurship and management of Admiral Hyman Rickover, the navy developed nuclear submarines and aircraft carriers, working most closely with Westinghouse and General Electric. The air force launched a program to develop an intercontinental ballistic missile system that could deliver atomic warheads to the Soviet Union. In the process, the air force created a new "systems-driven," high technology firm named TRW, led by former Bell Laboratories researcher Dean Woolridge and former General Electric Research

Laboratory member Simon Ramo. Long-range, high-altitude bombers were developed by several aircraft companies whose R&D capabilities and facilities were dramatically expanded. A computer-driven early warning system was developed by IBM to protect the United States from a surprise attack by Soviet bombers coming over the North Pole. This system was based on the wartime and immediate postwar research of the Servomechanisms Laboratory at MIT. Other new countermeasures were developed. New chemical and biological weapons emerged from laboratories. The list goes on, and to it one must also add the manned space program of the National Aeronautics and Space Administration (NASA). As several historians have noted, the creation of NASA was driven more by the exigencies of the Cold War than by any desire for a Columbus-like quest to explore the universe, and it led to the creation and expansion of numerous industrial firms acting as prime contractors and subcontractors to NASA.

Assessing the Cold War's full impact on industrial R&D is not possible in an essay of this scope, but a few of the salient aspects deserve mention. The Cold War drove federal spending for research almost entirely in the direction of the military. As Kevles notes in *The Physicists,* "For almost a quarter-century after 1945, defense research expenditures rose virtually exponentially, even in constant dollars, accounting through 1960 for 80 percent or more of the entire federal R&D budget. In 1950, it was estimated that there were 15,000 defense research projects; in the early 1960s, perhaps 80,000." The historian of physics Paul Forman has gone even further, writing that "through the 1950s, the only significant sources of funds for academic physical research in the U.S. were from the Department of Defense and an Atomic Energy Commission whose mission was *de facto* predominantly military." Forman argues that the entire development of quantum electronics in the postwar period can be attributed to military funding of research.

Industry, of course, was also affected by this development. As Forman notes, the electronics industry in particular came to depend on the military for its R&D funding. In 1960, for instance, the federal government (almost exclusively the military) paid for 70 percent of the R&D conducted by the electronics industry in the United States. With the military funding so much of its research, the electronics industry became increasingly conservative about the way it spent its own money in research. Most historians and electronics industry analysts agree that the United States lost its leadership position in consumer electronics in part because of its preoccupation with military electronics, which led companies to focus attention on performance objectives rather than market objectives.

The growth in military spending for R&D, the overwhelming role of military funding, and the nature of that funding in advanced electronics, aeronautics and space, nuclear weapons, and related areas meant that the costs of securing researchers mounted rapidly after 1947. This problem grew even worse with the start of the U.S. space program in response to the Soviet launch of *Sputnik* in 1957 and the panic about a "missile gap" that ensued. This panic reestablished the power that scientists had garnered in the highest levels of policy making during World War II, which had dissipated somewhat during the early 1950s. With renewed power, argues the historian Roger Geiger, scientists "propounded the ideology of basic research" and secured for themselves more money with fewer strings attached. Research monies in defense industries and defense projects flowed freely, driving up the bidding for scientific and technical talent. This left industries and firms that did not participate in Cold War research unable to compete for the best research talent. Contemporary accounts of this problem are legion. Du Pont in the chemical industry and Xerox in copiers, for example, found themselves unable to hire the researchers they wanted. The American utility industry was unable to continue to recruit high-caliber electrical engineers because work in electronics, computers, and space was far more appealing to students and their professors than was power engineering. Firms that had historically done commercially oriented R&D work but which won sizable military contracts in the Cold War found themselves reallocating their scientific and technical talent. A two-class system (military and nonmilitary) ultimately developed, with the best and brightest concentrated in the former.

Debates emerged about whether these effects were real or merely apparent. Some analysts stressed the idea of spillovers, arguing that any R&D work done for the military and with federal dollars would eventually be useful in commercial products. Others argued that excessive direction of R&D toward national security purposes was undermining the long-run commercial health of the nation's economy. Robert Solo challenged the spillover arguments in the pages of the *Harvard Business Review* in 1962, and Richard Nelson raised similar questions in a 1963 article in the *American Economic Review.* The 1965 *Report of the President's Committee on the Impact of*

Defense and Disarmament contained corresponding analyses. This last document, although accepting the idea of spillover, argued that the same benefits could have been attained "at substantially lower costs and with more certainty" if research had been governed by market forces in the civilian sector.

The role of military-related projects in funding industrial R&D became somewhat less dominant during the late 1960s and early 1970s, not in response to the kinds of concerns voiced by economists such as Nelson and Solo or the presidential commission but because of the growing political costs of continuing the same policies. The tenor of the nation gradually shifted from being largely supportive of the national security state, with all its scientific and technological trappings, to being quite suspicious of it. There was a sense that the "system" had come to resemble the state depicted in George Orwell's chilling dystopian novel *1984*. The Vietnam War, environmental concerns, urban crises, and the ho-hum public attitudes that beset NASA after the first few moon landings all contributed to the relative decline of federal support for industrial R&D, an era called the Social Priorities Period by one science policy scholar, Harvey Brooks, and the Crisis of Authority by another, Alexander Morin.

This shift was also attended by another among many of the largest industrial R&D spenders, including virtually all the R&D pioneers. For almost two decades firms had generously supported programs in fundamental research and managed fundamental researchers with kid gloves, as prescribed by the vast literature on the management of industrial research and development that appeared in the 1950s and 1960s. But by the late 1960s executives in many big firms had lost faith in the linear model. Many concluded that the money they had lavished on large, country-club-like research laboratories located in the exurbs had not been productive. Few, if any, blockbuster products had emerged from the fundamental research programs. GE had produced some exotic things in its laboratory, but the company had not earned much measurable return on its investment in academic-style research. Du Pont had no new nylons. Kodak had no radically new system of photography. RCA had lost many opportunities, and one of its Princeton lab's products had failed to gain management support. Managers and executives at IBM began to question whether it had been wise to separate research from development; as one IBM researcher wrote, the move "had gone too far, . . . work in research was so esoteric that it no longer had value to IBM." Many other corporate executives concluded that their firms had built ivory towers. In so doing, the argument went, they had neglected their older, existing businesses, which were still producing the majority of their sales and whose profit margins were now being squeezed. Those firms that had dedicated major resources to new product R&D—even those that had put new products on the market—often found these products failing commercially or in serious need of additional research to make them profitable.

Thus many corporations began to reallocate R&D monies from long-term to short-term objectives at the same time that federal spending for industrial R&D declined. Moreover, during the late 1960s and the first half of the 1970s—years of inflation—corporations held their overall R&D budgets flat, producing declines in R&D spending when counted in constant dollars. For the two generations of researchers who had grown up holding the values espoused in *Science—The Endless Frontier,* these changes produced an enormous amount of anxiety and malaise. The age of the great industrial R&D programs appeared to be waning rapidly. Images of twilight abounded in much of the literature on industrial R&D during this period. The shocks to the U.S. economy brought on by the OPEC oil embargo in the early 1970s simply compounded these problems and perceptions.

RESURGENCE OF RESEARCH: THE OLD OR THE NEW?

Yet in the late 1970s and throughout much of the 1980s, there was a remarkable return to the pattern of the late 1950s and early 1960s—what the science policy analyst Alexander Morin mockingly called the Return to Normalcy (of the Cold War). Federal spending for research performed by industrial firms went up once again, although it did not reach the heights it had attained in 1957. Moreover, industry expenditures on research rose by 14 percent per year during much of the first half of the 1980s and at a lower but still healthy rate during much of the second half. The defense buildup under President Ronald Reagan, symbolized most clearly by the Strategic Defense Initiative or "Star Wars" program, brought large-scale funding of military R&D back to levels reminiscent of the earlier period. The buildup also directed the magic 5 percent of these funds toward basic research—a percentage that some scholars have said is the price of university researchers' souls.

Writing in 1985, the historian Margaret Graham stressed that "while the funding scenario may look like a return to the Age of Big Science, in other respects the current era for industrial research promises to be quite different." She noted the degree to which the federal government had abandoned the Vannevar Bush model by "encouraging cooperation in R&D and transfer between sectors, industries, and companies, trying to avoid the perceived problems of research competition that emerged in the [1950s and 1960s]." Yet the swing toward military domination of the federal research budget, which Daniel Kevles termed "the remilitarization of research," greatly worried some policymakers. As director of the National Science Foundation from 1984 to 1990, Erich Bloch, a veteran of IBM development projects, launched and saw significant development of an extensive series of engineering and interdisciplinary research centers dedicated to building knowledge and capabilities that cut across firms and industries and that were of direct commercial relevance. Bloch maintained that these university-based engineering research centers were truly devoted to basic research. Such research differed from the "basic research" supported by mission-oriented agencies of the Department of Defense, NASA, and the Department of Energy, which he and others of different political persuasions argued was conducted principally within industry, inherently biased toward the missions of those agencies, and therefore not really very "basic."

The resurgence of industry-funded R&D spending in the late 1970s and 1980s was attended by another recognizable trend: big spending by firms on university research. Monsanto's unprecedented $23 million research grant to Harvard University in 1974 was the opening move of several large corporate grants to major research universities. Exxon's 1980 grant of $8 million to MIT, Du Pont's $6 million contract with Harvard Medical School in 1981, Hoechst's $50 million grant to Massachusetts General Hospital in 1981, and Mallinckrodt's $3.9 million contract with Washington University in 1981 suggested to some that a new trend was in the making.

A major study commissioned by the National Science Board, the governing body of the National Science Foundation, for inclusion in its 1982 annual report to the president and Congress, focused on these and less spectacular industry grants. The report also examined the whole range of university-industry research relationships. These included the NSF's formal grants program for university-industry research partnerships, an important prelude to Bloch's engineering research centers. This study was the first of many that were done in the 1980s and 1990s to track the major trends of industry-university research

relationships. A 1994 report on some eleven hundred university-industry research centers, performed by Carnegie Mellon University professors Wesley Cohen and Richard Florida, suggested that the federal government had been an active promoter of these centers, 60 percent of which were formed in the 1980s, by tying federal contributions to universities to industry participation. These university-industry research centers represented roughly 70 percent of industry's expenditures on academic R&D. Of the $4.1 billion spent in the centers in 1991, local, state, and federal governments contributed 46 percent and the universities themselves 18 percent. Industry contributed most of the remainder, with private foundations contributing a small fraction.

The big research agreements undertaken by Monsanto, Du Pont, Hoechst, Mallinckrodt, and others were part of a major strategy of firms, mostly in the chemical industry, to move their companies into biotechnology, the hottest area in industrial research from the late 1970s on. In some sense, the grants made by the firms represented the price of admission to the biotechnology drama that was unfolding in university laboratories. Companies not only wanted access to the latest science, but they also hoped to learn who the best scientists were, with the goal of recruiting them for their own new programs. Many university scientists, however, shunned big firms. Instead, they leveraged their university research to gain major equity in the numerous biotechnology start-up companies that dominated the scene.

Cooperation in the 1980s was not limited to the universities and industries, however. While pushing up federal spending for Star Wars and other defense-related research, the Reagan administration also began to dismantle much of the antitrust architecture that had been built up in the Justice Department since the late New Deal and that had so definitely shaped corporate strategies over the previous four decades. This effort culminated in the National Cooperative Research Act of 1984, which paved the way for research consortia such as Sematech and the Microelectronic and Computer Technology Corporation (MCC). These intraindustry cooperative research efforts, like the university-industry research relationships, were ostensibly geared to shoring up or restoring American industry and research capabilities as global competition mounted. But, as with university-industry research centers, the government—or more particularly the Department of Defense—proved to be the major supporter of Sematech and a large supporter of other such efforts. As the nation reached the final crescendo in the Cold War symphony, economic security and military security were inextricably bound together. The echoes of the Cold War symphony still resonated in the early 1990s, and so calls for a "civilian DARPA" (Defense Advanced Research Projects Administration) were hardly surprising.

Concern about the United States' competitiveness in the global economy and the natural desire to maintain many of the scientific and technical structures of the Cold War led Congress to pass key pieces of legislation. The Stevenson-Wydler Technology Innovation Act of 1980 sought to transfer federally owned or developed technologies to state and local governments and, ostensibly, to the private sector, but additional legislation was necessary to generate much enthusiasm for the process. The Federal Technology Transfer Act of 1986 and the National Competitiveness Technology Transfer Act of 1989 enabled, respectively, the National Laboratories and the federally funded research and development centers (contractor-operated laboratories) to transfer non–national-security-threatening technologies out of the confines of those institutions and into the marketplace. Agents for these organizations immediately began marketing their laboratories' knowledge, skill, hardware, and software. Many industrial firms, especially those with solid in-house capabilities, began shopping around these laboratories, looking for technological opportunities. Whether these technology transfer projects improved the nation's competitiveness in the short- or long-run or saved the National Laboratories in what people called "defense conversion" after the Berlin Wall came down in 1990 and the Soviet Union collapsed in 1991 remained unclear. Conversion suggested to some, however, that the labor market for R&D personnel would be restructured over time, reversing some of the effects of the Cold War buildup. Others maintained that it was only a matter of time before the government would begin to close some of the National Laboratories bred by the Cold War.

The Reagan administration's loosening of the antitrust statutes also stimulated another development that affected the management of industrial R&D in the 1980s and early 1990s: joint ventures. The 1980s and early 1990s witnessed a robust growth in the number of firms that undertook joint R&D projects, in theory combining the R&D capabilities of two or more firms while sharing costs and risks. Whether this joint-venture phenomenon represented merely the release of a pent-up demand that had grown over many years of strict enforcement of antitrust statutes, a strong secular trend, or simply a fad remained unclear.

This litany of Reagan-era developments, most of them initiated by the federal government but some supported vigorously by industry, should make clear that the 1980s brought about a crazy quilt of avenues, approaches, and opportunities for corporate R&D managers. The array of ways to spend money on R&D became staggering, especially in light of the increasing globalization of business, which was also affecting industrial research.

GLOBALIZATION OF R&D

The process of globalization of industrial research antedates the end of the Cold War. During the mid-1950s and early 1960s, many U.S. firms established research laboratories in Europe in anticipation of or in response to the formation of the Common Market, which emerged from the Treaty of Rome in 1957. They did so for several different reasons, including the desire to create means of recruiting highly qualified and talented European scientist and engineers for U.S. companies; the need to provide U.S. corporations with the know-how to modify their products for European markets; the desire to open windows to European scientific developments; the hope of building bridges to the European universities; and the imperative to lower the costs of research. In addition, some U.S. corporations simply inherited research organizations when they acquired European-based companies. The negotiations among members of the European Community (the former Common Market) that led up to the Maastricht Treaty of December 1991 and the anticipated effects of a "United States of Europe" that was to emerge in 1992 led to another wave of laboratory foundations or expansions in Europe by U.S.–based corporations. At the same time, the desire of U.S.–based corporations to penetrate Asian markets, from Japan and South Korea to Malaysia and especially China, resulted in a significant pattern of laboratory foundations in these markets in the late 1980s and early 1990s.

This pattern of U.S.–based firms establishing R&D laboratories all around their increasingly global markets was matched by the actions of Asian and European firms entering the American industrial R&D scene. By 1990, almost fifty Japanese corporations had built or acquired R&D laboratories in the United States, often in high-technology centers such as California's Silicon Valley or along Route 128 near Boston. Many Japanese firms had also built research alliances with leading U.S. universities such as Stanford and MIT. Most of the German chemical and electrical and electronics firms had done likewise, and some of their U.S.–based research divisions were larger than those in Germany. German chemical and pharmaceutical companies located their central laboratories for biotechnology research in the United States because of the increasing power of the ecologically motivated Greens political movement in Germany. The Greens had led the push for highly restrictive environmental and animal rights laws that made much research in biotechnology politically if not legally impossible there.

The globalization of industrial R&D raised new questions about the management of research in the modern corporation. It posed problems that transcended many perennial difficulties that corporations had faced almost as soon as they had established formal research programs in the early twentieth century. Dealing with different laws and social customs and different educational systems and work ethics challenged research managers seeking global knowledge and power. With globalization of business and research, the effects of changes in corporate strategy and well-being could be felt widely. For example, in the early 1990s the Eastman Kodak Company moved aggressively in establishing industrial research programs in Japan. A change in the leadership of the corporation, however, led the company to abandon its Japanese lab, leaving its Japanese researchers, many of them "defectors" from Japanese companies, high and dry, confused, and angry. In late 1992 and early 1993, IBM cut $1 billion—roughly 20 percent—out of its annual R&D budget, a cut that had repercussions throughout Europe, Asia, and the United States.

Globalization of R&D has also posed problems for those who are responsible for accounting for the United States' research and development budget. The phenomenon simply added fuel to the arguments made by the analyst and future secretary of labor Robert Reich in his paean to the global economy, *The Work of Nations* (1991). Detailing the global character of many products, Reich raised the apt question, "Who is us?" Nonetheless, the administration of President Bill Clinton committed itself in 1993 to pursuing a coordinated, effective industrial policy. The Clinton administration believed that the United States needed to improve its competitiveness in the world economy, to stave off the gains of foreign manufacturers in U.S. markets, and to help U.S.–based firms better penetrate foreign markets. These policymakers grew alarmed by the news that Japanese spending in R&D as a percentage of Gross National Product (GNP) had surpassed that of the United States in 1986 and had continued to widen the gap

into the 1990s. Moreover, when the calculation was run for *nondefense* R&D spending as a percentage of GNP, both Japan and Germany had since 1970 been spending considerably more than the United States: Japan almost 50 percent more in 1990, Germany roughly 30 percent that same year.

TOWARD A NEW EQUILIBRIUM?

The growth of industrial research has been one of the distinguishing features of the twentieth century. Firms that pioneered industrial R&D in the United States did so because they were threatened by competition, because they were engaged in a process of rationalizing their organizations (often in response to antitrust threats and actions), and because they saw benefits to internalizing R&D rather than relying on the market to direct these activities. Yet in internalizing these functions, the R&D pioneers and firms that emulated them were never completely free to do what they wanted vis-à-vis scientists and scientifically oriented engineers. Corporations were highly dependent on educational institutions and the elite cadre of university professors for their supply of researchers. Academic researchers often had competing agendas and possessed ideals that were sometimes hostile to industrial R&D. Thus industrial research was shaped by the American scientific community perhaps as much as or more than the reverse. The two world wars and the Cold War significantly influenced the course and nature of industrial research. Seeking support for "best science"—the unrestricted, unquestioned, and unaccountable support for a scientific elite housed in a relatively few American universities—the American scientific community used national security concerns to promulgate a linear model of technological development that rested squarely on basic research. The achievements of such wartime products as the atom bomb, radar, and the proximity fuse lent enormous credence to this model, which was adopted wholesale in the post–World War II period and quickened by the national security concerns of the Cold War. Industrial research therefore came to be skewed more and more toward basic or fundamental research. It was pursued with the faith that blockbuster products would inevitably flow out of this research, whether funded by firms themselves or by the largess of the national security state.

The linear model began to fall apart in the mid-1960s, and reductions in industrial research set in. During the later 1970s, however, concerns about the decline in U.S. industry's competitiveness and, after

Ronald Reagan's election in 1980, about the "evil empire" of the Soviet Union fueled a resurgence of industrial research, funded both by industry and the military. Some scholars saw this as the remilitarization of research or the return to the normalcy of Cold War research. Others saw it as providing a greater diversity of avenues in which firms could, and did, invest in research, whether through university research centers, joint ventures, private research laboratories, or research consortia. Perceived opportunities in biotechnology also gave this era a different feel from that of the 1950s and added considerably to the dynamic growth of industrial research, especially after the late 1970s.

Growth in the diversity of research opportunities was a major development of the 1980s and 1990s. After the disintegration of the Soviet Union, U.S. firms could even go so far as to contract for research in the former Soviet Union—for a fraction of what it would cost in the United States. Perhaps this development of flexibility in industrial research was closely related to the secular movement toward what economists Michael Piore and Charles Sabel called "flexible specialization" in their highly influential 1984 book, *The Second Industrial Divide,* which when logically played out meant the downsizing of firms and the out-sourcing of production (and research) to a great degree. But perhaps these developments were simply logical outcomes of the end of the Cold War. Where and when a new equilibrium might be reached were unclear. One thing was certain, however. The outcome would not be wholly determined either by American corporate decisionmakers or by global economic forces. If the past is any guide to the future, the scientific communities in the United States and the rest of the world would themselves have much to say about the conduct and future of industrial research.

SEE ALSO Large-Scale Scientific Enterprise; Computer and Communications Technology; Aerospace Technology; Medical Science and Technology (all in this volume).

BIBLIOGRAPHY

The New Deal's National Resources Planning Board became the first forum for the systematic study of the history of industrial research in the United States when it published Howard R. Bartlett's still-useful essay, "The Development of Industrial Research in the United States," in volume 2 of the three-volume *Research—A National Resource* (1941). Since then, no comprehensive historical survey of industrial research has appeared. However, Leonard S. Reich's *The Making of American Industrial Research: Science and Business at GE and Bell, 1876–1926* (1985) provides an excellent introduction to the subject that corrects a good deal of the always-interesting but overstated study by David F. Noble, *America by Design: Science, Technology, and the Rise of Corporate Capitalism* (1977). David C. Mowery and Nathan Rosenberg's *Technology and the Pursuit of Economic Growth* (1989) draws on these works and, while offering a reasonable if somewhat uneven survey of industrial R&D in the United States and Britain, responds to an important body of economic thought about the subject that will be covered below. Harold Vagtborg's *Research and American Industrial Development: A Bicentennial Look at the Contributions of Applied R&D* (1975), though not well documented, provides information not encapsulated elsewhere. How industrial research fits into the larger frame of corporate capitalism is treated in Alfred D. Chandler, Jr.'s *Scale and Scope: The Dynamics of Industrial Capitalism* (1990).

Several works open up the nineteenth-century context for the rise of industrial research in the twentieth century. On Germany, see John J. Beer's classic book, *The Emergence of the German Dye Industry* (1959); and the supplemental essay by Georg Meyer-Thurow, "The Industrialization of Invention: A Case Study from the German Chemical Industry," *Isis* 73 (1982): 363–381. On innovation in "system-driven" industries and firms in the last century, see Paul Israel, *From Machine Shop to Inventor: Telegraphy and the Changing Context of American Invention, 1830–1920* (1992); Steven W. Usselman, "Running the Machine: The Management of Technological Innovation on American Railroads, 1860–1910," (Ph.D. diss., University of Delaware, 1985); Steven W. Usselman, "From Novelty to Utility: George Westinghouse and the Business of Innovation during the Age of Edison," *Business History Review* 66 (1992): 251–304; and Thomas P. Hughes, *Elmer Sperry: In-*

ventor and Engineer (1971). The literature on Thomas A. Edison and his two laboratories includes William Pretzer, ed., *Working at Inventing: Thomas A. Edison and the Menlo Park Experience* (1989); and Andre Millard, *Edison and the Business of Innovation* (1990). On Edison's relationship with the professional scientific community in the United States, see David A. Hounshell, "Edison and the Pure Science Ideal in 19th-Century America," *Science* 207 (1980): 612–617. W. Bernard Carlson's *Innovation as a Social Process: Elihu Thomson and the Rise of General Electric, 1870–1900* (1991) provides a portrait of an Edison contemporary and rival, who also fashioned himself as an important scientist.

The history of an important sector of the U.S. scientific community is masterfully portrayed in Daniel J. Kevles's *The Physicists: The History of a Scientific Community in Modern America* (1978). See also the collection of essays in Alexandre Oleson and John Voss, eds., *The Organization of Knowledge in Modern America, 1860–1920* (1979); and Ronald Tobey, *The American Ideology of National Science, 1919–1930* (1971). More recently, Roger L. Geiger has included the scientific community as part of his studies of higher education in the United States, *To Advance Knowledge: The Growth of American Research Universities, 1900–1940* (1986), and *Research and Relevant Knowledge: American Research Universities since World War II* (1993). Although no historian has fully surveyed the relationship between industrial research and universities, Arnold Thackray's "University-Industry Connection and Chemical Research: An Historical Perspective," in the National Science Board's, *University-Industry Research Relationships: Selected Studies* (1983), opens the literature for that industry, as does John P. Swann's, *Academic Scientists and the Pharmaceutical Industry: Cooperative Research in Twentieth-Century America* (1988) for the pharmaceutical industry. For a survey of recent developments in university-industry research centers, see Wesley Cohen, Richard Florida, and W. Richard Goe, *University-Industry Research Centers in the United States* (1994). The history of the Mellon Institute and changing research environments is treated in John W. Servos, "Changing Partners: The Mellon Institute, Private Industry, and the Federal Patron," *Technology and Culture* 35 (1994): 221–257.

Perhaps the most penetrating work on industrial research is to be found in studies of individual companies. On General Electric, in addition to Reich's book noted above, see George Wise, *Willis R. Whitney, General Electric, and the Origins of U.S. Industrial Research* (1985); on Kodak, Reese V. Jenkins, *Images and Enterprise: Technology and the American Photographic Industry, 1839–1925* (1975); on Du Pont, David A. Hounshell and John Kenly Smith, Jr., *Science and Corporate Strategy: Du Pont R&D, 1902–1980* (1988); on Alcoa, Margaret B. W. Graham and Bettye H. Pruitt, *R&D for Industry: A Century of Technical Innovation at Alcoa* (1990); on RCA, Margaret B. W. Graham, *RCA and the VideoDisc: The Business of Research* (1986); on General Motors, Stuart W. Leslie, *Boss Kettering: Wizard of General Motors* (1983); on IBM, Emerson Pugh, "Research," in Charles J. Bashe et al., eds., *IBM's Early Computers* (1986), pp. 522–570; on various pharmaceutical companies, John Parascondola, "Industrial Research Comes of Age: The American Pharmaceutical Industry, 1920–1940," *Pharmacy in History* 27 (1985): 12–21; on U.S. Steel, Paul Tiffany, "Corporate Culture and Corporate Change: The Origins of Industrial Research at the United States Steel Corporation, 1901–1929," in David A. Hounshell, ed., *The R&D Pioneers* (forthcoming); and on Westinghouse, Ronald Kline, "The Origins of Industrial Research at the Westinghouse Electric Company, 1886–1922," in Hounshell, ed., *The R&D Pioneers.*

Industrial research during World War II has not been fully explored by historians, but see the Pulitzer Prize–winning book by James P. Baxter, *Scientists against Time* (1946); as well as Ronald Kline, "R&D: Organizing for War," *IEEE Spectrum* (November 1987): 54–60.

The relationship between the Cold War and industrial research is treated in a vast number of works, including Stuart W. Leslie's outstanding comparative study of Massachusetts Institute of Technology and Stanford University, *The Cold War and American Science* (1993); James L. Clayton, ed., *The Economic Impact of the Cold War: Sources and Readings* (1970); Paul Forman, "Behind Quantum Electronics: National Security as Basis for Physical Research in the United States," *Historical Studies in the Physical and Biological Sciences* 19, part 1 (1987): 149–229; and Margaret B. W. Graham, "Industrial Research in the Age of Big Science," in *Research on Technological Innovation, Management, and Policy,* Richard S. Rosenbloom, ed., vol. 2 (1985). For an insider's view of industrial research during the Cold War, see Simon Ramo, *The Business of Science: Winning and Losing in the High-Tech Age* (1988).

With the exception of Joseph Schumpeter, few economists were interested in industrial research and development until the Cold War. While working for the air force–funded RAND Corporation, several economists wrote seminal papers on the economics of R&D. These include Richard R. Nelson, "The Simple Economics of Basic Scientific Research," *Journal of Political Economy* 67 (1959): 297–306, and "The Economics of Invention," *Journal of Business* 32 (1959): 101–117; and Kenneth J. Arrow, "Economic Welfare and the Allocation of Resources for Invention," in *The Rate and Direction of Inventive Activity* (1962). Nathan Rosenberg's "Why Do Firms Do Basic Research (with Their Own Money)?" *Research Policy* 19 (1990): 165–174 provides an important critique to this earlier thought. Wesley M. Cohen and Richard C. Levin, "Empirical Studies of Innovation and Market Structure," in *Handbook of Industrial Organization,* vol. 2, R. Schmalensee and R. D. Willig, eds. (1989), provides a recent survey of the economics literature on industrial R&D.

The Cold War also shaped science policy in the United States, which in turn affected industrial R&D. Alexander J. Morin, *Science, Policy, and Politics* (1993), provides a short but incisive overview, as does Jeffrey K. Stine's *A History of Science Policy in the United States, 1940–1985* (1986). See also the perspective of Harvey Brooks, "National Science Policy and Technological Innovation," in *The Positive Sum Strategy: Harnessing Technology for Economic Growth,* Ralph Landau and Nathan Rosenberg, eds. (1986); and Bruce L. R. Smith, *American Science Policy since World War II* (1990). The assessment of then-director of the National Science Foundation, Eric Bloch, "Basic Research and Economic Health: The Coming Challenge," *Science* 232 (1986): 595–599, provides additional perspectives by the former IBM executive.

The rapid changes in industrial research that occurred in the late 1970s and throughout the 1980s have not yet been systematically treated by historians. But see Margaret B. W. Graham, "Corporate Research and Development: The Latest Transformation," *Technology in Society* 7 (1985): 179–185; John T. Scott, "Historical and Economic Perspectives on the National Cooperative Research Act," in *Cooperative Research and Development,* Albert N. Link and Gregory Tassey, eds. (1989); Gadi Kaplan and Alfred Rosenblatt, "The Expanding World of R&D," *IEEE Spectrum* (October 1990): 28–33; the annual *Science & Engineering Indicators* issued under the National Science Board of the National Science Foundation; and Trudy Bell, "From Monopoly to Competition: Long-Term Research is Vulnerable," *IEEE Spectrum* (October 1990): 46–50. Globalization of R&D is surveyed in Robert Ronstadt, *Research and Development Abroad by U.S. Multinationals* (1977); Mark Casson, ed., *Global Research Strategy and International Competitiveness* (1991); and Ove Granstrand et al., eds., *Technology Management and International Business* (1992). Edward E. David, Jr., "Science in the Post–Cold War Era," *The Bridge* 24 (1994): 3–8, provides some long-term perspectives on the present and future of industrial research. The Office of Technology Assessment's study, *Defense Conversion: Redirecting R&D* (1993), conveys an overview of how the end of the Cold War has affected the major National Laboratories and changed their relationship with both university and industrial research.

EVOLUTIONARY THEORY

Gregg A. Mitman and Ronald L. Numbers

In 1859 the British naturalist Charles Darwin published his epoch-making book *On the Origin of Species by Means of Natural Selection*. In opposition to the conventional view that biological species represented separate creations by God, he argued that "probably all of the organic beings which have ever lived on this earth have descended from some one primordial form." He suggested that the evolution of species had occurred primarily by means of natural selection, as organisms with differing traits struggled to survive and propagate. Although he at first skirted the sensitive topic of human origins, in *The Descent of Man* (1871) he declared that humans had evolved from a hairy, tree-dwelling quadruped with a tail and pointed ears, which itself had descended from "some fish-like animal."

In presenting his views to the public, Darwin wished not only to overthrow what he called "the dogma of separate creations" but to promote his theory of natural selection as the chief agent of evolutionary change. Among American scientists he quickly achieved his first goal. By the mid-1870s most American naturalists seem to have embraced some notion of organic evolution, and in 1899 the last surviving special creationist of scientific repute in North America, the distinguished geologist John William Dawson of Montreal, died. Darwin enjoyed noticeably less success in converting American scientific opinion to natural selection. Even his foremost American disciple, the Harvard botanist Asa Gray, urged a "special origination" in connection with the appearance of humans and harbored the "very anti-Darwin" view that variations in plants and animals were divinely directed. Well into the twentieth century the overwhelming majority of evolutionists in the American scientific community relegated natural selection to a secondary role in the evolutionary process, while relying instead on such mechanisms as the pressure of the environment to induce variations and the inheritance of characteristics acquired by use and disuse. Such positions were often lumped together under the label neo-Lamarckianism, after the early-nineteenth-century French naturalist J.-B. Lamarck.

The attitudes of nonscientists, most of whom left no trace of their opinions, are more difficult to assess. During the last quarter of the nineteenth century many liberal theologians and clergymen in the mainline Protestant churches joined their scientific brethren in espousing theistic evolution. In doing so, they abandoned a literal reading of Genesis and sometimes the very notion of a transcendent God. We do not know the views of most Protestant preachers, but it seems likely that the majority remained skeptical if not decidedly antagonistic to evolution, especially to the idea of human kinship with the apes. The great mass of American Protestants, though seldom expressing themselves on the topic, apparently saw no compelling reason to trade Moses for Darwin. Catholics, too, split over the issue of evolution. Although a small number of intellectuals, such as the controversial priest-scientist John Zahm, pushed for accepting the evolution of the human body (while insisting on the special divine infusion of the soul), the prevailing attitude remained hostile to evolution, as Zahm discovered when the Congregation of the Index banned his book, *Evolution and Dogma*, in 1898. American Jews faced the new century divided over the issue of evolution, with Reform Jews, the largest faction, tending to emphasize their conformity with the scientific spirit of the age, while the Orthodox, a smaller group made up largely of recent immigrants from eastern Europe, allied themselves with traditional beliefs.

THE DEATHBED OF DARWINISM

The opening of the twentieth century found scientific criticism of natural selection so intense that one German author devoted an entire book (published in English in Iowa) to reporting events occurring *At the Deathbed of Darwinism* (1904). Natural selection still had its strong defenders, but few could be found in turn-of-the-century America. Most American naturalists, though increasingly skeptical of claims regarding the inheritance of acquired characteristics, still tended to show a preference for theories that stressed the influence of the environment, the power of inherently progressive forces, or the role of mutations in effecting biological change.

Until the 1880s the notion of inheriting acquired characteristics had seemed commonsensible, even to Darwin himself. Then in the 1880s the German zoologist August Weismann mounted a sustained logical and experimental attack on the notion. He insisted that Lamarckian inheritance had never been demonstrated and that the germ plasm, or hereditary material, could not be affected by bodily or somatic influences. To test the Lamarckian theory, he cut off the tails of generations of mice and watched to see if their offspring grew shorter tails. They did not. Weismann believed that individual traits such as eye color and height resulted from the inheritance of elementary particles residing in the germ plasm. As the particles combined during sexual reproduction, they gave rise to chance variations, upon which natural selection acted. Weismann stressed the all-importance of natural selection in the evolutionary process, a position dubbed neo-Darwinism in 1888.

The ensuing debate between the admirers and critics of Weismann led the paleobotanist and social theorist Lester Frank Ward in the early 1890s to divide the biological community into two camps: the neo-Lamarckians and the neo-Darwinists. The former, loosely led by the vertebrate paleontologist Edward Drinker Cope, the entomologist Alpheus Packard, and the invertebrate paleontologist Alpheus Hyatt, came to be known for advocating the inheritability of organic changes brought about by either use or shifts in the environment. But their primary goal was to find natural, external explanations for the origin of variations, which Darwin had left unexplained and Gray had attributed to divine beneficence. Well before 1900 both Packard and Hyatt had quit defending the inheritance of acquired characteristics.

Few Americans openly identified with neo-Darwinism. Although Ward claimed that Weismann's "vigorous onslaught" on the inheritance of acquired characters had "probably aroused a greater amount of interest among scientific men than any other event that has transpired since the appearance of Darwin's *Origin of Species*," he named not a single American neo-Darwinist. The zoologists William Keith Brooks and Edmund Beecher Wilson led the American de-

fense of natural selection at the turn of the century, but even they at times expressed discomfort with the neo-Darwinist emphasis on purely fortuitous variations. Wilson, for example, confessed late in life to an aversion to the notion "that higgledy-piggledy can provide an adequate explanation of organic adaptations." The California naturalist Joseph Le Conte suggested another reason why American scientists hesitated to go all the way with Weismann. If Weismann is right, he said, "then alas for all our hopes of race improvement—physical, mental, and moral!—for natural selection will never be applied by man to himself as it is by Nature to organisms."

Shortly after the turn of the century the Stanford biologist Vernon L. Kellogg wrote a book titled *Darwinism To-Day* (1907), in which he surveyed scientific opinion on evolution, noting in particular the rapidly growing conviction among Americans that "the theory of descent had to be remoulded." In response to rumors about the death of Darwinism, he distinguished between the specific theory of natural selection, about which there was much debate, and the general theory of organic evolution, about which scientists had little doubt. Although he personally found Weismann's arguments against the inheritance of acquired characters to be convincing, he thought that the neo-Darwinists had failed either to destroy belief in neo-Lamarckism or to "make selection the all-sufficient and, indeed, sole factor in species-forming." Hence American scientists, especially paleontologists and pathologists, continued "mostly" to lean toward a weakened version of neo-Lamarckism. They did so not because of the empirical evidence in its favor, but because no satisfactory theory had yet emerged to take its place. "In fact probably a majority of biologists entertain a conviction . . . of the actuality of an influence on organic modification and descent directly exerted by those various external factors or conditions of organic life which we call, collectively, *environment*."

Kellogg went on to discuss several alternatives to natural selection, including the increasingly popular "mutation theory" associated with the Dutch scientist Hugo De Vries. In contrast to Darwin, who had favored slight variations, the Amsterdam botanist invoked "the occurrence of occasional, sudden, fixed, and often considerable changes or variations in the offspring of a plant or animal" to explain the origin of new species. To account for the transmission of these mutations from one generation to another, he appealed to the recently rediscovered work of the Austrian monk Gregor Johann Mendel, who in an obscure paper published decades earlier had spelled out the fundamental principles of heredity. Although Kellogg welcomed Mendel's "fruitful idea of unit species characters," he remained skeptical about De Vries's solution to the problem of speciation. "For my part it seems better to go back to the old and safe *Ignoramus* standpoint," he advised. "We are ignorant; terribly, immensely ignorant."

Confessions such as Kellogg's, whatever his intentions, undermined lay confidence in the scientific standing of evolution. Just two years before the appearance of his book, the American Bible League had published a pamphlet, *Collapse of Evolution* (1905), by the Methodist antievolutionist Luther T. Townsend. In view of the rising tide of criticism of Darwinism, Townsend urged American evolutionists to be "as honest and manly" as their German counterparts in conceding the shortcomings of the theory. The waning fortunes of Darwinism led some American creationists to charge liberal Christians with having embraced evolution prematurely. One conservative expressed the hope that, in the light of recent developments, those who had "abandoned the stronghold of faith out of sheer fright will soon be found scurrying back to the old and impregnable citadel, when they learn that 'the enemy is in full retreat.'"

Until after World War I, however, militant evangelicals who opposed modernism focused their attacks more on the higher criticism of the Bible than on evolution. Even *The Fundamentals* (1910–1915), the series of mass-circulated pamphlets that gave these conservative Christians their name, allowed that "some genetic connection" existed between higher and lower forms of life and refrained from the evolution-bashing that came to characterize the fundamentalist movement after World War I. Although the founding editor, A. C. Dixon, felt only "repugnance to the idea that an ape or an orang-outang" was his ancestor, he selected George Frederick Wright, a once-prominent Christian Darwinist who still harbored suspicions that humans and apes were related, to contribute an essay on "The Passing of Evolution." Wright chastised Darwin's modern disciples for teaching that all organic forms had arisen by strictly natural processes from one primordial speck, but he left the door open for the divinely guided evolution of species from originally created organic forms.

Even the most unbending antievolutionists of the early twentieth century, with few exceptions, readily accepted the paleontological evidence for the antiquity of life on earth, and virtually no one outside of a few marginal sects attached geological significance to Noah's flood. Bible-believing fundamentalists accommodated the findings of historical geology either by interpreting the days of Genesis 1 to represent vast ages in the history of the earth (the day-age theory) or by separating a creation "in the beginning" from a much later Edenic creation in six literal days (the gap theory). Both theories bore impeccably orthodox credentials, but the latter enjoyed greater popularity among rank-and-file fundamentalists. It did so in part because of its endorsement in the *Scofield Reference Bible,* a fundamentalist favorite. This version of the King James text assigned the creation story associated with the Garden of Eden to "B.C. 4004" in the margins but explained in an annotation that the original creation of "the heaven and the earth," mentioned in Genesis 1:1, "refers to the dateless past, and gives scope for all the geological ages." Although most fundamentalists identified Adam and Eve as the first humans, some went so far as to concede the existence of pre-Adamite humans.

During the early years of the century notions of organic evolution rapidly infiltrated the schools and churches of America. As public high schools mushroomed across the landscape, many of them adopted biology textbooks that treated evolution positively, if not extensively. These texts, argues historian Edward J. Larson, "carried evolution to an increasing number of America's youth for the first time, including the children of countless fundamentalist parents." Even Christian colleges in the South and Midwest began teaching evolution, in part because, as one president lamented, it was virtually impossible to find a science teacher or textbook that did not support organic development.

EVOLUTION, EUGENICS, AND THE GREAT WAR

At the annual meeting of the American Association for the Advancement of Science in 1917, the year of America's entry into World War I, the biologist Maurice Bigelow of Columbia University charged that neo-Darwinism served as the philosophical foundation of German militarism. The Germans, he alleged, had been using Darwin's notion of the survival of the fittest in a world dominated by ruthless struggle to justify their aggressive actions. In numerous presidential addresses and popular articles other American biologists—including such prominent figures as Leon J. Cole, Edwin Grant Conklin, David Starr Jordan, William Patten, Raymond Pearl, and William Emerson Ritter—joined Bigelow in condemning the German militarists for using what the Americans regarded as a distorted view of organic evolution to justify international war. Thus the debate over the mechanism of evolution expanded to include culture as well as biology.

The most compelling exposé of the horrors of German ideology and its underlying evolutionary philosophy was Vernon L. Kellogg's *Headquarters Nights* (1917), which first appeared in serial form in the *Atlantic Monthly*. Drawing on conversations he had had with the German high command while serving as the chief representative of the Commission for Relief in Belgium and northern France, the distinguished Stanford biologist argued that the war had resulted in part from the German people's enthusiastic acceptance of "the worst of Neo-Darwinism, the *Allmacht* (all-sufficiency) of natural selection applied rigorously to human life and society and Kultur." Kellogg particularly criticized the biologist Weismann and his followers for their dogmatic adherence to natural selection as the sole agent of evolutionary change, a view that contrasted with the tendency of American biologists to regard natural selection as only one of many evolutionary mechanisms. Thus the Americans could dismiss Germany's biological justification of war because it was founded on an erroneous understanding of evolution. "Nowhere in nature does natural selection, as indicated by modern careful study of the subject, operate with anything like that mechanistic precision which the German political philosophy postulates," wrote Raymond Pearl, a population biologist at Johns Hopkins University.

Followed to its logical conclusion, the neo-Darwinism of Weismann revealed a history of life on earth governed by purely naturalistic processes and blind chance. Mendel's laws of inheritance and De Vries's mutation theory, ideas espoused by the youthful advocates of the new experimental biology during the first two decades of the century, seemed to lend credence to such a mechanistic, materialistic outlook. But an older generation of American biologists, born in the decade surrounding the Civil War and trained in the descriptive and observational techniques of natural history and morphology, found it difficult to accept the possibility that the diversity of life on earth had resulted from random processes alone. They studied the natural world in part to find meaning and purpose in their own lives and in the course of Western civilization. For them, biology bore a religious significance they were unwilling to surrender easily. The paleontologist Henry Fairfield Osborn, director of the American Museum of Natural History, censured the disciples of Weismann for portraying life in fatalistic terms, devoid of improvement and progress. Although he stopped short of blaming

Weismann for World War I, Osborn viewed the conflict as the ultimate "horror of mechanism and materialism." William E. Ritter, director of the Scripps Institute of Oceanography, went even further, arguing explicitly that German biologists had turned Darwinism into a scientific justification for "militaristic brutism."

Confronted by such revulsive evidence of biology run amok, some American biologists sought to reinstill a sense of purpose and progress in nature's grand design. Fortunately for them, evolution could be used as easily to justify American democracy as to promote German militarism. These Americans blamed the wartime crisis of civilization not on evolution itself but on the Germans' misunderstanding and misuse of evolution. The root problem, as the Americans saw it, was the Germans' wrong-headed tendency to portray nature as the scene of a ruthless struggle for existence, in which fitness was equated with physical strength. Darwin had indeed envisioned an overpopulated world of organisms fighting over scarce resources; but, as the Russian prince Petr Kropotkin had pointed out in the 1890s, the struggle to survive often pitted an organism against its abiotic environment rather than against other organisms. On the basis of his observations of wildlife in the desolate steppes of northern Russia, Kropotkin had concluded that mutual aid and cooperation rather than competition allowed organisms to survive a harsh environment. As the Stanford ichthyologist David Starr Jordan remarked, such studies showed that "altruistic social adjustments are powerful factors in the struggle for existence in the life of animals as well as man."

The American appeal to mutual aid and cooperation in explaining evolution also derived in part from the writings of the British philosopher Herbert Spencer on social evolution. A committed neo-Lamarckian, Spencer battled with Weismann in the 1890s over the inheritance of acquired characteristics. For some nineteenth-century Americans Spencer came to represent the cutthroat competition and laissez-faire individualism that marked the Gilded Age. His memorable phrase "survival of the fittest" was adopted by the Yale economist William Graham Sumner, the steel magnate Andrew Carnegie, the oil baron John D. Rockefeller, and others as a convenient justification for their belief that a free-market economy with unrestrained competition would lead to economic progress. American biologists, however, tended to pick up on other aspects of Spencer's evolutionary theory. He portrayed evolution as a progressive development from the simple to the complex, from the homogeneous to the heterogeneous, with increasing specialization and integration marking the higher stages of individual and social life. "All kinds of creatures are alike," he wrote, "in so far as each exhibits co-operation among its components for the benefit of the whole; and this trait, common to them, is a trait common also to societies." This emphasis on progress through interdependence and cooperation impressed a number of American biologists, including Charles Otis Whitman, Edwin Grant Conklin, and William Patten, as being a key element in the evolutionary process.

A variation on this theme was the idea of emergent evolution, which the entomologist William Morton Wheeler, dean of the Bussey Institution at Harvard, popularized in America during the 1920s. Through the association of elements into an interdependent whole, such as hydrogen and oxygen in the formation of water, new properties appeared that were unpredictable from the behavior of the individual parts. Each level of organization, from the simplest chemical compounds to cells, organisms, and societies, represented an emergent property. Emergent evolution thus preserved a place for the progressive trend in evolution without appealing to some vitalistic force or active deity.

Seen in this light, evolution had much to teach Americans about the moral conduct of their society. Such theories of organic development not only undermined the stress placed on competition and conflict by German evolutionists abroad, but countered the negative images of evolution painted by fundamentalist antievolutionists at home. Evolution legitimated a Christian social ethic, not immorality. The themes of interdependence, cooperation, and mutual service also struck a responsive chord within the sociopolitical arena in the United States. By the turn of the century the transition from a rural, agrarian society to an urban, industrialized economy had left the invisible hand of a free market incapable of holding competing interests in balance. Reformers, politicians, and social scientists alike called on individuals to subordinate their own interests to the common good as a means of restoring the sense of community and order formerly provided by church and family.

Advocates of social cooperation frequently buttressed their arguments with appeals to the economy of nature. The Dartmouth biologist William Patten, for example, told his students in the first compulsory course on evolution for college freshmen that just as the parts of an organism cooperate to create something larger than themselves, so did "all the different parts and environments of the college work together

for its creation." Because the college constituted "a great living organism," it could thrive only if the students placed the good of the college above their own individual desires—just as the nation could prosper only when its citizens cooperated to attain collective goals. At Princeton, the biologist Edwin Grant Conklin preached a similar message: the need for a "new revolution which will enforce the duties of man as our former revolution emphasized the rights of man." As the writings of Patten and Conklin suggest, Spencer's emphasis on specialization and cooperation as companion principles of progress could be used to substantiate a need felt by American intellectuals such as Herbert Croly for an organic unity between self and society whereby the individual would become more subordinate to the common good. This message also appealed to American socialist intellectuals prior to World War I, who similarly appropriated Spencer's social organicism to legitimate their political cause. This cooperative rendition of evolution found its strongest scientific support in fields such as ecology, embryology, and physiology, where the impact of Mendelian genetics remained weak. But even biologists of a hereditarian stripe could find evolutionary grounds for denouncing war. Kellogg and Jordan, for example, appealed not to mutual aid or Spencerian evolution but to selection in criticizing militarism. In contrast to militarists who argued that war improved the human race by eliminating the weak and preserving the strong, the Stanford biologists pointed out that war killed off society's very fittest. Because the military selected the strongest and healthiest recruits and rejected the infirm, war disproportionally destroyed genetically worthy lives while leaving genetically less desirable members of society free to produce more offspring. Thus, unlike natural selection, war was maladaptive; it led to racial deterioration, not improvement.

Kellogg and Jordan's arguments for the dysgenic effects of war drew strength from the growing popularity of the eugenics movement in the United States. Darwin's cousin, Francis Galton, had coined the term "eugenics" in 1883 to describe scientifically informed efforts to direct human evolution by encouraging persons with high intelligence and admirable talents to breed while discouraging reproduction among persons deemed inferior. Although Galton's proposal at first met with little success, the rediscovery of Mendel's laws of inheritance in 1900 endowed it with a measure of scientific credibility. Enthusiasm for eugenics grew during the first decade of the new century with the discoveries that some human traits, such as color blindness and polydactyly, and certain metabolic diseases followed a Mendelian pattern of inheritance. Eugenicists reasoned that if single genes governed physical characteristics, then presumably mental and moral traits such as feeble-mindedness and alcoholism had a hereditary basis as well.

Mendel's laws of heredity attracted the interest not only of theoretically inclined biologists but practically minded agricultural scientists, often attached to agricultural colleges and experiment stations. In 1903 W. M. Hays, an assistant secretary in the U.S. Department of Agriculture, established the American Breeder's Association (ABA) to facilitate communication between academic biologists and practical breeders. Three years later the ABA created the first eugenics organization in America: a eugenics committee chaired by David Starr Jordan and charged with investigating human heredity with an eye toward emphasizing "the value of superior blood and the menace to society of inferior blood." Other such organizations soon followed, the most notable being the Eugenics Records Office (ERO), founded in 1910 by the Harvard-trained biologist Charles B. Davenport, who also directed the Society for the Study of Experimental Evolution. During its three-decade existence the ERO received over $1.2 million from various philanthropists and organizations such as the Carnegie Institution of Washington to carry out its work as a clearinghouse for scientific information on allegedly inheritable human traits ranging from weight and eye color to criminality and thalassophilia (i.e., love of the sea).

American interest in eugenics reflected widespread enthusiasm for applying scientific knowledge of heredity and evolution to the solution of plant, animal, and human problems. The eugenics movement offered biologists a welcome opportunity to apply their expertise and prove their social worth. Raymond Pearl captured his colleagues' sentiment in 1912 in his address to the First International Congress of Eugenics. "Hitherto, everybody except the scientist had a chance at directing the course of human evolution," he noted. "In the eugenics movement an earnest attempt is being made to show that science is the only safe guide in respect to the most fundamental of social problems." During the so-called Progressive period of the early twentieth century, American biologists commonly offered college students courses that combined evolution, genetics, and eugenics. The prospect of using science to manipulate human evolution harmonized with the Progressive spirit of the times, which advocated the employment of experts to improve society by rational planning and scientific management.

The paradox of modernity, viewed through the lens of Darwinian evolution, was that civilization had increasingly removed humans from the very forces of nature that had promoted human progress. The frontier, which the historian Frederick Jackson Turner identified as the builder of American character, had all but disappeared by the 1890s. Overcivilization was producing decadence and decay. The increasing number of eastern and southern European immigrants who began pouring into the United States in the 1880s seemed to threaten the established order and racial integrity dear to many white Anglo-Saxon Protestants, whose ancestors had conquered, populated, and developed the New World. Through artificial selection, society could ensure the preservation and further development of the characteristics deemed essential to success in white, middle-class American society: intelligence, physical prowess, and moral virtue.

In the opinion of American eugenicists, biology justified elevating the welfare of the race or society above that of the individual. As the Princeton biologist Edwin Grant Conklin put it, "race preservation, not self preservation was the first law of nature." Thus eugenicists felt few compunctions about recommending—in the interests of race betterment—the sterilization of criminals and the insane. Justice Oliver Wendell Holmes characterized the eugenic philosophy in a U.S. Supreme Court case, *Buck* v. *Bell* (1927), that challenged the states' authority to enforce sterilization laws. "We have seen more than once that the public welfare may call upon the best citizens for their lives," he remarked. "It would be strange if it could not call upon those who already sap the strength of the State for these lesser sacrifices . . . in order to prevent our being swamped with incompetence." Just as biologists interpreted Spencerian evolution to sanction the sacrifice of individual rights to the common good, so eugenicists elevated the good of the race above individual desires.

Although eugenic considerations spurred the passage of sterilization laws—in sixteen states by 1917—the most noted piece of legislation associated with the movement was the Immigration Restriction Act of 1924. In 1920 the U.S. House of Representatives Committee on Immigration and Naturalization appointed Harry H. Laughlin, superintendent of the ERO, to serve as a eugenics expert. Drawing on anti-immigrant sentiment in the wake of World War I, Laughlin cited "scientific" evidence to prove that the influx of "genetically inferior" eastern and southern Europeans, especially Jews, was leading to the decay and degeneration of the germ plasm within the

United States. Arguing that biological studies demonstrated the deleterious effects of race crossing, he called for a selective immigration policy to preserve the racial homogeneity of the Anglo-Saxon population. The resulting Immigration Act of 1924, which lowered the quota of immigrants from southern and eastern Europe, won the praise of the eugenics community for reflecting "biological wisdom."

Only one geneticist, the Johns Hopkins protozoologist Herbert Spencer Jennings, appeared before the Committee on Immigration and Naturalization to challenge Laughlin's biological arguments in favor of selective immigration. Although not opposed to the general aim of eugenics, Jennings took issue with Laughlin's conclusions. During the 1920s, as the eugenics movement drifted further and further from its scientific moorings, a number of prominent American biologists, including Thomas Hunt Morgan, Hermann J. Muller, Raymond Pearl, and Herbert Spencer Jennings, publicly distanced themselves from what was turning into a reactionary propaganda campaign. The rise of the Nazi race-hygiene movement in the early 1930s further tarnished eugenics, but developments in the field of genetics contributed as well. At Columbia University, Morgan and his coworkers, experimenting with the fruit fly *Drosophila,* discovered numerous mechanisms operating at the chromosomal level that confounded a simple one-to-one mapping of genes to traits. Throughout the 1930s and 1940s, developments in the fields of population genetics and systematics brought about a redefinition of the term species, which came to be seen not as an ideal type but as a population of individuals that display a range of variation and are united by their ability to interbreed. Nevertheless, in some circles eugenics remained respectable until after World War II.

THE ANTIEVOLUTION CRUSADE

Whereas American biologists responded to the Germans' use of evolution in World War I by stressing the cooperative rather than the competitive aspects of organic development, religious fundamentalists such as William Jennings Bryan replied by seeking to outlaw the offending doctrine. A Presbyterian layman and lawyer who had three times run unsuccessfully as the Democratic candidate for the presidency of the United States, Bryan had long believed in the silliness of monkey ancestors and the ethical danger of teaching young people that might makes right, but he rarely spoke out on the subject until Germany's wartime behavior—and books such as

Kellogg's *Headquarters Nights*—convinced him that Darwinism had dulled that nation's collective conscience. "The same science that manufactured poisonous gases to suffocate soldiers," he declared, "is preaching that man has a brute ancestry and eliminating the miraculous and the supernatural from the Bible." Bryan's suspicions about the dire moral consequences of accepting evolution, awakened by reports from wartime Germany, found apparent confirmation closer to home. In 1924, for example, newspapers reporting on the trial of Nathan Leopold and Richard Loeb for the cold-blooded kidnapping and murder of young Robert Franks linked their crime with the dulling effects of believing that humans were nothing but highly evolved animals. From various informants Bryan learned that American young people were succumbing in ever-increasing numbers to religious skepticism. When he investigated the cause, reported his wife, "he became convinced that the teaching of Evolution as a fact instead of a theory caused the students to lose faith in the Bible, first, in the story of creation, and later in other doctrines, which underlie the Christian religion." The surveys of the Bryn Mawr psychologist James H. Leuba lent credence to Bryan's contention. Leuba found that the longer students attended college, the less they espoused traditional religious beliefs.

Convinced of the connection between Darwinism and social decay, Bryan in 1921 launched a nationwide crusade to crush the offending doctrine as he had helped to crush the liquor interests in 1919. Although at times he sounded like a science-baiting biblical literalist, he privately confessed that he had little objection "to evolution before man," and he publicly repudiated the notion of a literal six-day creation. By adopting the day-age interpretation of Genesis 1, he was able to squeeze the fossil-bearing geological strata into the ages before the appearance of Adam and Eve in Eden. And by insisting that humans were the divinely created children of God rather than descendants of apes, he hoped to inspire them to behave accordingly. Confident that the overwhelming majority of Americans agreed with him, he urged them to overthrow the "scientific soviet" that dictated science policy and return control of the schools to the people. "Forget, if need be, the highbrows both in the political and college world, and carry this cause to the people," he suggested. "They are the final and efficiently corrective power."

Although Bryan enjoyed his greatest success among evangelical Baptists and Presbyterians in the South, his followers came from all walks of life and from all parts of the country. Among his chief lieutenants in the war against evolution were the Baptist preachers John Roach Straton of New York City, J. Frank Norris of Fort Worth, and William Bell Riley of Minneapolis. In 1919 Riley, a socially progressive Northern Baptist, had founded the World's Christian Fundamentals Association (WCFA). In the early 1920s Riley and Bryan joined forces to combat evolution. Partly as a result of their efforts, at least twenty state legislatures considered antievolution laws. Three—Tennessee, Mississippi, and Arkansas—banned the teaching of evolution in public schools; two others—Oklahoma and Florida, respectively—prohibited the adoption of evolution textbooks and condemned the teaching of Darwinism as "improper and subversive." Even the U.S. Congress debated whether to ban radio broadcasts favorable to evolution.

No event attracted greater attention to the antievolution crusade than the trial in 1925 of John Thomas Scopes, which pitted Bryan, representing the WCFA as a special prosecutor, against the free-thinking Clarence Darrow, who joined the team of defense lawyers assembled by the American Civil Liberties Union (ACLU). Scopes, a high-school teacher in Dayton, Tennessee, volunteered to serve as a guinea pig to test the new state statute banning the teaching of human evolution in public schools. Although the court in Dayton found him guilty and fined him $100, the Tennessee Supreme Court overturned the decision on a technicality (the fine should have been levied by the jury, not the judge) while upholding the constitutionality of the law. In the end neither side had much to celebrate. The ACLU had failed in its effort to get the Tennessee law declared unconstitutional, while the fundamentalists had taken a beating in the national press and had lost their aging leader, Bryan, a few days after the end of the trial. Nevertheless, rather than marking the demise of the crusade against evolution, the Scopes trial, by demonstrating that the courts would uphold antievolution laws, spurred the creationists on to renewed effort. Antievolution sentiment peaked in 1927 and remained sufficiently robust in 1928 to secure passage of a law in Arkansas. By then, however, both sides were growing battle weary, and opponents of evolution were abandoning their efforts to secure state laws banning the teaching of Darwinism.

The events of the 1920s prompted most publishers to dilute the coverage of evolution in their high-school biology texts. References to such inflammatory issues as the origin of life and the ancestry of the first humans virtually disappeared. Some textbook writers went so far as to delete the word "evolution"

entirely, cautiously replacing it with the more innocuous term "development." In one popular text Darwin's portrait, used as the frontispiece, silently vanished. Partially as a result of this "emasculation of textbooks," to use the words of one distressed evolutionist, an estimated 70 percent of the public high schools in America dropped the teaching of evolution from their curricula.

Although creationists opposed evolution primarily for moral and religious reasons, they often expressed scientific objections to the theory. Following some older philosophers of science and most modern dictionaries, which defined science as "classified knowledge," the creationists argued that evolution, a mere theory, fell outside the boundaries of true science. When the distinguished British biologist William Bateson confessed in 1921 that scientists had not discovered "the actual mode and process of evolution," creationists hailed his speech as "the swan song of Darwinism."

Despite the creationists' claims that most of the world's best scientists opposed evolution, they could name only one living biologist of repute, the German zoologist Albert Fleischmann, who rejected all theories of organic evolution. In North America not a single Ph.D.-possessing scientist publicly joined their ranks. Thus for scientific legitimacy they turned to such men as S. James Bole, a professor of biology at fundamentalist Wheaton College in Illinois, who had studied penmanship and fruit culture at the University of Illinois; Arthur I. Brown, an American-born surgeon from Vancouver, British Columbia, whose supporters billed him as the "greatest scientist in all the world"; and Harry Rimmer, a young homeopathic medical-school dropout turned Presbyterian evangelist, who established the home-based Research Science Bureau to support his ministry.

But the "principal scientific authority of the Fundamentalists," according to the journal *Science,* was the self-trained Seventh-day Adventist geologist and educator George McCready Price. Inspired by the visions of the Adventist prophetess Ellen G. White, Price developed an ultraliteral model of earth history that telescoped virtually the entire geological column into the one year of Noah's flood, thus at a single stroke depriving evolutionists of both the time and the evidence they needed for organic development. Having persuaded himself that 95 percent of the purported evidence for evolution came from geology, Price devoted relatively little attention to biological arguments for organic development. He believed that Mendelian genetics favored creation rather than evolution because it allowed for only "definite and pre-

Trial of John Scopes, Dayton, Tenn., 1925. Scopes is seated and leaning forward at the defense table, his left hand on his shirtsleeve. His defense attorney, Clarence Darrow, is leaning against the table (center). For a photograph of Darrow's adversary, William Jennings Bryan, see the article "Pacifism and Arms Limitation" (in this volume). PRINTS AND PHOTO-GRAPHS DIVISION, LIBRARY OF CONGRESS

dictable" variations within fixed boundaries, not the virtually unlimited variations required by natural selection. Unlike most fundamentalists, who employed the gap or day-age interpretations of Genesis 1 to accommodate the paleontological evidence of geological epochs, Price compressed the history of life on earth to about six thousand years.

Fellow creationists applauded Price's attacks on evolution and his defense of the deluge, but few of them saw the necessity of abandoning their accommodationist schemes for his radical flood geology. During the Scopes trial, for example, Bryan named Price as the one living scientist with whom he agreed but then promptly conceded the existence of geological ages, a concession abhorrent to Price.

As antievolution agitation abated in the late 1920s, conservative American Christians turned their energies inward; instead of trying to reform the nation's churches and schools, they sought to build up their own independent institutions. On the evolutionary front, they retreated from the legislative halls and began appealing to local school boards. Convinced that mainstream scientists would never grant them a fair hearing, they established their own alternative societies and began publishing their own journals. To some creationists, the most pressing need was the formation of a united front against evolution. As Dudley Joseph Whitney, one of Price's disciples, observed in the mid 1930s, fundamentalists were "all mixed up between geological ages, Flood geology and ruin, believing all at once; endorsing all at once." As long as they failed to agree on the correct meaning of Genesis 1, he reasoned, they could hardly expect to convert the world to creationism.

In 1935 Whitney, Price, and a handful of fellow creationists launched the Religion and Science Association specifically to find "a harmonious solution" to the exegetical discord within fundamentalism. Earlier antievolution groups had sought to outlaw the teaching of evolution, but this was the first to try to achieve a consensus within the fundamentalist community on the correct meaning of Genesis 1. Within a year, however, the leaders were squabbling over the Mosaic history—especially the possibility of a universal pre-Adamic cataclysm—and by 1937 the organization lay in shambles.

Saddened but not discouraged by the failure of the Religion and Science Association, Price and his fellow flood geologists in 1938 organized a more homogeneous group, the Deluge Geology Society. Although nominally nonsectarian, the society drew largely on Seventh-day Adventists in southern California and limited membership to persons who believed that the week of creation lasted no more than "six literal days, and that the Deluge should be studied as the cause of the major geological changes since creation." The deluge geologists undertook some of the earliest collective field research connected with creationism, including investigations of allegedly human fossil footprints found with dinosaur tracks and an abortive search for Noah's ark. Despite being in general agreement on the recent appearance of life on earth, the society split over whether the language of Genesis 1 allowed for the prior existence of a lifeless earth. It expired a short time later, before reaching its tenth anniversary.

Outside the small circles of the Religion and Science Association and the Deluge Geology Society, few Americans during the 1930s and 1940s displayed much interest in defending creationism. Liberal Christians, when they addressed the subject, typically endorsed evolution as the divine method of creation, and even evangelical Christians, who looked on organic evolution with suspicion because of its apparent conflict with Genesis, remained largely quiescent. The leaders of the American Scientific Affiliation, founded in 1941 by a small group of evangelical scientists, instinctively opposed evolution at first, but before long they were inspecting and evaluating it. Led by the geochemist J. Laurence Kulp and the anatomist Russell L. Mixter, affiliation leaders repudiated the strict creationism of fundamentalists such as Price and increasingly embraced the evidence for organic development over long periods of time, perhaps punctuated by divine interventions. A few became out-and-out theistic evolutionists. Such open-mindedness within the ranks of evangelicals

helped to spark a creationist counteroffensive in the 1960s.

THE DARWINIAN SYNTHESIS

While conservative Christians were squabbling among themselves over the correct interpretation of Genesis, American biologists for the first time were reaching a consensus about the efficacy of natural selection in evolution. During the years between the two world wars developments in the fields of population genetics and systematics led to a rapprochement between experimental biologists and field naturalists, who came to agree on the centrality of natural selection to the evolutionary process. The Darwinian synthesis, as the achievement came to be called, represented a belated victory, after nearly three-quarters of a century, for one of Darwin's key insights.

During the interwar years population geneticists, notably Ronald A. Fisher and J. B. S. Haldane in Britain and Sewall Wright in the United States, provided theoretical evidence that selection operating on random variations within a Mendelian population could give rise to evolutionary change. Although the three emphasized different aspects of the evolutionary process, they shared a common understanding of evolution as change over time in gene frequencies within a population.

Fisher's interest in applying mathematics to the problems of evolution stemmed from a lifelong commitment to eugenics. In 1930 he published a landmark contribution to the emerging field of population genetics, *The Genetical Theory of Natural Selection,* in which he offered mathematical proof of how natural selection operating on Mendelian variations within a population could effectively change the frequencies with which certain genes appeared over time. Two years later Haldane brought out *The Causes of Evolution,* which provided mathematical models of such evolutionary processes. Both men focused on the ways in which a population could become more fit by natural or artificial selection operating on a single gene, thus providing theoretical justification for the power of eugenics. Although Fisher remained a political conservative while Haldane moved from socialism to communism, they shared a common belief in the biological basis of class differences. With respect to race, Haldane admitted differences among groups but thought that no one group outshone all others; he regarded variation among individuals as being more important than the group to which they belonged.

While Fisher and Haldane were developing mathematical models of evolution occurring in large populations and operating on single genes, Wright was formulating a mathematical theory of evolution attentive to small populations in which selection operated on interactive systems of genes. A former student of W. E. Castle and E. M. East at Harvard, Wright spent over a decade with the U.S. Department of Agriculture before joining the zoology department at the University of Chicago in 1926. His familiarity with agricultural problems proved of importance in his later work on genetics. In the early 1930s he proposed a "shifting balance" theory of evolution, which focused attention on small semiisolated groups within a larger population, such as a species. Because of the small size of these groups, random fluctuations in gene frequencies would produce greater effects than would occur in the larger setting. Within each small group, inbreeding over the course of a relatively small number of generations would reduce the range of genetic variation, while random changes or "drift" within these groups would produce diversity within the species as a whole. Because some traits would be fixed within a group by chance rather than by selection, nonadaptive characteristics could survive within a species.

Part of the attractiveness of Wright's theoretical model was its conformity to what many systematists or taxonomists were seeing in nature. Throughout the 1920s and 1930s most naturalists believed that the differences separating races and closely allied species had no adaptive significance. During that period the Russian Sergei Chetverikov developed a new approach to the study of the genetics of natural populations that allowed Mendelian genetics to be integrated with natural history. By collecting wild *Drosophila* and breeding them in a laboratory, he demonstrated the existence of a large number of recessive mutations not otherwise observable. Theodosius Dobzhansky brought this Russian approach to America when he came to work with T. H. Morgan at Columbia in 1927. Over the course of the next decade Dobzhansky, sometimes collaborating with Wright, helped to forge a link between systematics and population genetics. His influential *Genetics and the Origin of Species,* published in 1937, inaugurated a series of important works, the Columbia Classics in Evolution, that formed the cornerstone of what came to be known as the modern synthesis. This series included such titles as Ernst Mayr's *Systematics and the Origin of Species,* George Gaylord Simpson's *Tempo and Mode in Evolution,* and G. Ledyard Stebbins's *Variation and Evolution in Plants.* Within

these works, natural selection, formerly held in contempt by many biologists, emerged as the most significant causal mechanism governing speciation and macroevolutionary change.

The accord reached by biologists contrasted markedly with the strife that engulfed the world at large. The rise of fascist regimes in Europe during the 1930s and the entrance of the United States into World War II in 1941 presented American biologists with an intellectual challenge similar to the one that had confronted their predecessors during World War I. Like the generation that preceded them, the biologists of the 1940s sought to mobilize science in defense of democracy. But they did so in novel ways and with new theoretical weapons.

Located at Columbia University, where the anthropologist Franz Boas had long been leading an attack on scientific racism, Dobzhansky used evolutionary science to condemn Nazi race theory and discredit the underlying assumptions of totalitarianism. During the 1930s he had accumulated experimental evidence documenting an abundance of genetic variation in populations of wild *Drosophila.* Studies of these fruit flies, he believed, had a direct bearing on the human condition. He presented the implications of his work for human society to the American civilization program at Princeton University during the academic year 1945–1946. Because all individuals, regardless of race, are genetically unique and because a given population includes a wide range of genetic variation, he argued, single racial types do not exist. Differing frequencies of blood groups in populations around the world, to which Dobzhansky assigned no adaptive significance, suggested that only the frequencies of some genes distinguished one race from another. Humans composed a single species with a common pool of genes; their ability to interbreed pointed to their underlying unity. This conception proved of special importance in the formulation of the 1950 UNESCO Statement on Race, authored by the physical anthropologist M. F. Ashley Montagu.

Dobzhansky argued that populations displaying a great deal of genetic diversity possessed a selective advantage over populations that did not. But not all geneticists agreed. For example, Herman J. Muller, a student of Morgan's who won the Nobel Prize in 1947 for work on the effects of x-rays on genetic mutation, insisted that most variations arising through chance mutations would be deleterious. Selection, therefore, eliminated diversity rather than preserved it. Muller, an ardent eugenicist, believed that civilization had largely isolated humans from the effects of natural selection. This isolation was leading to a dangerous increase in the load of deleterious mutations, which, if not reduced through artificial selection, would result in the extinction of the species. In the wake of Hiroshima and Nagasaki, Muller found an American public receptive to his passionate warnings about the harmful biological effects of atomic radiation and the dangers of nuclear testing.

In a book titled *Heredity, Race, and Society* (1946) Dobzhansky and a colleague, Leslie C. Dunn, defended democracy against the specter of totalitarianism by arguing that democracy most closely conformed to the ideals of genetic diversity found within nature. Because each individual has an equal opportunity in a democratic society, the realization of one's full genetic potential can be more readily achieved than in a nondemocratic society, where factors other than heredity determine one's fate. According to this way of thinking, democracy encouraged diversity by forcing individuals to find their particular social niches. Totalitarianism, in contrast, reduced diversity by emphasizing conformity. Although some scientists saw the social insects as biological exemplars for human society, Dobzhansky maintained that insects provided a bad model for humans because the genetic fixity of individuals within insect societies rendered them unable to respond to changing environmental conditions. In an influential article written with Ashley Montagu, Dobzhansky stressed the importance of developmental plasticity in order for humans to respond to their rapidly changing social world.

During the early 1950s both Dobzhansky and Montagu appealed to the writings of the University of Chicago ecologist Warder Clyde Allee to justify a benign view of nature that downplayed fierce struggles for existence. From 1921 until his death in 1955 Allee built a research program at Chicago intent on demonstrating the benefits of group life in the animal kingdom, from protozoa to humans. Animal aggregations, he believed, helped to ameliorate harsh environmental conditions and provided physiological benefits unattainable in solitary life. In a competition between groups possessing different degrees of cooperation, the more cooperative group would win. Allee's experimental findings lent support to the view that natural selection operated on populations as well as on individuals. With his Chicago colleagues Alfred Emerson and Ralph Gerard he taught the lessons of cooperation in nature to counteract the implication that war was rooted in human genes.

In emphasizing group integration, in ecological communities as well as in human societies, these Chicago biologists found themselves stepping on dangerous ground. The paleontologist George Gay-

lord Simpson, of the American Museum of Natural History, who did much to bring the evidence from the fossil record in line with a neo-Darwinian explanation of natural selection operating on small-scale random variations, scathingly attacked the "aggregation ethics" of the Chicago school because its "totalitarianist biology" threatened to undermine the importance of the individual, on which democracy rested. For Simpson, the individual, not the group, constituted the fundamental unit of selection and the essential component of democracy. In contrast to the Chicago biologists, who emphasized the selection of groups, Simpson viewed groups as mere amalgamations of individuals with no distinctive properties of their own. Any scheme that subordinated the interests of the individual to the group supported totalitarianism. For Simpson, evolutionary progress depended not on increasing levels of integration but on greater individualization. Thus he developed a naturalistic ethics that stressed the importance of the individual in both biological and social evolution.

Simpson's views reflected a hardening of the modern synthesis during the period of the Cold War, as evolutionary biologists increasingly came to embrace a rigid adaptationist program in which natural selection acted solely on individuals within a population. Indeed, by the late 1960s many biologists were suggesting that evolution operated not for the good of the group, but for the good of the individual. In the wake of World War II old arguments about evolution promoting the interests of the species or race no longer found a receptive audience. The horrors of Nazi Germany had called such conceptions into question, and the threat of totalitarianism abroad had led to an emphasis on the importance of the individual, not the group, as the pillar of democracy. During the Cold War American liberals identified the pluralist nature of American politics, with its diverse and competing interest groups, as the essential characteristic of American democracy, sheltering it from the threat of dictatorship. Difference, diversity, and conflict contributed as much to the political economy of the United States as they did to the economy of nature.

The synthetic theory of evolution, taken to its logical extreme, seemed to empty the organic world of meaning. The theory implied that life on earth had resulted from blind chance, not purpose or direction. But even some of the architects of the synthesis, such as Dobzhansky and Simpson in the United States and Julian Huxley in Great Britain, found this philosophical implication difficult to accept. Thus they undertook the challenging task of fashioning a worldview that preserved progress while adhering to a mechanistic and nonpurposive account of evolution. Simpson, for example, in *The Meaning of Evolution* (1949) pointed to the evolution of greater individual capacities within the human species as the source for a naturalistic ethics. Such attempts to find moral and spiritual values in nature prompted the historian John C. Greene to label them the "Bridgewater Treatises of the twentieth century," a reference to a popular series of nineteenth-century works on natural theology.

Religious conservatives anathematized such efforts, but at least some liberal churchmen joined their scientific brethren in enterprises such as the Institute on Religion in an Age of Science, founded in 1954, which sought to "reformulate the theory and practice of religion in the light of contemporary scientific knowledge." In 1966 Ralph Wendell Burhoe, a philosopher-theologian associated with the institute and with the Center for Advanced Study in Theology and the Sciences at Meadville Theological School in Chicago, began publishing *Zygon: Journal of Religion and Science.* The journal served as a forum for discussions of moral and spiritual values based on science rather than revelation. More recently, in the television series *Cosmos* the astronomer Carl Sagan introduced millions of Americans to the evolution-based philosophy of secular humanism.

No attempt to extrapolate normative guidelines for human behavior from studying the evolution of the animal kingdom attracted more attention than the Harvard entomologist E. O. Wilson's *On Human Nature* (1978), a work that popularized the ideas of his earlier and more academically oriented book *Sociobiology: The New Synthesis* (1975). Such renditions of evolutionary naturalism in the latter part of the twentieth century sought to imbue science with the authority of religion. But even Wilson recognized the limited impact of his ideas. "Scientists and other scholars, organized into learned groups such as . . . the Institute of Religion in an Age of Science, support little magazines distributed by subscription and organize campaigns to discredit Christian fundamentalism, astrology, and Immanuel Velikovsky," he wrote, referring to the controversial author of the best-selling *Worlds in Collision* (1950), but they "are vastly outnumbered by true believers, by the people who follow [astrologer] Jeane Dixon but have never heard of Ralph Wendell Burhoe."

THE CREATIONIST REVIVAL

The 1960s witnessed a creationist revival that continued unabated into the 1990s and that undermined the efforts of evolutionists to guide the moral lives of Americans. Unlike the antievolution crusaders of the early twentieth century, who had little quarrel with the geological evidence of an ancient earth, the so-called scientific creationists of the latter part of the century insisted that life on earth, and perhaps the universe itself, had existed for no more than ten thousand years. Following in the footsteps of George McCready Price, they squeezed virtually the entire geological column into the year or so spanned by Noah's flood and its aftermath.

The creationist revival coincided with the appearance in the 1960s of the federally funded Biological Sciences Curriculum Study textbooks, written in response to the Soviet Union's launching of the artificial satellite Sputnik in 1957, which shamed Americans into improving their teaching of science. Since the 1920s evolution had virtually disappeared from public high-school classrooms, but the BSCS texts featured it as "the warp and woof of modern biology." Creationists, aroused by this "attempt to ram evolution down the throats of our children," responded by promoting the teaching of creationism. Their revival gained momentum in the 1970s from its association with the new religious Right and from a suspicion in some circles that establishment science could not be trusted. But if such events help to account for the rising tide of antievolution sentiment, they tell us nothing about the reasons why so many creationists turned their backs on tried-and-true interpretations of Genesis that accommodated historical geology in favor of a theory that necessitated fitting all of earth history into a few thousand years. To answer that question, we must turn our attention to developments in the evangelical community beginning in the 1950s.

In 1954 the Baptist theologian and philosopher Bernard Ramm published an influential book, *The Christian View of Science and Scripture,* which argued that Bible-believing Christians did not need to insist on a young earth, a universal flood, or even the recent appearance of humans. Greatly overestimating the inroads that Price's flood geology had made among evangelical Christians, Ramm made a point of questioning the amateur geologist's competence, training, and integrity. Although many evangelicals applauded Ramm for liberating them from the "narrow bibliolatry" of the hyperfundamentalists, the targets of his attack reacted with understandable ill humor. One outraged reader, John C. Whitcomb, Jr., a young Princeton-educated biblical scholar who belonged to the Grace Brethren, resolved to devote his doctoral dissertation to rebutting Ramm and defending Price. When he approached a publisher with the completed dissertation, he was advised to seek a scientifically trained collaborator to help turn the dissertation into a book. Unable to find a single geologist who embraced Price's views, he turned to Henry M. Morris, a Baptist with a Ph.D. in hydraulic engineering from the University of Minnesota. Early in 1961 a small fundamentalist publisher brought out the product of their joint effort, *The Genesis Flood*.

Beginning with a testimony to their belief in the inerrancy and infallibility of the Bible, "verbally inspired in the original autographs," Whitcomb and Morris went on to marshal evidence from both scripture and nature that seemed to support a recent creation in six literal days and a universal deluge that remolded the surface of the earth. With Price, they shared a conviction that geology, not biology, held the key to unlock the mystery of origins. If the fossil-bearing strata had been deposited during the brief period of Noah's flood, they argued, then "the last refuge of the case for evolution immediately vanishes away, and the record of the rocks becomes a tremendous witness . . . to the holiness and justice and power of the living God of Creation!"

Although the appearance of *The Genesis Flood* went largely unnoticed by the scientific community, it ignited a heated debate among conservative Protestants. In contrast to Ramm and his scientific friends in the American Scientific Affiliation, who interpreted Genesis in ways compatible with considerable organic evolution, Whitcomb and Morris insisted that a correct reading of scripture required the acceptance of flood geology and ruled out belief in the widely held day-age and gap theories. If death had resulted from Adam's sin, as the Bible said, they reasoned, then how could fossils antedate the Edenic creation, as advocates of the day-age and gap theories believed?

One of the few affiliation members to side with Whitcomb and Morris was the Berkeley-trained geneticist Walter E. Lammerts, a Missouri Lutheran who, like Morris, had once belonged to the Deluge Geology Society. Frustrated by the refusal of the American Scientific Affiliation to give flood geology a sympathetic hearing, Lammerts led a revolt in 1963 that resulted in the formation of the Creation Research Society. The society stopped short of making the acceptance of flood geology a condition of membership, but there was never any doubt where it stood in the debate over Genesis. Partisans of geological ages and exegetical gaps were not welcome. Four decades earlier creationists had been unable to claim a single well-trained American naturalist on their side; in contrast, six of the ten founding members of the Creation Research Society possessed earned doctorates in biology or biochemistry and a seventh held a master's degree in biology. In ten years the society recruited nearly two thousand members, over 40 percent of whom claimed graduate degrees in pure or applied science. Along with Morris's Institute for Creation Research, founded in San Diego in the early 1970s, the Creation Research Society became the most influential promoter of young-earth creationism.

Besides publishing a quarterly journal featuring creationist research, often of a literary nature, the society prepared a high-school biology text based on creationist principles. Several state textbook committees approved its use; but when one district in southern Indiana decided to rely on just the creationist text, a state court banned further use in public schools on the grounds that the book presented "*only* the view of Biblical Creationism in a favorable light." This came on the heels of a Supreme Court decision in 1968 that struck down the 1928 Arkansas law banning the teaching of evolution in public schools and a bitter textbook controversy in California that opened the door for the teaching of creationism "in scientific terms."

In a casuistic attempt to alleviate such constitutional concerns about the separation of church and state, young-earth creationists in the early 1970s began repackaging their version of biblical creationism as "scientific creationism" or "creation science." Scientific creationism described the same sequence of events as biblical creationism—from a recent special creation to a worldwide flood that buried the fossils—but did so without any mention of such biblical characters as God, Adam, or Noah. "Creationism is on the way back," announced Morris, "this time not primarily as a religious belief, but as an alternative scientific explanation of the world in which we live." Instead of seeking to outlaw the teaching of evolution, as their predecessors had done in the 1920s, scientific creationists began advocating the teaching of two models of earth history—creation and evolution—each, they argued, bearing the imprimatur of science.

By the early 1980s two states, Arkansas and Louisiana, and a number of local school boards had adopted the two-model approach. The Arkansas law mandating "balanced treatment" in teaching creation and evolution spelled out the cardinal tenets of creation science:

(1) Sudden creation of the universe, energy, and life from nothing; (2) The insufficiency of mutation and natural selection in bringing about development of all living kinds from a single organism; (3) Changes only within fixed limits of originally created kinds

of plants and animals; (4) Separate ancestry for man and apes; (5) Explanation of the earth's geology by catastrophism, including the occurrence of a worldwide flood; and (6) A relatively recent inception of the earth and living kinds.

A half-century earlier virtually no creationist outside of Seventh-day Adventism would have insisted on the geological significance of a universal deluge, but for the new breed of scientific creationist the Genesis flood had come to represent "the real crux of the conflict between the evolutionist and creationist cosmologies." If George McCready Price's system of flood geology could be established "on a sound scientific basis," declared Morris in his handbook *Scientific Creationism* (1974), "then the entire evolutionary cosmology, at least in its present neo-Darwinian form, will collapse."

Evolutionists, not surprisingly, resisted the effort to sell creationism as science and denounced the scientific creationists as religious zealots in shabby scientific clothing. In contrast to the creationists, who tended to define science in ways that allowed their views to be included within the scientific domain, their critics drew the boundaries of science to exclude creationism. Frequently they employed Karl Popper's contention that all scientific statements must be falsifiable to argue that creationism was not science because its central claims could not be disproved. (On occasion these same critics attempted to disqualify creationism on the grounds that modern science had falsified it.) Convinced of the nonfalsifiability of creation science, the federal judge who ruled on the legality of the Arkansas "balanced treatment" act declared creation science to be religion, not science. Thus any law requiring that it be taught was unconstitutional because it violated the First Amendment requirement that church and state be separate. Merely showing creation science to be "bad science" would have been insufficient in this case, because the constitution does not ban the teaching of bad science in public schools. In 1987 the United States Supreme Court upheld the judge's decision, but left open the possibility of voluntarily teaching creation science, if done so with a clearly secular intent. Creationists consequently shifted their attention from legislators to science teachers and school-board members.

The 1981 trial in Arkansas graphically illustrated the fallacy of portraying the evolution-creation debate as simply a conflict between science and religion. As the presiding judge observed, the plaintiffs (who opposed teaching creationism) included "the resident Arkansas Bishops of the United Methodist, Episco-

pal, Roman Catholic and African Methodist Episcopal Churches, the principal official of the Presbyterian Churches in Arkansas, other United Methodist, Southern Baptist and Presbyterian clergy," and various Jewish organizations—as well as one high-school biology teacher and the National Association of Biology Teachers. The list of defendants (who favored teaching creation science) included no ministers or religious groups. During the trial itself a Methodist bishop, a Catholic priest, a Protestant theologian, and an evangelical church historian joined four scientists and other experts in opposing the law, while a number of scientists spoke in favor of it. Thus, in the opinion of the theologian-participant Langdon Gilkey, the trial pitted not science against religion but "elite" science and religion against "popular" science and religion.

The creationist revival sparked by the appearance of Whitcomb and Morris's *The Genesis Flood* elevated the deluge geology of George McCready Price to a position of fundamentalist orthodoxy and endowed special creationism with a measure of respectability unknown for over a century. Although most Americans and even many evangelical Christians remained untouched by the revival, the flood geologists exerted enormous influence on American thought during the last third of the twentieth century. At first the revival attracted little attention beyond the pews of America's fundamentalist churches. Most American scientists, when they thought about creationists at all, dismissed them as more of a nuisance than a threat. By the early 1970s, however, both the National Academy of Sciences and the American Association for the Advancement of Science were taking notice; and when more than twenty state legislatures began debating balanced-treatment acts in the early 1980s, the scientific establishment grew alarmed. "Creationism," reported the journal *Creation/Evolution,* "is breaking out from coast to coast." In 1984 the National Academy of Sciences issued a spirited defense of evolution, *Science and Creationism,* that sought to expose creationism as a threat to both science and society. "In a nation whose people depend on scientific progress for their health, economic gains, and national security," wrote the president of the academy with passion, "it is of utmost importance that our students understand science as a system of study, so that by building on past achievements they can maintain the pace of scientific progress and ensure the continued emergence of results that can benefit mankind."

The scientific creationists not only coopted the creationist label for their peculiar brand of creationism but set the terms of debate for most discussions of creation versus evolution. By the end of the century it was difficult to discuss the issue of origins without at least mentioning the views of the young-earth creationists. At first the creationist revival seemed confined largely to the sunbelt, but it soon spread throughout the country, indeed, throughout the world. The Korea Association of Creation Research, founded in 1980 after a visit by Morris, enjoyed such success that within a decade it had planted several branches in the United States.

Since the beginning of the century creationists had attempted to bolster their case against evolution by citing the writings of scientists who questioned the prevailing evolutionary dogma. The respected British biologist William Bateson, who proclaimed that scientists had not discovered "the actual mode and process of evolution," became a fundamentalist favorite in the 1920s, as did Austin H. Clark in the 1930s, Richard B. Goldschmidt in the 1940s, William R. Thompson in the 1950s, and Gerald A. Kerkut in the 1960s. Later in the century the scientific creationists invoked the "neocatastrophism" of the paleontologist Stephen Jay Gould and the geologist Robert H. Dott, Jr., to support a nonuniformitarian vision of earth history. In contrast to evolutionists who insisted on slow changes in the past, Gould employed the concept of "punctuated equilibria" to develop a theory of evolution by spurts, while Dott used the notion of "episodic sedimentation" to explain the relatively rapid formation of geological strata. Both scientists denied that their views lent any support to the catastrophism of the creationists, but that did not prevent the latter from appealing to their authority.

As we have seen, the creationist revival of the late twentieth century derived strength from a number of social and political developments, including the aggressive promotion of evolution in public-school classrooms and the growing political strength of the New Right. But why did so many creationists in opposing evolution feel the need to turn away from religiously orthodox old-earth interpretations of Genesis, which allowed them to accept the evidence of historical geology, and embrace the extreme young-earth views of the flood geologists? Socioeconomic factors, which might help to explain opposition to evolution in general, seem to have played little role in prompting evangelical Christians to adopt scientific creationism. Pentecostals, for example, presumably differed little from fundamentalists socially and economically, but their experiential orientation to religion made them less vulnerable than their fund-

amentalist brothers and sisters to the cerebral arguments of the scientific creationists.

Nothing accounts for the success of flood geology more than the publication of *The Genesis Flood* by Whitcomb and Morris and the authors' subsequent efforts to convince evangelical Christians that a correct reading of the Bible required giving up belief in hermeneutic schemes that accommodated scientific evidence of the antiquity of life on earth. By forcing scientific data to fit into a biblical framework, they appealed to Christians "fed up with articles and books which tried to make scripture conform to the latest theory." Flood geology required no assumption that Moses had meant an "age" when he wrote "day" or that he had overlooked eons of earth history when writing the first verses of Genesis. Biblical literalists who read in the last book of the Bible of the earth's imminent apocalyptic end took comfort from assurances that the first book described the earth's recent catastrophic beginning. As one admirer put it, "Tens of thousands of Christians have been convinced by Morris & Whitcomb's books because *they make sense of the Bible.*" And, as hundreds of creation scientists assured them, they could accept Morris and Whitcomb's claims without sacrificing one scientific truth.

CREATION AND EVOLUTION IN THE 1990s

A nationwide Gallup poll in 1991 showed that 47 percent of Americans, including a quarter of the college graduates, professed to believe that "God created man pretty much in his present form at one time within the last 10,000 years." Another 40 percent favored the theistic evolutionary view that "Man has developed over millions of years from less advanced forms of life, but God guided this process, including man's creation." Only 9 percent thought that "Man has developed over millions of years from less advanced forms of life" with God having no part in the process. African Americans, women, and the poor seemed most receptive to creationism.

These findings suggest that Darwinian evolution had not yet found a receptive home among large segments of the American public, even though it had become firmly entrenched within the academic scientific community. Although many American scientists, especially during the first half of the century, continued to espouse theistic evolution, they increasingly censored such sentiments from their professional pronouncements. As evolution, assisted by the modern synthesis, moved to center stage on the biological platform, appeals to evolution for moral and spiritual guidance, characteristic of an earlier age, became suspect. Many biologists still expressed wonder when contemplating nature's grand design, but they rarely did so at scientific meetings or in professional journals. For them, religion had become privatized.

SEE ALSO Protestantism (volume IV).

BIBLIOGRAPHY

There is no standard history of the responses of American scientists to evolution, but two useful introductions are Edward J. Pfeifer, "United States," in *The Comparative Reception of Darwinism,* ed. Thomas F. Glick (1974), pp. 168–206; and Peter J. Bowler, "Scientific Attitudes to Darwinism in Britain and America," in *The Darwinian Heritage,* ed. David Kohn (1985), pp. 641–681. For Protestant, Catholic, and Jewish reactions to Darwin in America, see, respectively, Jon H. Roberts, *Darwinism and the Divine in America: Protestant Intellectuals and Organic Evolution, 1859–1900* (1988); John L. Morrison, "A History of American Catholic Opinion on the Theory of Evolution, 1859–1950" (Ph.D. diss., University of Missouri, 1951); and Marc Swetlitz, "Responses of American Reform Rabbis to Evolutionary Theory, 1864–1888," in *The Interaction of Scientific and Judaic Cultures,* ed. Yakov Rabkin and Ira Robinson (forthcoming from Science Review Press). On the social implications of Darwinism, see Robert C. Bannister, *Social Darwinism: Science and Myth in Anglo-American Social Thought* (1979); and John C. Greene, *Science, Ideology, and World View: Essays in the History of Evolutionary Ideas* (1981).

The best introduction to evolutionary thought at the turn of the century is still Vernon L. Kellogg, *Darwinism To-Day* (1907). For a recent assessment, see Peter J. Bowler, *The Eclipse of Darwinism: Anti-Darwinian Evolution Theories in the Decades around 1900* (1983). Bowler has also written *The Mendelian Revolution: The Emergence of Hereditarian Concepts in Modern Science and Society* (1989), a brief survey that occasionally looks at the American scene. Two biographies of prominent early-twentieth-century American biologists who contributed to evolutionary theory are Ronald Rainger, *An Agenda for Antiquity: Henry Fairfield Osborn and Vertebrate Paleontology at the American Museum of Natural History, 1890–1935* (1991); and Garland E. Allen, *Thomas Hunt Morgan: The Man and His Science* (1978).

Daniel J. Kevles provides a readable and reliable overview of eugenics in America in *In the Name of Eugenics: Genetics and the Uses of Human Heredity* (1985). Hamilton Cravens, *The Triumph of Evolution: American Scientists and the Heredity-Environment Controversy, 1900–1941,* 2d ed. (1988), is especially insightful in discussing the decline of eugenics in America. Gregg Mitman, *The State of Nature: Ecology, Community, and American Social Thought, 1900–1950* (1992), describes the responses of American biologists to World War I and analyzes changing attitudes about the individual and community within American society. For a historical analysis of the use of evolutionary theory by American socialists, see Mark Pittenger, *American Socialists and Evolutionary Thought, 1870–1920* (1993).

Ronald L. Numbers, *The Creationists* (1992), upon which much of the preceding discussion of creationism is based, surveys the subject from 1859 to the present. The legal issues are discussed in Edward J. Larson, *Trial and Error: The American Controversy over Creation and Evolution,* updated ed. (1989). Maynard Shipley, a critic of creationism, provides a detailed, partisan account of the crusade against evolution in the 1920s in *The War on Modern Science: A Short History of the Fundamentalist Attacks on Evolution and Modernism* (1927). The best state-level history of the campaign is Willard B. Gatewood, Jr., *Preachers, Pedagogues, and Politicians: The Evolution Controversy in North Carolina, 1920–1927* (1966).

Henry M. Morris, *A History of Modern Creationism* (1984), tells the story of the creationist revival from the perspective of a leading advocate. For a more critical analysis, see James R. Moore, "The Creationist Cosmos of Protestant Fundamentalism," in *Fundamentalisms and Society: Reclaiming the Sciences, the Family, and Education,* ed. Martin E. Marty and R. Scott Appleby (1993), pp. 42–72. Dorothy Nelkin, *The Creation Controversy: Science or Scripture in the Schools* (1982), focuses on the educational debates between 1957 and 1982. On the place of evolutionary thought in the secular humanism of the Cold War period, see John Durant, "Evolution, Ideology, and World View: Darwinian Religion in the Twentieth Century," in *History, Humanity, and Evolution: Essays for John C. Greene,* ed. James R. Moore (1989), pp. 355–374.

William B. Provine explores the development of population genetics and its contribution to the modern synthesis in two works: "Adaptation and Mechanisms of Evolution after Darwin: A Study in Persistent Controversies," in *The Darwinian Heritage,* ed. David Kohn (1985), pp. 825–866, and *Sewall Wright and Evolutionary Biology* (1986). The standard history of the evolutionary synthesis is Ernst Mayr and William B. Provine, eds., *The Evolutionary Synthesis* (1980). However, two recent works have challenged the conventional view of population genetics and systematics coming together into an overarching theory of evolution: V. B. Smocovitis, "Unifying Biology: The Evolutionary Synthesis and Evolutionary Biology," *Journal of the History of Biology* 25 (1992):

1–65; and Joseph Allen Cain, "Common Problems and Cooperative Solutions: Organizational Activity in Evolutionary Studies, 1936–1947," *Isis* 84 (1993): 1–25. Dobzhansky's contributions to the evolutionary synthesis are discussed by John Beatty in "Dobzhansky and Drift: Facts, Values, and Chance in Evolutionary Biology," in *The Probabilistic Revolution,* vol. 2 of *Ideas in the Sciences,* ed. Lorenz Kruger, Gerd Gigernzer, and Mary S. Morgan (1987), pp. 271–311. For a history of the concept of progress in twentieth-century evolutionary biology, see Michael Ruse, "Molecules to Men: Evolutionary Biology and Thoughts of Progress," in *Evolutionary Progress,* ed. Matthew H. Nitecki (1988), pp. 97–128.

The authors wish to thank John Beatty, Edward J. Larson, and Jon H. Roberts for commenting on this essay.

THE HUMAN MIND AND PERSONALITY

Jon H. Roberts

During the twentieth century American intellectuals have sought to bring to the study of the human mind an approach comparable in rigor to that already employed in studying natural phenomena in the physical and biological worlds. This effort, informed by the conviction that a scientific understanding of human nature provides the most reliable means of promoting mental health and social progress, has led them to dismiss the psychological thought of their predecessors as barren speculation.

Such disdain underestimates the historical significance of the discussion of the human mind that preceded the advent of "scientific" psychology. Still, it is true that for much of the nineteenth century systematic psychological discourse in the United States was a largely descriptive enterprise closely associated with and often subordinate to philosophical and theological concerns. The most common forum for such discourse was a college course in mental and moral philosophy. Highly eclectic, the American thinkers who dealt with psychological issues prior to 1875 were most strongly influenced by Thomas Reid, Dugald Stewart, and other proponents of Scottish commonsense realism, but they also frequently employed the perspectives of English and, especially during the later years of this period, Continental thinkers. The resulting amalgam was a view of psychology as the "science of the soul." Underlying this view was the conviction that it made sense to posit a sharp distinction between mind and matter. The elaborately schematized descriptions that appeared in the numerous textbooks produced by Americans for use in college classrooms typically divided the human mind into a tripartite division of intellectual, emotional, and volitional powers, or "faculties." Although in practice their conclusions were often the product of deductive reasoning, academic psychologists characteristically embraced the principle that the interdependent operation of the mental faculties could best be understood through observation, by which they meant both introspection and analysis of behavior.

Many also believed that the mind's faculties were similar to muscles in that they could be strengthened and enlarged through appropriate exercise and discipline. Using the insights of psychology could thus foster the development of "character."

THE "NEW PSYCHOLOGY"

In their allegiance to empirical investigation and the idea that understanding human nature could pay rich practical dividends, "prescientific" academic psychologists anticipated the concerns of those who followed them. The same can be said of proponents of the less systematic psychological ideas, most notably mesmerism and phrenology, that were articulated outside American colleges during the period between 1800 and 1875. By the late nineteenth century, however, an increasing number of Americans had become convinced that a more concerted employment of the systematic, seemingly objective methods of scientific inquiry was the surest way to push back the frontier of ignorance and arrive at truth. Among these Americans was a growing number of "new psychologists" in the nation's burgeoning colleges and universities, who became convinced that it was time to separate psychology from speculative philosophy by applying methods associated with the natural sciences to the study of the human psyche. The theory of organic evolution, which implied that human beings were not utterly unlike other animals and that the human mind, like the human body, was a product of transmutation, did much to bolster their confidence that the mind was a legitimate object of scientific investigation. The work of European physiologists and psychologists was also significant in this regard, for it suggested the interdependence of mental and neurophysiological processes and provided American psychologists with some of the experimental techniques that they employed in subjecting consciousness to scientific examination and measurement.

The early partisans of the new psychology introduced scientific instruments and controlled experiments into their work. Those actions were of crucial importance in helping to define psychology as a scientific discipline, secure its independence from philosophy, and enhance its prestige. Actually, however, experimentalism most frequently supplemented rather than replaced philosophical speculation; the work of the pioneer generation of scientific psychologists remained strongly informed by assumptions drawn from philosophy and theology. Often, in fact, they sought to ingratiate themselves with college officials and gain the support of the American public by implying that psychological experimentation would foil those who wished to reduce the data of consciousness to neurophysiological processes. These thinkers tended to use their science less as a tool for eliminating metaphysics altogether than as a club for attacking those who embraced a metaphysical position with which they disagreed.

By the beginning of the twentieth century, in spite of continuing resistance from some philosophers, the new psychologists had managed to acquire for psychology most of the characteristic elements of an autonomous scientific discipline: professorships, laboratories, graduate programs, journals, a professional organization, and several textbooks treating psychology as a branch of natural science. Notwithstanding these successes, however, many other scientists continued to regard "mind" and "consciousness" as metaphysical terms resistant to scientific analysis and measurement. This prompted psychologists to redouble their efforts to establish convincing scientific credentials. As a result, psychology became afflicted with a sustained and particularly severe case of what has commonly been referred to as "physics envy."

Although most of the eminent spokespersons in academic psychology shared a commitment to the norms of scientific investigation, the discipline's unity and possibly its status as a science were undermined by disagreements concerning subject matter, goals, and methods of psychological inquiry. The 1890s witnessed the emergence of structuralism as the first clearly recognizable "school" of psychology in the United States. Proponents of this perspective, led by the English émigré and Cornell psychology professor Edward Bradford Titchener, were strongly influenced by German experimental psychology and based their approach to the mind on the models of anatomy and physical science. Through experiments employing carefully controlled stimuli and introspective reports of the sensations that those stimuli produced on the consciousness, structuralists sought to determine the fundamental constituents of the human mind and to establish what Titchener called "the laws of connection of the elementary mental processes."

Despite having the imprimatur of German experimentalism, structuralism gained few disciples in the United States. By 1900 most American psychologists, enthralled with the evolutionary theories of Charles Darwin and vividly aware of rapid changes in their social environment, regarded mind as an agency that contributed to the ability of organisms to adapt to their surroundings. This gave rise to a perspective that came to be known as functionalism. Whereas the structuralists regarded the analysis of the contents of the human mind as an appropriate end in itself, the research program of the functionalists, first articulated by William James in his *Principles of Psychology* (1890) and attaining its preeminent expression in the work of John Dewey and James Rowland Angell at the University of Chicago at the turn of the century, focused on what minds actually did and how they assisted organisms—animal and human alike—in adapting to their environments. Noting that both instincts and habits were frequently adequate to enable organisms to cope with their surroundings, proponents of functionalism reasoned that the primary function of consciousness, which comprised emotions, thinking, sense perceptions, and a wide variety of other mental activities, had arisen during the course of biological evolution as an instrument enabling organisms to deal with new, unfamiliar situations. In so doing—and functionalists such as John Dewey never tired of emphasizing the point—consciousness endowed organisms that possessed it with a measure of freedom and transcendence over the situations confronting them. Drawing intellectual nourishment from the work of American pragmatists, who emphasized the centrality of function and use in their analysis of truth, the functionalists regarded the behavioral manifestations of mental life as crucial, for it was behavior that ultimately determined the success of organisms in responding to their environment.

To suggest that the structuralists and functionalists were warring sects would imply the existence of more acrimony than actually existed. The commitment of both groups to the idea of approaching the mind as an object of scientific investigation was far more central to their self-image as psychologists than any of the issues dividing them. Moreover, some psychologists, such as Mary Whiton Calkins, the eminent partisan of "self psychology," held that both perspectives were necessary to the development of any comprehensive scheme of scientific psychology. Nevertheless, the divisions between structuralists and functionalists prevented psychologists from presenting a united front to the natural scientists, religionists, and other outsiders who challenged the rigor of their discipline.

By the first decade of the twentieth century, although few functional psychologists repudiated introspection in principle, many tended increasingly to base their own generalizations about consciousness on inferences from observable behavior. That such an agenda could be fruitful seemed amply confirmed by the work of animal psychologists. Comparative psychologist Edward Lee Thorndike's experiments in 1898 showing that animals tended to solve problems by means of trial and error rather than through insight, reason, or imitation of other members of their own species convinced some psychologists that consciousness was a uniquely human phenomenon. To be sure, Robert M. Yerkes, Margaret Washburn, and a number of other eminent animal psychologists continued to embrace the notion that consciousness was an appropriate object of inquiry for comparative psychology. Nevertheless, by the early 1900s most animal psychologists had disavowed the common earlier practice of drawing anthropomorphic inferences from the behavior of their subjects. Many concluded that observable behavior was sufficient to tell them what they wanted to know about the adaptation of animals to their environment and that drawing inferences from such behavior was a more rigorously empirical and scientific mode of procedure than discussing consciousness and employing introspective reports.

Because most psychologists continued to assume that psychology was primarily the study of human consciousness, animal psychology remained subordinate during the first decade of the twentieth century to those branches of psychology that dealt with human subjects. It is against this backdrop that the rise of behaviorism, which has been described by John M. O'Donnell in his book *The Origins of Behaviorism* (1985) as "the vindictive offspring of animal psychology," can best be understood. Early in his graduate school career at the University of Chicago, John Broadus Watson, the individual responsible for combining the disparate strands of the behaviorist outlook within a coherent framework, had abandoned the study of philosophy for experimental psychology. After briefly working with Jacques Loeb, a mechanistic reductionist and ardent materialist who endeavored to show that the behavior of organisms was the

product of physiological activity rather than consciousness, Watson wrote his Ph.D. dissertation under James Rowland Angell in the field of animal psychology. After receiving in 1903 a Ph.D. in psychology at the University of Chicago, Watson left that university in 1908 to become professor of experimental and comparative psychology and director of the psychological laboratory at Johns Hopkins University.

During the next few years Watson became increasingly impatient with the relative indifference of most psychologists to the contributions of animal psychology. By 1912 he had come to believe that the behavior of human beings, like that of many other animals, was the result of the formation of habits through association of stimulus and response. The next year, in a series of lectures at Columbia University and in his subsequent manifesto, "Psychology as the Behaviorist Views It," Watson went public with his views. He contended that if psychologists wished to realize their goal of making their discipline a "purely objective experimental branch of natural science," it would be necessary to base it on the kind of observable behavioral data used by animal psychologists. Such an approach would erase the "dividing line between man and brute" and give psychology data for objective study akin to those possessed by other natural sciences.

Watson reserved his most stinging invective for the notion that psychology was devoted to "the phenomena of consciousness." Not only was the notion of consciousness a speculative will-o'-the-wisp irrelevant to the "experimental attack on problems associated with the behavior of organisms," he asserted, but reliance on introspection was a profoundly unscientific mode of procedure. If psychologists truly wished to behave like scientists, it would be necessary for them to "discard all reference to consciousness," make a definitive break with metaphysics by eliminating "speculative" terms such as sensation, purpose, desire, thought, and emotion from their vocabulary, and confine their efforts to studying observable behavior. For his part, Watson expressed confidence that human psychology could be understood and described entirely in terms of stimulus and response, adaptation through the formation and integration of habits, and other behavioral categories.

Watson's goal was the discovery of natural laws of behavior that transcended individual species and applied to all organisms. In spite of the fact that he claimed to be severing all ties between psychology and philosophy, his disdain for mentalism and his view of human beings as "machines" were predicated on an interpretation of natural science that was rooted in positivistic, deterministic, materialistic, and mechanistic philosophical commitments.

Watson had articulated the concerns of many experimental psychologists in the face of continued skepticism from other scientists regarding the rigor of their discipline. He also presented a vigorous and forceful critique of psychology's commitment to the concept of consciousness and the methodology of introspection. Nevertheless, his views encountered resistance from many psychologists, who were unwilling to accept Watson's contention that the scientific legitimacy of their discipline required the total abandonment of introspection and the strict limitation of psychological inquiry to behavior. Indeed, some psychologists expressed doubts that Watson's research agenda was sufficiently broad to yield significant revelations about human nature. In retrospect, however, what is more striking than the opposition he encountered is the unwillingness of Watson's contemporaries to view his essay as the manifesto of a revolutionary. This may have been at least partly because Watson failed in that essay to promulgate a clearly articulated theoretical alternative to introspection. It was not until 1915, when he invoked the concept of the conditioned response developed by Ivan Pavlov and other Russian reflexologists, that Watson advanced a clear-cut alternative to introspection, and it was not until considerably later that the concept of conditioned reflex became central to his system. Even more fundamentally, however, it would appear that many younger psychologists saw in Watson's demands that psychologists focus on observable, publicly verifiable phenomena much that was appealing but little that was radically new. Those psychologists had already shifted their research efforts to behavioral problems. As time went on, that behavioral orientation became increasingly commonplace.

Watson also embraced another proposition that was already an important conviction among psychologists and destined to become more so: that psychology should prove itself useful to society. To be sure, when he declared in his 1913 manifesto that his ultimate goal was "the prediction and control of behavior," he was expressing a view of psychology's promise that far exceeded its performance. Still, with the exception of the structuralists, most American psychologists agreed with Watson's refusal to equate the genuineness of science with its purity. Joseph Jastrow expressed the sentiments of many, perhaps most, American psychologists when he declared in his 1900 presidential address to the American Psychological Association: "Psychology and life are closely related; and we do not fill our whole function if we leave uninterpreted for practical and public benefit the mental power of man."

During the first two decades of the twentieth century an ever increasing number of psychologists expressed interest not only in understanding and describing the human mind but also in explaining—and perhaps ultimately predicting—human thought and behavior. This interest was another element in academic psychology's ongoing quest for public support. It was also the product of both a venerable view of the social sciences that linked understanding human nature to improving society and a new, more "progressive" view that sought to use the power and authority of science to impose a measure of order over industrialism, urbanization, high rates of geographical and social mobility, and the other centrifugal forces of "modernity." Some psychologists, such as Columbia University's James McKeen Cattell, regarded the purity of scientific psychology as superior to the self-interest of politics as an agency of social improvement; others, such as John Dewey, sought to employ the results of psychological investigation for self-consciously political ends. Whatever their views, long after progressivism had lost much of its political clout, psychologists continued to join forces with other members of the cultural and managerial elites in attempting to use their science to combat social disorder and help determine the shape of society. In the process they helped to create a heightened role for themselves and their services within American society.

Some of the clearest manifestations of psychologists' desire to put their discipline to work could be found in the field of education. Indeed, by 1910 over a third of all the psychologists in America expressed an interest in the educational implications of psychology. Confronted by an explosion in the number and heterogeneity of the public elementary and secondary schools in the United States, American educators looked to the work of psychologists such as G. Stanley Hall, who endeavored to ascertain the "normal" course of childhood mental development, for assistance in evaluating pedagogy and curriculum. On a different front, a number of psychologists followed Lightner Witmer in creating psychological clinics designed to diagnose and treat the educational problems of children. Finally, educators responded enthusiastically to another program created in the name of applied psychology that actually transcended education in its range of applicability: mental testing. The idea underlying the mental testing movement was that it was both possible and desirable to use instruments of empirical science to determine the range of peoples' motor and sensory functions, cognitive and emotional development, and achievement in a variety of classroom subjects, and to measure and rank individuals within that range. As early as the 1890s mental testing was undertaken by James McKeen Cattell, but it was not until 1908, when Henry H. Goddard, director of psychological research at the Vineland Training School for the mentally retarded, published the first American version of the intelligence scale devised by the French psychologists Alfred Binet and Theodore Simon that the mental testing movement began to yield results that were widely regarded as valuable and interesting. In the twelve-year period following Goddard's publication, intelligence testing became the fastest growing professional specialty in the United States among both psychologists and educators.

From the vantage point of many would-be social engineers in the United States, the mental testing movement offered the promise of finding an objective, "scientific" means of classifying people in accordance with their abilities. In this way, the reasoning proceeded, leaders in education, industry, and other important institutions would be better able to place "normal" American citizens in niches appropriate to their skills and intelligence and to develop suitable segregated facilities for the others. Although later observers have concluded that the tests actually measured facility with the English language and familiarity with American middle-class culture rather than innate intelligence, psychologists committed to testing managed to convince many Americans that they were performing a valuable social service.

Some measure of the credibility mental testing achieved during the early twentieth century can be gleaned from the fact that during World War I the Committee on Classification of Personnel, an organization within the Adjutant General's Office, used psychological testing to place recruits in appropriate occupational specialties. In addition, the United States Army commissioned psychologists under the leadership of Robert M. Yerkes of Harvard to develop tests designed to measure the intelligence of recruits. During the course of the war almost two million of these "Alpha" and "Beta" tests were administered. Although these tests received more attention than the occupational tests, there is little evidence that the Army actually made use of the results. Nevertheless, the performance of psychologists during the war did much to convince important opinionmakers of the social value of psychology.

PSYCHOTHERAPY AND THE "AMERICANIZATION" OF SIGMUND FREUD

In the first two decades of the twentieth century the work of virtually all of the academic psychologists who aspired to serve science and society through their labors focused on understanding "normal" mental structures and processes. Yet, during this same time, some of the most important and provocative views of the human mind and personality were advanced by individuals who ministered to people afflicted with mental disorders.

The early twentieth century was a period of crisis in the understanding and treatment of mental illness in the United States. The prevailing somatic interpretation, which attributed mental disorders to the presence of brain lesions, lacked both a coherent theoretical structure and a record of effective therapy. Moreover, its failures could hardly have been more ill-timed. Not only were other medical specialties, bolstered by the germ theory of disease and other advances in knowledge, beginning to increase their ability to diagnose and treat patients, but in a middle-class culture increasingly preoccupied with what seemed to many Americans to be an epidemic of "nervousness" national in scope, neurologists and psychiatrists were increasingly finding themselves in competition with a variety of "mind cure" movements such as Christian Science and New Thought.

During the first decade of the twentieth century the failures of somatic medicine, coupled with the careful clinical observation of mentally ill patients and new work in hypnosis suggesting an ideational rather than physical cause of some mental disorders, impelled a growing number of neurologists and psychiatrists to give serious consideration to the merits of psychotherapy. The most notable were James Jackson Putnam, a professor of neurology at Harvard Medical School, and Adolf Meyer, a Swiss immigrant whose distinguished and fruitful career included the directorship of the Phipps Psychiatric Clinic at Johns Hopkins Medical School. Psychotherapy was predicated on the idea that mental and even physical disorders were sometimes caused by dysfunctional "mental states" rather than somatic factors and that those disorders could often be cured by changing those mental states. It appealed not only to physicians searching for more effective treatments of mental illness but also to a large number of other Americans who hoped to receive insight into those mysterious, hidden regions of the mind believed to be repositories of untapped "inner resources."

A variety of psychotherapeutic approaches—suggestion, persuasion, and reeducation, and other perspectives more or less aligned with Protestant churches—competed with one another for the respect and attention of the American people in the early twentieth century. By 1915 the approach that had become most influential within the medical community and the larger intellectual community alike was psychoanalysis. At the hands of Sigmund Freud and his disciples, psychoanalysis moved well beyond an emphasis on the treatment of mental disorders to become also a method of investigating the psyche, a comprehensive theory of human nature, and a professional movement.

By the early twentieth century, Freud's studies and his work with hypnotism, free association, dream interpretation, and conversations with his patients had convinced him that powerful, amoral, irrational instinctual drives—most notably the sexual drive—had evolved as a means of sustaining the life of the human organism and ensuring the survival of the species. Freud held that in attempting to gratify these primal impulses, people often galvanized desires, wishes, and ideas that were antithetical to the conventional, "civilized" standards embraced by their conscious minds. When this occurred—and it often occurred in the early years of life—individuals resisted those unacceptable thoughts by "repressing" them within the unconscious, a dynamic region of the psyche that served as the underlying source of all mental processes, the causal center of human behavior, and the repository of all memories. Unfortunately, however, this psychic defense mechanism was not always successful; sometimes repressed material did not remain entirely buried. It was the surfacing of this material rather than organic lesions or "hereditary degeneration," Freud maintained, that caused obsessions, hysteria, anxiety, sexual dysfunction, and other mental problems. There was, however, hope. With the guidance of their analysts, patients could attain knowledge of both the repressed material and the forces of repression generated by the "civilized" impulses within their consciousness. By thus bringing to consciousness that which was previously unconscious, they could free themselves of their neurotic conflicts and begin to choose their own goals and ambitions.

Freud, who in his early years had embraced the idea that mental illness was the result of physical causes, denied that his invocation of psychological rather than somatic factors in accounting for both the causes and cures of many mental disorders was anything other than rigorously scientific. Although he never rejected in principle the idea that it would some day be possible to reduce mental processes to neurophysiological variables, he insisted that this day had not yet arrived. By 1900 he had come to regard physiology and psychology as equally valid ways of organizing and interpreting experience, and he maintained that in his lifetime a comprehensive, "scientific" view of the mind would most likely be obtained by using psychological rather than physicalistic discourse. He was convinced that he had disclosed an underlying pattern and continuity within the mind and had extended the scope of determinism into the psychic arena by showing that all thought and behavior, no matter how seemingly inadvertent or irrational, was part of a causal nexus. From his perspective, these achievements provided ample evidence of his scientific scruples.

In 1909, at the invitation of G. Stanley Hall, the president of Clark University who had long been a student of genetic psychology and human sexuality, Sigmund Freud made his first and only visit to the United States to discuss his theories. At this date he could claim only a few ardent American disciples. Nevertheless, psychoanalysis had already received a good deal of attention in the scholarly journals. Moreover, in the five years after Freud's visit to the United States, his disciples engaged in concerted efforts to win converts. Their efforts paid rich dividends; by 1915 many American physicians sympathetic to functional interpretations of mental disorders had come to value Freud's work more highly than other psychotherapeutic approaches. The founding of both the New York Psychoanalytic Society and the American Psychoanalytic Association in 1911 gave Freud's ideas an institutional grounding and his followers a new sense of professional identity.

In the final analysis, however, institutional factors were less decisive in accounting for the favorable response of many psychiatrists and neurologists to psychoanalysis than Freud's banishment of mystery and his imposition of pattern on previously hidden areas of the psyche, his analogies between the mechanisms of the mind and the laws of physical science, his insistence on rooting human personality in the evolutionary process, and his appeal to deterministic causal principles. For many physicians the Freudian analysis of the human mind appeared to be a tough-minded system of scientific psychology. In its capacity for dealing with human emotions and irrational impulses, it not only rivaled other versions of psychology with its claims of scientific comprehensiveness, but it also seemed to be more responsive to the

Freud in America. In 1909, Sigmund Freud visited Clark University at the invitation of the psychologist G. Stanley Hall, who was the president of the university. *Front row, left to right:* Freud, Hall, Carl G. Jung; *back row, left to right:* Freud's American translator, A. A. Brill; Freud's British colleague, Ernest Jones; Freud's Hungarian colleague, Sándor Ferenczi. *Courtesy Clark University Office of Communications*

experiences and conflicts of human beings as they went about their daily lives.

Not everyone was infatuated with the scientific promise of Freud's ideas. Ironically, at the same time physicians were embracing Freud's views as an expression of tough-minded scientism, research psychologists, already hyperconscious of issues relating to scientific status, were rendering an unfavorable verdict on the scientific merits of his work. This is hardly surprising, for in spite of the fact that psychologists could endorse Freud's commitment to determinism and his desire for theoretical comprehensiveness, it would be difficult to find an approach and set of conclusions more antithetical to experimental psychology than psychoanalysis.

Until about 1916 psychologists were rather restrained in their response to psychoanalysis. This was at least partly because they regarded Freudianism less as a pretender to the throne of science than as simply

another variant upon a whole series of "mind cures" masquerading as science. When psychologists finally did examine Freud's work, they advanced two major indictments against it. The first, which was part of their growing antipathy toward introspective techniques, was that the Freudian method of relying on individual clinical cases and anecdotal testimony was antithetical to true scientific method, which they associated with public, experimental verification of hypotheses that were often described in quantitative terms. Underlying this attack on the methodology of the Freudians, who valued introspection and placed great emphasis on the personal interaction of the analyst and analysand, was research psychologists' equation of science with objectivity; to them, objectivity involved the self-conscious distancing of the observer from the observed.

The other major criticism advanced by psychologists was that Freud's view of the mind and motivation was dependent for its validity on the existence of an "entity"—the unconscious—that lay beyond the reach of experimental methods laid down by psychologists as normative. In contrast to his supporters, who rightly viewed Freud as a foe of supernaturalism, psychologists regarded his affirmation of the existence of an unobservable, unmeasurable unconscious as a capitulation to metaphysical obscurantism.

Freud's disciples within the medical community largely ignored the criticisms that his views received from academic psychologists and turned instead to the task of making converts within the larger culture. During the second decade of the twentieth century, largely as a result of their efforts, psychoanalysis received a great deal of attention in the media. Of particular importance was the association of Freud's work with the mental hygiene movement, which was launched with the publication of a book by a former mental patient, Clifford Beers's *Mind That Found Itself* (1908). In the process of trying to expose the evils of the prevailing institutional treatment of mental illness and press for more positive efforts promoting mental health, writers associated with the mental hygiene movement touted Freud's work for affirming the vast potential of all human beings. The publicity that Freud's views received was effective; in the period prior to 1920 some Americans associated the "new psychology" with Freudianism rather than academic psychology.

Although Freudian views hardly took the nation by storm, the pluralistic nature of American society enabled some groups to welcome them enthusiastically and quickly. On the other hand, pluralism did not ensure tolerance, and American proponents of psychoanalysis were therefore anxious to show that it could be harmonized with dominant medical and cultural views. As a result, they "Americanized" Freud's views by interpreting—or ignoring—them in accordance with other cultural priorities and imperatives. Generally speaking, most Americans who embraced Freudianism during the first two decades of the twentieth century placed less emphasis on Freud's therapeutic prescriptions than on his interpretations of the human psyche. Moreover, they characteristically refused to treat those ideas as a coherent theory of human nature. Instead, they were quite selective in what they adopted. American exponents of psychoanalysis characteristically placed far more emphasis on Freud's early work, which focused on the instinctual drives, resistance, and repression, than on his somewhat later views, which were characterized by a widened definition of sexuality and an increased emphasis on infantile and early childhood sexuality.

Proponents of psychoanalysis in the United States also maintained a more plastic view of human nature than Freud and tended to emphasize a hardy environmentalism that was not in total harmony with the spirit of Freudian thought. Although Americans, who had long been convinced that many of the roots of adult life could be found in earlier experiences, were receptive to Freud's belief in the significance of childhood for subsequent human development, most childhood specialists in the United States had maintained that adolescence and puberty played a particularly influential role, and Freud's supporters tended to disregard his claim that the decisive period of human development was the first five years of life. Finally, American commentators largely ignored Freud's emphasis on the intractability of instinctual drives and early childhood experiences, as well his acknowledgment of the incompleteness of knowledge about mental illness, in favor of a more optimistic assessment of both the range of mental disorders that psychoanalysis could treat and the prospects for cure that therapy offered.

In spite of the fact that American psychoanalysis possessed a somewhat less revolutionary cast than psychoanalysis in Europe, even after its Americanization Freudianism was strong stuff, and this was precisely why a number of writers and artists in the American avant-garde found it so appealing. To most of these intellectuals, psychoanalysis appeared to be an important agent of purification and self-knowledge. Residing in an age intent on eliminating barbaric laws and unjust institutions, they regarded psychoanalysis primarily as an instrument for allowing human beings to bring to heel at long last the irrational and bestial forces within them. By facing reality and attaining self-knowledge, individuals could also achieve a more effective sublimation, thereby equipping themselves to deal more effectively with the socioeconomic imperatives of life while at the same time contributing to the larger society.

Although most advocates of psychoanalysis within the American avant-garde focused on the role it could play in fostering social responsibility, some regarded the Freudian description of human personality primarily as a powerful weapon in their cultural war of liberation against "Puritanism" and rigid self-control in the name of modern values. These rebels had already been partly prepared for Freud's frontal assault on conventional views of human nature by the work of literary realists and naturalists, modern artists, and feminists. At the same time, muckrakers, progressive historians, and Marxists had convinced them that outward appearances were often illusory and that the real motives of human behavior—and often human oppression—were frequently hidden. Psychoanalysis, however, went even further, promising not only to tear away the veil of society's hypocrisy and sham but also to provide individuals with the scientific tools they needed to plumb the very depths of selfhood. The inference that some American writers and artists drew was that such an examination would enable individuals to attain a kind of secular salvation.

Partly, perhaps because of the intellectual company that it kept, Freud's views were subjected to a good deal of criticism from the guardians of conventional morality, who bitterly complained that psychoanalysis posited an immoral view of the mind. These critics appear to have found Freud's doctrine of the universality of eroticism more scandalous than his emphasis on the salient role of sex in accounting for neuroses. They were especially outraged by his doctrines of childhood sexuality and dreams, in large measure because those doctrines seemed to blur the established Victorian distinction between the "perverted" and the normal. Freud's assertion of the existence of a universal Oedipus complex also raised a storm of criticism, for it seemed to cast aspersions on the purity of women and children alike.

Notwithstanding such criticisms, by 1920 many of Freud's views had been embraced by a significant number of mental health professionals and avant-garde intellectuals alike. In fact, during the early twentieth century the United States proved far more receptive to psychoanalysis than any of the nations of Europe.

NATURE, NURTURE, AND THE TRIUMPH OF BEHAVIORISM, 1920–1945

After 1920 the connection between experimental psychology and applied psychology became more tenuous. Applied psychology, which concentrated on devising instruments and approaches intended to be immediately useful to the larger society, experienced a continued expansion in the number of practitioners employed, the instruments used, and the range of activities undertaken. Beginning in the twenties the use of batteries of intelligence, achievement, and personality tests became commonplace in American education. Industrialists, too, enamored of the "scientific management" movement pioneered by the engineer Frederick W. Taylor and increasingly aware that maximizing efficiency involved managing not

only the movements of workers but also their feelings and their attitudes about their jobs, became interested in psychology. The use of intelligence and aptitude tests and counseling services in business and industry reflected this interest. The experiments at the Hawthorne plant of the Western Electric Company in Chicago conducted by a team led by the psychologist Elton Mayo during the mid-twenties were only the best-known (if ultimately flawed) efforts to apply the insights of psychology to the workplace.

In spite—or perhaps at least partly because—of the growing interest in applied psychology, that branch of the discipline was sharply criticized in the period after 1920 by experimental psychologists in colleges and universities. Experimentalists complained that in their zeal to be useful, applied psychologists were doing nothing to advance the cause of science. For their part, academic psychologists remained divided over issues lying at the very heart of their discipline. One of the most significant of these was the relative importance of heredity and environment in determining human conduct. Much of the psychological thought of the first two decades of the twentieth century had been informed by the belief that there was a strong hereditarian component in human nature. This belief, though probably not unrelated to the fact that most psychologists were middle-class WASPs confident of the superiority of their subculture, was primarily the product of an assumption—to term it a reasoned conviction would be too strong—that the concept of evolutionary continuity implied that human beings were, like other animals, strongly influenced by hereditary factors. This assumption, coupled with the fact that performance on mental tests administered prior to 1920 seemed to be linked to such variables as race and ethnicity, convinced many psychologists that human nature was primarily the result of heredity.

From this perspective, the results of the "Alpha" and "Beta" tests given to military personnel during World War I seemed most disheartening. According to the report issued by Robert Yerkes after the war, almost half the white men who were drafted and a significantly higher number of African Americans and the "new" immigrants from southern and eastern Europe were, in the mental age assigned to them, equivalent to what Henry H. Goddard had earlier labeled "moron." Although some critics, most notably Walter Lippmann, showed that inferences drawn from the tests were groundless, many other Americans joined the eminent Harvard psychologist William McDougall, author of *Is America Safe for Democracy?* (1921), in expressing concern that the average level of intelligence in the United States might well be too low to sustain a viable democracy.

These conclusions not only provided additional justification for invoking the assistance of scientific "experts," but they also seemed to justify the convictions that greater restrictions should be imposed on the opportunities for southern and eastern Europeans to immigrate to the United States and that "inferior peoples" already living in the nation—in particular, the "feeble-minded" and certain delinquent groups—should be prevented from having additional children. There is, however, little evidence that the results of psychological tests or the testimonies of hereditarian psychologists were crucial in bringing about either the passage of the immigration restriction laws of the 1920s or the passage by 1930 of eugenics legislation in some thirty states providing for the compulsory sterilization of groups felt unfit. Bigotry was capable of accounting for the passage of those measures without psychology's assistance. Nevertheless, it is a telling commentary on the cultural authority of science during the period after 1920 that those laws were often justified and defended with hereditarian rhetoric.

Notwithstanding the power and influence of hereditarianism within American psychology, proponents of that perspective began to encounter opposition even before 1920. One aspect of this opposition was an all-out attack on the significance of instinct in human behavior spearheaded by animal psychologists who insisted that the gap between the human mind and that of other animals was wider than hereditarians had assumed. John B. Watson's experiments with infants also led psychologists to reconsider the significance of instinct in human thought. These experiments seemed to show that most patterns of human behavior attributed to instinct were actually conditioned reflexes. In 1917 Watson concluded on the basis of his researches that the responses of human beings to stimuli were more plastic, less fixed, than hereditarians tacitly assumed and that human personality was a collection of habit systems gradually constructed by conditioned reflexes. Not everyone shared Watson's belief that the only three human instincts were fear, rage, and what he referred to as joy or love. Nevertheless, his experiments, coupled with a new awareness that the conventional instinct theory lacked any experimental basis, helped convince most psychologists in the period between 1917 and 1925 that a more environmentalist interpretation of human behavior was necessary.

Reinforcing the inclination of many American psychologists to question the significance of heredity were ideas coming from outside the discipline. For example, in 1924 the sociologist Luther L. Bernard wrote an important and influential book attacking the idea that instinct adequately accounted for human behavior. Of even greater importance was the work of the Columbia University psychologist Franz Boas. Although Boas acknowledged that heredity played some role in shaping the lives of individuals, he emphasized that the line between heredity and environment was indistinct. Moreover, he made it clear that he was convinced that in accounting for the diversity of human activity, cultural factors were paramount.

At the same time that proponents of the importance of nurture were questioning the significance of heredity in shaping human behavior, they were also challenging the assumption that intelligence tests truly measured hereditary endowments. Environmentalists noted that even if it were granted that the tests effectively measured intelligence, they failed to differentiate the impact of heredity from that of the environment. The work of the psychologist Otto Klineberg, who had studied with Boas while doing graduate work at Columbia, was particularly important in showing the importance of cultural factors in all tests. These conclusions did not succeed in bringing an end to the use of intelligence tests. By 1930, however, a series of damaging technical criticisms of the tests' scientific legitimacy, as well as the success of behaviorists in disclosing the mechanics of learning and the role of cultural and socioeconomic variables in that process, had impelled testers to cease using IQ tests to establish the salience of heredity or to posit hereditary distinctions among racial and ethnic groups.

Like the hereditarians, spokespersons for a more environmentalist perspective drew support from larger streams within the culture for positions they believed they could justify on scientific grounds. By attributing the fortunes of peoples and groups to the environment rather than their biological makeup, proponents of nurture enabled all individuals, in theory at least, to acquire the resources necessary to improve their lives. By contrast, the attribution of people's conditions to heredity opened the way for society to deny to certain groups and individuals the opportunities and respect to which they ought by right to be entitled.

All of this is not to say that heredity ceased to play any role in discussions of human thought and behavior. Although virtually all discussion of instinct ceased, psychologists and social scientists continued to invoke inborn drives and impulses in accounting for human activity. Beginning in the mid-twenties the view that human nature was the product of the interaction of heredity and environment became increasingly dominant. Although in theory this view imposed on disciplines charged with the study of human thought and conduct the task of determining the relative influence of nature and nurture, in practice most students of the human sciences for the next thirty years centered their attention on trying to understand the relationship between environmental forces and learning.

Discussions of the relative significance of nature and nurture were closely related to a continuing debate among psychologists concerning the appropriate methodology and subject matter of their discipline. As of 1920, though psychologists wholeheartedly agreed on the desirability of pursuing their research in a scientific manner, the question of just how behaviorally oriented psychology should be continued to divide them. During the next decade, however, a steadily increasing number of psychologists concluded that mentalism was incompatible with an objective, scientific approach to the study of human nature. In taking this position, they found support in the work of a significant number of American philosophers. "New realists" and instrumentalists in the tradition of John Dewey joined forces in assailing the concept of a private consciousness peculiarly open to introspective interpretation.

By the end of the twenties, it had become clear that methodologically, at least, behaviorism had become the reigning perspective in American experimental psychology. Few psychologists were willing to join Watson in repudiating the very existence of consciousness, and many found his approach to behaviorism rather crude. Nevertheless, the long-standing desire of experimental psychologists to model their discipline on other natural sciences led most of them to agree that consciousness played no operational role in determining human conduct, that it was unnecessary to invoke data derived from introspection to account for human behavior, and that the objective study of observable behavior, symbolized by controlled studies of rats and other nonhuman species, was sufficient to tell them what they wanted to know about human nature. These individuals began to call themselves behaviorists or neobehaviorists. Hence, by 1930 a discipline that in 1900 had conceived its principal concern to be the scientific investigation of human consciousness had been driven by its essentially positivistic conception of natural science to forsake consciousness as an unworthy object of devotion.

Most psychologists who viewed themselves as advocates of a behaviorist perspective agreed that the central problems to be solved by experimental psychology revolved around learning, which they interpreted as the process by which organisms adapted to their environment. In addition, they shared an increasing tendency to express their conclusions in terms of a vocabulary and strategy of discourse derived from logical positivism. Behaviorists often differed quite sharply, however, in their formulations and their approaches to their data. For example, differences of opinion emerged in discussions as to what unit of behavior was most important for experimental analysis. Some behaviorists, such as Watson and the University of Washington psychology professor Edwin Guthrie, believed that behaviorists should focus on what came to be known as "molecular" processes, which involved specific, generally small, components of behavior, such as muscular responses to stimuli. Other behaviorists, such as Edward A. Tolman of the University of California and Clark Hull, a Yale psychologist and the most eminent experimental psychologist in the United States from 1930 to 1950, argued that examination of behavior at a more "molar" level, involving complex rather than single sets of stimuli and responses, would disclose relationships and patterns that escaped molecular interpretations.

Probably the most important philosophical disagreement among behaviorists centered on the status of purpose. Tolman, for example, acknowledged the reality of purpose but insisted that instead of being an inference from certain types of behavior, as mentalists claimed, it was instead an objective, "immanent" feature of behavior itself. By contrast, Hull and his numerous disciples maintained that purposeful behavior could be reduced to underlying mechanistic principles. Like Watson, Hull, whose intellectual hero was Isaac Newton, regarded human beings and other animals as essentially organic machines whose behavior was to be explained by means of the same mechanistic principles that physicists used to describe the operations of an inorganic machine. During the 1930s, Hull, anticipating a position held by many later cognitive psychologists, maintained that it should be possible to build machines that operated in ways that were indistinguishable from what was normally identified as purposeful behavior. During his later career, though his interest in machines abated somewhat, Hull persisted in attempting to develop a "mathematico-deductive" theory that would allow him to account for all of human behavior within the framework of a relatively few universal, mechanistic laws.

Finally, although Tolman and Hull agreed that it was necessary to acknowledge the existence of theoretical structures to link stimulus and response, the "intervening variables" that they invoked for this purpose were quite different. Tolman interpreted them as "cognitive maps" guiding behavior and enabling organisms to solve problems posed by their environment. By contrast, Hull's variables were, predictably, mechanistic "drives" and "strength of habit."

The dominant role of behaviorism in psychology was reflected in the credence given its findings by other disciplines charged with the task of understanding human affairs. By 1930, some sociologists, political scientists, and even economists used the behaviorist view of the mechanisms of human conduct in their formulations of quantitatively oriented models of social processes. Through such interdisciplinary institutions as the Yale Institute of Human Relations, which offered seminars in which Hull was a major instructor and guiding influence, students in the behavioral and social sciences were exposed to the ideas of the behaviorists and afforded the opportunity to learn how to apply scientific methods to their disciplines and to the larger society.

This is not to suggest that behaviorism enjoyed a monopoly among students of human thought and conduct. John Dewey, for example, concurred with the behaviorists' emphasis on learning but expressed concern that in their dismissal of consciousness and their insistence on defining human behavior in terms of stimulus and response, they were guilty of ignoring the significant creative role played by intelligence in responding to new situations and anticipating future consequences. On a different front, Karl Lashley, a student of both Adolf Meyer and John B. Watson, attained eminence in neuropsychology at least in part by assailing the idea that learning was nothing more than a "concatenation of reflexes" and resisting the equation of psychology with behavior.

Another view that differed from behaviorism was provided by Gestalt psychology, a perspective brought to the United States during the twenties and thirties by the German psychologists Max Wertheimer, Wolfgang Kohler, and Kurt Koffka. Unlike the behaviorists, the Gestalt psychologists sanctioned the use of introspection and continued to regard the human mind as an entirely appropriate object of psychological inquiry. Proponents of the Gestalt movement believed that the behaviorists were prevented by their atomistic analysis of perception, learning, and other processes from recognizing that as a result of the way the brain organized data perceived from the external world, the mind interpreted that world in terms of *Gestalten*—wholes, or configurations. In contrast to the behaviorists, who envisioned learning in terms of conditioning, the Gestalt psychologists held that it was the product of a restructuring of the mind's cognitive and perceptual structures that they referred to as "insight."

The Gestalt psychologists' critique of behaviorism was grounded in the conviction that a more holistic interpretation of the human mind not only comported more closely with experimental evidence but also expressed greater sensitivity to issues of value and meaning than more mechanistic approaches. A similar concern with meaning, values, and wholes informed the work of Gordon Allport, Henry A. Murray, Gardner Murphy, and other spokespersons for "personality theory," a branch of psychology that received formalization and attained field status during the 1930s. Personality theorists complained that in their all-consuming search for comprehensive laws of human conduct, the behaviorists had ignored a datum crucially important to psychology: the individual person. In examining the configuration of internal traits and/or psychodynamic properties that made up the principle of organization and source of continuity commonly referred to as "personality," they insisted on the need to use a variety of data and approaches that went beyond the limits of the experimental laboratory. Accordingly, they also drew eclectically on traditions of individualistic psychology and the social sciences. On the other hand, personality theorists did not eschew efforts to approach their data scientifically. Rather, they sought to create tests that would enable them to measure in a scientifically rigorous manner a determinate list of common personality traits and patterns without ignoring the life history and idiosyncrasies that made each individual unique and complex.

If, however, behaviorism did not go unchallenged, between 1920 and 1960 it nevertheless maintained a commanding position within experimental psychology and the social sciences alike. It played a less hegemonic role in the larger culture. John B. Watson retained easy access to the public forum and remained an aggressive campaigner for his radical version of behaviorism. In 1920, he was dismissed from Johns Hopkins University for moral turpitude following an affair with a graduate student collaborator. His departure from academe and subsequent entry into the advertising industry did little, however, to prevent him from continuing his behaviorist crusade. In fact it actually liberated him to make even bolder, more unqualified pronouncements on behalf of his cause. In the numerous magazine articles and books that he wrote for mass consumption during the twenties, Watson denounced consciousness as nothing more than an outworn relic of earlier theological doctrines relating to the soul, insisted that the burden of proof in determining the existence of consciousness lay with the mentalists, and held that behavioral science was much more dependable than the more conventional sources of religion and morality in molding human behavior. The proper use of the behaviorist principles of conditioning, he asserted, would not only enable individuals to reshape their own behavior but also confer upon experts the ability to remodel the larger society. His most famous statement of this provocative message was expressed in his popular work, *Behaviorism* (1924): "Give me a dozen healthy infants, well-formed, and my own specified world to bring them up in and I'll guarantee to take any one at random and train him to become any type of specialist I might select—doctor, lawyer, artist, merchant-chief and yes, even beggar-man and thief, regardless of his talents, penchants, tendencies, abilities, vocations, and race of his ancestors." In the sense that Watson's vision exempted no one from behaviorist redemption it was radically egalitarian. On the other hand, he was never entirely clear about what he believed were fitting goals for the behaviorist technocracy he advocated. Moreover, he seemed disconcertingly indifferent to the issue of just who would determine those goals.

In spite of the fact that Watson's words made good copy and impelled representatives of numerous intellectual positions to grapple with his ideas, his radical vision of behaviorism does not seem to have been terribly influential within the larger culture. Although more work needs to be done before confident assessments can be made, it would appear that most members of the American reading public realized that Watson had gone considerably beyond the evidence in making many of his assertions, and they found many of these profoundly counterintuitive, even offensive. Many of his ideas were subjected to a withering assault in the popular media by theologians, philosophers, social theorists, and psychologists alike. They maintained that Watson's behaviorism amounted to little more than an illicit attempt to establish a kind of secular religion predicated on a denial of human autonomy.

While many Americans found Watson's vision dangerous, most were ignorant of the more sober labors of the neobehaviorists and other experimental psychologists working in the controlled conditions of their laboratories. As a result, in the period between 1920 and 1945 most Americans who sought the counsel of scientific experts for insights into the human condition looked to psychoanalysis and its offshoots. In fact by 1940 the popular media were virtually ignoring experimental psychology altogether.

PSYCHIATRY AND PSYCHOANALYSIS IN THE INTERWAR YEARS

Like the Gestalt psychologists and most of the personality theorists, the supporters of psychoanalysis, who affirmed the central importance of intrapsychic phenomena, regarded the behaviorists' programmatic abandonment of the mind as an exercise in futility. During the twenties, however, the status of the psychoanalytic movement within the American medical community, on whom it depended for its scientific credentials, was insufficiently secure to permit it the luxury of sustained criticism of another discipline. Psychiatry and neurology continued to be arenas of fierce debates between supporters of functional and organicist views of mental illness. Most mental health professionals remained intent on finding physiological causes of mental illness and therapies designed to alter the physical state of the central nervous system, although, however inconsistently, many employed psychoanalytic psychotherapy in selected cases without regard to theory. Even among those psychiatrists who embraced the principles of psychotherapy, not all endorsed Freud's approach to psychodynamics. Physicians sympathetic with psychoanalysis characteristically employed it as only one of a variety of approaches in the therapeutic repertoire. Nevertheless, in the period after World War I the American medical profession remained more receptive than European medicine to Freud's views, and during the twenties, in spite of the fact that Freud himself opposed the medicalization of analysis, physicians attained a virtual monopoly on psychoanalysis in the United States.

During the next decade the link between psychoanalysis and psychiatry became institutionalized, and psychiatrists increasingly moved out of hospitals into private practices in urban offices. In addition, by the thirties analysts had apparently become more comfortable with their status in a pluralistic society, as they placed less emphasis on working within existing institutions and enthusiastically established separate, highly organized and often extremely rigid psychoanalytic societies and institutes. The thirties also brought an influx of European analysts into the United States, and these refugees brought new ideas, new energy, new faces, and a new emphasis on theory into the American psychoanalytic movement. The overwhelming majority of American psychiatrists did not receive formal analytic training. Moreover, few of those who had such training were able to limit their practice to analysis. Still, by 1940, the United States had become the major center of psychoanalysis in the world.

Like American research psychologists, Freudian thinkers became embroiled in the ongoing cultural dialogue concerning the role of heredity and environment in shaping human nature. Freud himself was an interactionist in that he attributed human behavior to the interplay of innate instinctual drives with life experiences. His insistence upon the decisiveness of early childhood made Freudianism the object of attack from numerous American social psychologists, who asserted that every individual's personality was the product of interrelationships that the individual had with other people throughout life. The most important figure in American psychiatry between the wars, Adolf Meyer, was one of those psychiatrists who refused on these grounds to support the Freudian vision wholeheartedly.

Yet some critics of Freud's emphasis on intrapsychic factors and the primacy of early experiences nevertheless conceived of themselves as participants in the major qualifications in the psychoanalytic tradition. The most notable of these were the "neo-Freudians"—Harry Stack Sullivan, Karen Horney, and Erich Fromm. These analysts deemphasized such fundamental Freudian doctrines as pansexuality and the Oedipus complex and accentuated the role of anxiety and other problems generated by interpersonal relations. At the hands of neo-Freudians of a leftist persuasion, such as Erich Fromm, this led to a comprehensive assault on the structure of society.

By the thirties even many analysts who did not dissent fundamentally from Freudian doctrine expressed great interest in reconciling the individual to the larger social environment. In that decade the theoretical contributions of the refugee analyst Heinz Hartmann and others served to extend and elaborate on Freud's own increasing interest in the ego and its adaptive mechanisms, and "ego psychology" became the primary orientation in American psychoanalysis. In contrast to Freudians who focused on the instinctual drives and defenses in their interpretation of human nature, ego psychologists viewed psychoanalysis primarily not as a doctrine of liberation but as a way of curbing primal impulses in the name of promoting civilization. For most of the analysts who emphasized the role of the ego, as well as for mental-health-care professionals sympathetic to the role of

environmental factors in shaping human personality and many proponents of "progressive education," the problem of facilitating the "adjustment" of the individual to the larger society became paramount. In fact, those professionals generally equated a healthy and mature personality with the ability to integrate successfully into the larger society and act productively and responsibly within it.

As in the early twentieth century, interest in Freud's work was not limited to analysts and their patients. After World War I, middle-class Americans seemed eager to glean from science and medicine as many revelations as possible concerning the nature of human personality. Encouraging this eagerness was the plethora of literature associated with the mental hygiene movement and the numerous discussions of nervousness and mental disorders that had occurred during the first two decades of the twentieth century. The effect of this publicity was to confer increased cultural authority upon psychiatrists and other mental health professionals. Indeed, most educated Americans regarded science as a crucial supplement to—and some even viewed it as a substitute for—religion, philosophy, and art in providing insight into the human condition.

During the twenties and to a lesser extent the thirties, the media, anxious to minister to Americans' fascination with science, popularized Freudian ideas, albeit often in oversimplified and distorted form, in books, magazine and newspaper articles, and even radio programs and films. As a result of their efforts, awareness of Freud's views expanded from select circles of the avant-garde to the larger public. Many accounts of Freud's ideas were hostile, and it is impossible to estimate with any accuracy just how many Americans actually embraced the major tenets of psychoanalysis. Nevertheless, it would appear that by 1930 the major elements of popularized Freudian thought had become familiar to most literate Americans.

As in the early twentieth century, discussions of psychoanalysis after World War I dovetailed with other, sometimes larger, cultural issues. Perhaps the clearest example of this can be seen in the popular literature dealing with the sexual themes in Freudianism, a subject that had evoked considerable interest even before 1920. Although it is possible to find in Freud's work complaints about sexual repression in modern societies, Freud himself was not in any meaningful sense a sexual radical. But because his views were received in a cultural environment characterized by a growing tendency on the part of middle-class Americans to confront sexual topics more openly, his emphasis on the primacy of the sex drive and its centrality in accounting for the psychoneuroses proved remarkably resonant. Sexual radicals used—and often distorted—Freud's ideas in the name of sexual liberation. Their opponents, on the other hand, regarded Sigmund Freud as one of the villains of modern civilization.

An equally important theme within the larger culture was Freud's contributions to the meaning of the self. In contrast to the analysts and other intellectuals who employed Freudian ideas to facilitate the adjustment of individuals to society, those who discussed the meaning of Freud's thought in the popular media after World War I centered on the contributions that psychoanalytic thought could make to a better understanding of selfhood. As zeal for large-scale political reform waned in the postwar period, the interest of many educated Americans shifted to self-fulfillment. Explorations of the "inner self" seemed integral to that interest.

During the 1920s, Freud's interpretation of the human psyche reinforced the vague, often unarticulated awareness of many Americans that underlying the *persona* that people exposed to the world was a more primal, often hidden self. Freud's work suggested that this self was at least partly composed of irrational, often primitive, impulses and that appeals to reason were characteristically "rationalizations" for those impulses. This prompted a minority of Americans, especially those who embraced a modernist artistic or literary perspective, to conclude that psychoanalysis promised to liberate individuals from convention and reason and provide them with additional power by releasing hidden inner resources. Yet, most American commentators on Freud within the public forum drew a different inference from his views—that by digging below surface appearances, it would be possible to release people from the shackles of unreason imposed by their hidden selves. For Americans who interpreted Freud's views in this manner, Freudian liberation offered the promise of greater rationality and self-control.

POSTWAR BEHAVIORISM, THE "COGNITIVE REVOLUTION," AND THE "BIOLOGIZATION" OF THE MIND

After World War II the behaviorist perspective continued to prevail in American experimental psychology. By 1960 the influence of Clark Hull's views had begun to wane, and B. F. Skinner became the preeminent behaviorist and the most famous psychologist in the world. Skinner, who had been inspired by his reading of Watson's works to become an experimental psychologist, embraced a radical behaviorism predicated on two ideas: that human beings were mechanisms conditioned by environmental forces and that the ultimate goal of psychology should be the control of human behavior. In contrast to most other behaviorists, Skinner was convinced that in describing behavior, psychology should no more employ "drives" and other physiological factors than mentalistic language. Nor was Skinner enamored of elaborate theoretical expositions. Rather, he was a rigorous experimentalist who assumed that the surest method for obtaining truth about the human species lay in correlating observable environmental variables with observable behavioral variables. Finally, like Watson, Skinner was intent on bringing his message to the public.

Skinner's major contribution to psychology and the foundation of his radical behaviorism was his concept of operant conditioning. This proceeded from his conviction that an adequate theory of behavior was obliged to account not only for reflex behavior, elicited by a determinate stimulus, but also for activities that could not be triggered by such a stimulus. Skinner referred to the latter variety of behavior, which people commonly referred to as "voluntary," as "operant." He held that while operant behavior cannot be elicited, the probability of bringing about its recurrence could be increased if it were followed by what he called a reinforcer. From Skinner's perspective, in everyday life operant behaviors that received reinforcement from the environment were characteristically strengthened, and those that were not were eventually extinguished.

Beginning with the publication of his popular utopian novel *Walden Two* (1948) and reaching more systematic expression in his *Science and Human Behavior* (1953) and *Beyond Freedom and Dignity* (1971), Skinner extended his interpretation of animal behavior to human beings. His belief that all behavior was determined by the environment prompted him to deny the ultimate value of such hallowed concepts as freedom and dignity. Although he acknowledged that the commitment of human beings to the value of freedom was a rational—and inevitable—response to humanity's experience with punishment by the state, he insisted that if governments had consistently used positive instead of negative reinforcement to accomplish their ends, the very idea of freedom would have been meaningless. Dignity, too, was ultimately unintelligible. Because all human actions were determined by the environment, human beings did not possess free will. Accordingly, the notions of praise and blame on which the concept of dignity rested were inappropriate. Convinced that human beings were creatures of their environment, Skinner held that the choice confronting them was whether they would allow ungoverned forces to determine their fates or whether they would seize control of the factors influencing them and govern them on behalf of the survival and happiness of the human species.

Not surprisingly, Skinner's position, perhaps the most consistent and rigorous exposition of the deterministic implications of behaviorism in the twentieth century, was enormously controversial. Within the academic community, a number of experimentalists regarded the research program espoused by Skinner as productive and rewarding, and his students exercised a good deal of influence. In the larger society Skinner's views were among the factors that led to the development of behavior modification techniques first employed in controlled environments, such as prisons, and later extended to individuals through counseling. Skinner's views received little support, however, among other social scientists, possibly because they could not bring themselves to dismiss the values central to Western civilization. For their part, some psychologists found Skinner's more radical claims outrageous and his efforts to popularize his views unseemly.

Among the factors limiting Skinner's influence may well have been increasing reservations about behaviorism itself. Beginning in the late 1940s and picking up steam during the 1950s and 1960s, a growing number of psychologists and other students of the human sciences came to believe that the dogmatic insistence of behaviorists on restricting inquiry to observable behavior had unreasonably constricted the boundaries of investigation. These restrictions precluded psychology from confronting head-on such crucial issues as the nature of human language, the process of planning and anticipation, and the nature of imagination. Indeed, given the importance of these topics, it is tempting to argue that behaviorism's dominance within psychology had as much to do with the widespread commitments of its practitioners to a philosophy of science—logical positivism—as with the viability of its research agenda.

Although most of the neobehaviorists had themselves acknowledged that an exclusive focus on observable behavior was inadequate by introducing "intervening variables" into their theoretical expositions, by the late 1940s a number of psychologists interested in cognition had begun to conclude that this compromise was insufficient. Between 1945 and 1960, pressures to focus more attention on what occurred inside the mind emanated from a number of sources. These included comparative psychologist Karl Lashley's claim in 1948 that the behavioral sequences involved in such commonplace activities as playing a musical instrument, playing tennis, and speaking occurred so quickly and were so complex that only advanced mental planning from a centralized mental agency was sufficient to account for them; the invocation by Jean Piaget, a European genetic epistemologist, of unobserved, mathematically describable mental structures in accounting for the ability of children to interpret the world; the contention of social psychologist Leon Festinger that expectations and beliefs within the mind prompted individuals afflicted with "cognitive dissonance" to change their behavior; the argument for a "New Look" in perception that conferred upon perceivers a more active role than behaviorists had allowed; psychologist Jerome Bruner's interpretation of concept formation as the result of an active intellectual process employing an overall strategy; and linguist Noam Chomsky's critique of the behaviorist theory of language and defense of the existence of innate linguistic rules. The most important elements underlying the "cognitive revolution" within American psychology, however, were the modern high-speed digital computer and the growing prominence of two technologically derived concepts that suggested ways of envisioning high-level mental processes in mechanistic terms. One of these concepts, information-feedback, enabled machines to replicate the kind of goal-directed behavior normally associated with human activities. The other concept, program, enabled psychologists to preserve the disciplinary autonomy of psychology while leaving intact the analogy of mind with machines by distinguishing the human mind—in effect, the human program—from its hardware, the brain.

Armed with these products of technological innovation, a number of cognitive psychologists began during the fifties to develop descriptions of the human being as machine that were far more literal-minded than those of their behaviorist predecessors. In effect, they characterized human beings as information-processing systems akin to computers. From this perspective, the task of psychology became that of investigating the ways in which human beings used their programs—the ideas, symbols, schemata, rules, images, and other representations found in the mind—to process information they received from the environment and respond accordingly.

During the 1960s and 1970s, assaults on behaviorism continued. Ethologists, for example, pointed out that the behavior of many animals in their natural habitats was more constrained by heredity than the learning theories developed by behaviorists on the basis of laboratory experiments implied. The work of animal researchers also suggested that a central "inner" source that was at least partly the product of heredity determined the degree to which animals managed to link chains of stimulus and response.

Meanwhile, the growth and further elaboration of cognitive psychology continued apace. By the sixties, a variety of different emphases was available to those who wished to embrace precepts of cognitive psychology. A small minority of cognitivists, for example, turned to Europe, where they drew on a flourishing tradition of structuralism associated with Claude Lévi-Strauss, Jean Piaget, and Michel Foucault. These cognitivists held that human behavior was ultimately the product of structural patterns embedded in the mind. Most cognitive psychologists in the United States, however, continued to pursue the idea of modeling the human mind on information-processing machines. By the late 1970s some psychologists interested in problems concerning the relationship between cognition, artificial intelligence, and computer simulation even began to break off from their discipline to join other interested parties in creating a new field called "cognitive science."

In recent years a number of historians have taken issue with the notion that cognitive psychology constituted a radical break from behaviorism. Important continuities between behaviorism and cognitive psychology unquestionably exist. Both approaches make examination of behavior a central concern. In addition, most behaviorists and cognitive psychologists embraced mechanistic models in describing human beings; the difference between thinking of people as "organic machines" and viewing them as computers is not particularly great. Neither behaviorism nor cognitive psychology devotes much attention to such issues as emotion and aesthetic experience. In the final analysis, however, the points of difference seem at least as significant as the elements of continuity. In contrast to the behaviorists, who regarded behavior as the psychological datum that needed to be explained, cognitive psychologists examined behavior primarily in order to draw inferences about mental processes and structures that could account for it. Moreover, though cognitive psychologists do not ignore the significance of the environment in shaping human responses, they put far more emphasis than the behaviorists on "internal" constraints on the responses. Finally, unlike the behaviorists, who found it necessary either to redefine in significant ways or to eliminate altogether such terms as thought, language,

meaning, purpose, imagery, and consciousness, the cognitivists appropriated those terms as they were commonly defined and made them once more scientifically useful.

During the 1980s, several intellectually sophisticated attacks were made on the analogy between artificial intelligence machines and human beings. It remains an open question whether the human mind can ultimately best be understood as a sophisticated information-processing device akin to a computer.

The renewed emphasis on cognitive processes was only one of the developments in the period after World War II leading to a greater emphasis on "interior" aspects of human nature. At a different level, new views of the relevance of evolutionary mechanisms for human behavior, coupled with advances in neuroscience, led to the claim that human personality was primarily a function of biological processes. Actually, for all the efforts of psychologists during the twentieth century to delineate for their discipline a territory distinct from biology and neurophysiology, there has always been an intimate, albeit sometimes only implicit, connection between psychology and those two sciences. In the period after World War II, however, a growing number of biologists and neuroscientists began to assert that it was impossible to understand the human mind without assimilating the results of their labors.

One of the most extreme statements of this position was expressed by exponents of sociobiology. Sociobiology began to emerge in the 1960s, when a number of biologists concluded that the sciences of genetics, ethology, neurophysiology, and neuropsychology had advanced to the point where it was both possible and necessary to biologize the human sciences. Convinced that mind and behavior were no less fundamentally determined by natural selection than morphological characteristics, these biological scientists reasoned that human beings who possessed the kind of genetic material that enabled them to think and behave in the manner most conducive to survival had been favored by the evolutionary process.

This view constituted an implicit repudiation of a consensus that had been achieved only after long years of wrangling about the social and psychological implications of Darwinism. By the mid-twenties natural scientists and social scientists had begun to treat biological and psychological evolution as essentially distinct processes and to regard the latter as primarily the product of culture rather than biology. By contrast, proponents of sociobiology rejected the notion that culture had liberated human beings from the power of heredity. Moreover, unlike functional psychologists earlier in the century, for whom adaptation to the environment had a plethora of value connotations having little to do with what evolutionary theorists meant when they used the term "survival," sociobiologists took quite seriously the Darwinian emphasis on procreation as the criterion of "fitness" and survival to procreate as the "goal" of the evolutionary process. Nothing in culture, they asserted, exempted human beings from that evolutionary imperative.

In 1975 the eminent evolutionary theorist Edward O. Wilson presented some of the speculations that resulted from efforts to biologize the human mind and behavior in the concluding chapter of his *Sociobiology: The New Synthesis* (1975). In this work and in subsequent accounts that he wrote for nonscientists, Wilson contended that sociobiology involved not only the study of behavior but also the construction of values and a more humane social order in accordance with the precepts of Darwinian fitness.

Since 1975 a number of other sociobiologists have joined Wilson in affirming the preeminent role of biology in shaping mind and culture. In turn, their views have been vehemently attacked by a legion of critics in the natural sciences, social sciences, and philosophy. Some have charged that both the intent and the effect of sociobiology is to provide a justification for attributes central to the sociopolitical status quo. Others have complained that the data thus far derived from biology simply do not justify most of the claims for genetic determinism made by supporters of a strong program of sociobiology. There would appear to be some justice to this claim; the current state of biological knowledge makes it impossible to obtain anything approaching a consensus among scientists concerning the validity of the sociobiological project.

Another effort to biologize the mind that has led to debates similar to those occurring in sociobiology took place in the area of mental testing. In 1969, on the basis of a review of testing literature, the University of California psychologist Arthur Jensen concluded that much of the difference between the scores of blacks and whites on intelligence tests was attributable to heredity. The furor that Jensen's article provoked in the popular media increased in 1971, when the Harvard psychologist Richard Herrnstein published an article in which he maintained that approximately 85 percent of intelligence was due to heredity. In the ensuing debates critics of testing made it clear that IQ tests were not infallible indicators of achievement in life and that performance was significantly affected by a multitude of environmental factors. In addition, many argued that IQ itself poorly measured the complex qualities referred to as "intelligence." Finally, critics made a strong case for the view that tests of IQ were socioculturally biased. Nevertheless, the controversy over intelligence testing has continued. So, too, have disagreements over whether verdicts of science should be as subject to political debate as other human enterprises or whether they possesses a privileged status that raises them above such debate.

Among the most clearly efficacious manifestations of the commitment to a biologized view of the mind have been a number of pharmacological breakthroughs in biological psychiatry. In contrast to the period prior to World War II, when psychotropic drugs did not exist as therapeutic agents, the postwar period witnessed the appearance of a number of drugs that dealt effectively with the symptoms of the schizophrenias, the manic depressive psychoses, nonsituational, endogenous depression, hyperactivity among children, and other mental disorders. Although these drugs—which included chlorpromazine, lithium, and a family of antidepressants—were first used to treat major illnesses, they subsequently proved beneficial in dealing with less serious, yet debilitating, conditions such as agoraphobia. The use of such drugs, coupled with economic considerations and pressure from social reformers, has facilitated a reduction in the length of hospital stays for many of the mentally ill, and more patients have been treated on an outpatient basis. Only recently has research discovered the specifics of how those psychoactive drugs affect the operation of neurotransmitters, the neurochemical agents responsible for brain function.

In spite of their rather clear success in dealing with mental disorders, the use of psychoactive drugs has generated controversy. Critics have emphasized that drug therapies fail to get at the underlying causes of the problems provoking the symptoms while discouraging patients from undertaking the kind of in-depth analysis of their environmental situation and/or life history on which any real hopes for cure depend. Notwithstanding such criticisms, however, the use of drug therapy and efforts to find biological causes for psychological conditions have continued, and it would appear that during the last twenty years pharmacological approaches to mental disorders have gained increasing support from the medical community and the public alike.

THE CHANGING FORTUNES OF PSYCHOTHERAPY

It is perhaps not altogether coincidental that the increasing tendency to employ drug therapy has coincided with increased doubts within the medical community as to the efficacy and legitimacy of psychoanalysis and an increased reliance among Americans on psychotherapeutic strategies that do not depend on the expertise of psychiatrists. These tendencies represent a marked change from the twenty-year period after World War II, when respect for psychoanalysis in the United States was at an all-time high. Possibly because of its success in explaining the prevalence of mental problems attending the war, and doubtless for other reasons thus far not discerned, psychoanalysis emerged from World War II as the dominant theory of personality and most exalted approach to therapy in psychiatry and clinical psychology alike. The interpretation of Freudianism preeminent within the American psychoanalytic institutes, which grew increasingly intolerant of dissent in the two decades after the war, concentrated on fostering the adjustment of the individual to social norms.

During the period between 1945 and 1965, Freudian views were respectfully received not only by mental health professionals but by the larger culture as well. Most American intellectuals conferred upon psychoanalysis much the same prestige that they attached to other expressions of science in general and medicine in particular. This status, coupled with the widespread disillusionment of postwar American writers and artists with political categories of analysis, their renewed interest in problems relating to selfhood, and their faith in the ability of the analytic method to plumb the depths of the human psyche, made psychoanalysis a major component of liberal establishment thought in the period between 1945 and 1965. Moreover, largely as a result of the widespread popularization of Freudian ideas in the postwar era, many literate Americans who were not part of the intelligentsia also concluded that psychoanalysis was an important source of enlightenment concerning the nature of the human condition. This conclusion converged with the growth of a middle class able and willing to spend discretionary income in the hope of solving personal problems.

Perhaps the most influential conduit of Freudian ideas during the 1940s and 1950s was Benjamin Spock, whose frequently revised guide to child rearing, first published in 1946, was purchased by millions of American readers. Although Spock employed little Freudian terminology, he clearly embraced Freud's view that the development of the human psyche was primarily the product of the interaction of biological drives with early social experience. From this perspective, he concluded that the primary responsibility of parents to children was to provide a nurturing

environment in which personality development could take place.

The period since the 1960s has seen a decline in the fortunes of psychoanalytic theory and practice. Philosophers of science have increasingly joined forces with psychologists in rejecting Freudianism's scientific credentials. In addition, a number of clinical investigations have raised serious questions about the therapeutic success of psychoanalysis. Finally, the declining status of psychoanalysis has reflected growing skepticism about what has seemed to be analysts' overweening emphasis on facilitating the adaptation of individuals to prevailing social norms. Since the fifties, many critics have complained that such an emphasis precludes individuals from effectively expressing their individuality.

In 1989 the settlement of a class-action suit led the American Psychoanalytic Association to open psychoanalytic training to nonmedical health professionals. In spite of the fact that this has resulted in a new wave of interest in analysis among would-be nonmedical practitioners, it remains to be seen whether the influx of new trainees will result in a sustained renewal of the vitality and status of psychoanalysis within the United States.

Challenges to psychoanalysis have done little to undermine the commitment of Americans to other psychotherapeutic approaches to self-understanding. Since 1945 the popularity of such approaches, which characteristically involve less of a commitment of time and money than that associated with analysis, has led—and in turn has responded—to an enormous increase in the number of mental health care professionals in the United States. Undoubtedly the most notable development in this area has been the rapid growth of clinical psychology, which prior to World War II had been a field of applied psychologists charged with the task of diagnosing and evaluating sensory and learning difficulties through the use of tests. The psychological needs of returning veterans, however, imposed strong pressures on clinical psychologists to offer psychotherapy, heretofore the preserve of psychiatry. Reinforcing these pressures were the continued efforts of psychologists to expand the purview of their profession. By the 1950s, psychotherapy had become the major function of clinical psychologists, and as a result of a continuing high demand for their services, the number of clinical psychologists increased at a much faster rate than that of academic psychologists. In the course of a mere decade psychology was transformed from a discipline principally located in colleges and universities and primarily concerned with experimental approaches to mind and behavior to a profession intimately concerned with the mental health and discomforts of the population.

Overseeing the work of professional psychologists in the period after World War II was the American Psychological Association. In 1937 the commitment of the APA to scholarly research had prompted professional psychologists to form their own separate organization, the American Association for Applied Psychology. During the war, however, the institutional rupture between academic psychology and applied psychology was healed when the American Psychological Association embraced a plan reorganizing that organization into a federation of autonomous divisions representing the major interest groups within psychology. The affiliation of clinical psychology and academic psychology within this federal structure was undoubtedly instrumental in leading clinical psychologists in the postwar years to embrace a scientist-practitioner model of professional training.

During the sixties, when a large number of Americans joined the assault on the cult of conformity, psychotherapeutic approaches associated with Abraham Maslow and Carl Rogers became increasingly popular. These approaches, which were characteristically juxtaposed under the rubric of "humanistic psychology," stressed the desirability of human autonomy, the existence of latent human capabilities, and the desirability of "self-actualization." Because they emphasized the realization of untapped potential rather than the grappling with serious mental distress, they became appealing to many middle-class Americans who felt capable enough of functioning within their society but vaguely dissatisfied with the quality of their lives.

Since 1970 psychotherapeutic approaches to fostering individual growth and assisting individuals in their efforts to reach their full potential have proliferated. Although these approaches have openly opposed mechanistic reductionism and the dominance of scientific objectivity, most of them have not viewed themselves as opponents of science per se, and many have explicitly invoked the authority of science in promoting their ideas. The common denominator uniting the programs in this so-called human potential movement has been a reluctance to discuss determinate ethical norms other than "growth," which is characteristically equated with an openness to change, and "authenticity," generally described as an uninhibited expression of feelings and an unabashed commitment to self-acceptance. As a result of the growing number of people in psychotherapy and the images generated by the popular media, psychological concepts and jargon have become increasingly pervasive within American culture.

These developments have been attended by a steady stream of books and articles questioning the therapeutic value, intellectual rigor, and social implications of psychotherapy. During the 1960s, the psychiatrist Thomas Szasz was one of a number of critics who maintained that the preoccupation with mental health and the construction of the term mental illness to stigmatize social deviance not only ratified the cultural status quo but also undermined faith in human freedom and moral responsibility. Since that time a number of other commentators have expressed concern that psychotherapy fosters the development and dissemination of a "victim mentality." Some critics have also argued that a preoccupation with self has placed obstacles in the way of more far-reaching, fundamental social and political change. Still others have pointed to numerous studies challenging psychotherapy's therapeutic efficacy. Although the difficulty of evaluating results when the goal is as elusive as "change of personality" or "enhancement of self-image" has precluded the emergence of a clear consensus, there does seem to be general agreement that unless the therapist is peculiarly gifted and well-trained, psychotherapy will be no more useful than discussions with a trusted friend or other forms of self-help. Notwithstanding such criticisms, however, the tendency of Americans to resort to psychotherapeutic categories in thinking about themselves and others continues, thus leading a number of students of American culture to suggest that the United States has become a "therapeutic society."

See Also Gender Theories (in this volume).

BIBLIOGRAPHY

Mitchell G. Ash and William R. Woodward, eds., *Psychology in Twentieth-Century Thought and Society* (1987), is an important and widely cited collection of articles dealing with a number of topics in the history of twentieth-century psychology in Europe and America. Josef Brozek, ed., *Explorations in the History of Psychology in the United States* (1984), is uneven in quality but provides useful background on many of the important movements in psychology. John C. Burnham, *Paths into American Culture: Psychology, Medicine, and Morals* (1988), is a collection of many, though not all, of the important essays written by the preeminent historian of American psychology and psychiatry. Although the last third of Carl N. Degler, *In Search of Human Nature: The Decline and Revival of Darwinism in American Social Thought* (1991), reads more like a polemic than a sober work of historical scholarship, the book manages ably to synthesize a large body of important material. Sigmund Koch and David E. Leary, eds., *Century of Psychology as Science: Retrospectives and Assessments* (1985), contains numerous essays that are pertinent to understanding psychological interpretations of human nature in the twentieth century. Thomas Hardy Leahey, *A History of Psychology: Main Currents in Psychological Thought*, 2d ed. (1987), is a readable, often insightful survey that focuses primary attention in its treatment of the twentieth century on developments in American psychology. R. W. Rieber and Kurt Salzinger, eds., *Psychology: Theoretical-Historical Perspectives* (1980), contains a number of solid essays describing topics germane to twentieth century psychology.

In spite of the fact that it was published more than a half century ago, Edna Heidbreder, *Seven Psychologies* (1933), is still a solid, readable discussion of the major "schools" of psychological thought in the early twentieth century. John M. O'Donnell, *The Origins of Behaviorism: American Psychology, 1870–1920* (1985), is, though not always entirely convincing, a highly sophisticated survey of American psychology in a crucial period. Michael M. Sokal, ed., *Psychological Testing and American Society, 1890–1930* (1987), contains a number of important essays relating to the testing movement in the early years. Donald S. Napoli, *Architects of Adjustment: The History of the Psychological Profession in the United States* (1981), is the most complete survey of applied psychology in the twentieth century, though there is definitely room for additional work on this subject.

Nathan G. Hale, Jr., *Freud and the Americans: The Beginnings of Psychoanalysis in the United States, 1876–1917* (1971), is the standard treatment of the early reception of Freud's work in the United States. F. H. Matthews, "The Americanization of Sigmund Freud: Adaptations of Psychoanalysis before 1917," *Journal of American Studies* 1 (1967): 39–62, is a provocative discussion of the way in which Freud's work was received within American culture. Jacques M. Quen and Eric T. Carlson, eds., *American Psychoanalysis: Origins and Development* (1978), is a helpful compilation of short essays. Fred Matthews, "In Defense

of Common Sense: Mental Hygiene as Ideology and Mentality in Twentieth-Century America," *Prospects* 4 (1979): 459–516, is a far-reaching, deeply nuanced treatment of the cultural implications of the mental hygiene movement. J. A. C. Brown, *Freud and the Post-Freudians* (1961), is the best survey of neo-Freudian thought with which I am familiar. David Shakow and David Rapaport, "The Influence of Freud on American Psychology" *Psychological Issues* 13 (1964), is the most complete treatment of the subject but probably underestimates the acrimony between psychologists and Freud. Gail A. Hornstein, "The Return of the Repressed: Psychology's Problematic Relations with Psychoanalysis, 1909–1960," *American Psychologist* 47 (1992): 254–263, is a superb, albeit brief, account of a crucial subject.

Kerry W. Buckley, *The Mechanical Man: John Broadus Watson and the Beginnings of Behaviorism* (1989), is an excellent treatment of the life of John B. Watson and the cultural context of his work. Franz Samelson, "Organizing for the Kingdom of Behavior: Academic Battles and Organizational Policies in the Twenties," *Journal of the History of the Behavioral Sciences* 21 (1985): 33–47, is a solidly researched study that should serve to qualify claims that behaviorism took psychology by storm. Samelson's, "The Struggle for Scientific Authority: The Reception of Watson's Behaviorism, 1913–1920," *Journal of the History of the Behavioral Sciences* 17 (1981): 399–425, is the best treatment of the early response to Watsonian behaviorism. Hamilton Cravens, *The Triumph of Evolution: American Scientists and the Heredity-Environment Controversy, 1900–1941* (1988), is an intelligent treatment of a crucial topic in American intellectual history. Laurence D. Smith, *Behaviorism and Positivism: A Reassessment of the Alliance* (1986), not only shows that the indebtedness of the neobehaviorists to the logical positivists has been exaggerated but provides very able summaries of the ideas of Tolman, Hull, and Skinner.

Michael M. Sokal, "The Gestalt Psychologists in Behaviorist America," *American Historical Review* 89 (1984): 1240–1263, is a well-written, perceptive survey of an important topic. Calvin S. Hall and Gardner Lindzey, *Theories of Personality*, 2d ed. (1970), provides an overview of the major personality theorists of the twentieth century.

Albert R. Gilgen, *American Psychology since World War II* (1982), is a solid, though superficial, survey. Virginia Staudt Sexton, "Clinical Psychology: An Historical Survey," *Genetic Psychology Monographs* 72 (1965): 401–434, is not profound but is still the best survey of this crucial subject. Howard Gardner, *The*

Mind's New Science: A History of the Cognitive Revolution (1987), is a well-written, nontechnical, and intelligent account of the multifarious strands comprising developments in cognitive science since 1945.

Nancy C. Andreasen, *The Broken Brain: The Biological Revolution in Psychiatry* (1984), provides a useful summary of recent findings in neuropsychology and neurophysiology. Howard L. Kaye, *The Social Meaning of Modern Biology* (1986), is an intelligent discussion of sociobiology and other biological issues that relate to the behavioral sciences.

The author wishes to thank the following persons who read and commented on an earlier draft of this essay: John C. Burnham, Donald Fleming, David Hollinger, Ronald L. Numbers, Sharon Roberts, Dorothy Ross, Michael M. Sokal, James Turner, and William R. Woodward. They are of course not responsible for the errors of fact or interpretation that remain.

GENDER THEORIES

Jill Morawski

New theses about the nature of men and women flourished in the twentieth century; not just in the academy but in all professions, from accounting to social work, in courts, schools, work environment, and homes. Within the academic realm virtually no discipline or movement was exempted from what appears to have been a pressing quest to comprehend the sexes and their differences. Initially sought as an answer to the "woman question," a multifaceted inquiry into the status of women which was posed during the nineteenth century, gender theories were anticipated to resolve problems of human rights, legal reform, mental health, labor concerns, personal anxieties, and intimate relations. With this initial focus on women as the question, early gender theories often centered (and many still do) around femaleness or femininity, setting maleness or masculinity as unquestioned terms or implicit norms.

Given the diverse sites in which theories of gender were demanded and proposed, and their proliferation both outside and within the rapidly expanding professions of science and social science in the present century, an exhaustive history would be voluminous. This account primarily represents theories and other relatively formal conjectures about gender that were produced within the sciences and social sciences, leaving largely untreated the vast realm of popular or "folk" theories generated in everyday life or the popular media, and theories that emerged from literary projects, those conceived in fiction and literary criticism. By situating the development of gender theories within the context of social, economic, and political events relevant to the matter of the sexes the impact of cultural conditions can be considered. How theorizing was influenced by the changing landscape of the scientific and social scientific professions, notably their increasing specialization and inclusion of women as both practitioners or producers and subjects of science, is also examined.

Twentieth-century theories of gender have been at once ubiquitous and varied in their explanatory bases. All have necessarily proceeded from observed differences between the sexes, although there has been considerable variation in what differences were identified for analysis and what interpretive lens—economic, biological, psychological—was employed to examine these differences. While some theorists (the earliest being evolutionists and the most recent the sociobiologists) grounded their investigations on the presumed centrality of sex difference in reproductive functions, fitting the differences to biological notions of determined function, other theorists proceeded by analyzing sex differences in psychosocial activities and investigated features of the social world—institutions and customs—that both caused, perpetuated, and gave meaning to the differences.

Despite ongoing variations in theoretical forms, they have been influenced in relatively systematic ways by dominant political and intellectual forces. There are detectable trends in theorizing that roughly correspond to three chronological periods. In the early years of the century the theories bore the mark, sometimes implicit and at other times quite obvious, of nineteenth-century science and its efforts to locate natural causes for the observed differentiation of the sexes. However, liberal political movements of the early twentieth century, and the changes they initiated in social institutions, altered the investigative landscape and ultimately gave rise to a theoretical dualism whereby the origin of gender was ascribed either to nature (in accordance with the predominant scientific attitude of the nineteenth century) or to culture (a stance compatible with Progressive politics). From the 1920s until the 1950s, theories of gender lost many vestiges of nineteenth-century thinking as they increasingly were accommodated to the interests and ideologies of the professional specialties in which they were constructed. The controversy between nature and nurture explanations of sex differences did not disappear; rather, the quest to understand the differences between the sexes became entangled in disciplinary debates such as those over adequate empirical methods for observation and procedures for verification. The very project of theorizing gender through a rational scientific system itself eventually came under challenge as a possible product of gender differences: however, although these challenges were voiced throughout the earlier two periods, it was only in the 1960s that they were seriously applied to the study of gender. For the next thirty years, some researchers nevertheless eschewed such concerns and continued to construct theories, while other researchers undertook critical and reflexive analyses of the gendered bases of gender theories, making the disciplines themselves a subject of study.

A note on the use of the term *gender* is warranted before proceeding with this historical review. For most of the century, *sex* was the term used to refer to the categories of male and female as well as characteristics designated as masculine and feminine. *Gender* was an auxiliary term typically employed either as a synonym or to denote attributes of the male or female sex. The critical interrogations of theorizing initiated in the 1960s spurred an intensive reevaluation of these language practices: both terms were found to convey surplus meaning and confuse analyses. In some instances the problems encountered in debates over an adequate terminology led to the design of disciplinary norms to guide word usage. There still is no consensus on their meanings, although most often *sex* is used in reference to biological factors pertaining to males and females and *gender* is used in all other circumstances. In order to register the historical variations in language use, this account uses, whenever possible, the terms *sex* and *gender* as they were deployed in the particular theories being described.

THE LIMITS OF NATURALISM

Havelock Ellis's *Man and Woman*, published in 1894, was claimed as the first comprehensive survey of scientific research on sex differences, and the conclusions to that volume presaged the general climate of theorizing about sex differences for the next thirty years. Given the complexity of his lengthy review, Ellis warned readers that "Sometimes a sufficiently wide induction of facts . . . suffices to show us what is artificial and what is real; at other times . . . the wider the induction of facts the more complex and mobile become our results." His assertion was more than a statement on the occasional equivocality of scientific facts, for he continued with a challenge to the common naturalist presupposition that the human world is as stable as the physical universe: "We have to recognize that our present knowledge of men and women cannot tell us what they might be or what they ought to be, but what they actually are, under the conditions of civilization." At once Ellis's study exemplified the rapidly expanding belief that scientific methods could yield veridical knowledge about the social world and a slower growing skepticism about the limits of the naturalist premises underlying that scientific attitude. With such faith in naturalism, it was held that scientific studies would lay "the axe at the root of many pseudo scientific superstitions" and generate knowledge for the design and execution of social policy. But Ellis's accompanying doubts about this faith were shared by many intellectuals who were also beginning to question whether all human actions were natural, historically stable, and unmodifiable. Thus, the very moment that promised scientific truth about the puzzling and sometimes tortuous problems of the sexes also bore at least an undercurrent of uncertainty about that promise.

While containing gestures of skepticism, Ellis's *Man and Woman* nevertheless conveyed the then dominant attitudes of naturalism: a belief that human actions had natural bases (rather than rational, idealist, or supernatural) and that, therefore, the methods of empirical science were the appropriate means to study humans. It was the prevalent conjunction of naturalism and evolutionary theory that guided many researchers in their studies of gender and particularly sex differences. Both in its specific analyses of the sexes and in its general descriptions of human evolution, Darwin's writing had multiple influences on how gender was examined and explained. His emphasis on the biological origins of human temperament fostered studies that explained gender psychology in biological terms. Thus, aggression in men was interpreted as a biological mechanism for survival and certain social inclinations in women were seen as expressions of maternal instinct to protect the young. Darwin's theory also initiated an interest in individual differences both as measures of natural variations in the species and as means for evolutionary changes (which were often defined as progress). In turn, the focus on individual differences affected the study of the sexes in two ways: it provided theoretical and methodological frameworks for studying sex differences in a wide range of psychological and physiological attributes and it undergirded discussions of the relative superiority (in evolutionary terms) of one sex over the other.

By the time of Ellis's project to synthesize the known differences between males and females, researchers committed to naturalism and evolutionary theory had generated numerous working hypotheses. Among these conjectures was the existence of different brain structures in males and females, and the greater variability of man in all attributes (thus explaining the predominance of male geniuses and identifying males as primarily responsible for species variations that determine evolutionary progress). Added to these hypotheses were notions that female reproductive functions (menstruation, pregnancy, and menopause) were biological processes that had behavioral and psychological consequences, notably in making them unfit for public life and suited to domestic activities.

Ellis relied on these conjectures yet established a more complex portrait of sex differences. He theorized that sexual differences were matters of both biological and social evolution; they represented either natural differences (those genetic in origin) or artificial differences (those rendered through social custom and practices) respectively. He also expanded Darwin's categorization of primary and secondary sexual characteristics to include a category of "tertiary" sexual characteristics. Primary characteristics are those (glands and organs) essential to reproduction; secondary characteristics are auxiliary but important to the propagation of the race (by making the sexes more attractive to each other) and include such features as breasts, body hair, and voice. Tertiary characteristics are only indirectly related to primary and secondary sexual differences but are nevertheless important; these include such attributes as skull size, intelligence, and metabolism.

From the data amassed, Ellis tentatively concluded that women were more childlike in attributes ranging from large head size, delicate facial configuration, small bones, degree of hairiness, as well as in psychic characteristics of engagement in the immediate practicalities of life, youthful interests, and general positive temperament. Men, by contrast, were more like the aged or the savage in their relatively smaller head size, more body hair, interests in remote and abstract ideas, and tendency to dominate nature and others around them. Ellis's findings corroborated Darwin's observations that men varied more in their physical dimensions; yet Ellis held that infantile characteristics actually represented highest evolution (i.e., large skull size) and that, therefore, women were evolutionary leaders, so to speak.

Man and Woman contained yet another conjecture from evolutionary theory that was widely employed by theorists at the turn of the century. Evolution frequently was interpreted in terms of *progress* toward more adapted or efficient forms, and with the assertion of some desirable endpoint of evolution, studies of variation and difference were available for making what can now be seen as undeniably political

claims. Just as he recognized both biological and social evolution, so Ellis subscribed to notions of biological and social progress. And although he was an advocate of social reform for women's rights, *Man and Woman* asserted nature's eventual power over social experiments. The permanence of any social changes in the organism, including reforms in the respective treatment of the sexes, ultimately were to be determined by natural law.

If one were to describe a prototypical theory of gender at the start of the twentieth century, it would contain the primary components of Ellis's study: naturalism, evolutionary theory, and a politically informed conception of human progress. With the Darwinian emphasis on variation (difference) and function, along with the scientific commitment to uncovering the "real" through the tools of science (notably experimental and quantitative techniques), researchers interrogated the phenomena of gender. They worked not so much to challenge the separate spheres of the sexes, which were idealized in nineteenth-century culture and proclaimed in the loosely scientific theorizing of Herbert Spencer among others, as to definitively locate and inscribe the boundaries of those spheres through systematic testing and measuring. Most of the studies concurred in describing woman's nature as being physically vulnerable, less rational, more emotional and expressive, passive, and suited to interpersonal occupations—to domestic or private life. Man's nature, by contrast, was consistently found to be physically robust, rational, instrumental, active if not aggressive, and suited to mastery of objects in the world—to public life. Few adopted Ellis's position that women had the evolutionary advantage but, rather, viewed the progress of civilization and human nature as a result of male attributes.

Experiments in biology and psychology, statistical analysis of census and anthropological data, and evolutionary theory were not the only scientific tools applied to the question of the nature of the sexes. Advances in nineteenth-century medicine, particularly neurophysiology and reproductive biology, were similarly employed to distinguish the sexes. Patricia Vertinsky (in *The Eternally Wounded Woman*) has documented how extant knowledge of bodily functioning was extended to describe and prescribe women's capacities, eventually locating physical and psychical limitations in female reproductive organs. Even the science of physics, with its theory of the conservation of energy, was engaged to explain how the reproductive processes of women's bodies consumed energies that otherwise would be available for fueling higher mental functions. These studies generally represented female characteristics first, as a deviation from some human (male) norm and, second, as a lack or deficit; gender was routinely perceived in terms of difference with the qualities of the male sex presented as the desirable term in this theoretical dichotomy.

By the turn of the century the expanding array of scientific theories of gender had become inextricably bound up with a popular social concern that had become known as the "woman question." Numerous events throughout the nineteenth century—including the religious revivalism of the early part of the century, abolition, suffrage movements, and increased industrialization—each in varied ways raised questions about the rights of women and the social conventions which structured their lives. For some intellectuals, like the scientist G. T. W. Patrick, the authority of science was at odds with social and legal programs for the advancement of women. In *The Psychology of Women*, Patrick provided evidence for women's evolutionary role as caretakers of the generations, asking in the end whether that role is "too sacred to be jousted roughly in the struggle for existence, and that she deserves from man a reverent exemption from some of the duties for which his restless and active nature adapts him?" G. Stanley Hall, the developmental psychologist and founder of the American Psychological Association, took a comparable stance, drawing upon evolutionary doctrine to define and delimit women's social sphere and intellectual capacities. Hall generated such theoretical accounts even as late as the 1920s when he proposed that the flapper, despite her image as resisting feminine attributes and demanding equality, actually represented the appearance of a newer and more progressive womanhood devoted to childbearing and nurturance. However, the new authority of science was not always of one voice on policy matters regarding the woman question. While Hall used evolutionary naturalism to argue for the formal if special education of women who, after all, would have responsibilities educating their young, Edward Clarke, called upon related medical models of women's capacities to make the contrary claim that higher education would harm the bodies and consequently the reproductive fitness of women.

The woman question, however, was not merely a topic for popular debate: it encompassed a host of practices and projects through which the dominant ideology of the sexes, including the doctrine of separate spheres, was being scrutinized and at times transgressed. By the beginning of the twentieth century, industrialization, urbanization, and immigration had produced changes in social institutions such that the pairing of male and female life with public and private domains respectively was even less appropriate, if it ever had been. Women's participation in the labor force was substantial and their admission into institutions of higher education, among other things, significantly changed the social relations of the sexes. Given the saliency of the woman question and its presence in Progressive reform movements, it is not surprising that many among the first generation of women to receive university training chose to study the nature of the sexes. And perhaps it is more than a bit ironic that women who studied the social sciences at the time were, according to Dorothy Ross (in *The Origins of American Social Science*), entering fields whose practitioners, with their "realist desire to eliminate subjectivity as well as the desire for scientific authority have repeatedly cast the social scientific enterprise in masculine terms." Yet despite the rational and instrumental nature of science, and the similarly masculine accoutrements of realism and scientism, the social scientific professions, like the sciences, afforded opportunities (albeit restricted ones) for women to advance in intellectual pursuits. And despite such inhospitable conditions, women were prominent among those early-twentieth-century researchers examining the sexes: they produced theories both within the profession and as independent scholars without official positions in research institutions.

In part owing to this new female constituency in higher education who challenged Victorian social ideals, and in part due to a growing suspicion that naturalism was inadequate to the task of deciphering the complex causes of human behavior, the theories proposed in the first decades of the century were heterogeneous, often conflicting, in their claims about the origins and nature of gender. The decision to seek an understanding of gender either in biology and evolution or, alternatively, in social conditions such as history, economics, and social structure, was also conditioned by the maturation of the social sciences into distinct disciplines with their own logic of inquiry and theoretical interests. Thus, theories of gender developed during the period were heterogeneous, sometimes mutually incompatible, and multitudinous in their discipline-specific forms.

Studies of gender conducted in psychology exemplify the effects of both distinct disciplinary practices and the presence of women researchers, and the resultant concepts of gender in that field aptly illustrate the theoretical quandaries that were emerging. By the twentieth century, American psychology was considered thoroughly scientific: as a hybrid product of nineteenth-century German psychophysics and evolutionary naturalism it honored the traditions of scientific experimentation and strict quantitative measurement. However, influenced by the social reform movement and prodded by the necessity of justifying its social relevance, psychology extended its mission and did not proceed with a clear separation of scientific and social interests. The pressing questions of the sexes stand as one instance where psychologists expanded their scientific commitments by bringing their new methodological rigor to matters of immediate social concern. An impressive number of laboratory experiments were conducted to ascertain the differences between men and women on every imaginable psychological dimension from memory to color preference, from motor efficiency to fear responses. The results of these many experiments often were equivocal, with males performing better in some instances, females in others, and in many studies no sex differences were found at all. For instance, in studies of mental abilities the reigning assumption of male intellectual superiority frequently was not confirmed. In his first major experiments with the revised Binet-Simon Intelligence Scale conducted between 1910 and 1914, Lewis Terman tested one thousand school children and found slight superiority of girls; these results led him to reconsider why women had not attained eminence in public life and ultimately to posit, in *The Measurement of Intelligence*, that their failure "may be due to wholly extraneous factors."

The first generation of women psychologists was highly represented among those researchers who explored the psychic vicissitudes of sex, and most of them were convinced by the experimental reports that sex differences merited little further attention except as a phenomenon caused by social conditions. They contributed to the growing number of experimental studies which examined sex differences in diverse mental activities including reaction time, smell and taste perception, motor abilities, reading comprehension, memory, and problem solving. The results of these experiments were equivocal: while some reported that men excelled on a task, others found women to excel, and still others found no significant sex differences. Leta Hollingworth (in "Comparison of the Sexes") found differences reported in experimental studies were so slight that any reviewer who restricted himself to assessing sex differences on mental traits would "automatically tend to do himself out of his review. He would have little to report." Many of these researchers reached the general conclusion that the environment was a

primary determinant of sex differences. Some researchers, like Beatrice Hinkle writing in the *Psychoanalytic Review*, even doubted the adequacy of such experiments until that time "when the tradition of women's inferiority has completely disappeared and the children of both sexes are given the same training and freedom, with the same privileges and responsibilities."

Within psychology the new experimental findings on sex differences were leading many researchers toward a theoretical position that explained those differences in terms of prevailing social conditions, in terms of "nurture" rather than biological "nature." However, the experimental program ultimately provided no final test of theory, no conclusive explanation or indication of whether differences were environmentally or biologically determined. And because certain variables were beyond control through laboratory manipulations, the critical experiment to ascertain whether differences were biologically or socially caused could not be conducted. As Helen Thompson noted as early as 1903 (in her dissertation, *The Mental Traits of Sex*), the entire life conditions of males and females had to be controlled to perform any "trustworthy investigation of the variations due to sex alone." She skeptically remarked that "complete fulfillment of these conditions, even in the most democratic community, is impossible." Such conclusions about sex differences did not, in themselves, constitute a coherent theory of the social causes of these differences or even a composite of what these differences actually were. However, they did support an environmental position and at the same time challenged beliefs both in naturalism and scientism by indicating the inaccuracy of biological models as well as the limitations of laboratory experimentation.

Other psychologists were undaunted by the new experimental findings and sought to refine notions of psychological sex differences as real and locatable correlates of biological ones. For these researchers, the experimental findings of undetermined or no differences were unconvincing; they urged further investigation into the reality of sex differences. Writing about the unexpected findings of no gender difference on the I.Q. tests, G. Stanley Hall claimed that "our Simon-Binet tests can grade and mark, at least for intelligence, but here they falter, stammer, and diverge." The conviction about substantive psychological sex differences led such psychologists to seek sex differences in some deeper structures or processes of the mind. Reasserting a faith in evolutionary naturalism, investigators like Joseph Jastrow, in "The Feminine Mind," held that since other human sciences, notably anatomy and physiology, reveal man as man and woman as woman, then "What reason is there to suspect psychology to enter a dissenting opinion." Such suspicions about the hidden but real nature of men and women (and their differences) were not dissimilar from many late-nineteenth-century claims: both described woman's nature as emotional, nurturing, and dependent and man's as rational, assertive, and independent.

Although in the first quarter of the twentieth century psychology produced no comprehensive theory of gender, it did present alternative possibilities, thereby cementing a polarity in theorizing that would endure through the remainder of the century. Gender could be explained as a biological phenomenon that could account for sex differences in every realm of human functioning; conversely, it could be explained as a socially caused phenomenon with a similar range of explanatory power. What the case of psychology illustrates is how diverse gender theories were devised and contested and yet, despite this diversity, how these theories contained no substantial disagreement about what was seen as constituting feminine and masculine behaviors or types. The matter of what constituted male and what female often remained a theoretical given that mirrored cultural norms regarding gender, even while the matter of what caused these polar types was actively debated.

Researchers in other fields had somewhat different opportunities to examine gender. Less constrained by a scientific warrant to employ experimental techniques and adopt naturalist doctrine, some anthropologists and sociologists nevertheless engaged the woman question with the attitude of scientism, thereby attempting to resolve social anxieties concerning gender with objective empirical investigations, often through the quantification of observations. Theorists like William Thomas and George Herbert Mead provided conceptual vantage points from which more empirically minded sociologists could investigate sex characteristics using a distinctly social as opposed to naturalistic or biological framework. Adopting this theoretical purchase, Jessie Taft conducted research on the social circumstances that gave rise to unique feminine traits and situations. In studies of both educated women and criminal women she found female roles encompassed conflicts between self development and social oppression. Trained in sociology and anthropology, Elise Clews Parsons used empirical ethnographic techniques to contest the popular social-evolutionary argument that women's characteristics were designed to serve the maintenance of private, notably family life. Par-

sons's studies of primitive societies underscored the cross-cultural ubiquity of the social restrictions on women's lives: these studies led her to question why sexual classifications were so common, central, and resilient in so many cultures. Here Parsons took a more theoretical bent, postulating how sexual categories and ultimately sexual differences resulted from deep psychological processes. More specifically, women's subjugation derived from a general human fear of the unlike along with a need to classify the social world; these tendencies were coupled with the force of discriminatory social structures of power. "Social rule," she argued, in a 1916 book with that title, is the primary function of social classifications and serves that classificatory and regulatory aim well by restricting women's power, for "as long as they are thought of in terms of sex, and are the weaker and more submissive, they are subject by hypothesis to control. Just as soon as women are considered not as creatures of sex, but as persons, sex regulations cease to apply." Although probably inspired by Progressive reform ideals, Parsons's research and theoretical writing eventually intimated dismal prospects for redirecting what she saw as human tendencies toward power and security; her theory contained no simple prognosis for altering women's unhappy social and psychological situation.

Other sociological studies, similarly motivated by reform impulses, reached somewhat different conclusions. Survey and interview studies of marriage, sexual behaviors, birth control, prostitution, and family patterns occasionally became the bases for locating the social restrictions that both shaped women's public and private lives and fostered antagonisms between the sexes. For some researchers, these studies also provided the groundwork for arguing that the oppressive social position of women required remediation. Research on the sexuality of men and women, however, did not lead all investigators to such liberatory conclusions, and the varied ways in which the research was used to support both liberal and conservative policies attests to the ongoing tensions between professionalism and activism that underlaid social science of the period. Nevertheless, as Rosalind Rosenberg concluded in her historical review of sex research (in *Beyond Separate Spheres*), the groundbreaking knowledge about sexual life fostered by this research "between about 1900 and 1920 gave women something that was essential to their eventual liberation: a broader conception of their own physical needs and a greater confidence in their ability to control their physical destiny."

During this period gender was gaining prominence: just as it gained attention in the academy as a salient social category so it also became more apparent as a social anxiety if not a crucial social problem. And given the popular absorption with the "woman question" and the "new woman" issues, theorizing the nature of gender was not an undertaking restricted solely to American professional science and social science. In fact, two of the most visible and enduring theoretical projects, Charlotte Perkins Gilman's economic theory of gender distinctions and Sigmund Freud's psychoanalytic theory, were largely conceived outside the academic context. In varied ways, Gilman's and Freud's writings contained perspectives on gender that had no notable counterparts within academic social science. While both theories were inspired by cultural tensions and anxieties as well as by the effervescent scientific spirit of the era, they comprise substantially different, evidently oppositional, explanations of gender and diagnoses for the social ills thought to be related to gender.

Charlotte Perkins Gilman, a notable feminist lecturer and writer, advanced a theoretical perspective on gender relations that was informed at once by evolutionary doctrine and economic thinking. In *Women and Economics* (1898), Gilman proposed that what is seen as women's nature is in fact the product of restrictions on their bodies, actions, and thoughts. What evolutionists referred to as secondary sex characteristics (physical characteristics differentiating the sexes but not crucial to reproductive functions) was believed by Gilman to result from social and economic conditions wherein females are economically dependent on males. Because of this dependence on men, women consequently develop excessive sex-related characteristics to curry favor and receive continued support, and they do so basically to survive. Although these excessive characteristics have evolved socially, they are actually unnatural and cannot be corrected simply by natural selection processes because the particular dependence relations that created them persist. Through inequitable relations between men and women, female development is arrested and women are "checked, starved, aborted in human growth." Thus, Gilman argued that men and women are very different in their social and psychological natures: culture produces and reflects these differences. Gilman's theory rests, first, on an understanding of the current social order as structurally and functionally masculine and, second, on a belief that civilization is and should be evolving toward cultural forms that embrace the nurturance, cooperation, and pacifism of the feminine as well as the aggressiveness, conflict, and individualism of the masculine. In *The*

Man-Made World, or Our Androcentrism (1911) Gilman refined her theory of sex differences, recommending that the future evolution of civilization depends on the termination of male-centered social organizations, notably the patriarchal family and private life (known as the home). This transformation ultimately requires an end to women's economic subordination and dependency, along with the introduction of matriarchal values into the organization of society.

Gilman's theory essentially subverts, by inversion of dominant values, the conventional evolutionary account of sex difference. While other theories of the period make similar use of evolutionary doctrine, Gilman's was probably the most successful (although not the first) theory to register the societal and personal damages brought on by androcentrism, and to describe the virtues of organizing society according to the feminine values of caring, love, altruism, and materialism. As a prescriptive theory it demanded the abolition of the home and family as it was then known while preserving certain values of private life by their institutionalization in the public sphere.

The writings of Sigmund Freud also originated far from the terrain of North American social science, but were to eventually have a lasting impact on most of those professional disciplines. Freud's psychoanalytic theory was constitutively a theory of sexuality and, hence, matters of sex differences or gender attributes are considered in many of his essays and texts. As a student of late-nineteenth-century medicine, Freud drew from scientism a persuasive axiom that reality has different attributes from those it appears to have, and that science comprises the only viable route to access that less apparent, underlying reality. Regarding psychological phenomena, Freud thus was devoted to looking beyond conscious experiences and visible appearances in order to locate hidden mechanisms of psychic life. Similarly influenced by nineteenth-century studies of energy and evolution, Freud located psychic mechanisms that guide consciousness and behavior, tracing the development of those mechanisms in both the lives of individuals and the history of the race. The primary psychic mechanism is sexual drive, or the libido, which in early infancy is undifferentiated and only with maturation becomes connected with specific objects and aims (receiving satisfaction initially from anal and oral and then genital stimulation). At first boys and girls differ neither in libidinal energies nor in the satisfaction of those drives. However, in the developmental stage in which children recognize the penis as an attribute of only one sex (around three years of age), the psychic development of girls and boys begins to diverge: girls then perceive their lack of something, consequently experience jealousy and, later, the desire for substitutes to fill their lack, and boys perceive their differentness from the mother (from women), and then identify with the sexual persona and ego ideals of the father.

Freud's theory of psychosexual development is complex, but in terms of gender identity it clearly asserts emerging and permanent differences between females and males. Although girls maintain an essentially masculine libido until puberty, it is during the phallic stage that sex differences emerge and further growth is toward differentiated sexual and psychological types. In his early writings, such as "Three Essays on the Theory of Sexuality" (1905), Freud was uncertain about these differences, often equating female sexual nature with the male norm; even in his later writings he admitted a modicum of ignorance, calling the sexual life of adult women a "dark continent" for psychology. Nevertheless, in his lectures "Femininity" and "Some Psychical Consequences of the Anatomical Distinction Between the Sexes," Freud made elaborate distinctions between the psychology of men and women, deploying a biological-determinist explanation for the existence and permanence of those differences. In "Some Psychical Consequences" Freud postulated that the difference between males and females "is an intelligible consequence of the anatomical distinction between their genitals and of the psychical situation involved in it; it corresponds to a castration that has been carried out and one that merely has been threatened." For boys, learning of the physical difference at once determines their future relations to women, often prefiguring relations of contempt for women, and through complex psychological processes gives rise to super-ego development, to conscience and morality. For girls, learning of their physical difference as absence is immediate and leads to either psychological refusal, and thus a masculine complex, or acceptance and ultimately self-contempt, jealousy, and eventual rejection of clitoral (or masculine) sexuality. These psychological experiences mean that women's super-ego is less well-developed: "Their super-ego is never so inexorable, so impersonal, so independent of its emotional origins as we require it to be in men." Freud believed that his theory and observations confirmed historically recurrent claims that women "show less sense of justice than men, that they are less ready to submit to the great exigencies of life, that they are more often influenced in their judgments by feelings of affection or hostility." In "Femininity" Freud elaborated on these psychological differences

beginning with assertions of similar libidinal developments in early life: "the little girl is a little man." Once girls discover the fate of their genitals, however, the sameness ends. The anger toward and rejection of the mother is the impetus for hostility and self-hate, and the female's ultimate acceptance of her impoverished state leads to the growth of normal femininity. Not only is her superego arrested but her shame and self-hate tends her toward masochism, lower libido, and narcissism such that "to be loved is a stronger need for them than to love." Finally, given women's particular resolution of the Oedipal situation attending the phallic stage, men's aptitude for sublimation and, hence, for achievement in the world, is superior such that "A man of about thirty strikes us as a youthful, somewhat unformed individual, whom we expect to make powerful use of the possibilities for development opened up to him by analysis. A woman of the same age, however, often frightens us by her psychical rigidity and unchangeability. Her libido has taken up final positions and seems incapable of exchanging them for others. There are no paths open to further development."

Freud's theory of psychosexual development had elements in common with other psychological theories of the period, especially in its use of biological, particularly evolutionary tenets to explain apparent differences between the sexes. His rendition of the qualities of male and female psychic life recapitulated dominant cultural understandings of the constitution of males and females. However, his emphasis on sexuality, coupled with the complexity and inaccessibility of the rudimentary psychic processes of gender development that he had identified, not only challenged prevalent social mores but, more than any other contemporaneous theory, intimated that the matter of the sexes was not always what we believed or desired it to be. This latter claim was to have enduring and complicating effects on later efforts to theorize gender, particularly when psychoanalytic thinking gained more legitimacy within the academy.

By the 1920s, persons interested in the woman question or the "battle of the sexes," as it was coming to be called, had at their disposal a variety of theses about gender from which to support nearly any personal or political stance. The intense social interest in gender had already resulted in a market offering a diverse assortment of theories. The components of the available theories could be sorted into several binary categories, including the biological or social (nature or nurture), the androcentric or gynocentric, conservative or reformist, and realist or nominalist. For at least the next thirty years these polarities would be reenacted in revised and new theories of gender, sometimes spawning debate but more often simply serving as the grounding for empirical studies of sex and gender.

DEFINING THEORIES: GATHERING EVIDENCE

By 1930 the quest to decipher gender, sex, and their social dynamics had lost its urgency. Suffrage had been won by 1919 and the women's movement had lost its cohesiveness, although many of its supporters believed that considerable work remained to be done to ensure women's rights. The reform spirit that had motivated many investigations of the sexes seemed to be a passion of the past. Especially in light of the economic depression by then evident throughout the world, concerns with women's rights or ideal family relations were either discredited or overshadowed by the multiple social crises ensuing from economic collapse. Over the next thirty years, what was termed the woman question would on occasion attain a degree of political volatility but never to the extent it had in the first two decades of the century. The precarious and restricted presence of women in the academy further muted the previously ascendant interest in questions of sex and gender.

Between 1930 and the mid-1960s, scientists and social scientists continued their efforts to define sex and sex differences and, to a lesser extent, to discover their origins. Although these efforts may not have been as directly connected with popular culture and politics as they had been earlier, they nevertheless reflected a spectrum of theoretical positions and, consequently, a wide range of social policy implications. The politics of theorizing became subdued, however, because during this period the sciences and social sciences sharpened the separation of professional work and activism, primarily through distinctions between fact and value in research, insistent claims that they were concerned only with the factual, and the concordant adoption of a positivist metatheory that eschewed the making of evaluative statements. Added to this change was achievement of a greater autonomy of the disciplines that simultaneously lessened conversation between fields and fostered discipline-specific theorizing. Therefore, theories of gender were frequently tied to larger theory projects within various disciplines and were submitted to the empirical fact-gathering of more positivist inquiry.

Among the disciplines that made gender a subject of inquiry, psychology continued to lead in the execution of studies mandated by a commitment to scientific method, specifically to objective observation, control, and measurement of phenomena. Despite decades of empirical research indicating the equivocality of psychological sex differences, researchers persevered in their attempts to locate the "real" essence of maleness and femaleness; they designed new experiments and tests that would definitively isolate that essence which had seemingly eluded detection by common sense and earlier experimentation. The most successful of these ventures, one that was to have a longstanding impact on the psychology of gender, was conducted by Lewis Terman and Catherine Cox Miles. Their decade-long study was devoted to the construction of a psychological test that would quantitatively assess an individual's level of femininity and masculinity. Their project was grounded in what had become a psychological axiom that "if something exists then it exists in some quantity and if it exists in some quantity then it can be measured." *Sex and Personality*, published in 1936, reports Terman and Miles's attempt to rectify the masculinity-femininity problem with a formula similar to that used in the classification of intelligence, namely "a quantification of procedures and concepts." The result was a 910-item test (containing subtests in areas such as word association, ethical responses, and cultural interests) that successfully discriminated between males and females. The test and its results indicated that masculinity is associated with interests in adventure, machinery, and physical phenomena and with emotional dispositions of aggressiveness, self-assertion, and roughness, whereas femininity is associated with interests in aesthetic objects, domestic affairs, and sedentary or ministrative activities and with emotional dispositions of compassion, timidity, emotionality, and fastidiousness.

Terman and Miles's masculinity-femininity test became a commonplace research instrument and eventually was integrated into (or imitated in) many scales of personality and personal adjustment. The test was designed not simply to give quantitative value to the relative psychological attributes but also to detect the hidden facets of a person's sex since, for instance, "We have not learned the art of discovering what is beneath the roughneck apparel of the swaggering male who would disguise his femininity." Terman and Miles also structured their test to serve as a diagnostic tool in the detection of two supposed behavioral "correlates" of masculinity and femininity: homosexuality and marital adjustment. Thus, although Terman and Miles hesitated to theorize about the origins of sex-related attributes, they provided a theoretical claim about the consequences of psychological sex traits: if a person's psychological sex does not match his or her biologically assigned sex, then mental health is jeopardized. Given that homosexuality and marital failure were thought to be indicators of maladjustment, Terman and Miles applied their tests to individuals in these groups to assess the degree of misfit between what was assumed to be psychological and biological sex.

Just as psychologists' construction of tests of sex difference illustrates the prevailing commitment to scientific methodology, so these efforts signify two predispositions toward gender: the suspicion that the essence of gender is determinable but is not detectable at the surface of social life and the belief that sex differences somehow are connected with sexuality. Both theoretical premises probably owed much to psychoanalysis, but in North American social science the debt was not always acknowledged directly and the research bore little outward resemblance to psychoanalytic work. The study of sexuality, in particular, consisted largely of paradigmatic empirical research: counting, sorting, classifying and otherwise statistically analyzing all known sexual behaviors. The research of Alfred Kinsey came to be seen as the most comprehensive of these routinized tallies of sexual activity. Many, although not all, of the studies of sexuality or sexual behavior were grounded in a construal of normal sexuality, first, as "complimentary" or comprising opposite sexes and, second, as requiring "correspondence" or a match between participants' physical (biological) and psychological sex. Both assumptions led to the implication that homosexuality was abnormal, if not pathological. Research on sexuality contributed to an emerging tenet of individual psychology that considered the match between one's biological sex and psychological sex to be a mainstay of normal development and that assumed categorical distinctions between the "normal" and the "deviant."

Despite the tacit presence of assumptions about normal sex development, and the growing tendency to avoid direct discussion of the origins of sex and gender phenomena, there was no consensus among theorists. Divergent perspectives were generated even among researchers who abandoned biology or evolutionary naturalism as explanatory tropes and who instead focused primarily on the social world. The comparative example of the respective work of the anthropologist Margaret Mead and the sociologist Talcott Parsons exemplifies the substantial contrasts among such social theories. Mead undertook anthropological fieldwork in the 1920s and for the next four decades collected data on cultural variations of social life, including sex roles and relations. These studies indicated the cultural plasticity of sex roles and led to a cultural theory postulating that while all cultures display patterns of sex-specific behaviors and customs, these patterns vary tremendously across cultures. Mead's *Coming of Age in Samoa* (1928) compared the adolescence of girls in Samoa and the United States, finding that the psychological stresses experienced by North American girls were not experienced by the Samoan girls, and concluding that such experiences are cultural and not physiological in origin. In *Sex and Temperament in Three Cultures* Mead reported a comparison of the emotional and behavioral repertory of men and women in three societies: among the findings was the fact that while in one society neither sex was aggressive, in another both sexes were. The results of this study led her again to propose a theory that sex-related characteristics varied across cultures and were, therefore, socially determined. Through the use of empirical counterexamples, Mead challenged the vestigial theories of evolutionary sex differences. With these examples she likewise garnered material for a trenchant critique of the cultural norms for sex-appropriate behaviors in North America and provided documentation of their damaging effects on human potential.

Talcott Parsons, like Mead, purportedly rejected the idea that sex roles and differences are biologically determined. By extending his functional model of social systems specifically to the family unit, Parsons proposed that sex differences in social behavior and personality serve the maintenance and continuation of the nuclear family, a social function that he deemed important to society. Parsons's 1955 *Family, Socialization and Interaction Process* entails a refined version of his functional theory of sex differences and the social roles they served. Men and women, he argued, develop two distinct profiles that could be called respectively "instrumental" and "expressive" personality styles: the instrumental type is rational, assertive, independent, and suited to leadership while the expressive type is emotional, interdependent, and suited to interpersonal tasks. These personality styles are complementary in that they function together harmoniously; they also are socially significant inasmuch as they are integrally part of the composition of all social systems, not just the private domain of the family. However, the family is the chief producer of these styles, just as it is the primary site for the socialization of children. Parsons (loosely) engaged psychoanalytic theory to account for personality differentiations according to sex, linking them to the special roles of women in childbearing and lactation and the specific social-interaction patterns resulting from this role specialization. Although Parsons acknowledged the precariousness of the family as a social system in modern society and noted the special strains it imposed on women's lives, he questioned neither the appropriateness nor the continuation of that system. In the end his functionalist analysis implied the biological as well as social necessity of marked differences in the personalities and social status of men and women. Thus, although working from a social perspective on human capacities that resembled Mead's premises, Parsons formulated a theory of gender that described the existence, uniformity, and desirability of differences between the sexes (rather than their potential commonalities).

The dramatic contrasts in gender theorizing in mid-century America were due in some part to the achievement of autonomy in science and social science fields whereby theories were generated and evaluated mainly with discipline-specific criteria. Like the research conducted earlier in the century, these theoretical projects also were influenced by the presence (or absence) of women practitioners—professionals who brought their own personal interests and sometimes feminist orientation to the questions about gender. Finally, the variations in theorizing were further accentuated by a general tendency in the human sciences to utilize one of two dichotomous models, the biological or environmental (social), to account for the vicissitudes of social life, along with a set of dualisms that posed male and female as opposite terms and oppositional character types.

Two additional theoretical projects during this period exemplify the variations in gender theories: the maturation and mutations of psychoanalysis and the appearance of commentaries that criticized the values and objectives of much of the intellectual work on sex and gender. The first enterprise is relatively well known; it comprised a proliferation of schools of psychoanalysis that variously modified Freud's basic theories. In these reconstructions, notably those fashioned by Melanie Klein, Carl Jung, and Karen Horney, the origins of sex differences and of psychological masculinity and femininity are locatable in early life experiences, and in this sense their writings remained consistent with Freud's work. However, the activation and dynamics of these differences were not always attributed to a basic sexual instinct as was the case in Freud's theory, but rather were related to various other motivations such as power, ego, or universal conditions of the unconscious. For instance, Jung eschewed Freud's primary emphasis on sexual

drives for an explanation of psychic sex characteristics that looked at the origins of these differential traits in the unconscious. "Anima," the feminine (nurturing and emotional) part of the unconscious, and "animus," the masculine (analytic and rational) part, are the bases for psychological gender. The effect of these new theoretical reformulations was not a fundamental challenge to Freud's biological determinism; in fact, whatever the interest of the respective theorists, the general effect of their work was to reaffirm deep and essential differences between women and men, differences compatible with traditional (dualist) understandings of femininity and masculinity.

These elaborations of psychoanalytic thought, particularly in their focus on early life experiences, converged with and probably reinforced a postwar interest in children and the development of gender attributes. Especially within experimental psychology there emerged a project to locate the first appearance of gender-linked attributes and to trace the developmental processes through which they evolved toward adult manifestations of gender. By the early 1960s developmental psychologists had ascertained that a child acquires gender awareness as early as two years old and that ensuing (healthy) psychological developments involve the application of these perceived differences to assess self and others, internalization of the social norms associated with appropriate gender behaviors, and modeling of those appropriate behaviors. For these researchers the questions of what constituted gender-appropriate attributes and how they came to be were of little interest as they were concerned primarily with documenting the actual appearance of gender and gender differences and charting the process of their unfolding.

The second trend in theorizing about gender concerned not the design of explanatory models but the articulation of a critical consciousness about such theorizing. Alongside the discipline-specific theories and psychoanalytic work there emerged an awareness among some writers that such theories had not realized the value-free qualities claimed to undergird the scientific enterprise. These critical responses to the theories and science of gender grew in number especially in the years immediately after World War II. It is probably no coincidence that these criticisms increased at a time when women who had entered the workplace during the war were urged to return to the homefront, enabling men to gain employment and ensuring the resumption of the nuclear family structure as it had been known. The transition back to the purportedly appropriate roles of women and men was to some extent supported by theories of gender such as Parsons's and, in a more sensational vein, Philip Wylies's popular psychoanalytic account posed in *A Nation of Vipers*. The criticism of androcentric culture and theories took many forms, from the debunking of extant research to the construction of counter-theories. Ruth Herschberger's *Adam's Rib*, published in 1948, employed journalistic style to reveal the discrimination against women perpetuated both in society and in science, while Georgene Seward's 1946 *Sex and the Social Order* used a scientific format and empirical evidence to argue that contemporary women's roles not only constrained their lives but also restricted further progress of society. By employing the canonical techniques of social science, some of these critics (most of them women) offered alternative explanations of sex differences in personality, problems with marriage and the family, and social distress generally. Helen Hacker argued that what was taken as the normal feminine personality was actually a dysfunctional personality; her 1951 "Women as a Minority Group" suggested that the social status and treatment of women was the cause, not the consequence, of their sex-specific and self-debilitating traits. Other researchers found in their empirical investigations evidence that female sex roles were hazardous for women as well as for social well-being more generally. For instance, Mirra Komarovsky demonstrated how adolescent girls directly face cultural contradictions when they confront an unavoidable decision to be feminine and socially successful or nonfeminine and socially unacceptable.

The most influential of these critical studies, and one that was to symbolize a sea change in both the popular and scholarly work on gender, was Betty Friedan's *The Feminine Mystique*. Friedan reaffirmed the theoretical orientation of early-twentieth-century writers who insisted that the nature of the sexes, in the end, was a matter of equality and economics. In describing the pathology of normative sex roles and in arguing for the creation of conditions of sex equality, her book came to denote the beginnings of the "second wave" of American feminism. It also extended analyses of sexism to address the very achievements of the human sciences, particularly psychoanalysis. Friedan found in the writings of Freud and his successors, as well as in much of the social scientific research on women's adjustment, a powerful system of ensuring women's inferiority, passivity, and self-denigration. Scientific theory had cultivated a "feminine mystique" that "elevated by Freudian theory into a scientific religion, sounded a single, over-protective, life-restricting, future-denying note for women."

Friedan's analysis, and a voluminous literature of critical reassessment that followed, established a new intellectual criterion whereby the project of designing theories of gender would be accompanied by examination of the effects of those very theories on gender arrangements and, vice versa, the effects of gender on the making of theories. The sober and, in retrospect, simple efforts to construct value-free and empirically verifiable theories that characterized research of the preceding thirty years did not come to an end with these critiques but they did become obviously problematic by the 1960s. As a consequence, gender theorizing became even more diverse as theories began to differ not only in their relative emphasis on nature or relative nurture, on the individual or society, but also on the degree to which they were or were not constructed upon deeply grounded sexist premises.

GENDER AS AN ESSENTIAL CATEGORY

The critical interrogation of theories of gender, increasing in visibility and frequency after World War II, precipitated a virtual revolution in the understanding of gender. The awareness that personal opportunities, constraints, and, ultimately, experiences (such as those traditionally associated with gender) are at least partly determined by cultural mores and political conditions eventually evolved into an extensive, cross-discipline exploration of the connections between personal and political life and between social experience and formal systems of knowledge. Sensitivity to the evaluative nature or interestedness of all knowledge-seeking inspired inquiries into the extent to which knowledge was androcentric, or male-biased. These studies, in turn, raised difficult new questions about the possibility of knowing anything outside of a gendered framework. In many instances the search for a veridical theory of gender gave way to an inward (or reflexive) examination of how theoretical pursuits were themselves the product of specific gender relations. Over the next twenty-five years there unfolded a wholesale scrutiny of the various assumptions that had undergirded gender research: these critical evaluations ranged from analysis of the putative dichotomies of male and female, nature and culture, real and artificial, to scrutiny of the very concepts of gender, men, women, and science.

The revival of feminism, simultaneously a political and intellectual movement, undoubtedly motivated this critical awareness, but feminism was not a totalizing force and certainly did not affect every attempt to examine gender; nor was it the only new condition affecting these intellectual pursuits. Feminism certainly inspired much intellectual work; it also influenced the increased participation of women in professional occupations, academics included, for it led to the creation of equal opportunity and affirmative action programs that monitored employment situations for women. However, the 1960s also was a period of enhanced concern with human rights more generally, and in the academy this interest was manifested in critical examinations of the core tenets and political implications of conventional social theory. At the same time, members of many disciplines undertook comprehensive evaluations of their field's philosophical as well as ideological foundations, exercises that resulted sometimes in rejection of these foundations (and a consequent turn to postempiricism or postmodernism) while at other times in nothing more substantial than a flurry of critical exchanges. It is not surprising to find that throughout this period of intellectual unrest, political activism, and apparent social change, the theories of gender that were advanced were varied, even discordant, with some of them continuing an established tradition of explanatory formula and some taking critical interrogations to their conceptual and logical limits.

Several theories of the period, most of them produced in the 1960s, merely extended one or another of the theoretical frameworks introduced in the preceding decades. Erik Erikson, for instance, in "Inner and Outer Space: Reflections on Womanhood," combined psychoanalytic premises about the connections between anatomical sex and psychological states with insights into the effects of historical change on individual psychology to formulate a theory of female and male differences. After rejecting the strict equation of women with passivity that Freud and some of his successors had maintained, Erikson instead proposed that women's psychic life is determined by her "inner space," her womb, and the concomitant "fear of being left empty or deprived of treasures, of remaining unfulfilled and of drying up." Given the drive to fill and nurture this inner space, girls develop personalities that are compassionate, caring, emotive, and more tolerant of pain (previously described as "masochistic"). Men's psychic life also is organized by morphological differentiation: Erikson described their genitals as external, erectable, and intrusive. Their identities are characterized by that "outer space" of assertiveness, intrusion, and activity. However, Erikson added the factor of history to that polar anatomical theme, acknowledging the historical reasons why "man, in addition to having a body, is *some*body; which means he is an

indivisible personality *and* a defined member of a group." With history factored in, Erikson granted that woman might not "live only in this extended somatic sphere" of inner space but is increasingly coming to act also as a citizen and worker. Nevertheless history can only modify what is laid down: "since woman is never not-a-woman, she can see her long-range goals only in those modes of activity which include and integrate her natural dispositions."

Erikson's revision of psychoanalytic doctrine made only minimal modifications to its understanding of females and males. Some researchers in psychology similarly reformulated both nature- and nurture-oriented theories of sex differences. From theorists subscribing to environmental or "nurture" explanations came more sophisticated experiments on "social learning," specifically on the environmental conditions—the rewards and punishments—that socialized girls to enact feminine traits and boys masculine ones. From new studies of cognition came an interesting twist to these socialization theories: Lawrence Kohlberg proposed that not only do children learn to distinguish and value what is sex-appropriate, but due to the size differences between men and women they also eventually equate males with power. By borrowing a psychoanalytic belief in the force of anatomy, Kohlberg designed a more complex, and an essentially biological-determinist theory of sex-role acquisition, a theory that diverged from the staunch environmentalism of then-prevalent learning theories that emphasized the socialization of roles.

While some psychoanalytic, learning, and cognitive theorists applied or extended the dominant explanatory modes that had been introduced earlier, other researchers amended these dominant genres through critical appraisals, sometimes transforming those orientations beyond their recognizable forms. Starting from knowledge about the fundamental androcentrism of canonical theory, along with a political consciousness of women's subjugated position in society, these theorists unearthed erroneous and dubitable tenets of research practices and reformulated theories through the application of nonsexist or feminist premises.

The reevaluations of social learning and culture theories, theories that assumed that social conditions determine gender, eventually led to refinements of that assumption. The reappraisals also triggered refutation of several central dualisms—those of nature and nurture, public and private, and masculine and feminine. The work of anthropologists such as Michelle Rosaldo and Sherry Ortner revealed that even cultural theories of gender depended on ideological categorizations such as nature and culture. As Ortner claimed in "Is Female to Male as Culture Is to Nature?" women's "pan-cultural second-class status could be accounted for, quite simply, by postulating that women are being identified or symbolically associated with nature, as opposed to men, who are identified with culture." By continued emphasis on women's bodily functions and her domestic roles (considered to be lower order culture), and by repeated assertions that the psychic life of women ensues from their reproductive functioning and lesser social roles, women are seen to be closer to nature. This symbolic representation of gender is sustained by (just as it sustains) a cultural distinction between public and private life, between the world of action and the domestic realm. The constructed oppositional categories, nature versus culture and public versus private, are what makes and gives meaning to gender and gender differences: both the activities of men and women and the rhetoric employed to describe them depend on such invented and dualist categorizations.

Researchers in other disciplines also discovered the operation of dualist categories and traced the numerous contradictions that were perpetuated through such core dualisms. Although social-learning theorists (and functionalists generally) had cited the family as fundamental to the maintenance and production of gender roles and psychological sex differences, closer analyses revealed dysfunctions and contradictions within that putatively essential social system. Phyllis Chesler's 1973 landmark book, *Women and Madness*, amassed statistical data to demonstrate the relation between women's psychological problems and the institution of marriage. That text is but one of many studies that challenged the appropriateness, complementarity, and normality of culturally dominant gender roles and gender-based institutions like the nuclear family. Other investigations examined the normative assumptions about human nature underlying the technical assessment of female and male differences: they found how constructs of mental health, decision making, occupational success, and intelligence were male-biased in their repeated equation of adequacy with personal qualities that are conventionally associated with men. Further, by using such male-centered constructs in empirical research, what are detected as female differences are then interpreted as deviations or are problematized as non-normative, while male characteristics continue to be taken as normative. Carol Gilligan's *In a*

Different Voice (1982) located these biased operations in moral decision-making research: not only had investigators constructed theories of moral decision making according to masculine standards, privileging the styles normally practiced by men, but they also neglected other, primarily feminine styles that engaged different standards and processes of decision making.

A quite different avenue of investigation extended analyses of cultural contradictions and biases to the very categories of masculine and feminine, to the central terms that were routinely used to denote differences between men and women. In 1973 the psychologist Sandra Bem questioned the fundamental dualism of sex-difference research in psychology by proposing that psychological gender is not necessarily of two types, masculine and feminine, but may take other forms. Bem, among other social scientists, employed the term *androgyny* to designate a third gender type that incorporates both masculine and feminine characteristics: androgynous beings, whether biologically female or male, exhibit traits that are most functional for the specific situation in which they are immersed, and do not restrict themselves to traits conventionally ascribed to their gender.

Yet another means of reevaluating the central categories of gender theories entailed scrutiny of the very concepts of gender and sex, investigating whether they represented natural classifications or socially constructed ones. For instance, in the 1978 book *Gender: An Ethnomethodological Approach*, authors Suzanne Kessler and Wendy McKenna proposed that the ascription of one gender to a person is entirely a social process whereby individuals use social rules to make decisions and hence where "a world of two 'sexes' is a result of the socially shared, taken-for-granted methods which members use to construct reality." Thus, distinctions of female and male are made, not found, in the world. Even the distinction between sex and gender that by the late 1970s had become routine social-scientific terminology for differentiating natural or biological phenomena (sex) from cultural or social phenomena (gender) is explainable as the accomplishment of cultural mappings of the world, and not of some natural, verifiable categorization of that world.

The critiques, analyses, and reformations of several core tenets of gender theories transpired across the human sciences; they addressed psychoanalytic and popularized interpretations as well as theory-building programs within disciplines. Although psychoanalysis had no single home within a discipline, by the 1960s its maxims had permeated, sometimes tacitly and other times more explicitly, a vast range of intellectual enterprises. By the 1970s, feminist critics had begun to dismantle the androcentric edifice of psychoanalysis, concentrating primarily on its attitudes of misogyny, male-centered accountings, and its fatalistic determinism regarding the conditions of the sexes. Two landmark texts, both appearing in 1970, guided this critical project. Kate Millett's *Sexual Politics* and Shulamith Firestone's *The Dialectic of Sex*. Both understood Freud's work not simply as a scientific production but as a political backlash against women's struggles toward emancipation. While Millett offered counterexamples of Freud's ideology of women, citing their active and assertive characteristics, Firestone challenged the very social reality that Freud took as a given. Suggesting that his world was not a necessary or permanent one, Firestone revealed another side to this reality: she described the family and love as mechanisms for maintaining women's oppression and hiding men's primary and emotionally infantile interests. Just as men are "emotionally warped by the sublimation process" so women are emotionally dependent on men. With this description of the everyday pathology of current gender arrangements, Firestone departed from Freud's determinism, and she went on to propose utopian measures that would free women from this arrangement, suggesting the use of technological innovations (in reproduction) to liberate women from their biological roles in reproduction.

The dazzling yet often trenchant critiques, like those of Millett and Firestone, were succeeded by the introduction of feminist-psychoanalytic theories of gender, projects that drew selectively upon psychoanalytic doctrines to present alternative explanations of gender and gender relations. Writings such as *The Reproduction of Mothering* (1978) by Nancy Chodorow and *The Mermaid and the Minotaur* (1976) by Dorothy Dinnerstein preserved the notion that psychoemotional characteristics were established through early life experiences and were distinctly different for men and women. Yet rather than privilege the masculine personality, these theories uncovered the mutual strengths and weaknesses of female and male characteristics. In a world where infants first experience social interaction with women, usually their mothers in a nuclear family arrangement, boys acquire a sense of self that is partly based on a separation from and rejection of females—they develop toward autonomy, distance, and masterly con-

trol. Girls acquire a sense of self that retains emotional connections to females—they develop toward social interdependence, emotional expressivity, and nondirectiveness if not collusion with powerful others. In these theories, dominant social life forms—not biology—are destiny, and the psychodynamics of gender are shown at once to reflect and ultimately maintain that dominant order as men enact their rational, disconnected interests in the public realm and women enact their affective, dependent interests in the private world of interpersonal relations and the family. Thus gender characteristics are simultaneously a product and a cause of social relations and structures, reproducing oppressive relations and troubling contradictions in personal lives.

Regardless of conceptual or disciplinary orientation, the critical revisionings spawned in the mid-1960s eventually produced a distinctly new awareness about gender. Among the new precepts of gender research is an understanding that knowledge itself may be constituted by the forms and processes of gender. This precept constitutes a reflexive move that insists on the interrogation into how the world exists through gender (not just how gender exists in the world); it calls for gender analysis of those very systems dedicated to producing knowledge of that world. Such a reflexive turn has led scholars who are searching for an adequate theory of gender to consider just how gender itself structures those scholarly pursuits and, ultimately, to examine core constructs of theorizing that previously had been taken-for-granted ingredients in the construction of knowledge about the human sciences generally (and not just gender theories). Constructs of the family, sex, and equality had long been subjected to critical analyses, but it has become apparent that gender-biases and presuppositions also pervade such putatively neutral intellectual constructs as citizenship, personhood, labor, rationality, objectivity, cognition, emotion, agency, and experience. With these realizations, for instance, literary theorists have reconsidered the very notions of "author" and "reader" in terms of gender, and historians similarly have reassessed the "subject" of history. Even that domain of intellectual work believed most immune from social conditions, the natural sciences, has been found inextricably dependent upon gender. The analyses of Ruth Bleier, Donna Haraway, Sandra Harding, Evelyn Fox Keller, and Hillary Rose among others have revealed manifestations of gender in the methods, epistemology, imagery, organization, and findings of science. In her 1985 *Reflections on Gender and Science*, for instance,

Keller traced the historical and psychological association between the ideal of objectivity in modern science and masculine psychic life, finding that the cognitive norms of science have emerged out of an emotional substructure that in certain ways parallels male psychology. Mirroring the psychic dynamics of masculinity, science relies on a division of "subjective" and "objective" forms of knowing and "the scientific mind is set apart from what is to be known, that is, from nature." The scientific mind is a masculine one characterized by autonomy, separation, and distance as well as control, mastery, and power.

Attention to the interdependence of gender relations and knowledge claims has radically altered and enriched the understanding of gender. If this awareness has interrupted the realization of elegant or generalizable theory, two of the ideals guiding classical theory construction, it has not been the only complicating concern. Other events and intellectual currents have challenged theoretical pursuits. The philosophies of deconstruction and post-modernism have generated questions about the objects of "truth" and the universality of knowledge claims; they also have initiated debates over concepts central to the tradition of gender theories, namely the coherence and historical uniformity of the individual, identity, difference, and subjectivity. Social groups who have been notoriously underrepresented and misrepresented in social theories as well as in the academy generally have raised crucial questions about the universality of those theories. For example, in the area of gender research, women of color and lesbians have criticized the exclusionary and culture-bound conceptions of women, identity, and sexuality that had been mainstays of gender theorizing. With these varied challenges, as with the above-mentioned reflexive analyses, the stakes for theory making have been raised even higher, but so have been the opportunities for more innovative and comprehensive work.

In the final decade of the century, the interest in explaining gender is at least as intense as it was in the first decade: just as knowledge continues to be shaped by pressing personal and political directives, so it is also prefigured by interests in the status and utility of professional knowledge making. Surveying the development of theories of gender provides illustrative evidence of the power of dominant cultural forms, along with the tensions and anxieties accompanying them. The pursuit of knowledge about human nature, including knowledge about gender, has been and continues to be highly institutionalized. The history of gender theories makes apparent the continued difficulty in acknowledging the mutualities of social life and knowledge production. The prolonged practice of ignoring these relations has fostered either uncritical repetition of abstract tenets or blind accommodation of cultural stereotypes and ideologies. Yet comprehension of the relations seems to lead, at best, toward formidably complex demands on theory construction, or to a seemingly paralyzing regression where social conditions and knowledge claims are taken as a series of back and forth reflections of each other.

However, such difficulties, as revealed in the history of gender theories, are largely problems for contemporary theorists. The chronicle of twentieth-century gender studies serves as historical testimony: it documents the fate of a prominent movement in the human sciences that has attempted to configure individuals as physical bodies, psychological entities, and as social actors and, then, to coordinate or classify these configurations into a meaningful composite of personhood. The reign of scientism, despite repeated antiscience reactions, and the privileging of technological research devices (statistics, tests, medical assessment tools, and so on) have dominated this mission, such that the human sciences have tended to seek knowledge largely if not entirely by codifying, classifying, and measuring phenomena such as gender. One result has been a preoccupation with the display of gender within individuals—in their bodies, behaviors, and internal mental states. Most of the theories produced during this century take gender to be an (essential) attribute of individuals that exists in one of two forms, female or male. In the final decades of the century, these patterns of theorizing were subjected to scrutiny, generating bold questions about whether there are only two genders, whether gender inheres in individuals or in social interactions, whether persons are always just one gender, or whether it is possible to inscribe the experiences of gender or merely its artifactual norms. Yet, however transgressive, these inquiries remained grounded in the beliefs that gender is a basic category of human affairs, and that it too can be classified and coded as a meaningful characteristic of persons and social life. As long as gender remains a salient feature of social life, guiding the way people act and judge, these beliefs will remain significant.

SEE ALSO The Human Mind and Personality (in this volume); Gender Issues (in volume I).

BIBLIOGRAPHY

The very category of gender, in both its biological and social forms, is critically and historically examined in Judith Butler, *Gender Trouble: Feminism and the Subversion of Identity* (1990); Denise Riley, *"Am I That Name?" Feminism and the Category of Women in History* (1988); and Suzanne Kessler and Wendy McKenna, *Gender: An Ethnomethodological Approach* (1978). There are also numerous critical analyses of the concepts and understanding of gender specific to intellectual disciplines: on history see Joan Scott's *Gender and the Politics of History* (1988); and on psychology see Corinne Squire's *Significant Differences—Feminism in Psychology* (1989); and Rachel T. Hare-Mustin and Jeanne Maracek's *Making a Difference* (1990).

Feminist thinking has had an extensive effect on theories of gender, offering both critique and constructive alternatives to classical social theories. An excellent source on the history of modern American feminism is Nancy F. Cott, *The Grounding of Modern Feminism* (1987). Historical surveys of the influence of feminism on disciplines, including its effect on gender theories, are contained in Allison M. Jaggar, *Feminist Politics and Human Nature* (1983); Terry R. Kandal, *The Woman Question in Classical Sociological Theory* (1988); and Susan M. Okin, *Women in Western Political Thought* (1979). More general histories of the professions and their treatment of gender both in their membership and as an analytic category include Ellen Fitzpatrick, *Endless Crusade: Women Social Scientists and Progressive Reform* (1990); Rosalind Rosenberg, *Beyond Separate Spheres: Intellectual Roots of Modern Feminism* (1982); and Patricia Vertinsky, *The Eternally Wounded Woman: Women, Doctors, and Exercise in the Late Nineteenth Century* (1990). Dorothy Ross's *The Origins of American Social Science* (1991) provides a synthetic history of the cultural forces shaping the social science profession, while excellent accounts of the pre-twentieth-century attitudes and theories of gender can be found in Thomas Lacqueur, *Making Sex: Body and Gender from the Greeks to Freud* (1990); and Carroll Smith-Rosenberg, *Disorderly Conduct: Visions of Gender in Victorian America* (1985). Two accessible and lively surveys of the recurrent biases in modern scientific studies of gender are Anne Fausto-Sterling, *Myths of Gender: Biological Theories about Women and Men* (1985); and Carol Tavris, *The Mismeasure of Woman* (1992).

915

SOCIETY

Howard Brick

Like so much of the intellectual apparatus of the twentieth century, the concept of "society" is largely a creation of modern times in the West. According to the British cultural critic Raymond Williams, "the primary meaning of *society*" when it first came into use in English was "companionship or fellowship," the human experience of being among and in league with others. From the sixteenth to the eighteenth centuries, there emerged the distinct idea of society as a substantive entity, a broad-based milieu of human association and an object of reflection having a definite structure accessible to observation and analysis. Not until the mid- to late nineteenth century, however, did "society" become the main focus of inquiry by several leading writers, and only around the turn of the twentieth century, with the rise of social science disciplines in the modern research university, did formal speculation about the nature and constitution of society become a concerted enterprise.

As a general term for forms of human association beyond the level of kin groups, society in some sense had been an object of reflection long before the early modern period. Plato and Aristotle considered the terms of human association in their discussions of the *polis,* where the conjoint exercise of citizenship enabled humans to realize their true nature as rational beings. This traditional, political concept of society was communal and moral in character, focused on local, proximate institutions of participation and on the "virtue" of self-conscious, civic individuals. In Roman thought, reflection on social organization at large remained more or less focused on the nature of statesmanship, the qualities of virtue, and the problem of public corruption. On the other hand, *societas* in Latin referred not to society in a broad, structural sense but to voluntary and purposeful collective enterprise, such as the *societates* organized to maintain roads or provide other public services.

To reach the more abstract, modern concept of society, concerning the involuntary relations which form the framework and substance of life for large aggregates of people, several innovations were required. As Anthony Pagden has shown in *The Fall of Natural Man* (1982), early modern Christian scholars in Spain helped to universalize the classical doctrine of political society by insisting that membership in a community and the rational capacities associated with it *(civitas)* were features of all human experience rather than an achievement of some (the civilized) and not others (the barbarians). The French philosopher Jean Bodin, writing at the end of the sixteenth century, similarly broadened and generalized the prevailing concept of society by challenging the classical definition of commonwealths (or republics) as "societies of men assembled to live well and happily together." Bodin insisted instead that large human communities constituted "commonwealths" whether or not people therein dwelled happily or were governed well. As Peter Manicas points out in *A History and Philosophy of the Social Sciences* (1987), it was with reference to such a generalized condition of associated living, and to the boundaries of distinct "commonwealths," that early modern theorists like Hobbes, Locke, and Montesquieu examined the nature and form of society.

The appearance in early modern Europe of several large territorial units of associated living, each knit together by internal markets and centralized administration, gave rise to the new, substantive concept of society. According to Eric Wolf in *Europe and the People without History* (1982), accelerating trade, the accumulation of wealth, and its centralization in a few hands occurred in synchrony with, and at the service of, mounting financial demands posed by expansive monarchies that sought power over "internal" sources of faction (fractious nobility) as well as external bodies of people. The dual dynamics behind the formation of the great European nation-states then provided the main prototypes—the generalization of market relations or the purposeful coordination of state resources—for thinking about social being. For Hobbes, Locke, and Montesquieu, thinking about society turned toward the pivotal issues of government and statecraft. A current of nineteenth-century sociology (notably the work of Auguste Comte in France and Lester Frank Ward in the United States) likewise remained focused on the state-building dynamic of Western social development, emphasizing political functions of leadership, order, and organization as essential to maintaining society as such. Nonetheless, over the long term, thinking about "society" tended to move beyond both of its early prototypes, differentiating "society" first from the polity, and second, by the mid-twentieth century, from the economy.

During the eighteenth and nineteenth centuries, the concept of society became more clearly differentiated from political institutions. David Hume distinguished society as a "system of common life" from the state as "an organization of power," echoing the attempt of his friend Adam Smith to mark off economy as an autonomous sphere of relations ideally separate from politics. Other figures of the Scottish Enlightenment, Adam Ferguson and John Millar, likewise described "civil society" as an entity whose evolution was understood primarily in terms of economic development. The rise of bourgeois social relations fostered this sense of society's proximity to economy and distance from the polity. The same dichotomy figured in middle-class radical politics of the time. In *Common Sense* (1776), Thomas Paine counterposed society and government, the former the sphere in which people acted freely to satisfy their wants by exchange, the latter a sphere of constraint.

"Society," in this nonpolitical sense, was not always so narrowly identified with economic action. When Paine's associate, Mary Wollstonecraft, referred to "the constitution of civil society" in *A Vindication of the Rights of Woman* (1792), she had in mind matters such as education, morality, personal character, and manners. In these areas a new middle class committed to individualism hoped to find the key to an orderly way of life, while battling the mores of an old society founded on "rank," prestige, and hierarchical authority. At the same time, conservative currents of thought, including Burke in England, Joseph de Maistre and L. G. A. de Bonald in France, and F. K. von Savigny and others in Germany, struck historicist and organicist notes that would prove crucial to the dawning sense of society as an inherited order of habitual interpersonal relations. In any case, neither the liberal idea of society as a unit composed of independent persons rather than segmented "estates," nor the conservative sense of society as an order shaped by rank, can be understood apart from

the bourgeois revolutions which posed new questions about the structure of social life.

With the further development of commercial and industrial capitalism in the nineteenth century, "society" was understood in terms clearly referring to the primacy of economy in modern life. "Society" figured prominently in the work of the early utopian socialists—particularly Robert Owen, Charles Fourier, and their American followers in the 1840s and 1850s—both as an indication of the determining force that the social environment (as opposed to innate factors) had over human behavior and as an antipode to the disruptive force of economic competition. The latter claim could also be adopted by conservative opponents of the liberal Enlightenment, as in George Fitzhugh's *Sociology for the South* (1854), with its argument that the hierarchy of the slave system better met the prerequisites of social order than the competitive individualism of the northern wage system. On the other hand, the market economy provided a ready model or prototype for conceiving social relations, and the key dimensions of Herbert Spencer's thought—the definition of social change as something independent of political decision, the evolutionary tendency to enhanced differentiation of functions, and the teleological "social state" geared to wholly voluntary relations among individuals—clearly mirrored the putative autonomy of economy from state, the increasing division of labor, and the market ideal of universalized exchange relations.

THE EARLY DEVELOPMENT OF FORMAL SOCIAL THEORY IN THE UNITED STATES

The concept of society achieved genuine ascendancy only in the 1870s. The change of a single word, from the publication of Henry Maine's *Ancient Law* in 1861 to the appearance of Lewis Henry Morgan's *Ancient Society* in 1877, suggested the growing tendency to move beyond political categories of large-scale organization and perceive sources of order in the distinct sphere of society as such. Other key works on "society" and "sociology," such as Herbert Spencer's *The Study of Sociology* (1872) and Ferdinand Toennies's *Community and Society* (1887), appeared around that time. Among the factors fostering a new, systematic discourse about society was the growing repute of science, indicated by the development of the research university in the United States and the formation of new social science disciplines, led by the "marginalist revolution" in economics. More generally, heightened attention to social forces stemmed from startling advances of the 1870s in industrial development, market integration, and state-building, particularly in the United States and Germany.

The concept of "society" by this time implied alienation, something sensed as distant from the individuals making it up. The objective character of "society" had something in common with the alienated and alienating force of the market—a mechanism composed of purposive individuals yet having effects on them which they did not, and could not, control. The experience of modern economic crises, phenomena unintended by human action and yet not determined by forces of physical nature, lent force to the notion of "society" as a thing apart. In the United States, furthermore, the economic slump of the 1870s and the strikes of 1877 so pointedly raised the "social problem" of poverty and class struggle that a cohort of young, religiously minded political economists trained in German universities, including Richard T. Ely, John Bates Clark, and Henry Carter Adams, promoted a new "social" sense of collective responsibility for the general welfare. Experiences of national revolution and reconstruction in this period also pointedly raised the question of society as an entity. Reflecting on the emancipation of the slaves, George Woodbridge of Vermont declared, "New social and political relations have been established. Four million people have been born in a day." Thus he suggested how profoundly Reconstruction in the United States laid bare the very stuff of social order and the mystery of its foundations. Half a world away, unification of Germany under Bismarck posed similar conditions for reflection on the elementary substance of social relations and unity at the very moment American students of social science flocked there.

Still, the 1870s marked only the beginning of a surge in social thought, the start of a prolonged transition toward the notion that "society" had to be understood as an entity founded on genuinely collective human relations and experiences. Much of what went by the name of "social science" in mid-nineteenth-century America, Thomas Haskell has argued in *The Emergence of Professional Social Science* (1977), was rooted in the melioristic campaigns of antebellum reform and the doctrine of moral individualism that guided them. Reformers recognized the force of social conditions on personal life, but almost wholly in the negative sense of evil surroundings corrupting the individual; the institutions they built (schools, orphanages, asylums, prisons) were in-

tended to foster moral aptitudes in the individual (of self-control, thrift, etc.), since these were believed to be the fount of both personal achievement and social order. By the end of the nineteenth century, however, the moral individualism of antebellum reform gave way to a concept of society governed by the notion of the "interdependence" or "organic" integration of parts, better reflecting the extent of organization and complexity in a nation-spanning industrial order. At the same time, a generic "social science" gave way to separate, professional organizations of specialized practitioners (academic economists, sociologists, etc.) who claimed to examine and understand, in various ways, the workings of this complex organization from the outside, objectively.

The work of William Graham Sumner, who offered courses in "political and social science" at Yale University in 1873 and wrote explicitly on "sociology" by 1881, as well as that of Lester Frank Ward, who entered government service in the 1870s and published *Dynamic Sociology* in 1883, emerged from the watershed of the 1870s and straddled the divide between the old and the new social science. Clearly, Sumner's stout defense of laissez-faire principles was firmly rooted in moral individualism. As Richard Hofstadter wrote, for Sumner, "human progress is at bottom moral progress, and moral progress is largely the accumulation of economic virtues." On the other hand, Sumner argued strenuously for a kind of evolutionary realism that bordered on historical relativism, debunking "natural laws" as nothing but the mores of a particular time fitted to particular social circumstances. He implied a principle of social determinism, which grasped society as a "superorganism" having its own course of development before which individual wishes and actions were helpless. The contradiction between his extreme determinism and the individualism of his moral foundations, as well as the contradiction between the dawning relativism of his sociology and the universalism claimed by classical economics, did not appear to trouble Sumner too much. With a comparable degree of contradictory allegiances, Lester Ward endorsed government intervention in social affairs and mocked laissez faire while also seeking to maximize the free play of desire in human action, a sign of the "radical subjectivism" that linked him to older styles of "free thinking" individualism. Nonetheless, Ward's emphasis on the role that conscious human intent played in guiding social, as opposed to natural, evolution went part of the way toward highlighting emergent properties of social organization as such.

In the years of rapid industrialization (1880–

1920), the centrality of the economic sphere in modern life could not be ignored, and economic relations remained a focal concern in all discussions of society as such. During the Progressive Era in the United States, "society" was understood, for the most part, as something constituted by economic relations. The most dynamic currents of thought insisted on the determinant impact of economic interests and economic institutions on politics and history, as in E. R. A. Seligman's *The Economic Interpretation of History* (1902) and Charles Beard's *An Economic Interpretation of the Constitution* (1913). Much of what went under the name "sociology" before World War II was closely wedded to the study of institutional aspects—the context and consequences—of economic activity. Writing retrospectively in 1940, the sociologist Charles Hunt Page found that the "older school of writers" in American sociology, from William Graham Sumner to Edward A. Ross, had made issues of socioeconomic class—of class divisions, conflict, consciousness, and compromise—in their examination of society. George Edmund Haynes, the first African American to receive a Ph.D. in sociology (Columbia University, 1912), published *The Negro at Work in New York City: A Study in Economic Progress* (1912). Dorothy Swaine Thomas, associated with the University of Chicago sociologist William F. Ogburn, wrote *The Social Aspects of the Business Cycle* in 1927. Given these conceptual affiliations, sociology was often taught within economics departments as well as in departments of "social ethics."

By the 1890s, however, the concept of "society" was closely associated with the reform impulses of a segment of the middle class aiming to modify, ameliorate, constrain, or overcome the communally destructive impact of expanding market relations. Although arguments on the incompatibility of the market and society had earlier been embraced by conservatives like Fitzhugh, now the "new liberal" reformers took up the issue, deriding market norms as insufficiently integral means of achieving necessary social order, control, or harmony. Much of U.S. social thought around the turn of the century consisted of a polemic against the atomistic assumptions of nineteenth-century economic ideology (monadic individualism and a one-sided rationalist psychology). By emphasizing, for instance, the role played by cooperative relationships in forming something so ostensibly private as the self, the social psychology of writers such as George Herbert Mead and Charles Horton Cooley challenged economic individualism and suggested a mildly anticapitalist social ethics. At the same time, thinking about "society" often took a holistic cast, suspicious of the partial description of human motives in economics and intent on grasping the multiple dimensions of human experience and collective organization in a common framework of thought.

By 1900, the dispute between Sumner and Ward was played out again in the tension between the two leading sociologists of a subsequent generation, Franklin Giddings at Columbia University and Albion Small of the University of Chicago. Giddings began his career as a journalist and an advocate of workers' cooperatives. Like other middle-class reformers, he sought at first to emphasize the moral elements of social interaction which classical economic theory ignored in its emphasis on rational egoism. Subsequently, however, he was seduced by marginalist economics and its emphasis on the role of subjective factors in determining value (i.e., price as a function of the intensity of wants). Marginalism gave Giddings a vision of social order arising as the equilibration of wants, a combination of free will and destiny that appealed to his orthodox Calvinist temperament, according to Robert Bannister in his *Sociology and Scientism* (1987). To be sure, Giddings developed as well a notion of noneconomic bonds at work in society—the idea that a growing "consciousness of kind" (or the measure of sympathy uniting like with like) knit persons together in social groups of increasingly large scale—but that notion appealed to him primarily as an alternative to the objectionably interventionist state proposed by Ward's reformism. Wanting to emphasize the nonpolitical sources of order, Giddings's "consciousness of kind" served to explain solidarity given his economistic assumption that individuals existed first in a state of mutual independence.

Albion Small was far friendlier to positive state action and acknowledged his debt to the political tradition of Lester Frank Ward, though like Giddings he sought to discover "harmonizing processes" that were, as Dorothy Ross puts it in *The Origins of American Social Science* (1991), "imbedded in society itself" rather than bestowed by the polity. Small was an ordained Baptist preacher who emphasized the "social teachings" of Jesus, understood as a call for "a regenerated society whose constitution is cooperative" (rather than individualistic), and regarded his religious commitments as fully compatible and integrated with his scientific aspirations. He wanted to grasp society as a whole. From his position as head of the Chicago sociology department and first editor of the discipline's flagship, the *American Journal of*

Sociology, Small often defined sociology as the study of "the total structure and relations of a human population having common bonds" and hence the "queen" of the social sciences comprising all others. As Fred Matthews pointed out in *Quest for an American Sociology* (1977), however, this holistic vision of sociology alternated with Small's narrower definition of sociology as the field of specialized research into the structure of institutions such as family, school, church, and neighborhood. Throughout, he was motivated by a polemic with economic theory. Along with other sociologists who had personal origins in dissenting politics, like Edward A. Ross, Small sought to deny the universal force of possessive, competitive individualism by locating other institutional sources of action and order.

A writer only a few years younger than Small and Giddings provided an alternative vision of the study of society. The work of Thorstein Veblen has retained theoretical merit in ways far surpassing theirs. Social theory today still refers respectfully, for instance, to Veblen's thesis on the advantage of the "late starter" in industrial development; and his fundamental observation of the division of ownership and management in modern corporations laid the basis for a train of diverse writers in economic history and economic sociology. Furthermore, while Small described sociology as the "queen of the social sciences," Veblen avoided such grand, imperialistic claims as he worked from within the discipline of economic studies to build a holistic theory (an anthropological economics) that challenged the presumptions of economic orthodoxy, particularly its universalism and its identification of markets with efficiency.

Reared in a rural immigrant community, Veblen was always conscious of being an outsider in the academy. Motivated by Edward Bellamy's "nationalism" and the populist movement to turn his attentions from philosophy to social studies, Veblen maintained a lively interest in European socialism and American workers' movements while cultivating his expertise in the financial structure of business enterprise during the great merger wave beginning in the late 1890s. Veblen found an affinity between technological development and the "workmanlike" inclination of popular consciousness, and he was a withering critic of the upper classes as a backward-looking social force. Relying on collectivist notions of culture drawn from the emerging field of anthropology, he derided economic presumptions that humans were universally motivated by hedonist or rational principles and challenged the conventional idea

that economic growth as such constituted social progress.

Veblen's approach, however, failed to generate a program for further theoretical development. While his writings appealed to a general audience interested in social criticism, his academic following (so-called "institutional economists") jettisoned most of Veblen's critique and relied instead almost wholly on his empiricist methodology to build a program of statistical research in economics, contributing little to the theory of society. Small's sociological imperialism, on the other hand, could not stand in the face of a backlash from the other social-scientific disciplines and the desire among practitioners in his own discipline for a clear empirical program. The struggle to develop a theory of society thereafter sought not to incorporate economics but to imagine society "beyond" economics.

TOWARD A DIFFERENTIATED CONCEPT OF SOCIETY

The history of thinking about society in the twentieth century can be understood largely as a movement toward a concept of society differentiated from economics. The concept of society had a close, historical association with the emergence of economy as an ostensibly autonomous sphere of human activity apart from the state; the impulse to transcend economics arose in turn from the suspicion reform-minded intellectuals at the turn of the century bore toward the laissez-faire ideal of the market. This was an inherently ambiguous project. To challenge economic ideology was to deny the prevailing assumptions that contemporary market relations were fixed in human nature and that they provided sufficient grounds for social order. To recognize the significance of the noneconomic aspects of social existence helped justify, consequently, more or less extensive and intrusive means of social control over market processes. On the other hand, to deny the practical centrality of economic relations in a modern capitalist society was to obscure something of its essential character. This ambiguity in the relation of reform-minded social theory to contemporary economic life would pose fundamental problems for the concept of society throughout the twentieth century.

Economism was not, in any case, the only naturalistic doctrine advocates of a new, differentiated concept of society sought to combat. Besides economy, biology constituted another traditional pole of attraction for thinking about social relations. While a strong individualistic bias in American culture made it difficult to think in terms of human groups as significant aggregates, prevailing practices of racial domination introduced into common parlance naturalistic terms for judging collective behavior and thus a predilection for biological determinism in explaining social affairs. Deeply entrenched notions of "separate spheres" in family and gender relations as well as Darwinian notions of "sexual selection" introduced another naturalistic element in conventional social thought. The movement toward a differentiated concept of society therefore entailed, besides a polemic with economics, a struggle to build a concept of society beyond biology, taking the form of a mounting challenge to the assumed significance of race and sex in governing behavior and structuring human relations.

This challenge motivated the early sociological work of W. E. B. Du Bois, whose field study, *The Philadelphia Negro* (1899), was intended to demonstrate that the problems of poverty, crime, and family disorder in the African American district of the city had social, not racial, causes. Women activists and scholars also played a significant role in promoting a differentiated concept of society. The settlers at Hull-House in Chicago, driven by ideals of social organicism and social healing, introduced forms of urban social research (surveys, demographic maps, and participant observation) that influenced the sociologists and social psychologists at the University of Chicago. The subjects that settlers and social workers investigated—the organization of urban neighborhoods, structures and patterns of family life, problems of relations among different ethnic groups—became the characteristic topics of the early professional sociologists. Women with settlement-house experience such as Edith Abbott and Sophonisba Breckinridge joined the early sociology faculty at the University of Chicago, before moving to the School of Social Work there in 1920.

Around the same time, as Rosalind Rosenberg indicates in *Beyond Separate Spheres* (1982), other women shifted their scholarly affiliation from sociology to anthropology or psychology, where they found a friendlier reception. In these new areas, some noted women scholars, such as Elsie Clews Parsons and, later, Margaret Mead began investigating the cross-cultural variability of women's roles and thus built an argument for social, rather than biological, determinants of gender norms. In this sense, the concept of culture emerging in anthropology, particularly under the influence of Franz Boas at Columbia University, helped foster an idea of social phenomena beyond economics and biology. Boas's notion of cul-

ture as something holistic and plural (that is, his emphasis on examining different "cultures," each an integral way of life, instead of presuming that all human development followed a single trajectory toward "culture" per se) challenged race as a primary determining force in human behavior as it rejected the model of evolutionary linearity that had a deep affinity with classic liberal ideas of economic growth. The Boasian culture idea would find its most popular voice in the work of one of the paramount women in American social science, Ruth Benedict, who described different societies as each a product of a peculiar configuration of cosmological assumptions, moral values, and motives—that is, a "cultural pattern."

Nonetheless, strong forces in the early twentieth century continued to pull conceptions of society back to biology and economy. Racialism remained a strong element in the social thought of figures such as Edward A. Ross, who had begun his career as a radical critic of capitalism, regarded "social control" (a counterweight to the market) as the keynote of sociology, and considered immigration restriction a salutary exercise of it. Hereditarian ideas—as indicated in doctrines of fixed racial types, instinctual bases of human psychology, intelligence testing, and the campaign by eugenicists for sterilization laws—remained strong in the United States throughout the Progressive Era and in the wake of World War I, losing their luster only in the 1930s and 1940s. The difficulty of moving beyond economics, furthermore, can be witnessed in the case of the Chicago school of sociology. Chicago sociology became a "school" as the research program in urban affairs first cultivated in the university's collaboration with Hull-House was developed further by Robert Park, Ernest Burgess, and Ellsworth Faris, all of whom joined the department there between 1914 and 1919. It was exemplified best by the work that became the touchstone of American sociology for much of the 1920s and 1930s, William I. Thomas and Florian Znaniecki's *The Polish Peasant in Europe and America* (1918–1920).

The key terms Thomas and Znaniecki used in *The Polish Peasant* were not those of economics (self-interest, income, accumulation), but terms of a distinct social-psychological character, having to do with motives, attitudes, and values. Nonetheless, the way Chicago sociologists viewed the problems posed by contemporary social life—and the modes of action they thought responded to and promised to resolve those problems—were profoundly economic in character. Heavily indebted to Spencer and Sumner, William I. Thomas and Robert Park thought of social development in terms of a stark contrast between traditional and modern societies and defined the latter in economistic terms, marked by the primacy of market relations, the growing salience of individualism, and the priority of rational, interest-oriented action. Marked by these traits, modern urban life ruptured the traditional modes of exerting social control over persons, namely their involvement in extended families, primary (face-to-face) groups in neighborhoods, local communities, and so forth.

Sociology, for Thomas and Park, was largely defined by its preoccupation with this problem of "disorganization" and the modes of "adjustment" that promised to reconstruct social ties in a new form. In this sense they furthered the counter-economic impulse embedded in the new concept of society, but their diagnoses of urban relations and prognoses of social development revealed the continued strength of the economic imagination. The "ecological" approach Thomas and Park developed for studying processes of conflict and accommodation between and among social groups suggested an economic model of "interests," competition, and unregulated balance. Furthermore, the kinds of action they endorsed as checks on the market-driven forces of social disintegration paradoxically remained largely individualistic and economic in character. As Eli Zaretsky pointed out in his introduction to an edited version of *The Polish Peasant,* Thomas and Znaniecki repeatedly found forms of "social adjustment" in their subjects' tendencies to form farmers' cooperatives, pursue education and make improvements, save wages, and budget family resources—actions of a self-interested, economic-rational sort.

The further growth of universities and research foundations in the 1920s fostered a number of other writers, "schools," and trends to contend with Chicago's dominance of the discipline. In *Sociology and Scientism* (1987), Robert Bannister focused on the self-conscious attempt by figures such as William Ogburn, Stuart Chapin, Luther Bernard, and others to develop a "scientific sociology" after World War I, based on the objectivist view that sociological science ought to examine only "the observable externals of human behavior" and that "human volition and subjective consciousness have no place in social science." Influenced by Albion Small's social organicism, Luther Bernard tried to revive the approach of Auguste Comte by advocating a "positive" science of society and asserting that such a science could provide moral leadership in the reform of social relations. In contrast to Bernard and his "realist" view

of society as a "self-existent, and organic and self-perpetuating unity," those objectivists trained by Franklin Giddings at Columbia University such as Ogburn and Chapin adopted the "nominalist" position that "society" was merely a convenient term for an aggregate of individuals, whose actions could be understood scientifically in terms of statistical generalizations. Regardless of such differences, however, all these advocates of a rigorous "science of society" failed to build a robust concept of society firmly differentiated from economy.

Bernard was a quirky radical who saw economic relations as little more than chicanery and feared hedonic individualism as an impetus to moral chaos. Social control was something to be established on the basis of a set of standards suited to the maintenance of society as a whole, standards that could be derived by scientific observers. Committed to social reform and progress, he sought to combat the idea that fixed biological propensities governed social action. Given his hostility to individualism and the subjective vagaries of personal life, however, he refused to replace "instinct" with any notion of purpose, interest, wish, or desire at the heart of behavior, and insisted instead that behavior be understood as "reactions" to an environment. Assuming that human actions could be explained in behaviorist terms of stimulus and response, Bernard suggested that a program of manipulating the social environment in ways determined by sociological knowledge (changing the stimulus to draw different responses) could help shape behavior to the demands of a rational order. But of what did "society" consist if not the persons whose interactions made it up or the sense of belonging they shared? Blocked by his social realism and objectivism from taking either of these tacks, Bernard could hardly define the substance of "society" except as something whose order depended on economic coordination to be imposed by a government of expert planners.

The other camp of objectivists was also forced back to economic models of society. Chapin and Ogburn were committed to the goal of "social control" or the conquest of divisive tendencies in modern industrial society. Ogburn in fact had shown some sympathy with radical movements like the Wobblies, proponents of workers' solidarity, before World War I, but wartime hysteria led him to doubt the public's ability to embrace rational change and order. His book of 1922, *Social Change,* suggested an early embrace of "new era" capitalism, where the promise of social order lay in the ability of individuals to find meaning not in a shared, public world but in the "good life" of private consumption. In effect, this solution restated Giddings's acceptance of marginal economics as a system establishing order based on the equilibration of freely varying personal wants. Ogburn's acceptance of an economic model of order (in a new consumer society of relaxed morals) was mirrored by the "living room scales" devised by Chapin, who would assess individuals' class identity by toting up the points allotted to the ensemble of their domestic possessions.

Throughout this period, various other figures composed an "antipositivist" camp devoted to the realm of social theory and the significance of consciousness in society. In American university departments of sociology, there emerged an institutional pattern of balancing theorists and empiricists. After Giddings retired in 1928, Columbia brought in a theorist to head the new regime in sociology, Robert MacIver of Scotland, who was soon joined by Robert Lynd, former secretary of the Social Science Research Council, coauthor with Helen Merrill Lynd of *Middletown* (1929), and advocate of scientific sociology. Sociology at Harvard University was also to be led by a "theorist." A late starter in the field, Harvard's search for a "big man" to lead a new sociology department ended with the 1931 appointment of Pitirim Sorokin, a Russian émigré recently employed at the University of Minnesota who had made a mark with his compendious survey of 1928, *Recent Sociological Theories.* Sorokin tried to achieve a kind of theory/empiricist balance at Harvard by bringing with him from Minnesota the rural sociologist Carle Zimmerman. Harvard, however, had not one but two theorists, for Sorokin's leadership was challenged by the young Talcott Parsons. Parsons was to take a more decisive step toward a differentiated concept of society than did other figures of the interwar period. Schooled outside the American sociological tradition, Parsons began as Veblen did with a problem from within the economic sphere and moved outward toward a more thorough critique of economic logic than any achieved by the older sociologists.

Son of a minister active in the Social Gospel movement, Parsons entered Amherst College in 1920 where the progressive educational ideas of President Alexander Meiklejohn prevailed, Veblenians Walton Hamilton and Clarence Ayres presided over the social sciences, and the spirit of radical prewar reform movements survived, at least until around 1924. While there, Parsons learned, as he put it at the time, that "the economic and social order was a matter of human arrangements, not one of inevitable natural law, and hence that it was subject to human control."

With a group of like-minded students, Parsons organized an independent major under the title, "Control in the Economic Order." Parsons chaired his college chapter of the Student League for Industrial Democracy (SLID), the successor of the war-wounded Intercollegiate Socialist Society. After graduation, in an attempt to gain a holistic understanding of modern economic society, Parsons went abroad to England—to meet the leading social-democratic intellectuals Harold Laski and R. H. Tawney—and then to Germany.

Parsons's encounter with Max Weber's legacy at the University of Heidelberg in 1925–1926 marked a crucial turning point. Parsons returned to the United States the next year, at a time when Veblen's repute was declining rapidly and orthodox economics was consolidating its sway over academic departments throughout the United States. Influenced by Weber's attempt to mediate the German *Methodenstreit* between neoclassical economics and the "historical school" of economics, Parsons now accepted the validity of formal economic theory, while insisting that its applicability in social analysis was limited and that the theory per se entailed no endorsement of the prevailing capitalist organization of society. Thereafter, with the help of arguments borrowed from Max Weber and Émile Durkheim, Parsons challenged the anticollectivist dogma of market economists Friedrich Hayek and Ludwig von Mises on the grounds that the moral regulation of social action through institutions like the learned professions could drive economic activity as well as, and perhaps better than, egoistic interest in monetary accumulation.

The questions posed in this debate about the nature of "economic motivation" in modern life remained at the heart of Parsons's theoretical concerns in the 1930s, concerns he knew were bound up with pressing contemporary issues of social reform. Parsons's monumental treatise of 1937, *The Structure of Social Action,* can be understood in these terms. The book began with a long critique of "the utilitarian theory of action," a transparent reference to classic market theory, based on atomistic individualism and the assumptions that ends of action are given exogenously and that the means of action are solely determined by norms of efficiency. In a long and subtle argument, Parsons showed how this theory tended to deride human capacities for reason and free will by explaining social action either in behaviorist terms of adaptation to given conditions or in biologistic terms of instinctual drives. Parsons's desire to preserve human capacities for reason and freedom as modern society moved steadily toward more organized forms of existence signaled his attempt to intervene against the threat of increasingly coercive forms of organization in his time (fascism). His insistence on the central significance of "common-value integration" in society was intended as a body blow against the metaphysical individualism of the liberal tradition and as an argument for more collectivist values in the sphere of economic action.

Paradoxically, the arguments developed by Parsons in order to justify certain forms of social reconstruction in economic life served thereafter to catapult Parsons beyond the realm of economics entirely. In the mid-1930s he sought to relativize the market system and justify reform of economic institutions by refusing to identify social process as a whole with the economic calculus of utilitarianism; by grasping the "value" element of motivation that both complemented and countered the prevalence of economic self-interest; and by perceiving the continued salience of nonmarket communal organization and orientation (such as those of the professions) in modern society. By the early 1940s, however, the same arguments served, in Parsons's hands, to suggest that society could not be defined adequately in economic terms at all and that "capitalism" had lost meaning as a social definition and diagnosis of contemporary life.

Further development of genuinely social explanations of relations between "racial" groups also helped promote a more differentiated concept of society during the interwar period. The great migration of African Americans from the rural South to the urban North and West began in the wake of World War I just as academic social research was coming of age as a professional endeavor. At the same time, racial liberalism, signaled by the critique of racialist doctrine by Franz Boas, was steadily infusing, and finally dominating, academic intellectual life. Chicago's Robert Park made a long stride toward treating race relations as a social process, regarding twentieth-century African Americans as a typical "peasant" people experiencing the same disorientation as other groups of immigrants who had to adapt to modern urban norms and assimilate a new and unfamiliar national culture. He also opened professional doors to a new group of distinguished African American social scientists. Park, however, still held to residual biologistic notions of a "racial temperament" which, in the case of African Americans, he described as sunny, cheerful, and practical-minded. His view that African Americans as a type were disinclined to abstract thought even suggested old notions of blacks' "limited educability." Regardless of these prejudices, Park's black students saw him as a friend and patron

of black intellectual talent and serious, unbigoted research on race. Black students of Park and of Chicago's social anthropologist W. Lloyd Warner contributed to an outpouring of major studies on African American life: *The Negro Family in the United States* (1939) by E. Franklin Frazier, *Black Metropolis* (1945) by Horace Cayton and St. Clair Drake, and *Deep South* (1941) by black anthropologist Allison Davis with Burleigh Gardner and Mary R. Gardner.

THE BEHAVIORAL CONCEPT OF SOCIETY

By mid-century, the formal study of "society" had found new affiliations and coordinates. Rather than being wedded as it once was to the older social sciences of economics and politics, sociology after World War II was more likely to be associated with cultural anthropology and social psychology. The years from 1940 to 1970 were marked by the preeminence of a new conception of social studies—sometimes called "behavioral science"—focused on the construction of motivation in common behavior and the part played in that process by institutions such as family, school, church, neighborhood, and small group interaction. This view, cited for instance in Robert Berkhofer's book, *A Behavioral Approach to Historical Analysis* (1969), and clearly distinguished from stimulus-response behavior*ism,* defined society largely in terms of the associations and interactions that molded human action through the media of subjective phenomena such as personality, roles, values, orientations, perceptions of reality, sentiments of solidarity, and the like.

This marked the heyday of "society" as a noneconomic concept and signaled a profound "paradigm shift" in modern social thought. Earlier figures, such as Charles Horton Cooley and Albion Small, had occasionally defined the object of sociology as those "social institutions" that arose in concentric circles around the family and prevailed in a sphere apart from direct economic activity, but the mid-century shift in this direction implied something new. By this time, the definition of a noneconomic "social" sphere had been freed from its polemical engagement with economics. Suspicion of economic assumptions (individualism and rational motivation) remained a tacit orientation of sociology and anthropology, but for practitioners in these fields it was no longer urgent to wage battle in pursuit of the high ground in social studies. The point was no longer to challenge the social assumptions of economics but simply to leave economics aside in exploring other concerns. The new prestige of the fields which took a "behavioral" approach to society—sociology, anthropology, and psychology—suggested, however, that economics had lost its dominant position in explaining social affairs broadly speaking. This theoretical trend was compounded and sustained by the contemporaneous ideology of the "welfare state," which suggested that advanced societies had entered a new stage of development where (as British sociologist T. H. Marshall put it) "social rights" to security, health, and education had achieved primacy and economy had been reduced to the status of a mere instrument in the pursuit of such public aims.

The shift began in the 1930s. As the economic crisis was compounded by political crisis in Europe, there arose the overarching question of the "fate of modern society." Such an apocalyptic moment called forth various holistic attempts to understand social processes of order and change. Meanwhile, although the Depression made questions about the economic substructure paramount in estimating the nature and future prospects of society, it also cast doubt and suspicion on the discipline of economics and the primacy of economic action. More collectivist phenomena in the realms of culture and social psychology consequently attracted attention. The fever pitch of the European Right and the approach of another cataclysmic war confirmed this new emphasis, for many observers felt such irrational phenomena as fascist mass movements were inadequately understood if regarded in strictly economic terms. Thus, the interdisciplinary trend in social thought of the 1930s came to focus particularly on cross-fertilization between the theory of society and theory of culture, that is, between anthropology and sociology. Anthropology in the United States, as it was described in Ralph Linton's volume *The Study of Man* (1936), began to incorporate greater attention to "social structure" in the sense of a systemic arrangement of "roles" and "statuses." At the same time, mainstream sociology drew on the older Boasian notion of "cultural patterns" to grasp the distinctive characters of different societies. Another ingredient in the trend toward interdisciplinary work during the 1930s was the marked development of greater interaction between American and European social thought. American social thought had never been quite so provincial as some critics of American culture claimed: the early academic sociologists in the United States studied the work of the German historical economists and knew some of Georg Simmel's work in English translation before 1910. Nonetheless, the new world stature of the United States after World

War I assured even greater transatlantic communication in the social sciences, fostered by exchange programs organized by the new research foundations. Furthermore, the reverse flow of refugee European scholars after 1933 introduced to the United States a variety of European theoretical currents including Karl Mannheim's sociology of knowledge, the existentialism of Martin Heidegger and Karl Jaspers, Edmund Husserl's phenomenology, psychoanalysis, and the radical currents later dubbed Western Marxism. The work of Max Weber, in particular, found several exponents in the United States besides Talcott Parsons: Hans Gerth at Wisconsin introduced a "critical," antibureaucratic version of Weber to C. Wright Mills; Alexander von Schelting at Columbia promoted Weber's work in social science methodology; somewhat later, Reinhard Bendix at Berkeley presented Weber as a theorist of social conflict. Émile Durkheim's work enjoyed a growing audience in the late 1930s, too, and had influence as a source for the sociology of knowledge, the structural-functionalism of British anthropologist A. R. Radcliffe-Brown (which understood particular social practices and institutions in terms of how they helped to maintain the order of society as a whole), and later the structural anthropology of Claude Lévi-Strauss, the French scholar of kinship and myth who spent the war years as a refugee in New York City.

Moreover, in the early 1940s, many liberal social scientists in the United States focused their attentions on the problem of "national morale," understood as a sense of solidarity needed to sustain the war effort. Insofar as "morale" demanded a Durkheimian respect for collective needs, it militated against economic individualism and incorporated the liberals' suspicion of market norms. At the same time, the problem of "morale" turned attention away from economic issues per se and helped reorient the prevailing concept of society. The campaign for "national morale" helped turn Talcott Parsons away from the question of "capitalism" in American life toward issues of American national identity and, consequently, studies of "culture and personality." By 1942, Parsons's growing interest in psychoanalysis and in cultural patterns led him toward new disciplinary allies. His new Department of Social Relations, unveiled in 1946, combined sociology, cultural anthropology, and social psychology but conspicuously left economics (as well as government) out of its conception and organization of holistic social research. The same tripartite organization cropped up in other interdisciplinary efforts, such as Chicago's core program in social science, "Self, Culture and Society," and in Howard P. Becker's textbook, *Man in Reciprocity: Introductory Lectures on Culture, Society, and Personality* (1956).

Publication of *An American Dilemma* in 1944 by the Swedish sociologist Gunnar Myrdal signaled both the new degree of transatlantic collaboration and the impact of the war. Myrdal wedded the racial liberalism of the interwar years to the issue of national morale by insisting that the binding force of a central "American creed" would impel change toward greater racial equality. With its thorough rejection of residual racialist ideas, Myrdal's book surpassed Robert Park's work. Its clear denunciation of white supremacy as a moral disgrace and its prophecy of Jim Crow's imminent fall went well beyond any previous academic study, including John Dollard's *Class and Caste in a Southern Town* (1936), which had already painted a scathing portrait of segregated society as a regime of terror. Although later critics suggested that Myrdal's account of African American culture (as merely a variant, and a "pathological" one at that, of general American culture, without any significant ties to African culture) was "racist," the book's principled opposition to Jim Crow garnered the support of the most left-wing figure among black graduates of Chicago sociology, E. Franklin Frazier.

Myrdal's study also adopted a functionalist framework like that which would dominate postwar sociology, for his argument highlighted the significance of "strain" in the American mind and the pressures to establish a better balance in the values and social organization of American life. The best-known postwar exponent of this approach, however, was Talcott Parsons, whose second major work, *The Social System* (1951), helped make "structural-functionalism" one of the main currents of sociological discourse in the 1950s and 1960s. Its emphases on the so-called pattern variables in defining a society's typical roles (a matrix of simple dichotomies, such as achieved versus ascribed statuses, universalist versus particularist norms), along with themes of functional integration, deviance, "strain," and re-equilibration of systems were more or less easily grasped, adopted into the lexicon, and subjected to a few sharp critiques. Parsons's influence in the discipline prevailed for various reasons other than the intrinsic merits of his theory, including the Harvard cachet, the grandeur of Parsons's attempt at creating a universal theory of all social systems, and the vigor of Parsons's loyal students. In any case, the theoretical model Parsons presented in *The Social System* was only a waystation to a more embracing grand theory that he developed in the late 1950s and continued to probe through

the rest of his life—the so-called four function model, where functions of managing resources, determining collective goals, integrating differentiated social roles, and replicating basic value-patterns were understood to be the most fundamental aspects of a social system—each one linked to, and interdependent with, the others. In this respect, Parsons was a leader in importing systems theory, and the notion of cybernetic controls, into the description of society, suggesting that cultural processes (the maintenance and replication of value-patterns) served to "regulate" activities carried out at more energy-intensive or material levels of social practice.

Parsons's leading student of the 1930s, Robert K. Merton, went on in the 1940s and 1950s to found a related but distinct "school" of sociological research at Columbia University. Merton differentiated himself from Parsons by defining the nature of "social structure" less in terms of the global coordination of society as an integrated system than in terms of more particular and proximate relations among limited sets of institutions. Merton's "functional" analysis emphasized such partial linkages, and proved attractive to students who granted a significant role in social affairs to group conflicts, contradictions between various social demands, and ambivalence in motivation—who recognized, that is, a considerable degree of openness and slippage in the coordination of institutions. Institutions, furthermore, were regarded here as concrete, discernable things of the social world (political parties, professions and occupations, schools or scientific disciplines, families, etc.) rather than as abstract, functional aspects of systems ("the family"). Nonetheless, both Mertonian and Parsonsian functionalism put "basic values" at the heart of the constitution of society. Both were concerned with the moral norms, or ethos, defining such modern institutions as science and the professions. Both regarded "strain, tension, contradiction or discrepancy between the elements of social and culture structure" as the source of social change, according to Charles Crothers in his profile *Robert K. Merton* (1987). Together, and in roughly equal proportions, Parsons and Merton were by far the most cited authors in postwar sociology textbooks until the 1970s.

The behavioral concept of society fostered other sorts of theory as well, particularly the interactionist and phenomenological perspectives developed by Erving Goffman, Harold Garfinkel, and others in the 1960s. Goffman's work was a late offshoot of one dimension of Chicago sociology, indebted to W. I. Thomas's emphasis on subjective elements of social experience and the pragmatist philosopher George

Herbert Mead's emphasis on interaction. Simply put, Mead had argued that human individuals became persons in a process of interacting with others and assimilating the others' expectations: one achieved personality, then, by gaining the capacity to look at oneself as others did, in the looking glass of society (to use Charles Horton Cooley's phrase). Personality development was tantamount to the skill of role-taking, developed in children through simple play and (later) organized games. This perspective encouraged the study of social action as a process in which human actors exchange with each other meaningful cues about their intentions and perceptions, the phenomenon of "symbolic interaction."

Mead's argument was a powerful rejoinder to methodological individualism, for it insisted that persons were profoundly social products. Goffman's work was also determinedly social. Among the writers he cited most often was Durkheim, who insisted on the reality of "society" as a supraindividual entity, indeed the source of individuality itself since humans became distinguishable persons only as society made them something other than creatures of instinct and impulse. The radically social perspective of Goffman was indicated by the assertion made by his book *Asylums* (1961) that the character of the mental hospital patient was determined by "his institution, not his illness." Goffman's approach to social interaction—best known in terms of his "dramaturgical" model in which all persons, like stage actors, conduct their social life by donning and doffing various masks and learning to "manage impressions"—tended to flatten perspectives, however. There appeared to be no "inner" person (or "true self") behind the masks of social presentation, nor any large-scale social structures (beyond immediate situations of interaction) which constrained or motivated behaviors. The perspective seemed cold, even cynical, for while there was no use searching for an "authentic" personality behind impression-management, there was no point either in describing "society" as the site of fulfillment, as earlier social psychologists had. Rather, "society" seemed to be a milieu of mortification, a system of conventions that confined the individual.

Goffman's mordant irony was evident in his choice of the mental hospital as a case study in the social construction of personality, for the routines of the institution *made* a person (the patient) whose behaviors were then regarded as pathological symptoms. He was coy, too, for though he distinguished the "total institutions" he studied (hospitals, prisons, or army camps) from the "civil" or "civilian" society on the outside, he still implied that the modes of control he found in the former case were analogous to those prevailing at large. There was, however, another more poignant side of Goffman's critique, for he borrowed Durkheim's notion that modern society rested on a "cult of the individual," and he castigated the total institutions he investigated for trampling over the normal ritual practices of interaction which did honor to the self. In so doing, he upheld the integrity of the individual as a sacred value, notwithstanding that—indeed perhaps because—there was no discrete "substance" at the heart of personality. (It is worth recalling that the sacred, according to Durkheim, was defined solely by the prohibitions that marked it off, not by its intrinsic qualities, and thus was an "empty" category too.) In this way, Goffman defended the maintenance of the "social fabric" as the inevitable grounding of persons.

Garfinkel's "ethnomethodology" had origins different from those of Goffman's program. As a student of Parsons, Garfinkel had learned the Weberian emphasis on subjective motivation and the priority of "understanding" *(Verstehen)* in social observation. He went further, however, by relying on the work of the phenomenological sociologist Alfred Schutz to argue that "explanation [in social science] comes to be regarded as a matter of connecting action to its sense rather than behavior to its determinants." Thus for Garfinkel social action is understood as a performative gesture aimed at constructing and sustaining a sense of reality shared with others. Indeed, Schutz's phenomenology suggested not merely that a "sense of reality" but that "reality" as such was a social construction. Such an argument has been criticized as an extreme form of sociologism, idealism, and relativism—a reduction of knowledge to a purely social, hence arbitrary, artifact. In any case, Goffman, Garfinkel, and phenomenological sociology may be regarded as part of the general "behavioral" frame of social studies after 1940. Goffman's training entailed the combined fields of sociology, cultural anthropology, and social psychology, and "ethnomethodology" by its very name likewise linked sociology closely with the work of anthropology.

While issues of women's rights and women's equality were temporarily suppressed in the wake of World War II, the new behavioral concept of society brought a new focus to those realms of activity where women's activities had traditionally been paramount (family, church, neighborhood, and school, as opposed to the male-dominated realms of institutionalized economic and political practice). The beginnings in the 1930s of formal university instruction and research on the topic of "marriage and the fam-

928

ily" led, in combination with Parsonian and Mertonian functionalism, toward growing interest in family structure, gender roles, and sexuality in personality development. Attention to differential roles in the family led to Parsons's formulation, with the help of Robert Freed Bales, of the value distinction between "expressive" and "instrumental" norms in women's and men's activities, respectively. Later feminist critics often considered this work a manifestation of conservative 1950s domestic ideology, since it suggested this division was "functionally" necessary for family and social stability; other feminists, such as Nancy Chodorow, recognized the Parsonian model as a social, rather than natural, explanation of behavior and thus part of the trend which rendered "gender roles" contingent and open to criticism. The functionalist milieu spawned other work regarding gender roles. Studying worldwide changes in family and social structure during the late 1950s and early 1960s, William Goode of the Columbia sociology department emphasized a long-term trend toward equality of the sexes, though he noted persistent values and behavior (particularly men's) that diverged from the widespread ideology of sex egalitarianism. He served as an adviser to Betty Friedan as she wrote her landmark book, *The Feminine Mystique* (1963). The Columbia University milieu included others—such as Mirra Komarovsky, who wrote *Women in the Modern World* (1953) and *Blue-Collar Marriage* (1964), and Rose Laub Coser, a Merton associate who wrote on the structure of family life in the early 1960s.

Although Mary Jo Deegan has described the years 1920–1965 as "the dark era" for women as practicing scholars and researchers in sociology, the number of women trained in the field actually increased in the 1940s and 1950s. They were slow to be heard since many of them married and bore the burden of domestic duties and deferred careers. It was precisely this dilemma of advanced training and limited outlets for professional expression that led Alice Rossi to write her 1964 critique, "Equality between the Sexes: An Immodest Proposal," and launched her career as a leading feminist sociologist of the 1960s and 1970s. Her struggle against professional subordination led Rossi "to rethink the functionalist sociology I had swallowed whole from Columbia"; others, such as Rose Laub Coser and Miriam Johnson, considered their training in Mertonian and Parsonian functionalism to be valuable in focusing attention on family institutions and gender differentiation and not incompatible with a feminist critique of gender roles.

At the same time, the 1950s and early 1960s saw a decline in extensive studies of U.S. race relations, compared to the great studies of the 1930s and 1940s by Abram Harris and Sterling Spero (*The Black Worker* in 1931), Frazier, Myrdal, and Drake and Cayton. The behavioral concept of society, which emphasized the psychocultural elements of social experience, was nonetheless well-suited in some respects to grapple with issues of race and gender, especially as these came to be regarded as matters of social construction and insofar as they were defined in relation to social problems of prejudice. According to a cultural reading of racism and sexism, prejudice may be regarded as a social process in which certain kinds of differences are marked as things apart from the acceptable norm. Goffman's 1963 book, *Stigma,* concerned practices of extrusion from normal social regard, an analysis that could be applied to an understanding of racial prejudice. His later study, *Gender Advertisements* (1979), addressed the social reproduction of sexism and male domination by means of detailed conventions of everyday interaction (the meaningful character of posture, gesture, and the like). In an intriguing case study of transsexual surgery, Garfield investigated gender as a narrative of "normal" identity that figures prominently in a person's self-presentation.

THE CRISIS OF THE SOCIAL SCIENCES

The rise of social criticism and disruptive political action in the 1960s eventually posed a substantial challenge to the postwar paradigm, the behavioral concept of society. The so-called "crisis of the social sciences" arose around 1970 with the formation of radical caucuses in all the major disciplines and a crescendo of criticism suggesting that "Western social science" had been willfully blind to the causes and persistence of gross social problems, particularly marked social inequality. Critics focused on the alleged failure of behavioral science to examine the part played by differential *powers* and *interests* in constructing social relations: the absence of political and economic analysis, that is, seemed to have disabled the social diagnosis of social problems. In the wake of this crisis, social theory in the United States witnessed a revival of Marxism and other historical theories of large-scale social change, a heightened attention to forces disrupting social order, a pursuit of full-fledged multidimensional accounts of social process as a whole, and the introduction of a vocal feminism bolder than any since the early twentieth century.

The first salvos in the controversy over the character and prestige of social science were fired in the

1950s by C. Wright Mills, the Columbia University sociologist. Mills had begun his intellectual career as a radical around 1940, regarding social theory as a tool for social criticism. Like much of the left-wing intelligentsia in the 1940s and early 1950s, he drifted toward a more liberal politics (supporting Adlai Stevenson for president in 1952), due in part to his conviction that power had become so concentrated during the war that sharp conflict and the possibility of dramatic change in modern American society had lapsed. The difference between Mills and the other radical-cum-liberal intellectuals, however, was that he maintained his sharp dislike of the static social order he described and made that known in a series of books that set a standard for acid social criticism in the 1950s.

That series culminated in his book *The Sociological Imagination* (1959), which focused much of his ire on Talcott Parsons. Mills was not alone in criticizing the ostensibly conservative elements of Parsons's theory—the focus on the mechanisms that check behavioral deviations from conventional roles and help maintain the homeostatic "equilibrium" of a social system. Ralf Dahrendorf, Lewis Coser, Donald Levine, Reinhard Bendix, and others had made similar criticisms of Parsons for pinning a theory of society on the conception of order or stability, rather than conflict and change. Mills however went further to mount a full-scale jeremiad against his own discipline and the social sciences in general for having given up the humanistic tasks of criticism that led the giants of social theory (Marx, Weber, Durkheim) to pose "big questions" regarding the nature and direction of modern society and the prospects for freedom and dignity within it.

A decade later, Mills's arguments appeared to achieve predominance in a current of self-styled "radical sociology." Much of this new radicalism was determinedly empirical in focus, reacting against the abstract formalism of systems theory in favor of more "realistic" or "practical" applications of research. An early volume of "Radical Perspectives in Sociology" was entitled *Where It's At* (1970), evoking the contemporary phrase for "real experience." This brand of radical sociology sought to redirect attention to "social problems" (poverty, discrimination, violence) while insisting that their explanation and solution lay in "social structure" or "systemic" forces—that poor children's failure in school, for instance, was due not to motivational problems of the poor but to the failure-producing effects of the school system.

Concentrated attention to problems of social class, once an unavoidable topic in studying a society marked by the stresses of industrial development, urban growth, and group conflict, had not been prominent in the postwar behavioral sciences. Functionalism tended to regard class as an aspect of modern society (in terms of "stratification") but not as a fundamental, constitutive, or disruptive element of it. Also, rising interest in issues of race, from World War II–era liberalism to the civil rights agitation of the 1950s and 1960s, often served to reinforce the disregard of *class* cleavages in American life. As an exception, Oliver Cromwell Cox, a black Marxist sociologist who persistently emphasized the interpenetration of race and class, remained an obscure, marginal figure throughout the postwar period. By the late 1960s, however, a new generation of black sociologists appeared, including figures such as William Julius Wilson, who redirected attention toward the structure and uses of power in American society, suggesting that social class was an inescapable element in any theory of U.S. race relations. Under the influence of the radicalized movements for racial justice in the mid and late 1960s, especially as attention turned from the "anomaly" of southern segregation to the plight of the urban black poor in the North, this cohort reasserted the lost link between economic phenomena and social process.

The new sociology of race and class suggested a dramatic turn away from the postwar assumptions of the "new social sciences," that is, their focus on motivation and action in coherent systems considered apart from matters of interest, power, and historical change. A black sociologist, Robert G. Newby, remarked that his adoption of a "class view of the world" at an urban university in the mid 1970s made his recent Stanford University dissertation on "the impact of [black] racial consciousness on black–white interaction in small groups" suddenly seem "irrelevant." In some respects, all the "behavioral" disciplines were under attack from critics within, and most of the critics sought some connection between their specific discipline and political economy, understood as the sphere (broadly speaking) of relations of power and interest. So in anthropology, there was a certain movement to reconnect the study of cultural systems with economic systems and to criticize the ties between the development of anthropology as a discipline and Western imperialism.

Even though radical sociologists, such as the contributors to *Where It's At,* took an empiricist approach to issues of power, wealth, and race, they also put a priority on the "commitment" of the scholar (rebutting the norm of value-neutrality in social-science scholarship) and on "redefining" the contours of debate on contemporary social problems (thus raising questions about the status of basic concepts and categories in the pursuit of social knowledge). Thus they helped turn attention to questions of ideology and theory. In *The Coming Crisis of Western Sociology* (1970), which described sociological functionalism as the image of a society organized in such a way as to contain problems, deflect conflict, and reproduce itself indefinitely, Alvin Gouldner called for a new "reflexive" sociology that would be conscious of sociology and sociologists as themselves products of social forces and actors in social affairs. Although his interpretations of the social place and meanings of social theories were often heavy-handed and his clarion calls for a return to Hegelian dialectics dumbfounded many of his unphilosophical colleagues, Gouldner helped to foster a new attention, among academic radicals in particular, to "theory" in the large.

Marxism, following a period in which it had been widely considered an obsolete form of economic reductionism, enjoyed a dramatic revival in the wake of the "crisis." It was given credit for its insistence on the role of political economy, its emphasis on comprehending the "totality" of social relations, and its examination of the role of the observer and political actor in understanding society. It should be emphasized that Marx's critical category of "mode of production" cannot be reduced to "the economy": relations of a "social" and "political" character figure in it at the most basic level, since forms of property and ways of organizing labor entail both the formation of groups and the exercise of power in official and unofficial ways. Furthermore, while Marx used the concept of the "mode of production" to abstract the most fundamental ways humans act in concert and in antagonism to reproduce themselves, he also sought (but never elaborated) a way of understanding its articulation with the various forms of human action and expression (including "cultural" phenomena) that make up whole societies. Thus Marxism held out the prospect of a genuinely synthetic theory of social relations, encompassing all the various fields that had been established as separate social sciences.

Marxist thought itself, however, had been subject to the general trends bifurcating the social sciences and producing the "behavioral" concept of "society" apart from political economy. Antonio Gramsci's work in the 1930s, for instance, which aimed at a theory of "civil society" and "hegemony," can be understood as an analog within Marxism to the "behavioral" revolution in mainstream social science. Gramsci argued that social order (the maintenance of oppressive class society) could not be explained wholly in economic and political terms but rested on the ideas about authority and deference to it which were maintained in the "social" institutions (family, school, church, etc.) of everyday life. Likewise, the work of the Institute of Social Research (first in Frankfurt and then, in exile, at Columbia University during the 1930s and 1940s) illustrated the inclination of mid-century "Western Marxism" to turn attention to the "subjective" elements of social existence (social-psychological and cultural) in hopes of understanding the failure of revolutionary movements. Before the crisis of the social sciences around 1970, one of the best-known Marxist intellectuals working in the United States, Herbert Marcuse, published *Eros and Civilization* (1955) and *One-Dimensional Man* (1964), which were "cultural and characterological" in approach.

Consequently, the reinvigoration of Marxism in the United States took two forms. On the one hand, especially under the sway of the early New Left, whose worldview was still largely dominated by the "behavioral" definition of society, there was a concerted attempt to recover (and translate) key works of "Western Marxism" and extend the approach of Marxism to questions of "subjectivity" (culture and personality, alienation, the construction of motivation under exploitative social relations, etc.). On the other hand, by the 1970s, the revival of Marxism entailed a concerted attack on the postwar paradigm by emphasizing the central significance that social class formation, class struggle, economic crisis tendencies, state administration and repression, and so forth, had for understanding the development of society as a whole.

The most vigorous work in American Marxism took the form of concerted studies in sociology, economics, and political science which examined the organization of work (historical processes of de-skilling, transfer of authority from workers to supervisors and managers, the evolution of "split" or "segmented" labor markets, etc.); the nature of contemporary economic crisis (the role of the profit rate, of rising wages, or of inadequate popular consumption); the significance of class (the concentrated and enduring character of inequality); and the nature of the state (the forms of repression, the management of consensus, the relation of government to business and workers movements). Some attempts were made to bridge questions of political economy and social-cultural affairs, particularly regarding the nature of schooling, the structure of family life, and (in a historical vein) the significance of working-class culture for the conduct of the labor movement. There was also in this new Marxism clearer attention to the nature and significance of ideology, such as the emphasis (in the work of James O'Connor among others) on the "legitimation" functions that adjoined the repressive and managerial functions of the state.

Nonetheless, the revival of Marxism was weakest on points of "subjectivity." Debates about the role of consciousness in Marx's theoretical system played a considerable part in relatively abstract philosophical discussions, but Marxists produced relatively little in terms of empirical studies of personality and culture. The influence of Marxism in anthropology during the 1960s and 1970s directed attention toward reasserting the place of productive relations and historical change in structuring societies, rather than addressing the construction of "culture" as understood by the mainstream of anthropology (norms, values, attitudes, symbols, rituals). A few distinct currents from abroad have moved more decisively toward an integration of political economy and culture. "Cultural studies" in Britain, closely associated with the work of Richard Hoggart and Raymond Williams in the 1950s and 1960s and carried on by Stuart Hall in the 1970s and 1980s, has tried to bring a Marxian sense of class structure and struggle to the study of symbolic and experiential aspects of life in contemporary Western society, particularly with regard to schooling, youth culture, and popular entertainments. In France, more formal and empirically rigorous exercises in a class-oriented sociology of culture have been carried out by Pierre Bourdieu, whose work began to have widespread influence in the United States during the late 1980s.

At the same time and especially since the late 1970s, the work of Max Weber again became the focus of extensive theoretical discussion. Neo-Weberians such as Randall Collins and English sociologist Anthony Giddens revived key Weberian criticisms of Marx—for promoting an unduly limited emphasis on economic determination and class conflicts, for endowing history with too fixed a developmental trajectory, for neglecting the role of distinctly political and cultural forms of power, and for failing to put sufficient emphasis on the subjective element of understanding and purpose in human action. As Weber achieved a new measure of clout, however, it was nonetheless a more "Marxian Weber" that appealed to young sociological theorists, compared to the idealist version of Weber most commonly accepted in the postwar period. Theorists after the "crisis of the social sciences" rediscovered the historical Weber, who had devoted enormous energy to studying the role of economic interests and conflicts, the pursuit of and maintenance of power by specific social groups, and the problem of explaining epochal social change. Out of the conjoint renewal of interest in Marx and a more historical Weber came an explosion since the 1960s in "historical sociology," which examined how social structure was constructed over time by human action and the way significant attempts to challenge, alter, or overturn an established order were spawned, promoted, and limited by specific forms of social structure.

Barrington Moore, Jr.'s *Social Origins of Dictatorship and Democracy* (1966) was a lodestar for virtually a generation of American academic radicals committed to "historical sociology." Like Mills, Moore referred to the heritage of Thorstein Veblen, not so much for his critique of theoretical formalism as for his ventures in economic sociology and broad, developmental generalizations. In a comparative study of English, French, and American democracy, Chinese communism, Japanese militarism, and the anomalous development of postcolonial India, Moore accomplished a wide-ranging revision of modernization theory, highlighting the place of social class in relation to the organization, rupture, and reconstitution of arrangements of political power. Moore criticized "cultural explanations" of social development which failed to offer a causal account for the persistence of culture itself, and he argued that conflict and rupture (indeed revolutionary violence) were, paradoxically, essential elements in founding whatever stability and endurance Western "democratic society" had achieved.

Historical sociology challenged some key presuppositions of the postwar paradigm, particularly that society could be examined more or less as a coherent, unitary body and that normative consensus played an essential role in binding it together. More attuned to conflict and disruption and, in some cases, to such transnational developments as imperial domination or economic integration and dependency in a "world system," historical sociology tended to doubt the significance of common consciousness in maintaining social order. Although some historical sociologists, such as Moore and his student Theda Skocpol, tended to slight the role of consciousness in society, other writers in the field did not. For instance, the British Marxist historian E. P. Thompson, who had some influence in the United States on those seeking to apply social theory to problems of explaining historical change, highlighted the normative element in social action. In *The Making of the English Working Class* (1963), he sought to redefine the Marxian concept of class in largely voluntarist terms—as a body of people who, in the flux of economic activity, welded themselves together on the basis of a shared worldview and in pursuit of certain morally valued ends.

Another profound element in the crisis of the social sciences was the rise of feminist research. Emerging from the women's liberation movement of the late 1960s, feminism proposed a new focal element in the construction of society, namely the oppression of women and their pursuit of liberation from pervasive domination by men. One of the first tasks assumed by feminists was to challenge the "invisibility" of women in the portraits of social process and order drawn by most of the social sciences. Since the early twentieth century, women had a more secure place in American anthropology than in other social-science disciplines, particularly sociology, and consequently feminist anthropologists such as Michelle Rosaldo, Louise Lamphere, and Sherry Ortner played a leading role in raising questions about sexual inequality in human social experience. In anthropology, the "invisibility" of women was evident in such common themes as the "Man the Hunter" hypothesis about the origin of social cooperation. Beyond correcting invisibility, however, feminist research in anthropology and other disciplines helped to make "gender" (or the social-cultural construction of masculine and feminine identities and relations) a new paramount category of social inquiry.

Feminism also helped promote a thoroughgoing interdisciplinary scholarship on social relations. As noted above, the attention of postwar social theory to realms of experience outside economy and polity had already gone beyond those disciplines which could assume a generic male actor insofar as they focused on institutionally distinct spheres dominated by men. Later feminist gender studies, however, had the signal impact of drawing concepts heretofore customarily restricted to politics and economy—interests, conflict, power, and domination—into the "social" sphere where the postwar paradigm had assumed a kind of harmony, or normative integration, crucial to the reproduction of social relations. Feminist scholarship went further to challenge conventional definitions of political and economic spheres as purely male preserves. Anthropologist Jane Collier, for instance, insisted that "politics" referred not merely to central institutions of statecraft but also to the varied, often hidden, ways in which women, acting in the "private" reaches of family life, struggled to achieve influence and power over social decisions.

The pursuit of a genuinely holistic perspective also motivated a number of noted writers who worked in the field of "grand theory." Anthony Giddens wrote of ways to recognize both "agency" and "structure" (subjective will and free action, on the one hand; external forms and limiting constraints, on the other). American Jeffrey Alexander began a virtual campaign in the 1980s to resurrect Talcott Parsons's sociology as a "multidimensional" program aimed at overcoming the breach between "positivistic" theories that emphasized social conditions over consciousness and "idealistic" theories that emphasized consciousness over conditions. In quite a different venture, *Revolution in the Development of Capitalism* (1987), Mark Gould took the Parsonsian heritage back to the concerns of historical sociology in a theoretically informed account of the English civil war. By applying Parsons's notions of the role of deviance and functional strain to the Marxian problem of social revolution, Gould made a bold attempt to bridge normative and structural concerns in a single view.

MOVING BEYOND THE CONCEPT OF SOCIETY

Aspirations for a genuinely holistic theory in the social sciences have not been successful in dominating the field of social theory. Different attempts to build interdisciplinary bridges among the human sciences have pulled in different directions, reproducing the polar division in the social sciences between studies of "interests" and "meanings." On the one hand, the development (particularly by James S. Coleman since the 1970s) of a "rational choice" theory of society attempts to understand social processes as general outcomes of rational action by individuals to maximize utility. At the other pole is the contemporaneous elaboration of culturalism, best known in the emblematic work of Clifford Geertz. Geertz argued that the task of social science must be one of understanding and interpretation—examining the ways of thinking, perceiving, valuing, and symbolizing that construct worlds of meaning for human actors—rather than explanation, that is, discovering causal relations among human actions. Contrary to "rational choice" theory, culturalism would draw the behavioral sciences (sociology, anthropology, and psychology) not toward the "old social sciences" of economics and politics but toward an alignment with the humanities.

Either association, with economy or with culture, potentially provides new understandings of society, but difficulties arise when the competing partners each strive for an exclusive, dominant position. In the extreme, the attempt by rational choice theory to bring together economics and sociology has led to "economic imperialism," or the claim that economic methods (market models) explain any social phenomenon adequately. At the other extreme, the culturalist bias has encouraged the adoption of critical methods (more or less loosely termed "postmodern") which would treat social relations as *textual* relations full of unresolvable ambiguity. While these two "imperialistic" currents of rational choice theory and postmodernism appear to be diametrically opposed to each other, they share a deep suspicion of the "social" category. Rational choice theory returns to the methodological individualism of orthodox economic theory, turning the tables on the long historical polemic that thinking about society had waged against economic premises. "Society" again appears as the field of unintended consequences or aggregated results of individual actions—these latter being considered primary and most real. And in the hands of postmodern theorists extending the principles of textual deconstruction to social analysis, the notion of an order of things in social relations likewise becomes suspect, the very idea of "society" suggesting an unwarranted imposition of coherent meaning on a dispersed field of practices and symbolic acts.

The rise of imperialistic theories eroding the concept of "society" itself and its centrality in the general theory of the human sciences reflects the long duration of the theoretical "crisis" begun around 1970. A single dominating theory of society—really a broad consensus on a "behavioral" definition of society—fell from its reigning stature, and no other dominant "paradigm" has emerged to replace it. It is possible the long-term suspension of paradigmatic unity in the social sciences indicates a change in the character of general intellectual life, an expansion and diversification of professional scholarship and formal reflection which defies organization under a common rubric. More concretely, however, the loss of theoretical coherence is a consequence of the rapid decline of the radical academic and extra-academic movements that first undermined the liberal consensus. Rather than leading to a reinvigoration of the Left as a major force in American politics and social life, capable of refashioning prevalent ways of thinking about society, the radical upsurge of the late 1960s and early 1970s quickly gave way, as the political Right surged to promote promarket and "traditional" values. The absence of vital social and political forces outside the academy committed to "society" as such (by promoting social services and communal belong-

ing) has hobbled the pursuit of holistic social theory. Liberal and radical intellectuals inside the academy have been unable to recover the kind of confidence the postwar generation possessed, which rested on a widespread conviction that the aims and methods of social science were functionally bound up with the given course of social progress. In the absence of such institutional confidence in the role and meaning of social science, it has been impossible to restore consensual principles for pursuing knowledge.

The history of rational choice theory in the United States can be dated to the early work of Gary S. Becker, a University of Chicago economist who published *The Economics of Discrimination* (1957), *Human Capital* (1964), and *The Economic Approach to Human Behavior* (1976). Becker's project was to apply principles of economics—the assumed propensity of individuals to rationally maximize utility—to a wide range of issues and problems in behavior and social policy. Even the sleeping habits of Americans could be examined and explained as the outcome of rational choices made by individuals about the utility of sleep in their own overall "economy" of behavior, according to researchers at Michigan State University in 1989. Another early influence on rational choice theory in sociology was George Homans, a Harvard sociologist who had begun his career studying the Italian economist Vilfredo Pareto, and who showed an early interest in historical sociology as well as small-group studies, and in the 1950s and 1960s advocated an "exchange theory" of social action based on methodological individualism and behaviorism. The rational choice model gained more adherents in the 1980s, in part due to the turn of prevailing social policy toward an emphasis on markets as arbiters of resource use. It has reached its pinnacle in the publication by James S. Coleman of *Foundations of Social Theory* (1990), a massive work often compared in its scope and aspirations to Talcott Parsons's *Structure of Social Action*.

In the 1950s, Coleman had been a student of Robert Merton and a contributor, with Seymour Martin Lipset and James Trow, to *Union Democracy,* one of the landmark studies of organized labor as an institution. In the 1960s, he was a prominent figure in the Great Society–era application of social science to public policy, author of the famous 1966 report bearing his name which claimed racial integration of schools had a positive effect on the educational achievement of black schoolchildren. Even then, Coleman was interested in importing economic methods to sociological research, and he began systematically in the 1970s to rebuild sociological theory on the basis of a rational choice paradigm, while working close by Gary Becker at the University of Chicago. The project was immensely ambitious, for Coleman made it clear he intended not to reduce social research to an explanation of individual choices, but rather to move from the level of purposive actions by rational individuals to explain the nature of collective processes themselves. Thus there are, for Coleman, truly social phenomena such as trust and authority, which involve decisions by individuals to confer resources, or surrender their autonomy, to the guidance of others. These phenomena, Coleman argued, should be understood as the general result of choices made by individuals who perceived an advantage to themselves in such arrangements. Beyond such elementary collective phenomena as trust and authority, Coleman recognized there are such things as "norms" and "social structure," which likewise appear to be "problem-solving inventions" demonstrably useful to the persons who accept them.

Coleman was motivated by a sharp revulsion against the more reified notions of "systems" that some critics saw in Parsons's functionalism. Against the idea that "persons behave in accordance with social norms" and thus are "bearers" of a social "system" whose formal, functional needs govern institutional change over time, Coleman resorted to a model of purposive individualism in order, he wrote, to comprehend and preserve capacities for personal choice, moral criticism, and willful action shaping the future. Like a host of more historically minded writers, Coleman emphasized "agency" in social process. Given his adoption of economic models of behavior, however, he eschewed most of the preoccupations of the other social sciences, especially those that had played a key part in the postwar paradigm—psychology (and the notion of some "interior" regions of the personality that had to be investigated to understand action), anthropology (and the significance of overarching "values" or cultural patterns in defining motivation and behavior), and much of "role theory" in sociology. At the same time, Coleman's theory manifested a benign portrait of social life, a disinclination to recognize the uses and efficacy of coercive power in human history, and significant difficulties in explaining large-scale historical changes in the structure of social orders. Thus, despite his attempt to rescue voluntarism from the sway of Parsonsian functionalism, Coleman's theory was saddled with some of the very same weaknesses ascribed to his predecessor.

There was also considerable irony in Coleman's diagnosis of modern society and the remedies he proposed for it. The social structure that had emerged as a set of "problem-solving inventions" serving the interests of self-seeking individuals consisted by now of large-scale organizations (corporations and government) with fictive identities (as legal persons) and concentrated capacities for decision and action dwarfing those of concrete individuals. At the same time, the traditional substance of personal life (what Coleman called "primordial" social organization in family, clan, ethnic group, neighborhood) was eroded, almost wholly robbed of function. Consequently, modern society faces the loss of those social resources (in family, neighborhood, and ethnic community) by which people protected themselves from those results of self-interested behavior which were unanticipated and undesirable. The only solution Coleman had to offer, however, was the introduction of further utility-maximizing incentives to guide individual behavior in ways he regarded as socially reproductive. Thus he suggested that parental solicitude and provision for the young and their education could be assured by passing laws requiring that a portion of adult children's earnings be returned to their parents. Not only did such solutions require a kind of benevolent dictatorship of policymakers at odds with the voluntarism of Coleman's methodological assumptions, but they also reasserted the kind of behavior (rational egoism) which was itself, he believed, responsible for eroding social infrastructure.

At the other pole of social theory was the further development of culturalism in social science. Here the idea of "interests" in human action gave way almost wholly to the priority of "meaning," and the idea of "explaining" social affairs in cause-and-effect terms surrendered to the insistence on "interpretation" as the true province of the human sciences. Humans were, no doubt, purposive beings, but their action was better appreciated as symbolic rather than instrumental, oriented toward the significance rather than the utility of the world. As French anthropologist Claude Lévi-Strauss put it, humans typically regarded the things of the world as "good to think" rather than "good to eat." Lévi-Strauss's "structural anthropology," which sought to discover a universal logic governing the "transformations" of basic myths into their manifold variants, represented a French analog to the postwar behavioral current in the United States: its emphasis on the collective properties of mind perpetuated a polemic against the methodological individualism and voluntarism of economics, while reducing social existence largely to its psychocultural dimension. It assumed, furthermore, systematic coherence in the social organization of human life. Nevertheless, Lévi-Strauss entered U.S. social discourse more or less as a part of French semiotics and cultural criticism, a wave of influence growing in the late 1960s and 1970s and persisting beyond the onset of the crisis in social science.

The dominant American figure in the culturalist trend of the 1970s and 1980s was likewise a veteran of the postwar academy, a student of Talcott Parsons, and advocate of "Weberian" approaches in anthropology. Clifford Geertz's influence grew widely among the human sciences in the mid 1970s, following publication of his collection of essays, *The Interpretation of Cultures,* in 1973. In the keynote essay of that collection, "Thick Description: Toward an Interpretive Theory of Culture," Geertz made clear that he departed from a concept of culture as a whole "way of life" including instrumental as well as ceremonial beliefs and practices. Rather, his was a determinedly "semiotic" concept of culture, based on the assumption that "Man is an animal suspended in webs of significance he himself has spun." Geertz's meticulous reconstruction of ritual and symbol in such widely read essays as his "Balinese Cock Fight" impressed readers for the extraordinary empirical rigor and particular detail that Geertz wove into ethnography. Such arduous exercises at reconstruction were driven by some idea of holism in culture— that "thick description" of particular practices yielded something of the "logic and singularity" of a culture. In later essays, Geertz tended more to emphasize the difficulty of reaching a whole view, precisely because the multiplicity of meanings in a particular practice implied that "significance [spread] out profusely in an embarrassment of directions." Increasingly, as Steven Weiland shows in *Intellectual Craftsmen,* Geertz adopted the mode of contemporary literary theory and treated the various artifacts of culture (including "rituals, palaces, technologies and social formation") as "texts to be read," though he did not accept wholly the skepticism of contemporary literary theory and insisted that good ethnography told readers something "about" another culture.

In the context of "blurred genres"—Geertz's term for the trend drawing social science toward the humanities—contemporary currents of literary criticism, particularly deconstruction, began to have an impact on social theory. In its approach to "texts," deconstruction denied the possibility of interpretation in the sense of locating a definite meaning at the heart of writing. Language is "opaque" rather than "transparent," referring not to some anterior reality outside it but carrying in itself a load of meanings, suggested in profuse allusions to and contrasts

with other signifiers. Texts were thus by nature dispersive rather than coherence-making things. In anthropology, such conclusions led to a new degree of skepticism about ethnography, and culturalist currents after Geertz have very largely eschewed empiricist claims of cultural description. They insist instead on examining the "dialogic" and "reflexive" relations between the cultural observer and the observed, for these were allegedly all that ethnography really disclosed.

The influence of such "postmodern" ways of thinking about the social sciences and their objects went further in the 1980s to touch on the notion of "society" itself. Self-consciously "postmodern" views promoted deep hostility toward theories which presumed to describe entities as having definable coherence, core meanings, or central mechanisms. Thus postmodernism would challenge the understanding of "society" as something whole and bounded. The presumption of order in describing or analyzing a "society" as such appeared to be a suspect imposition of meaning. Emphasizing the "indeterminate" or profusely varied character of human action or aggregate phenomena, postmodern approaches to social science would be reluctant to claim functional linkages or a hierarchy of determining factors "underlying" action and its consequences. Not infrequently, however, implicit generalizations about social structure—such as claims about the universal sway of "commodification" in contemporary life—crept back into postmodern accounts.

In some cases, postmodernists such as Jean Baudrillard offer an empirical argument about social development to justify the preeminence of cultural analysis, viz., that a universal commodification of life marked by the bombardment of "consumers" with messages, status symbols, claims, counterclaims, and an endless regress of allusions to other signs of consumption, tended toward the "triumph of signifying culture" and thus "the end of the social" as such. "Society," furthermore, suggested to Baudrillard an order of excessive constraint, and he applauded forms of resistance—"resistance to work . . . resistance to medicine, resistance to schooling, resistance to security, resistance to information . . . resistance to the social in all its forms." In a similar move, Jean-François Lyotard, the French theorist of "the postmodern condition," promoted the undisciplined, "wild" impulses of experimental method as a hedge against the concentrated power of those institutions that accumulated and utilized knowledge in the new "post industrial" society. In the pursuit of such a new, unbounded style of discourse, Lyotard foresaw the "atomization of the social into flexible networks of language games."

The late-twentieth-century flight from the social takes its most extreme form in the guise of sociobiology. If rational choice theory virtually overturns the long-running attempt in the twentieth century to build a theory of society independent of economic models, this development tends to work against the other dynamic of differentiation in the twentieth-century concept of society, the movement beyond biology. The imposing development of sociobiology in the last twenty years aims to uncover the instinctive or genetic bases of behavior and thus provide naturalistic causes for the forms of social action and order.

With the resurgence of rational choice theory and the contrary drift to determinedly culturalist readings of social affairs, there remains a sharp split between different camps of social theory. Here there are still dichotomous notions of individualism and collectivism, of interests and meanings, which continue to frustrate attempts to build a genuinely holistic concept of society which would recognize the centrality of political economy while also offering access in a nonreductive manner to matters of personality and culture (including gender and race). Furthermore, the general disenchantment with "the social" marked by methodological individualism, postmodern criticism, and sociobiology raises the question of whether social theory will go "beyond 'society.'" In fact, there are, besides these trends, still other, possibly more convincing reasons to question the foundational implications of the concept, "society." The anthropologist Eric Wolf has argued that the concept of "society" implied a "state of internal cohesion or boundedness in relation to the external world" that ideologically served to uphold the authority of particular national elites and helped prevent understanding of the dynamic complexity of relationships among different peoples on a world scale—particularly the phenomena of colonialism and imperialism which shaped both conquered and conqueror in modern times. The sociologist Michael Mann has asserted also that " 'societies' themselves are neither unitary nor bounded totalities but heterogeneous, overlapping networks of social interaction, without fixed edges." World-historical perspectives thus demand a dramatic reconsideration of the concept of society, but they also entail retaining some notion of "structure," or the enduring patterns of relations between and among individuals and groups, patterns which channel and constrain actions. A holistic theory of social relations founded on world-historical understanding would entail both attention to subjective aspects of human action (in phenomena of personality and culture), which dominated the behavioral sciences after World War II, and recognition of the force plied in human affairs by differential interests and powers. If such an approach were possible, history would join the theory of the constitution of social relations and help to reveal the rough edges and interdependencies, the rigidity and the openness, the ways that social groups large and small interpenetrate and engender movement and friction in unfixed, but not indecipherable or wholly unpredictable, courses of change.

SEE ALSO Ethnicity and Immigration; Gender Issues; Class; Family (all in volume I).

BIBLIOGRAPHY

There are many general studies of Western social thought. Tom Bottomore and Robert Nisbet, eds., *A History of Sociological Analysis* (1978), is a useful compendium of authoritative essays by sociologists on various theoretical schools and empirical fields in the discipline. Two studies treating early developments in the concept of society, by a philosopher of science and a sociologist respectively, are Peter T. Manicas, *A History and Philosophy of the Social Sciences* (1987); and Göran Therborn, *Science, Class, and Society: On the Formation of Sociology and Historical Materialism* (1976).

Historians have brought various perspectives to understanding the evolution of the concept of society. Anthony Pagden, *The Fall of Natural Man: The American Indian and the Origins of Comparative Ethnology* (1982), examines sixteenth-century Spanish debates regarding indigenous peoples of the Western hemisphere which spawned a rudimentary kind of cultural relativism. Focusing on a later period, around the turn of the nineteenth century, Wolf Lepenies, *Between Literature and Science: The Rise of Sociology* (1988), situates the origin of modern social sciences in the contest of liberal revolution and conservative reaction. Adam Kuper, *The Invention of Primitive Society* (1988), elucidates ideas about "primitive society" that emerged in the 1860s and 1870s (and lost credibility after the 1960s). A provocative collection of recent historical essays examining the intellectual assumptions, institutional contexts, and social applications of the social sciences is JoAnne Brown and David K. van Keuren, eds., *The Estate of Social Knowledge* (1991).

The best general history of social thought in the United States is Dorothy Ross, *The Origins of American Social Science* (1991), a bold, wide-ranging study examining the development of political science, economics, and sociology in the United States to 1929. James Kloppenberg, *Uncertain Victory: Social Democracy and Progressivism in European and American Thought, 1870–1920* (1986), a massive study of about a dozen key writers who promoted experimental ethics, self-critical but not skeptical epistemology, and radical social reform, provides a thorough and cogent account of the general intellectual scene at the time of the origins of modern social theory in the United States. An older, still instructive account is Morton White, *Social Thought in America: The Revolt against Formalism* (1949). Among the studies concerning racialist thought (which can be regarded as a backdrop to social thought in the United States), Thomas F. Gossett, *Race: The History of an Idea in America* (1963), offers a general survey; and George Frederickson, *The Black Image in the White Mind: The Debate on Afro-American Character and Destiny, 1817–1914* (1971), analyzes the crescendo of white racist attitudes toward African Americans. Du Bois's role in early American social science can be traced in David Levering Lewis, *W. E. B. Du Bois: Biography of a Race, 1868–1919* (1993). Manning Marable, *W. E. B. Du Bois: Black Radical Democrat* (1986), serves as a concise introduction to Du Bois's intellectual and political career.

The significance of gender in the organization and practice of American social science has become a growing concern among intellectual historians. Ellen Fitzpatrick, *Endless Crusade: Women Social Scientists and Progressive Reform* (1990), is an expert and readable account of efforts by four early women graduates of the University of Chicago to combine social research, social welfare, and social reform. Early-twentieth-century research by women scholars on the cross-cultural variability of gender roles is the concern of Rosalind Rosenberg, *Beyond Separate Spheres: Intellectual Roots of Modern Feminism* (1982), which ends with a portrait of Margaret Mead's work in the 1920s. Mary Jo Deegan, *Jane Addams and the Men of the Chicago School, 1892–1918* (1988), is an innovative, if somewhat tendentious, account of how Jane Ad-

dams's thinking and activism helped shape the pragmatic philosophy and sociological research that developed at the University of Chicago. Deegan has also edited a useful reference tool, *Women in Sociology: A Bio-Bibliographical Sourcebook* (1991), featuring short biographies of fifty-two women active in the development of sociology, mostly in the United States during the twentieth century.

Studies of particular figures or "schools" in early-to mid-twentieth-century American sociology and anthropology include George W. Stocking, Jr., *Race, Culture and Evolution: Essays in the History of Anthropology* (1968), a collection of pathbreaking essays including studies of Franz Boas and his contribution to the modern, pluralistic concept of culture; Fred Matthews, *Quest for an American Sociology* (1977), an interpretive biography of Robert Park and his urban research program at the University of Chicago; Eli Zaretsky's superb historical and interpretive essay introducing an abridged version of William I. Thomas and Florian Znaniecki, *The Polish Peasant in Europe and America* (1984); and Robert C. Bannister, *Sociology and Scientism: The American Quest for Objectivity, 1880–1940* (1987), which examines objectivist sociologists between the wars who derided the role of consciousness in society.

Historical studies of mid-century developments in American social theory are only beginning to appear in significant numbers. One of the most accomplished is Walter Jackson, *Gunnar Myrdal and America's Conscience* (1990), a magisterial account of Myrdal's long career and the social, political, and intellectual conditions under which *An American Dilemma* was written. Steven Weiland, *Intellectual Craftsmen: Ways and Works in American Scholarship, 1935–1990* (1991), includes a half-dozen informative essays on key figures in American social science after World War II. Works by sociologists examining major figures in their discipline include Jeffrey C. Alexander's *Theoretical Logic in Sociology*, vol. 4, *The Modern Reconstruction of Classical Thought: Talcott Parsons* (1983), an extremely lucid review, defense, and critique of Parsons's social theory over the whole span of Parsons's career; and Charles Crothers, *Robert K. Merton* (1987), a concise argument that Merton established a "school" of functional theory with its own distinctive propositions and methods. Anthony M. Platt, *E. Franklin Frazier Reconsidered* (1991), emphasizes the persistent radicalism of this African American sociologist.

More recent trends have been examined in a wide range of current literature. Several volumes published as "antitextbooks" around 1970 examined the "crisis" occurring at that time in different social science disciplines, such as Dell Hymes, ed., *Reinventing Anthropology* (1972); Philip Green and Sanford Levinson, eds., *Power and Community: Dissenting Essays in Political Science* (1970); and Barton Bernstein, ed., *Towards a New Past: Dissenting Essays in American History* (1968). Michelle Rosaldo and Louise Lamphere, eds., *Women, Culture, and Society* (1974), is an early set of essays by women anthropologists on the causes and character of women's subordination to men in various human societies. Ellen DuBois et al., *Feminist Scholarship: Kindling in the Groves of Academe* (1985), coauthored by five women in different fields, emphasizes the profoundly multidisciplinary character of contemporary feminist scholarship. Bertell Ollman and Edward Vernoff, eds., *The Left Academy,* vol. 1 (1982), explored the currents of Marxist scholarship in the social sciences that had emerged since the 1960s. An example of neo-Weberian work in the United States is Randall Collins, *Weberian Sociological Theory* (1986). Stemming from both Marxian and Weberian sources, an enduring strain of historicism has emerged, discussed in Dennis Smith, *The Rise of Historical Sociology* (1991).

Carl Degler, *In Search of Human Nature: The Decline and Revival of Darwinism in American Social Thought* (1991), surveys the triumph of the culture concept over biological notions of race and sex in early-twentieth-century social sciences and the renewed rise of sociobiology since the 1960s. Discussions among social scientists about the rise of rational choice theories figure prominently in Richard Swedberg, *Economics and Sociology: Redefining the Boundaries* (1990). In *Post-Modernism and the Social Sciences: Insights, Inroads, and Intrusions* (1992), Pauline Marie Rosenau reviews different types of postmodern argument in contemporary social science.

MEDICAL SCIENCE AND TECHNOLOGY

Susan E. Lederer

Over the course of the twentieth century, advances in the medical sciences have transformed the theory and practice of medicine. In the first half of the twentieth century, laboratory research and clinical experimentation produced unprecedented therapeutic benefits, including insulin therapy for the treatment of diabetes, the discovery of hormones and vitamins, and, above all, the introduction of penicillin and other antibiotics. After World War II, new medical technologies—such as radiation therapy, respirators, and kidney dialysis—and an impressive array of powerful drugs revolutionized the delivery of medical services and the experience of and expectations about health and disease in the United States.

What is medical science? In the twentieth century, the term encompasses both the basic medical sciences (anatomy, biochemistry, microbiology, pathology, pharmacology, and physiology) and the clinical sciences. In the last quarter of the nineteenth century, medical science emerged as an important vehicle for the transformation of the American medical profession, as a small number of academic medical scientists sought to recast medicine as an experimental science.

Some physicians resisted the replacement of the family physician by a scientist at the bedside. "When you enter my wards," the medical educator Samuel Gee informed his students in 1888, "your first duty is to forget all your physiology. Physiology is an experimental science—and a very good thing in its proper place. Medicine is not a science, but an empirical art." By the first decade of the twentieth century, however, Gee's position was no longer tenable.

Even before medical science delivered on its promise to enhance medical practice, D. W. Cathell, author of an enormously popular guide to success in medical practice, advised physicians that working with the microscope would not only bring fees and lead to valuable information but would also give "popularity and professional respect, by investing you, in the eyes of the public, with the benefits of a scientific reputation." By the 1920s, physicians had more than a scientific reputation; they could point to such dramatic therapeutic advances as diphtheria antitoxin and insulin, products that resulted from research conducted in the laboratory and at the bedside. In the 1930s and 1940s the development of sulfa drugs and antibiotics dramatically enhanced the therapeutic capabilities of the physician and made possible the tremendous strides in the medical sciences in the decades after the Second World War.

By mid-century, medical scientists had made impressive discoveries in the field of cancer research. In addition to laboratory work into viruses and other carcinogens, American researchers developed considerable expertise with radiotherapy and chemotherapies for cancer. After the first two atomic bombs were dropped in 1945, radioactive isotopes, such as iodine, phosphorous, and cobalt, were harnessed in the war on cancer. As the American Medical Association's lay magazine, *Hygeia,* noted in 1947, "medically applied atomic science has already saved more lives than were lost in the explosions at Hiroshima and Nagasaki." Another legacy of the war was the application of toxic chemicals to the treatment of cancer. In the years 1946 to 1950, scientists at Sloan-Kettering Institute in New York tested over 1,500 types of nitrogen mustard gas and other agents for their chemotherapeutic potential. Although such research did not produce a "magic bullet" to cure all cancers, researchers in the 1950s and 1960s discovered an array of chemicals to treat cancers, including drugs effective against such systemic conditions as leukemia or Hodgkin's disease that had been untreatable by surgery or radiation. By the 1980s, experts estimated that cancer drugs saved nearly 3,000 patients under the age of thirty every year.

PRIVATE AND FEDERAL FUNDING OF MEDICAL RESEARCH TO WORLD WAR II

Changes in the organization and funding of medical research are critical to understanding the development of medical science in the twentieth century. Before World War II, medical scientists received little support from the federal government for research in human health and disease. Ironically, more federal money was available for the study of animal disease than human disease. As the historian Richard H. Shryock noted, most Americans did not favor investment in medical research, "partly because human welfare brought no direct financial return. Hogs did." In the late nineteenth century, the Hatch Act, passed by Congress in 1887, guaranteed each state $15,000 to establish an agricultural experiment station (the appropriation was increased to $30,000 in 1906 with the stipulation that money be applied for original research). Although initially established to aid farmers, experiment stations became an important locus for research on human biology and nutrition. Cattle feeding experiments at the Wisconsin experiment station, for example, helped clarify the role of trace elements in foods. The discovery of vitamins benefited dairy farmers; it also enabled physicians to understand dietary deficiency diseases in human beings. Studies in animal husbandry, sponsored by the Bureau of Animal Industry, illuminated the role of insect vectors in the spread of such animal diseases as Texas cattle fever, and facilitated the understanding of insect vectors in human disease.

The federal government, in addition to limited support for research at agricultural experiment stations, sponsored scientific investigations in the armed services and in the U.S. Public Health Service. Military physicians studied a number of problems related to military medical needs. In 1900, for example, Surgeon General George Miller Sternberg appointed a commission of military medical officers to study the disease problem in Havana, Cuba. Headed by Walter Reed, the Yellow Fever Board established the Aedes mosquito as the vector of yellow fever. Efforts to control the mosquito population not only contributed to the safety of American troops in Havana, but made possible American-sponsored building of the Panama Canal (opened in 1914). In addition to yellow fever research, army physicians studied such tropical diseases as leprosy that affected populations in the newly acquired Hawaiian Islands and in the Philippines. Although leprosy afflicted few Americans in the continental United States (only 278 recorded cases according to a 1901 survey), the prevalence of the disease in the Philippines encouraged General Leonard Wood to establish a research center and leprosy colony in the 1920s. During World War I, American military researchers studied the problems associated with chemical warfare, as well as surgical

shock and blood transfusion. Amid the influenza pandemic of 1918–1919 (which caused the deaths of more than half a million Americans and an estimated 20 million people worldwide), military researchers joined civilian investigators in the search for the cause of the disease and a means to control its harmful effects.

The development of new technologies encouraged military physicians to undertake studies of the physiological limits of human beings. The introduction of powered aircraft and the rapid development of airplanes after World War I made the investigation of the physical demands on aviators a vital interest of the military. In addition to screening potential flyers, military physicians investigated the effect of higher altitudes and speeds on the human body, and worked with engineers to find the means to enable humans to transcend these apparent limitations. Most research was undertaken to resolve practical questions related to military effectiveness rather than to extend medical knowledge.

Practical solutions were also sought by scientists at federally sponsored medical laboratories. In the first part of the twentieth century, disease outbreaks continued to disrupt the lives of many Americans. In response to various epidemics, Congress authorized small appropriations for original medical research to investigate the causes of disease. In 1901, the Hygienic Laboratory of the Marine Hospital Service (reorganized as the U.S. Public Health Service in 1912) received a federal appropriation of $35,000 to establish a laboratory for original research in infectious diseases and conditions relating to the public health. Public Health Service investigators conducted research on such infectious diseases as typhus, Rocky Mountain spotted fever, yellow fever, and plague. In 1913, federal funds allowed the PHS to establish a hospital for pellagra research in South Carolina. One of the first tasks of the newly appointed PHS investigator Joseph Goldberger was to investigate whether the disease, which raged in southern states, was contagious as many believed. Through investigations at southern orphanages, prisons, and mental hospitals, Goldberger established that pellagra resulted from poor diets rather than microorganisms.

Another southern health problem prompted a different approach on the part of Charles Wardell Stiles, the first director of the Division of Zoology at the Hygienic Laboratory of the Marine Hospital Service. In 1902 Stiles studied hookworm infestation in the American South. When he realized the extent of parasitic infestation, responsible for a staggering degree of morbidity among poor whites, Stiles developed strategies to alter the conditions under which the parasite flourished. Although the subject of disposing of human excrement earned him derision (Harvey Wiley dubbed him the Privy Counselor), Stiles worked tirelessly to improve rural sanitary conditions. Unable to obtain the necessary funding from the federal government, Stiles enlisted the financial support of John D. Rockefeller, whose wealth from the oil and gas industry was already being used to fund medical research. Amid widespread suspicion of Rockefeller's motives for underwriting such a campaign, the Rockefeller Sanitary Commission, working with the health departments of thirteen southern states, spent over a million dollars to eradicate hookworm disease in the South.

Rockefeller's role in funding the campaign against hookworm illustrates the significant role that private individuals played in the funding of medical research in the first half of the twentieth century. The scarcity of funds for research in medical schools and universities encouraged physicians, scientists, and administrators to solicit funds from wealthy patrons, who provided large sums of money. Why did wealthy men and women endow medical research and education? Although some historians have argued that philanthropic contributions to medical research represented attempts to legitimize the fundamental social structure of capitalist society and to provide for its technical needs, the historian Kenneth Ludmerer has more accurately characterized philanthropists' motives as a mixture of genuine altruism, pragmatism, and a self-serving desire to escape the taint associated with "robber barony." For their part, wealthy benefactors preferred to identify their gifts as philanthropy rather than charity. Persuaded that medical science showed increasing promise, they were willing to invest large sums in medical research and education.

John D. Rockefeller was perhaps the most ambitious benefactor. Approached by Harvard Medical School in 1901, Rockefeller contributed $1 million to the school's capital campaign and then embarked on building his own medical research establishment. Prompted by his adviser Frederick T. Gates, the oil magnate provided $20,000 in 1901 for grants to medical researchers. In 1902 he donated a million dollars for the establishment of the Rockefeller Institute for Medical Research. By 1920 Rockefeller had increased his donations to $23 million and by 1928 his gifts to the institution totaled more than $65 million. Like Rockefeller, steelmaker Andrew Carnegie donated large sums of money for research and education in the first part of the twentieth century. In 1885 an appeal from his personal physician led Carnegie to donate $50,000 to build a research laboratory at the Bellevue Hospital Medical College. In 1902 he donated $10 million to establish the Carnegie Institution of Washington, where investigators pursued research in the physical sciences, embryology, and nutrition.

The foundations established by Rockefeller and Carnegie aided the reforms in American medical schools in the first three decades of the twentieth century. The Carnegie Foundation funded Abraham Flexner's survey of American medical education. Although the shocking descriptions of the low standards and inadequate facilities of most medical schools in the Flexner Report (1910) persuaded Carnegie not to give additional money to medical education, the General Education Board (established by Rockefeller in 1902) made substantial contributions to the medical schools deemed worth saving. By 1930 the Board had donated $82 million to selected medical schools across the nation.

Grants from these foundations enabled some medical schools to support full-time faculty and to invest in laboratory equipment and facilities for research. Despite the largesse of benefactors like Rockefeller, funds for medical research at academic institutions remained meager before World War II. Academic researchers received small grants from such organizations as the Commonwealth Fund, the Milbank Memorial Fund, and the Rosenwald and Josiah Macy, Jr. Foundations. As part of its effort to improve medical science, the American Medical Association instituted a research grant program in 1903, which provided small grants to investigators. By the 1920s, the rise of voluntary health societies provided some additional funds for research. Perhaps equally important, these groups began to lobby congressional leaders for greater federal support for medical research. The National Association for the Study and Prevention of Tuberculosis, founded in 1904, raised funds for public education and to establish tuberculosis clinics. Beginning in 1921, the organization (which became the National Tuberculosis Association in 1918) offered investigators funding for medical research in tuberculosis and lung disease.

The other significant source of funding for medical research in the first half of the twentieth century was the pharmaceutical industry. Although drug companies had little interest in funding medical science before the twentieth century, by 1945 pharmaceutical companies spent an estimated $40 million in research. The reform of American medical education in the early twentieth century had furnished an institutional base for basic scientists within medical school departments. Researchers in newly established departments of pharmacology, biochemistry, and physiology taught medical students, and pursued research in their disciplines. In the 1920s and 1930s some academic scientists developed mutually beneficial relationships with drug companies, in which university workers received economic and intellectual support for their research. Advances in the medical sciences and the realization that research could lead to profitable new drugs encouraged collaboration between drug companies and academic scientists. In addition to providing stipends to fund scientists in university departments, several leading pharmaceutical companies in the 1930s established special research units where basic research and clinical trials were conducted. In the interwar years, these joint ventures produced a variety of significant therapies, including anesthetics, hormones, sedatives, and anticonvulsants.

PHARMACEUTICAL RESEARCH

One of the issues that confronted medical researchers and pharmaceutical companies was the decision to patent a medical discovery. Before the 1920s few academic researchers patented their discoveries. Distrust of patents harked back to nineteenth-century fears of secret remedies and medical exploitation. The monopoly of a medical discovery in relationship to the public health made patenting more problematic for physicians than chemists or engineers. In 1891, when the bacteriologist Robert Koch initially withheld the formula for his alleged cure for tuberculosis, American physicians were openly critical of his ethical lapse. (Hopes that tuberculin would cure the disease soon evaporated, but the extract became a useful diagnostic test.) By the 1920s, researchers had become interested in patenting as a means of controlling their discovery in the public realm. Holding a patent became especially useful as a means of quality control and as a method of generating additional revenue to fund medical research.

Concerns that the newly discovered insulin would be released on the market without adequate safety testing and quality control helped researchers at the University of Toronto to overcome their scruples against patenting the hormone in 1922. Although patenting resolved some problems, it certainly created others. Commercial arrangements between the Eli Lilly Company and the University of Toronto proved problematic when researchers became concerned that the Americans were attempting to usurp their patent rights. The importance of insulin as a treatment for a life-threatening disease made the Canadian researchers, F. G. Banting, Charles H. Best, and J. J. R. McLeod, reluctant to give the pharmaceutical company sole American rights. The Lilly Company ultimately accepted the conditions but only after extracting a series of economically advantageous concessions. The patent struggles could not detract from the spectacular clinical success of insulin. Immediately hailed as a miracle cure, the drug literally brought people back from the edge of death, and represented a dramatic return on public investment in medical science.

The success of medical research was further enhanced by the discovery of another extract to treat a life-threatening disease, pernicious anemia. Following the successful collaboration between Lilly and the University of Toronto, the Lilly Company entered into a series of less formal arrangements with researchers at Harvard University and the University of Rochester to produce and market liver extracts. In the 1920s, the discovery that liver was an effective food to restore anemic dogs to their normal states gave clinicians hope for the treatment of pernicious anemia. In early clinical trials, sick patients consumed a daily half-pound ration of lightly-cooked (or preferably raw) liver and experienced dramatic improvements. With financial support from the Lilly company, scientists searched for the active agent in liver to produce a more efficient (and more palatable) product for widespread distribution and sale. From the 1920s to the 1950s, funds from the Lilly Company supported a broad program of research at the University of Rochester, as well as scholarship programs for medical students. Harvard University scientists also received large grants that supported basic research into blood disorders as a compensation for their contribution to the development of liver extract. Although liver extract was not essential to the treatment of the disease in the way that diabetics required insulin (anemia patients could continue on the raw liver diet), the extract was an important addition to the therapeutic arsenal of physicians.

The lucrative nature of medical patents made them increasingly attractive to medical researchers, if not to research institutions. The University of Wisconsin, for example, did not anticipate problems when they developed a patent agreement for the vitamin researcher Harry Steenbock. In 1924, Steenbock discovered that the sun's ultraviolet rays produced vitamin D, which played an important role in preventing rickets. The Quaker Oats Company immediately offered Steenbock a million dollars for patent rights to his discovery. After consultations with university officials, Steenbock instead assigned patent rights to the newly founded Wisconsin Alumni Research Foundation. By 1931, WARF had received nearly $400,000 from the patent, and in turn reinvested the money in research projects at Wisconsin. In the 1930s, a growing number of public health professionals criticized the patent arrangement on the grounds that it had increased the cost of irradiated milk. Amid the poverty of the Great Depression, the argument that parents could not provide milk for their children was especially compelling. Attempts to defend infringements on the Steenbock process and other patents held by WARF damaged the foundation's public image.

Collaborations between industry and academic scientists declined in the 1950s and 1960s. With the advent of recombinant DNA techniques in the 1980s and the development of the biotechnology industry, these ventures have once again become significant. At the same time, concerns about the scientific consequences of and the moral questions raised by patenting genetic information have resurfaced.

The American entry into World War II brought important changes in the funding of medical research. In 1941 President Franklin D. Roosevelt signed the executive order that established the Office of Scientific Research and Development (OSRD) to coordinate the nation's medical response to the war. Headed by Vannevar Bush, the OSRD consisted of two parallel branches, the Committee for Medical Research (CMR) and the National Defense Research Committee. Charged with "mobilizing the medical and scientific personnel of the nation," the CMR, under the direction of the pharmacologist A. Newton Richards, administered 450 contracts to universities and 150 to research institutes, hospitals, and other organizations. Between 1941 and 1947, the CMR granted $25 million for research in medicine, surgery, aviation medicine, physiology, chemistry, and malaria.

The investments in medical research produced impressive results. The development of penicillin, cortisone, gamma globulin, blood substitutes, and other drugs and techniques impressed both Congress and the American public. National expenditures for medical research rapidly expanded in the years after World War II. When the CMR was disbanded in 1945, the National Institutes of Health administered the remaining wartime contracts. Created in 1930, the National Institute of Health had superseded the Hygienic Laboratory of the Public Health Service. With the addition of the National Cancer Institute in 1937, the NIH, which focused on chronic diseases

like heart disease, began to award grants to outside researchers. Although federal appropriations steadily increased between 1931 and 1945, the available research funds remained limited. At the end of World War II, new institutes (National Institute for Mental Health, 1946; National Heart Institute and National Dental Institute, 1948) expanded the Public Health Service's administration of medical research and the growing importance of the National Institutes of Health (the name became plural in 1948). By 1951 the seven institutes—microbiology, arthritis and metabolic diseases, and neurological diseases and blindness had joined the list—operated with an annual budget of $60 million and awarded research grants in excess of $16 million. Appropriations for biomedical research grew substantially in the 1950s and 1960s. By 1952, the federal $73 million investment in medical research outstripped funding from industry ($60 million) and philanthropy and other sources ($40 million). Between 1955 and 1960, the NIH budget rose from $81 million to $400 million.

Research expenditures at NIH encompassed a broad range of activities. Research included laboratory work on basic cellular processes, clinical epidemiology (such as the demonstration of the link between cigarette smoking and lung cancer), and clinical trials of new drugs and procedures on patients. At the Clinical Center, a research hospital established at NIH in 1953, patients and normal volunteers participated in tests of new cancer treatments and other therapies.

Philanthropic sources continued to play a significant role in the years after World War II. Money from the National Foundation for Infantile Paralysis helped finance research and development of an effective vaccine for polio. An outgrowth of the Presidential Birthday Balls Commission honoring the nation's most famous polio patient, Franklin Delano Roosevelt, the National Foundation raised huge sums of money for polio research and treatment for those crippled by the disease. From $1.8 million dollars raised in 1938, contributions to the Foundation increased to nearly $5 million in 1942, over $12 million in 1944, and almost $20 million in 1945. Grants from the foundation enabled researchers to purchase expensive laboratory equipment and research animals.

In the 1940s, the only experimental animals suitable for the study of polio were monkeys and chimpanzees. Unlike rats, mice, and rabbits, primates were not only difficult to acquire but extremely expensive to purchase and maintain. Already compromised by the long shipboard journey from Asian countries, the animals in the laboratory experienced high rates of disease, which hindered their use in research. The prohibitive cost of primates had already played a role in the tragic history of two earlier polio vaccines. In the 1930s, both the live-virus polio vaccine (developed by physician John Kolmer) and the formaldehyde-treated killed-virus vaccine (developed by Maurice Brodie and William H. Park) were administered to children after experimentation involving only sixty-two monkeys. In 1935, field-testing of the Kolmer vaccine revealed that rather than creating immunity to the disease, the vaccine infected children with polio. After the deaths of nine vaccinated children, Kolmer withdrew his vaccine. Additional testing on monkeys demonstrated that the Brodie vaccine did not induce polio in children but neither did it provide protection from the disease. According to polio researcher John R. Paul, the outcome of these early vaccine trials, involving more than 20,000 children, had a chilling effect on polio research for nearly two decades.

In the 1940s, the National Foundation attempted to address the primate problem in polio research by establishing Okatie Farms in South Carolina. After importing monkeys and chimpanzees from Asia, the animals were shipped to the farm for conditioning before being sent to laboratories. All researchers funded by the National Foundation were instructed not only to purchase their research animals from the farm, but also to buy the specially formulated monkey chow developed at Okatie. When the discovery in 1948 that poliovirus could be successfully grown in the laboratory in non–nervous-system human tissue dramatically reduced the need for experimental animals, the Foundation continued to provide funding for animal studies, and the tissue culture and tissue typing programs that eventually produced Jonas Salk's successful vaccine.

The research on polio did not come cheap. In 1953, a year after polio cases reached an all-time high in America, the Virus Research Laboratory at the University of Pittsburgh spent $63,000 on monkeys, $16,000 on chimpanzees, $18,000 on mice, $12,500 on animal food, and an additional $30,000 on such expendable supplies as glassware, dry ice, and chemicals. That year the National Foundation provided $2 million for polio research, the National Institutes of Health $72,000. When Salk proposed field trials of his killed-virus vaccine, the Foundation provided $7 million and helped to coordinate the logistics of a trial involving nearly 2 million school children (the Polio Pioneers) and 217 health districts in 44 states. At the conclusion of the field trial, an estimated

20,000 physicians, 40,000 nurses, 15,000 principals, and 200,000 other volunteers had participated in the administration and evaluation of the Salk vaccine. The Foundation's role did not end with the announcement on 12 April 1955 that the Salk vaccine worked. In the subsequent months, the Foundation organized a public education campaign to encourage people to obtain the vaccine. The staff scored a coup when, after considerable persuasion and a number of telephone calls to his mother, Elvis Presley agreed to a public polio vaccination.

Disease advocacy groups continued to play an important role in funding medical research. The American Heart Association (incorporated in 1924), although unable to contribute funds for research in its first two decades, began to support research at significant levels in the 1950s. By the 1960s, the AHA was awarding over $10 million a year to support research in cardiac physiology and heart disease. In addition to fundraising, voluntary organizations like the American Cancer Society (the revamped American Society for the Control of Cancer) became a powerful lobby for Congress to increase federal appropriations for medical research.

In the years after World War II, medical researchers relied on a variety of funding sources. The development of the birth control pill in the 1950s illustrates how funds from governmental sources, pharmaceutical companies, and private donors combined to produce results. After forming the Worcester Foundation for Experimental Biology in 1944, the researchers Gregory Pincus and Hudson Hoagland received financial support from the Searle Company for their work on hormonal control of reproduction. Small grants from the National Research Council's Committee for Research in Problems of Sex and from Planned Parenthood further supported their work. Conducting the massive field trials to establish the safety and efficacy of the oral contraceptive, however, required even larger sums of money, and was eventually provided by a wealthy benefactor. Katherine Dexter McCormick, who had earlier donated money to study the biochemistry of schizophrenia, contributed more than one million dollars to research on contraception. Successful field trials in Puerto Rico, largely funded by McCormick, led to FDA approval of the first birth control pill in 1960.

In the late 1960s, conflicts over whether Congress should fund basic research or support applied research to discover treatments for diseases began to slow the rate of increase for medical research funding. The expansion of the federal investment in medical research became the subject of controversy in the

1970s and 1980s. Part of the criticism directed at rising research expenditures reflected debate over what kind of research the federal government should fund. Should medical researchers target clinically significant problems and diseases or should they pursue knowledge about basic mechanisms of life in health and disease? What are the appropriate battlefields in the war on cancer (declared by President Richard Nixon in 1971) and who should determine national research priorities? The allocation of funds for research was never free of politicking. In the 1980s, the AIDS epidemic introduced new features to what were once mannerly discussions between policy makers, patient advocates, and researchers. Aggressive lobbying by AIDS activists and HIV-infected people not only induced the pharmaceutical company Burroughs Wellcome to lower drug prices for the antiretroviral agent AZT, but encouraged Congress to allocate large sums of money ($1.7 billion in 1992) for AIDS research.

The apparent success of AIDS activists prompted advocates for patients with other diseases to adopt similar tactics and strategies. In the 1980s women with breast cancer emerged as an outspoken and increasingly militant lobby. Advocates for funding in breast cancer research promoted their cause by comparing the federal investment in AIDS research with the monies slated for research into the disease that killed more than 43,000 American women in 1990. AIDS received twenty times the sum allotted for breast cancer. The rise in activism for breast cancer has been accompanied by a demand that the medical establishment pay more attention to women's health issues in general. In response, the National Institutes for Health created the Office of Research on Women's Health. In 1993, NIH introduced new requirements for the inclusion of women and minorities in research in federally funded clinical studies. Because the inclusion of women raises a host of ethical, legal, scientific, and social issues, the Institute of Medicine, a constituent society of the National Academy of Sciences, convened an advisory committee to recommend policies to enhance inclusion of women. In 1994 the committee issued its policy recommendations, including means to ensure the participation and protection of pregnant women and their fetuses.

In light of continuing pressures on the federal budget and potential declines in funding for medical research, some health economists have explored the potential for philanthropies to provide once again a greater share of the funding of medical research. In the 1980s, for example, the Howard Hughes Medical Institute and the Markey Charitable Trust donated substantial funds to medical research. How medical research will be funded, amid the development of a national health policy during the Clinton presidency, remains to be seen.

THE SOCIAL ORGANIZATION OF MEDICAL SCIENCE

The tremendous increase in expenditures for medical research is one facet of the changes in the medical sciences since 1900. Another feature of the dramatically altered landscape is the social organization of medical science. For most of the century, medical science was overwhelmingly male and white. Between 1920 and 1974, fewer than 10 percent of graduates from American medical schools were women. Since the 1970s, the number of women entering medicine has dramatically increased; in 1993, 42 percent of first year medical students were women. In the first part of the twentieth century, obstacles for women scientists were formidable. After their struggle to obtain medical or scientific training, many women found the doors of universities and medical schools closed to them. Lack of access to postdoctoral training and restrictions on membership to professional societies hindered the careers of women scientists. In the years 1920 to 1938, 254 of the 1,194 doctorates (21.3 percent) in the medical sciences were earned by women. However, women received only 14 of the 250 National Research Council fellowships awarded in medicine (5.6 percent). Some women were able to conduct research in such female-dominated disciplines as home economics or nutrition. A small number found positions as research associates, where they received little credit for their contributions. In the years between 1960 and 1990, the number of women earning science degrees rose steadily. By 1991, women made up nearly 30 percent of the 32,079 Ph.D. researchers employed in the medical sciences.

The number of women in medical science has risen, but minorities, especially African Americans, remain significantly underrepresented in medicine. Blacks have traditionally lacked access to medical training. In 1915, as the Flexnerian reforms in medical education took hold, the number of black medical schools dropped from eight to three. In 1923, only two schools remained—Meharry Medical College and the School of Medicine at Howard University. Before 1940 white medical schools that accepted black applicants produced altogether no more than twenty black physicians a year. These medical graduates often found themselves excluded from residency and internship programs.

As the first black resident to be trained at Presbyterian Hospital in New York City, Charles Richard Drew became accustomed to the color line in American medicine, and experienced it directly in his efforts to establish major blood plasma projects in the 1940s. An expert on methods and techniques of blood procurement and processing, Drew headed the plasma drive for the Blood for Britain project in 1940 and served as medical director of the first American Red Cross Blood Bank. Drew was troubled when, in 1941, the American Red Cross established a policy of excluding black blood donors in the blood drive to aid American soldiers. In 1942, when the agency permitted blacks to donate blood for the war effort, they continued to segregate blood along racial lines. These policies reflected social preferences rather than scientific realities, and did much to discourage both African American physicians and donors. Although segregation of blood was discontinued during the Korean conflict in 1950–1951, integrating hospital staffs and patients took much longer, especially in the South. By 1965 federal courts and the 1964 Civil Rights Act compelled southern hospitals to begin the process of integrating medical personnel and patients. Despite increased access to higher education in medicine and the sciences, the number of African American Ph.D.s remains low. In 1991, black Ph.D.s represented only 3.2 percent of the 99,329 medical scientists employed in American laboratories.

Over the course of the twentieth century, medical science was transformed from a largely individual activity into a collaborative enterprise, often involving large numbers of personnel from a variety of fields, backgrounds, and institutions. Patterns of authorship in biomedical journals illustrate the increasingly collective nature of medical science. In 1916, 91 percent of the articles published in the *New England Journal of Medicine* were by individual authors; by 1946, the percentage dropped to 46 percent. In 1976 and 1977, 96 percent of the articles had multiple authors. The evaluation of new chemotherapies for cancer, for example, now routinely involves the participation of sizable numbers of patients, clinicians, biostatisticians, drug company sponsors, other funding agencies, members of the institutional review board, and federal regulatory agencies like the Food and Drug Administration.

The growth of collaboration in medical science developed in part from innovative methods for evaluating the efficacy of new therapies. Since the numerical studies of the French clinician Pierre Louis, who tested the effectiveness of bloodletting for pulmonary disease in the early nineteenth century, physicians have attempted, with varying success, to introduce quantitative assessments to their evaluation of medical therapies. In the twentieth century, medical acceptance of statistical approaches to the evaluation of therapies and understanding disease grew appreciably after World War II. As early as the 1920s, however, clinical researchers had attempted to amass and standardize large groups of patients to evaluate the bewildering array of treatments for syphilis, a national disease priority.

The Cooperative Clinical Group's investigations of syphilis (1928–1935) required that clinicians agree on uniform standards for selecting, classifying, treating, and evaluating patient response to therapy before reliable comparisons could be made and conclusions drawn. As historian Harry Marks has shown, the group's early trials were plagued with conceptual and practical problems (the introduction of penicillin as an effective treatment for syphilis in the 1940s largely rendered the treatments for tertiary syphilis unnecessary.) The early and halting attempts to evaluate therapies prepared the way for the randomized clinical trials, which became, after World War II, the gold standard for evaluating the safety and efficacy of a therapy. In the contemporary controlled clinical trial, statistically significant groups of patients are randomly assigned to treatment groups, including a control group of patients who typically receive a placebo instead of the active drug. Neither the patient nor the researcher knows which therapy the patient receives, and independent observers evaluate patient response.

The collaborative style and the competitive nature of medical science may have fostered a disturbing trend in the late twentieth century, an apparent increase in scientific misconduct. Although the extent of scientific fraud is unknown, the problem has received increasing attention in the 1980s and 1990s. In 1989 a survey of the problem from the Acadia Institute found that approximately 40 percent of the deans of major American graduate schools acknowledged confirmed cases of scientific misconduct in their own institutions within the previous five years. A report from the American Association for the Advancement of Science similarly noted that personal experience with scientific misconduct was not rare. Of scientists surveyed by the organization, 27 percent reported they had personally encountered research they believed to be either fabricated, falsified, or plagiarized. A growing number of cases of misconduct in the medical sciences generated considerable interest in the 1980s.

Whether fraud in medical science is more common or receives greater attention because of the public interest in medicine and health is not known. Media coverage of cases of misconduct in medical science and fears that loss of public confidence would create serious consequences led the National Institutes of Health to organize the Office of Scientific Integrity (OSI) in 1989. Investigating cases of scientific misconduct has proven difficult. The OSI became embroiled in controversy amid the accusations of misconduct against a prominent AIDS researcher at the NIH. The investigation of the charges that Robert Gallo had falsified his patent application for the blood test for HIV infection created tensions between the OSI and Dr. Bernardine Healy, the director of NIH, whose former institution was also undergoing investigation into charges of scientific misconduct. In 1993, in response to growing tensions over the Gallo proceedings, OSI was moved from NIH and reorganized as the Office of Research Integrity in the Office of the Assistant Secretary of Health in the Department of Health and Human Services. As the number of accusations against medical scientists increased, some observers expressed fears that the public would lose confidence in medical research. The revelation in early 1994 that a Canadian researcher had falsified patient records as part of a large clinical trial comparing survival rates among women undergoing lumpectomy for breast cancer versus women who had mastectomies produced anger and outrage. Such problems underscore the difficulty inherent in a clinical trial involving large numbers of patients, researchers, and institutions.

In an effort to stem a growing tide of misconduct cases, some research institutions have taken steps to remedy the problem of scientific fraud. In the 1980s, Stanford Medical School and Harvard Medical School established formal, comprehensive guidelines for the proper conduct of research. Some schools proposed adoption of a different standard for promotion and tenure that emphasized quality of research papers over quantity. In 1990, the National Institutes of Health enacted new requirements for institutions receiving training grants. The regulations required schools to provide all trainees with instruction in the principles of scientific integrity, including the recording and retention of data, codes of conduct, conflict of interest, and responsible authorship.

RESEARCH ON ANIMAL AND HUMAN SUBJECTS

The use of experimental animals has also created problems for the medical research community over the course of the twentieth century. American opposition to animal experimentation began in the late nineteenth century, but was relatively weak in the first half of the twentieth century. As funding for medical research escalated in the postwar years, the number of animals used in research rose dramatically. In the period between 1959 and 1965, the numbers of rats, mice, and rabbits used in laboratories reportedly rose from 17 to 60 million per year. Even though dogs and cats constituted only a small percentage of the animals in laboratories, the use of pet animals in research created public interest and concern. In the 1940s and 1950s, antivivisectionists and the research community engaged in a series of volatile battles over the use of pound animals—abandoned cats and dogs—in medical research. In 1966, amid reports of organized pet-theft rings, Congress passed the Laboratory Animal Welfare Act, regulating the sale and transfer of research animals to laboratories. One indication of the public investment in dogs was the response to military use of beagles for testing toxic substances. In 1973, the Pentagon received more than 30,000 letters from outraged Americans—more mail than was generated by any single issue since President Harry Truman fired General Douglas MacArthur in 1951. As a result, the U.S. Army suspended procurement of beagles and began an intensive review by the offices and agencies of the Department of Defense. Opposition to animal experimentation intensified in the 1970s and 1980s, even though the use of research animals was steadily declining. In 1994 scientists from Tufts University reported that laboratory animal use had dropped by 50 percent since 1968.

Clinical investigators have had to confront a different set of issues, relating to the participation of human beings in medical research. Over the course of the twentieth century, physicians and patients have grappled with the ethical questions of consent, benefit, and risk in human experimentation. Although most Americans have granted the necessity for trying innovative therapies on the desperately ill, using normal subjects in medical experiments has been more controversial. In the early twentieth century, for example, accusations that physicians used "orphans as guinea pigs" fostered official inquiries into the ethical limits of experimentation with human beings. Unlike Walter Reed's research on the transmission of yellow fever conducted on adult volunteers, the pediatrician Alfred F. Hess and his colleagues studied scurvy in infants at the Home for Hebrew Infants by withholding orange juice until the children developed the characteristic lesions of the disease. In 1921, when the journalist Konrad Bercovici challenged the morality of such research, physicians defended the necessity for scientific research that did not endanger the lives or well-being of the children and that also gave the orphans the opportunity to repay their debt to society.

American investigators continued to rely on orphans and other institutionalized populations as research subjects during World War II. With America's entry into the war, participation in medical experiments became a patriotic duty. Few investigators experienced qualms about subjecting orphans, the mentally ill, prisoners, and conscientious objectors to hazardous experiments related to the war effort. Indeed access to such institutionalized populations enhanced an investigator's application to the Committee for Medical Research.

As part of the war effort, American soldiers participated in tests of chemical weapons and research on the new atomic weapons. By the end of World War II, an estimated sixty thousand servicemen had been involved in experiments on chemical weapons. Although most apparently experienced little harm from slight exposures to mustard gas and Lewisite (an arsenic-containing gas), many of the nearly four thousand soldiers and sailors who received more severe exposures in tests conducted in gas chambers and other conditions developed severe burns and other injuries. In 1991, the U.S. government formally acknowledged the participation of American soldiers in military research projects, and began providing compensation for those injured in experimentation.

In addition to tests of chemical weapons, American military investigators studied the effects of germ warfare on American civilians. After the atomic explosions at Hiroshima and Nagasaki, government investigators studied the effects of radiation on both soldiers and civilians. In the 1950s and 1960s, as part of the Cold War search for a mind-controlling agent, the United States military and the CIA funded studies on lysergic acid diethylamine (LSD) at a number of leading American and Canadian university medical schools. Although American servicemen were induced by offers of leave and other privileges to participate in the tests, some experiments on civilians occurred without the knowledge or consent of the subjects.

In the 1960s, some American physicians expressed concern about the disturbing trend in clinical research. One of the leading figures in the movement to reform clinical research ethics was Henry Knowles Beecher, a Harvard anesthesiologist and medical educator. In 1966, in a widely quoted article in the *New England Journal of Medicine,* Beecher claimed that not only was unethical experimentation not uncommon, but ethical errors in clinical research were increasing in numbers and variety. To bolster his case, Beecher cited twenty-two studies in which American medical investigators had "risked the health or the life of their research subjects," without the permission or knowledge of the patients or their families. Two of Beecher's examples—the Willowbrook hepatitis studies and the live cancer cell injections at the Jewish Chronic Disease Hospital—generated extended public controversy.

In the 1950s, in order to develop an effective vaccine and treatment for infectious hepatitis, the pediatrician Saul Krugman and his colleagues at New York University purposefully infected with the disease strain residents at the Willowbrook State School, a New York institution for severely mentally retarded children. Physicians obtained permission from parents for administration of oral virus or intramuscular injections to their children, but critics charged that few parents understood that their children were being given the disease for research purposes. Critics also challenged the coercive nature of the consent process. In 1964, amid the severe overcrowding at the Willowbrook school, parents were only able to have their child admitted to the institution by agreeing to enter the child on the experimental protocol. In the Jewish Chronic Disease Hospital case, the physician Chester Southam injected elderly hospital patients with live cancer cells for a study of immunity in cancer. Patients were informed that they were receiving injections, but they did not learn about the nature or purpose of the study. In 1963, following an investigation, the Board of Regents of the State University of New York censured Southam and his colleague for unprofessional conduct. Found guilty of misconduct by the state medical examiners board, the investigators received suspended sentences.

Beecher's disclosures and the public discussions about human experimentation had an immediate effect on the leadership of the National Institutes of Health and the Food and Drug Administration (FDA). Already sensitive to congressional pressures and anxious to preserve the levels of funding for medical research, officials at these agencies, as the historian David Rothman has argued, quickly responded to concerns about human experimentation. In 1966, the NIH issued a set of guidelines for federally funded human experimentation, mandating institutional review of research projects and requiring documentation of patient consent for experimentation. The same year, the FDA, the agency responsible for insuring the safety and efficacy of medicinal drugs, developed regulations for the testing of investigational drugs on human beings.

Disturbing revelations about abuses of human subjects continued. The most notorious case of experimental exploitation, the forty-year study of untreated syphilis conducted by researchers at the United States Public Health Service, brought increased congressional scrutiny to clinical research. On 25 July 1972, it was disclosed that since 1932 physicians from the Venereal Disease Division of the United States Public Health Service had studied the natural history of syphilis in a population of four hundred African American men in rural Alabama. The men, who participated in the study believing they were being treated for their "bad blood," were subjected to diagnostic tests and actively prevented from receiving treatment for syphilis. Government doctors provided a series of small incentives for the men, who received hot meals and free rides to the clinic in a government car. The families of the men also received a burial stipend of $50 (later raised to $100) if they allowed government doctors to perform an autopsy. The study, although marred by procedural problems and the fact that some of the men received inadequate treatment for syphilis, confirmed that untreated syphilis increased the likelihood of serious disability and premature death.

Reports that government doctors had deliberately misled the men about their disease and the available treatments, most notably penicillin after 1945, provoked outrage in the public press. At hearings on human experimentation conducted by the congressional subcommittee on health of the committee on labor and public welfare in February and March 1973 came other disclosures. Senator Edward M. Kennedy described a study in San Antonio, Texas, in which Mexican American women unknowingly participated in the testing of the efficacy of a new contraceptive. Believing they were receiving birth control pills, some women were given placebos without their knowledge. Other congressional committees heard testimony about the studies commissioned by the U.S. Army and Air Force in which enlisted men received hallucinogenic drugs, including LSD, without their knowledge or consent.

The hearings and the concerted pressure of Senators Kennedy, Jacob Javits, and Walter Mondale produced legislation regarding human experimentation. In 1974 Congress passed the National Research Act, which created the National Commission for the Protection of Subjects of Biomedical and Behavioral Research. Composed of eleven members from the general public and the fields of medicine and the

humanities, the commission was superseded in 1978 by the President's Commission for the Study of Ethical Problems in Medicine. In addition, the 1974 Act converted the guidelines for human experimentation from the Department of Health, Education and Welfare (responsible for the NIH, FDA, and the Public Health Service) into federal regulations. The regulations mandated institutional review boards composed of both medical professionals and lay persons to evaluate proposals involving human beings and required written consent forms for human subjects.

Since 1974, the regulations have undergone some modification but the basic machinery of institutional review boards remains intact. The new protections for human subjects have not satisfied all critics of medical experimentation. Controversial experimental therapies such as the implantation of a baboon heart into a dying infant, critics charge, demonstrates the need for some type of national review board to protect patients and their families. In the 1990s, Senators Edward Kennedy and Mark Hatfield proposed legislation to create a national bioethics commission to investigate such controversial research as embryo cloning and to advise the Department of Health and Human Services whether such research should be allowed to proceed or be discontinued. Although similar proposals have foundered in Congress, the new proposal gained momentum in the light of public outrage over the revelation in late 1993 of radiation testing on American citizens during the Cold War.

In response to growing media coverage of radiation testing involving retarded children and pregnant women in the 1940s, 1950s, and 1960s, Energy secretary Hazel O'Leary announced her intention to declassify information about the nuclear weapons industry and ordered the Department of Energy (DOE) to release all information in its possession relating to radiation testing on human beings. In December 1993 the DOE hotline for people who believed that they were involved in government-funded radiation research was swamped with calls from anxious Americans. Like the Tuskegee Syphilis Study, many of the radiation experiments had been openly published in medical journals; they were not secret. Surviving investigators found themselves trying to account for their decades-old experimental practices. The level of public concern led President Clinton in January 1994 to create a Human Radiation Interagency Working Group to coordinate government efforts to investigate federally funded research involving radiation and to appoint an advisory panel to make recommendations about compensation for those injured by their participation.

THE DEVELOPMENT OF AND RESPONSE TO MEDICAL TECHNOLOGY

The radiation experiments renewed public fears about nuclear weapons, nuclear energy, and nuclear medicine. In the first half of the twentieth century the American public celebrated the marvels of medical technology; since World War II, Americans have expressed greater ambivalence about technology. The mass media have both reflected and transmitted American investment in the wondrous mysteries of medical science. In the 1920s and 1930s, research in suspended animation and resuscitation led some Americans to confidently anticipate the end of death itself. In the 1960s, the tide turned. Where Americans once celebrated the machines that made life possible, a growing number of Americans began to express concern about the tyranny of medical technology. The growing number of patients maintained by artificial life support raised new questions about the definitions of life and death. The advent of organ transplantation in the 1960s raised the specter that doctors would harvest organs before death occurred. At the same time, proponents of euthanasia and death with dignity have criticized doctors for not allowing patients to die. For perhaps the first time, as the historian Martin Pernick has observed, Americans have expressed fears of being wrongly declared dead or alive. Since the 1970s, critics have expressed additional concern about medical technologies. The introduction of machines to measure physiological states and to maintain life support has adversely affected the relationship between doctors and patients. Medical technologies have also been implicated in the spiraling costs of medical care.

The pace of technological change is one of the characteristic features of twentieth-century medicine. In the 1990s patients and their families encounter a striking array of medical technologies, from fetal monitors and ultrasound images at the beginning of life to respirators and life-support machines at the end of life. In Michigan, the controversial pathologist Jack Kevorkian has gone one step further, offering chronically ill individuals an innovative death technology, the assisted-suicide device.

The development of medical technology did not begin in the twentieth century. The introduction of the stethoscope in the early nineteenth century (initially a wooden instrument, later modified for hearing in both ears) and the thermometer began to alter the physician's relationship with the patient. The stethoscope in particular provided doctors with an objective recording of physiological function not accessible to the patient. The thermometer, which became a standard instrument for American physicians in the late nineteenth century, offered a numerical reading of a formerly subjective estimation of body temperature.

In the late nineteenth century, the introduction of the x-ray dramatically influenced the physician's approach to the human body. William Roentgen's discovery of x-rays offered physicians a radically different view into the inner structure of the human body. American physicians and their patients greeted the x-ray with enthusiasm. Following a pattern that would be repeated over the century, the x-ray was applied with abandon until reports of radiation-related injury, including sterility and cancer, began to appear.

Over the course of the twentieth century technologies increasingly dominated the definition and management of human disease. The understanding of heart disease illustrates the hegemony of medical technology and the staggering pace of innovation. As deaths from infectious disease declined in the first part of the twentieth century, physicians focused more on chronic illness, especially cancer and heart disease. An array of new instruments and devices redefined medical understanding of heart disease. The diagnosis of coronary heart disease, argues the historian Joel Howell, has been profoundly influenced by the availability of technical measurements of heart disease and heart function.

The electrocardiograph was the first in a series of devices to describe heart function. Invented in 1902 by Willem Enthoven, the instrument, which produced graphic tracings of the heartbeat, was by 1912 considered essential to clinical evaluation of the heart by Thomas Lewis, a leading British cardiologist. By the 1920s, the EKG machine was fast becoming a routine feature of hospital care for diagnosis and treatment of cardiac patients.

By the 1950s, the treatment for heart disease had undergone a profound transformation. Improvements in the diagnosis of heart disease and advances in surgical techniques made heart surgery possible. Critical to the success of open-heart surgery was the development of the heart-lung machine. First conceived by the surgical researcher John Gibbon in 1930, the heart-lung machine offered surgeons the opportunity to work on damaged hearts by having a machine take over the pumping function of the heart and the oxygenating function of the lung. Gibbon received little outside financial help for his groundbreaking research; two grants for $4,000 from the Josiah Macy Foundation helped fund his early work. After the creation of the National Heart Institute in 1949, Gibbon received more substantial support for his research. A relationship with International Business Machines (IBM) was critical to the endeavor. Engineers from IBM helped Gibbon transform his experimental (cat-sized) device into a machine that could be used for human beings in a sterile operating room.

In the 1960s, the introduction of coronary arteriography heralded a new era for surgical treatment of heart disease. Through the injection of radioactive dyes, cardiologists were able to see a coronary obstruction and to bypass the area through grafts of arteries or veins. Coronary artery bypass surgery became a growth industry in the 1970s and 1980s. By 1980 the operation, which cost an estimated $10,000 to $25,000, accounted for 1 percent of the total health care costs in the United States. In the 1980s, bypass surgery has received increasing criticism as questions about cost and efficacy continue to mount. The development of clot-dissolving drugs and the refinement of coronary balloon angioplasty (both less invasive and less costly) have made bypass surgery less attractive.

For more seriously damaged hearts, cardiac surgeons have pursued more radical solutions. Surgeons have replaced defective hearts with harvested hearts from human cadavers, with organs obtained from animals, and with artificial organs. Efforts to transplant organs date from the late nineteenth century. In the 1910s and 1920s physicians transplanted testes and ovaries (from animals and from human cadavers) into men and women, seeking to restore hormonal secretions. Working at the Rockefeller Institute for Medical Research, the French surgeon Alexis Carrel pioneered methods of kidney transplants on dogs and other animals. In the 1930s, together with the American aviator Charles Lindbergh, Carrel developed a glass heart to demonstrate the feasibility of replacing defective or badly damaged hearts. The advent of the heart-lung machine spurred the search for replacement organs. The success of kidney transplants and kidney dialysis (an artificial kidney) and the optimistic predictions of investigators encouraged the federal government to invest massive sums of money into the search for an artificial heart. In 1968 the world was startled by the announcement from South Africa of the first human heart transplant. Performed by the surgeon Christian Barnard, the transplant procedure was subsequently adopted by surgeons around the world.

In 1985 an advisory panel for the National Heart, Lung Blood Institute ratified the decision to invest in a totally implantable artificial heart and recom-

mended federal expenditures of approximately $130 million over a thirteen-year period. The artificial heart, the panel enthusiastically noted, would allow a significant increase in lifespan for those individuals under seventy afflicted with heart disease. The panel did address some of the issues raised by the costs of the artificial heart. The investment in the artificial heart (if successfully developed) would not greatly exceed the total monies spent on such life-extending technologies as kidney dialysis. The panel estimated that the average cost per recipient of the artificial heart (over $200,000) was also consistent with the costs of bone marrow transplants (around $100,000) and heart transplants (estimated at $130,000).

Unlike the development of new drugs, which have been subjected to federal regulation since the 1938 Food, Drug, and Cosmetic Act, medical device makers have had less governmental oversight. In 1975, reports that the Dalkon Shield, introduced as a contraceptive method in 1970, was linked to miscarriages, pelvic infections, and at least sixteen deaths prompted Congress to pass the Medical Device Amendments in 1976. Before placing a new device on the market, the manufacturer is required to provide evidence of safety and efficacy. Before permission to establish a device's utility in human trials is granted, the FDA requires an applicant to disclose data from experimental animals.

Protecting the public from unsafe medical devices has been problematic. Policy decisions must often be conducted in the face of medical uncertainty. In some cases, risks of medical devices have only become clear after decades of use. When the medical device amendments were enacted in 1976, for example, silicon gel breast implants were already on the market. By the 1990s, a number of the 2 million women who had received implants had experienced some difficulties. Problems with the implants included contracture (hardening), bleeding of the gel into surrounding tissue, and rupture of the gel-containing sac. But estimates of the frequency of such problems varied enormously; contracture, for example, reportedly occurred in 10 to 70 percent of women who received the device. Citing the failure of the manufacturers to establish proof of safety and efficacy of their product, the FDA in 1992 restricted access to the device to women who required breast reconstructive surgery willing to enter a clinical trial. The FDA's decision sparked considerable controversy. In light of medical uncertainty, should American women be prevented from obtaining a device they deem important to their well-being? Should American women be coerced into entering a clinical trial of the safety of the device? In 1994, the manufacturers of silicon gel implants settled a class action suit on behalf of women injured by their implants. The settlement does not address the continuing need of physicians, patients, and public health advocates to act responsibly in the face of scientific uncertainty.

THE FUTURE OF MEDICAL RESEARCH

The costs of medical technology have increasingly been implicated in the spiraling costs of medical care. In the 1990s, the multibillion-dollar medical device industry may account for as much as 40 percent of the health care bill ($660 billion in 1990; 12 percent of the gross national product). The adoption of such new technologies as electronic fetal monitoring has a direct impact on the overall costs of medical services. Because American health insurers have generally provided reimbursement for standard, rather than experimental, procedures or applications, there is considerable pressure on manufacturers and physicians to obtain validation as a standard therapy. In some cases, such evaluations have been made by panels of medical experts, who have considerable experience with the equipment and hence are more likely to perceive the technology as necessary. Efforts to restrain medical costs will have to take the medical device industry and the public desire for medical technologies into account.

At the end of the twentieth century, the extraordinary optimism that Americans reserved for medical science and technology has been tempered. The availability of reproductive techniques—both new and old—have called into question social definitions of parenthood and kinship. In the 1980s and 1990s the availability of in-vitro fertilization, in which male and female gametes are combined outside the body, and then implanted in the uterus, and surrogacy arrangements in which an unrelated woman carried a fetus to term for a fee have been debated in courtrooms and state capitals. In 1993 reports that a new technique would allow ova to be recovered from an aborted female fetus and used for in-vitro fertilization shocked Americans. The rate of technological innovation in medicine increasingly seems to have outpaced changes in cultural norms.

Perhaps more than any other event, the AIDS epidemic has taught Americans that medical science cannot solve all physical ills. Acquired immune deficiency syndrome (AIDS) was first identified in 1981 by the Centers for Disease Control in Atlanta. Spread by sexual contact and through blood, the disease, which cripples the body's immune response, has been reported in 138 countries around the world. In 1992, the number of HIV-infected people around the world had grown to an estimated 12.9 million.

Initially, hopes for a vaccine and an effective treatment were high. The identification of the HIV retrovirus in 1983 prompted considerable optimism that AIDS, like plagues of time past, would soon be vanquished by medical science. Reports that Jonas Salk, the developer of the polio vaccine, was working on AIDS buoyed public hopes that the disease would be relegated, like polio, to the pages of medical history. The development of a blood test to detect the virus enabled physicians to protect the blood supply, but not before a majority of American hemophiliacs had been infected. The mounting death toll has damped the optimism that characterized the first decade of the AIDS epidemic.

In the twentieth century America was transformed from a scientific backwater into the leading center of biomedical research in the world. What was once the solitary and marginal activity of a small cohort of committed medical scientists has given rise to a medical-industrial complex of considerable sophistication and complexity. The next decades will determine whether the medical science establishment can sustain its current level of growth and funding and recapture public confidence in the products of scientific research.

Advances in medical science and technology have revolutionized the lives of American patients and their physicians. New drugs, new devices, and new conceptual approaches to disease have altered the American experience of birth, sickness, health, and death. Medical science has made considerable inroads against the infectious diseases that ravaged Americans in the nineteenth century; researchers have also done much to reduce cancer mortality and heart disease. In the last decade of the twentieth century, the AIDS epidemic offers a compelling reminder that new diseases and new threats to physical well-being will continue to confront physicians and patients. That may be the safest prediction for the century to come.

See Also Large-scale Scientific Enterprise; Industrial Research and Technology; Computer and Communications Technology; Health and Disease; Health Care Delivery; The Human Mind and Personality; Gender Theories; Evolutionary Theory (all in this volume).

BIBLIOGRAPHY

Richard H. Shryock, *American Medical Research: Past and Present* (1947), is the classic starting point for understanding the development of American medical research. Charles E. Rosenberg, *No Other Gods: On Science and American Social Thought* (1976), examines several facets of the growing hegemony of science in American thought at the beginning of the twentieth century, including the funding of agricultural science. Kenneth M. Ludmerer, *Learning to Heal: The Development of American Medical Education* (1985), analyzes the intersection of clinical research and medical education. For the interrelationship of government, industry, and medical education, William G. Rothstein, *American Medical Schools and the Practice of Medicine* (1987), provides a useful overview. Margaret Rossiter offers a perceptive analysis of the education and employment patterns of women researchers in *Women Scientists in America: Struggles and Strategies to 1940* (1982).

For understanding the growth of biomedical research institutions, a good survey is A. McGehee Harvey, *Science at the Bedside: Clinical Research in American Medicine, 1905–1945* (1981). The histories of particular institutions are also valuable, especially George W. Corner, *A History of the Rockefeller Institute* (1964); and Victoria A. Harden, *Inventing the NIH: Federal Biomedical Research Policy, 1887–1937* (1986). For governmental research policies, see Stephen Strickland, *Politics, Science and Dread Disease: A Short History of United States Medical Research Policy* (1972). Eli Ginzberg and Anna B. Dutka, *The Financing of Biomedical Research* (1989), provide a valuable overview of the funding of medical science. For the intersection of hospitals and medical research, Charles E. Rosenberg, *The Care of Strangers* (1987), is essential reading.

Histories of disease, an increasingly active area of historical research in the past two decades, are an important resource for understanding research patterns and developments. A useful survey is Harry F. Dowling, *Fighting Infection: Conquests of the Twentieth Century* (1977). A more nuanced history is John Ettling, *The Germ of Laziness: Rockefeller Philanthropy and Public Health in the New South* (1981), which analyzes the intersection of private funding and research in the battle against hookworm disease. The scientific efforts to trace the source of the influenza pandemic are explored in Alfred Crosby, *America's Forgotten Pandemic: The Influenza of 1918* (1989). Victoria A. Harden, *Rocky Mountain Spotted Fever: History of a Twentieth-Century Disease* (1990), provides important insights into governmental scientific efforts. Keith Wailoo, "'A Disease *sui generis*': The Origins of Sickle Cell Anemia and the Emergence of Modern Clinical Research, 1904–1924," *Bulletin of the History of Medicine* 65 (1991): 185–209, offers a provocative analysis of the structures, practices, and values of the clinical research community in the first part of the twentieth century. A number of historians have examined the history of polio research: two important sources are Naomi Rogers, *Dirt and Disease: Polio Before FDR* (1992); and Jane Smith, *Patenting the Sun: Polio and the Salk Vaccine* (1990).

Two biographies offer another valuable resource for the history of American medical research. Saul Benison, *Tom Rivers: Reflections on a Life in Medicine and Science* (1967), traces the career of the eminent virologist and Rockefeller medicine man. In addition, Benison's biography of the Harvard physiologist Walter Bradford Cannon (written with A. Clifford Barger and Elin L. Wolfe), *Walter B. Cannon: The Life and Times of a Young Scientist* (1987), provides important insights into the career paths for medical researchers in the first half of the twentieth century. For the development of specific medical scientific disciplines, see John Parascandola, *The Development of American Pharmacology: John J. Abel and the Shaping of a Discipline* (1992); Robert E. Kohler, *From Medical Chemistry to Biochemistry: The Making of a Biomedical Discipline* (1982); and W. Bruce Fye, *The Development of American Physiology* (1987).

Marcel C. LaFollette reviews issues relating to scientific fraud in *Stealing into Print: Fraud, Plagiarism, and Misconduct in Scientific Publishing* (1992). The history of the complex issues concerning intellectual property are analyzed in Charles Weiner, "Patenting and Academic Research: Historical Case Studies," *Science, Technology, and Human Values* 12 (1987): 50–62. Tensions between animal experimenters and lay critics are examined in Susan E. Lederer, "Political Animals: The Shaping of Biomedical Research Literature in Twentieth-Century America," *Isis* 83 (1992): 61–79; and Andrew N. Rowan, *Of Mice, Models, and Men: A Critical Evaluation of Animal Research* (1984).

Susan E. Lederer, *Subjected to Science: Human Experimentation in America before the Second World War* (1995), examines the rise of public and professional discussion about the use of human beings as research subjects. For the development of clinical trials, see Harry M. Marks, "Notes from the Underground: The Social Organization of Therapeutic Research," in *Grand Rounds: One Hundred Years of Internal Medicine,* ed. Russell C. Maulitz and Diana E. Long (1988), pp. 297–336. David J. Rothman, *Strangers at the Bedside: A History of How Law and Bioethics Transformed Medical Decision Making* (1991), argues that human experimentation became the point of entry for the modern bioethics movement. James H. Jones, *Bad Blood: The Tuskegee Syphilis Experiment* (1981), and Allan M. Brandt, "Racism and Research: The Case of the Tuskegee Syphilis Study," *Hasting Center Report* 8 (1978): 21–29, offer essential insights into the Tuskegee Syphilis Study.

For the history of medical technology, the best starting point is Stanley Joel Reiser, *Medicine and the Reign of Technology* (1978). Also useful for the broad perspective on medical technology in the twentieth century is Susan Bartlett Foote, *Managing the Medical Arms Race: Innovation and Public Policy in the Medical Device Industry* (1992); and Joseph Bronzino, Vincent H. Smith, and Maurice L. Wade, *Medical Technology and Society: An Interdisciplinary Perspective* (1990). Martin S. Pernick offers important insights into the attitudinal shift toward medical technology in "Back From the Grave: Recurring Controversies over Defining and Diagnosing Death in History," in *Death: Beyond Whole Brain Criteria,* ed. Richard M. Zaner (1988), pp. 17–74.

For the development of x-rays, a useful starting point is Ruth and Edward Brecher, *The Rays: A History of Radiology in the United States and Canada* (1969). The role of technology in managing heart disease is examined in Joel D. Howell, "Machines and Medicine: Technology Transforms the American Hospital," in *The American General Hospital: Communities and Social Contexts,* ed. Diana E. Long and Janet Golden (1989), pp. 109–134. The history of open heart surgery is reviewed in Ada Romaine-Davis, *John Gibbon and His Heart-Lung Machine* (1991). For analysis of the artificial heart, see Diana B. Dutton, *Worse than the Disease: Pitfalls of Medical Progress* (1988); and Michael J. Strauss, "The Political History of the Artificial Heart," *New England Journal of Medicine* 310 (1984): 332–336.

The history of pharmaceutical research and development is effectively told in John P. Swann, *Academic Scientists and the Pharmaceutical Industry: Cooperative Research in Twentieth-Century America* (1988); and Jonathan Liebenau, *Medical Science and Medical Industry: The Formation of the American Pharmaceutical Industry* (1987). Indispensable for understanding the insulin story is Michael Bliss, *The Discovery of Insulin* (1982). For the history of antibiotics, arguably the most important discovery of the twentieth century, see David P. Adams, "Wartime Bureaucracy and Penicillin Allocation: The Committee on Chemotherapeutic and Other Agents, 1942–1944," *Journal of the History of Medicine* 44 (1984): 196–217; and James C. Whorton, "'Antibiotic Abandon': The Resurgence of Therapeutic Rationalism," in *The History of Antibiotics: A Symposium,* ed. John Parascandola (1980), pp. 125–136. Harry M. Marks, "Cortisone, 1949: A Year in the Political Life of a Drug," *Bulletin of the History of Medicine* 66 (1992): 419–439, offers perspective on the challenging intellectual and political climate in medical research after World War II.

The development of the birth control pill is analyzed in Linda Grant, *Sexing the Millenium: Women and the Sexual Revolution* (1994). Some of the social implications of the new reproductive technologies are addressed in Barbara K. Rothman, *The Tentative Pregnancy: Prenatal Diagnosis and the Future of Motherhood* (1986).

The politics of research funding for AIDS is discussed in Robert M. Wachter, "AIDS, Activism, and the Politics of Health," *New England Journal of Medicine* 326 (1992): 128–133. A valuable collection of essays analyzing the AIDS epidemic is Elizabeth Fee and Daniel M. Fox, *AIDS: The Making of a Chronic Disease* (1992).

HEALTH AND DISEASE

Richard A. Meckel

In concluding his presidential address to the delegates attending the 1901 American Public Health Association conference, the Pennsylvania sanitarian Benjamin Lee suggested that the twentieth century would represent a new epoch in the history of America's experience with disease and death. Noting that death rates had been dropping for more than a decade, that the threat from epidemics of smallpox, cholera, and yellow fever had all but disappeared, and that the new science of bacteriology held great promise for controlling the microorganisms responsible for endemic killers such as tuberculosis, diphtheria, and typhoid, Lee predicted that in the coming century life expectancy, especially among the young, would steadily rise as infectious diseases posed an ever diminishing threat to the American people. He also predicted that as this happened, a smaller percentage of total deaths would occur among the young and a larger percentage among the old, who would succumb to the degenerative diseases associated with advanced age.

Although Lee's prediction seems to have been based as much on optimism as on evidence, it has proved surprisingly correct. When he made it, life expectancy at birth was less than fifty years, infants and children died in massive numbers, and the three leading causes of death were infectious diseases. Nine decades later, as the century comes to a close, life expectancy at birth is more than seventy-five years, infant mortality is less than 8 percent of what it was at the turn of the century, child death, while not unknown, is rare, and only one infectious disease, pneumonia, is among the top ten causes of death in the United States. Moreover, as the century has progressed, the burden of death has shifted from the young to the old, who now die primarily from such degenerative diseases as heart disease, stroke, and cancer.

Often referred to as the latter stages of epidemiologic and mortality transitions that began in the developed nations of the West, respectively, around the middle of the seventeenth and eighteenth centuries, the sharp rise in life expectancy, especially among the young, and the substitution of chronic and degenerative diseases for infectious diseases as the principal causes of death represent one of the most profound and fundamental ways in which life has changed for Americans during the course of this century. Constituting a dramatic shift in the timing, cause, and risk of death, the twentieth-century mortality and epidemiologic transitions have helped reshape the age composition of the population, necessitating a redefinition of social, economic, and political relations, and, perhaps most important of all, have fundamentally altered the way Americans think about, behave toward, and experience living, dying, sickness, and health. Outlining the essential configurations of these transitions, explaining how and why they occurred, and discussing their consequences for the health of the nation is the focus of this essay.

MEASURING MORTALITY: DATA AND STATISTICS

Measuring U.S. mortality levels and trends over the course of the twentieth century is neither simple nor precise, principally because data for the early years are incomplete. Prior to 1933, U.S. mortality data include only deaths that occurred in the Death Registration Area, an area created in 1880 that initially consisted of a few states and cities where death registration was deemed at least 90 percent accurate. By 1900 the Death Registration Area included ten states, the District of Columbia, and 153 registration cities outside the registration states, and encompassed 41 percent of the national population. By 1910 that percentage had risen to 58.3, by 1920 to 82, and by 1930 to 96.2. After 1932, U.S. mortality data include data from the entire United States.

Aside from their incompleteness, the major problem with the Death Registration Area data is their lack of representativeness. Especially in the first decade, the Death Registration Area was disproportionately northeastern and urban. Indeed, in 1900, 70 percent of the Death Registration Area population lived in towns and cities of 2,500 or more residents. For that reason a number of statistical tables and charts subsequently published by the Census Bureau describe mortality only in the registration states, which contained a smaller proportion of the total population than did the entire registration area but were less disproportionately urban. Readers should thus take note which of the statistics cited below refer to the total Death Registration Area and which refer only to the Death Registration States.

The initial incompleteness and unrepresentativeness of the Death Registration Area data do not invalidate them, but do skew them in certain directions. Because urban mortality was higher than rural mortality, death rates for the Death Registration Area are probably slightly higher than those for the entire United States. More significant, the early Death Registration Area death rates for African Americans are probably considerably higher than they were nationally. At the beginning of the century the vast majority of African Americans lived in the rural South and likely had lower death rates than those living in northern and southern cities. Yet because the rural South was not initially included in the Death Registration Area, it is the mortality experience of urban African Americans that is reflected in the early registration area figures.

If the early data on the number of deaths are somewhat problematic, those on the cause of death are even more so. At least before the era of life-support machines, the difference between life and death was relatively easy to establish and was rarely the subject of interpretive arguments outside the areas of theology and philosophy. Cause of death, however, was quite another matter. Although diagnostics had greatly improved since the advent of death registration in the mid-nineteenth century, it remained an inexact science through the early decades of the twentieth century. For instance, while fewer infant and child deaths were ascribed to such nebulous causes as teething and wasting away, some still were; and a significant proportion of infant death was attributed to convulsions, which were probably the result of electrolyte imbalance due to acute diarrhea and enteritis. Indeed, in 1900 more than 4 percent of all deaths were classified as being from ill-defined causes. Moreover, the official and internationally accepted system of classifying deaths has been revised nine times during the twentieth century.

What do we mean when we speak of changing mortality? Given, as the old adage has it, that death along with taxes is an absolute certainty, it seems paradoxical to talk of changes in mortality. Since death is certain, the number of people who die will always be equal to the number of people born. What we mean when we speak of a change in mortality is thus not a change in the certainty of an individual's eventual death, but a change in both the pervasiveness of death within a society and in the risk of dying faced by members of that society at specific times.

Several statistics are used to describe this pervasiveness and risk. Among these are annual death rates, which are the ratio of those dying to those living in a given year. For the entire population, two such death rates are commonly used: the crude death rate and the age-adjusted death rate. The first is the number of deaths recorded in a particular year per 1,000 population at mid-year. For instance, in 1900, 343,217 deaths were recorded in the Death Registration States, which had a mid-year population of 19,965,446. Hence, the crude death rate for the Death Registration States in 1900 was 17.2. Although it fluctuated in the early decades, the crude death rate has dropped dramatically over the course of the century and in 1992 it was 8.6.

While the crude death rate is a good measure of changes in the pervasiveness of death, it is not a good measure of changes in the risk of dying due to health conditions at different periods because it is sensitive to changes in the age composition of the population it is describing. Specifically, because the old die more frequently than the young, an increase in the proportion of the population that is elderly will mask the extent to which mortality is actually dropping at the various ages. Because the age composition of the U.S. population has changed in just that way during the twentieth century, demographers prefer to use a second statistic, the age-adjusted death rate. Like the crude death rate, this statistic is the ratio of annual deaths to the midyear population, but reflects the actual risk of dying at the various age intervals and adjusts the overall population so that its age composition remains constant over time. As shown in figure 1, the age-adjusted death rate at the beginning of the century was higher than the crude death rate, but since about 1930 has fallen much more sharply than the crude death rate, which has been biased upward by the aging of the U.S. population. Given its greater accuracy in representing actual change in the risk of dying across time, the age-adjusted death rate will be used in the following pages to illustrate overall U.S. mortality trends since the beginning of the century.

958

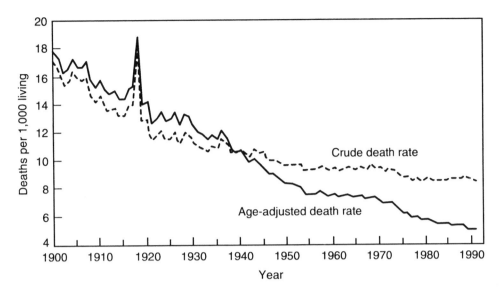

Figure 1.   Crude and age-adjusted death rates: Death-registration states, 1900–1932; United States, 1933–1991. (Source: data from three publications of the National Center for Health Statistics: *Vital Statistics of the United States, 1988* vol. 2, *Mortality* [1990], part A, sec. 1, pp. 3–6; "Advance Report of Final Mortality Statistics, 1989," *Monthly Vital Statistics Report* 40 [7 January 1992], p. 14; "Births, Marriages, Divorces, and Deaths for January 1992," *Monthly Vital Statistics Report* 41 [28 May 1992], p. 13.)

Other mortality statistics used in this essay are age-specific death rates, cause-specific death rates, infant, neonatal, and postneonatal mortality rates, and maternal mortality rates. The age-specific death rate is the ratio of those dying in a particular age group per 1,000 midyear population of that age group. The cause-specific death rate is the ratio of those dying from a specific cause per 100,000 midyear population. The infant mortality rate is the annual number of deaths of infants, defined as less than one year of age, per 1,000 annual live births. It is important to distinguish the infant mortality rate from the age-specific infant death rate, which is the ratio of infant deaths to infants living and is usually somewhat higher. The neonatal mortality rate is the annual number of deaths of infants less than twenty-eight days old per 1,000 live births; the postneonatal mortality rate is computed similarly but describes the death rate of infants twenty-eight days to one year old. The maternal mortality rate is the ratio of annual deaths of women due to complications of pregnancy and childbirth per 100,000 annual live births.

The other major measure of changing mortality used here is current life expectancy, both at birth and at specific ages. Life expectancy values, computed from the age-specific death rates at a particular time, are the average number of years of life that a person can expect to live if he or she reaches a certain

age and is exposed for a lifetime to the age-specific death probabilities existing in that year. It is important to note that life expectancy is a measure of the overall effect of mortality on a given population at a specific time and is not a prediction of how much longer a person who is born or reaches a particular age in a specific year will actually live. For instance, U.S. life expectancy at birth in 1989 was 75.3 years, but because age-specific death rates continue to decline, someone born in 1989 can, on average, expect to live longer (figure 2).

A CENTURY OF DECLINING MORTALITY

At the beginning of the twentieth century, life in the United States was precarious. Seventeen of every 1,000 Americans living in the Death Registration States failed to survive the year. Life expectancy at birth was only forty-seven years. Tuberculosis and typhoid ravaged the population, killing tens of thousands. Pneumonia struck down tens of thousands more, especially the very young and the very old. The great epidemics of the previous century—smallpox, cholera, and yellow fever—had receded as threats, but fatal epidemics had not yet become a thing of the past. In 1918 a pandemic of influenza struck the United States, killing more than a quarter million

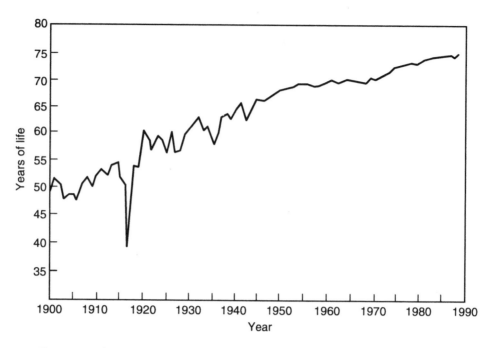

Figure 2. Life expectancy at birth: Death registration states, 1900–1932; United States, 1933–1992. (Source: data from two publications of the National Center for Health Statistics: *Vital Statistics of the United States, 1988,* vol. 2, *Mortality* [1990], part A, sec. 6, pp. 18–19; "Advance Report of Final Mortality Statistics, 1989," *Monthly Vital Statistics Report* 40 [7 January 1992], p. 1; *Statistical Abstract of the United States,* 1994.)

people in the Death Registration States alone. Polio was a growing threat, killing 6,000 people and crippling thousands more, many of them children, during a 1916 epidemic outbreak. Measles, diphtheria, whooping cough, and scarlet fever were childhood rites of passage that thousands of children failed to survive. Diarrhea and enteritis were endemic, regularly incapacitating adults and older children and cutting a deadly swath through the infant population, especially during the hot summer months. Indeed, between 10 and 13 percent of all U.S. residents died within the first year of life, some 18 percent never reached the age of five, and nearly 23 percent died before age twenty. Adulthood was safer, but not safe. For women, giving birth was both a frequent and risky experience. For men, working in agriculture, industry, or mining could bring sudden death from accident or slow death from breathing or ingesting coal dust, lead and other toxins. Among both sexes, tuberculosis and other infectious diseases killed extraordinary numbers. Rather than coming at the end of a long life, death was a frequent visitor at all periods of the life cycle.

The precariousness of life in the United States at the turn of the century was not unusual for the time. In poorer, undeveloped, and nonindustrial countries of the world, the risk of dying was significantly greater. In the wealthier industrial countries it was nearly the same as in the United States. Indeed, the United States ranked somewhere in the middle of the major industrial nations, with a life expectancy at birth that was lower than that in Australia, Denmark, Holland, Norway, and Sweden, but higher than that in England, Germany, France, Switzerland, Italy, and Japan.

Nine decades after the century began, the U.S. age-adjusted death rate has declined sharply from around 17 to just above 5, and life expectancy at birth has risen correspondingly to more than seventy-five years. Most of the childhood diseases are less frequently contracted and rarely fatal. Typhoid is no longer a significant threat; and tuberculosis, although lately evidencing a resurgence, especially among individuals with compromised immune systems, remains but a shadow of the scourge it once was. Similarly, while AIDS has become pandemic, causing an ever increasing number of deaths each year, and the recent emergence and spread of Lyme disease and some deadly disorders caused by new strains of streptococcal and *E. coli* bacteria offer vivid reminders that the microbial threat to health in the United States has not been banished, infectious disease in general is no longer the handmaiden to death that it was at the beginning of the century.

In particular, infectious disease has dramatically decreased among the young and among childbearing women. The annual epidemics of diarrhea and enteritis that swept away thousands of infants each summer no longer occur and, although infancy is still a period of risk, that risk has decreased over twelvefold. Today, only 0.9 percent of all infants born fail to reach age one. And, where at the turn of the century almost a quarter of all Americans died before age twenty, now less than 2 percent do. Women face less than 1 percent of the risk of dying in childbirth than they did ninety years ago; and outside of accidents, homicide, and suicide, young adults of both sexes face few risks of death. Death still occasionally calls upon the young, but in 1990, 72 percent of deaths occurred among Americans more than sixty-four years of age.

While it is readily apparent that mortality has declined significantly through the twentieth century, it is less apparent when that decline began. Because of the absence of reliable national-level mortality data for the United States prior to 1900, estimates of nineteenth-century mortality rates and trends have been based on inference from other types of data or extrapolated from the experiences of the very few states or cities that kept relatively accurate death records for at least part of the century. Predictably, these estimates, and the theories of mortality change built on them, vary widely. One theory has mortality declining after 1840 as income began rising. A second has it declining in the initial part of the century and then increasing again during the middle decades as the negative effects of urbanization and industrialization offset the positive effects of rising income. A third, based on Massachusetts records, has mortality remaining relatively stable between 1790 and 1860. Yet, whatever mortality was doing during most of the nineteenth century, it seems relatively certain that it was declining by the 1890s and, although the decline probably began earliest in rural areas, it was most rapid in cities, particularly large cities. It also seems certain that death rates from some of the major infectious diseases, particularly tuberculosis, had already begun to decline significantly by the beginning of the twentieth century.

By 1900, U.S. mortality levels had already been set on the course they would follow through the coming century. In figure 1, the relentless downward direction of that course is apparent, yet it is also apparent that mortality's descent has not been uniform across time. Prior to the late 1930s, the reduction of mortality was marked by significant short-term fluctuations and reversals, especially in 1918 when the influenza pandemic drove death rates to their highest point in the century. After 1937 the fluctuations and reversals began to flatten and by the early 1940s had almost disappeared. It is also apparent from figure 1 that the rate of decline has not been uniform, with certain periods seeing more rapid decline than others. Excepting 1918, age-adjusted death rates fell relatively sharply between 1907 and 1920, after which they fluctuated, but did not significantly decline, for a decade and a half. In the latter part of the 1930s, they began another period of rapid descent, which lasted until the early 1950s. In 1968 they again began to fall sharply and continued to do so until the early 1980s.

In addition to not being uniform across time, the twentieth-century decline in mortality has not been uniform across all segments of the U.S. population. While all U.S. population groups have benefited from the decline in mortality, they have not benefited at the same rate and time, or to the same degree. Rate, timing, and degree of benefit have differed considerably according to age, sex, race, place of residence, and socioeconomic status, as well as to various combinations of these variables.

Perhaps the greatest variation has been by age. Although all age groups have experienced significant declines in mortality, some have seen their death rates fall farther than others, in part because their death rates started higher. In 1900, death came most frequently to those at the very end and the very beginning of the life cycle; that is, to the extreme aged over eighty-four and to infants under one year of age. The death rates of both groups have fallen dramatically over the course of the century, with that of infants falling the most. Sizeable, although smaller, declines were experienced by the elderly (those sixty-five to eighty-four) and by young children, and even smaller declines were experienced by older adults, young adults, adolescents, and older children (table 1).

Size or distance of decline is only one way to measure the relative mortality reductions among the different age groups. Another way is to look at the percentage decline in the mortality rates of each group. The data in table 1 show that, proportionately, mortality declined most among children aged one to four, then older children and infants, followed by adolescents, young adults, middle-aged adults, the elderly, and the extreme aged. Hence, with the exception of infants and young children, the rate of decline has been greatest among those age groups

Table 1.   AGE-SPECIFIC DEATH RATES AND PERCENTAGE DECLINE
DEATH REGISTRATION STATES, 1900 AND 1930; UNITED STATES,
1960 AND 1990

Age Group	Age-Specific Death Rate[a]				Decline, %
	1900	1930	1960	1990[b]	1900–1990
<1	162.4	69.0	27.0	9.4	94.2
1–4	19.8	5.6	1.1	0.4	98.0
5–14	3.9	1.7	0.5	0.2	94.9
15–24	5.9	3.3	1.1	1.0	83.1
25–34	8.2	4.7	1.5	1.4	82.9
35–44	10.2	6.8	3.0	2.2	78.4
45–54	15.0	12.2	7.6	4.6	69.3
55–64	27.2	24.0	17.4	11.8	56.6
65–74	56.4	51.4	38.2	26.1	53.7
75–84	123.3	112.7	87.5	60.8	50.7
≥85	260.9	228.0	198.6	148.0	43.3

[a] Age-specific death rate = deaths within age group per 1,000 mid-year population of that age group.
[b] Rates for 1990 are provisional.
SOURCE: National Center for Health Statistics, *Vital Statistics Rates in the United States, 1940–1960*, by Robert
    D. Grove and Alice Hetzel (1968), Table 56, p. 325, and "Births, Divorces and Deaths for January 1992,"
    Monthly Vital Statistics Report 41 (May 28, 1992):13.

that across the century have faced the lowest risk
of death.

The reduction of mortality among the different
ages also varied by timing. Just as the mortality of
the entire U.S. population declined faster and farther
in some periods than in others, so too did the mortality of each age group. The proportion of each age
group's mortality reduction that occurred during the
periods 1900–1930, 1930–1960, and 1960–1990 is
presented graphically in figure 3. A distinct pattern
is evident. Children under fourteen achieved their
greatest mortality reduction during the first part of
the century, with improvements ranging from just
under 60 percent for those five through fourteen
years of age to over 70 percent for those aged one
to four. Significantly smaller gains were achieved by
these age groups in the second period and the smallest
in the last, although infants, more than children, have
experienced a significant decline in mortality since
1960. The first part of the century was also the period
in which mortality declined the most for adolescents
and young adults, aged fifteen to thirty-four. But
this age group also experienced a mortality reduction
of almost equal proportions in the second period,
while their mortality improved little if any since
1960.

Among adults thirty-five to forty-four, mortality
dropped the most during the middle period, although as was true with the younger ages, a significant mortality decline occurred during the first part
of the century. For middle-aged and younger elderly

adults, forty-five to seventy-four, the middle period
was also the time of greatest improvement. Unlike
younger adults, however, middle-aged and younger
elderly Americans achieved their next greatest mortality reduction during the most recent years of the
century. Finally, among the older elderly and the
extreme aged, mortality declined most after 1960,
although significant mortality reductions were registered in the two earlier periods.

Aside from illustrating that the twentieth-century
mortality decline has varied in timing among the
different ages, figure 3 also shows a clear pattern to
that variation. As we move up through the life cycle,
the period of greatest mortality reduction moves correspondingly up from the beginning decades of the
century to the latter decades. The one exception to
this pattern, as shown in figure 4, occurred in the
group consisting of those within the first year of life.
There the pattern is reversed. Postneonatal mortality,
or the mortality of older infants, fell most rapidly
during the first half of the century and has been
relatively stable since around 1970. However, neonatal mortality, or the mortality of those in the first
month of life, has declined significantly since the
late 1960s.

The rate and timing of mortality decline during
this century has also varied by sex (figure 5).
Throughout the century women have experienced
lower death rates and have lived longer than men.
But beginning in the 1920s, the death rates of U.S.
women began declining more rapidly than those of

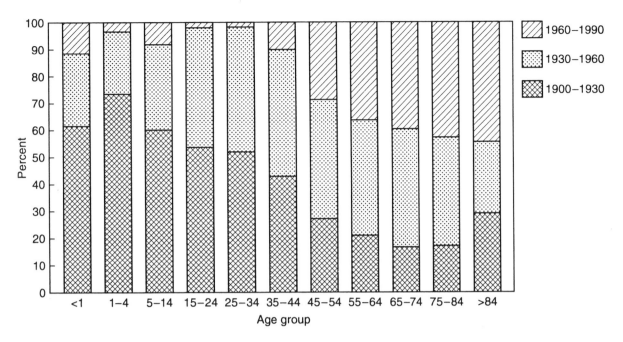

Figure 3. Proportion of total mortality decline at each age occurring during three periods: 1900–1930, 1930–1960, 1960–1990. (Source: data from two publications of the National Center for Health Statistics: *Vital Statistics Rates of the United States, 1940–1960,* by Robert D. Grove and Alice Hetzel [1968]; "Births, Marriages, Divorces, and Deaths for January 1992," *Monthly Vital Statistics Report* 41 [28 May 1992], p. 13.

U.S. men, and continued to do so until the 1970s, after which the differential seems to have diminished slightly. Although the difference in the death rates of the two sexes is apparent at all ages, it has consistently been greatest in early adulthood and in the years between fifty-four and seventy-five.

Along with age and sex, race has also been an important variable in the twentieth-century mortality decline. In 1900 U.S. residents classified as nonwhite had a significantly higher death rate than those classified as white (figure 6). Ninety years later the disadvantage persists, but has shrunk. Between 1900 and 1989 the ratio of the nonwhite to the white age-adjusted death rates decreased from 1.6 to less than 1.4. Significantly, much of that shrinkage seems to have resulted from an extraordinary decrease in mortality among nonwhite women. In 1900 the death rate for nonwhite women was 47 percent higher than for white men and 61 percent higher than for white women. Today it is fully 20 percent lower than for white men, and only 37 percent higher than for white women.

For African Americans, the most numerous of those classified as nonwhite, the pattern of mortality decline mirrors that of the larger nonwhite race category. Even though the Death Registration States data

exaggerate the level of African American mortality in the early decades of the century, it is fairly certain that in both absolute and relative terms mortality among U.S. blacks has declined faster and farther than it has among whites, although it remains significantly higher, especially for certain age groups. For instance, although the infant mortality rate of black babies has fallen dramatically since the beginning of the century, it remains more than twice that of white babies. As with all those classified as nonwhite, the greatest improvement has been among black females. In 1900–1902, life expectancy at birth was 32.5 years for African American males and 35.0 for African American females, compared with 48.2 for white males and 51.1 for white females. By 1989 white male life expectancy had increased 24.5 years to 72.7 and white female life expectancy 28.1 years to 79.2. During the same period, black male life expectancy increased 32.3 years to 64.8 and black female life expectancy 38.5 years to 73.5. Significantly, though, the sharp decline in mortality among African Americans seems to have leveled off, and, indeed, during the last few years mortality has actually increased among African American males.

Mortality rate and trend differentials between the races in twentieth-century America have varied ac-

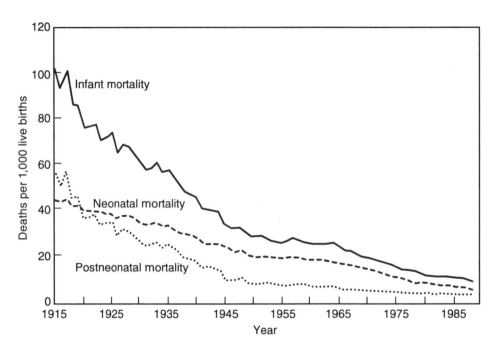

Figure 4.   Infant, neonatal, and postneonatal mortality: Birth-registration states, 1915–1932; United States, 1933–1989. (Source: data from four publications of the National Center for Health Statistics: *Vital Statistics of the United States, 1988,* vol. 2, *Mortality* [1990], part A, sec. 2, p. 1; *Vital Statistics Rates of the United States, 1940–1960,* by Robert D. Grove and Alice Hetzel [1968], pp. 206–207; "Advance Report of Final Mortality Statistics, 1989," *Monthly Vital Statistics Report* 40 [7 January 1992], p. 14; "Births, Marriages, Divorces, and Deaths for January 1992," *Monthly Vital Statistics Report* 41 [28 May 1992], p. 19.)

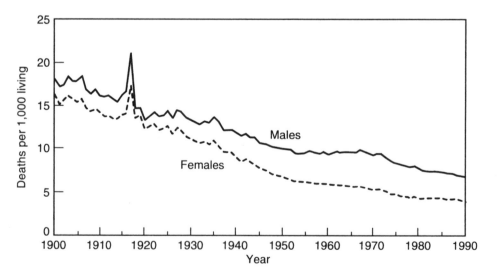

Figure 5.   Age-adjusted death rates by sex: Death-registration states, 1900–1932; United States, 1933–1991. (Source: data from three publications of the National Center for Health Statistics: *Vital Statistics of the United States, 1988,* vol. 2, *Mortality* [1990], part A, sec. 1, pp. 5–6; "Advance Report of Final Mortality Statistics, 1989," *Monthly Vital Statistics Report* 40 [7 January 1992], p. 14; "Births, Marriages, Divorces, and Deaths for January 1992," *Monthly Vital Statistics Report* 41 [28 May 1992], p. 13.)

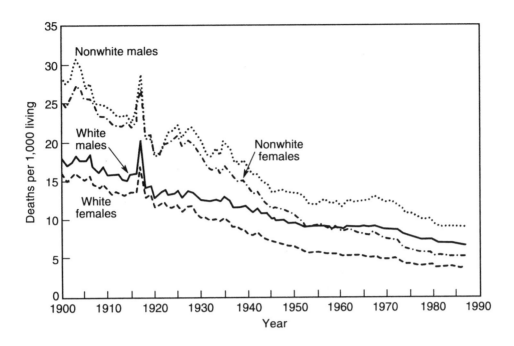

Figure 6.   Age-adjusted death rate by sex and race: Death-registration states, 1900–1932; United States, 1933–1989. (Source: data from two publications of the National Center for Health Statistics: *Vital Statistics of the United States, 1988,* vol. 2, *Mortality* [1990], part A, sec. 1, pp. 5–6; "Advance Report of Final Mortality Statistics, 1989," *Monthly Vital Statistics Report* 40 [7 January 1992], p. 14.

cording to age, as well as sex. Since 1930, when the Death Registration Area was large enough to make nonwhite mortality figures representative of the national nonwhite population, the mortality differential between the races has consistently been higher at certain ages than at others (table 2). Starting at a peak

among infants less than one year old, the differential declines through childhood and adolescence before peaking again among young adults aged twenty-five to forty-four. After the second peak, the differential declines steadily with advancing age and inverts among the older elderly. Indeed, although a portion

Table 2.   RACE DIFFERENTIALS IN MORTALITY: RATIO OF NONWHITE TO WHITE AGE-SPECIFIC DEATH RATES; DEATH-REGISTRATION STATES 1900 AND 1930; UNITED STATES 1960 AND 1988

Age Group	1900	1930	1960	1988
<1	2.09	1.72	1.96	2.09
1–4	2.24	1.78	1.90	1.58
5–14	2.36	1.63	1.50	1.40
15–24	2.02	2.86	1.60	1.40
25–34	1.49	3.05	2.67	2.02
35–44	1.47	2.73	2.42	2.17
45–54	1.64	2.39	1.94	1.79
55–64	1.56	1.79	1.24	1.44
65–74	1.23	1.26	1.28	1.22
75–84	0.98	0.92	0.86	1.10
≥85	0.82	0.89	0.68	0.81

SOURCES: Computed from data in National Center for Health Statistics, *Vital Statistics Rates in the United States, 1940–1960,* by Robert D. Grove and Alice M. Hetzel (1968), pp. 328, 331, and *Vital Statistics of the United States, 1988,* vol. 2, *Mortality,* part A, sect. 1, pp. 7–8.

of this observed inversion may be due to the misreporting of ages, it is arguable that through most of the century nonwhites over seventy-five have enjoyed lower death rates than whites. The age variation in the mortality differential between the races also holds true within the first year of life. Since 1930, nonwhites and especially blacks have experienced significantly higher rates and slower declines in neonatal mortality than have whites.

The rate, trends, and timing of the decline in mortality in twentieth-century America have also varied according to the size and population density of places of residence. Because the risk of death in the past from infectious disease was greater in places where people were crowded together and where there was a constant stream of new arrivals, the death rates in cities in the United States were always higher than death rates in less populated and more isolated rural areas. This certainly was true at the turn of the century. The crude death rate in the urban areas of the Death Registration States in 1900 was 18.9 while in the rural areas it was 15.2. Accordingly, life expectancy at birth for rural white males in 1901 was ten years greater than it was for their urban counterparts; and for rural females it was seven years greater.

Mortality was higher in all urban areas, but particularly so in the largest cities. In 1900, New York's crude death rate was 20.6, Boston's 20.4, Philadelphia's 20.9 and Baltimore's 21.4. Moreover, in the poorer sections of cities—where substandard housing was the rule, where sewerage, water supplies, and garbage disposal were invariably the worst, and where population density was greatest—death rates were usually considerably higher. In particular, those sections of cities occupied by newly arrived immigrants or by African Americans had among the highest death rates in the United States at the time.

A risky place to live for people of all ages, cities seemed especially dangerous for the young. While some 12 percent of all infants born in the Registration States in 1900 died before reaching age one, over 18 percent of those born in New York City failed to survive the year, and this was down considerably from the almost 25 percent who had regularly perished each year in New York during the 1870s and 1880s. Little wonder that the *New York Times* would lament in 1876: "There is no more depressing feature about our American cities than the annual slaughter of little children of which they are the scene." Indeed, much of the difference between urban and rural mortality at the beginning of the century appears to have been due to the greater risk of death faced by urban infants and children.

Starting with the highest death rates, the largest U.S. cities seem to have been the earliest urban areas to register significant declines in mortality. Between 1880 and 1900, the crude death rates of the ten largest U.S. cities declined from 10 to 30 percent. Less populous cities experienced smaller or no declines, but overall urban mortality rates at the turn of the century appear to have been falling faster than rural mortality rates. This trend continued until the third decade of the century when the rates of decline for urban and rural areas converged. Since 1960, no clear trend is apparent. Some large cities, due in part to differences in the age composition of their populations, have lower crude death rates than the nation as a whole, while others have higher rates. It seems fairly certain, however, that many of the poorer sections of large cities remain unhealthy places to live. While infant mortality is dramatically lower than it was ninety years ago, it is still considerably higher in such areas than elsewhere. For instance, as late as 1986, the infant mortality rate in central Harlem was more than two-and-a-half times the national rate. Rates of mortality among the adult urban poor are also higher, from virtually all the leading causes of death and particularly from violence. Indeed, among poor, urban, young adult males, and especially among those who are African American and reside in racially segregated sections of cities, violence now ranks as the most frequent cause of death.

Last to be considered are the ways in which mortality levels and trends have varied over the course of the century in relation to economic status. While wealth and poverty are necessarily relative and the connection of each to mortality levels is complex, it has long been axiomatic that, historically, the economically well-off have faced a lower risk of dying than the economically disadvantaged. The reasoning behind this axiom is straightforward. Research into contemporary mortality patterns worldwide has shown that the ability to secure safe and sanitary housing, to purchase sufficient amounts of nutritious food, to get timely and skilled medical advice and care, to avoid the most dangerous occupations and most violence-prone neighborhoods, and to achieve the educational and cultural competency that encourages healthful behavior are all directly related to income level. It is thus not surprising that a leitmotif running through analyses of twentieth-century U.S. mortality rates and trends has been the assertion that throughout the century economic status has consistently been one of the most important determinants of mortality rates and trends.

That assertion is supported by considerable evidence, ranging from the data collected early in the century by the Children's Bureau, which linked infant mortality levels to fathers' incomes, to more recent data on family resources and relative risks of death. Yet, while the evidence demonstrates that economic factors have been important throughout the century in establishing mortality levels, it has not demonstrated that the importance of economic factors has been constant across time. The case can be, and has been, made that since Medicaid, Medicare, and other sociomedical assistance programs became available in the 1960s, the correlation between economic status and mortality has weakened.

In addition, a few historical demographers have recently argued that economic factors were considerably less powerful as determinants of death rates at the beginning of the century than they subsequently became. Demonstrating that in turn-of-the-century America the professional classes did not have significantly lower child death rates than other groups, these demographers have theorized that the ability to purchase health care is an advantage only if that health care is effective. In their view, the way in which resources translate into mortality levels has changed considerably over the course of the century as the medical care and advice those resources can make available has improved.

It should be clear from the preceding discussion that while U.S. mortality levels have dropped dramatically since the beginning of the twentieth century, they have done so with great variation across time and across different population groups. Significant fluctuations and short-term reversals marked the earliest part of the decline. More rapid rates of descent marked the decline during the 1910s, 1940s, and 1970s. In absolute terms, the decline in mortality has been greatest among the very young and very old, but in relative terms improvement has been greatest among children, adolescents and young adults. For the young, the greatest reduction in death rates took place in the first three decades of the century. For the middle-aged, it was the period between 1930 and 1960 that was most important. And for the old, mortality declined most dramatically after 1960. Both sexes have experienced greatly reduced death rates as the century has progressed, but, especially after 1920, mortality has fallen faster among females than males, although the difference seems to be leveling out. Those classified as nonwhite have seen their death rates drop faster and farther than those classified as whites, although nonwhites still suffer significantly higher mortality levels, especially in infancy and

Table 3. LEADING CAUSES OF DEATH, DEATH-REGISTRATION AREA, 1900

Cause of Death	Rate[a]	% of All Deaths
1. Influenza and Pneumonia	203.3	11.6
(Pneumonia, all forms)	(180.4)	(10.3)
(Influenza)	(22.9)	(1.3)
2. Tuberculosis (all forms)	201.2	11.3
3. Diarrhea and Enteritis	133.2	7.6
4. Heart Disease	111.2	6.3
5. Nephritis (all forms)	89.0	5.1
6. Congenital Malformations and Diseases of Early Infancy	88.4	5.0
7. Accidents and Injuries[b]	78.9	4.5
8. Cerebrovascular Disease[c]	67.5	3.8
9. Cancer	63.0	3.6
10. Diphtheria	34.1	1.9

[a] Deaths from specified cause per 100,000 mid-year population.
[b] Exclusive of injuries at birth, homicide, and suicide.
[c] Apoplexy.
SOURCE: Calculated from data contained in U.S. Census Bureau, *Mortality Statistics, 1900–1904* (1906), pp. 82–89.

young adulthood. While both rich and poor have benefited from the decline in mortality, the rich may have benefited more because the importance of their greater material resources seems to have grown as the effectiveness of purchasable medical services has increased.

THE CHANGING CAUSES OF DEATH

Intimately related to the variations that marked the profound decline in U.S. mortality during the twentieth century has been an equally profound change in the principal causes of death, for both the total population and the different age groups. Through 1960 at least five major trends in this epidemiologic transition are evident. The first and most significant is a shift in the principal causes of death from infectious diseases, which strike all ages but are particularly deadly among the young, to chronic and degenerative diseases which cause death most often among those over forty-five. The second is a gradual and uneven increase in the importance of external causes of death—accidents and injuries, homicide, and suicide—as killers of children, adolescents, and young adults. The third is an increase in the proportion of infant mortality attributable to congenital malformations and anomalies, prematurity, and other so-called diseases of early infancy and a corresponding decrease in the proportion of infant mortality caused by digestive and respiratory diseases. The fourth is a dramatic decrease in maternal mortality, not only from puerperal septicemia but also from all other causes. The fifth is an increasing concentration of the vast majority of all deaths among fewer and fewer causes.

In 1900, the three leading causes of death were infectious diseases: tuberculosis, pneumonia, and diarrhea and enteritis. Together they accounted for close to one-third (30.5 percent) of all deaths recorded in the Death Registration Area. Although certainly not limited to infants, children, adolescents, and young adults, these three diseases were responsible for a greater proportion of deaths among those under forty-five than among those forty-five and over (table 3). Diarrhea, enteritis and other gastrointestinal diseases were the leading killers of infants and one-year-olds, pneumonia of young children, and tuberculosis of older adolescents and young adults. Other infectious diseases also caused large numbers of deaths among the young. Diphtheria, which ranked as the tenth leading killer overall, measles, whooping cough, scarlet fever and meningitis cut down thousands of children aged one to fourteen. Typhoid killed thousands of adolescents and young adults. And puerperal septicemia was responsible for the deaths of almost half of all women who died in childbirth.

Conversely, those causes of death that were not infectious diseases accounted for a comparatively small percentage of all deaths. Chronic and degenerative diseases such as heart disease, cerebrovascular disease, and cancer ranked well down on the list and together accounted for less than 19 percent of all deaths. This does not mean that turn-of-the-century Americans did not develop such diseases; it only means that they did not die from them as frequently as they did from infectious diseases. It is arguable that had infectious diseases not been so prevalent and fatal, older Americans at the beginning of the century would have died from chronic and degenerative diseases as frequently or more frequently than they do at the end of the century. External causes such as accidents, homicide, and suicide produced less than 6 percent of all deaths. Congenital malformations and anomalies and the diseases of early infancy were responsible for just over a quarter of all infant deaths (table 4).

By 1930, the preeminence of infectious diseases as the major killers of Americans had faded considerably. The death rates due to both typhoid and diarrhea and enteritis had declined over 80 percent, that due to tuberculosis over 60 percent, and that due to pneumonia over 50 percent. The childhood diseases had also become dramatically less deadly. Death rates

Table 4. LEADING CAUSES OF DEATH, DEATH-REGISTRATION STATES, 1930

Cause of Death	Rate[a]	% of All Deaths
1. Heart Disease	213.5	18.8
2. Influenza and Pneumonia	102.7	9.0
(Influenza)	(19.5)	(1.7)
(Pneumonia)	(83.2)	(7.3)
3. Cancer	97.2	8.6
4. Nephritis	90.8	8.0
5. Cerebrovascular Disease[b]	88.8	7.8
6. Accidents and Injuries[c]	80.6	7.1
7. Tuberculosis	71.5	6.3
8. Congenital Malformations and Diseases of Early Infancy	60.9	5.4
9. Diarrhea and Enteritis	26.3	2.3
10. Diabetes Mellitus	19.0	1.7

[a] Deaths from specified cause per 100,000 mid-year population.
[b] Includes embolism and thrombosis.
[c] Exclusive of injuries at birth, homicide, and suicide.
SOURCE: U.S. Bureau of the Census, *Mortality Statistics, 1930* (1934), p. 11.

from diphtheria and scarlet fever had fallen over 80 percent, from measles over 70 percent, and from whooping cough over 60 percent. The risk of death from puerperal septicemia faced by women in childbirth had also begun to fall, to near 60 percent of what it had been at the turn of the century, although overall maternal mortality remained high.

Accompanying the fall of death rates from infectious diseases was an increase in death rates from chronic and degenerative diseases, from external causes, and from problems specific to early infancy, along with a corresponding increase in the proportion of all deaths accounted for by these causes. Heart disease became the leading killer of Americans; its death rate nearly doubled and the percentage of all deaths for which it was responsible tripled. Cancer ranked number two, nephritis number three, and stroke number four. Of all the infectious diseases, only pneumonia remained among the top five causes of death.

Equally significant, the percentage of all deaths attributable to accidents and injuries had increased, especially among the young. In 1900 accidents and injuries caused 2.5 percent of all deaths among those one through fourteen. Thirty years later, accidents and injuries were responsible for 15.7 percent of all deaths in that age group. During the same period, the proportion of infant deaths attributable to congenital malformations and the diseases of early infancy rose from approximately 27 percent to just under 50 per-

Table 5. LEADING CAUSES OF DEATH,
UNITED STATES, 1960

Cause of Death	Rate[a]	% of All Deaths
1. Heart Disease	369.0	38.7
2. Cancer	149.2	15.6
3. Cerebrovascular Disease	108.0	11.3
4. Accidents and Injuries[b]	52.3	5.5
(Motor Vehicle)	(21.3)	(2.2)
5. Congenital Malformations and Diseases of Early Infancy	49.6	4.2
6. Influenza and Pneumonia	37.3	3.9
(Influenza)	(4.4)	
(Pneumonia)	(32.9)	
7. General Arteriosclerosis	20.0	2.1
8. Diabetes Mellitus	16.7	1.8
9. Cirrhosis of the Liver	11.3	1.2
10. Suicide	11.0	1.1

[a] Deaths from specified cause per 100,000 mid-year population.
[b] Exclusive of injuries at birth, homicide, and suicide.
SOURCE: National Center for Health Statistics, *Vital Statistics of the United States, 1960,* vol. 2, *Mortality,* part A, sec. 1, p. 23.

cent. Finally, where in 1900 the ten leading causes of death accounted for some 60 percent of all recorded deaths, in 1930 they accounted for over 73 percent (table 5).

By 1960, the transition was complete. Of the formerly deadly infectious diseases, only pneumonia remained a major killer. All the other principal causes of death were either chronic and degenerative diseases, external causes, or problems related to early infancy. Moreover, the three leading causes accounted for a lion's share of all deaths. Heart disease, cancer, and stroke killed over 65 percent of all Americans who died that year; and, altogether, the ten leading causes were responsible for over 85 percent of all deaths. Both the death rate due to accidents and injuries and the percentage of total deaths for which they accounted had fallen, but the relative importance of accidents and injuries as killers of children continued to increase. Over 38 percent of all children who died in the United States in 1960 did so from these two causes. Similarly, although both the infant and neonatal mortality rates had dropped since 1930, the percentage of infant deaths taking place in early infancy increased significantly. Finally, between 1930 and 1960 maternal mortality dropped dramatically, from more than six hundred to only thirty-seven deaths per 100,000 live births (table 6).

After 1960, however, the trend is less clear. Death rates from traditional infectious diseases continued to fall. Among the major turn-of-the-century infec-

tious killers, only pneumonia and influenza continued to cause a significant number of deaths, although by 1989 they accounted for barely 3.6 percent of all U.S. fatalities. Yet as the last decade of the century began, there were disturbing signs that infectious diseases might be making a comeback. Affecting a dramatic reversal of what had been a seemingly inevitable trend since the late nineteenth century, a new and frighteningly deadly infectious disease had appeared and quickly spread. Labelled acquired immune deficiency syndrome (AIDS), a name by which it is still most popularly known, and then more precisely human immunodeficiency virus infection (HIV infection), the disease at first seemed largely limited to male homosexuals and intravenous drug users. But while the morbidity and mortality rates remained highest among these two groups, the disease slowly spread to other segments of the population and by 1989 ranked as the eleventh leading killer of Americans and as the third leading killer of those aged twenty-five to thirty-four. Having played a major role in reversing a century-long trend of rising life expectancy among young adult males, the HIV infection epidemic has already had an impact on the pattern of U.S. mortality surpassed in the century only by that of the 1918 influenza pandemic.

Less visible but perhaps more portentous has been a resurgence of infectious disease in general. Some of this resurgence involves the reemergence of such familiar and successfully controlled diseases as child-

Table 6. LEADING CAUSES OF DEATH,
UNITED STATES, 1989

Cause of Death	Rate[a]	% of All Deaths
1. Diseases of the Heart	295.6	34.1
2. Cancer	199.9	23.1
3. Cerebrovascular Disease	58.6	6.8
4. Accidents and Injuries[b]	38.3	4.4
(Motor Vehicle)	(19.2)	(2.2)
5. Chronic Bronchitis and Emphysema	34.0	3.9
6. Pneumonia and Influenza	30.8	3.6
7. Diabetes Mellitus	18.9	2.2
8. Suicide	12.2	1.4
9. Chronic Liver Disease and Cirrhosis	10.8	1.2
10. Homicide and Legal Intervention	9.2	1.1

[a] Deaths from specified cause per 100,000 mid-year population.
[b] Exclusive of injuries at birth, homicide, and suicide.
SOURCE: National Center for Health Statistics, "Advance Report of Final Mortality Statistics, 1989," *Monthly Vital Statistics Report* 40 (7 January 1992), p. 5.

hood measles, and can be attributed to public, professional, and government complacency in regard to public health measures, particularly immunization. Some involves the emergence of new or more virulent pathogens that result from the rapid genetic mutation and recombination that microorganisms continually undergo. And some is attributable to the evolution of pathogens resistant to existing chemotherapeutic interventions. For instance, in the last decade researchers have documented the existence of drug-resistant strains of the microorganisms that cause tuberculosis and certain types of streptococcal and pneumonococcal infections. Finally, some of the observed resurgence seems to be associated with the changing natural environment and humanity's relation to it. The recent appearance and spread throughout much of the United States of Lyme disease, which is caused by a spirochete transmitted by ticks that live on deer, has been traced to the reforestation of previously cleared farmlands and the increasing penetration of those reforested areas by Americans seeking recreation and wooded home sites. Similarly, increasing human penetration and settlement of previously isolated ecosystems, particularly in the subtropics, combined with ever growing global commerce and transportation, seems to be introducing onto the world stage an unfamiliar array of zoonotic diseases; that is, diseases of animals that are transmissible to humans. AIDS, which many researchers believe is zoonotic in origin, is thus far the only such disease to have had a significant impact on the U.S. population. But time may change that.

The post-1960 trend in fatalities from chronic and degenerative diseases is also mixed. The death rate from heart disease, which had peaked in the 1950s, dropped slowly but steadily, initially among the middle-aged and then among the elderly. Much of this decline was due to a sharp decrease in deaths from myocardial infarction (heart attack). The death rate from cerebrovascular disease dropped even more dramatically, again first among the middle-aged and then in the 1970s and early 1980s among the elderly and extreme aged. Other major chronic and degenerative diseases also became less fatal. The death rate from arteriosclerosis decreased more than 60 percent and that of chronic liver disease and cirrhosis 5 percent. On the other hand, the death rate from cancer has continued steadily upward with a very significant increase in deaths due to lung cancer. However, with the possible exception of breast cancer among women, cancer's rising death rate has been limited to those over fifty-five. Indeed, among children, adolescents, and young adults, the risk of death from

cancer has declined since 1960. Significant increases have also been registered in deaths from diabetes mellitus and especially from chronic bronchitis and emphysema, which like lung cancer, are associated with smoking.

Deaths from external causes also followed a path that is not clear. Such causes continued to account for a steadily increasing proportion of all deaths among the young, in 1989 causing 60 percent of all deaths of those aged one to thirty-four and 70 percent of all deaths of those aged one to twenty-four. Yet between 1960 and 1989 the risk of death from accidents actually dropped for the young, in large part because the death rate from motor vehicle accidents fell. At the same time, however, the risk of death from violence rose significantly, especially for older adolescent and young adult males. Also, between 1960 and 1989 the suicide death rate among those fifteen to twenty-four rose 156 percent, with young males four times as likely to kill themselves as females and white males more than twice as likely to kill themselves as black males. During the same period the homicide death rate rose 186 percent with murder becoming the leading cause of death for young black men.

The trend in maternal and infant deaths has been clearer. After hitting a plateau in the late 1950s and early 1960s, the maternal mortality rate dropped almost 75 percent between 1965 and 1982, after which it has fluctuated. There continues, however, to be a major race differential in the rates, with African American women over three times as likely to die as white women. Infant mortality has followed a similar trend. After leveling off during the 1950s and early 1960s, it declined rapidly, from 24.7 in 1965 to 9.1 in 1990. Significantly, a large portion of this decline was due to a sharp decrease in deaths during the neonatal period; that is, from deaths associated with early infancy. From the beginning of the century through the late 1960s, mortality among infants in the first month of life fell more slowly than it did among infants one month and older. As a result, the ratio of neonatal mortality to postneonatal mortality rose from 0.8 in 1915 to 2.8 in 1968. After 1968, however, neonatal mortality fell more rapidly than postneonatal mortality with the ratio between the two decreasing to 1.7 by 1990.

These trends in changing causes of death help explain the variations noted earlier in the timing and rate of the twentieth-century mortality decline. The short-term fluctuations that characterized mortality rates in the early part of the century were in large part due to the prevalence of infectious disease. Even when endemic, infectious diseases, and especially those that confer immunity, tend to surge and ebb, raging through the susceptible members of a population and then retreating until a critical mass of new susceptible members develops. Thus, as infectious diseases ceased to be major killers of Americans, the short-term fluctuations in the U.S. death rate disappeared.

The sharp decline in fatalities from infectious disease during the first third of the century also helps explain why the death rates of the young dropped more sharply during that period than did the rates of other ages. Because the greatest proportion of deaths that occurred among the young in the early twentieth century were from infectious diseases, the greatest proportion of the young's decline in mortality coincided with the decline in the prevalence and fatality of such diseases. Similarly, the decline in death rates among the middle-aged and elderly that took place in the second half of the century was in large part produced by the concurrent decline in the death rates from heart disease and stroke.

Along with the decline in maternal mortality, the substitution of chronic and degenerative diseases for infectious diseases as the major killer of Americans helps explain why the death rate of women has fallen faster than that of men. Although some research suggests that women have greater immunity to infectious disease, in late-nineteenth- and early-twentieth-century America such diseases accounted for a larger proportion of female deaths than of male deaths, especially at the younger ages. In 1900, for instance, pulmonary tuberculosis was responsible for 33 percent of all deaths in the Death Registration Area among females aged ten through twenty-nine, whereas it caused only 27 percent of the recorded deaths of males the same age. Moreover, while the chronic and degenerative diseases cause fatalities among both sexes, women thus far have proven much less likely to develop and die from such diseases than men. In particular, heart disease, lung cancer, cirrhosis of the liver, and occupation-related neoplasms have been much more common and deadly among men. The same is true of deaths from external causes, especially motor vehicle accidents, suicide and homicide. And it has also proven true for HIV infection. Indeed, in 1989 the death rates for all fifteen leading causes of death were higher for males than for females.

The changing causes of death also help explain why blacks have experienced a greater drop in mortality than whites. At the end of the nineteenth and early part of the twentieth centuries, African American adults suffered dramatically higher death rates

from tuberculosis than did whites. Hence, as mortality from that disease declined, black mortality declined apace. Similarly, African Americans have benefited more, proportionately, from the declines in infant mortality and maternal mortality. Benefit, of course, should be understood relatively here. That African Americans still suffer higher death rates from virtually all the major causes of death stands as testimony to the persistence of those inequitable social and economic arrangements that made their mortality at the beginning of the century so much higher than that of other Americans.

UNDERSTANDING THE TRANSITIONS

It is important to understand why this epidemiologic transition took place. Why did infectious diseases cease to be the major killers of Americans and why was their place taken by chronic and degenerative diseases and external causes? The answer has two parts. The first is straightforward and has been subject to little debate. The second is quite complex and remains the focus of considerable disagreement.

The straightforward part to the answer describes the ways in which the epidemiologic transition has been a consequence both of the mortality transition and of itself. The decline of death rates among the young meant that with each year a greater percentage of those born in the United States were making it into the older adult years. Combined with a concurrent decline in fertility rates, this produced a shift in the age composition of the U.S. population. As the century progressed, the population aged, with an ever greater proportion of Americans occupying the upper reaches of the life cycle where they faced a higher risk of degenerative and chronic diseases than they did earlier in life. For instance, in 1900 infants and children less than fifteen years of age accounted for almost 24 percent of the population of the Death Registration States, while adults forty-five and over accounted for less than 18 percent. By 1990 the proportion of the U.S. population younger than fifteen had declined to 20 percent, while that of those forty-five and over had risen to over 31 percent. This increase in the percentage of the population who were older and elderly, combined with an overall decrease in the risk of dying from infectious diseases, inevitably drove upward the death rates from chronic and degenerative diseases. In a similar manner, the rising percentage of the young dying from external causes was a function of the decline in deaths from infectious diseases. Because the young face a comparatively low risk of dying from natural or biological causes other than infectious diseases, the decline in mortality from such diseases shifted an ever increasing proportion of responsibility for death to external causes, even while death rates among the young from all causes were falling.

The changing age composition of the U.S. population, however, provides only a partial explanation of the epidemiologic transition. It does not indicate what caused mortality from infectious disease to decline so dramatically, or why the death rates from other diseases have risen and declined over the century independent of shifts in the populations most at risk. The answers to these questions are complex; and, indeed, especially in regard to the early part of the century, have prompted substantial debate among demographers and medical historians.

One way to appreciate the source of that debate, as well as the complex amalgam of factors that affect the pattern of mortality and causes of death in twentieth-century America, is to separate the various determinants of the causes and fatality of disease into four broad categories. The first of these categories can be called ecobiologic determinants, which encompass the many ways in which the biology and virulence of disease agents and the effectiveness of human resistance constantly change as they interact with each other and with the social and physical environment. The second category of determinants includes those that indicate general socioeconomic status or standard of living; that is, levels of income and wealth, quality of shelter and degree of population density, and sufficiency of nutrition. The third category comprises cultural and behavioral determinants such as general hygiene, habits and behavior, and knowledge of and value placed upon health-enhancing life-styles. Medical, public health, and political determinants make up the fourth category and include specific and purposive preventive and curative measures adopted to combat and manage disease as well as political steps taken to devote resources to those measures.

Perhaps the greatest amount of debate has centered on the latter part of the nineteenth and first part of the twentieth centuries and has concerned the relative importance of each of the four categories of determinants in the decline of mortality from infectious disease in developed, industrialized nations such as the United States. For at least two decades, the dominant theory of that mortality decline has been a materialist one, most recently and cogently articulated in the work and arguments of T. R. McKeown. Focusing on England and Wales, McKeown has suggested that the decline in mortality during the late nineteenth and early twentieth centuries was due principally to the reduction of deaths from infectious disease, especially tuberculosis, and that the main determinants of this reduction were ecobiologic and socioeconomic. In particular, McKeown has argued that rising living standards, and especially improvements in diet, which led to greater human resistance, were the chief catalysts of the early part of the mortality transition. He has also attributed some, although lesser, importance to improvements in hygiene and public sanitation, as well as to possible changes in the virulence of disease agents, particularly in the case of scarlet fever. But McKeown has given little or no credit to medical practice or to public health immunization programs prior to the second third of the twentieth century. His materialist interpretation has been applied to American mortality trends by a number of scholars who have argued that only rising living standards and better diet can most adequately account for the decline in airborne infectious diseases, such as tuberculosis, that began in the latter half of the nineteenth century.

Although dominant, the materialist interpretation is hardly unassailable. It is quite probable, as a few analysts have noted, that the disease pattern prevailing in the United States at the end of the nineteenth century was not identical to that in England and Wales and that falling death rates from diarrheal diseases may have made up a larger proportion of the mortality decline here. It is also quite probable that the link between rising wages, better nutrition, and increased resistance to disease is more complex than allowed for in the materialist interpretation. While there seems little doubt that improvements in diet since the latter half of the nineteenth century have led to greater disease resistance among Americans, and particularly among the poor, it is unclear how and to what degree such improvements have been tied directly to changing socioeconomic standards. For instance, income did not rise steadily through the late nineteenth and early twentieth centuries, but, rather, fluctuated dramatically due to a number of severe economic disruptions and depressions. Yet the observed decline in death rates from infectious diseases seems to have been little affected by the widespread impoverishment that accompanied these disruptions and depressions. Moreover, while at the end of the nineteenth century many poor Americans, especially children, suffered from nutritional disorders such as rickets, anemia, and (in the rural South) pellagra, all of which could and did lower resistance to other disease, significant decline in the incidence of these diseases did not come about until well into the current century and was at least as much due to scientific discovery of the nutritional role of vitamins and minerals as it was to rising incomes.

Finally, it has been argued that because food was comparatively abundant and inexpensive in the United States at the turn of the century and because death rates among the well-off were not significantly lower than among the disadvantaged, it seems highly unlikely that rising incomes alone could so dramatically affect the quality of diet as to be primarily responsible for precipitating a mortality decline. In short, the major problem with the materialist interpretation is that it is somewhat simplistic and reductionist, especially in its treatment of economic development, dietary improvement, and disease reduction as directly linked and separable from numerous other far-reaching social, cultural, political, and technological changes occurring at the same time. Indeed, a more plausible interpretation of the initial part of the twentieth-century mortality and epidemiologic transitions would be that death rates from infectious disease declined in the United States for a wide variety of reasons, including but not limited to rising living standards and improved diet.

Among the most important of those reasons are the extensive and varied public health activities undertaken by states and cities in the early part of the century. In the years following the Civil War, many of the larger municipalities in the United States created public health departments, gave them statutory control over environmental sanitation, and granted them access to some of the tax revenues accruing from urban economic expansion. On the sanitary principle that dirt and pollution generated disease, water supply and sewerage systems were constructed, street cleaning and garbage disposal were initiated, and regulatory statutes were enacted concerning the handling and marketing of food and the sanitary condition of tenement houses and public buildings. Through the 1870s and 1880s the effectiveness of these measures proved relatively limited. In all but a few cities and towns, fecal contamination of drinking water remained a serious problem, in part because the newly constructed sewers often drained directly into the adjacent lakes and rivers which were the sources of drinking water. Both corruption and the pace of urban growth made street cleaning and garbage disposal irregular and inefficient. Especially in hot weather, towns and cities were suffused with the stench from horse manure, rotting garbage, and decaying animal carcasses that littered streets, alleys, and vacant lots. Regulatory measures were resisted and

ignored, or eviscerated by city and state legislatures unwilling to face the ire of landlords, homeowners, and businesses. Nevertheless, especially in large cities, the 1870s and 1880s witnessed some improvement in the sanitary environment and, perhaps more important, saw the creation of a bureaucratic, regulatory, and physical infrastructure that would subsequently support more effective public health activities.

A large step toward effectiveness was taken in the last two decades of the nineteenth century when public health professionals began embracing the germ theory of disease causation and started to develop methods for testing food and water for bacterial contamination and for positively diagnosing individuals infected with certain communicable diseases. Although this new microbiologic basis of public health was resisted by some health officials who remained wedded to miasmic theories of disease, it eventually had an enormous impact. The testing of water led to the development of effective filtration and purification methods, which, combined with efforts to redirect sewer outlets away from water supplies, ultimately had a dramatic effect on the transmission of deadly waterborne diseases such as typhoid. The recognition that it was bacterial contamination and growth that made food and drink dangerous gave specificity to regulatory measures controlling the production and handling of foodstuffs, and, perhaps more important, gave powerful impetus to the innovation of technologies to kill bacteria in food or impede its growth. The widespread adoption of ice boxes for the home and market and the design and use of refrigerated cars for food transport found strong support in the microbiologic revolution. So too did the development of milk pasteurization and the compulsory pasteurization laws that most cities and states ultimately enacted.

Public health's embrace of the germ theory in the late nineteenth and early twentieth centuries probably also had an eventual impact on the transmission of some airborne childhood diseases such as diphtheria and tuberculosis, although the death rate from the latter had been declining at least since the 1860s. While physicians in general were slow to incorporate the germ theory into their everyday practice, the establishment of diagnostic laboratories where cultures could be analyzed allowed for the positive identification of infected individuals. So too did the development and increasing use, especially on school children, of the tuberculin skin test. Combined with laws that prohibited school attendance by sick children and that required families with a sick individual to be quarantined, the development of positive diagnostic techniques promoted the isolation of contagious children, thereby reducing the risk of infection through human contact.

Embrace of the germ theory also prompted research in immunology and serology. Admittedly, most of the products of that research would not become available until after 1930, but at least one—diphtheria antitoxin—was being commercially produced by the late 1890s. That diphtheria death rates remained relatively high had less to do with the effectiveness of the antitoxin than with its uneven and slow deployment and with initial uncertainty over appropriate dosage levels. Where it was widely deployed and where the dosage levels were effective, as in New York City, the impact on diphtheria deaths was significant.

Turn-of-the-century microbiologic developments also enabled public health to identify and target specific vector-borne diseases such as malaria. With the identification of the *Anopheles* mosquito as the agent by which the malaria-causing parasite was transmitted to humans, programs for draining swamps were given a scientific rationale. Similarly, gradual recognition that flies were important vectors for the transmission of both typhoid and the nonspecific bacteria that caused much infant and childhood diarrhea and enteritis led to programs aimed at destroying the breeding grounds of flies as well as to the gradual adoption of window screens.

Early-twentieth-century public health also vastly expanded the scope of its activities, moving into the areas of medical and social welfare and health education. Health departments began hiring nurses to visit the sick and to instruct their families on the basics of care and hygiene. They also disseminated rudimentary health information by circulating flyers and pamphlets and by conducting health demonstrations and sanitary fairs. Infants and children were especially targeted. During the first two decades of the century there was an intensive and broad-based public health campaign aimed at reducing the appalling rates of infant mortality. Infant welfare stations were opened in which babies were weighed and examined and mothers were given instruction and clean milk. Nurses were sent to the homes of newborns, information was circulated widely, and clinics were opened where sick infants could be brought for examination and treatment. In the larger cities, these and a host of related activities were overseen by newly established bureaus of child hygiene. States also eventually established such bureaus, and the federal government, which had thus far devoted more funds to safeguarding the health of livestock than of

humans, established a national Children's Bureau in 1912 and gave it responsibility for researching the causes of infant mortality.

To improve the health of older children, state and municipal health departments began working with school committees and boards of education to establish school health programs in which schoolchildren were periodically examined for disease and health problems, special classes were established for the tubercular and handicapped, and, in the larger towns and cities, clinics were opened to diagnose and sometimes treat minor skin, eye, ear, and teeth ailments. School systems also adopted regulations prohibiting children who were sick with or exposed to infectious diseases from attending school for a specified period, made hygiene a part of the curriculum, and eventually began providing free or subsidized school lunches.

In pursuing infant welfare, school health, and the myriad other social and medical welfare activities in which they involved themselves in the first decades of the twentieth century, public health departments worked in conjunction with a wide variety of philanthropic organizations. Some, such as local associations for improving the condition of the poor, had been around for several decades, but others were of recent origin and their creation demonstrated a new development within U.S. philanthropy: the appearance of national voluntary associations focusing on specific health problems or diseases. In 1904 the National Association for the Study and Prevention of Tuberculosis was formed, marking the beginning of a two-decade period that witnessed the creation of similar organizations dedicated to combating infant mortality, deafness, insanity, venereal disease, paralysis, heart disease, blindness, and cancer. Bringing together physicians, public health professionals, social workers, and philanthropists, these organizations funded and operated a wide array of clinics and programs and, through the popular media and their own publications, mounted an unprecedented health education campaign.

Newly established private foundations also dedicated themselves to improving public health. The Rockefeller Foundation established programs to combat malaria and hookworm in the South and subsequently was a major force in promoting rural health. Others, such as the Milbank Fund, the Commonwealth Fund, and the Rosenwald Fund, sponsored health demonstrations and funded various types of clinics, programs, and research. So too did a few major corporations. Convinced that keeping its policyholders alive was good business, the Metropolitan

Life Insurance Company hired an army of part-time nurses to visit and instruct those whom it insured.

Was this proliferation of public health activities primarily responsible for the early-twentieth-century decline of mortality from infectious disease? Of course not, but the evidence does suggest that such activities played a meaningful role, at least where they were present. In New York, where milk regulation was stringent and infant welfare programs probably the most extensive, the infant diarrheal death rate plunged from 47.6 per 1,000 live births in 1905 to 15.8 in 1919. Moreover, the fatal summer epidemics of infant diarrhea that as late as 1910 had made most American cities during the hot months killing grounds for babies had all but disappeared by 1920. Similarly, in cities where effective water filtration and purification systems were put in place, deaths from typhoid dropped dramatically. Progress came slower to small-town and rural America and to most of the South, but it did come. Especially after the Sheppard-Towner Act (1921) and New Deal programs began channeling federal funds into public health activities, waterborne and vector-borne disease fatalities began to drop. While the evidence is less clear for fatalities from airborne diseases, it does suggest that measures to identify and isolate the sick had a positive effect.

Yet it is important not to consider developments in public health independently of other changes that were taking place in the United States. Indeed, public health activities were intimately related to a number of far-reaching political, scientific, cultural, economic, and general environmental changes. The construction of water and sewerage systems, the enactment and enforcement of regulations on food and beverages, the establishment of infant welfare and school health programs, and the myriad other activities undertaken or overseen by public health departments in the late nineteenth and early twentieth centuries would have been impossible without the concurrent growth of government's willingness and court-defined right to take responsibility for and devote resources to such activities. That growth came slowly and unevenly, following a course marked by political battles and court cases. It also occurred within the North before the South and West, and first within municipal and state government and only belatedly within the federal government. It also was incomplete. Geographic inequities persisted. So too did racial inequities. Even after federal funds became available, the public health services extended to African Americans in the South and Mexican Americans in the Southwest remained extremely limited. Moreover, faced with unrelenting opposition from private

medicine and fiscal and ideological conservatives, public health activity in the United States rarely if ever included the types of health care services ultimately sponsored by government in most of the other industrialized nations. Beginning with restrictions placed on municipal clinics, extending through the narrow mandate granted the Children's Bureau, and culminating with the strict limits placed on activities funded by the Sheppard-Towner Act and the Social Security Act, the health care activities allowed public health were largely confined to diagnosis and advice. Treatment was left to the private sector. Indeed any judgment of the effectiveness of public health activities in early-twentieth-century America must be tempered with an appreciation of how little of what could have been done was actually done.

Public health activities in the first third of the century were also shaped, made possible, and complemented by a host of technological and scientific developments: in the mechanics of water filtration, in sewerage and domestic plumbing, in heating and ventilation, in food transport and refrigeration, in disinfection and sterilization, in dairy practice, and in the broad area of biomedical science. Indeed, although biomedical researchers would not begin producing effective drug therapies until the third and fourth decades of the century, their earlier work, especially in bacteriology and epidemiology, provided a solid basis for preventive measures and advice. For instance, the discovery that milk could and did transmit typhoid, scarlet fever, diphtheria, strep throat, and tuberculosis provided specific justification for regulations and other measures designed to guarantee a milk supply free of dangerous pathogens. Similarly, research connecting nonspecific bacteria with infant diarrhea and enteritis reshaped the advice given to new mothers. Recommendations that mothers wash their hands after contact with infant feces, launder bedclothes, diapers, and garments in hot water, and sterilize feeding containers and nipples, were both new and etiologically sound.

Public health activities in the early twentieth century, especially popular health education, were both fostered and reinforced by what must be termed a simultaneous revolution in health awareness among the American people. Since the mid-nineteenth century there had been emerging, initially among the urban middle classes, a culture of personal and domestic hygiene. Rooted in morality and evolving class consciousness as much as secular science, the culture of hygiene promoted individual and household cleanliness as a sign of social worth. By the turn of the century that culture had incorporated the germ theory of disease causation and was spawning both an ethos of asepsis and a host of consumer products designed to facilitate living by that ethos. The design of kitchens and bathrooms increasingly mirrored that of laboratories and operating rooms. And in between articles on hygienic living that were becoming standard fare in the popular periodicals aimed at the middle classes, were advertisements for disinfectants and germicides, easy to sterilize toilets and sinks, home water filters and baby bottle sterilizers, hot water heaters, washing machines, and linoleum floorings.

The first decades of the century also witnessed an explosion of interest in the hygiene of infant and child care. Popular magazines such as *Harper's Bazaar* and *The Ladies' Home Journal* began featuring articles on specific diseases and their management, established regular infant and childcare columns, and competed with each other to sign on as writers the best known experts in the emerging specialty of pediatrics. In an effort to safeguard their offspring and improve their management, parents began purchasing infant and childcare manuals in sufficient numbers to make some of the authors both wealthy and famous. Pediatrician L. Emmett Holt's *The Care and Feeding of Children,* first published in 1894 but revised and reissued several times after 1900, approximated during the first third of the century the popularity and influence that Benjamin Spock's *Baby and Child Care* did during the second. Women's clubs and other voluntary associations sponsored lectures and seminars; state and municipal health departments conducted demonstrations and fairs and circulated pamphlets on infant feeding and child care; the U.S. Children's Bureau assisted private groups and municipal agencies in organizing "baby weeks" and between 1914 and 1921 distributed free more than one-and-one-half million copies of its basic advice pamphlet, *Infant Care.*

As with the emergence of a culture of domestic cleanliness, rising interest in promoting and managing child health was most pervasive among the middle classes. In some respects the two can be viewed as part of the process by which the middle classes reinvigorated their distinguishing sense of child and domestic centeredness by reinforcing its nineteenth-century moral foundation with a cast constructed of tenets derived from twentieth-century biomedicine. But it would be a mistake to view them only as such. For neither was limited to the middle classes. While they may have upheld the conventions of social class, they also provided a number of effective prophylactic strategies that were widely used to combat the transmission of infectious disease. Cleanliness and some of the regimens of infant and child hygiene were exceedingly useful in an environment where fecal contamination of water, food, and beverage was responsible for killing a large percentage of all those who died.

It would also be a mistake to view the developments discussed above as unrelated to or divorced from economic development and rising living standards. Late-nineteenth- and early-twentieth-century economic expansion in the United States produced a host of environmental and social problems, but it also produced the tax revenues that were needed to support public health activity. Moreover, it generated wealth sufficient and widespread enough to create a demand for the design and supply of better housing and the domestic technologies that made housing more hygienic. Indoor plumbing and window screens are effective prophylactics against waterborne and vector-borne diseases, but only if householders have the means to purchase them. Similarly, without increasing wealth it is doubtful whether either a culture of cleanliness or an ethos of scientific childcare would have developed, since both depend on a level of access to and consumption of products and knowledge that require a certain threshold of general wealth.

No single reason can therefore be isolated as the primary reason for the early-twentieth-century decline of mortality from infectious diseases. Rather, it seems probable that the decline came about because a number of social, cultural, economic, scientific, and governmental developments combined to transform the unequal relationship that Americans had traditionally had with disease and disease agents. Armed with a more effective understanding of the etiology of disease, adopting patterns of behavior and value rooted in that understanding, showing a willingness to devote private and public resources to controlling the transmission of disease, and having the economic wherewithal to do so, early-twentieth-century Americans, along with the inhabitants of other developed nations, were able to loosen the grip in which they had long been held by the natural disease environment. In so doing, they initiated what would be a century-long shift in the balance of power between humans and disease.

It is worth noting that this shift in power took place against a backdrop in which changes in the basic patterns of living and working were making life less hazardous. The early twentieth century saw a concerted reform effort to improve occupational and industrial safety. The regulations and work practices that emerged from that movement, combined with new technologies, initiated a slow but eventual reduction in the number of deaths and disabilities due to work-related accidents. Similarly, the first third of the century saw significant improvement in preventing fires in homes, factories, and public buildings. The enactment of fire safety codes, the replacement of gas lighting with electric lights, the development of new building designs and materials, the production of safer stoves and heating apparatus: all worked to reduce deaths from accidental fire. Deaths from scalding, falls, and innumerable other accidents also began to decline. Indeed, the death rate from non–motor vehicle accidents was almost halved between 1900 and 1930.

For many of the same reasons it had declined through the first third of the century, mortality continued to decline through the second third. Beginning in the 1930s, however, the development and application of specific medical interventions and technologies played an increasingly important role in driving death rates downward and life expectancy upward. In the earlier period the advances that had been achieved in controlling death from infectious disease were largely ecobiologic and prophylactic; that is, they involved natural increases in human resistance and an array of environmental and behavioral changes that reduced the risk of infection by decreasing the possibility that individuals would come in contact with infectious agents. With the exception of smallpox vaccine and diphtheria antitoxin, little progress had been made in medically immunizing individuals against infection or in increasing an individual's chance of survival once infected. Significant improvement in these areas did not occur until the years between the late 1930s and late 1950s, when a number of new and effective immunizations and drug therapies were made widely available. Particularly important were the development and commercial production of antibacterial drugs, first sulfonamides and then antibiotics such as penicillin and streptomycin. Ineffective against viruses and a few types of bacteria, these new drugs were extremely effective in reducing fatalities from bacterial pneumonia, scarlet fever, bacterial meningitis, tuberculosis, and a host of other bacterial infections including the streptococcal or wound infections resulting from accidents, surgery, and childbirth. Although the introduction and use of sulfonamides and antibiotics is not the only reason why mortality dropped so rapidly in the 1940s, it is probably the most important. Along with the development and application of effective chemotherapies, the middle third of the century also

saw significant improvements in both the techniques and the technologies available to detect and manage potentially fatal diseases and to cure or manage nonfatal diseases and health conditions that weakened resistance to more dangerous disease. Many of these techniques and technologies had their origins in earlier research and experimentation, but came into widespread use only after 1930 when health care services dramatically improved in quality and availability. Among the more important of these innovations were the use of electrolyte and fluid therapy to counter acidosis and dehydration in infants suffering bouts of diarrhea and enteritis; the increasingly sophisticated preventive and therapeutic use of vitamins and minerals to aid metabolism and combat such diseases as rickets, pellagra, and pernicious anemia; and the development and refinement of safe and effective surgical processes to correct the consequences of injury and congenital malformation. Indeed, it is safe to say that between 1930 and 1960, scientific medicine came fully of age in the United States and attained a level of effectiveness and availability that drove death rates significantly below what could have been achieved by prophylaxis alone. Hence, while not responsible for initiating the decline of mortality from many diseases, medical measures kept that decline going beyond the point where it probably would have leveled off.

It is important to note that the many social, scientific, and environmental developments that drove down death rates from infectious disease in the first half of the century were accompanied by others that proved to have a negative impact on the health and life expectancy of Americans. Both alcohol consumption and cigarette smoking increased, sowing the seeds for degenerative disease in later life. The automobile brought physicians and health care facilities within reach of isolated rural residents and rid city streets of the tons of horse manure that attracted flies; but it also fouled the air with toxic pollutants and, more significant, made the nation's roads and highways scenes of an accidental carnage of unprecedented dimensions. Rising wealth brought better housing and a host of other benefits; but it increased sedentary living and the consumption of fatty foods—both of which have been linked to cardiovascular disease. And while science was busy making the environment safer by eliminating many pathogenic bacteria and controlling insect vectors, it was also making the environment dangerous by contributing to the production of a host of new chemicals, many of which would subsequently be identified as carcinogens. Moreover, although chemotherapy proved extremely effective in fighting many infections, it also spawned a number of new, drug-resistant pathogens. Indeed, while the negative impact of twentieth-century social, scientific, and technological developments has not been anywhere near sufficient to block continuing mortality decline, it has produced a new disease environment in which many of the risks of death can now be called human made.

By the 1960s, death rates among infants, children, and younger adults, especially from infectious diseases, had reached such a low level that many analysts began to caution that the mortality decline begun late in the nineteenth century had bottomed out and that any future improvements would proceed at a snail's pace. As support for their warnings they pointed to the leveling off of death rates that had occurred in the late 1950s and noted that the major killers were now congenital, degenerative, and chronic diseases and impairments and that the burden of death had been shifted to those who were congenitally unfit to survive or who had nearly reached what was assumed to be the biological limit of life. No sooner had this caution been issued, however, than mortality again began to drop, particularly among congenitally disadvantaged neonates and among older and elderly adults afflicted with chronic and degenerative diseases. Indeed, the decline has been so significant that a few analysts are now suggesting that it qualifies as a new stage in the epidemiologic transition, one in which all but the most congenitally impaired infants will be saved and in which, at the other end of the life cycle, death will be postponed longer and longer.

What caused this latest mortality decline? For neonates, an answer is readily apparent. In the early 1960s national embarrassment that infant mortality rates had leveled off in the United States while continuing to decline in other advanced industrial nations prompted an intensive, government-funded effort to design and implement sociomedical programs and to develop specific techniques and technologies for preventing neonatal deaths, which by then constituted the bulk of deaths within the first year. That effort resulted in the government provision of nutritional, prenatal, and natal care to many women who qualified for public assistance, in the perfection of diagnostic techniques and drugs that have proven effective in managing pregnancy and preventing premature labor, and in the development of sophisticated and effective surgical, therapeutic, and intensive care techniques and technologies to correct congenital deformities and to counter the risks faced by low birthweight or premature babies. As a consequence,

neonatal mortality declined 60 percent between 1965 and 1985.

Among older Americans, as previously noted, much of the improvement in life expectancy was due to declines in death rates from cardiovascular diseases, principally heart disease and stroke. Behind these falling rates are several causes. Reductions earlier in the century of childhood syphilitic and streptococcal infections probably reduced the percentage of Americans who reached middle and old age after the 1960s with damaged heart muscles and valves. Changes in diet and a decline in smoking may have also played a role. But undoubtedly, the most important reason for the decline in cardiovascular death rates has been the development of an expanding array of effective drugs, therapies, and surgical and intensive care techniques for managing and correcting the physiological causes and consequences of cardiovascular disease and for improving the survival chances of those who suffer heart attacks and strokes.

Developments since the 1960s in chemotherapy, surgery, and intensive care have also been critically important in reducing death rates from certain types of cancer and from other degenerative diseases. So too have been the development of such technologies as pacemakers, dialysis machines, and life-support systems that supplant or assist organ function. Moreover, government has played an important part in increasing access to these developments, by funding the construction of health care facilities in areas where none existed and by providing health insurance (Medicare) for those sixty-four and older. As a consequence, since the late 1960s, many older and elderly Americans who in the past would have died relatively quickly from organ dysfunction and other degenerative health problems have been granted a temporary reprieve. Combined with other innovations in gerontological medicine, this has made the latest reduction in mortality one in which life expectancy was increased largely through the medical postponement of death at the very end of the life cycle.

Building on earlier ecobiologic and prophylactic change, scientific medicine in the United States since the 1930s has thus played an increasingly important and effective role in pushing mortality rates downward and life expectancy upward: first by acquiring the ability to reduce the risk of death from infectious disease and then by developing effective techniques and technologies to correct or manage the consequences of congenital abnormalities and degenerative and chronic diseases. It has not, of course, played that role perfectly. Scientific medicine has tended to slight prevention in favor of activist therapeutics and has too often dehumanized life while preventing death. Access to its rewards has historically been unequal and still is. And control over its delivery has in large part remained monopolized by those who practice it. And yet, scientific medicine, for all its biases and problems, has been remarkably successful in loosening the grip in which natural disease had long held humans. Indeed, that success is a major reason why the current AIDS epidemic has proven so frightening. In many respects, AIDS forcibly returns us to an earlier era. An infectious disease that primarily strikes down those in the bloom of life, that is transmitted through something so basic to life as blood, and for which no effective immunizations nor therapies have yet been devised, AIDS serves as a terrible and tragic reminder that while the grip of natural disease has been loosened, it has not been broken.

A HEALTHIER NATION?

It takes but a moment's reflection to appreciate that the twentieth-century mortality and epidemiologic transitions have profoundly transformed American life by changing when and from what Americans can expect to die and by dramatically altering the age structure of society. But have they produced a significant improvement in health; that is, are Americans living at the end of the twentieth century healthier than those living at the beginning? The common-sense answer to this question is yes. Intuitively, it seems so obvious that declining mortality would necessarily be accompanied by declining sickness or morbidity that few people would question the assertion that Americans are healthier today than they have ever been. Yet analysts of twentieth-century morbidity trends have long been aware of a seeming paradox, characteristic not only of the U.S. experience but also of that of other developed countries. Even granting the difficulty of accurately tracing morbidity patterns across the century, data from the distant and recent past strongly suggest that as mortality rates have fallen, sickness rates and health care spending have risen.

How can this counterintuitive paradox be explained? Accounting for the rise in health care spending can be done readily, if not completely, by noting that as the century progressed Americans have had greater access to physicians and health care facilities, due in part to the introduction of private and government-sponsored health insurance and to the proliferation of hospitals and clinics; that this greater access has been accompanied by rising physician and hospi-

tal fees and by both a greater reliance on expensive technologies and procedures and a shift from less costly short-term health problems to costly long-term ones; that steadily improving diagnostic techniques and technologies has led to earlier and more comprehensive discovery of diseases and health problems; and that Americans are more likely today than in the past to seek medical help for their ailments. Accounting for the rise in health care spending, however, does not account for the observed rise in sickness. Thus, the question remains why morbidity has increased as mortality has decreased.

One way to answer that question is to claim that the observed rise in morbidity is not biologically real but rather the consequence of changing social and cultural conceptions of health and sickness. Those who make such a claim often argue that as the century has progressed Americans have become more and more obsessed with their health and as a consequence have defined an ever widening array of physical, emotional, and mental conditions as sickness. To the extent that such arguments reveal the ways in which changing social and cultural configurations help determine at what point health shades into sickness on a continuum between feeling wonderful and being at death's door, they have some validity. But they are on far shakier ground in claiming that rising sickness rates are principally the product of a dramatic increase in national hypochondria and in the progressive medicalization of physical, emotional, and mental conditions. Indeed, while it is probable that Americans today have higher expectations of being free from disease and debility, it is unlikely that they are significantly more obsessed with their health than were past generations. A quick perusal of any popular turn-of-the-century periodical, with its abundance of advertisements for medicines, nostrums, corrective devices, and health manuals, is enough to dissuade one from believing that Americans in the past spent little time worrying about their health. Moreover, there is little evidence to suggest that Americans today are more likely than past generations to interrupt normal activity due to ill health or sickness.

The paradox thus cannot be explained away simply; it can only be disentangled by identifying the various trends that produced it. In doing so, it is first necessary to establish what analysts of morbidity trends generally mean by a state of sickness or ill health. While acknowledging that any definition is at least in part socially and culturally relative, most analysts use a definition similar to that used in current sickness surveys such as the U.S. National Health Interview Survey, which has been conducted yearly since 1957. In such surveys a state of sickness is distinguished by two criteria: the presence of an acute or chronic condition; and an accompanying incapacitation or significant reduction of normal physical activity. Morbidity is thus judged to be rising if either or both of the following are present: (1) a growth in recorded acute and chronic conditions or (2) an increase in the disruption of normal activity due to the presence of some physical condition.

It is also necessary to make a distinction between getting sick and being sick, between contracting a disease or developing a health problem and being in a state of sickness or ill health. Although one leads to the other, getting sick and being sick are not identical measures of health because the first is dependent on the incidence of disease at a given time while the second is dependent on both the incidence and duration of disease. Incidence of disease is determined both by the prevalence of disease agents in the environment and by the age composition of the population, since the risk of getting sick or developing a health problem has always been and continues to be greater at certain ages than at others. Duration of disease is determined by type of illness and by the effectiveness of available therapies in curing or managing illness. By definition, acute infectious diseases are short-term. They have also proven relatively responsive to therapeutic cures. Conversely, chronic and degenerative diseases are generally long-term and are more easily managed than cured. The number of people in a society that get sick during a given time is thus a function of demographics and disease environment, both of which determine the risk of contracting or developing an illness. How many people in a society are sick at a given time is a function not only of the risk of getting sick but also of the duration of sickness, since the greater the duration of sickness the greater will be the number of people who get sick and remain sick.

It is also useful to consider that there are different levels of severity and depth to being sick. The most obvious measure of severity is case fatality rates, how often being sick results in death. Case fatality rates, however, are sometimes problematic, as with long-term chronic or degenerative diseases among the elderly. Thus another useful measure of severity is incapacitation. Depth of disease recognizes that people can and do simultaneously suffer from more than one disease or health problem. Hence, the depth of disease in a society refers to the extent to which the sick members of that society may be suffering a number of different diseases simultaneously.

Distinguishing between the risk of getting sick and being sick and recognizing that the severity and depth of disease can change over time somewhat independent of sickness rates, allows us to grasp the multidimensionality and complexity of the observed rise in morbidity and to see it for what it is: an amalgam of different trends. If we consider the history of sickness in the twentieth century only in terms of getting sick, then it is apparent that at least two countertrends occurred. Accompanying the decline in mortality from infectious disease was a less dramatic but still significant decline in the risk of contracting an acute illness, especially among the young. That the risk of dying once sick fell more sharply than the risk of getting sick is due in large part to ecobiologic and medical developments lowering case fatality rates. Conversely, the risk of getting sick with chronic and degenerative diseases has increased consonant with the increase in the proportion of the population at those ages where the likelihood of developing such diseases is highest.

The risk of getting sick with chronic and degenerative diseases may have also increased for a number of other nondemographic reasons. Modern medicine's increasing diagnostic capability to detect and identify diseases has certainly increased the number of physical conditions that are now considered specific illnesses or health problems. And its progressively improving ability to keep alive those who in later life face increased risk due to earlier sickness, injury, or constitutional debility may have contributed to the rising incidence of chronic and degenerative diseases. So too may have an increase in carcinogens and other toxins in the environment, although this would be difficult to substantiate because turn-of-the-century Americans—surrounded by lead paint and arsenic-cured wallpaper, consuming beverages and foods preserved or adulterated with formaldehyde, mercury derivatives, and a host of other additives, drinking water conveyed through lead pipes, and breathing air fouled with smoke and the fumes of ill-vented furnaces and stoves—can hardly be said to have lived in a toxin-free environment.

The long-term trends in the severity of sickness also present a mixed picture. If severity is measured by case fatality rates, then it would seem that, especially among infants, children, adolescents, and younger adults, sickness has become less severe. Infants still suffer bouts of diarrhea and enteritis, but, unlike in the past, few die, thanks in large part to the effectiveness of available fluid and electrolyte therapy. Similarly, infectious respiratory diseases, such as pneumonia, bronchitis, and influenza, although less prevalent than in the past, still routinely strike the young and the healthy; but now cause comparatively few deaths. The probability of dying has also dropped for those who suffer injury, congenital anomalies, and chronic diseases. Burns and wounds, which early in the century often led to death, pose far less of a threat today. Blocked intestines and other congenital malformations are now routinely repaired. And such chronic diseases as severe asthma no longer impose an almost certain sentence of early death.

If severity is measured by degree of incapacitation, however, the trend is less clear. Drug and other therapies have in many cases shortened the course of some diseases, but in other cases have lengthened it by keeping alive those who in the past would have quickly expired. Similarly, while medical and surgical interventions have proven increasingly effective in enabling the physically restricted to lead normal lives, they have also been increasingly successful in keeping alive the severely incapacitated who in the past would have died relatively quickly.

A different, although equally complex, picture emerges of the history of morbidity in the twentieth century if morbidity levels and trends are determined by how many people are sick at a particular time. Although the evidence for the first half of the century is neither abundant nor easily interpreted, it seems probable that, overall, the percentage of Americans who can be considered sick has risen as mortality has dropped. One important reason for believing this is that the average duration of illness—that is, the time spent being sick by those Americans who get sick—has increased significantly through the century. Why? First, as we have already seen, declining mortality and rising life expectancy have produced a progressive increase in both the proportion of Americans reaching advanced age and the years Americans live at advanced age. This factor, combined with the development and use of medical technologies and therapies capable of keeping the aged alive while not curing them of their ailments, has led to a consonant increase in the percentage of the population suffering from long-term and often intractable chronic and degenerative diseases.

The decline in the prevalence and fatality of infectious disease has also contributed to lengthening the duration of sickness among those who get sick. Early in the century those who were born with or developed long-term chronic or degenerative diseases often did not survive long, but rather soon died from pneumonia or some other infectious disease to which their weakened state made them vulnerable. With the development of drug and other therapies effective in combating and managing secondary in-fections, the length of time which the chronically and degeneratively ill are able to survive has increased significantly.

That an aging population combined with life-extending medical therapies and technologies would increase the proportion of Americans who are sick is neither difficult to grasp nor counterintuitive. If this alone constituted the twentieth-century rise in morbidity, then the observed paradox would not be so unsettling. But since national morbidity data began to be collected in the 1950s, they have shown an unmistakable rise in sickness at all ages. Why this has occurred is by no means clear and remains subject to considerable debate. One partial explanation is that improved diagnostic techniques have led to the earlier and more comprehensive detection of disease, thereby increasing the duration of sickness as well as expanding both the number of physical conditions considered sickness and the proportion of the population considered sick. Another explanation is that the point where health shades into sickness has shifted somewhat, and thus Americans are earlier and earlier considering themselves sick and curtailing their activity. The evidence for this second explanation, however, is not firm. A third, somewhat Darwinian, explanation is that as medicine has enjoyed increasing success in keeping alive those born with chronic conditions or who in early life suffer debilitating injury or disease, the number of sick at all ages has increased.

Also unclear and subject to debate is whether the first half of the century witnessed a rise in being sick among the nonelderly similar to that recorded since 1957. A number of analysts believe that it did, but again the evidence is difficult to interpret. An equally good case can be made that the current rise in sickness rates among the young was preceded by nearly a half century of decline prompted by changes in the depth of sickness. While it is probable that the depth of sickness in the United States has increased overall—in large part due to the increase in the proportion of the population who are older and elderly and most likely to suffer multiple health problems—it is equally probable that the depth of sickness has decreased among the young. As noted earlier, in the first third of the century many children suffered from chronic nutritional diseases and dietary deficiencies. Lead poisoning was common, especially among urban children. Also widespread were bacterial, parasitic and viral skin diseases, such as boils, impetigo, head lice, scabies, pinworms, hookworm, and pityriasis, for which treatment was rudimentary and often ineffective. Among young adults as well as children, bouts of diarrhea and other gastric ailments seem to have been frequent. Crippling or semicrippling incapacitation due to the now often correctable effects of injury or disease was also common. So too was the continued discomfort of chronic urinary tract infections and unrepaired lacerations associated with childbirth. With dentistry rudimentary and the fluoridation of water not even a dream, tooth decay was a part of life for all but the most genetically blessed. As records from the medical exams given to early-twentieth-century schoolchildren and World War I draftees make abundantly clear, tooth and gum disease were more the norm than the exception. Indeed, whether or not they significantly restricted their activity, younger Americans in the first decades of the century lived with a level of pain and discomfort largely unknown to their late-twentieth-century counterparts.

What should be evident from the preceding discussion is that there is no clear and simple answer to the question: Are Americans at the end of the twentieth century healthier than they were at the beginning? Although we can generalize about the entire population, such a generalization is problematic given the divergent trends that emerge when we differentiate between getting sick and being sick, focus on specific age groups, and consider both the depth and severity of sickness. However, at least one generalization seems justified. While the twentieth-century mortality and epidemiologic transitions may not have been accompanied by a profound reduction in sickness, they have been accompanied by a profound alteration in the way Americans experience sickness, conceptualize it, and attempt to avoid it. In the beginning of the century, the experience of sickness was largely acute, attended by a significant risk of death, and shared by all ages. One fell sick, was sick for a short and intense period, and then either recovered or died. As a consequence sickness was largely conceived of as a short-term but life-threatening surprise attack that one could either attempt to avoid by limiting exposure to disease agents or prepare for by building up the body's ability to fend off or defeat the disease. Intemperate eating and drinking, smoking, and lack of exercise were avoided by health conscious turn-of-the-century Americans, less because they planted the seeds for degenerative disease in later life than because they weakened the body and made it less capable of successfully defending itself.

At the end of the twentieth century, Americans of all ages still get sick with acute diseases, but consider them temporary incapacitations from which recovery is almost certain. The diseases that now most frequently bring death, and thus are the focus of greatest concern and fear, are largely degenerative, have incubation periods extending for years and even decades, and are associated with the later stages of life. Rather than as a short and intense surprise attack that can come at any time, potentially fatal disease is thus conceived of by contemporary Americans as the end result of a slow and cumulative infiltration that may take years to accomplish. For health conscious Americans in the late twentieth century, preventing fatal disease has thus become a matter of, on the one hand, avoiding toxins and behaviors that can initiate or quicken degeneration, and on the other, pursuing activities that can reverse or prevent it.

INTO THE TWENTY-FIRST CENTURY

The past is a notoriously inadequate tool with which to predict the future, and historians are generally poor prognosticators. But it seems both appropriate and irresistible, after reviewing mortality and morbidity trends during this century, to speculate briefly on what the initial part of the next century might bring. Given current mortality trends, it is probable that the age-adjusted death rate will continue to fall, although the recent leveling off of the post-1968 reductions in mortality among neonates and the aged tempts one to caution that we may be approaching biologic limits to which premature life can be made viable and degenerated life extended; and thus that future gains in life expectancy will be small and slow in coming. Yet, as we have seen, such cautions were issued in the past and proved unwarranted. Indeed, recent innovations in biogenetics suggest new possibilities for yet a fourth significant reduction in mortality and increase in life expectancy in a little over a century. Where the initial sharp drop in mortality was due to ecobiologic and prophylactic change, the second, largely due to chemotherapeutic developments, and the third, due to new technologies and intensive care techniques, the next may follow from effective manipulation of the genetic codes of both humans and disease agents.

More certain is that the population will continue to age, especially in the early part of the twenty-first century as the baby boomer cohort reaches advanced age. Hence, it seems likely that the causes of death will further compress, with the chronic and degenerative diseases of old age accounting for an ever greater percentage of all deaths. It is also likely that the further aging of the population will increase the total level of sickness among Americans. However, whether that increase will be as great as that which occurred during the second half of the twentieth century is uncertain. Some analysts believe it will be, noting that the incidence, if not the fatality, of degenerative disease among the aged has remained relatively constant. Others, however, are more optimistic. Even if biogenetics does not live up to expectations, they argue, environmentalist measures that reduce exposure to toxins plus dietary and lifestyle change among the health-conscious baby boomers promise a future elderly population who will reach advanced age less damaged than the aged of today.

More troubling is the possibility that racial differences in the levels and rates of morbidity and mortality will persist and, perhaps, grow greater. Indeed, the recent leveling off in the decline of black infant mortality and the rise of death rates, especially from violence, among young African American males, suggest that this possibility may be a probability. Many changes have occurred over the course of the century in regard to U.S. morbidity and mortality; unfortunately, the importance of race as a determinant of death and sickness levels has not been one of them.

Also troubling is the observed recent resurgence of infectious disease, both in the United States and worldwide. Indeed, such is the concern this development is causing that in the spring of 1993 the U.S. Centers for Disease Control and Prevention introduced a new series, "Emerging Infectious Diseases," as part of its *Morbidity and Mortality Weekly Report.* In explaining its decision to devote a specific section of its weekly report to the resurgence of infectious disease, the CDC warned that the U.S. public health system was facing a serious challenge from the emergence of new, more virulent pathogens, or drug-resistant diseases and syndromes and from the reemergence of a number of diseases thought to be under control.

At this point it is impossible to gauge with any accuracy the seriousness of the threat posed by this resurgence of infectious disease. Most analysts of U.S. health trends, citing the profoundly greater capabilities of scientific medicine today, doubt that it holds the potential to make infection in the early twenty-first century the scourge it was in the early twentieth. Others are less sanguine, and warn that complacency could lead to national catastrophe. What is possible to predict is that the disease environment in which Americans live and die will continue to evolve, and will do so in ways that are neither completely manageable nor foreseeable. Over the course of the twentieth century we have gained considerable ability to manipulate our relationship with the disease environment, but we are still very far from gaining mastery over the outcomes of that relationship.

SEE ALSO Medical Science and Technology; Health Care Delivery (both in this volume).

BIBLIOGRAPHY

A standard text that explains the theory, techniques, and sources of demographic calculation and analysis is U.S. Bureau of the Census, *The Methods and Materials of Demography,* by H. S. Shryock, J. S. Siegel, and Associates (1971). Aggregated twentieth-century U.S. mortality statistics can be found in U.S. Bureau of the Census, *Mortality Statistics* (1906–1938), an annually published multivolume series that contains data on the numbers and rates of mortality broken down by cause, sex, race, region, and age in the Death Registration Area and States. The first volume covers 1900–1904 and the last 1936. The series has been replaced by one titled *Vital Statistics of the United States,* first published annually by the Bureau of the Census and then by the U.S. Public Health Service, National Office (now Center) for Health Statistics. The most up-to-date statistics can be found in the *Monthly Vital Statistics Report* put out by the National Center for Health Statistics. For the late nineteenth and early twentieth centuries, U.S. Bureau of the Census, *United States Life Tables: 1890, 1901, 1910, and 1901–1910,* by James Glover (1921), is widely considered the most authoritative source of data on mortality and life expectancy within the Death Registration States and is especially valuable for the data on African Americans and the foreign born.

Erwin Imhof, "From the Old Mortality Pattern to the New: Implications of a Radical Change from the Sixteenth to the Twentieth Century," *Bulletin of the History of Medicine* 59 (1985): 1–29, helps to place the twentieth-century mortality transition within its long-term historical context. So too does Stephen J. Kunitz, "Mortality Change in America, 1620–1920,"

Human Biology 56 (1984): 559–582, which also argues that mortality began declining in the late nineteenth century first from named, specific endemic diseases and then from unnamed, nonspecific respiratory and gastrointestinal infections.

Various patterns of mid-nineteenth-century mortality and its determinants are presented in Richard A. Meckel, "Immigration, Mortality, and Population Growth in Boston, 1840–1880," *Journal of Interdisciplinary History* 15 (1985): 393–417; Richard H. Steckel, "The Health and Mortality of Women and Children, 1850–1860," *Journal of Economic History* 47 (1988): 333–345; and Maris Vinovskis, "Mortality Rates and trends in Massachusetts before 1860," *Journal of Economic History* 32 (1972): 184–213.

Late-nineteenth-century and early-twentieth-century levels, trends, and differentials of U.S. mortality are discussed in Gretchen A. Condrun and Eileen Crimmins, "Mortality Differentials between Rural and Urban Areas of States in the Northeastern United States, 1890–1900," *Journal of Historical Geography* 6 (1980): 179–202; Douglas Ewbank, "History of Black Mortality and Health before 1940," *Milbank Quarterly* 65 (1987), suppl. 1: 100–128; Michael R. Haines, "Mortality in Nineteenth-Century America: Estimates from New York and Pennsylvania Census Data, 1865 and 1900," *Demography* 14 (1977): 311–331; Robert Higgs, "Mortality in Rural America, 1870–1920: Estimates and Conjectures," *Explorations in Economic History* 31 (1973): 177–195; Robert Higgs and David Booth, "Mortality Differentials within Large American Cities in 1890," *Human Ecology* 7 (1979): 353–370; and Edward Meeker, "The Improving Health of the United States, 1850–1915," *Explorations in Economic History* 9 (1972): 353–373.

While focusing primarily on the second half of the century, Donald J. Bogue, "Mortality," in *The Population of the United States: Historical Trends and Future Projections* (1985), offers an invaluable overview and analysis of twentieth-century U.S. mortality trends, differentials, and causes along with a discussion of the population consequences of declining mortality. Eileen M. Crimmins, "The Changing Pattern of American Mortality Decline, 1940–77, and Its Implication for the Future," *Population and Development Review* 7 (1981): 229–254, analyzes mortality levels and trends during the middle part of the century according to age, race, sex, and cause of death.

U.S. Public Health Service, National Center for Health Statistics, *Trends and Current Status in Childhood Mortality,* by Lois Fingerhut and Joel Kleinman (1989), surveys the twentieth-century mortality ex-

perience of the population aged one through nineteen, paying special attention to mortality among the young from violence and other external causes since 1950. Robert D. Retherford, *The Changing Sex Differential in Mortality* (1979), provides a good introduction to and overview of the changing ways in which sex has correlated to differences in the causes and levels of mortality. More specific is Lois M. Verbrugge, "Gender and Health: An Update on Hypotheses and Evidence," *Journal of Health and Social Behavior* 26 (1985): 156–182, which reviews and analyzes the data and theories concerning historical and current sex differentials in U.S. mortality. Irvine Louden, *Death in Childbirth: An International Study of Maternal Care and Maternal Mortality, 1800–1950* (1992), is both exhaustive and provocative. A standard work on socioeconomic status as a determinant of twentieth-century morbidity and mortality patterns is Evelyn Kitagawa and Philip M. Hauser, *Differential Mortality in the United States: A Study of Socioeconomic Epidemiology* (1973), which should be updated with Gregory Pappas, Susan Queen, Wilbur Hadden, and Gail Fisher, "The Increasing Disparity in Mortality Between Socioeconomic Groups in the United States, 1960 and 1986," *New England Journal of Medicine* 329 (1993): 103–109. Racial Mortality differentials and the interaction of race and socioeconomic status are treated in Colin McCord and Harold P. Freeman, "Excess Mortality in Harlem," *New England Journal of Medicine* 322 (1990): 173–177; Vincente Navarro, "Race or Class Versus Race and Class: Mortality Differentials in the United States," *Lancet* 336 (1990): 1238–1240; Lloyd B. Potter, "Socioeconomic Determinants of White and Black Males' Life Expectancy Differentials, 1980," *Demography* 28 (1991): 303–321; and Richard G. Rogers, "Living and Dying in the U.S.A.: Sociodemographic Determinants among Blacks and Whites," *Demography* 29 (1992): 287–303.

Abdel Omran's "The Epidemiologic Transition," *Milbank Fund Memorial Quarterly* 49 (1971): 509–539, is a seminal essay defining three major stages in the epidemiologic history of modern nations and expounding an epidemiologic transition theory that links changing patterns of health and disease to their demographic, economic, and sociologic determinants. His "Epidemiologic Transition in the U.S.," *Population Bulletin* 32 (1977): 3–42, applies the epidemiologic transition theory to the U.S. experience.

Jay Olshansky and A. Brian Ault, "The Fourth Stage of the Epidemiologic Transition: The Age of Delayed Degenerative Diseases," *Milbank Quarterly* 64 (1986): 355–391, reviews the dramatic decline in mortality and increase in life expectancy among the aged since 1968 and argues that it qualifies as a new and fourth stage of the modern epidemiologic transition.

Thomas McKeown, *The Modern Rise in Population* (1976), offers the most comprehensive statement of the author's influential thesis that rising living standards and especially improvements in diet were primarily responsible for mortality reduction prior to the 1930s. John B. McKinlay and Sonja M. McKinlay, "The Questionable Contribution of Medical Measures to the Decline in Mortality in the United States in the Twentieth Century," *Milbank Memorial Fund Quarterly* 55 (1977): 405–428, applies the McKeown thesis to the United States and, focusing on death rate trends from five major diseases, argues that medical and public health interventions contributed little to the overall decline in mortality during the first half of the century. S. Szreter, "The Importance of Social Intervention in Britain's Mortality Decline c. 1850–1914: A Reinterpretation of the Role of Public Health," *Social History of Medicine* 1 (1988): 1–37, offers a compelling critique of and counter interpretation to McKeown's argument that public health activities were relatively unimportant as an influence on the late-nineteenth- and early-twentieth-century decline of mortality in Great Britain. So too does Gretchen A. Condrun and Rose A. Cheney, "Mortality Trends in Philadelphia: Age and Cause Specific Death Rates, 1870–1930," *Demography* 19 (1982): 97–123, which offers a strong argument that mortality declined in late-nineteenth- and early-twentieth-century America because of a complex amalgam of interrelated ecobiologic, socioeconomic, cultural, medical, and public health developments. A complementary argument is offered in Samuel H. Preston and Michael R. Haines, *Fatal Years: Child Mortality in Late Nineteenth-Century America* (1990), which provides a sophisticated and exhaustive analysis that identifies race, size of place, and region as the major determinants of child mortality levels and differentials at the turn of the century, questions the degree of importance accorded by historical demographers to socioeconomic status, and contends that it was lack of know-how more than lack of material resources that made the levels of child mortality so high. Another recent critique of the McKeown thesis, and one focusing specifically on declining mortality from tuberculosis, is Leonard G. Wilson, "The Rise and Fall of Tuberculosis in Minnesota: The Role of Infection," *Bulletin of the History of Medicine* 66 (1992): 16–52.

Medical and public health measures and campaigns that contributed to declining mortality from infectious disease during the first half of the century have been examined in numerous articles and monographs. John Duffy, *The Sanitarians: A History of American Public Health* (1990), provides a useful overview of the evolution of public health institutions and activities from the seventeenth century through the present. Howard D. Kramer, "The Germ Theory and the Early Public Health Program in the United States," *Bulletin of the History of Medicine* 22 (1948): 233–247, presents a good discussion of the adoption of the germ theory by public health officials. Stuart Galishoff, "Triumph and Failure: The American Response to the Urban Water Supply Problem, 1860–1923," in *Pollution and Reform in American Cities, 1870–1930*, ed. Martin V. Melosi (1980), offers a brief but good overview of the construction and extension of urban water supply systems in the late nineteenth and early twentieth centuries. Richard A. Meckel, *Save the Babies: American Public Health Reform and the Prevention of Infant Mortality, 1850–1929* (1990), provides a detailed illustration of the breadth and multidimensionality of one of the major twentieth-century public health campaigns. Nancy Tomes, "The Private Side of Public Health: Sanitary Science, Domestic Hygiene, and the Germ Theory, 1870–1900," *Bulletin of the History of Medicine* 64 (1990): 509–539, argues that the late nineteenth century witnessed a cultural and behavioral hygienic revolution directly related to changing scientific concepts of disease. David McBride, *From TB to AIDS: Epidemics among Urban Blacks since 1900* (1991), provides a provocative and nuanced interpretation of the twentieth-century African American morbidity patterns and the response they provoked from government, social reformers, and the medical profession.

A good survey of the major developments in medical therapy since the 1930s is Paul B. Beeson's "Changes in Medical Therapy during the Past Half Century," *Medicine* 39 (1980): 79–99.

James C. Riley, *Sickness, Recovery and Death: A History and Forecast of Ill Health* (1989), analyzes recorded and projected mortality and sickness trends from the mid-seventeenth through the twenty-first centuries in Britain, Western Europe, and the United States and asks and attempts to answer the question: has the decline in mortality and the reduction of risk of death posed by episodes of illness meant ever longer and healthier lives? Lois M. Verbrugge, "Longer Life but Worsening Health? Trends in Health and Mortality in Middle-Aged and Older Persons," *Milbank Memorial Fund Quarterly* 62 (1984):

475–519, focuses on the experiences of Americans forty-five and older between 1958 and 1981 and discovers a decline in acute conditions but a rise in restricted activity associated with those conditions. S. Ryan Johansson, "The Health Transition: The Cultural Inflation of Morbidity during the Decline in Mortality," *Health Transition Review* 1 (1991): 39–68, offers a thoughtful and informed discussion of the role that changing cultural conceptions of health and disease may have played in the seemingly paradoxical recorded rise in morbidity that has accompanied declining mortality among modern populations. Charles E. Rosenberg, "Disease and Social Order in America: Perceptions and Expectations," in *Milbank Memorial Quarterly* 64, suppl. 1 (1986): 34–55, provides a good introduction to the changing social constructions of disease and to how medical historians have dealt and do deal with that construction. A. J. Barsky, *Worried Sick: Our Troubled Quest for Wellness* (1988), argues that the observed rise in sickness accompanying the twentieth-century decline in mortality is primarily due to the medicalization of mental, emotional, and physical conditions that previous generations did not consider forms of ill health.

Joshua Lederberg, Robert E. Shope, Stanley C. Oakes, Jr., eds., *Emerging Infections: Microbial Threats to Health in the United States* (1992), a report prepared under the auspices of the Institute of Medicine, details the resurgence of infectious disease at the end of the twentieth century and recommends what might be done to lessen its impact.

HEALTH CARE DELIVERY

Vanessa Northington Gamble

On 5 November 1991 Democrat Harris Wofford, a political newcomer, won Pennsylvania's senatorial election by beating Republican Dick Thornburgh, the state's former governor and the former U.S. attorney general. At the outset of the campaign, Wofford's chances appeared slim. He trailed in the polls by forty points against the better financed and more widely known Thornburgh. Running on a platform that promised national health insurance, Wofford's candidacy steadily gained momentum. Wofford's ability to translate dissatisfaction with America's health care system into votes contributed significantly to his upset victory.

The Pennsylvania senatorial election helped make health care reform a major issue in the 1992 presidential election. Throughout the campaign, it became increasingly clear that discontent with the nation's health care system was not limited to the voters of Pennsylvania. Nationwide, American citizens criticized the escalating costs of health care and the inaccessibility of adequate medical care. Many felt trapped by job situations they could not leave because they did not want to lose their health insurance. Many became aware that approximately 37 million Americans, many of whom were employed, did not have health insurance.

Criticism came from several sources. Large businesses criticized the increasing amount of their revenues that went toward their employees' medical benefits and maintained that these costs had hindered their ability to compete in the global economy. Physicians decried the further intrusion of government in the practice of medicine. Members of Congress, operating under the specter of the burgeoning federal deficit, called attention to government's rising health care expenditures. In 1960, federal expenditures for health care totaled $2.9 billion; thirty years later they had risen to $195.4 billion. In 1960, health care spending represented 5.3 percent of the gross national product; thirty years later it represented 12.2 percent. Despite his narrow margin of victory, President Bill Clinton portrayed his election as a referendum on national health care reform. Indeed, one of his first presidential actions was the appointment of a task force, under the direction of Hillary Rodham Clinton, to develop strategies to reform the American health care system.

Concerns over the delivery of health care did not originate in the 1990s and contemporary efforts at health care reform cannot be understood outside of a historical context. An examination of the history of the twentieth-century American health care delivery system underscores the complexities involved in health care reform. A relatively uncomplicated system centered on the individual doctor-patient relationship evolved into a far more intricate one influenced by a myriad of institutions and participants.

This essay focuses on two major topics in the history of the twentieth-century American health care delivery system: financing and hospitals. An analysis of these topics delineates important characteristics of the system, including (1) the development of an array of uncoordinated public and private financing programs; (2) public ambivalence over who should be responsible for the payment of health care; (3) the integration of health services into the market economy; (4) an increasing role of government in health care; (5) the influence of a wide range of groups, including physicians, businesses, and private insurers, on health policy; (6) the dominance of medical specialization; and (7) the preeminence of the hospital as the primary locus of medical care.

A historical analysis of these two topics, financing and hospitals, also makes plain that factors external to the practice of medicine have profoundly affected its delivery. These social factors include urbanization, the Great Depression, the Cold War, the civil rights movement, and unionization. Furthermore, it is clear that the health care system has not been exempt from the dilemmas and tensions raised by issues of race, class, and gender.

Unlike most industrialized countries, the United

States does not have national health insurance—a government-sponsored health insurance system that provides universal or near universal coverage to its citizens. Instead, most Americans are covered by private plans that they receive as part of their employee benefits packages. Government programs are reserved for limited segments of the population—the elderly, the poor, the military, veterans, and Native Americans.

There have been several attempts to reform health care in the twentieth century, especially to develop a form of national health insurance. Previous efforts have ended in failure or the adoption of incremental solutions that accommodated special interests and did not challenge the organizational structure of the existing system. An examination of the calls for national health insurance that intermittently appeared throughout the twentieth century reveals that there has been a lack of consensus over the dimensions and financing of a mandatory government health insurance program. Although the inability of the United States to enact national health insurance has been the subject of much historical work, we must not let this question, as Daniel Fox warns us, be the primary lens through which we examine the history of health care financing. Our analysis must include the study of programs that did develop to respond to the medical care needs of the American people.

The sociologist Paul Starr, in his Pulitzer Prize–winning history of the American medical profession, *The Social Transformation of American Medicine* (1982), offers a useful conceptualization for analyzing the development of health insurance. Starr maintains that the politics of health insurance revolve around four sorts of costs: (1) individual losses of income; (2) individual medical costs; (3) the indirect costs of illness to society; and (4) the social costs of medical care. During the twentieth century, health care reformers have shifted the attention that they paid to the categories of costs. Proposals introduced during the early twentieth century focused on income maintenance and national efficiency. Those introduced between 1930 and 1960 concentrated on expanding the access of Americans to increasingly expensive medical services. Since 1970, the emphasis has been on cost containment and institutional reform. It should also be noted that throughout the century, the question of who should be responsible for the payment of medical care has been frequently raised. The answer has not been consistent. Individuals, businesses, and the government have all been identified as the responsible parties.

HEALTH CARE DELIVERY AND FINANCING, 1900–1920

At the turn of the century, the practice of medicine was a dyad: a private relationship between a patient and physician. Rarely did organizations outside of the medical profession dictate the terms of a physician's compensation. Physicians were entrepreneurs who billed and collected fees for services directly from patients. In many communities, local medical societies established schedules of minimum fees as guidelines and urged members not to engage in the "unethical" practice of undercharging. Practitioners charged patients for each service they provided. This arrangement, known as fee-for-service, was the dominant form of payment for most of the twentieth century. Class shaped the dimensions of payment. Poor patients were often treated free of charge by physicians while patients with means were held responsible for their bills.

Medical practice for many physicians did not offer financial security. Patients often lacked funds to pay them in a timely fashion—if at all. In rural communities physicians often bartered their services for produce and livestock. In 1913 the American Medical Association (AMA) estimated that only 10 percent of physicians in the United States earned "a comfortable living." Although the AMA may have been exaggerating the problem, there is evidence that many physicians were not well off. For example, in 1914 fewer than 60 percent of Wisconsin's physicians earned enough to be eligible for tax payments.

At the beginning of the twentieth century, physicians practiced mainly in the homes of their patients. Hospitals were peripheral to the provision of medical care, medical education, and medical research. They operated primarily as traditional welfare institutions that cared for a variety of indigent and dependent persons, including (but by no means restricted to) the sick. Hospitals offered limited therapeutics and functioned, in part, to maintain the social order by isolating the socially marginal and by serving as loci for moral as well as medical care.

Poverty and dependence were the main criteria for hospital admission. Hospitals did not charge indigent patients for their care, but subsidized it through voluntary and governmental contributions. Municipal hospitals, such as New York City's Bellevue and Philadelphia's General, began their institutional lives as medical departments in almshouses. The social elite in many cities had established voluntary or not-for-profit hospitals as charities to keep the "worthy poor" out of the almshouse and to protect them from the stigma and demoralizing influence of the almshouse. Principles of Christian stewardship regarding upper class obligations to the poor prompted the development of most voluntary hospitals and even governed their day-to-day operations.

The home continued to serve as the dominant site of medical care for persons with resources and roots in the community. Most Americans relied on self-medication or care from other family members, usually women. Physicians, when called, not only provided care in the home, but even performed major surgeries there, often in the kitchen. As therapy in both locations consisted primarily of food, rest, warmth, and tonics, hospital care offered no therapeutic advantages over domestic care. People avoided hospitals both out of pride, because of their identification as charitable institutions, and out of fear of contracting hospital-originated infections and fevers.

At the beginning of the twentieth century, hospitals also played an insignificant role in the professional development of the average practitioner. Medical education did not require clinical training in hospitals nor did contemporary medical practice demand that physicians serve internships, residencies, or hold hospital appointments. The average physician could complete his or her medical education and have a successful practice without setting foot in a hospital. Hospital appointments were limited to a small group of elite, urban physicians. Those physicians who did practice in voluntary hospitals did not receive any financial remuneration for their services. Their rewards came from the knowledge and reputations that they gained from hospital work and the resulting fees that they could charge their private patients.

At that time, most Americans did not have any form of insurance to pay for the costs of medical or hospital care. Those who did purchased it from trade unions, commercial insurance companies, or fraternal organizations. The number of Americans covered under such plans is not known. But in 1919 the health insurance commissions of Pennsylvania and Illinois estimated that approximately one-third of all workers had voluntary health insurance. Fraternal organizations, established in working-class and immigrant communities, provided the bulk of the coverage. These societies offered members sickness insurance to reduce financial hardships from lost wages that resulted from illness; their primary purpose was income maintenance. Benefits, however, were limited. The insured received a small cash payment of five to ten dollars a week for up to thirteen weeks.

A few of the programs sponsored by fraternal organizations also provided a fixed cash benefit for medical expenses and medical services. These prepaid medical services offered restricted services that were supplied by physicians who were under contract to the organizations. This type of contract practice was harshly criticized by organized medicine because it violated the traditional doctor-patient relationship by allowing organizations outside of medicine to invade private practice. The method of compensation for these contract physicians was also a point of criticism. These physicians were not paid on the professionally sanctioned fee-for-service basis, but rather on a capitation basis (that is, a fixed sum per patient per year). Despite the opposition from organized medicine, financial necessity forced some physicians to accept such work.

During the early twentieth century, a few industries, most notably, railroad, mining, and lumber companies, offered health insurance to their employees. These plans were usually financed by mandatory payroll deductions and by employer contributions. The geographical isolation of these companies often prompted them to provide health care to their workers. However, their desire to build up employee loyalty as a strategy to stop union organizing cannot be discounted. The choice of physicians was controlled by the industries who hired them. It is clear that the allegiances of these physicians rested with the employers. Physicians often represented the company's interest in damage suits that employees brought to court. But the provision of health insurance by companies was rare. For the most part, industrial medicine consisted of taking care of accident victims and providing employment examinations.

During the first decades of the twentieth century, state and federal governments also limited their endeavors in the financing of health care. Their activities consisted primarily of the provision of direct assistance rather than of insurance. Governmental agencies paid for the health and hospital care of special groups within American society. Before World War I, these groups included the indigent, Native Americans, merchant seamen, and patients with particular diseases such as mental illness and tuberculosis. For example, in many large cities governments provided care to the poor by operating hospitals themselves or by giving subsidies to voluntary hospitals. The cities also operated dispensaries or outpatient departments for indigent patients.

Across the Atlantic in Europe, a different picture of government involvement in the financing of medical care had started to emerge by the end of the nineteenth century. In 1883 Germany established the first national system of compulsory sickness insurance as a component of a general program of social insurance. Government plans to cover sickness, old age, unemployment, and disability shared a common goal—to safeguard individuals against the loss of earnings. These plans initially protected workers only and did not extend to their dependents. The benefits of the sickness insurance included medical care, medicines, and sick pay. The program was jointly financed by contributions from employees and employers.

By 1913 nearly every European nation, including Great Britain, Austria, Hungary, and the Netherlands, had legislated some kind of compulsory health insurance. Other countries, such as France, Italy, Denmark, and Switzerland, granted subsidies to the mutual benefit societies that workers had established. At times political discontent prompted the state's actions, especially in the adoption of compulsory social insurance programs. Chancellor Otto von Bismarck, for example, had introduced the plan in Germany to gain worker loyalty and stem the tide of socialism.

The first push for compulsory health insurance in the United States came in 1912 from the American Association for Labor Legislation (AALL). The organization, composed primarily of academics, social workers, and economists, had been founded in 1906. It had been active in campaigns launched during the Progressive Era to establish workers' compensation, child labor laws, and unemployment relief. In 1912 the AALL established a Committee on Social Insurance to prepare model legislation for the enactment of compulsory medical insurance by state legislatures. As was the case in Europe, the AALL saw medical insurance as a form of income maintenance. It argued that such a program would relieve the poverty that illness often caused. Invoking the rhetoric of the Progressive movement, the organization also maintained that the insurance would increase efficiency by decreasing the costs of illness. In 1915, the AALL presented its plan. Coverage was to be limited to the working class, those making less than $1,200 a year, and their dependents. Benefits included medical aid, sick pay, maternity benefits, and death benefits. The plan would be financed jointly by employees (40 percent), employers (40 percent) and state governments (20 percent). By 1917 twelve states were considering bills to provide health coverage.

Physicians, in the words of Ronald L. Numbers, were "almost persuaded" to support compulsory health insurance. Indeed, many initially promoted the idea. The *Journal of the American Medical Association* hailed the AALL legislation, as did the state medical societies of Pennsylvania, Wisconsin, and New York.

Financial considerations influenced the physician response. In 1915 their incomes averaged $2,000. Compulsory health insurance would provide a fixed income and eliminate the nuisance of collecting unpaid bills.

However, by 1917 physicians' sentiment started to shift, again because of economic factors, and they emerged as vocal opponents of compulsory health insurance. Physicians increasingly came to believe that their incomes would decline, not grow, under the AALL plan. A false rumor that practitioners' salaries would be limited to $1,200 proved especially damaging. The proposed per capita reimbursement mechanism also came under fire.

Opposition to the AALL plan was not limited to physicians. Other critics included organized labor, business, and insurance companies. Labor leaders, especially Samuel Gompers of the American Federation of Labor, denounced government-sponsored health insurance as an unnecessary and paternalistic program that they feared would lead to state supervision of individual health matters. Unions also opposed it, as well as other forms of social insurance, on the grounds that a government insurance system would infringe upon labor's right to organize. Labor opposition would continue until Gompers's death. Business representatives rejected the argument that the program would increase efficiency. They contended that the provision of sick benefits would have an opposite effect and would encourage malingering. Commercial insurance companies vigorously opposed the AALL plan, specifically the burial benefit, because they believed that it threatened their profitable life insurance plans.

Other factors contributed to the defeat of the first American campaign for compulsory health insurance. For one, it fell victim to rising anti-German sentiment. The country's entry into World War I led to allegations that compulsory health insurance was "un-American" because it had been "made in Germany." The AALL had not been able to generate any broad-based public support for the program. In 1919 California held the only state referendum on compulsory health insurance and voters defeated it by a wide margin. Compulsory health insurance, it appeared, had no political viability.

THE TRANSFORMATION OF THE HOSPITAL

The first twenty years of the twentieth century also witnessed major changes in the status, mission, financing, and organization of the hospital. It evolved from a benevolent institution that served primarily poor patients to a medical workshop that served patients of all classes. Hospitals became central to medical education, medical care, and clinical investigation.

An interplay of medical and social factors led to this transformation. The rise of scientific medicine played a major role. Medical accomplishments included the establishment of the germ theory of disease, breakthroughs in therapeutics and diagnostics, such as diphtheria antitoxin and the Wassermann test for syphilis, made possible by advances in serology and immunology; the developments of technologies such as the x-ray; and the growth of surgery as a specialty because of the advent of asepsis, anesthesia, and new surgical techniques. Social factors such as urbanization, immigration, and industrialization also cannot be discounted. For example, migration to large cities led to an increase in the number of people without families to care for them. In addition, the smaller homes and apartments associated with urban living did not provide the space to care for sick people. Thus a need grew for institutions to provide medical care to urban residents.

By 1920, hospitals became essential for patient care and medical practice. The institutions had evolved into integral components of the new scientific medicine as sites of clinical practice for all physicians, not just those of the urban elite. In hospitals, physicians could exchange professional knowledge and have access to expensive hospital-based technologies. In other words, as Charles E. Rosenberg has argued, "the hospital had been medicalized" and "the medical profession had been hospitalized." The advances of scientific medicine led to increases in the prestige, power, and reputations of hospitals, as upper- and middle-class patients' perceptions changed because of tangible evidence that the institutions could benefit them.

Hospitals also became indispensable for medical education. In 1910, the Carnegie Foundation for the Advancement of Teaching released a survey of American and Canadian medical schools that had been conducted by Abraham Flexner. The Flexner Report provided a description of each school and depicted in graphic detail the horrible conditions, including poorly equipped laboratories and the presence of inadequately trained professors, that existed at many of the institutions, especially the proprietary ones. Flexner considered these schools were insufficient to meet the demands of the new scientific medicine. He argued that medical schools needed to follow the model set at Baltimore's Johns Hopkins. This school had well-equipped laboratories, a medi-

cal-school-controlled teaching hospital, a curriculum that emphasized both the basic and clinical sciences, and a full-time faculty.

Several significant reforms occurred in American medical education during the years surrounding the publication of the Flexner Report. One key change was a new emphasis on clinical training as an integral component of medical education. The hospital was central to this program. The American Medical Association's Council on Medical Education recommended in 1905 that medical school graduates complete an internship as part of their basic medical education. By 1914, an estimated 80 percent of medical school graduates served an internship; five medical colleges required an internship as a prerequisite for a medical degree; and one state board, Pennsylvania's, required it as a prerequisite for licensure. Seven years later, every surviving medical school had established an affiliation with a hospital. A lack of hospital facilities had become a death knell for many schools.

The reforms in medical education also led to efforts to improve the quality of postgraduate training. In 1919, the Council on Medical Education started issuing "The Essentials of an Approved Internship," a list of minimal criteria that internships had to meet. In addition to the internship, specialty training and other forms of hospital-based medical training began to expand.

The increased complexity in the practice of medicine engendered by the advancements of scientific medicine also influenced the growth of medical specialization. At the beginning of the century most physicians were general practitioners. In fact, specialization was frowned upon. However, this had changed by the 1920s. In 1923, over 15,000 physicians listed themselves as full-time specialists; six years later the number had grown to 22,000. Including part-time specialists, approximately 30 percent of American physicians considered themselves specialists. By the early twenties, twenty-three specialty fields existed and the hospital was the base for much of this practice.

The number of hospitals increased exponentially during the first two decades of the twentieth century. In 1873, the first hospital survey had located only 178; fifty years later, almost 5,000 facilities were in operation. Facilities often developed in response to community needs and values rather than according to national medical standards. For example, racial and religious discrimination was one factor that fueled the growth of hospitals. In the face of social hostilities, various ethnic and religious groups established their own institutions. Catholics and Jews founded denominational hospitals because they feared religious conversion and had encountered religious intolerance at Protestant institutions. The desire of Jewish patients to keep kosher when hospitalized and the wishes of Catholic patients to receive the sacraments were major factors in the establishment of sectarian hospitals.

Racial discrimination prompted the creation of black hospitals. In some instances, whites established the institutions to provide at least some hospital care for black people, all the while maintaining the color line. The motives behind the creation of these facilities varied. Some white founders expressed a genuine, if paternalistic, interest in supplying health care to black people and offering training opportunities to black health professionals. However, white self-interest was also at work. The newly accepted germ theory of disease acknowledged that "germs have no color line." Thus the theory mandated attention to the medical problems of African Americans, especially those whose proximity to whites threatened to spread disease.

The African American community also founded hospitals in order to meet its particular needs. Black patients often found their access to hospitals severely restricted. Hospitals—in both the North and South—either denied them admission or accommodated them, almost universally, in segregated wards, often placed in undesirable locations such as unheated attics and damp basements. In Newport News, Virginia, for example, black patients were housed in the city jail until the 1914 establishment of a black hospital. Black nurses and physicians also encountered discriminatory customs. Few hospitals offered them training or practice opportunities. By 1919, approximately 118 black hospitals had been established, 75 percent of them in the South.

At the turn of the century, no formal criteria governed the provision of hospital care and the management of hospitals. However, in concert with the transformation of the hospital, efforts began to standardize and improve hospitals. For example, the American College of Surgeons, founded in 1912, established national yardsticks for the evaluation of hospitals. It hoped that adherence to these guidelines would upgrade or eliminate inferior hospitals. In 1919, the College issued a set of rules that specified minimum standards for staff, equipment, facilities, and basic operating procedures. These guidelines had to be met before a hospital could be placed on the American College of Surgeons' list of approved hospitals.

As a result of the standardization movement and the growth of scientific medicine and industrialization, the costs of operating hospitals significantly increased. Hospitals now needed to maintain laboratories and expensive technologies such as x-ray machines and electrocardiograms. Aseptic surgery required the purchase of rubber gloves, sterile bandages, and sterilization equipment. Hospitals also had to provide electricity, purchase coal, and meet safety codes. Consequently, hospitals could no longer be maintained primarily by the financial contributions of wealthy donors; they had to develop new sources of funding. One mechanism was to expand the number of paying patients, either by increasing the number of middle-class patients or by charging poor people for services that had previously been free. As hospitals moved away from their traditional charitable functions toward a system based on ability to pay, hospital care increasingly became a commodity to be bought by those who could afford it.

THE EVOLUTION OF VOLUNTARY HEALTH INSURANCE

Concerns over the rising costs of medical care and the inability of many Americans to pay for such care prompted new debates over health insurance. In the years between the two world wars, discussions shifted from income maintenance to the removal of economic barriers to medical care. It had become increasingly clear that financial considerations restricted the access of not only poor people, but also middle-class individuals who were too affluent to enter charity wards but not prosperous enough to pay for private care. The Depression only exacerbated the situation.

The problems of the high costs and maldistribution of medical services were underscored in the 1932 final report of the Committee of the Costs of Medical Care (CCMC), an independent body that included fifty physicians, economists, public health specialists, and consumers. The group, with financial support from several foundations, had been created in 1927 to examine the organization and availability of scientific medicine.

During the course of its five-year existence, the CCMC published twenty-seven research reports that offered the first comprehensive examinations of the American health care system. For example, they provided the first reliable estimates of national health care expenditures. The CCMC found that in 1929, 4 percent of the gross national product, or $3.66 billion, was spent on health care. Over 53 percent of the total went to pay doctor and hospital bills.

The CCMC presented a vivid description of

inequities in the provision and costs of medical care. It reported that approximately 4 percent of the families incurred 80 percent of the costs. It also found that income greatly influenced the provision of medical care. In a survey of 8,500 white families the CCMC discovered that 14 percent of families with incomes greater than $10,000 had no medical care within the course of a year; but 47 percent of those making less than $1,200 had no such care. Although the CCMC did not conduct a similar study with black families, it acknowledged in its final report that inequities in the delivery of health services were more severe for African Americans.

The contention of the CCMC that the benefits of scientific medicine should be available to every American, regardless of financial status, ran counter to the prevailing market ethos that services should be distributed by ability to pay. The CCMC saw maldistribution of resources, not the lack of resources, as the major impediment to access. As the committee's staff director put it, "What exists is not so much a system as a lack of a system." The CCMC's final report recommended a reorganization of medical practice in the United States, calling for the establishment of hospital-based group practices and of voluntary group insurance plans. Specialty practice in the organizations would be limited to those who had advanced training and hospitals would be coordinated by local and state planning boards.

The CCMC did not reach a consensus on how to reform the health care system (only thirty-five of its fifty members supported its recommendations). A group composed almost exclusively of general practitioners voiced the harshest criticism. It viewed group practice as a threat to their livelihoods because it would restrict specialization. The dissenters also portrayed the proposed reorganization of medical practice as a technique of big business that was antithetical to the personal doctor-patient relationship. In addition, they feared that it would establish a medical hierarchy that would cause physicians to lose their autonomy. The critics opposed voluntary health insurance because they feared it was a bridge to compulsory health insurance. The AMA backed the dissenters, calling the recommendations socialistic and inimical to the best interests of the American people.

Despite initial objections from organized medicine, voluntary health insurance programs proliferated throughout the 1930s and 1940s and insurance companies began to assume important roles in health care delivery. The Depression proved to be the initial catalyst. At the time, many hospitals found themselves financially vulnerable because their main source of income, direct payments by patients, sharply declined. Charitable contributions to the institutions also decreased. Hospitals, therefore, had to develop new fiscal strategies. One response was the encouragement of voluntary hospital prepayment plans for those with some means. The government would be responsible for providing medical relief to the poor. Prepayment plans would give hospitals a guaranteed source of income and would offer an alternative to compulsory health insurance with its potential for government intervention.

At first, commercial insurance companies showed little interest in developing such plans because of actuarial and financial concerns. Traditionally, the companies insured against losses, such as theft, fires, and death, that were unambiguous and measurable. Many insurers doubted that medical care was an insurable risk because of the difficulty of predicting losses accurately. They pointed to the financial ramifications of possible adverse selection, that is the purchase of insurance by those most likely to become sick. They also expressed concern that many of the costs associated with health insurance were within the control of hospitals and physicians who could potentially profit by dispensing additional services.

The reluctance of insurance companies to design health insurance programs and the adverse impact of the Depression on the financial lives of hospitals and consumers provided the impetus for the creation of the first Blue Cross plan. As the law professor Sylvia A. Law has stated, "Blue Cross is the child of the Depression and the American Hospital Association." Throughout the 1920s and 1930s all hospitals grappled with the problem of financing. Governments and insurance companies infrequently paid for hospitalization and the Depression greatly reduced the institutions' incomes. Charitable contributions, which had earlier in the century been a major source of revenue, steeply declined. The financial calamity forced many people to forego hospitalization or, if they did require admission, to enter as charity rather than pay patients and to seek admission to public rather than private facilities. These threats to the viability of voluntary hospitals prompted hospital administrators to seek new sources of revenue. One strategy was to encourage voluntary hospital insurance for those able to afford it.

The history of Blue Cross began with the efforts of Dr. Justin Ford Kimball, an administrator at Baylor University Hospital in Dallas, Texas, to develop a plan to cover the hospital expenses of teachers admitted to the hospital. He enrolled 1,250 teachers in a program to prepay 50 cents a month in exchange for twenty-one days of semiprivate hospitalization at the institution. The plan was not insurance in the traditional sense. Enrollees did not receive the usual indemnity benefits, but service benefits. The plan's subscribers made payments directly to the hospital, rather than to the patient, who would then pay the hospital. Thus subscribers would not have to file claims for reimbursement.

The Baylor program attracted considerable attention as a strategy to help financially distressed hospitals and similar plans developed nationwide. However, its requirement that enrollees be restricted to one hospital prompted criticism. Critics charged that such an arrangement severely limited the options of patients and physicians and led to unneeded competition among hospitals. Consequently, "free-choice" plans that included a number of hospitals in a community emerged. In 1932, for example, all the hospitals in Sacramento, California, jointly offered hospital service contracts to employed persons. State insurance commissioners had viewed the establishment of single-hospital plans as the sale of prepaid hospital services and not as insurance. Thus these plans were not subject to the legal requirements of insurance companies such as the maintenance of cash reserves. However, they regarded the establishment of the multi-institutional plans as a form of insurance that required state regulation.

In response, the American Hospital Association (AHA), initiated a lobbying campaign to convince state legislators that hospital service plans differed from insurance. It argued that these independent plans were nonprofit corporations that fulfilled a public need by providing hospital care to low-income patients. The hospital organization contended that the existence of these plans would supplant the use of funds from public coffers or private charities to hospitalize these patients. In 1934 the AHA won a significant victory when the New York state legislature passed enabling legislation that exempted hospital service plans from state insurance regulations and designated them as charitable organizations. Since hospitals would underwrite the plans, the bill also required that a majority of the directors of the plans be hospital representatives. In exchange, the plans pledged to serve the entire community and to assure the availability of insurance to persons of moderate and low income. By 1939 similar legislation had passed in twenty-five states. Because of their tax exempt status and close connections with hospitals, Blue Cross plans rapidly grew throughout the 1930s. By 1940, there were fifty-six plans with a combined

total of 6 million subscribers. Each program was autonomous and locally controlled.

The success of the Blue Cross model prompted the commercial insurance companies to reevaluate their stance on health insurance and in 1934 they began to offer group hospitalization insurance. Six years later, they provided hospital insurance to 3.7 million Americans.

Several characteristics, however, distinguished the commercial plans from Blue Cross. These included indemnity coverage, limited enrollment, and experience rating. Private insurance carriers reimbursed or indemnified the patient for covered services up to a specified dollar amount. It was the responsibility of the hospital to collect the money from the patient. Blue Cross plans practiced open enrollment, in which any individual could purchase coverage, regardless of health status. Commercial insurers charged at-risk applicants, such as the elderly and chronically ill, higher premiums or denied them coverage. Blue Cross plans traditionally established premiums by community rating. This meant that everybody in the community paid the same premium. By this mechanism, well consumers subsidized sick consumers who used physicians and hospitals more frequently. In contrast, commercial insurers used experience rating in which the rate of each group was based on that group's historic costs. The healthier the group the lower the premiums.

Many members of organized medicine had initially viewed the establishment of voluntary insurance as the first step toward compulsory insurance. However, in 1938 the AMA endorsed voluntary group hospital programs as long as they did not include physicians' fees. Organized medicine considered payment of physicians' services by a third party an infringement of the doctor-patient relationship. It viewed medical care as a private and personal matter. In addition, the medical profession did not want a third party to set reimbursement rates; it wanted to retain that responsibility. However, by the late 1930s medical societies created programs that would cover the costs of physician services and would be controlled by physicians. In 1943, the AMA established Associated Medical Care Plans, the precursor to Blue Shield. Blue Shield differed from Blue Cross in that it covered the costs associated with physician services while Blue Cross covered those associated with hospital costs.

Two factors significantly influenced organized medicine to change its position on voluntary health insurance. First, because of the Depression, many physicians found themselves under financial strains.

994

During the first year of the Depression, the net income of physicians dropped by 17 percent. Health insurance would provide them with some measure of financial security by stimulating the use of physicians' services and by helping patients pay their bills. Second, organized medicine had come to view voluntary health insurance as a viable alternative to an increasing government role in health care financing and a revived push for compulsory health insurance. In her book, *In Sickness and in Wealth: American Hospitals in the Twentieth Century,* the medical historian Rosemary A. Stevens exhaustively demonstrates the factors underlying this shift. She notes that starting in the 1930s the major medical and hospital organizations "used voluntarism as a major, unifying rhetoric, allowing them to present a common front against the threat of increased government intervention." "The language of the 'voluntary way,' " she argues, "became the antithesis to 'socialized medicine.' "

THE FEDERAL GOVERNMENT AND HEALTH CARE DELIVERY

The Depression had indeed led to an expanded federal role in health care delivery, most notably for the poor. Responsibility for indigent care increasingly shifted from hospitals and charities to governmental agencies. Federal efforts originated before the stock market crash when in 1921 Congress passed the Sheppard-Towner Act. This legislation established the first grants-in-aid to state health agencies for the direct provision of services, specifically for maternal and child health programs. The AMA regarded this measure with alarm. The medical organization perceived it as opening the door to government encroachment on private practice. AMA opposition led to the demise of the Sheppard-Towner Act in 1929. (For a summary of important legislation affecting health care and medicine, see table 1.)

Despite the failure of the Sheppard-Towner Act, the financial exigencies of the Depression led to greater legitimation of a state and federal role in providing medical care to the poor. Medical care became recognized as an essential element of relief efforts. For example, under the auspices of the Federal Emergency Relief Administration (FERA), the federal government made funds available to states to pay the medical expenses for Americans on relief. However, most states only covered emergency medical and dental services. The FERA program did not survive the Depression.

The Depression set a precedent for increased federal financing of medical care, but just for specific and restricted populations. This trend continued during the 1940s. By 1944 the War Food Administration had established health centers and clinics in 250 areas for poor farm workers. To meet the health care needs of service families, the federal government in 1943 launched the emergency medical and infant care program (EMIC). The program, administered by the Children's Bureau through state health departments, provided obstetrics, hospital, and pediatric care at military bases. It served 1.1 million maternity cases before its termination in 1946.

The federal government also continued to provide veterans with medical services and to operate a national hospital system to care for them. The government involvement in the delivery of health care to this population had begun with the enactment of the War Risk Insurance Act of 1917 and 1918. This bill provided veterans, disabled by service-related diseases and injuries, with medical, surgical, and hospital services. Initially, they received their care in government hospitals (such as those run by the Public Health Service) and in voluntary hospitals that had contracted with the federal government. However, the end of World War I brought hordes of ex-soldiers who needed care. Their sheer numbers overwhelmed the existing institutions. Many veterans found that they could not receive the services that had been guaranteed them. In response, the American Legion and Veterans of Foreign Wars launched an effective lobbying campaign. They reminded members of Congress of nation's obligation to the men and women who had served valiantly in the "War to End All Wars." They publicized stories of shell-shocked veterans sent to hospitals for feeble-minded children and of tubercular ex-soldiers sent to marshy districts detrimental to their health.

In March 1921 Congress finally appropriated $18.6 million to create a national hospital system for veterans. Shortly thereafter, Secretary of the Treasury Andrew W. Mellon appointed a committee of medical experts, the Consultants on Hospitalization, to advise him on its development. The group worked for two years to develop a hospital system that was not only national, but rational. It held hearings and heard testimony from over 100 groups—all interested in having a veterans hospital located in their area. In addition, it painstakingly collected and analyzed data on the number of veterans, their medical needs, and the number of hospitals that would be required to care for them. It sought to make its recommendations based on statistics, not political considerations.

But the Consultants on Hospitalization were not immune to the racial politics of the time. In their

Table 1. TWENTIETH-CENTURY LEGISLATION IN HEALTH AND MEDICINE

Title	Year Enacted	Description
Biologics Control Act	1902	Provided for the inspection and licensing of vaccine, antisera, and antitoxin manufactories, to insure product safety and potency.
Pure Food and Drugs Act	1906	Gave the Department of Agriculture authority to inspect and regulate food and drug producers in order to protect against adulteration, contamination, and fraudulent sales.
War Risk Insurance Act	1917	Basic package of World War I veterans' benefits. Provided for low-cost voluntary insurance against death or disability, compensation for service-connected disabilities and for dependents of the dead, vocational rehabilitation for the disabled, and medical and hospital care.
Sheppard-Towner Maternity and Infancy Protection Act	1921	Provided matching federal grants-in-aid to states for the purpose of promoting child and maternal health services; provided for instruction through public health nurses, visiting nurses, consultation centers, child care conferences, and literature distribution.
Social Security Act	1935	Provided for federal old-age insurance benefits, federal-state unemployment insurance, federal grants-in-aid for old-age assistance, Aid to Dependent Children (ADC, later AFDC); omits provision for health insurance.
Hospital Survey and Construction Act (Hill-Burton Act)	1946	Provided matching funds to states for hospital construction based on state assessments of local needs.
Social Security Amendments of 1965 (Medicare and Medicaid)	1965	Included a hospital insurance program for elderly Social Security recipients, funded from payroll taxes, and voluntary medical service insurance for the same group, funded by small premiums and general revenues; and expanded the Kerr-Mills program for all medically indigent individuals.
Public Health Service Amendments of 1972	1972	Established a mechanism for Professional Standards Review Organizations (PSROs); mandated that hospitals receiving federal funds conduct Certificate of Need Reviews.
Health Maintenance Organization Act	1973	Authorized federal grants and loans to finance establishment of HMOs
Omnibus Budget Reconciliation Act of 1981	1981	Collapsed funding for many categorical grant programs into block grants to states; reduced funding for all health services programs; and increased local and state governance over remaining programs.
Tax Equity and Fiscal Responsibility Act	1982	Tightened regulations on Medicare and Medicaid; introduced Medicare reimbursement based not on costs or charges, but on set rates for diagnostic related groups (DRGs).

SOURCE: Adapted from *Encyclopedia of the United States Congress* (New York: Simon & Schuster, 1995), pp. 804, 958, 1849, 2040.

final report, published in 1923, they recommended that a separate national hospital for black veterans be established at Tuskegee, Alabama. Earlier that month, Congress had appropriated $18.6 million for the hospitals and President Woodrow Wilson on his last day in office had signed the law (P.L. 66-384). These new facilities would be organized and financed by the federal government and initially would be re-

stricted to those veterans with service-related diseases and injuries.

The growing emergence of national health insurance programs that covered specific groups did not stop attempts to develop one that would cover the entire population. Efforts were made throughout the 1930s and 1940s. The Depression revived interest in social insurance. In 1934, President Franklin Delano

Roosevelt appointed the Committee on Economic Security to comprehensively examine the issue and to recommend legislation. Its deliberations included old-age pensions, unemployment insurance, and health insurance. However, the specter of compulsory health insurance in the proposed social security legislation provoked renewed efforts by organized medicine to lobby against it. In February 1935, the AMA's House of Delegates met in special session, the first time since World War I, to reaffirm its opposition. When President Roosevelt sent the report of the Committee on Economic Security to Congress, it did not include any recommendation on health insurance. Fears that opposition to it would endanger passage of the entire Social Security Act greatly influenced the President's action. Although the final social security legislation did not include health insurance, it did include provisions that continued the government role in the financing of health care. It provided grants-in-aid to states for maternal and child care, aid to crippled children, aid to the blind, the aged, and other health-impaired people.

Despite the failure to include health insurance as part of the Social Security Act, efforts continued throughout the New Deal to broaden the government's role in health care. In 1937, the Roosevelt administration named a Technical Committee on Medical Care to formulate a national health program. The committee in its final report recommended an expansion of federal subsidies to states for medical activities rather than the establishment of a national health insurance system. Specifically, it called for (1) the augmentation of existing public health and maternal and child health services under the Social Security Act; (2) the establishment of federal disability insurance; (3) the provision of grants for hospital construction; (4) the expansion of medical assistance programs for welfare recipients; and (5) the "consideration" of a general medical program supported by either taxes or insurance contributions for the rest of the population.

In 1938, President Roosevelt convened a national meeting to announce the committee's findings. The meeting, attended by over 150 representatives of labor, social welfare, and medical professions, strongly supported the report. The next year, Sen. Robert F. Wagner (D-N.Y.) introduced a bill that incorporated many of the report's recommendations. Congress took no action on the bill. This did not deter Wagner. In 1944, he joined forces with Sen. James E. Murray (D-Mont.) and Rep. John D. Dingell, Sr. (D-Mich.) to introduce a bill providing medical and dental insurance to all persons paying social security taxes as well

as to their families. The first of a series of Wagner-Murray-Dingell bills differed significantly from legislation that Senator Wagner had initially introduced. It proposed compulsory health insurance on a national basis with social security taxes, not on a state-by-state basis with federal grant to states. The two bills shared a similar fate: the latter proposal died in a congressional committee.

Several factors contributed to the failure to establish a program of national health insurance during the New Deal. The issue never received a strong mandate from the White House. Roosevelt's support, at best, was weak. The entry of the country into World War II diverted attention from domestic policy issues. In addition, while organized medicine remained adamant in its opposition, supporters had not been able to mount a successful campaign. Divisions existed, even within the administration, over the scope and content of proposals. For many supporters, national health insurance was not a priority. For example, although labor had reversed its traditional position and no longer opposed health insurance after Gompers's death in 1924, the issue remained a secondary one. The movement for compulsory health insurance also did not attract a groundswell of public support. Public opinion polls conducted in the late 1930s and early 1940s indicated that Americans increasingly saw the provision of health insurance as a government responsibility, but displayed ambivalence over the financing and control of medical services. For example, 58 percent of those surveyed in 1943 thought that social security should pay for physician and hospital services; two years later, 68 percent agreed. However, support dropped to 44 percent and to 51 percent, respectively, when respondents were asked whether they would support a rise in social security taxes to finance such a program. Public reluctance to finance national health insurance by increasing taxes is a trend that has persisted throughout the twentieth century.

THE CONTINUING DEBATE OVER COMPULSORY HEALTH INSURANCE

The campaign to establish national health insurance that was universal, comprehensive, and compulsory gained new momentum in the years after World War II. For the first time, the effort received strong presidential support. In November 1945, three months after the end of the war, President Harry S. Truman sent a message on health legislation to Congress. He called upon it to adopt a national program that assured Americans the right to adequate medical care and protection from the economic fears of sickness. The President's four-point program included (1) the expansion of hospitals; (2) increased support of public health and maternal and child care services; (3) federal aid for medical education and research; and (4) a comprehensive, prepaid health insurance system that would include all Americans. The medical insurance program would be financed through a 4 percent rise in the Social Security Old Age and Survivors Insurance Tax. Poor people not covered by social security would be covered by payments from general federal revenues. The President's plan was incorporated into the second Wagner-Murray-Dingell bill. Again, no action was taken on the legislation.

The sociologist Paul Starr has pointed out the expansionary nature of Truman's proposal. He writes, "It aimed to expand access to medical care by augmenting the nation's medical resources and reducing financial barriers to their use, and it promised doctors higher incomes and no organizational reform." The President acknowledged that his program would cost money. But he contended that the country could afford to spend more money on health services because medical services absorbed only 4 percent of the gross national product.

Compulsory health insurance became a campaign issue during the 1948 presidential election. Truman blamed the "do-nothing" Republican Congress for his inability to get health insurance legislation passed. He promised to continue to push for it if he were reelected. Emboldened by his upset victory and by the return of both houses of Congress to Democratic hands, President Truman kept his promise. In his 1949 State of the Union Address he once again called for compulsory national health insurance.

Hearings on the legislation provoked bitter debate and intense lobbying. The AMA launched a vigorous and well-organized campaign against "socialized medicine." It contended that the legislation represented an attack on individual fee-for-service medical practice, and with it the entire free enterprise system. Compulsory health insurance, it argued, would eventually lead to governmental control of the profession.

In response to Truman's proposals, organized medicine became even more outspoken in its support of voluntary health insurance, which it believed represented less of a threat to the professional autonomy of physicians. Whittaker and Baxter, a California public relations company, spearheaded the AMA charge. The firm had already waged a successful battle

in its home state against a compulsory state health insurance program. The AMA set up a $3.5 million war chest to defeat the national legislation. Its strategies included conducting a campaign to "educate" the American public about the virtues of voluntarism and the evils of socialism, and donating campaign contributions to politicians who backed its position. Organized medicine did see a restricted government role in health care delivery. It supported Republican-sponsored legislation that authorized federal grants to states to subsidize voluntary health insurance for the poor.

Other health care organizations split over the issue of compulsory health insurance. The American Hospital Association opposed the Truman plan; although not as vehemently and as vocally as the AMA. It favored a three-pronged strategy to avoid compulsory health insurance: (1) government support for the poor; (2) encouragement of voluntary health insurance; and (3) government support of a hospital construction program. On the other hand, the American Public Health Association (APHA) endorsed compulsory health insurance. In 1944 it adopted a set of principles on comprehensive health care for all Americans that would be financed through Social Security and/or general taxation revenues.

Despite strong presidential support, compulsory health insurance failed to be enacted during the Truman administration. To be sure, massive lobbying by the AMA played a major role, but several factors contributed to its defeat. The AMA lobbying proved so effective because it was able to taint the campaign for health insurance with the rhetoric of Cold War politics. The links between national health insurance and socialism became so strong that even those who supported it spoke of "socialized medicine." Political realities also cannot be discounted. The legislation never produced a groundswell of public support. In 1949, only 36 percent of Americans endorsed the measure. Although the Democrats controlled both houses of Congress, internal divisions plagued the party. Southern Democrats, the so-called Dixiecrats, angry at Truman's stance on civil rights, withheld legislative support. Some historians have also contended that Truman's weak legislative skills contributed to the plan's defeat.

HEALTH INSURANCE AND THE WORKPLACE

The exponential rise of voluntary health insurance coverage that followed World War II also hindered the push for compulsory health insurance. In 1940 only 9 percent of the civilian population had coverage for hospital costs, 4 percent for surgical costs, and 2 percent for in-hospital physicians' costs. Ten years later, 51 percent had coverage for hospital costs, 36 percent for surgical costs, and 14 percent for in-hospital physicians' costs.

Government policies helped to fuel this growth. During World War II the federal government imposed wage and price controls in order to combat inflation. However, in 1942 the War Labor Board exempted fringe benefits from these restrictions. At a time of severe labor shortages, employers increasingly supplemented wages with fringe benefits, including health insurance, in order to attract employees. Later government actions promoted the growth of employer-financed health insurance. The 1935 National Labor Relations Act (Wagner Act) required that management bargain with labor over "wages and conditions of employment." The act did not make clear whether fringe benefits fell under its scope. In 1948 the National Labor Relations Board ruled, in a dispute between the United Steelworkers' Union and the Inland Steel Company, that fringe benefits were indeed subject to collective bargaining. A year later, in the *Inland Steel* case, the United States Supreme Court reaffirmed this decision. As more union members gained medical insurance coverage through their jobs, labor had less impetus to push for universal national health insurance.

Tax policies also encouraged strong links between health insurance coverage and the workplace. Federal legislation enacted in 1954 excluded business revenues used to pay insurance premiums from corporate taxes; and employees were not taxed for the health insurance benefits that they received from their employers.

Health insurance for most Americans throughout the latter half of the twentieth century has remained a condition of employment and the responsibility of their employers. Employers, however, are under no legal obligation to provide this fringe benefit. Between 1948 and 1950 the number of workers covered by negotiated health insurance plans increased from 2.7 to 7 million. By the end of 1954, the numbers had grown to 12 million workers and 17 million dependents. In 1988, 153 million Americans, 73 percent of those with insurance, obtained coverage through their employers. The proportion of businesses offering health insurance is directly related to size: the larger the business, the more likely it is to provide it. A 1991 survey revealed that only 27 percent of the firms with fewer than 10 employees of-

fered it as opposed to 98 percent of those with over 100 employees.

The growth of employer-financed medical coverage helped to spur the involvement of commercial insurers into health-related areas. Between 1945 and 1949 commercial group hospital policies rose from 7.8 to 17.7 million. By 1953 commercial carriers provided hospital insurance to 29 percent of Americans, Blue Cross to 27 percent, and independent plans to 7 percent. Commercial insurers used experience rating to set premiums and could offer companies lower rates than Blue Cross on healthy, low-risk workers. Thus many businesses had come to favor them. However, by the end of the 1950s most Blue Cross plans dropped their traditional community rating system and adopted experience rating. They feared that they would not be able to compete with the commercial insurers if their pools included a large number of high-risk individuals. Their action reflects the realities of the integration of health insurance into the market economy.

POSTWAR GOVERNMENT HEALTH POLICY

Although the movement for compulsory health insurance failed, the trend toward increasing federal involvement in medical programs did not. Support for these programs often allowed the opponents of compulsory health insurance to demonstrate their commitment to health care delivery. In 1946 Congress passed the Hospital Survey and Construction Act (Hill-Burton Act) that provided federal monies to public and voluntary hospitals for construction. As opposed to their stance on national health insurance, the AMA and AHA supported the legislation. The AHA even took an active role in structuring the bill. Parts of the initial legislation had been written by its executive director, George Bugbee. The organization established a multimillion-dollar education fund to push for the legislation. Both the AMA and AHA believed that the proposed law would benefit their members, but without sacrificing professional and institutional autonomy. The act provided federal funds for the construction of hospitals, but prohibited government intervention in hospital policy.

The impetus behind the act was concern about disparities in the provision of hospital services. A shortage of acceptable hospital beds plagued many areas in the country. An estimated 40 percent of counties, many located in rural areas, did not have hospital beds. More than 50 percent of the hospitals in use in the 1940s had been built before 1920.

Surgeon General Thomas Parran estimated in 1944 that 25 percent of all facilities were obsolete.

The Hill-Burton Act appropriated money for states to conduct hospital surveys and to develop state plans for hospital development. It also provided states with funds to assist in the construction of voluntary and public hospitals. A state's federal allocation was based on a formula that benefited states with low per capita incomes. However, within those states it favored hospital construction in middle-class areas because communities had to pay two-thirds of construction costs. In addition, hospitals supported under the plan had to be financially viable.

The Hill-Burton program ended in 1974, but its impact was significant. It greatly expanded the number of hospital beds in the country. In addition it helped to secure the centrality of the hospital in the health care delivery system, at the expense of outpatient and long term care facilities. Between 1947 and 1971 it allocated almost $4 billion to finance 30 per cent of the hospital projects in the United States.

In order to address the needs of the poor, the legislation required that recipients of Hill-Burton funds provide a "reasonable volume of services to those unable to pay." Enforcement of this free care obligation was weak. In 1970 lawyers for the poor brought suit to have hospitals honor this obligation. In *Cook* v. *Ochnser Foundation Hospital* they claimed that ten Louisiana hospitals that had received Hill-Burton funds did not provide a reasonable amount of free care. As a result of this suit, the Department of Health, Education, and Welfare issued new charity regulations in 1972. These new regulations set guidelines for charity care—5 percent of a hospital's estimated patient revenues. Lax enforcement also followed these new regulations.

The Hill-Burton legislation also made a feeble attempt to address the problem of hospital segregation. It contained an antidiscrimination clause that stipulated that hospitals receiving funds could not discriminate on the basis of race, creed, or color. However, communities could obtain waivers to this policy if they maintained "separate-but-equal" facilities and many did so. Dr. Vane M. Hoge, chief of the Division of Hospital Services of the U.S. Public Health Service, hailed these inclusions as concrete steps toward improving hospital service for African Americans. His optimism did not convince black physicians. Leaders of the National Medical Association, a black medical society, contended that the separate-but-equal clause would encourage the continuation of segregation and inequality in hospital

care. They pointed out that interpretation of the clause was under state, not federal control and that the act had been championed as a states' rights bill in the Senate by one of its sponsors, Lister Hill (D-Ala.). The predictions of black physicians proved correct. Hill-Burton monies were widely used to build racially exclusive hospitals. By March 1964, the program had assisted in the construction of 104 segregated hospitals, 20 black and 84 white.

Federal support of medical research exploded after World War II. Prior to the war, private institutions such as the Rockefeller Institute for Medical Research and pharmaceutical companies sponsored most of the country's medical research. This began to change in 1941 when President Roosevelt created the Office of Scientific Research and Development (OSRD). Its Committee on Medical Research coordinated and funded research projects related to the war and national defense. The committee linked the work activities of investigators in the government, university, and industry. Its work led to the development and wide distribution of a number of pharmaceuticals, including penicillin, sulfonamides, gamma globulin, and cortisone. The success of wartime research efforts, particularly the Manhattan Project and the discovery of penicillin, augmented the public's faith in the promise of scientific research. Scientific achievements came to symbolize the nation's dominance as a world power. Consequently, funding for scientific research increasingly became a federal responsibility. Between 1941 and 1951 the federal budget for medical research climbed from $3 million to $76 million.

THE CREATION OF MEDICARE AND MEDICAID

As we have already seen, government policies fostered the development throughout the latter half of the twentieth century of an American health care system in which employer-financed voluntary health insurance became dominant. The federal government, however, continued its practice of providing or funding medical services for populations deemed particularly vulnerable or entitled. In 1950, amendments to the Social Security Act set up an administrative framework for a welfare medicine program. They provided matching funds, called vendor payments, to the states for direct payments to doctors and hospitals for medical services to welfare recipients. Previously, those on welfare received direct payments for general living expenses, including a small amount for medical care. These amendments extended government financing of health services for the poor that had steadily increased since the Depression. This assistance covered only those poor who received support from four federal-state public assistance programs. Thus many poor Americans were left out. The federal government also expanded its funding of veterans hospitals. The health care financing system in the United States had become a patchwork of private and public plans. The private system was primarily reserved for those well-off or well-organized, the public one maintained for a limited number of people. This state of affairs left many Americans without protection, including the elderly, the unemployed, and the chronically ill.

By the 1950s the inadequacy of existing public and private programs to provide for high-risk groups such as the elderly became increasingly apparent. Consequently, arguments increased for government intervention to take care of them. The failure of supporters of compulsory health insurance to win passage of any legislation forced them to develop a new, more incremental tactic. They retreated from their advocacy of a universal, comprehensive program to one restricted to national hospital insurance for the elderly. They hoped to establish a model for national health insurance with one population and then later extend it to other groups.

Several factors underlay the new emphasis on the elderly. The number of Americans over sixty-five years of age had steadily grown over the century. In 1900 they made up 4 percent of the population; by 1950 the percentage had more than doubled. Supporters of the proposed plan pointed out that the elderly represented an especially needy and deserving segment of society. In 1950, approximately two-thirds of the elderly had annual incomes of less than $1,000 and only about 12 percent had health insurance. Thus they did not have the means to meet the rising costs of medical care. Hospital prices, for example, had doubled during the 1950s. In addition, the elderly, burdened with the chronic diseases and conditions associated with aging, utilized a disproportionate amount of medical services.

Political considerations also influenced this new focus on the elderly. Because of demographic changes the group had begun to emerge as a powerful and politically active special interest group. Supporters of compulsory health insurance used the population's special needs to their political advantage. As Oscar Ewing, head of the Federal Security Agency, put it when he announced the plan, "It is difficult for me to see how anyone with a heart can oppose this type of program."

In 1965, Congress did ultimately pass the Medicare legislation to address the health care delivery needs of the elderly. But an examination of the history of this legislation reveals the continuing struggle over defining the role of the government in health care delivery and finance. In 1957 Rep. Aimee Forand (D-R.I.) introduced one of the first pieces of legislation to cover the aged beneficiaries of social security. It called for payment of up to 120 days of hospital and nursing home care and would be paid for by an increase in social security payroll taxes. In a concession to organized medicine, the bill did not cover physicians' services.

As had been the case with earlier efforts to institute compulsory health insurance, the Forand bill provoked a heated response. Supporters included organized labor, the American Nurses Association, and liberal Democrats. Opponents included the AMA, many Republicans (including President Dwight D. Eisenhower), and most business and insurance groups. By the 1960 presidential election, the bill had surfaced as a major campaign issue. The eligibility criterion proved to be a major source of contention. Critics argued that not all of the elderly needed assistance and proposed alternative legislation that covered only the poor elderly. In 1960 two powerful members of Congress, Sen. Robert S. Kerr (D-Okla.) and Rep. Wilbur D. Mills (D-Ark.) introduced such a bill. A few months later Congress passed the Kerr-Mills bill (Title XVI of the Social Security Act), which provided additional federal matching funds to the states for vendor payments under the Old Age Assistance Act. In addition it created a new public assistance category—the medically indigent, people who did not need assistance for general living expenses, but for their medical bills. The objective of this aid was to keep people financial solvent during a medical crisis and off the welfare rolls. Inequities in state action and financing limited the impact of the program. In 1963, for example, five industrial states, with one third of the nation's population, received 90 percent of the funds.

The limitations of the Kerr-Mills bill and the continuing failure of the existing voluntary system prompted the continuation of the campaign to extend the Social Security Act to provide hospital insurance for its elderly beneficiaries. In February 1961, during his first month in office, President John F. Kennedy called for such legislation. Later that year, Sen. Clinton Anderson (D-N.M.) and Rep. Cecil King (D-Calif.) introduced a bill that embodied the new president's proposal. As the political scientist Max J. Skidmore has pointed out, both sides of the debate used rhetorical and inflammatory terms to argue that their program fit more appropriately with perceived American ideals such as self-reliance, pragmatism, equality, and individual responsibility. Opponents portrayed the program as un-American, the entering wedge of socialism. Supporters countered that socialism was un-American, but that the proposed measure was American, an extension of a venerable American institution—social security.

Between 1961 and 1965 much political maneuvering surrounded the provision of health insurance for the elderly. Grassroots activism by the elderly and political jockeying by both parties helped to keep it at the forefront of the national agenda. Policies to assist the elderly gathered overwhelming public support. The issue became not whether there would be a government program to assist the elderly with their medical needs, but what form such a program would take. In addition to the King-Anderson bill, which only covered hospital services, other proposals surfaced. The AMA, in an effort to stop a compulsory insurance, introduced "Eldercare" to help the elderly pay for hospital, physician, and drug bills. This plan called for a federal-state program to subsidize the purchase of voluntary health insurance policies. Republicans, led by Rep. John W. Byrne (R-Wis.), introduced a similar bill. Its "Bettercare" proposal sought to establish a program under federal, rather than state, auspices to help the elderly obtain coverage through the private sector. Action on these various measures lingered for several years. The turning point proved to be the 1964 Democratic sweep of the White House and Congress. Medicare emerged as one of the highest priorities of President Lyndon B. Johnson's Great Society programs.

In 1965 Congress finally adopted amendments to the Social Security Act that established a government-sponsored program to take care of the health care needs of the elderly. The legislation combined elements of the three approaches to the problem that had been bandied about throughout the 1950s and 1960s. It contained the Democratic plan for a compulsory hospital insurance program under social security (Medicare Part A). It also included the Republican proposal to provide government-subsidized voluntary insurance to cover physicians' bills (Medicare Part B). Congress, in a separate amendment, increased federal funds to the states to assist the poor with a program called Medicaid.

Although passed at the same time, major distinctions existed between Medicare and Medicaid. Medicare mirrored past social insurance legislation and enjoyed its legitimacy and popularity. The program would be financed by mandatory contributions from employers and employees. Eligibility for benefits criteria would not be determined by income, but by age or social security status. A means test to determine an individual's financial status would not be employed. Benefits would be established at the national level and would not be based on one's state of residence. Under Medicare, physicians would be allowed to charge their "usual, reasonable, and customary" fees. In contrast, Medicaid reflected previous welfare medicine measures. Income determined eligibility. Benefits substantially varied from state to state. In addition, physicians did not receive full reimbursement for their services. Medicaid also carried the stigma and political vulnerability attached to welfare and public assistance.

HEALTH CARE DELIVERY AND THE CIVIL RIGHTS MOVEMENT

President Johnson's Great Society program also included the enactment of civil rights legislation. The health care delivery system was not exempted from the campaign to integrate American society and institutions. Medical civil rights activists had initially selected the Veterans Administration hospital system as one of their first targets. It was a shrewd choice. Segregation in this federal system especially underscored America's hypocrisy with regard to the rights of African Americans. Approximately 1.2 million black men and women had served valiantly in a war allegedly to defend democracy against fascism and Nazism, but upon its conclusion, they found themselves either segregated in or barred from many veterans hospitals.

Efforts to desegregate veterans hospitals began shortly after World War II. In October 1945, representatives of civil rights groups and black medical and nursing organizations met with the medical director of the Veterans Administration. Black leaders demanded the complete integration of the agency's hospitals. It took them eight years to achieve their goal, but in 1953 the Veterans Administration ordered an end to segregation in all its hospitals, including the one at Tuskegee, Alabama. Shortly after this order was issued, white patients were admitted to the hospital.

The medical civil rights activists also used the courts in their battle to desegregate the health care system. They used the antidiscrimination clause of the Hill-Burton Act that had proven to be ineffective as the tool to chip away hospital segregation. *Simkins* v. *Moses H. Cone Memorial Hospital* was the pivotal case. In 1962, a group of black physicians, dentists, and patients from Greensboro, North Carolina, filed the first suit designed to challenge the separate-but-equal clause of the Act. They argued that it should be declared unconstitutional on the grounds that it violated the due process clause of the Fifth Amendment and the equal protection clause of the Fourteenth Amendment.

The plaintiffs' case revolved around the racially discriminatory practices at Moses H. Cone Memorial Hospital and Wesley Long Community Hospital, voluntary hospitals that had together received $2.8 million in funds. The hospitals openly discriminated in both patient admissions and in staff appointments. Cone Hospital refused to admit any black patients except those who required services not available at L. Richardson Memorial Hospital, a voluntary black institution. Cone and Long excluded black physicians and dentists from their staff and Long completely barred black patients.

A district court dismissed the case, but in November 1963 the Fourth Circuit Court of Appeals reversed the lower court's decision. It found that voluntary hospitals receiving funds were instruments of the state because such facilities were integral parts of a state and federal plan to allocate resources effectively for the promotion and maintenance of the public's health. The Court issued an injunction prohibiting the hospitals from discriminatory practices in staff appointments and patient admissions. It also declared the separate-but-equal clause of the Hill-Burton Act unconstitutional. Since the Supreme Court refused to hear the case on appeal, the decision of the lower court stood.

The *Simkins* decision represented a significant victory in the battle for medical civil rights. It extended the principles of the *Brown* v. *Board of Education* decision to hospitals, including those not publicly owned and operated, although its authority was limited to those hospitals that received funds. A 1964 federal court decision, *Eaton* v. *Grubbs,* however, broadened the prohibitions against racial discrimination to include hospitals that did not receive such funds.

Later, the 1964 Civil Rights Act would extend these judicial decisions. The next year, the Department of Health, Education, and Welfare issued regulations that mandated that hospitals had to comply with Title VI of the Civil Rights Act in order to be eligible for federal assistance or to participate in any federally assisted program. The 1965 passage of Medicare and Medicaid legislation made virtually all hospitals potential recipients of federal funds and therefore obligated to comply with federal civil rights legislation.

THE ESCALATION OF HEALTH CARE COSTS

The passage of the Medicare and Medicaid legislation also heralded a new era of escalating health care costs, which began to consume an increasingly larger percentage of the nation's gross national product. Whereas in 1960 they represented 5.3 percent of GNP, by 1970 they represented 7.3 percent, by 1980, 9.2 percent, and by 1990, 12.2 percent. In 1960, national health care expenditures totaled $27.1 billion; thirty years later they had grown to $666.2 billion. In 1990, the largest percentage, approximately 40 percent, went to hospital care. Health care costs increased by over 51 percent between 1984 and 1989, nearly three times the period's rate of inflation.

The federal government's involvement in the financial aspects of health care delivery also grew rapidly after the passage of Medicare and Medicaid. In 1965, the federal government paid 13 percent of the nation's health care costs; by 1987 it paid 29 percent. Health care spending climbed to 16.7 percent of all federal expenditures in 1991, up from 15.3 percent in 1990. Much of this increase in federal health care spending can be attributed to Medicare and Medicaid. In 1991 the two programs were responsible for funding two-thirds of all federally financed health care. That year they spent $216.7 billion in providing health care services to over 63 million aged, disabled, and poor Americans and another $6.6 billion in administration. The increasing financial burden of health care was not limited to the federal government. For state and local governments, health spending climbed to 14.1 percent of total expenditures, up from 12.9 percent in 1990. Between 1965 and 1987, businesses saw the percentage of the average company's payroll committed to health care increase from 2 to 6 percent.

Several factors contributed to these rising health care costs. The Medicare reimbursement mechanism has played a major role. In order to win the cooperation of hospitals and physicians for the program, President Johnson agreed to allow cost-plus reimbursement for hospitals and usual, customary, and reasonable fees for physicians. Both concessions encouraged higher costs. Hospitals received payment not only for the direct cost of the specific service provided, but for indirect costs such as labor, capital investment, maintenance, medical education, and technology acquisition. In addition, since hospitals were reimbursed on the basis of their costs, institutions that reduced costs would decrease their incomes. Records of past costs affected future reimbursement levels. The Medicare reimbursement scheme gave hospitals incentives to maximize reimbursement rather than decrease costs. As Rosemary Stevens has put it, "Medicare gave hospitals a license to spend."

Medicare's usual, customary, and reasonable payment mechanism for physicians also encouraged inflation of medical fees. Medicare determines an allowable charge for a particular procedure by selecting the lowest of three amounts: the customary charge prevailing in the community, the usual charge by a particular provider, or the actual charge billed. Approved charges, which vary by procedure and provider, are updated annually. As was true with hospital reimbursement, past fees influenced future reimbursement levels. Therefore the system gave physicians incentives to increase their charges and benefited those who practiced in higher priced areas. Physicians also received higher compensation for hospital-based procedures than for outpatient ones. The usual, customary, and reasonable reimbursement system also did not provide mechanisms that translated technological advancements into financial savings. For example, if the time needed for a particular procedure declined, the physicians' fees usually remained at the prevailing level set at the time when the procedure took longer.

Other factors also played prominent roles in the rapid escalation of health care costs that began in the mid-1960s and continues to plague the nation. These include a growth of medical technology; an increase in the number of health care workers; rising medical malpractice insurance premiums; duplication of medical services; increased administrative costs such as claims processing to pay medical bills, marketing, and eligibility determination by third-party payers; an excess of hospital beds; an increase in the number of medical specialists; and rising expectations and demands on the part of patients.

Throughout most of the twentieth century, the emphasis had been on the expansion of health care services. However, by the 1970s the focus began to shift toward containment of health care costs. Between 1965 and 1970 total health care expenditures increased from $139 to $169 billion and per capita expenditures increased from $198 to $334. These rising costs prompted fears that health care spending would eventually threaten other goods and services that society needed. Proposals soon emerged to contain these escalating costs. One strategy was to promote alternatives to traditional fee-for-service medicine. The premise behind this idea was that increased competition would contain costs.

By the early 1970s increased attention began to be paid to the development of so-called managed care programs such as health maintenance organizations (HMOs) as mechanisms for cost containment. HMOs are prepaid group practices that integrate the financing and delivery of medicine. In an HMO, consumers pay a fixed monthly premium for which they can receive complete medical care services, regardless of how much they use. Under traditional fee-for-service practice the provider's income is directly related to the number of services rendered. With a fixed payment per enrollee, the HMO's income is inversely related to the number of services provided. This principle provides strong incentives for physicians employed by the HMO to reduce the number of unnecessary procedures.

Prepaid group health plans had originated earlier in the century. One of the largest, Kaiser Permanente, had been established in 1942 by industrialist Henry Kaiser to care for the employees of his shipyards in California and Oregon. Three years later, Kaiser opened the doors to the public. By 1955, the plan covered approximately five hundred thousand people. Other plans established after World War II included the Health Insurance Plan in New York City, Group Health Cooperative of Puget Sound, and Labor Health Institute in Saint Louis. Organized medicine criticized the establishment of group health practices. It viewed them as threats to solo fee-for-service medicine and to physician autonomy.

Despite this opposition, in February 1971 President Richard M. Nixon called for a "comprehensive health policy for the 1970s." HMOs would be the cornerstone of this policy. The President's actions had been prompted in part by political considerations. He recommended this policy as a response to the proposal by Sen. Edward M. Kennedy (D-Mass.) and Rep. Martha W. Griffiths (D-Mich.) for national health insurance. In 1973 Congress passed the Health Maintenance Organization Act, the federal government's first effort to develop an alternative to fee-for-service medicine. The law authorized federal grants and loans to finance the establishment of HMO plans and required employers of more than twenty-five workers to offer HMO coverage if such plans were available in the area and met federal requirements. Memberships in HMOs have since skyrocketed. Between 1980 and 1991 enrollment increased from 10.2 million to 39 million.

The Medicare legislation specified that there

should be "prohibition against federal interference" with the practice of medicine. The program was established to finance hospital and medical care for the elderly without attempting to alter or significantly influence the delivery of health care. Medicare was viewed rather narrowly as a reimbursement program that would provide funds for the purchase of additional access to services. However, this is no longer the case. Since the enactment of the bill, the federal government has evolved into the single largest payer for health services. And, it has not hesitated to use the programs that it finances as mechanisms to make changes in the system that it deems necessary.

The federal government has used its financial muscle to attempt to control health care costs. In 1972 Congress, over the bitter opposition of organized medicine, adopted amendments to the Social Security Act that established professional standards review organizations (PSROs) to review the quality and appropriateness of care rendered to the recipients of federal health programs. Eleven years later, Congress passed legislation that introduced prospective payment as the mechanism for hospital reimbursement. Under this system, hospitals are no longer paid according to the number of individual services they provide or the number of days that a Medicare beneficiary is hospitalized. Instead, they now receive a fixed amount of money for each admission. That sum is determined by the admitting diagnosis, which is assigned to a diagnosis related group (DRG). The rationale behind prospective payment is to make hospitals more efficient and to avoid unnecessary hospital stays.

The private sector has also joined the battle to contain health care costs. For example, private insurers have implemented utilization review and employers have provided incentives for consumers to join HMOs. These public and private initiatives have not been able to brake escalating health care costs, which have continued to rise throughout the 1980s and 1990s.

THE ROAD TO HEALTH CARE REFORM

By the 1980s, the health care delivery system faced another problem—an increase in the number of uninsured Americans. Between 1979 and 1984, the number of uninsured jumped from 28.8 to 37.3 million; for 1992, estimates ranged from 31 to 37 million. The uninsured include the near-poor under sixty-five, children, those unable to purchase individual coverage because of preexisting conditions, and the unemployed. However, most people who lack

health insurance in fact have jobs. One 1987 survey found that of the uninsured population, 70 percent were employed or the dependents of employed persons.

Several factors have contributed to this decline in health insurance coverage. One major element is an erosion of workplace coverage. Although the number of employer-subsidized health plans grew substantially after World War II, the recession of the 1980s resulted in a loss of jobs in the manufacturing sector and an increase in those in the service sector. Service industries have traditionally offered fewer employee benefits than those in manufacturing in part because of their lower level of unionization. The recession of the early 1980s also led to a larger number of unemployed Americans. Many of those fortunate to have employment found it in small businesses that do not provide health insurance. High premiums hinder the efforts of individuals who are not eligible for group rates to purchase health insurance. Thus, many Americans, including the middle class, complain of "job lock"—an immobilization resulting from fear of losing their health insurance. The tightening of eligibility criteria for Medicaid, a move taken during the Reagan administration to control health care costs, has also contributed to the growing numbers of uninsured.

The goals of the Clinton administration's efforts at health care reform are to control costs and to provide universal insurance coverage. However it is becoming increasingly apparent that access to health care involves more than financial considerations. Nonfinancial barriers to care must also be taken into account. These include availability of providers, their geographic proximity to patients, length of wait before securing an appointment with a physician, and length of provider-patient contact. Also important is how one is treated once one is in the clinical encounter. There is a growing body of medical literature that points out that even when African Americans have health insurance, racial disparities to access persist. African Americans are less likely to have access to specific technologies such as coronary artery bypass grafts and kidney transplantation. Other studies have indicated that gender disparities exist in women's access to particular procedures. Such disparities cannot be explained solely by biological differences. President Clinton's goal to increase the financial access of all Americans will at best narrow but not erase racial and gender disparities in health care. They must be attacked on a broader political and social level.

In a 1989 review of previous proposals for national health insurance, Samuel Levey and James Hill concluded that past actions could be characterized as "the triumph of equivocation." They described the reluctance of special interest groups and the American public to push for reform of the health care system. Changes have consisted primarily of minor tinkering. President Clinton's proposed health care reform package, announced in September 1993, has been widely debated, criticized, and analyzed by various special interest groups. As the package winds its way through the many Congressional committees that have jurisdiction over health care, it is not clear what the nature of health care reform will be. It has become apparent, as has happened so many times throughout the twentieth century, that no consensus exists among Americans over what the role of government in health care should be.

SEE ALSO Medical Science and Technology; Health and Disease (both in this volume).

BIBLIOGRAPHY

Paul Starr, *The Social Transformation of American Medicine* (1982), provides the best introduction to the evolution of the American health care system. Odin Anderson, *Health Services in the United States: A Growth Enterprise since 1875* (1985), offers a brief and very descriptive examination of the history of health care. Judith Walzer Leavitt and Ronald L. Numbers, eds., *Sickness and Health in America: Readings in the History of Medicine and Public Health,* 2d ed. (1985), is a useful collection that includes several articles on the history of twentieth-century American medicine and public health. Susan Reverby and David Rosner, eds., *Health Care in America: Essays in Social History* (1979), contains several essays that focus on social and political factors that have influenced the development of health care in the twentieth century.

Ronald L. Numbers, *Almost Persuaded: American Physicians and Compulsory Health Insurance, 1912–1920* (1978), examines the first American campaign for compulsory health insurance. Daniel S. Hirshfield, *The Lost Reform: The Campaign for Compulsory Health Insurance in the United States from 1932 to 1943* (1970), analyzes the second campaign during the presidency of Franklin D. Roosevelt. Monte M. Poen, *Harry S. Truman versus the Medical Lobby: The Genesis of Medicare* (1979), focuses on Truman's health insurance proposals. Max J. Skidmore, *Medicare and the American Rhetoric of Reconciliation* (1970), illuminates how various groups during the political debates over the creation of Medicare used rhetoric to advance their position. Theodore R. Marmor, *The Politics of Medicare* (1970), analyzes the legislative history of Medicare and places it in the context of American social welfare policy. Ronald L. Numbers, ed., *Compulsory Health Insurance: The Continuing American Debate* (1982), is a useful collection of essays on the attempts to institute compulsory health insurance in the United States. Sylvia A. Law, *Blue Cross: What Went Wrong?* 2d ed. (1976), is a highly critical analysis of the program. Samuel Levey and James Hill, "National Health Insurance—The Triumph of Equivocation," *New England Journal of Medicine* 321 (1989): 1750–1753, examines the reasons behind past defeats of national health insurance.

Charles E. Rosenberg, *The Care of Strangers: The Rise of America's Hospital System* (1987), provides an excellent analysis of the origins of the American hospital. Rosemary Stevens, *In Sickness and in Wealth: American Hospitals in the Twentieth Century* (1989), offers a comprehensive study of twentieth-century American hospitals and health policy. Diana Elizabeth Long and Janet Golden, eds., *The American General Hospital: Communities and Social Contexts* (1989), includes essays that survey the history of the community hospital. Virginia Drachman, *Hospital with a Heart: Women Doctors and the Paradox of Separatism at the New England Hospital, 1862–1969* (1984), analyzes the forces that have influenced the development of women physicians and their hospitals. Morris Vogel, *The Invention of the Modern Hospital: Boston, 1870–1930* (1980), uses Boston as a case study to demonstrate the interplay between medical and social factors in the transformation of the hospital. David Rosner, *A Once Charitable Enterprise: Hospitals and Health Care in Brooklyn and New York, 1885–1915* (1982), examines the economic pressures that forced hospitals to abandon their traditional functions and move toward a system based on ability to pay. Harry F. Dowling, *City Hospitals: The Undercare of the Underprivileged* (1982), traces the history of municipal hospitals. E. H. Beardsley, *A History of Neglect: Health*

Care for Blacks and Mill Workers in the Twentieth Century South (1987), focuses on inequities based on race and class that have influenced the delivery of health services. Vanessa Northington Gamble, *Making a Place for Ourselves: The Black Hospital Movement, 1920–1945* (1995), examines the role of race in the development of the American hospital system and the efforts of African American physicians to improve the medical and educational programs at black hospitals. Kenneth M. Ludmerer, *Learning to Heal: The Development of American Medical Education* (1985), describes the development of modern medical education and the rise of the teaching hospital.

Daniel M. Fox, *Health Policies, Health Politics: The British and American Experience, 1911–1965* (1986), compares government health policies in the United States and Great Britain. Rosemary Stevens, *American Medicine and the Public Interest* (1971), examines the history of twentieth-century health policy and the growth of medical specialization. Victoria A. Harden, *Inventing the NIH: Federal Biomedical Research Policy, 1887–1937* (1986), traces the evolution of the federal government's involvement in medical research. Stephen P. Strickland, *Politics, Science, and Dread Disease: A Short History of United States Medical Research Policy* (1972), analyzes the explosion of government-sponsored medical research that followed World War II and the role of special interest groups in this growth.

5